KEEP OUT!
BUG OFF!
TOP SECRET
INSIDERS ONLY
GO AWAY! THIS MEANS YOU!!
PRIVATE
CRUISES
AIRFARES
CAR RENTALS
HOTELS
AL-ROD

INSIDER TRAVEL SECRETS

You're NOT Supposed to Know!

Tom Parsons

Best Fares USA, Inc.
www.bestfares.com

Library of Congress Catalog Card Number: 96-83477

ISBN 0-9650960-1-7

Book and cover design by Lisa Leonard-Koger.
Illustrations by Al Rod.
Map illustrations by Mike Ellis.
Thanks to the entire *Best Fares* team. Special acknowledgement to *Best Fares'* Editorial staff, headed by Carol Kaminski and including Bill Brasher, Teena Carter, Kenneth Coleman, Nicole Crawford, Cynthia Duran, Andrew Harman, Lisa Harman, Elaine Hewlett, Sharon Manns, Maxine Manor, Jake Rigdon and Nena Tran.

The information published in *Insider Travel Secrets* is derived from industry sources which are considered reliable at the time of publication. Promotions and fares are subject to change and withdrawal without notice; therefore, it is the responsibility of the consumer to verify reliability on an individual basis based on specific consumer needs. *Insider Travel Secrets* assumes no responsibility, and extends no guarantees, for discount promotions, fares, or changes in travel industry programs listed in this publication. Chart data was compiled in April of 1998, except for the Kids Fly Solo chart, which was updated on June 4, 1998.

This edition of INSIDER TRAVEL SECRETS is dedicated

to my mother, Margie Harman,
for teaching me the true value of a buck;

to my father, John Harman, who passed away
last year but who continues to remind me:
"Tom, don't let the travel industry put anything
over on the consumers;

to my children, Stephanie, Michael and
Bryan, for giving me a good reason to spend
everything I've saved;

and to Southwest Airlines,
the number one low-cost carrier in the U.S.,
for continuing to prove
that you can give passengers a fair deal
and still make a fine profit.

About the Author

Tom Parsons has spent the past 16 years earning an unparalleled reputation as an expert in bargain travel. He appears on 80 to 100 radio and television shows each month and is often quoted by major newspapers and magazines. He has provided consumers with one-stop discount shopping in *Best Fares Discount Travel Magazine*, a publication that has earned accolades for 15 years. He created *Best Fares* Online (www.bestfares.com) in 1996, as a venue for providing consumers with daily updates on travel deals and tomorrow's travel news today. The site is updated several times a day, seven days a week and is taking the lead as the most bargain-friendly travel source on the internet.

Parsons grew up in South America where wheeling and dealing is woven into the culture. He earned his degree in Criminal Justice (specializing in white collar crime) and was a military investigator in Vietnam. He worked for a major international corporation as a specialist in tearing systems apart to uncover embezzlement and other corporate theft. His ability to be innovative and create new and unique ways of looking at things helped form an effective corporate investigative division known as the "Can Do Unit."

When Parsons became a frequent business traveler, his company handed him a corporate credit card and left him on his own. The airline industry had recently been deregulated. Before deregulation, all fare comparisons were apples-to-apples. After deregulation, a new world of discounts, price wars, frequent flyer programs and special promotions was created. Airlines offered fares so varied that no one seemed able to keep up with them.

After putting his best efforts into getting the lowest possible fare, Parsons learned that a co-worker purchased a ticket for the same itinerary for travel three days later and paid $100 less. He vowed to never let that happen again and decided to use his investigative skills to figure out how the new systems worked and how he could use them to his advantage.

Then, as now, there were literally tens of thousands of possible fares on any given day—several hundred on one route alone—all subject to change at a moment's notice. Parsons poured over airline guides, computer reservation systems, fare rules, market trends and industry promotions. He soon realized that even though most travel agencies try to find low fares, they work under handicaps: a commission-based system that provides no direct financial benefit for locating low fares, a computer reservation system geared toward major carriers' interests rather than those of consumers and an ever-changing array of discount offers and promotions.

His corporation offered a significant bonus to anyone who could reduce travel costs. "Can do," he replied and proceeded to cut corporate travel expenses by $800,000 in 14 months. He received the bonus and an award naming him "The Man Least Likely To Give Up A Buck."

His two-page travel tip newsletter (part of his cost-cutting strategy) was distributed within the company and soon became in demand by friends and associates of management. The mailing list grew to 300 people and, in 1983, Parsons began publishing *The DFW Report*, a regional newsletter for cost-conscious travelers in the Dallas/Fort Worth area. He anticipated a subscription base of 800 to 1,000, but subscriptions kept coming in along with requests from travelers in other parts of the country who wanted to know about travel, Parsons' style. In 1987 *Best Fares Discount Travel Magazine* made its debut. It now serves over 80,000 subscribers.

Parsons regularly consults with executives of most major airlines. He believes that business deserves to profit but he is adamantly pro-consumer. He takes a stand when he sees something wrong with the industry; he is equally quick to praise the airlines when they do something right.

He is a tenacious watchdog of the travel industry, often first to inform the national media of changes that affect consumers. "The Guru of Cheap Airfares" continues to be a sought-after guest on national and local radio and television, as he gives millions of people across the United States a free course on how to reduce travel costs. Many stations report that Parsons is their most requested return guest. His knowledge of hidden discounts and travel industry secrets is regularly featured on shows including *Good Morning America*, *The Today Show*, *CBS This Morning*, *CNBC*, *CNN* and *Nightline*; in newspapers such as *The Wall Street Journal*, *The New York Times* and *USA Today*; in magazines including *U.S. News And World Report*, *Fortune* and *Money*; online at sites including abcnews.com, expedia.com and travelocity.com. Over 2,000 online sites have links to Parsons' world of travel and over one million online visitors per month benefit from his advice. He has also shared his opinions and insights on air travel by invitation from the United States Congress.

INTRODUCTION

The first edition of *Insider Travel Secrets* earned rave reviews and sold out faster than we could re-order. When we began to update the book in preparation for a true second edition printing, we knew we had a winning formula. We thought it was a matter of a few tweaks and updates here and there. Many months later, we have documented evidence of the amount of change inherent in the travel industry. This edition comes to you with changes on every page, a new chapter on travel by rail and road, and many new additions brought about by the increasing importance of the internet in the world of travel.

This is the book for everyone who has ever called every airline for prices and checked with travel agents only to find that the person sitting next to them was flying on a much cheaper ticket. It is the book for hotel guests who notice that desk clerks circle the rate you're paying when you check in, rather than confirming it out loud—standard policy to avoid alerting you to the fact that the next person in line may be paying half as much. It is the book for people who were content with a free cabin upgrade on a cruise until they talked to someone who sailed on the same ship a week or two later on a two-for-one deal. It is the book for people paying high dollar for a rental car while others get better vehicles and more bonus miles at a much lower rate. *Insider Travel Secrets* exposes the two worlds of travel—one in which consumers pay what they're told to pay and one in which rates are discounted by as much as 70 percent (sometimes even more). We will tell you about hidden travel deals and show you how to use them to slash your travel costs.

Here is an example of deals that are noticed too infrequently and often missed entirely by the most experienced travelers. Tom was on a Delta flight from Los Angeles to Dallas. His seat mate was a seasoned traveler who flew Delta several times a week. He thought he knew all the bargain travel tricks and he did—to a point. Midway through the flight, Tom told him that he could take his spouse or one of his children with him on any Delta flight (including roundtrips to Hawaii or Europe) for just $25. He could do it without cashing in tens of thousands of frequent flyer miles.

There were three clues on the flight. The two-minute video preceding the in-flight movie mentioned this ticket bonanza but, like many seasoned travelers, Tom's seat mate had tuned it out. The in-flight magazine and display cards on the dinner trays also promoted the deal. AT&T was offering a free companion ticket to people who signed up for their 500-number service (a number that can reach you anywhere in the United States). After $25 worth of calls—calls paid for by the people placing them—the subscriber received a two-for-one certificate valid on any Delta roundtrip worldwide.

Not surprisingly, Tom's seat mate took the AT&T service and he subscribed to *Best Fares*. Tom also gave his new friend his own 500 number, knowing that his call would help Tom reach his own $25/free ticket goal. On the same flight, Tom asked the flight attendants if they were ever asked for free tickets. Most of them said yes, but none of them knew about the AT&T promotion even though they were the ones who loaded the video, distributed the magazines and served the meals.

It is impossible for most of us to notice everything in our busy worlds. In this information age we are constantly exposed to input and we have to screen some of it out just to survive. That's where *Best Fares* Magazine, www.bestfares.com and *Insider Traveler Secrets* come to the rescue. We have dozens of pairs of expert eyes constantly looking for the best hidden travel deals and presenting them to consumers.

Tom's highest motivation and his favorite reward comes from subscribers who take the time to tell him how much money they saved or how his insight and strategies helped make their travel dreams come true. His primary goal is for all travelers–no matter their income–to travel like kings and queens without paying a kings ransom.

This book provides the foundation needed to locate and use the deals that are best for you. The book has two major missions: to reduce your travel costs and to show you how to get as many free perks as possible. There are other travel books that paint pretty pictures of the advantages and details of specific travel destinations. This book shows you how to go where you want to go for less. If you want to fly First Class at Coach prices or fly a college student home for half the usual cost, we'll show you how. Whether you fly 200,000 miles a year or would like to travel more often if only you could afford to, you will benefit from this book.

Most chapters begin with savings maximizers—our all-around favorite ways to save. We'll show you how to save on major travel expenses, and how to continue the savings theme throughout your trip. There are deals and there are *better* deals. Don't settle for ten percent off when you can save 50 percent, and don't settle for 50 percent off when you can literally purchase travel for ten-cents on the dollar.

Flexibility is important but, in many cases, you may not need to change a thing in your travel patterns to substantially reduce your costs. In other cases, a minor change produces great savings. This book will give you consumer power in the form of the knowledge necessary to get lower prices no matter how, when and where you prefer to travel.

Sit back and relax as you read the pages of this book and learn that finding bargains is neither as complicated nor as time consuming as you may think. You don't have to dedicate your life to tracking down bargains; you just need a friend who can share the insider secrets most travelers never know. Learn the methods that will consistently bring you the thrill of beating one of the world's most complicated pricing systems. Any game is fun when you are an expert at playing. *Insider Traveler Secrets* will take you to the winner's circle of a game that pays off in cash.

TABLE OF CONTENTS

AIRLINES

Hotels

Car Rentals

CRUISES

Travel By Rail & Road

More Dollars & Cents

Travel Guide

KNOW WHO TO CONTACT

Don't Let The Airlines Take You For A Ride

Insider Travel Secrets can give almost anyone a Travel 101 course in the basics of air travel, plus tricks, hidden deals and strategies that keep air travel costs down. Those who read it carefully will earn the equivalent of a Ph.D. in bargain travel. This chapter begins with six savings maximizers:

Snooze You Lose fares that can save leisure and business travelers up to 80-90 percent, with very few restrictions or blackout dates. *Best Fares* publishes them three times a day, seven days a week at **www.bestfares.com**.

Use of the internet to cut the cost of airfares, get free or reduced companion travel and access bonus offers that make your frequent flyer accounts soar.

Special coupon promotions offering free tickets and major discounts. Some are yours for the asking; some come as bonuses with purchases that can be as little as $5; some are yours with purchases you make routinely.

Low-cost airlines, niche airlines and alternate airports that can cut fares by up to 75 percent.

Fare wars that offer sale fares that can be discounted even more by using double and triple whammies.

Creative ticketing methods that are carefully hidden but perfectly legal.

Since the first edition of *Insider Travel Secrets* was published, most airlines have posted record profits and devised dozens of ways to charge more for air travel. Airline pricing departments move quickly, initiating, altering and pulling sale prices with the speed of a Concorde in flight. This year, *Best Fares* Online headed the airlines off at the pass. When airfares changed dramatically at midnight, the information was on **www.bestfares.com** by dawn. We told you about fare wars before they were announced and published hundreds of Snooze You Lose fares. We don't ruffle the airlines' wings because we disagree with profit; we do it because we are committed to giving consumers every possible advantage in the confusing world of airfare prices. This chapter will show you how you can save money on virtually any ticket you purchase; how you benefit from low-cost carriers; how to lower the inflated prices travelers in major hub cities pay and much, much more.

We are embarking on an era of actual and proposed alliances between major airlines: Continental and Northwest; American and US Airways. Delta (the #1 carrier in passengers boarded) and United (the #1 carrier in revenue passenger miles). The past year also brought an increase in single airline monopolies at some airports. Delta became the first airline to board over 100 million passengers in a single year. Marketing efforts directed at business travelers increased. The American AAdvantage program added a new tier of elite frequent flyer status—Executive Platinum—with benefits including upgrade confirmation within 100 hours of departure and deferred mileage expiration. TWA increased the number of First Class seats on domestic flights by 60 percent. Air New Zealand launched a promotion offering a $747 rebate on some premium class travel.

Some low-cost carriers had difficulty this past year, notably Western Pacific, Carnival and Pan Am. The victories, however, were greater than the defeats. Southwest, the king of low-cost carriers, continued its winning ways and became our fifth largest airline in number of passengers boarded. They now bring low-fare service to 53 U. S. cities. If you question low-cost carriers' ability to fly safely while charging low fares, take a look at Southwest's 26 years of flying without one fatality. Low-cost carriers are one of the biggest single factors helping to keep airfares from rising at an even faster rate. They kick off fare wars in specific markets, and the major airlines are forced to match. They offer unique promotions: Vanguard's free tickets in exchange for a case of food donated to the local food banks; AirTran's $35 standby fares for students; Vanguard's $25 companion fares.

After you have studied this chapter, you will know how to recognize a good fare, how to make one appear when it seems next to impossible and how to take a low fare and reduce it even more. Some people would be more willing to travel if they knew how to make it more affordable. Others travel almost every day of their lives and want to be rescued from exorbitant business fares. Whether you are a small business owner carefully watching your bottom line, a grandparent who would like to see your grandchildren more often, a CEO who is tired of travel costs eating away at your bottom line or an adventurer dreaming of your first trip to Europe—this chapter will get you where you want to go for less.

FOUR KEY EVENTS IN AIR TRAVEL

The Biggest Innovation

The internet has opened more doors to bargains than any single innovation in the history of air travel. Used wisely, the internet gives you unprecedented access to fare and discount information. Accept an online fare quote without evaluating it, however, and you could pay more than you have to for many tickets. There are an estimated 300,000 travel sites on the internet. Some provide valuable information; others can be a waste of your time. Major airline, credit card, online booking and other sites publish special deals, but without hours each day to devote to surfing the web, they can sail right by you. When we developed *Best Fares* Online, we focused on features that would provide maximum benefit for travelers, including one-stop shopping for all travel discounts. After 14 years of publishing *Best Fares* Magazine, we were delighted to have a way to communicate discounts and hidden travel deals that came and went between magazine publication dates; to bring our subscribers deals as soon as they broke, so they would have first chance at limited availability usually applied to many special offers. Our **www.best fares.com** site hits hard and heavy with up to 50 special bargains every day.

The Biggest Consumer Windfall

Low-cost carriers continued to have a positive impact on airfares. Their success made major carriers respond with lower fares in competing markets. Southwest continued its amazing track record and came up with the best deal of the year: $25 one-way fares on all published routes nationwide. They also strengthened their frequent flyer program and introduced Southwest Standard and Gold Visa cards, demonstrating their ability to be a major carrier in ways that count the most to consumers. Delta Air Lines created Delta Express (point-to-point fares and a low-cost carrier ticket structure) and enjoyed a very successful first year. ProAir came to Detroit and provided new competition for market-giant Northwest. ValuJet and AirTran merged and put the accent on low-cost business travel. US Airways created MetroJet, a low-fare, limited range airline-within-an-airline.

The Best Non-Airfare Bargain Secret

Where does lost luggage (and cargo) go when it remains unclaimed? In many cases, it's shipped to Scottsboro, Alabama and placed on sale in a flagship store that covers a square-block area, or at one of two satellite stores. This is the flipside of the lost luggage coin—the chance to pick up fantastic bargains on items that were never able to find their way home. The Unclaimed Baggage Center has an extensive web site at **www.unclaimedbaggage.com**. You can read about current availabilities (portable CD players, carry-on luggage, video cameras, diamond rings and much more), learn how the center came to be and get detailed directions on how to get there from all four nearby airports. The flagship store in Scottsboro is open from 8 a.m. to 5 p.m. Monday through Thursday; 8 a.m. to 6 p.m. Friday and Saturday. Call **205-259-5753**. The Boaz store is open 9 a.m. to 5 p.m. Monday through Friday; 9 a.m. to 6 p.m. Saturday. Call **205-593-4393**. The Decatur store is open 9 a.m. to 5 p.m. Monday through Saturday. Call **205-350-0439**. Visiting any one of them is our idea of a great getaway weekend for bargain hunters!

Number of passengers who flew on U.S. carriers in 1997: 598,895,000.

The Biggest Industry Windfalls

Airlines took what Uncle Sam gave up. It started at the end of 1996 when airlines raised most domestic fares by ten percent. When the airline ticket tax expired on January 1, 1997, (a tax "coincidentally" at ten percent on domestic tickets) consumers paid the same fare amounts they were used to paying, but the airlines received what used to go to Uncle Sam. When the ticket tax structure changed in October of 1997, the airlines repeated their financially lucrative tactic.

Domestic airlines (quickly followed by most international carriers) cut travel agent commissions from ten to eight percent. Agents experienced a 20 percent drop in revenue (with no advance warning) and many began initiating service fees. Agents have been hurt, but consumers will take the biggest blow through service fees and through having fewer travel agents willing or able to take the time to shop for the lowest fares. We'll be watching to see what this does to airline profits. The first year after commission caps, they added a total of $630 million dollars to their profits, directly attributed to commission cuts.

Airlines also increased profits by continuing to reap the benefits of increased concern over airport security. Since domestic passengers must now show ID, people with non-refundable tickets (who used to sell them for half-price or equal dollar) were stopped in their tracks. The tickets are now truly non-transferable. Airlines also continued to profit from ticketless travel and online bookings that eliminated the need to pay travel agent commissions.

The Biggest Trend To Watch

Travel scams; currently a $12 billion a year industry. We hit them hard in the Scam Watch section of **www.bestfares.com**, in our magazine and in this book. Your best protection is knowing exactly how scammers work so you can identify them the moment you are approached by phone, mail, fax or e-mail. Your second line of protection is access to the thousands of legitimate travel bargains available to consumers. Why risk the unknown when you have so many legitimate bargains at your disposal?

OTHER SIGNIFICANT EVENTS

Single-airline dominance at major airports increased. In ten years Delta went from controlling 51 percent of the Atlanta market to 74.02 percent; Delta and Comair control over 90 percent of the Cincinnati market. Let's not single them out; other carriers are playing the dominance game too. American controls 63.5 percent in Dallas/Fort Worth and 63.97 percent in Miami. United controls 59.7 percent in San Francisco and 69.94 percent in Denver. US Airways controls 89.61 percent in Pittsburgh. Continental controls 77.19 percent in Houston and 51.41 percent in Newark. Northwest controls 78.62 percent in Detroit and 84.45 percent in Minneapolis. TWA controls 67.45 percent in St. Louis. As we go to press, the U.S. government is stepping in to help make the Big Seven airlines play fair, in terms of competition with low-cost carriers.

The skies became safer and overall safety improved. Keep in mind that there are more

Number of passengers who flew on U.S. carrier domestic flights in 1997: 546,157,000.

people flying than ever before. In the past five years there has been only 0.509 fatal accidents per million flights. Odds are even better on specific itineraries with 0.166 per million on U.S. and Caribbean flights; 0.463 on European flights. The catastrophic nature of some airline crashes has an enormous impact, but you can walk on a plane with more confidence today than ever before. Airlines are finally being forced to spend $400 million to equip 3,700 jet aircraft cargo holds with fire detectors. Wiring issues are being addressed. Keeping seat belts on throughout every flight will soon be the rule of the industry.

Low-cost carrier travel to Europe expanded, even though Sir Freddie Laker's groundbreaking Laker Airways stopped their Florida-London service. Several carriers offering service between the U.S. and Europe expanded their routes and offered some great fares, including bargains on one-way and premium class travel. CityBird was the standout new entry with $99 one-way promotional fares between Brussels and six North American cities. Southwest began codeshares with Icelandair. Martinair, Tower and LTU (among others) continued their aggressive pricing.

Asia became a hot international market and one of the best travel bargains due to the drop in the Asian stock market. Fares dropped by as much as 60 percent and special offers abounded.

The Wright Amendment was seriously challenged. It was enacted in 1979 to protect the then-fledgling Dallas/Fort Worth International Airport from competition at Dallas Love Field. It limited flights out of Love Field to airports within Texas and in adjacent states. Now, additional nonstop flights from Love Field to Alabama, Kansas and Mississippi are allowed. Legend Airlines (and any other carrier who chooses to enter the market) will be allowed to reconfigure DC-9 aircraft to carry 56 passengers (the Wright Amendment exemption limit) and begin flights out of Love Field. Legend plans to target business markets in the Midwest, East and Southeast. Even though the legal battle over Love Field continues, change is definitely on the wing.

This year's level of change in basic airline policies is notable. Some airlines experimented with cancelling confirmed reservations if travel agents did not ticket them within one hour. Revalidation stickers for changes in flight schedule were banned. Lost ticket fees went up. Many airlines increased their fee for pre-paid tickets. Policies for children flying alone changed on many airlines.

***Friends Fly Free* became a teaser.** After years of taking Southwest's two-for-one program for granted, passengers were given specific booking windows for *Friends Fly Free*. This change affected many other airlines' companion fares as they played their usual game of follow the leader.

Travelers accumulated more and more miles but found it harder and harder to use them. There wasn't a marked decrease in award travel availability, just more and more passengers vying for the seats. American AAdvantage, for example, has over 30 million members. If only 1/2 of one percent elected to use their miles for travel to Hawaii, the airline would have to fill two DC-10s per day with award ticket travelers–and they would still leave passengers at the gate. Almost a third of all award tickets issued now involve the payment of a fee for things like changing an itinerary, not booking at least three weeks

Number of passengers who flew on U.S. carrier international flights in 1997: 52,738,000.

in advance or cancelling your flight and requesting that your miles be moved back into your account. Many airlines began auctioning dream trips, trying to erase some of the miles from the debit side of their ledgers. America West kept domestic award tickets for frequent flyers at 20,000 miles, 5,000 miles less than other major carriers. TWA offered a 15,000 mile award ticket for shorthaul roundtrips but raised their longhaul award travel cost to 25,000 miles. Northwest continued to offer 20,000 mile award travel during specific seasons. United came up with reduced award travel for two people flying together on shorthaul routes. Southwest maintained their status as the only major airline that keeps award travel wide open. If there is an available seat on the flight, it's yours.

The percentage of jets on regional routes doubled and will continue to grow. This was the key issue in the American Airlines strike and one that is being decided in the consumer's interest. On more and more routes, you will either find all jet service or you will have a choice between turboprop and jet service if you are willing to be flexible about flight times.

In-flight amenities expanded as part of the fight for improved market share. Coach passengers experienced an increase in the availability of in-flight phones and, on a few airlines, improvements in meal service after last year's cutbacks (passenger feedback *does* have an effect). Premium class travelers were given more leg room, improved seating, even better meals, powerports for laptops and competitive amenities that went as far as limousine transportation to and from the airport. Technological improvements began to reach to the back of the cabin.

The DOT went to bat for passengers. The Department of Transportation mandated that all airlines and travel agents make *Conditions of Contract* more available to consumers opting for ticketless travel, stopped airlines from requiring a 48-hour notice from physically challenged passengers flying on 19 to 30 seat aircraft, began investigating predatory pricing policies and took a long overdue look at frequent flyer programs.

One of the negative side effects of crowded skies became very evident in the form of a dramatic increase in unruly and even violent passenger behavior. Airlines began to get tough on obnoxious or dangerous behavior in-flight after a year that brought incidents including a businessman defecating on a food cart and a passenger hitting a flight attendant with a wine bottle after not receiving the special meal he had ordered.

AirTran began offering First Class seats for only slightly more than Coach travel. Their merge with the former ValuJet gave business travelers a new range of options for low-cost premium class travel.

America West dropped senior airfare coupons entirely, then brought them back several months later. Four airlines deleted the cost-effective eight coupon option. TWA and Continental are currently the only two major carriers that still give you a choice of four or eight coupons. Continental, Delta, Northwest and United introduced or expanded senior discount programs that, in many cases, offered better value than senior coupons and often included dramatically discounted First Class travel. American and Delta introduced senior discount membership programs.

America West added First Class cabins to its entire fleet, then launched the new additions with special *Go First* fares for First Class travel. These promotional fares offered

U.S. cities with the largest 1997 increase in airfares: Richmond and San Diego.

confirmed First Class at full fare Excursion rates—a savings of 50 to 80 percent. They lasted through the summer then came back on special promotional routes.

American Airlines had to rebound from a 28-minute pilots' strike that had a major impact on consumer perception of the airline. They started with a 50-percent-off fare sale and added double miles and free space available upgrades to AAdvantage members. They also offered the cheapest one-way of the year: $22 for Indianapolis-Chicago (seniors paid just $19). The legendary Robert Crandall took early retirement and left American Airlines under the leadership of Don Carty.

Continental added new flights to Birmingham, Dusseldorf, Lisbon, Moscow, Rio de Janeiro and Sao Paulo and continued to score high in consumer Frequent Flyer surveys.

Delta became the number one U.S. carrier for transatlantic travel (in terms of passengers flown) and offered more international flights than any of its competitors. They also offered the cheapest coast-to-coast roundtrip of 1997: $98 for Miami-Seattle, published as a **www.bestfare.com** Snooze You Lose deal.

Northwest permanently cut 21-day advance leisure fares by up to 40 percent. This was one of the boldest moves since Bob Crandall of American Airlines introduced value pricing in April of 1992 (since then, there have been over 38 fare increases). The biggest plus to this new pricing structure is that it allows travelers heading to hot destinations to get a fare discount without waiting for a fare war and the blackout dates that come with it. The biggest negative: systemwide fare war discounts have not been as generous, though fare wars targeting specific markets continue to offer outstanding reductions.

Southwest won its fifth consecutive Triple Crown award, a distinction unmatched by any other carrier. They acknowledged the honor by painting the name of every Southwest employee on a specially-commissioned 737.

Southwest and America West won the title of most aggressive discounters in coast-to-coast markets. Southwest often came in at $196 roundtrip; America West at $238. They forced their competitors to match their aggressive pricing.

TWA became the first airline to award frequent flyer miles for miles flown and for each dollar paid for a full fare ticket. This ongoing offer is part of an aggressive strategy to lure more high revenue business travelers to the airline. Passengers flying on unrestricted full fare tickets (C, F or Y) are also allowed access to 23 TWA Ambassadors Clubs on their days of travel. They also dropped almost all 747 service, leaving Tower Air as the only airline offering 747 service coast-to-coast.

USAir became US Airways, revamped its frequent flyer program, dropped jet service to 11 cities and announced MetroJet low-cost airline, flying routes under 1,000 miles.

The skies became more crowded than ever before. Major airlines reported all- time record load levels. In November 1997 (the month that includes the busiest travel day of the year) several airlines posted all-time records. Four airlines recorded their highest passenger load level for a single day on the Sunday following Thanksgiving: America West, Continental (an amazing 90.7 percent), United and US Airways. Other airlines, including Midwest Express and TWA, posted record load levels for the month.

U.S. cities with the largest 1997 decrease in airfares: Denver and Detroit.

Passenger screening went into effect. Some passenger/bag matching now occurs on domestic flights and some passengers are singled out for additional screening. For security reasons, the exact criteria used to single out passengers and the number of passengers per flight who will be subject to extra scrutiny are not disclosed. We can reasonably assume that passengers flying on one-way tickets and passengers purchasing tickets by cash or check will have increased odds of being scrutinized. Frequent flyers are least likely to be singled out, but no one can consider themselves exempt from profiling. To help avoid the possibility of terrorists trying to beat the system by figuring out profiling criteria, some passengers on each flight will be selected at random. The Federal Aviation Administration has not yet made profiling mandatory but most (if not all) major airlines are expected to comply voluntarily. Smaller carriers (with less sophisticated computer systems) will follow.

Several major carriers lowered carry-on limits from two per passenger to one. United kicked it off with the announcement of a test limit in Des Moines and followed up with systemwide restrictions. Northwest announced a limit for travelers on bargain tickets: one carry-on plus a briefcase, laptop or purse. We may be looking at almost across-the-board standards, counting laptops against carry-on limits. The squeeze is definitely on.

> *"My favorite use of **www.bestfares.com** is bringing consumers travel bargains. I also like to use it to help consumers stay on top of the many changes in the industry, particularly those that directly affect the way you fly and the price you pay for a ticket. In the early days of our site, we were tested by the American Airlines pilot strike and we rose to the challenge, not only scooping many major media outlets, but offering practical options for travelers who would be affected by the strike. We took a pervasive consumer-oriented view and helped out cruise travelers booked on American for travel to their embarkation port, passengers heading to the Caribbean on routes dominated by American and travelers mystified about future travel planning. When Pan Am and Western Pacific shut down, we outlined passenger options and posted them within minutes of the shutdowns. When re-issue fees began creeping up, we let travelers know about each airline as it joined the price increase bandwagon. We even established links to let passengers know which movies would be shown on their flights. Our goal is to keep you informed on every change and every bit of information you need to keep you flying high on a cheap ticket."*

GETTING THE BEST BANG FOR YOUR BUCK

SNOOZE YOU LOSE FARES

Snooze You Lose Deals are unique to **www.bestfares.com** and represent the very best in air travel deals, with savings of up to 90 percent off standard 21-day excursion fares and inexpensive no Saturday stay fares for business travelers. For years, the airlines have dramatically reduced select fares in one another's key markets (as a way to communicate with one another) but consumers had no way to know about them. *Best Fares* Online took these marketing signals and made them available to air travelers. Were the airlines shocked when people began booking these mystery fares? You bet. We received letters and e-mail from people who had airline reservation agents tell them that fares this low didn't exist. Since we include the fare codes in each Snooze You Lose deal, consumers knew the magic numbers and were able to get almost unbelievable roundtrip fares (many not requiring Saturday night stays):

- Dallas/Fort Worth-Belize at $130
- Atlanta-Honolulu at $339
- Houston-New York at $67
- Salt Lake City-New York at $88
- Denver or Dallas/Fort Worth to

Honolulu at $170

- Dallas/Fort Worth, Houston or Atlanta to San Jose (Costa Rica) at $188
- Coast-to-coast from 11 West Coast cities to nine East Coast cities for $159
- Dallas/Fort Worth, Cincinnati, Atlanta or Miami to San Francisco or Seattle for $98
- Los Angeles-Hong Kong at $399
- New York-Cairo at $499 (a regular $1,500 fare)
- Boston, New York or Washington to Honolulu at $298

INTERNET BARGAINS

The past year has brought about an explosion of airfare deals by internet. We're proud to say that *Best Fares* Online leads the pack with the most comprehensive travel bargain information in existence. We've received accolades from The *Washington Post* and *USA Today*. Our site is updated several times each day, and offers travelers hundreds of ways to save.

***Best Fares* Online also tracks** airfare promotions, publishes a Wednesday summary of major airline weekly internet discounts and packs the subscriber side of the site with Hidden Travel Deals that offer free and reduced companion fare tickets, two-for-one travel and the most complete information on airline discount coupons in existence. A great deal of this information is available to the general public. Additional airline bargain information is offered on a subscriber only aspect of the site.

An ever-growing number of travel news and bargain sites appeared in the past two years. We believe that **www.bestfares.com** gives you the most comprehensive array of bargains, but here is a list of sites we always check:

- **www.abcnews.com** (click on travel)
- **www.expedia.com**
- **www.frommer.com**
- **www.travelocity.com**
- **www.previewtravel.com**
- **www.biztravel.com**
- **www.webflyer.com**
- **www.usatoday.com**
- **www.itn.com**
- **www.1travel.com**

Weekly major airline airfare discounts by internet offer another great source for bargain air travel. Airlines look over their load factors for the coming weekend, and slash fares on routes in need of passengers. What started as simple Wednesday internet postings or e-mail has grown into a maze of offers appearing on different days of the week and sometimes allowing travel weeks or months in the future—not just for the coming weekend. *Best Fares* Online covers them all, including a Wednesday afternoon summary of all major airline offers, listed by city. We provide the easiest way to access these discounts. You don't have to wade through pages of e-mail to find the departure city you need. It's not unusual for us to post 650-750 internet airfare specials each week.

Following is a summary of all airline weekly internet discount programs. For the most part, travel can originate in any city posted that week. Exceptions include international travel (which usually must originate in the U.S.), some internet specials to Hawaii (which usually must originate on the mainland) and US Airways fares which must originate in a specified city.

First airline to offer online redemption of frequent flyer award miles: US Airways.

INTERNET PROGRAMS		
AIRLINE	**TRAVEL DATES**	**SPECIAL NOTES**
Air Canada Websavers 800-776-3030 www.aircanada.ca	Depart Friday on or after 7 p.m. or any time Saturday; return the following Monday or Tuesday.	Released each Wednesday by e-mail. You must be enrolled in the Websaver e-mail program or have access to the e-mail of a member. Includes Avis, Hertz, Hilton, Radisson and Fiesta Americana discounts in select cities.
Alaska Web Specials 800-307-6946 www.alaskaair.com	Depart Saturday; return the following Monday or Tuesday.	Posted each Friday online, giving you a week's lead time. Includes U.S. and Mexico destinations. You must book by phone and use e-ticketing.
America West Surf 'n Go 800-325-9292 www.americawest.com	Purchase by Friday for Saturday departure; return the following Monday or Tuesday.	Posted each Wednesday. Online booking is required.
American Net SAAvers 800-344-6702 www.aa.com	Depart Friday after 7 p.m. (Friday travel may not be available in all markets) or anytime Saturday; return the following Monday or Tuesday.	Released each Wednesday by e-mail. Includes discounts for American Fly AAway Vacations; Hilton and Alamo discounts are available in select cities.
American International Net SAAvers 800-344-6702 www.aa.com	Depart Thursday and return the following Monday or depart Friday and return the following Monday or Tuesday.	Released each Monday by e-mail. Travel must originate in the U.S. Includes Alamo, Avis, Fiesta Americana, and Wyndham discounts in select cities.
American Trans Air 800-435-9282 www.ata.com	Reduced one-way fares are announced for as many as eight city pairs; travel on specific dates that may extend one to three weeks in the future.	Posted each Wednesday online. Roundtrip travel is not required.
Canadian Web Speci@ls 800-665-1177 Canada 800-426-7000 U.S. www.cdnair.ca	Depart Friday on or after 7 p.m. or any time Saturday; return the following Monday or Tuesday.	Posted online each Wednesday. A coupon code specific to each itinerary is required.

First U.S. carrier to offer direct online booking via its home page: Alaska.

INTERNET PROGRAMS		
AIRLINE	TRAVEL DATES	SPECIAL NOTES
Continental Online (CO.O.L.) 800-642-1617 www.flycontinental.com	Depart Saturday and return the following Monday or Tuesday.	Released each Wednesday by e-mail. Hilton, Radisson and National discounts are available in select cities.
Continental International Online 800-642-1617 www.flycontinental.com	Depart Monday through Thursday and stay a maximum of six days on some itineraries.	Released Fridays by e-mail. Includes Fiesta Americana discounts in select cities.
Delta Escape Plan www.delta-air.com	Limited to members in specific cities (Atlanta, Cincinnati, Dallas/Fort Worth and New York).	Released by e-mail each Sunday. Check *Best Fares* Online for the latest enrollment opportunities.
Kiwi International Internet Specials 800-538-5494 www.jetkiwi.com	Discounts travel on one to three city pairs.	Posted online each Wednesday. One-way travel is allowed.
Northwest CyberSavers 800-692-6961 www.nwa.com	Depart Saturday and return the following Monday after 11 a.m. or Tuesday before 11:59 p.m.	Posted each Wednesday online. Radisson and National discounts are available in select cities.
Southwest Net Specials www.southwest.com	Usually valid for travel for several months; includes selections from all 53 Southwest Airlines cities.	Released each Tuesday with a 72-hour booking window. Online booking required.
TWA Hot Fares 800-221-2000 www.twa.com	Purchase by Friday; depart Saturday and return the following Monday or Tuesday.	Posted each Tuesday online. Includes discounts for Getaway Vacations; Hilton and Alamo discounts are available in select cities.
TWA Hot Fares International 800-221-2000 www.twa.com	Purchase by Saturday for Saturday departure and return the following Tuesday or Wednesday.	Posted select Tuesdays as part of domestic internet specials. Travel must originate in the U.S.
United E-Fares www.ual.com	Depart Saturday and return the following Monday or Tuesday.	Posted Wednesday. Online booking required.
US Airways E-Savers 888-359-3728 www.usairways.com	Depart Saturday and return the following Sunday, Monday or Tuesday.	Posted Wednesday. Travel must originate in listed US Airways hub and mini-hub cities.

Month in which Microsoft Expedia hit $1 million in weekly online sales: February 1997.

Major airlines also use the internet for target market discounts. American periodically offers discounts for college students. Delta (with a weekly internet discount program for subscribers only) periodically posts sale fares for the general public for travel to and from a specific city. Most airlines promote online booking by offering bonus miles or points.

Low-cost and niche carriers also use the internet to post special sale fares. AirTran, posts on Wednesdays. Southwest pops up on Tuesdays. LTU and other low-cost international carriers offer discounts by e-mail.

SPECIAL PROMOTIONS

Airfare coupons are the buried treasure of airline discounts. Clipping grocery coupons to save fifty-cents is one thing; acquiring an airline coupon worth as much as several hundred dollars quite another. Some coupons provide free or discounted companion tickets; some give you free upgrades. Others are like hundred dollar bills attached to commonly purchased products. Often, it's worth buying a nominally priced product just to get the airline coupon. You can even use them on most fare war prices.

The newest version of airline discount coupons is the $99 or free companion ticket offer. You get the deal by booking a roundtrip ticket online. American, Delta and Northwest have offered these promotions off and on all year. They're trying to compel you to purchase more tickets online. Is it as simple as checking their sites? Not really. Sometimes you get the deals only on a specific online booking engine separate from the airline's online booking site.

Every major U.S. airline and many international airlines issue discount coupons. Some deals recur year after year. Some coupon offers pop up in surprising places: attached to a pair of boxer shorts, for example, or a preschooler's toy. Thousands of stores at any given point in time have airline discounts hidden in their merchandise, but you have to know where to look. Take your film to Joe's drugstore one week and you get a $100-off airline coupon. The next week, the deal may have moved to Rosie's pharmacy down the street. No single traveler can keep up with all the deals. For 14 years we have included the best of them in *Best Fares* Magazine and now, on *Best Fares* Online.

If you travel often, you're going to find a time and place to use almost any major airline coupon. If you travel less frequently (or if your business travel is covered by your company) you want to be sure that the coupon you're after covers the travel you want to do. That means heading for the fine print before you commit. If you come across a coupon promotion and all fine print details aren't there, note the promotion code and call the airline. They can fill you in.

- **Check travel and blackout dates.** Look for extended travel periods and coupons that allow travel on some dates during peak summer and holidays travel periods. Note advance purchase and minimum/maximum stay requirements. Most coupons require a Saturday stay. Coupons without that requirement are highly desirable. Two-for-one coupons that can be used with a Saturday stay can be extremely valuable to business travelers.

- **Check the classes of travel** covered (or excluded). Delta promoted a $99 companion deal recently that excluded L class—one of the most frequently used bargain fares. The coupon is still

Radio spots Southwest Airlines purchased to advertise their first off-peak fare: one.

worth having, but it is a limitation worth knowing.

- **On coupons for incremental discounts** based on ticket price, make sure travel out of your hometown isn't subject to special rules. Continental frequently limits coupon discounts for travel out of Cleveland, Houston or Newark to $25; Northwest coupons may exclude travel to or from Minnesota and Michigan; TWA coupons may limit discounts on travel in or out of St. Louis.
- **If you have to send for the coupon** and want to use it for a specific trip, make sure you have time to receive it and meet any advance purchase requirement.
- **Determine how many passengers** can use the coupon. Most allow either one, two or four passengers; a few allow as many as seven.
- **If a coupon comes with a purchase,** you are usually free to give it to anyone who can use it. Some discount coupons are issued with your name printed on the coupon. These may not be transferable but read the fine print; some of them are.

TRACKING THE HOT PROMOTIONS

We don't want you to feel bad about what you missed, but we do want you to know the wide variety of bargains at your disposal when you keep on top of discount deals. Many of these promotions appear for a limited time each year. If you don't know when they're in effect, you miss out. It doesn't matter where you want to go or which airline you prefer—there is usually a deal that can get you there for less. Here is a small sample of hidden travel promotions that *Best Fares* recently revealed.

Free Ticket Offers

Free American roundtrip with the purchase of a $299.95 Sony satellite system.

Free roundtrip to Vancouver with the purchase of a discounted $729-779 roundtrip to Hong Kong.

Free Virgin Atlantic companion roundtrip to London with the purchase of a $55 golf kit.

Free Aeromexico or British Airways roundtrip for flying premium class and writing a letter explaining why you did not believe their service was the best.

Free TWA companion roundtrip to any destination worldwide, First Class or Economy Coach, with enrollment in a $100 per year preferred guest program.

Free American domestic roundtrip with the purchase of a pro hockey season ticket.

Children fly free to Europe on Aer Lingus with adult fares purchased at sale prices.

Free Virgin Atlantic companion roundtrip to London for buying seven music CDs.

Free China Airlines companion roundtrip to passengers flying on their birthday and accompanied by a full fare passenger.

Two-for-one Business and First Class international travel on 14 airlines for American Express Platinum cardmembers.

Free Virgin Atlantic companion roundtrip to London to American Express cardmembers who have a special code.

Free roundtrip air to Hawaii when you book seven hotel nights and pay with

American Express.

Kids fly free on Delta Shuttle with the purchase of one adult fare.

Free Aeromexico roundtrip to resort cities with the purchase of a roundtrip ticket.

Kids fly free to Hawaii with the purchase of two adult roundtrips.

Free companion roundtrips on Lufthansa to over 35 European cities.

Reduced Companion Tickets

$99 American companion roundtrips with a $49.95 membership in *AAdvantage Exclusives*, a club that offers frequent flyer benefits.

$99 Delta companion roundtrips for filling out a brief survey and charging your ticket on American Express.

$199 Coach/$399 First Class Continental companion roundtrips for visiting one of 110 West Coast health clubs.

$99 American companion roundtrips with a single stay at any participating Fairmont or Loews Hotel.

Half-price Qantas or Air New Zealand companion roundtrips with the purchase of a published fare ticket.

Half-price Delta companion fares for SkyMiles members who sign up for the Delta American Express Optima card.

Half-price US Airways companion roundtrips to Florida plus over $500 in additional travel discounts.

Discount Zone Fares

Continental discount roundtrips starting at $198 with a $25 purchase at Northeast malls.

Northwest discount roundtrips starting at $258 when you charge your tickets on Visa.

America West discount roundtrips starting at $108 with a $50 food store purchase.

United discount roundtrips starting at $109 (for up to seven passengers traveling together) with an AT&T True Rewards promotion.

TWA discount roundtrips starting at $180 with a $75 department store purchase.

America West discount roundtrips starting at $109 with a coupon available from a long distance carrier.

TWA discount roundtrips starting at $168 with a financial transaction at any of 20 Chicago-area banks.

Two $159-239 Continental roundtrips for travel anywhere within the U.S. plus three additional discounts for students acquiring a no-fee credit card.

Northwest discount roundtrips starting at $188 with a $100 purchase at Kroger food stores.

TWA discount roundtrips starting at $178 with a $100 grocery purchase.

America West discount roundtrips starting at $130 when you join a credit union.

TWA discount roundtrips starting at $148 for students attending nationwide Health & Fitness Fairs.

Midway discount roundtrips starting at $149 with a $50 grocery purchase at East Coast food stores.

Other Valuable Promotions

Up to $300 off American with the purchase of a $35 piece of luggage from a nationwide retailer.

Northwest's 1993 promotion: "Adults Fly Free" (with each child's ticket purchased).

Up to $125 off Continental with a coupon tucked in any of 12 videos.

Instant TWA elite frequent flyer status and a $200 discount coupon after one night's hotel stay.

Free Delta upgrade worldwide for filling out a brief survey and charging your ticket on American Express.

Free Virgin Atlantic inter-Europe roundtrip, Eurostar train or Avis rental car when you book a transatlantic flight.

$50 off America West or a free upgrade plus a $198 companion fare certificate with a free Best Western guide.

$299 coast-to-coast on American with no Saturday stay, for a $100 grocery purchase.

Free companion ticket or airfare discount on multiple airlines when you upgrade your credit card or are accepted for a new card.

Free Reno Air First Class upgrade when you travel on your birthday.

Instant elite frequent flyer status on several airlines for travelers holding elite status on any other carrier.

Up to $4,100 in American and Continental discounts in a regional discount directory priced at $38-48.

Up to $2,000 in American and Canadian Airlines discounts with the purchase of a $43 travel discount directory.

Up to $100 off each of two roundtrips on your choice of airlines with the purchase of a $17.95 commemorative baseball.

Up to $150 off US Airways plus five gifts when you book a fly/drive package to Orlando and pay with Visa.

Up to $100 off Continental when you book one night at any Super 8 Motel.

25 percent off Kiwi full fare tickets for saying the code word "Yankee."

Up to $500 off America West roundtrips originating in Alaska.

$50 off United in a counter display at hundreds of car rental, hotel and camera shop locations.

$25 off any Southwest fare with a $25 Advantage rental car.

Up to $100 off each of four Continental roundtrips with any luggage purchase from a nationwide retailer.

Up to $100 off TWA with a $100 purchase at any of 80 U.S. or Canada Sportsmart Superstores.

Up to $200 off United when you join a travel club at a $1 trial membership fee.

Up to $150 off each of two American roundtrips with a $299 Magnavox purchase.

Up to $125 off Northwest or KLM with a $100 grocery purchase.

$50 off American for opening a department store charge account.

$25 off Southwest with a $75 luggage purchase.

> *"My favorite way to use discounts is to pile them up. Double whammies—two discounts on one ticket—are terrific. Triple whammies almost make buying airline tickets fun. Wait for a fare war (discount #1), find an alternate city routing that offers a significantly lower price (discount #2) and use one of the free companion tickets or dollars-off coupons you've been collecting (discount #3)."*

Year in which the Civil Aeronautics Board formally approved "Super Saver" fares: 1977.

Up to $100 off Continental for processing one roll of film at any of 3,000 stores nationwide.

$25 off United with a $25 Starbuck's purchase.

$50-75 off Aeromexico when you charge your tickets on American Express and mention a promotion code.

Up to $125 off Northwest to members of Marriott Honored Guest Awards.

LOW-COST & NICHE AIRLINES

One of the best ways to get the lowest fares is to keep up with where all low-cost and niche and airlines fly. These dynamic carriers allow us to create our own system of airfare options. They can even help when you are traveling to some cities without low-cost or niche service by providing a low-cost alternate airport option. Low-cost carriers offer point-to-point pricing and simplified fare structures. Major airlines usually match low-cost carrier fares. As a result, overall prices go down, sometimes by as much as 75 percent during promotional periods. This has happened even in cases where just one low-cost airline serves a market. When Southwest Airlines originally entered Baltimore, fares went down and traffic went up. Now Baltimore is a vital low-cost airport. Florida was once a high-ticket destination. Now, with the presence of Southwest, AirTran, Delta Express and MetroJet it can be one of the most value-priced destinations in the U.S.

Low-cost and niche airlines offer great one-way prices because they don't penalize you for not purchasing a roundtrip. This is a big plus for business travelers who prefer not to stay over a Saturday night, or leisure travelers seeking a cheap one-way ticket. You can even get good last-minute fares because their walk-up rates are far lower than the fares majors charge when advance purchase requirements are not met. Low-cost and niche airlines also tend to allocate a higher percentage of seats to their lowest prices than do their major carrier competitors.

Some low-cost and niche airlines base their fares on advance purchase and peak and off-peak times, varying by airline. Others use inventory-controlled pricing: a certain number of seats are sold at the lowest price, then the fare goes up to the next increment. Inventory-controlled fares are not usually affected by advance purchase requirements, but your chance of getting the lowest fare improves when you can book in advance.

First Class travel on low-cost carriers can be a definite bargain. AirTran, Tower, ProAir and Reno offer premium class travel for as little as $25 more per direction. In 1997, America West offered promotions with discounts of up to 70 percent on First Class published fares.

> *"The General Accounting Office tracked the percentage of decrease in airfares created by the entry of a strong low-cost carrier into particular markets. Some examples: Albuquerque/32.4 percent, El Paso/31.5 percent, Harlingen/20.1 percent, Houston Hobby/28.3 percent, Kansas City/25.1 percent, Las Vegas/32.2 percent, Midland/31.1 percent, Phoenix/32.4 percent, Reno/21.1 percent, San Diego/24.1 percent, Seattle/27.1 percent and Tucson/22.7 percent."*

Highest ranking woman at a major U.S. airline: Colleen Barrett, Southwest.

Low-cost carriers are also available for international travel. For travel to Europe, options include CityBird, Icelandair, LTU, Spanair and Tower. Within Europe options include Air Europa, British Midland, Debonair and Spanair.

Low-cost and niche airlines tend to be dynamic, adding new routes frequently. *Best Fares* Magazine and *Best Fares* Online monitor these changes and the introductory airfare offers they bring. Low-cost carriers also tend to be very creative with promotions. For example, Kiwi offered free roundtrip Fourth of July travel to anyone whose name matched the name of any of the original signers of the Declaration of Independence.

The following information updates low-cost carrier routes and is accurate at press time. *Best Fares* Magazine publishes a monthly update. *Best Fares* Online publishes changes, as they occur. We include several scheduled charter airlines: Myrtle Beach Jet Express, SunJet and Sun Country. Each listing includes the types of aircraft used by the airline, the hub city or cities (in italics) and contact information.

Low-cost carrier frequent flyer programs are offered by America West, Aspen Mountain Air/Lone Star (via American AAdvantage), Corporate Express, Delta Express (Delta SkyMiles), Eastwind (business travelers only), Frontier & Gulfstream (via Continental OnePass), Kiwi, Mesa, MetroJet (via U.S. Airways Dividend Miles), Midway (via American AAdvantage), Reno (its own and American AAdvantage), Southwest, Tower and Vanguard.

AirTran Airways

800-247-8726 or 800-825-8538

Aircraft types: 737s and DC9s

Akron/Canton, Albany, Allentown, *Atlanta*, Bloomington (IL), Boston, Buffalo, Chicago Midway, Dallas/Fort Worth, Dayton, Des Moines, Flint, Fort Lauderdale, Fort Myers, Fort Walton Beach, Greensboro (NC), Greenville/ Spartanburg, Houston Hobby, Islip, Jacksonville, Knoxville, Memphis, Mobile, Moline, Newburgh, New Orleans, Newport News/Norfolk, New York LaGuardia, Omaha, *Orlando*, Philadelphia, Raleigh/Durham, Richmond, Rochester (NY), Savannah, Syracuse, Tampa, Toledo, Washington Dulles & West Palm Beach

America West

800-235-9292

Aircraft types: 737s, 757s, A320s and B19s

Acapulco, Albuquerque, Atlanta, Austin, Baltimore, Boston, Burbank, Chicago Midway & O'Hare, Cleveland, Colorado Springs, *Columbus (OH)*, Dallas/Fort Worth, Denver, Detroit, El Paso, Fort Lauderdale, Fort Myers, Houston Intercontinental, Indianapolis, Ixtapa, Kansas City, *Las Vegas*, Long Beach, Los Angeles, Los Cabos, Manzanillo, Mazatlan, Mexico City, Miami, Milwaukee, Minneapolis, Newark, New York JFK & LaGuardia, Oakland, Omaha, Ontario (CA), Orange County, Orlando, Palm Springs, Philadelphia, *Phoenix*, Portland (OR), Puerto Vallarta, Reno, Sacramento, St. Louis, Salt Lake City, San Antonio, San Diego, San Francisco, San Jose, Seattle, Tampa, Tucson, Vancouver, Washington Dulles & National, West Palm Beach & Wichita

American Trans Air

800-225-2995

Aircraft types: 1011s, 727s and 737s

Cancun, *Chicago Midway*, Dayton, Des Moines, Fort Lauderdale, Fort Myers,

Grand Rapids, Honolulu, *Indianapolis*, Lansing, Las Vegas, Los Angeles, Madison, Maui, Milwaukee, Montego Bay, Nassau, New York JFK, Orlando, Phoenix, St. Petersburg/Clearwater, San Francisco, San Juan & Sarasota

Aspen Mountain Air/Lone Star

800-877-3932

Aircraft types: DC30s and M23s

Abilene, Aspen, Austin, Brownwood, Chihuahua City, Corpus Christi, *Dallas/Fort Worth*, Del Rio, Denver, Eldorado/Magnolia, El Paso, Enid, Harrison, Hot Springs, Jonesboro, Knoxville, Mountain Home, Pensacola, Ponca City, Roswell & Ruidoso (NM), St. Louis, Santa Fe (NM), Torreon (Mexico) & Tyler

Atlantic Airlines

800-879-0000

Aircraft type: Turboprops

Baton Rouge, Beaumont, Gainesville, Gulfport/Biloxi, Houston Hobby & Intercontinental, Jacksonville (FL), Lafayette, Lake Charles, Lakeland (FL), Mobile, New Orleans, *Orlando*, Panama City, Pensacola & Tallahassee

Cape Air

800-352-0714

Aircraft type: C402s

Boston, Fort Lauderdale, Fort Myers, *Hyannis*, *Key West*, Marthas Vineyard, Nantucket, Naples (FL), New Bedford, Providence & Provincetown

CityBird

888-248-9247

Aircraft type: MD11s

Brussels, Cancun, Los Angeles, Mexico City, Miami, Newark, Oakland, Orlando & Puerto Vallarta

Corporate Express

800-555-6565

Aircraft type: J32s

Atlanta, *Nashville* & Tri-Cities (TN)

Delta Express

800-325-5205

Aircraft type: 737s

Boston, Columbus (OH), Fort Lauderdale, Fort Myers, Hartford, Indianapolis, Islip, Louisville, Nashville, Newark, *Orlando*, Providence, Raleigh/ Durham, Tampa, Washington Dulles & West Palm Beach

Eastwind

800-644-3592

Aircraft type: 737s

Boston, Fort Lauderdale, Greensboro, Orlando, Tampa, *Trenton* & Washington Dulles

Frontier

800-432-1359

Aircraft type: 737s

Albuquerque, Baltimore, Bloomington (IL), Boston, Chicago Midway, *Denver*, El Paso, Los Angeles, Minneapolis/St. Paul, New York LaGuardia, Omaha, Phoenix, Salt Lake City, San Francisco & Seattle

Gulfstream

800-992-8532

Aircraft type: T9s

Fort Lauderdale, Freeport, Gainesville, Jacksonville, Key West, Marsh Harbour, *Miami*, Nassau, North Eleuthera, Orlando, Tallahassee, Tampa, Treasure Cay & West Palm Beach

Unique name of regional airline in the U.K.: Suckling Airways.

Kiwi International

800-538-5494

Aircraft type: 727s

Aguadilla, Atlanta, Boston, Chicago Midway, Las Vegas, *Newark*, Orlando, San Juan, Tampa & West Palm Beach

Mesa

800-637-2247

Aircraft types: B1900s and J50s

Albuquerque, Almogorda, Carlsbad (NM), Clovis, Colorado Springs, Durango, Farmington, Hobbs, Las Cruces, Little Rock, *Nashville*, Roswell, Silver City (NM), Tupelo & Wichita

MetroJet

888-638-7653

Aircraft types: 737s

Baltimore, Cleveland, Fort Lauderdale, Jacksonville (FL), Manchester (NH), Miami & Providence

Midway

800-446-4392

Aircraft types: Airbus, F100s and J9s

Atlanta, Baltimore, Boston, Cancun, Charleston, Fort Lauderdale, Hartford, Myrtle Beach, Nashville, Newark, Newburgh, New York LaGuardia, Norfolk, Orlando, Philadelphia, *Raleigh/ Durham*, Savannah, Tampa, Washington National, West Palm Beach & Wilmington

Mountain Air Express

800-788-4247

Aircraft type: M9s

Long Beach & Mammoth

Myrtle Beach Jet Express

800-386-2786

Aircraft types: DC9s, MD80s, 727s and 737s

Boston, Chicago Midway, Cleveland, Detroit, *Myrtle Beach,* New York JFK & Newark

Paradise Island Airlines

800-786-7202

Aircraft types: 737s and A320s

Fort Lauderdale, Miami, Orlando, Paradise Island (Bahamas) & West Palm Beach

ProAir

800-939-9551

Aircraft type: 737s

Baltimore/Washington, *Detroit*, Fort Myers, Indianapolis, Milwaukee, Newark & Orlando

Reno Air

800-736-6247

Aircraft types: MD80s and MD90s;

Anchorage, Atlanta, Chicago O'Hare, Colorado Springs, Detroit, Gulfport/ Biloxi, Las Vegas, Los Angeles, Oklahoma City, Orange County, Portland (OR), *Reno*, St. Petersburg, San Diego, San Francisco, *San Jose*, Seattle, Tucson & Vancouver

Southwest Airlines

800-435-9792

Aircraft type: 737s

Albuquerque, Amarillo, Austin, Baltimore, Birmingham, Boise, *Burbank*, Chicago Midway, Cleveland, Columbus, Corpus Christi, *Dallas Love*, Detroit Metro, El Paso, Fort Lauderdale, Harlingen, *Houston Hobby* & Intercontinental, Indianapolis, Jackson (MS), Jacksonville (FL), Kansas City, Las Vegas, Little Rock, Los Angeles,

Number of U.S. airline pilot strikes since deregulation: four.

Louisville, Lubbock, Manchester (NH), Midland/Odessa, *Nashville*, New Orleans, *Oakland*, Oklahoma City, Omaha, Ontario (CA), Orange County, Orlando, *Phoenix*, Portland (OR), Providence, Reno, Sacramento, *St. Louis*, *Salt Lake City*, San Antonio, San Diego, San Francisco, San Jose, Seattle, Spokane, Tampa, Tucson & Tulsa

Spirit

800-772-7117

Aircraft type: DC9s

Atlantic City, Boston, Chicago Midway, Cleveland, *Detroit*, Fort Lauderdale, Fort Myers, Myrtle Beach, Newark, New York JFK, Orlando, Pittsburgh & Tampa

Sun Country

800-752-1218

Aircraft types: 727s and DC10s

Boston, Chicago O'Hare, Cleveland, Dallas/Fort Worth, Detroit, Fort Lauderdale, Harlingen, Houston, Laughlin, Los Angeles, Margarita (Venezuela), Miami, Milwaukee, *Minneapolis/St. Paul*, New Orleans, New York JFK, Phoenix, Porlamar (Venezuela), St. Louis, Salt Lake City, San Antonio, San Jose (Costa Rica), Sarasota & seasonal Caribbean destinations including Aruba and St. Maarten.

SunJet

800-478-6538

Aircraft types: 727s, 737-300s, A320s and MD80s

Dallas/Fort Worth, Fort Lauderdale, Long Beach, *Newark*, Orlando & St. Petersburg/Clearwater

Tower Air

800-348-6937

Aircraft type: 747s

Athens, Las Vegas, Los Angeles, Miami, *New York JFK*, Paris, San Francisco, San Juan, & Tel Aviv

Vanguard

800-826-4827

Aircraft type: 737s

Atlanta, Chicago Midway, Dallas/Fort Worth, Denver, *Kansas City*, Minneapolis/St. Paul, New York JFK & Pittsburgh

FARE WARS

Plan far enough in advance and you can almost always take advantage of a fare war. Recently, we've seen a new domestic fare war begin approximately two to three weeks after each previous fare war ended. If you plan at least 60 days in advance, you have a very good shot at being able to get fare war prices. When Northwest introduced "permanently" lowered 21-day advance fares (usually identified by E21 in the fare code), we began to see lower percentage discounts on fare war travel. The need to analyze each fare war has grown increasingly more important. There are regional fare wars, systemwide fare wars and mini fare wars that affect just one city pair. *Best Fares* Online helps you tell them apart.

Ask your travel agent to compare any fare war price with the E21 fare published by Continental, Northwest or United. (American and Continental currently still maintain old and new E21 levels that can be confusing.) If the fare war price is 50 percent off the E21 fare, you may want to jump on it. If it's 60 percent off (or more), don't wait; purchase immediately.

Fare wars pop up regularly because yield management people send out the word that sales need a boost. They're usually initiated at the beginning of the week. One airline starts a fare war by lowering prices on select flights (highly competitive routes are most likely to be the prime focus). Within hours other airlines in competitive markets fall in line. They might match the fares the leader initiated, or they might undercut them. Fare wars increase the already mind-boggling array of prices available on any flight. One recent fare war resulted in a total of over 250 different fares for a New York-Los Angeles roundtrip, ranging from $290-2,334.

During the first hours of a fare war, travel agents can be placed at a disadvantage by the airlines. Information on their computer systems may be incomplete. The sale fares may be listed, but the travel agents may not be able to access the fare rules or may be unable to ticket.

Book a fare war ticket too soon and you may pay too much. Airlines update fares three times a day (Monday through Friday) usually at 12:30 p.m., 5 p.m. and 8 p.m. EST. On weekends they update at 5 p.m. Saturday and 3 p.m. Sunday. When a major airline starts a fare war they try to take advantage of the 8 p.m. weekday or 3 p.m. Sunday update so the competition is prevented from matching fares until the following update time—12:30 p.m. the next day. This gives the originator a 24-hour price and advertising advantage. It can pay to wait a day or so after a fare war starts to allow the airlines time to scramble, meet prices, open up seats and try to come up with advantages that scoop the airline that initiated the price cuts.

Don't be fooled by airline ads that say they'll honor a lower fare if ticket prices go down. What they fail to mention is that you generally have to give them $60-75 in processing fees (sometimes waived if you accept the difference in airline vouchers). Alaska and Reno charge $35. Southwest has no change penalty. Unless your fare goes down dramatically, you may not come out ahead. Ask your travel agency if they will void your ticket at no cost if the fare goes down before they submit their weekly Airline Reporting Commission (ARC) report and reissue the ticket at the lower fare.

Don't assume that a fare war price is the lowest available price. A low-cost carrier may have driven the ticket price even lower on a specific daily flight. An airline not even in the fare war may offer a ticket price below the publicized discount rates. For example, Hawaiian Airlines recently offered roundtrips to Honolulu at $80 less than other carriers' fare war prices. Don't settle for a fare war discount alone. In many cases, you can use a discount coupon to bring the fare down even lower.

Mini-fare wars get less media play but can save you a lot of money. Many of them appear as *Best Fares* Online Snooze You Lose deals. They occur when two carriers enter into competition in a specific market. Big Air lowers a fare to Huge Air's hub city. Huge Air strikes back. By communicating by computer, airlines slip through a legal loophole in regulations forbidding them to discuss fares among themselves. You can take advantage of these fares if you move fast.

Some fare wars are repeated each year. For example, fare wars designed to fill the last remaining seats for holiday travel.

Amount of data being handled by American Airlines computers at any given time: six terabytes.

These deals can get you bargains on tickets for holiday travel with just a one-day advance or with no Saturday stay requirement. The 1997 Thanksgiving holiday period had feathers flying. American launched one fare war, Southwest stepped to the plate with one-way sale fares and several other fare war changes followed, all within one week. You will usually find special fares for Christmas, the Fourth of July, Labor Day, Memorial Day, Thanksgiving, New Year's and even Elvis' birthday. This past year, American offered holiday, spring break and summer roundtrip bargains for college students. We also saw Valentine's Day and Veteran's Day specials.

International fare wars recur in approximately four- to five-week cycles. There are more fare wars to Europe than to any other international destination. Plan trips to Europe at least 90-120 days in advance to help ensure a fare war reduction of 20-40 percent. By using a wholesaler, such as World Travel Network (**800-576-2242**), you could save another five to 30 percent. By combining both discount opportunities (the fare war and the wholesaler), you get a double discount.

You can know when international fare wars occur by checking your daily newspaper. Look at the front page of the business section and check for display ads that often announce major fare war initiatives. Many are also announced on radio and television news shows.

Some deals have a very limited booking window; others are more extensive. There are also internet discounts for international travel: discounts for travel the following weekend and special offers designed to fill seats on low passenger load flights. All of these deals have one thing in common: limited availability. A certain number of seats are set aside for sale fare tickets. Some peak flights may have zero availability, even when the fare sale is first announced. Travelers who are among the first to know about international fare wars (and those who can be flexible on their travel dates) have the best chance of booking the best sale fares.

> *"I have a pretty good record of predicting fare war activity. Each time one is announced, I can be found thoroughly checking fares, rules and competitors' reactions. Here is one of my favorite fare war stories. On December 3, 1997 America West announced a fare sale. Because information on new fares must be posted in airline reservation systems very quickly (competitors are always nipping at one another's heels) the person entering the data made a mistake. The sale fares were meant to be offered for travel through March 11, 1998. A slip of the finger entered them as available for travel through March 11, 1999. I found the error and posted it at **www.bestfares.com** without delay. Many travelers who could plan in advance were able to book some very good deals. Later that day, the airline caught the error (quite possibly when our online subscribers and guests called to book their tickets) and entered the correct expiration date. I empathize with the person at America West who made the error. As hard as we all try to bring you accurate information, errors happen any time you try to combine speed and accuracy. In this case, consumers profited."*

When airlines started offering two fare categories: the 1940s, with discount seats at the front of the cabin.

CREATIVE TICKETING

HIDE THIS BOOK

This is the area where airlines post their *RESTRICTED ENTRY* signs. Dracula flinches at the sight of a cross; most airlines will have the same reaction if they see you carrying this book and this section is one of the main reasons why. What is going to be extra green to you can be like a red flag to airline gate agents.

Airlines have tried to intimidate consumers and travel agents into believing that creative ticketing is a black and white situation. It's really full of shades of gray, like the tax loopholes most of us use every year. There are ways to use creative ticketing and still meet every airlines' rules. In this section, we either legitimately counter the airline's claim that creative ticketing is wrong or give you ways to use creative ticketing while staying within the boundaries of each airline's rules. The airlines won't always be happy, but you'll be walking around with a much healthier bank balance.

Many travel agents are leery of creative ticketing because the airlines have tried to fill them with fear of reprisal if they take one step outside of what the airlines want them to do. The airlines' contracts with travel agents mandate that they cannot offer creative ticketing methods to their customers, even if it saves hundreds of dollars on a single ticket. Travel agencies can't afford to lose their contract to write tickets so they often hesitate to offer creative ticketing options. We'll tell you how to use these methods without jeopardizing your agent's standing with any airline.

ALTERNATE AIRPORTS

Using alternate airports is a form of creative ticketing that no airline really objects to, but they will not offer alternate airport options when you call for reservations or book online. If you tell them you want the lowest fare from Chicago to San Francisco, that's what you'll be quoted, even if the fare to Oakland (11 miles away)

A General Disclaimer

"Many creative ticketing methods ruffle the airline's wings. We've received letters from airline legal departments stating that these practices violate their rules. They refer to Conditions of Contract, documents most air travelers never even see. We have studied these documents carefully and believe that each ticket is a separate contract. If you choose to use multiple tickets for one itinerary, you meet your responsibility as long as you abide by the rules on each individual ticket. We don't believe airlines are accurate in claiming that they have the right to guess how you will combine tickets and then react, based on an assumption. Both the Department of Justice and the Department of Transportation state that creative ticketing options are legal. They also state that airlines can deny you boarding or charge you more for your ticket if they allege that you are using certain forms of creative ticketing. Know the limits!"

is 40 percent less. If you're looking for a low one-way fare to Los Angeles and call any major airline, they are certainly not going to tell you about a low-cost carrier flying into nearby Long Beach for just $99.

A reasonable change in departure or arrival airports (or both) can save you hundreds of dollars. This can be due to a price war in a certain market, a low-cost carrier that's causing prices to fall or other market factors. Alternate airports can also get you to popular destinations at peak times, such as New Orleans' Mardi Gras. Baton Rouge is just 65 airmiles away, but when most people think about booking Mardi Gras tickets, they don't give Baton Rouge a thought. If you're heading for the nation's capital, your best bet may be Baltimore, just 30 airmiles away.

More distant alternate airports can still provide big advantages. You can save enough to pay for a private limo to your actual destination; you can use a commuter flight to get there; or you can rent a car and trade several hour's time for several hundred dollars in savings. Compare the savings against any possible inconvenience, then decide. Is $50 in savings worth an 80-mile drive? What about a $350 savings and an 80-mile drive? For example, Dallas-Cincinnati roundtrips are going for $450. Dayton, Columbus, Louisville and Indianapolis are all approximately two hours or less from Cincinnati. The airfare to any of these cities could save you up to 80 percent.

Cities served by airlines including Southwest, AirTran, and (for longhaul service) America West offer potential alternate airport savings.

The alternate airport theory also works for international travel.

- **U.S. departure airports**: Check fares from major U.S. gateway cities. If you live in Philadelphia, for example, check the fares out of New York City. Be aware of U.S. departure cities for international low-cost carriers including CityBird, LTU and Tower.
- **European arrival airports**: If you are going anywhere near London, consider using the low fares almost always available to that city, coupled with rail travel or intra-Europe air passes. Virgin Atlantic offers $69 rail or air travel within Europe when you purchase specific 21-day advance transatlantic tickets. El Al offers roundtrips from the East Coast to London's Stansted airport year-round at under $300.
- **Flights to Scandinavia**: Flying into Germany puts you 100 miles from Denmark with easy access by rail and ferry. Your ticket is likely to be a lot cheaper than if you booked a flight directly to the Scandinavian country.
- **Icelandair flies into Luxembourg** (near Belgium, France and Germany). Its fares are almost always bargains, and the airline will even assist you in discount train travel to Paris or Zurich.
- **CityBird offers great Economy and Premium fares** to Brussels, a great gateway to Europe. You can book CityBird flights for one-way travel, with no penalty.

Find alternate airports by taking out a map and looking for nearby cities. Travel agents' computer reservation systems will list alternate airports. Check cities served by low-cost carriers. Don't forget to combine alternate airport fares with discount coupons for maximum savings.

This chart lists commonly used domestic alternate airports with airmile distance from the primary airport in parentheses.

Percentage of airline fines levied by the FAA (1990-1996) that were reduced by negotiation: 80 percent.

ALTERNATE CITIES (AIRMILE DISTANCES IN PARENTHESES)	
PRIMARY AIRPORT	**ALTERNATE AIRPORTS**
AKRON	Cleveland (36); Pittsburgh (70); Columbus (99); Detroit (162)
ALBANY	Hartford (80); New York City (140)
ATLANTA	Chattanooga (106); Birmingham (134); Knoxville (152)
ATLANTIC CITY	Philadelphia (55); Newark (93); Baltimore (142)
AUSTIN	San Antonio (70); Houston (143); Dallas/Fort Worth (183)
BALTIMORE	Washington National (30); Washington Dulles (43); Harrisburg (70); Philadelphia (90); Richmond (120)
BANGOR	Portland (111); Manchester, NH (189); Boston (201)
BATON ROUGE	New Orleans (65); Pensacola (236)
BOSTON	Manchester, NH (45); Providence (49); Hartford (91)
BOISE	Salt Lake City (291)
BUFFALO	Rochester (55); Toronto (68); Pittsburgh (186); Cleveland (192)
BURBANK	Los Angeles (18); Ontario (44)
BURLINGTON (VT)	Montreal (75); Manchester, NH (137); Hartford (177);
CHARLESTON (SC)	Columbia (95); Charlotte (168); Atlanta (259)
CHARLESTON (WV)	Columbus (131); Pittsburgh (165); Cincinnati (173); Louisville (226)
CHARLOTTE (NC)	Greensboro (82); Greenville/Spartanburg (84); Raleigh (130); Atlanta (227)
CHATTANOOGA	Knoxville (87); Atlanta (106); Nashville (113)
CHICAGO	Milwaukee (75); South Bend (75)
CINCINNATI	Dayton (64); Louisville (83); Indianapolis (98); Columbus (116)
CLEVELAND	Akron (36); Toledo (102); Columbus (112); Pittsburgh (124)
COLORADO SPRINGS	Denver (67)
COLUMBUS (OH)	Dayton (72); Akron (99); Cleveland (112); Cincinnati (116)
CORPUS CHRISTI	Harlingen (110); San Antonio (135); Houston Hobby (187)
DALLAS/FORT WORTH	Oklahoma City (175); Austin (183)
DAYTON	Cincinnati (64); Columbus (72); Indianapolis (110)
DAYTONA BEACH	Orlando (50); Jacksonville (97)
DENVER	Colorado Springs (67)
DES MOINES	Omaha (117); Kansas City (165)
DETROIT	Toledo (49); Flint (54); Lansing (74); Grand Rapids (120)

Average amount of FAA fines paid by the airlines after negotiation: 25 percent.

ALTERNATE CITIES (AIRMILE DISTANCES IN PARENTHESES)	
PRIMARY AIRPORT	ALTERNATE CITIES
EUGENE	Portland (106)
EVANSVILLE (IN)	Louisville (98); Nashville (141); St. Louis (161)
FLINT	Lansing (45); Detroit (54)
FORT LAUDERDALE	Miami (21); West Palm Beach (42)
FORT MYERS	Sarasota (71); Tampa (104); Fort Lauderdale (112)
FRESNO	Oakland (152); San Francisco (159); Sacramento (167)
GRAND RAPIDS	Lansing (48); Detroit (120); Chicago (134)
GREEN BAY	Milwaukee (107); Chicago (181)
GREENSBORO	Raleigh (67); Charlotte (82)
HARLINGEN	Corpus Christi (107); San Antonio (235)
HARRISBURG	Baltimore (70); Washington National (81); Philadelphia (83); Washington Dulles (94)
HARTFORD	Providence (66); Boston (91); New York City (108)
HILTON HEAD	Savannah (31); Charleston (62); Jacksonville (133)
HOUSTON	Austin (143); San Antonio (191)
HUNTSVILLE (AL)	Birmingham (74); Nashville (97); Atlanta (151)
INDIANAPOLIS	Cincinnati (98); Dayton (110); Louisville (111)
JACKSONVILLE (FL)	Daytona Beach (93); Savannah (117); Orlando (143)
KALAMAZOO	Grand Rapids (47); Lansing (62); Detroit (113); Chicago (116)
KANSAS CITY (MO)	Omaha (152)
KEY WEST	Miami (126); Fort Lauderdale (144)
KNOXVILLE	Nashville (152); Atlanta (152); Greenville/Spartanburg (261)
LANSING	Flint (45); Grand Rapids (48); Detroit (74)
LEXINGTON	Louisville (63); Cincinnati (70)
LINCOLN	Omaha (55); Kansas City (152)
LITTLE ROCK	Memphis (130)
LOS ANGELES	Burbank (18); Long Beach (18); Orange County (36); Ontario (47)
LOUISVILLE	Cincinnati (83); Indianapolis (111); Dayton (147)
MADISON (WI)	Milwaukee (74); Chicago (119)
MANCHESTER (NH)	Boston (45); Portland (73); Providence (84)

Southwest Airlines' passengers who book shorthaul, nonstop flights: 80 percent.

ALTERNATE CITIES (AIRMILE DISTANCES IN PARENTHESES)	
PRIMARY AIRPORT	ALTERNATE CITIES
MC ALLEN	Harlingen (37); Corpus Christi (119); San Antonio (232)
MEDFORD	Portland (222)
MEMPHIS	Little Rock (130); Nashville (200)
MIAMI	Fort Lauderdale (21); West Palm Beach (62)
MILWAUKEE	Chicago (75)
MOBILE	Pensacola (64); Birmingham (216)
MONTREAL	Burlington (82); Manchester, NH (209); Boston (254)
NAPLES (FL)	Fort Myers (26); Sarasota (98); Fort Lauderdale (101); Tampa (134)
NASHVILLE	Memphis (200); Atlanta (214)
NEW ORLEANS	Baton Rouge (65); Pensacola (186)
NEW YORK	Newark (14); Philadelphia (93); Hartford (108); White Plains (204)
NEWARK	New York (14); Philadelphia (81); Hartford (115); Baltimore (179)
NORFOLK	Newport News (23); Richmond (75); Washington (142); Raleigh (160)
OAKLAND	San Francisco (11); San Jose (30); Sacramento (75)
OKLAHOMA CITY	Tulsa (111); Wichita (156); Dallas (175)
OMAHA	Des Moines (117); Kansas City (152)
ONTARIO (CA)	Orange County (30); Burbank (44); Los Angeles (47); Palm Springs (65)
ORANGE COUNTY	Long Beach (19); Ontario (30); Los Angeles (36); San Diego (76)
ORLANDO	Daytona Beach (50); Tampa (80); Gainesville (98); Jacksonville (143)
PALM SPRINGS	Ontario (65); San Diego (85); Orange County (86); Los Angeles (110)
PENSACOLA	Mobile (64); New Orleans (186)
PHILADELPHIA	Newark (81); Baltimore (90)
PHOENIX	Tucson (110)
PITTSBURGH	Akron (70); Cleveland (124); Columbus (144)
PORTLAND (ME)	Manchester, NH (78); Boston (95)

U.S. regional airline routes that will have jet service by 2002: one-third.

ALTERNATE CITIES (AIRMILE DISTANCES IN PARENTHESES)	
PRIMARY AIRPORT	ALTERNATE CITIES
PORTLAND (OR)	Seattle (129)
PROVIDENCE	Boston (49); Hartford (66); New York (146); Manchester, NH (84)
RALEIGH	Greensboro (67); Charlotte (130)
RENO	Sacramento (112); Oakland (180); San Francisco (192)
RICHMOND	Newport News (52); Norfolk (75); Washington (97); Baltimore (120)
ROANOKE	Greensboro (85); Raleigh (120); Washington (192)
ROCHESTER (NY)	Buffalo (55); Syracuse (79); Toronto (106)
SACRAMENTO	Oakland (75); San Francisco (86); Reno (112)
SAGINAW	Flint (43); Lansing (58); Detroit (98)
ST. LOUIS	Indianapolis (229)
SAN ANTONIO	Austin (70); Houston (191)
SAN DIEGO	Orange County (76); Palm Springs (86); Long Beach (96); Los Angeles (109)
SAN FRANCISCO	Oakland (11); San Jose (30); Sacramento (86)
SAN JOSE	San Francisco (30); Oakland (30)
SARASOTA	Tampa (40); Fort Myers (71); Orlando (109)
SEATTLE	Vancouver (127); Portland (129)
SHREVEPORT	Little Rock (182); Dallas/Fort Worth (190)
SOUTH BEND	Chicago (75); Indianapolis (137); Detroit (157)
SPOKANE	Seattle (224)
SYRACUSE	Rochester (79); Buffalo (134); Toronto (175)
TAMPA	Sarasota (39); Orlando (80); Fort Myers (105)
TOLEDO	Detroit (49); Flint (96); Cleveland (102); Columbus (121)
TUCSON	Phoenix (110)
TULSA	Oklahoma City (111)
VANCOUVER	Seattle (127)
WASHINGTON	Baltimore (30); Richmond (96)
WEST PALM BEACH	Fort Lauderdale (42); Miami (62); Orlando (142)
WICHITA	Oklahoma City (156)
WORCHESTER	Providence (44); Boston (45); Hartford (47)

First U.S. commercial flight: Philadelphia's Navy Field to Hoover Field, Washington, DC (July 16, 1926).

BACK-TO-BACK TICKETS

The Monster The Airlines Created

Back-to-back tickets are the airlines own monster. They created the need for back-to-backs when they decided fares should not be based on distance flown. Here's how they work:

- You purchase two roundtrip tickets.
- Roundtrip A originates in your actual departure city; roundtrip B originates in your destination city.
- On your first trip, you fly on the first segment of roundtrip A and return on the first segment of roundtrip B.
- On your second trip, you use the second segment of roundtrip B for your departing flight; the second segment of roundtrip A for your return.

Many business travelers use back-to-back tickets to deal with the inordinately high price of no Saturday stay tickets. Who can blame them? As long as airline pricing people do their confusing loop-the-loops and business tickets cost several times the price of excursion fares, travelers will use back-to-back tickets. Today, a business traveler would have to pay $1,584 for a no Saturday stay roundtrip between Dallas/Fort Worth and New York. United Airlines offers a $193 seven-day advance roundtrip. The business traveler who goes to New York infrequently, can purchase two roundtrips, throw away the second part of each ticket and still pay just $386, as opposed to $1,584—a $1,198 savings. A business traveler who makes the trip frequently can turn the two $193 tickets into two back-to-backs, saving $2,396.

Technically, back-to-backs purchased

Location of a 1980's retreat attended by top executives from all major airlines: Wyoming's A Bar A Ranch.

from the same carrier violate airlines' *Conditions of Contract* on most major airlines. Hard-working travel agents who want to do their best for their clients rightly claim that the airlines are asking them to abide by rules airline reservation agents don't always follow. The airlines say their agents shouldn't be issuing back-to-backs either, but the practice continues. We believe that each ticket you purchase is under a separate contract. If you choose to use multiple tickets for one itinerary, you meet your responsibility as long as you abide by the rules on each individual ticket. Airlines believe otherwise, invoking the cross-ticketing clause that says you must complete one ticket before beginning travel on another. There is nothing illegal about using back-to-backs. The airline police aren't going to carry you away. The worst case scenario is that you end up paying what you would have had to pay anyway.

You can use back-to-back ticketing without violating any airline policies and without placing your travel agent in jeopardy. There is one cardinal rule for intelligent use of back-to-back tickets and several other factors to keep in mind. Always purchase each roundtrip on separate airlines. You avoid any risk of being questioned at the gate or charged a higher fare. If you buy one ticket from Mega Air and the other from Maxi Air, you have stayed completely within each airline's rules.

Keep your Saturday night stay in your home city and make the back-to-back process less complicated by buying a one-way ticket for the first leg of your first trip. You may have to bite the bullet and purchase a high dollar one-way ticket for the first leg of your trip or you may be able to book a low-cost or niche carrier to keep the price of your initial one-way ticket down. Use the first part of your back-to-back roundtrip ticket to fly home, saving the return segment for your next flight.

Use the two airline strategy and combine back-to-back tickets with open jaw ticketing for even more flexibility. This is helpful when you plan to travel to two separate cities. You can do this with any routing that meets the primary rule of open jaw ticketing: your return flight must be more than half the distance of your originating flight. If you're traveling, for example, on a 1,381 mile flight, your open jaw return flight must be 691 miles or more.

Use your flight coupons in order. You can't travel on the return segment of a roundtrip ticket, until you have used the departure segment.

The return dates on both roundtrips can be changed by payment of a nominal fee, giving you even more flexibility.

"Know the rules of the type of ticket you are purchasing, if you are using seven-, 14- and 21-day advance fares. Higher priced Excursion fares can give you up to 365 days to complete your return trip. The added flexibility may well be worth the extra cost, particularly if you fly between your two cities every month or every other month. You will still save, as compared to purchasing no Saturday stay tickets. If you make two trips to the same city within a 30-day period, less expensive tickets may fill the bill."

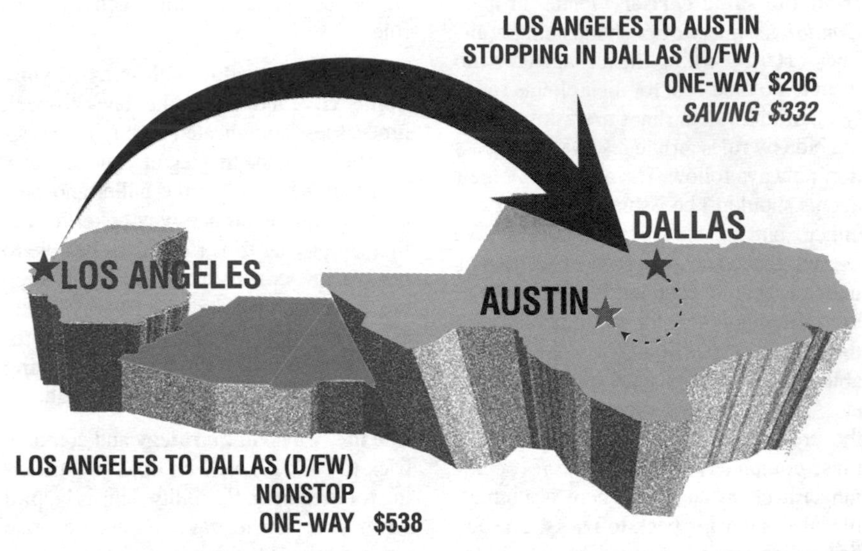

HIDDEN CITIES

Most airlines no longer base fares on distance flown. They've hidden the cities that provide the best ticket values, and we have to find them. Say you want to fly from Los Angeles to Dallas. You're quoted the "lowest" fare. What you're not told is that a flight originating in Austin, with a change of planes in Dallas, costs $361 less. The airlines expect you to pay more even though you're not flying as far. In this case, Dallas is the hidden city.

Hidden cities came from deregulation. The Civil Aeronautics Board (CAB) set tariffs prior to deregulation and allowed what were called "Point Beyond" fares—the predecessor of hidden cities. The CAB highly recommended Point Beyond fares because they believed it was unfair for people on the same plane to be able to fly farther for less than passengers who deplaned at stopover cities. Travel agents could legitimately issue a ticket from Point A to Point B, but charge the lower fare for Point A to Point C. They simply circled the fare on the flight coupon to let the airline know they were using a Point Beyond calculation. The airlines even offered advice on how to get the best Point Beyond fares. After deregulation, they were allowed more pricing freedom, and decided Point Beyond fares were not in their best interest.

Hidden cities can lower fares by as much as 80 percent—sometimes even more. Anytime you are flying one-way to a major airline's hub city, are not planning a Saturday stay or have no advance notice, you're likely to save by using hidden city ticketing. Airlines often lower fares on flights that connect through their hub cities. They do it to counter competition from other carriers at the originating airport. You book a ticket to the scheduled city, but get off the plane when it makes its stop at the hub. Remember to take carry-on luggage only, and make your exit as unobtrusive as possible.

Only use hidden cities for the first segment of your ticket, and only use them for one-way travel. If you try to use the second segment without having checked in for your first flight, you're likely to find that your entire ticket was cancelled as a no show. If you live in Dallas and want to travel to Chicago, a Dallas/Fort Worth-Toronto roundtrip on sale for $190 can save you $290 over the $480 cost of a Dallas/Fort Worth-Chicago one-way. When the airline notes that you have not flown the Chicago-Toronto segment, nor checked in for the Toronto-Chicago segment of the return flight, it will cancel your reservation. That isn't a problem if what you wanted was an inexpensive one-way ticket to Chicago. It's a small disaster if you actually had planned to use a return flight. In a word, don't.

Never call and cancel any flight you don't plan to use. It's technically fraud, because it comes under the definition of altering a ticket. Even if you never plan to board, let the reservation stand.

Respect your travel agencies reticence to book hidden cities. Many agencies will not book them since the airline can try to collect the fare difference by debit memo. Purchase directly from the airlines, making sure not to mention hidden cities, or from a travel agent who knows how to use hidden cities without running afoul of the airlines.

You can help determine hidden city possibilities by being aware of major airline hubs and low-cost carrier bases of operation.

> *"I've used hidden city ticketing properly for over 15 years. To date, I have never been directly challenged. The key is to use creative ticketing correctly, in ways that protect you from any repercussions from the airlines."*

AIRLINE HUBS

AIRLINE	HUBS
ALASKA	Anchorage and Seattle
AMERICA WEST	Columbus (OH), Las Vegas and Phoenix
AMERICAN	Chicago, Dallas/Fort Worth, Miami and San Juan
CONTINENTAL	Cleveland, Houston and Newark
DELTA	Atlanta, Cincinnati, Dallas/Fort Worth, Orlando and Salt Lake City
NORTHWEST	Detroit, Memphis and Minneapolis/St. Paul
SOUTHWEST	Burbank, Dallas Love, Houston Hobby, Nashville, Oakland, Phoenix, St. Louis and Salt Lake City
TWA	New York JFK and St. Louis
UNITED	Chicago, Denver, San Francisco and Washington Dulles
US AIRWAYS	Baltimore, Charlotte, Philadelphia, Pittsburgh and Washington National

Most widely used aircraft in the United States: the 737.

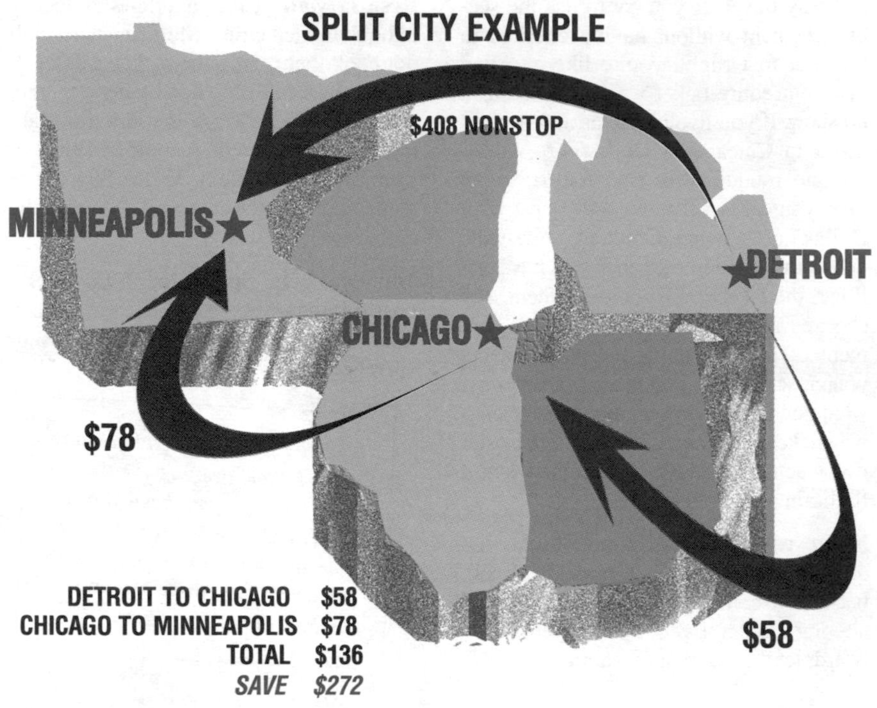

SPLIT CITIES

Save up to 70 percent and avoid the financial trauma of one airline's route monopoly by splitting your ticketing in half and buying two tickets: one to the intermediate city and one to your final destination. In many cases you can do this with separate tickets on the same airline. On other routes, you will have to use two airlines. Your extra effort could pay off with hundreds of dollars in savings per flight.

For example, a student flies from Detroit to her hometown in Minneapolis as often as possible. It's hard to plan in advance and last-minute fares are prohibitive. Using split cities, she books Detroit-Chicago roundtrips on one airline and Chicago-Minneapolis roundtrips on another. The total of her two separate roundtrips is less than a 21-day advance Detroit-Minneapolis roundtrip and up to 70 percent less than a last-minute roundtrip.

A strong low-cost carrier presence in a market can significantly increase your split city options. Book one leg of your trip on the low-cost carrier and you frequently get close enough to your destination city to get an inexpensive major airline ticket for the second leg. Low-cost carriers' walk-up fares are higher than their advance fares, but the ratio of increase is far less than it is for major carriers. On low-cost carriers using inventory-controlled pricing, you may even be able to get their lowest fare for last-minute travel, particularly if you fly during off-peak periods.

Use major carriers for split cities by using a separate carrier for each segment of your trip. This is possible when one of two factors is in play:

- **Competition** keeps fares low on a particular route, either through the presence of a low-cost carrier or major airline competition for dominance.
- **Fare war prices**, not in effect for the roundtrip you want, are in effect for one segment of your flight.

Use split cities for international savings. If you're going to Europe, check East Coast gateways like New York, Boston and Washington. Check roundtrip fares to London and roundtrips from London to your actual destination. If you're going to South America, check Miami departures. If you're going to the South Pacific or the Orient, check Los Angeles, Seattle and San Francisco departures. If you get a good promotional fare (or a great consolidator fare) you can add a separate roundtrip from your home city to the international departure city, and still come out way ahead.

There are two U.S. cities you can travel to at low fares that don't require Saturday stays—Reno and Las Vegas. The required minimum stay is two days—any days of the week. This is true even on the lowest priced 21-day Excursion fares. You can use this little-known fact to your advantage on many itineraries. You want to fly from New York to Los Angeles, for example, without a Saturday stay. Route your split city flights through Reno or Las Vegas and you can save 75 to 80 percent off published mid-week fares. Purchase a New York-Las Vegas roundtrip and a Las Vegas-Los Angeles roundtrip. If you have the time, take advantage of low hotel and meal costs in Reno or Las Vegas, and enjoy a stopover vacation.

LAST FLIGHT IN/ FIRST FLIGHT OUT

Gain another advantage most air travelers never know about by using last flight in/first flight out flexibility. You can fly to your connecting airport on the last flight of the day, overnight in that city, and catch the first flight to your destination in the morning.

Let's say you live in Dallas and need to be in New York City for a 10 a.m. meeting Tuesday. Your Monday schedule is full and you need every available moment in Dallas, and even plan to work well into the night. The first Tuesday Dallas-New York departure is at 7 a.m., a time that makes it impossible for you to be on time for your meeting. The last Dallas-New York flight on Monday night departs at 7:40 p.m. Your Monday schedule makes that flight unacceptable. Even if you rushed through your work, you don't want to check into a New York City hotel at 1 a.m. Using creative ticketing, you book the last Dallas-Atlanta flight on Monday night, departing at 11 p.m. You layover at an airport hotel, get a good night's rest and take the first morning flight to New York. You arrive in plenty of time to make your meeting. In this case, Atlanta is in the same time zone as New York City. It's also a Delta hub and offers frequent flights beginning early enough to get you to Manhattan with time to spare. You don't have to pay the airline extra for the layover since this is considered a connecting flight.

You can also use last flight in/first flight out when low priced fares to your destination are sold out. Say you want to fly from Orlando to New York City, but the cheapest available seat for a late afternoon flight is $700. There is a $200 fare open on the last flight of the day, because most

Cost of America West's new Tempe headquarters: $37 million.

travelers never even consider an overnight on a connecting flight. By booking that flight, and connecting to a 6 a.m. Atlanta-New York flight with many available seats since it leaves too early for other feeder flights, you've saved $500 minus your airport hotel stay.

> *"Rates at hotels near most hub airports are usually much lower than those in major metropolitan city centers. A $70 overnight near Atlanta Hartsfield sure beats a $225 rate in Manhattan—a rate you'd have to pay on top of the high roundtrip fare had you opted for the $700 late afternoon flight."*

BACKHAULING

Sometimes flights that take a circuitous route offer lower fares to fill empty seats and attract passengers from more direct flights. You usually need a very good travel agent to locate these deals. They're called backhauls because you fly *away* from your destination for part of your trip. For example, a Dallas/Fort Worth-Los Angeles fare can sometimes be lowered significantly by routing it through St. Louis.

STANDBY TRAVEL

Long gone are the days when you could officially fly standby on any type of ticket on any airline. Now, if you're flying on a cheap ticket, you'll encounter varying rules and that powerful thing called "gate agent discretion." Standby travel may work when you are holding a ticket for a future date and want to fly between the same city pairs (or their codeshare airports) prior to your ticketed travel dates. Alaska Airlines insists that your ticket be for travel on the same day you're attempting standby. The best you can hope for is an earlier flight that same day. Others, including American and TWA, will let you fly standby when you hold a ticket for future dates. A few low-cost airlines have been offering standby travel promotions, usually limited to ages 18 through 25.

Your chances for standby travels are enhanced if you opt for earlier flights booked significantly under capacity. A good travel agent can check this out for you before you head for the airport. Standby travel is usually not confirmed until ten minutes before departure, allowing all passengers ticketed for that specific flight and any latecomers purchasing tickets for that flight to board.

There are other types of standby travel most often attainable on (but not limited to) international routes and for passengers 25 and under. Ask about these options when you call for ticket quotes.

Some domestic coupon travel such as youth and senior coupon booklets permit standby travel on a space available basis. This is one of the best uses of flight coupons.

Virgin Atlantic, Air Canada and Icelandair frequently discount international tickets purchased one day or less before travel, but only on select flights with a decent percentage of empty seats.

THROW-AWAY TICKETS

Throw-away tickets are the easiest form of creative ticketing. They're used when you want to fly one-way and can't get a fare you can live with using a niche carrier, alternate airports or hidden cities. You simply buy a roundtrip ticket, use the outbound segment(s) and throw away the return ticket. You save money because roundtrip Excursion tickets (requiring a Saturday night stay) are usually substantially cheaper than any major airline's one-way ticket. Never throw away the first portion of a ticket and attempt to use the return segment(s). Your outbound reservation will be cancelled and the airline can legitimately charge you a full fare, one-way ticket when you arrive at the airport for your "return" flight.

OPEN JAWS

Open jaws are assets in several forms of creative ticketing. If you draw a simple diagram of open jaw routing, it looks exactly like its name. Use it when you want to fly to one city and return from another. The fare is calculated by taking half of the roundtrip fare to each destination and combining them. You can use open jaws on almost any fare basis. There are two types of open jaw tickets:

- **The origin and final cities are the same,** but the open jaw cities are different. Flying from Houston to Newark, for example, and returning from Boston to Houston.
- **The destination city is the same** but you originate in one city and return to another. Flying from Milwaukee to Boston, for example, and returning from Boston to Detroit.

Open jaw ticketing requires that your entire itinerary is on the same airline. A Saturday stay is usually required. There are geographical limits. On domestic travel, the mileage on your return flight must be half or more the distance of your originating flight. For example, flying New York City-Salt Lake City and returning New York City-Los Angeles can be done as an open jaw; returning from Chicago won't work.

Open jaws can provide particularly good options for international travel. You'll probably pay more than you'd pay for the cheapest ticket in and out of the same city, but you'll gain flexibility and avoid backtracking if you plan to cover several cities or countries.

CIRCLE TRIPS

Circle trips let you visit two cities at half the cost of the lowest roundtrip Excursion ticket between destinations. They offer destination options you can't get on open jaws, due to geographical restrictions. You must make your entire trip on the same airline and your trip must include a Saturday night stay. You can't make three or more stops without giving up the benefits circle trips offer. A sample circle trip itinerary: New York City to Denver, Denver to Dallas/Fort Worth and Dallas/Fort Worth to New York City.

Each airline has its own rules on circle trips. In general, the first leg must be the farthest point from your originating city and the first leg destination must be where you take your Saturday night stay. Delta, however, allows the Saturday stay requirement to be met on any portion of the trip. United allows you to choose your Saturday stay city on some itineraries.

FREE STOPOVERS

Travel within the 48 states and you have up to four hours between connecting flights. Anything over that bases your fare on one-way prices. The four-hour rule gives you a window that can be useful for quick family visits, brief meetings at airport club facilities or even city tours in connecting cities you've never visited. A business traveler flying from Los Angeles to New York, for example, may have clients in Dallas/Fort Worth or Memphis. Route your travel through a hub city, and you're likely to have your choice of sever-

When passenger jets began using recirculated cabin air: the mid 1980s.

al connecting flights, all within the four-hour rule. You can have a quick meeting with your client in Memphis without adding a penny of cost to your Los Angeles-New York City trip.

Get two free stopovers by using the four-hour rule on your outbound and on your return flights. Continuing with the previous example, stop in Dallas/Fort Worth on your way back. You've just seen three clients for the price of one. Ask your travel agent to review the rules and pull up proper connection cities on the computer. All approved cities should show up.

America West allows stopovers in Columbus (OH), Phoenix or Las Vegas for $60, a 50 percent increase over their old $30 fee. On select flights, Reno Air allows free stopovers in Reno. Continental has been allowing free stopovers in Los Angeles or San Francisco on flights to California. Fly to Los Angeles and add a free stopover in San Francisco.

Connect time allowed on international flights is frequently 12 hours, but check each route and airline for variances. Sometimes you can get a 24 hour stopover at no additional cost and enjoy two destinations for one price.

Some major airlines offer international fares that give you a six month window of travel and allow two stopovers (one in each direction) for an additional $100. United's BKXPK fare basis is just one example. These are premium-price tickets that should only be used when you have to travel internationally with short notice. Ignore your stopover option and you ignore the possibility of major savings. Used wisely, the stopover option gives you two one-way domestic flights, normally selling for several hundred dollars each (you paid just $50 each). You still have to purchase the other half of your domestic travel for both itineraries, but the $1,000-1,500 (or more) you save by using the stopover option goes a long way toward covering the cost. You need a savvy travel agent to help make this one work. Your hometown, your international destination and the domestic cities you travel to often are the key factors that could make this strategy work well for you.

> *“Here's another plug for travel agents—potentially one of your best allies in airline ticketing. I believe that every traveler should understanding the basic of how airline pricing works. I also believe that a savvy professional can help you form an unbeatable team.”*

OTHER WAYS TO SAVE

COMPANION FARES

Two-for-one can be the best deal of all, but there are some things you need to know to evaluate these offers. Companion fares, in some cases, are based on higher priced ticket categories. You save when you divide the cost of the paid ticket by two and get what is usually the lowest possible per-ticket price. Companion fares require that both people travel together on all segments of the flight. Sometimes they are limited to travel on specific days of the week. They almost always have blackout dates.

Not all airlines offer companion tickets consistently. They tend to pop up in certain markets when load factors are down, or in response to a competitor's offer. Make sure your travel agent checks down to the bottom of the computer screen where companion fares, family fares and other deals may hide. Then do the math and compare all your options. Many senior fares permit a companion of any age to fly at the same ticket price. College/student programs (such as American Airlines') offer free or discount coupons for companion travel. American Express Platinum cardmembers receive two-for-one international premium class travel.

Check companion fare availability to alternate cities. They may not be available for your exact destination, but a nearby airport may work. For example, companion fares may be offered to Oakland, but not San Francisco; to Chicago Midway, but not Chicago O'Hare; to Providence, but not Boston; to Dallas

U.S. carrier on which all pilots are captain-qualified: Southwest.

Love Field, but not Dallas/Fort Worth International Airport.

WEEKEND DISCOUNTS

Some discounted weekend fares can be booked in advance. American Airlines BreakAAway fares lead this category. BreakAAway fares represent savings of up to 85 percent. They are frequently available out of six locations: Dallas/Fort Worth, Chicago, Miami, Nashville, Los Angeles, and New York. Recently prices varied from $79-269 roundtrip, depending on the destination. A Memphis-Dallas/Ft. Worth roundtrip, can be $99; Dallas/Ft. Worth-Newark can be $199. TWA has also been aggressive this year in weekend fare promotions to and from their St. Louis hub. United, US Airways and other majors are also following American's weekend discount lead. Don't forget weekend discounts by internet, detailed at the beginning of this chapter.

Niche carriers, and therefore their competitors, customarily discount off-peak travel. Off-peak is likely to be after 7 p.m. weekdays and all day Saturday and Sunday. Holiday travel is often excluded.

EARLY BIRDS & NIGHT OWLS

Sometimes you can save on airfares just by choosing an early morning or late evening flight. American Airlines DAAyBreak fares, for example, can cut the cost of travel between Dallas/Fort Worth or Chicago and select U.S. cities. Take-off for both departing and return flights must occur between 5 a.m. and 8:30 a.m. Sunday through Friday. Night flight discounts are offered on airlines including America West. These bargains are offered on select routes. You may find some fare war prices are lower for time-specific flights.

GROUP FARES

Group and meeting fares must be booked by calling a separate reservation desk. Different deals require a different minimum number of travelers. Standard group and meeting discounts are ten percent. You will also find some zone fare programs. This year's group discount innovations included:

- **American, Delta and United** added an additional five percent to the standard ten percent discount. Advance purchase (up to 60 days) is required.
- **Midwest Express and Skyway Airlines** reduce group fares (eight or more travelers) during periodic specials. These deals usually apply to select off-peak flights for travel to or from five cities: Milwaukee, Cleveland, Columbus, Kansas City and Omaha.

CONSOLIDATORS

Consolidators sell discount tickets released to them in bulk by the airlines. Often you pay as little as half the published fare. International consolidator tickets are technically forbidden by a 1958 law stating they cannot be sold below their published price, but that law has not been enforced in almost 40 years (rather like laws against riding horses down Main Street on Sunday). In fact, some consolidators are actual partners with the airlines whose discount seats they sell.

- **Consolidator prices are rarely exactly as advertised**—but good consolidators will get very close. If there is a big discrepancy, ask for an explanation. Always compare a consolidator rate to the airline's quote, making sure you're comparing prices for the same ticket.
- **Consolidator tickets don't require**

Cruising speed of a 21-passenger 1935 DC-3 aircraft: 180 mph.

advance purchase, except for the time needed to get the ticket to you if you're purchasing by phone.

- ***Minimum/maximum stay requirements**, often attached to other discount tickets, can be waived. Many fare war prices permit a maximum of 30-45 days to complete travel. Many consolidator tickets allow 90-365 days to complete travel.*
- **Consolidator tickets may be non-endorsable**, meaning you won't be placed on an alternate carrier in case of extremely delayed or cancelled flights. On some consolidator tickets, you forego frequent flyer points, advance seat assignments and special meal options. Some consolidator tickets include all these extras.
- **Always deal with reputable consolidators** and always pay by credit card. Double check your tickets by calling the airline direct 24 hours after you've purchased your consolidator ticket. If the airline does not show your reservation, call the consolidator immediately.

*"World Travel Network (**800-576-2242**) is a consolidator I know and trust. They have a data base that tracks dozens of consolidator sources. You can also check local Sunday travel sections from gateway cities. If you're flying to Europe, check the New York Times and the Boston Globe. If you're flying to South America check the Miami Herald. If you're flying to the South Pacific or the Orient, check the Los Angeles Times and the San Francisco Chronicle. Most major city libraries will carry these out-of-town papers so you can review them for free."*

OFF-SEASON SAVINGS

Internationally, a small change in departure could save you big bucks. International fares, in most cases, are determined by the date of the outbound leg of your flight. Save hundreds of dollars simply by booking your departure a few days earlier or later when you travel near seasonal breaks. Always ask your travel agent if your travel dates are in or near high, low or shoulder season. The exact date breaks vary by destination. This past year, we have seen almost unbelievable deals for outbound travel between September and May, with discounts of up to $800 roundtrip.

Some of the best domestic airfare deals can be acquired during the busiest travel seasons if you can be flexible and wait until the last minute to book. Travel for the Christmas holidays, for example, can become very affordable if you travel Christmas Day. Special Fourth of July sales this year came in two varieties—roundtrips completed entirely on the 4th of July and roundtrips that allowed you to stay two to four days. There is usually an initial set of sale fares, followed by competitive variations.

Remember that consolidator fares can be up to 50 percent less than published fares in all seasons of travel. Consolidator fare contracts and new prices are usually released twice a year: in September and October for travel November 1 through March 31; in late January and February for travel April through October.

Leading manufacturing source for large, commercial jets: the United States.

SENIOR DISCOUNTS

The traditional ten percent senior discount, available on most domestic and international airline tickets, is usually extended to companions of any age. You can often get a senior discount on very low promotional fares (like *Best Fares* Snooze You Lose deals). Recently a major airline offered a $114 Dallas/Fort Worth-Washington roundtrip. Our art director's parents booked it at $102.60, using the ten percent senior discount.

When American Airlines announced their senior discount membership program, a mad flurry of competitive pricing occurred and it still hasn't abated, even though membership in the club is now closed. Northwest began undercutting American's senior membership fares, forcing other carriers to lower their senior fares as well. If you book through the airlines, have them check for special senior fares. Keep in mind that these special fares will not be available in all markets and will come and go quickly. Visit **www.bestfares.com** for daily updates.

Senior Freedom Passports

Continental Airlines has a deal for travelers ages 62 and above who plan to do a lot of concentrated traveling or would like to do more if it was affordable. You pay one price for an array of travel benefits, and companion passports (at the same price) are available for people traveling with the primary passport holder—regardless of age.

- **The *Freedom Passport*** allows travel within the 48 states and to St. Thomas. The four-month pass is $999/Coach; the 12-month pass is $1,999/Coach or $3,499/First Class. Travel noon Monday through noon Thursday and all day Saturday. You are allowed a single one-way per week. A Sunday stay is required. Travel to the same destination a maximum of three times. Add-on destinations expand the value and companions may purchase the same (or fewer) add-ons as the senior. Add-on prices for Coach/First Class: Alaska (limit one) $400/$550; Hawaii (limit one) $400/$550; the Caribbean (limit two) $250/$400; Central America (limit one) $300/$450; Mexico (limit two) $250/$400; Europe (limit one) $500/$1,000.
- **The *Global Passport*** covers domestic travel plus one roundtrip to each of three destinations—Hawaii, Alaska and Central America; two roundtrips to each of three additional destinations—Europe, Mexico and the Caribbean. A Coach *Global Passport* is $4,499; First Class is $6,999. All *Global Passports* last for 12 months. Travel to Europe is permitted Monday through Thursday and on Saturday.
- **Some travel periods require** a seven-day advance; others require as little as

one-hour advance, subject to availability. There are some holiday blackouts as well as other limits on availability and you won't earn frequent flyer miles. The bargain value of *Freedom Passports* depends on the amount of travel you do. For example, if you take six roundtrips on a four-month domestic Coach Passport, you pay an average of $166 per trip. If you take 20 domestic roundtrips on a 12-month Domestic First Class Passport, you pay an average of $175 per roundtrip—an unheard of price for First Class travel. Get a free brochure detailing your passport options, including an application form by calling **800-576-2242**.

Senior Membership Clubs

There are three major airline membership clubs for seniors. As we go to press, two of them have closed membership (United's *Silver Wings Plus* is the sole exception), but savvy travelers will jump when enrollment reopens, or when new senior discount membership programs are offered.

- **American's *AActive American Traveler Club*** (62+) required a $40 membership ($60 to include a companion of any age). The initial enrollment period covered discounted domestic travel through May 31, 1998; international travel Tuesdays through Thursdays through May 28, 1998.

- **Delta's *Senior Select Savings Plus*** (62+) offered domestic Coach roundtrips starting at $98; domestic First Class roundtrips starting at $298. Enrollment was closed faster than anyone anticipated, but it should reopen sometime in 1998. This program is exceptional because it has no blackout dates and it allows members to travel one-way for an additional $10. No minimum or Saturday stay is needed. The annual membership fee is $40 and members could enroll up to three additional travelers over age 62 or between ages two and 12 for a total of $70.

- **United's *Silver Wings Plus*** (55+) is $75 for a two-year membership; $225 for a lifetime membership. Quarterly mailings include airline discounts and discounted zone fares. As we go to press, offers include *USA Collection* discount zone fares. You purchase four roundtrip coupons for $25 and use them to access fares like Washington-Chicago at $158 and Los Angeles-Denver for $168; 50 percent off an SAS companion ticket; and $60 off Air Canada. An upgrade program allows members to purchase a Business Class upgrade for $1,000 and combine it with any Economy Class roundtrip fare, resulting in a total price of as little as 25 percent what a standard Business Class fare could cost. Call **214-760-0022**; go online at **www.silverwings.com**.

Senior airfare coupon books

Senior airfare coupon books have been through a lot of changes this past year. Some airlines that offered cost-effective eight-coupon options now only offer a four-coupon option. We found, in checking coupon prices each month, that reservation agents with some airlines gave out information in a way that made comparison shopping difficult. As we go to press, Northwest and United tend to quote senior airfare coupon prices without including the ten percent ticket tax. If you think you're getting a deal, you may see your savings disappear when you show up at the airport for your first flight, and are asked to pay ten percent of the total coupon book price.

Senior coupons are available to passen-

Artist who played the piano in 1970's American jumbo jet lounges: Frank Sinatra, Jr.

gers 62 and above and are valid for one year from date of purchase.

- **A 14-day advance is required.** Standby travel is allowed (many airlines permit standby travel even on the day of purchase) and you do receive frequent flyer miles, equal to what you would receive on any purchased ticket.
- **A limited number of seats per flight** are set aside for senior coupon travel. If the senior inventory is used up on a particular flight, you cannot use coupon travel. Your best bet is to allow as much advance booking time as possible. Also ask about blackout dates.
- **Each coupon book is valid for one year** from the date of purchase and each coupon allows one-way travel to or from your destination. Some long-haul destinations require two coupons per direction.
- **When deciding which senior coupon book to buy**, take into consideration the cities serviced by each airline and compare their routes to destinations you are most likely to use. Focus on destinations that provide real senior coupon value.
- **Don't use senior coupons when** you can beat the price with a separate ticket. Be particularly careful on shorthaul trips, and always check fare war prices, *Best Fares* Online Snooze You Lose deals and special promotions to see if they beat your per-coupon cost.
- **Always carry proof of age and identity** when you travel on senior coupons.
- **Seniors may only need to be 60** for some international flights, including Canada, Mexico and some Caribbean destinations. Check with each program for clarification.
- **Coupon books can be purchased** from the airlines or from travel agents. *Best Fares* subscribers receive a four percent rebate on many senior airfare coupon books.
- **Southwest** offers low senior fares on individual tickets to travelers 65 and above, available on all flights with no capacity limit. One-way tickets go for as little $29-99 for Monday through Thursday travel.
- **TWA offers the most favorable four-coupon rates**. Continental and TWA offer eight-coupon options that give you the best per-flight rate of all. TWA also allows you to purchase companion coupons for travelers of any age, at a slightly higher rate and throws in a coupon valid for 20 percent off select European flights. US Airways allows up to two children two-11 flying with a senior to use the same coupon book.

> *"If you purchase senior coupons by phone from your travel agent, you will be mailed an MCO (Merchant's Cash Order) which you will give the airline in return for your coupon book. Guard this piece of paper as if it was cash. If you lose it, you will find that some airlines have very stiff policies on honoring your purchase."*

The chart on the following page lists current senior airfare coupon options. Availability is limited to a specific number of seats on each flight. All major airline coupons cover destinations within the 48 states and to destinations listed in column three.

SENIOR COUPON BOOKS			
AIRLINE	COST PER BOOK & PER COUPON	48 STATES AND...	TWO COUPON ONE-WAY ITINERARIES
AMERICA WEST Senior Savers 800-235-9292	4 coupons: $548 ($137)	N/A	N/A
AMERICAN Senior TrAAvler 800-237-7981	4 coupons: $596 ($149)	Puerto Rico & the U.S. Virgin Islands	Hawaii
CONTINENTAL Freedom Trips 800-248-8996	4 coupons: $579 ($144.75) 8 coupons: $1,079 ($134.88)	Mexico, Montreal, Toronto & the Caribbean	Alaska & Hawaii
DELTA Young At Heart 800-221-1212	4 coupons: $596 ($149)	Canada, San Juan & St. Thomas	Alaska & Hawaii
MIDWAY Senior Travel Booklet 800-225-2525	4 coupons: $390 ($97.50) Companion: $440 ($110) Raleigh/Durham: $350 ($87.50) Companion: $385 ($96.25)	N/A	Cancun
NORTHWEST UltraFare Coupons 800-225-2525	4 coupons: $540 ($135) *Price does not include tax!*	Canada	Alaska & Hawaii
TWA Senior Travel Pak 800-221-2000	4 coupons: $548 ($137) Companion: $648 ($162) 8 coupons: $1,032 ($129) Companion: $1,132 ($141.50)	Jamaica, San Juan, Santo Domingo & Toronto	Hawaii
UNITED Silver TravelPac 800-633-6563	4 coupons: $541.80 ($135.45) *Price does not include tax!*	Canada & San Juan	Alaska & Hawaii except Seattle to Anchorage or Fairbanks
US AIRWAYS Golden Opportunities 800-428-4322	4 coupon book: $579 ($144.50)	Canada, San Juan, St. Croix & St. Thomas	N/A

Number of New Yorkers who gathered in 1927 for Lindbergh's parade: 4,000,000.

DISCOUNTS FOR CHILDREN, STUDENTS & FAMILIES

The big news this past year was the availability of 50-percent-off fares for children under two. Even though the little ones can fly free, an increasing number of parents prefer to book seats for their infants and toddlers. The primary benefit is increased safety when an approved child safety seat is used. Consumer groups have pushed for discounted seats and the use of safety seats because "lap babies" face a much higher risk of injury than restrained children. Secondarily, on crowded flights, parents are assured of a little elbow room and spared a child in arms for two solid hours (or longer). American Airlines was the first major carrier to make this discount available, following discounts initially offered by Southwest. You get the discount on any published fare, including advertised discounts. Each adult traveling may purchase an unlimited number of under two discount tickets. This discount is available for domestic flights and those between the U.S. and Canada.The child must travel in an approved safety seat that you provide. International travel for children under two flying with adults costs ten percent of the cost of the adult ticket and a separate seat is not guaranteed.

Student and youth fares come from three sources: consolidators, student membership programs (sometimes co-sponsored by an airline) and directly from the airlines. *Best Fares* Magazine and *Best Fares* Online detail many of these offers, as well as special promotions that can lower student travel costs considerably. These special promotions offer great savings on family travel. For example, Vanguard Airlines frequently offers a 25 percent discount for children two through 12 flying with a paying adult (18 or older). El Al's family plan fares give discounts that increase incrementally for each additional child in your family. American Airlines has offered great holiday travel discounts for students. Ongoing programs and special promotions include:

> *"Airlines do some things to make life easier for people traveling with infants and toddlers but they do not provide diapers (except on some international flights), changing tables (except on larger, newer aircraft) or refrigeration for bottles. Airport play areas and privacy rooms for nursing mothers are available at some major airports. Collapsible strollers are supposed to be checked baggage, but if you "forget," you can use it all the way to the boarding gate and the flight attendant will find a place for it. If you do check the stroller it won't count against your baggage limit. Always do a "gate check" and ask flight attendant to put a special tag on the stroller. The stroller will be delivered right to your arrival gate."*

Airline covering most of the $200 million cost of doubling Midway's terminal: Southwest.

- **American Airlines**: Enroll in the *College SAAver* e-mail plan (**www.aa.com**) and you will receive periodic e-mails offering discounted fares just for members. You must be a U.S. resident, a full-time college student and at least 18 years old. Sign up for a no-fee Citibank Visa or MasterCard and get eight free discount certificates when you are approved. You get four domestic zone fare certificates allowing discounted roundtrip travel within the 48 states and to Canada, a companion certificate allowing you and a friend or family member of your choice to fly at the zone fare and three international certificates offering discounts on travel to Europe; the Caribbean, Central or South America; and Mexico or Hawaii. Apply online at **www.americanair.com** or call **800-359-4444**.

- **America West:** Ten-percent discount to students 17 through 25 years of age on flights from the U.S. to Mexico on all published fares.

- **Delta:** Families with children ages two through 12 can take advantage of newly reduced rates for membership in Delta's *Fantastic Flyer* program, providing up to $1,000 in added values and discounts. U.S. residents pay $19.99 per child; residents of Canada and the Caribbean pay $24.99 (US). Membership for each additional child is only $9.99. New member bonuses include a certificate valid for $25-200 off (the discount depends on the ticket price) on each of three tickets for passengers booking and traveling together. One of the travelers must be a *Fantastic Flyer* member and another must be an accompanying adult family member. Travel roundtrip within the 50 states or between the 50 states and Bermuda, Canada, the Caribbean and Mexico. You also receive an additional $25-off travel certificate, valid for one traveler; two in-flight coupons for parents; two in-flight coupons for the *Fantastic Flyer*; and several discount offers including Radisson, select Hilton Resorts, Alamo, Avis, Hertz, National and Delta Dream Vacations. Call **800-635-9949**; enroll online at **www.delta-air.com/fantastic**.

- **Delta:** College students were offered a $35 per year *Extra Credit* program that provided unlimited use of discount zone fares in the 48 states at $109-299 roundtrip. Membership is currently closed but we expect it to reopen in the future.

- **Kiwi's *Student Standby Book*** offers six coupons, each valid for one-way travel. This offer is available to students 18 and above with ID. The coupon book sells for $320, including taxes and PFCs, making your average cost per flight $53.33. Coupons are fully transferable to other students. Use them for flights within Kiwi's route network, including Aguadillia, Atlanta, Boston, Chicago Midway, Newark, Orlando, San Juan and West Palm Beach.

- **Midwest Express:** Students 17 through 26 were offered special fares allowing up to 180 days to complete travel, giving college students ample time to complete a semester. Tickets are non-refundable, but there is no change penalty, so you get return date flexibility—useful in case of family emergencies, a little bit of freshman homesickness or just a taste for mom's (or dad's) hot apple pie. The promotion code for this special fare is KEGRAD. A seven-day advance is required.

- **TWA:** The *Student Travel Pak*, avail-

Airline logo prominent in the Beatles first U.S. press conference: Pan Am.

> *“When the whole family is flying together, particularly on international flights (including Mexico, Canada and the Caribbean), you may have some money-saving clout. Companion tickets and family fares can be two of the best options. The best family discounts are graduated, with each subsequent family member getting a larger discount off the published fare. Families flying to Tel Aviv on El Al, for example, may be able to take advantage of a frequently offered promotion: the first child pays full fare; the second gets 25 percent off; the third gets 50 percent off; additional children get 75 percent off. Always ask if a family discount is available.”*

able to students 14 through 24 provides five flight coupons. The first four permit one-way travel among the 48 contiguous states and San Juan; the fifth is valid for a 20 percent discount on travel to Europe. The current cost is $548, an average $137 purchase per one-way trip. A 14-day advance reservation is required, but students are allowed to attempt standby travel. Call **800-221-2000**.

Children Flying Unaccompanied

Each year, millions of children fly unaccompanied in the U.S. Whether you are placing your children on their first unaccompanied flight, or their tenth, knowing how the system works is the best way to help guarantee that everything will go as smoothly as possible. It will certainly be less expensive to send your child on an unaccompanied flight than it would to add two roundtrips for yourself. Because we think your child's well-being in this situation is of paramount importance, we are going to give you quite a few tips to make this way to save worry-free.

Summer rivals only the December holiday season as the peak travel period for children flying alone. Some are heading to grandparents or summer camp; some are going for extended visits with mom or dad. Just when airline staffs are stretched to their maximum, a steady stream of young flyers appears, many needing extra attention and escorts to connecting flights. Some airlines meet the demand by hiring interns and college students. They look for people who have worked with children as teachers, childcare workers or camp counselors. Others assign solo kids to regular staff members who must fit in the extra service with their regular job responsibilities.

Airline policy considers 12-year-olds adults. They pay adult fares and neither require nor receive special services. As any parent with children in this age group knows, 12-year-olds and teenagers can seem almost grown up one moment and far from grown up the next.

Most airlines will provide an escort for children 12 and over if you request it. The fee is worth it if you have any doubt that your children are ready for solo travel. You may have, for example, a 14-year-old with a learning disability or a 15-year-old who is extremely shy and hesitant about new situations. Explain the circumstances to the airline and be sure they document them in their record. If they still won't accommodate you, choose another airline. If you arrive at the airport with a child 12 or older, and you are told escort service can't be provided, you can refer them to your record and get what you need.

Cans of orange juice consumed by America West passengers per year: 1,350,000.

Major airline policies and fees for children flying solo can vary dramatically. Delta and Northwest now charge $60 per direction on connecting flights. One fee covers all related children booking and traveling together, except on Alaska, with a maximum of three children covered by one fee. The minimum age for nonstop flights remains five years of age, across the board. Here is the complete rundown, by airline. All fees are per direction.

AIRLINE POLICIES ON CHILDREN FLYING ALONE

AIRLINE	MINIMUM AGE/ CONNECTING	FEE FOR NONSTOPS	FEE FOR CONNECTING
ALASKA	Five	None	$30
AMERICA WEST	Eight	None	$30
AMERICAN	Eight	None	$30
CONTINENTAL	Eight	None	$30
DELTA	Eight	$30	$60
NORTHWEST	Five	$30	$60
SOUTHWEST	Twelve	Escorts not offered; special boarding is accorded.	Not Applicable
TWA	Five	$30	$30
UNITED	Eight	$30	$30
US AIRWAYS	Eight	None	$30

When children fly unaccompanied (nonstop and connecting flights) you must provide the following information:

- **The names of your children,** their ages and any relevant medical considerations. You will also be asked to sign an agreement to signify that you understand that the airline is not assuming any special responsibility or guardianship.
- **The name, address and phone numbers for the adult(s)** who will pick up your children at the arriving airport. Be sure to have that person carry legal identification. No matter how happily your children greet grandma and grandpa, the airline is not obligated to release the children without confirming identification.
- **Make sure the reservation record includes** all contact information for you—not just a home telephone number. Include your business number, your cellular number, your pager number—even the phone number of a relative who will be home while your child is in transit.

If the designated adult is not waiting for your children when their flight arrives, the airline generally takes one of two options:

- **Supervise the children** for a reason-

Number of cans of Coca Cola used by United each day: 40,000 regular; 26,000 diet.

able (brief) period of time while calls are made to try to locate the adult designated to pick them up. They have no legal liability to do this, however.

- **Turn the children over to child welfare authorities** or the local police department. This option may seem extreme, but several airlines (including Southwest) do it as a matter of policy, believing that it is in the best interest of the child.

Here are ten tips to help you enjoy the money-saving advantages of children flying unaccompanied while eliminating risk and worry.

1. Try to avoid sending young children unaccompanied if it is their first flight. It could be an exciting experience, but it could also be a disaster. Even a quick commuter flight experience will help them feel more at ease.

2. Don't ignore medical conditions that could present problems in flight. The stress of a flight could trigger an asthma attack in some children. The barely noticeable pain of a minor ear infection can intensify dramatically in flight. Chronicle any vital medical information, make it part of the reservation record and place it in the hands of the flight attendant. If your child has drug sensitivities or allergies, is diabetic or has another condition that would be pertinent in the unlikely event that emergency care is needed, document it. Don't count on any airline employee being allowed to hold or administer medication prescribed for your child, or any over-the-counter medication. You may be able to request that service when you make your reservation. The agent will send it to the airline's Special Assistance Department, where the decision will be made. Allow plenty of advance time.

3. Nonstop flights are best, even if you must pay a little more. If you must book a connecting flight, try to route through a city where you have close friends or relatives in case weather or mechanical difficulties prevent your child from leaving the connecting city. Make their contact information a part of your child's record.

4. In winter, try to avoid a connection in cities prone to snow or sleet. Don't put children on flights departing late in the day, particularly if they are making a connection. A cancelled flight could place your children in a strange city overnight. Remember El Nino and Murphy's Law.

5. Send a little cash to cover incidental expenses, like an orange juice between flights, popcorn or even a meal if a connecting flight is delayed. Your child's airline escort probably is not highly paid and couldn't afford to treat your hungry child to those expensive $4 airport hot dogs. Send an extra $10 for emergencies.

6. Be explicit about what your children should do if the behavior of any stranger makes them uneasy. Stress that the appropriate people to approach for help are people in uniform—recognizable airline employees, airport security or police officers. Be confident that you child will follow your directions before booking solo travel.

7. Use the options and special services the airline offers. Enroll your child as a frequent flyer. Delta has the *Fantastic Flyer* program just for children. They get a quarterly magazine, birthday cards and other kid-friendly treats; you get special bonus offers. British Airways offers *Skyflyers*. All airlines that provide meals offer special children's meals but you must order them

in advance. Options include favorites such as chicken nuggets, hamburgers and pizza. United offers McDonald's Happy Meals on many flights, with a toy that's usually Ronald McDonald flying a 747.

8. Ask to board the plane with your children to get them situated and point out special features of the plane. It's the perfect time to point out restrooms, how to fasten and unfasten the seat belt and how to summon a flight attendant. Think back to your first flight and how even simple things seemed confusing. They can be even more confusing to children.

9. Make sure the person meeting the flight has accurate flight information and will call the airline for flight updates.

10. If weather conditions are bad on the day of the flight, and you have some flexibility, call and ask the airline if you can reschedule without penalty. They're not obligated to do it, but since it could keep your child from being stranded due to late or cancelled flights, they may be happy to accommodate you. Check the weather conditions in the connecting and destination cities. Some airlines deny boarding to unaccompanied children if weather conditions are too bad.

E-tickets can present special considerations and you're probably going to be better off requesting a paper ticket in most cases.

- **Children five through 11:** Most airlines will allow the adult dropping off the unaccompanied minor and the adult picking up the unaccompanied minor to pick up e-ticket boarding passes at the airport. Since their information is already in the record, you are covered. American Airlines does not allow unaccompanied minors under 12 to fly on e-tickets; United allows it but requires that you purchase e-tickets for unaccompanied minors at United ticket offices.

- **Children 12 and older:** These children can technically travel alone without any requirement of adult drop off or pick up, but you're faced with another problem: whose ID will be accepted at the airport? Many children between 12 and 17 do not have official IDs. Policies for children in this age group using e-tickets vary by airline. Northwest, for example, doesn't require an ID. Southwest Airlines requires a birth certificate copy or a school ID. In calling the airlines, we've received different answers from different reservation agents. It all goes back to our initial comment on children flying on e-tickets— get a paper ticket and avoid potential problems.

BEREAVEMENT FARES

When you're faced with a critically ill family member or the death of a family member in a distant city, negotiating a good airfare is the farthest thing from your mind. You may assume that bereavement/compassion fares offered by all major airlines are the best you can do with no advance and an uncertain return date. That is not necessarily the case.

- **In the case of an illness,** you will likely be asked to provide the hospital's name and phone number and the name and number of the attending physician.

- **In the case of a death,** you must supply the name and number of the funeral home. Some airlines verify the information before they issue your ticket.

- **Each airline has its own policy** on

family relationships deemed acceptable for bereavement fares. Most will not offer a bereavement fare for the death or illness of a close friend nor will they allow a friend to fly with you at bereavement rates.

Airlines say they take 50 percent off full Coach fares and Northwest says they offer a 70 percent discount. These percentages seem to vary. In checking three bereavement fares, we found no clearly discernible pattern. Here, for example, is what we were quoted for San Francisco-Washington (DC) roundtrips on a recent fare shop. Please note that there is no difference in cost quoted for bereavement and compassion fares.

ROUNDTRIP BEREAVEMENT AND COMPASSION FARES

AIRLINE	NO ADVANCE RT	BEREAVEMENT RT	COMPASSION RT
AMERICA WEST	$1,192	$904	$904
AMERICAN	$1,892	$946	$946
CONTINENTAL	$1,892	$959	$959
DELTA	$1,151	$530	$530
NORTHWEST	$1,892	$876	$876
TWA	$1,892	$1,170	$1,170
UNITED	$1,892	$951	$951
US AIRWAYS	$1,892	$541	$541

When you need a bereavement fare, a savvy travel agent can be your best ally. A good agent will make the phone calls for you and present you with your best option. A great agent will go the extra mile, look at special fares, three-day advance fares, weekend fares and internet discounts.

Low-cost and niche airlines could provide the best solution of all. Many of their fares are based on one-way travel, so you don't have to lock in your return date. Some offer one- and three-day advance fares or capacity controlled fares where the rate you pay is determined by seats available, rather than advance booking. These alternate fares also relieve you of the burden of providing the airline with personal information to document the need for a bereavement fare.

MILITARY FARES

The prime advantages of military fares are flexibility and possible savings on last-minute flights or one-way travel. If you have advance booking time, you will probably do better with a fare war ticket or a 21-day advance fare. Military fares are available to active duty military and, in some cases, military dependents. Tickets generally cost $25-50 less than seven-day advance fares. Remember to also check niche carriers, split city options and special promotional coupon offers for last-minute flight savings.

Military fare tickets cannot be mailed, require military ID at the time of ticketing and at check-in and are only available within the U.S.

Recently Southwest introduced military

fares in all 53 cities it serves. The fares can be purchased for the use of active military personnel and their dependents. You must make a reservation, but there is no minimum advance. The airline has set aside a specified number of seats per flight, with some peak and holiday blackouts. Tickets are fully refundable.

FREE AND LOW-COST UPGRADES

There's nothing democratic about the free upgrade process. Checking in early won't necessarily earn you a single advantage. Gate agents determine who will be upgraded based on frequent flyer status and the fare paid. Sometimes qualified travelers are chosen for a upgrades just because the gate agent likes them; infrequently, they are even chosen because they've been overly insistent and the gate agent is tired of dealing with them. We think charm usually works better than insistence.

Can you charm your way into Business or First Class? It doesn't happen regularly, but passengers with winning personalities have been upgraded for handing a bunch of flowers to the gate agent, claiming to be on a honeymoon or mentioning a real or imagined injury that would make sitting in Coach an uncomfortable prospect.

Special deals for upgraded travel include:

- **Continental OnePass members** in the their first year of membership can purchase an *Executive Pack* ($64.95) that includes four one-segment upgrades valid on any published fare, plus a $99 Coach companion ticket certificate. The *Prestige Pack* ($99.95) also includes 7,500 bonus miles and six one-segment space available upgrade certificates. Call **800-441-1135** to enroll; **713-952-1630** to purchase.
- **Midwest Express** offers all Business Class style service, with two-across seating and the best domestic meal service at Coach prices. They service dozen of cities through hubs in Milwaukee, Omaha and Kansas City.
- **Northwest's *ConnectFirst*** offers a free space available upgrade on many flights connecting through Detroit, Minneapolis/St. Paul and Memphis.
- **TWA's *Y-Upgrade*** is confirmed when you purchase your ticket. It's available on flights through St. Louis to the continental U.S., Honolulu and Toronto and on most nonstops to and from New York JFK. They also offer upgrade deals on some flights departing after 7 p.m.
- **Reno Air offers $25 space available upgrades** to First Class, very useful for travel between their 19 Western cities plus Chicago and Detroit.
- **AirTran offers $25-35** one-way upgrades.
- **Air Jamaica offers space available upgrades** for as little as $50 each way. They'll also give you a free First Class roundtrip after you complete six paid roundtrips.

> *"CityBird offers $250 one-way, space available upgrades on your day of travel. With one-way fares to Europe often at $149-199, they represent a fantastic bargain."*

Use a low-cost carrier for deeply discounted, confirmed Business Class fares. Fly CityBird to Brussels, for example, and pay just $1,478 roundtrip from Miami or Orlando; $1,398 from Newark; $1,758 from Los Angeles or Oakland; $1,938 from Mexico City. Major airline fares on the same routes are $4,092, $3,498, $4,768 and $3,350 respectively.

Breaking your fare can save you thousands of dollars on upgraded travel. Say you're flying from Denver to Honolulu with a First Class fare of $3,260. Fly Coach to the West Coast, then pick up a low-cost upgradable ticket to Honolulu for $700-900. You get the comfort you want on the flight that matters most.

The American Express Platinum Card (800-428-0252) offers two-for-one international Business Class fares on 14 airlines. Members can use the program as often as they like. The $300 annual fee pays off handsomely.

ITT Sheraton Club International Gold (800-247-2582) has welcomed new members with two one-way American Airlines upgrades, confirmed when you book your tickets. Even American AAdvantage Gold and Platinum members have to wait for confirmation on many of their upgrades. I've seen people walk out of meetings or pick up their cell phones when that magic 72-hour deadline arrives. The $50 Sheraton membership fee can bring you a much better upgrade deal than the $200-300 airline upgrade that leave you hanging until three days before you travel.

Weekly internet specials for First Class travel are offered each Wednesday by American Airlines for travel the following weekend; each Friday by Alaska Airlines for travel one week from the following Saturday. TWA and other carriers include them from time to time.

Use frequent flyer miles to upgrade according to the policies of your membership plan. Most carriers charge a minimum of 10,000 miles, so reserve them for longhaul and international flights. Elite frequent flyers are often upgraded at no charge on a space-available basis. Some programs allow you to request the upgrade in advance. Others will only take requests at the gate. You can get a low-cost upgrade if you are a frequent flyer using a full Coach fare. The upgrade will be much less than the cost of purchasing a First Class ticket. Upgrade costs are usually based on flight lengths. Airlines offering this form of pricing include Alaska, America West, Canadian, Continental, KLM, Northwest, TWA, US Airways and Virgin Atlantic.

Purchased miles, while not a good deal for domestic travel, can be a gold mine for international flights. For example, purchase a $650 roundtrip fare war ticket for Los Angeles-London, then use 40,000 purchased miles (at an $800 cost) to upgrade. A total cost of $1,450 looks much better to me than $6,790 (the current British Airways Business fare). Your corporation can purchase miles directly from the airlines. Never purchase them from mileage brokers. It's against airline policy, you won't save a dime and you run the risk of being yanked off the plane. Why risk it? Check *Frequent Flyer Twists & Turns* for details.

***Best Fares* Air Travel Plus** offers special excursion First Class fares for just $300 more than standard 21-day advance tickets. This subscriber only offer covers travel within the 48 states and to Hawaii, with some restrictions. *Best Fares* International Air Travel offers deep discounts for Business Class travel to Asia and Europe. Since these business fares represent one of the biggest price gouges in the airline industry, we negotiate very hard for deals that can dramatically lower your costs.

Year in which London Gatwick opened: 1958.

TICKET REBATES

Some travel agencies offer rebates on airline tickets; usually four percent or less. There will be a minimum ticket amount. The full amount of the ticket is charged to your credit card. The rebate check is either issued with your ticket or you're asked to mail your boarding pass in after you've flown. Agencies that use the second method know a high percentage of people will not take the time to mail in their rebate request. Most rebate clubs have had to lower their rebate percentage to accommodate the airlines' commission reductions.

A rebate on a standard airline ticket is not a good deal unless a more significant discount is simply not available. Use rebaters primarily for reservations you've made with the airlines, either for airfare only or for vacation packages. By giving the agency the ticket designator or reservation number, your reservation can be pulled up and ticketed, and you can get the rebate.

The biggest error travelers make when first attempting to receive a rebate is giving their credit card number to the airline, then calling an agency and requesting the rebate. You only get it when you allow the agency to do the ticketing.

COUPON BROKERS

There are three main ways in which discount coupons and flight certificates change hands.

- **Frequent flyers have been selling their award tickets** ever since the program began. Some very frequent flyers could not possibly use all their miles and selling their benefits seems logical. The airlines prohibit it, and all litigation has backed them up. Airlines want to avoid offending their best customers, but they want to protect their bottom line even more. They've become more aggressive every year in trying to stop the selling of flight coupons. If you want to avoid trouble, don't do it.
- **Discount coupons from special promotions** can legally be given away, but they can't be sold. If your neighbor has a $100 off coupon or a companion coupon that she doesn't plan to use, she can give it to you but, according to airline rules, no money can change hands.
- **Coupon brokers** make a business out of wheeling and dealing in coupons. If you're going to use them, you'd better use caution. You're violating airline rules to attempt to gain a financial advantage you can as easily acquire through legitimate means. Airlines have bounties on broker tickets; some pay their gate agents to discover them. If you're challenged and lose, your ticket is confiscated and you end up paying full fare.

> *"Remember that your ID is going to be checked now, even on domestic flights. There is simply no sense in trying to fly on a ticket in another person's name. You won't get where you are trying to go and your entire investment will be lost. Use legitimate ways to cut the cost of travel. What used to be a moderately effective tactic is now completely out of the question."*

CLASSIFIED ADS

Many legitimate agencies, particularly those dealing in consolidator tickets, run classified ads or small display ads in travel and business newspaper sections. This form of low-cost advertising provides an effective means for discounters (who often operate on thin profit margins) to advertise their wares. If you are unfamiliar with the source, check it out as carefully as you would check out any new travel source.

Scam ads attempt to sell stolen and illegal tickets. Scammers can be in and out of a market in a few weeks. They get all the money they can, then disappear. The buyers don't discover that they're trying to fly on illegal tickets until they get to the airport.

COURIER TRAVEL

Courier travel made a good name for itself years ago and, in many hopeful travelers' minds, the good name lives on. In reality, free courier travel is almost nonexistent. Discounted courier travel is harder to find than ever and the discounts are not as favorable as in the past. About 20,000 passengers out of the 550 million total fly as couriers each year and many of them pay far more than you would imagine.

In the past (before overnight delivery services became prevalent), bearer bonds, documents and other timely materials had to be carried over the ocean by couriers. Companies bought wholesale tickets and offered them at deep discounts to those who agreed to serve as couriers. Now, most companies send their material via established delivery systems; those few who want material hand-carried very often send their own employees.

There are other disadvantages to courier travel, over and above the difficulty in getting a courier flight.

- **Many companies require that you pay a membership fee and a deposit** (usually non-refundable in case you decide not to take the flights that are offered).
- **It's next to impossible to travel with a companion** unless they pay for a high-dollar, last-minute ticket.
- **Most, if not all, of your luggage allowance may be consumed** by the material you're being asked to transport.
- **You are likely to be charged** as much as one-third to one-half the unrestricted Coach fare. Some last-minute courier flights may go for as little as $100, but they are the exceptions. The closer it is to the departure date, the less you will have to pay. In many cases, you can beat these deals with discount fares and special promotions.
- **You have to be in a major gateway city** (or be able to get to one cheaply). Most North American courier flights depart from Chicago, Dallas, Detroit, Los Angeles, Miami, Montreal, New York, Newark, San Francisco, Toronto and Vancouver.
- **You're stuck on someone else's schedule.** When you arrive at your destination, your return ticket may be confiscated by a representative of the company. You are not allowed to fly back at any time other than that which is ticketed. If you have a family emergency and want to go home early, tough luck. If you're having a great time and want to stay longer, tough luck.

The most frequent destinations for courier flights departing from North America are major cities in Europe, Asia, South America, Australia, New Zealand, Mexico, Jamaica, Puerto Rico and Guatemala City.

Courier opportunities are advertised in the telephone yellow pages under Air

Area of Hong Kong's new Chek Lap Kok Airport: 3,120 acres.

> *"If you're really interested in courier travel, you may want to check out the current state of the market on your own. See if your local library carries up-to-date books on the subject. Be sure to thoroughly check out any company offering courier opportunities. Ask how many flights they flew the previous year; ask how many were cancelled. The cancellation figure should not be more than one to two percent. Make sure the courier company has at least a year's track record and, of course, never agree to courier anything if you have any doubt about the legality."*

Courier Services, in travel sections and in classified newspaper advertising.

Other points of view on courier travel (and additional information):

- **A free audio cassette** on international courier flights from The International Association of Air Travel Couriers (IAATC), **561-582-8320**. They have a vested interest in putting a good spin on courier travel since it is their business. Write to IAATC Air Courier Cassette, 8 South J Street, P.O. Box 1349, Lake Worth, FL 33460.
- ***The Insiders Guide To Air Courier Bargains*** by Kelly Monaghan. Send $17.45 to Upper Access Publishing, Box 457, Hinesburg, VT 05461; call **800-356-9315**.
- ***The Courier Air Travel Handbook*** ($13.45) by Mark Field. Order from Book Masters, **800-507-2665**; P.O. Box 388, Ashland, OH 44805. You can also check your library or local bookstore (ISBN #0-9630613-1-3).

U.S. AIRLINE PASSES

U.S. airlines offer a selection of passes that will provide price advantages over single tickets, if you use them wisely. One disadvantage: most coupon books are non-refundable. Losing one is like losing cash. Most airlines allow a ten percent discount on pass purchases for seniors.

- **Aloha Airlines AlohaPass (800-367-5250)**, offers the Island Hopper with seven days of unlimited travel during off-peak hours for $299.
- **ATA Passbooks (800-225-2995)**, offer savings on select routes. There are three Passbooks available, each containing six one-way flight coupons. The *Bronze Pass* covers flights between Chicago, Indianapolis or Milwaukee and Florida cities in B, K or Q with some peak and holiday limits—the $696 cost averages $116 per coupon; The *Silver Pass* covers ATA routes within the continental U.S., excluding California—the $1,194 cost averages $199 per coupon; The *Gold Pass* covers all ATA routes systemwide (including Hawaii)—the $1,794 cost averages $299 per coupon.
- **Delta Connection-Comair Weekend Traveler (800-532-4777)**, provides four coupons for $299, valid for travel on weekends, Mondays until noon and during some holiday periods. Their base cities are Orlando and Cincinnati. Flights under 500 miles require one coupon. Flights over 500 miles, and all flights connecting through Cincinnati, require two coupons. Travel is valid to U.S. destinations and the Bahamas. Comair will send you a free booklet detailing the Weekend Traveler deal.
- **Hawaiian Airlines AirPass (800-367-**

Percentage of 1997 flights within Europe arriving more than 15 minutes late: 20 percent.

5320), has four coupons valid for unlimited flights during the period of validity. A five-day pass is $179, a seven-day pass (with the eighth day free) is $199, a ten-day pass is $239 and a 14-day pass (with the 15th day free) is $279. Seniors and children receive a $10 discount. Purchase requires proof of inbound travel from the continental U.S. and a confirmed return reservation. The Commuter AirPass allows unlimited travel for one month for $799. Commuter passes are only good from the first through the 31st of each month. They can't, for example, run from the 15th to the 15th. You also get two transferrable First Class upgrades for travel to the West Coast, access to airport lounges and 10,000 bonus miles.

- **Kiwi Commuter Coupon Books (800-538-5494)**, come in two varieties, each providing ten segments of travel on designated routes. On medium-range routes, the cost is $1,208 (tax included), averaging $120.80 per coupon. On long-range routes, the cost is $1,505 (tax included), averaging $150.50 per coupon. Coupons are valid for one year with a three-month extension available for $25. Standby travel is allowed. The coupons are non-refundable.

VISITOR AIRFARES & INTERNATIONAL PASSES

Visitor Airfares and International Passes consist of sets of one-way coupons or a pass for unlimited travel within a specified time period. They are only available to visitors; residents cannot purchase them. For coupon travel, there is usually a minimum and maximum coupon requirement, with the price often decreasing for higher quantities. Use them wisely and you can save 25 to 70 percent, as compared to individual tickets. This form of travel carries various restrictions. Have your travel agent or the airline read and explain them to you thoroughly before you purchase. Common restrictions on pass travel include:

- **Passes usually must be purchased in the U.S.** in conjunction with an international flight. Some require that your transoceanic travel is booked on a specific carrier. Many are not available if your international ticket comes from award miles or a consolidator. Passes are non-refundable once your trip has begun.
- **You must be a resident of a country other than** the one(s) you will use for pass travel.
- **Children's passes** generally cost 67 to 75 percent of adult fares; infants without an assigned seat pay ten percent of the adult fare.
- **Time allowed for travel varies** and is often linked to the dates of your international ticket.
- **Passes usually allow just one stopover per city** unless you use that city for a connecting flight. Each coupon covers one flight segment (except where noted); connections require two coupons. Save by choosing a carrier with routing and partners that keep you from having to fly back to a hub city. Most passes do not allow backtracking or travel to the same city twice, except for connections.
- **You cannot transfer to another carrier** if your scheduled flight is cancelled or delayed. Pass travel is not covered by interline agreements.
- **Some passes are seasonal** and either cost more or are unavailable during peak travel times.

Message painted on a Virgin Atlantic plane: "No way AA/BA."

> *"Many of these international coupon books and passes can be purchased by Best Fares subscribers at an added discount simply by purchasing through Best Fares International Air Travel. Be sure to check* ***www.bestfares.com*** *for internet deals including Cathay Pacific's All Asia Pass for $899 covering travel to Hong Kong plus 17 additional cities."*

Here is a listing of select international air travel passes. Because prices and specifics change often, be sure to confirm all pertinent information before you purchase. A few passes include transoceanic travel. Following the name of each pass is the airline offering it. You can call direct (check our *Know Who To Contact* section for phone numbers) but we recommend booking through your travel agent. If a specific carrier is required for your flight to/from the U.S., that entry begins with the carrier required.

Asia

Discover Asia Airpass/SilkAir
$129 per flight between Singapore and select cities in Indonesia, Malaysia or Thailand; $229 between Singapore and select cities in Burma, Cambodia, China, Indonesia, Laos or the Philippines. Maximum stay is 90 days.

Discover India Fare/Indian Airlines
$500 for 15 days of unlimited travel within India; $750 for 21 days of travel. (One Delhi-Calcutta flight alone costs about $225 without the use of this visitor fare.) The best source for this pass is Hari World Travel at **212-997-3300**; go online at **www.hariworld.com**.

Wonderfares/Indian Airlines
Price based on region of travel. For example, pay $300 for seven days of travel within one region. You must purchase in India using foreign currency.

Visit Indonesia Decade Pass/Garuda
Get the cheapest rate by flying internationally on Garuda (add $50 if you use another airline). Pay $330 for three flights; $550 for five flights; $110 for each additional flight (maximum seven). Minimum stay is three days; maximum is 60 days. Purchase in the U.S. or within 14 days of arrival in Indonesia.

Discover Malaysia Pass/ Malaysia Airlines
Pay $99 for up to five flights within the Malaysian Peninsula; $199 for up to five flights anywhere within Malaysia. Valid for 28 days. Purchase in the U.S. or within 14 days of arrival in Malaysia.

Discover Thai/Thai Airways
$259/four coupons; additional coupons $70 each. Maximum stay of 60 days. Destinations must be chosen in advance; $25 per change. Date/time of first flight must be confirmed in advance. Others may be left open.

Australia, New Zealand & The South Pacific

Boomerang/Qantas
$144-172 per segment (based on zone travel) for two to ten coupons for travel throughout Australia, Fiji and New Zealand. Valid for the length of your international ticket. First two destinations must be booked in advance. Purchase additional destinations after travel begins if you have at least one remaining coupon. Change dates in advance without charge; $50 fee per destination change.

Visit Australia and New Zealand/ Ansett

Two to ten segments for $160-200 each, depending on travel zones. Valid during the dates of your international ticket. Destinations and dates can be changed without penalty.

Explore New Zealand/ Air New Zealand
Three coupons/$336; four/$448; five/ $560; six/$672; seven/$784; a maximum of eight/$896. Valid during the dates of your international ticket.

New Zealand Air Pass/Ansett
Purchase this pass for travel within New Zealand (this pass can be purchased after you arrive in New Zealand as well as from the U.S.). Minimum purchase is three coupons/$315; maximum is eight coupons/$798.

Discover Fiji/Fiji Air
$236 for four segments of travel. Additional segments $50 each with no maximum. May be used within 30 days of the first segment flown. $50 fee per routing change. No fee for date changes.

Paradise Pass/Air Vanuatu
Visitor ticket on Air Vanuatu. Pay $399 for two segments within 30 days to locations including Auckland, Brisbane, Fiji, Melbourne, New Caledonia and Sydney. Some single fares on these routes are as much as $500.

Polypass/Polynesian Airlines
Fly any carrier from the U.S. to American Samoa, Australia, Fiji, New Zealand, Tonga or Western Samoa. $999 covers travel to five locations. Add Honolulu for $150. 30 days maximum travel time. Backtracking not allowed. Destinations cannot be changed. One date may be changed without penalty; others incur a $50 fee.

Visit The Pacific Pass/Air Nauru
Visitor ticket on Air Nauru. Covers destinations in Australia, Guam, Manila and Micronesia. $400 for three flights and $75 per additional flight within a nine day period. Unlimited stopovers in Nauru.

Discover Solomon/Solomon Airlines
This pass is valid for travel to 24 islands. $249 for four segments; additional segments (no limit)/$50 each. Valid 30 days. Backtracking allowed for connections only. Destinations must be chosen in advance; $50 per change. Date/time of first flight must be booked in advance.

Visit South Pacific Pass/ Several Airlines
Visitor ticket on Air Caledonia International, Air Nauru, Air Niugini, Air Pacific, Air Vanuatu, Polynesian Airlines, Qantas, Royal Tongan Airlines and Solomon Airlines. $150- 300 per coupon (based on zone travel) for travel between Australia, Cook Islands, Fiji, Kiribati, the Marshall Islands, New Caledonia, New Zealand, Niue, Papua New Guinea, the Solomon Islands, Tahiti, Tonga, Tuvalu, Vanuatu and Western Samoa. Two segments minimum/eight maximum. Six months maximum allowed for travel. First flight must be confirmed in advance. Subsequent dates may be left open, but destinations must be chosen in advance. $50 per routing change, plus any fare difference.

Baltic States

Visit Baltic/Scandinavian Airlines
Fly SAS to Copenhagen or Stockholm. Two to four segments are $110 each. Fly to Estonia, Latvia and Lithuania. Destinations must be chosen in advance; changes are $50. No charge to change date or time of travel. Valid during the dates of your international ticket.

The Caribbean

Butterfly Fare/BWIA International
Unlimited travel to most major Caribbean

Anti jet lag service offered by London's Gatwick Hilton: aromatherapy.

cities. Valid for 30 days. Travel must begin and end in the same location. Purchase in the U.S. or the Caribbean. Destinations, but not dates, must be chosen in advance. $20 fee per change.

Super Caribbean Explorers/Liat
Seven day advance required. Valid for 30 days of travel to any of 27 islands/one stop per island. $35 fee per change. A second pass allows three stops for $270 and must be purchased in the U.S. Segment credit on Liat.

Europe

Also see individual country listings.

Discover Europe/British Midland
Fly any carrier from the U.S. to any British Midland city. Segments under 90 minutes/$109; longer flights/$139. Valid one year. No maximum purchase. Backtracking allowed. First flight must be confirmed in advance. No charge for changing dates/$50 per destination change.

Discover Europe/Lufthansa
Fly any nonstop U.S.-Germany flight. Three coupon minimum/$375, $420/ peak. Up to six additional coupons at $105 each, $125/peak. Validity determined by the dates of your international ticket. Destinations (not dates) must be picked in advance. $50 per itinerary change.

Euro Flyer/
Air France or Czech Airlines
Fly any carrier to Paris or Czech into Prague. $99 per segment; $120/peak. Minimum of three segments/maximum of nine. Minimum of seven days/maximum two months. Most major European cities included. Destinations and the date of your first flight must be chosen in advance. $60 for changes.

Eurogreensaver/Aer Lingus
Fly transatlantic with Aer Lingus to purchase this pass for $99 per segment to cities including Amsterdam, Brussels, Copenhagen, Dusseldorf, Frankfurt, Milan, Paris, Rome and Zurich. Travel within the U.K./$60 per segment. No maximum segment purchase. Travel within six months. $20 per itinerary change.

EuroPass/Iberia
Fly transatlantic with Iberia. $125/segment to most destinations in Europe; $155/Cairo, Moscow and Tel Aviv. Two segment minimum/no maximum. Maximum travel time is three months. $50 per re-route; no fee to reschedule.

Europe Airpass/British Airways
Three coupon minimum/12 maximum. Zone 1/$82: inter-U.K. and inter-France; U.K.- Belgium, Ireland, Luxembourg, the Netherlands and Paris; Gibraltar-Tangier. Zone 2/$107: inter-German; U.K.-Denmark, France (excluding Paris), Germany, Portugal, Spain and Switzerland; Germany-Italy; Gibraltar-Morocco (excluding Tangier); Greece-Italy. Zone 3/$133: U.K.-Austria, Bulgaria, the Czech Republic, Finland, Gibraltar, Greece, Hungary, Italy, Norway, Poland, Romania and Sweden; France-Greece or Scandinavia; Germany-Norway; Spain-Sweden; London-Tangier; Germany-the Czech Republic and Switzerland. Zone 4/$166: U.K.-Azerbaijan, Cyprus, Israel, Madeira, Russia, Tunisia, and Turkey; Denmark-Spain; Germany-Latvia, Lithuania-Russia; Greece-Norway; Italy-Sweden; U.K.-Morocco (excluding Tangier). Most flights connect through London. Seven-day minimum; three months maximum. Destinations must be booked in advance. No re-routing; $40 per reschedule.

Europlus Air/Alitalia
Fly transatlantic with Alitalia. Three coupons for $299; additional coupons $100 each/no quantity limit. Minimum and maximum stays determined by inter-

Bonus offered by Alaska to the first airline to establish nonstop service to Japan: $1 million.

national ticket. Destinations and dates must be pre-set. $50 per itinerary change. Includes most major European cities. Backtracking allowed.

The Hungarian Pass to Europe/ Malev Hungarian
Fly transatlantic on Malev to most capital cities in Europe. All flights connect in Budapest. Three coupons for $330 or $420/peak; four for $379 or $479/peak; five for $454 or $579/peak; six for $529 or $679/peak; seven for $599 or $797/peak. Additional coupons to a maximum of nine are $90 each, $110/peak. Destinations must be chosen in advance and cannot be changed. Dates do not have to be chosen in advance and can be changed. Valid for the duration of your transatlantic ticket. Points on Malev after one transatlantic and one inter-Europe flight.

Passport to Europe/KLM or Northwest
Three coupons/$300-390, depending on season. 12 coupon maximum. Coupons four and five/$80 each, $110 peak. Six-12/$70 each, $100 peak. Season determined by date of first coupon flight. Includes most major European cities except to/from Dublin. Date validity determined by your international ticket. Three destinations and dates must be chosen before you depart the U.S. Destinations may be added. $50 per change in dates or destination. Most flights connect through Amsterdam.

“Several U.S.-based carriers also offer European travel passes. Check TWA's Inter-Europe and Delta's Discover Europe, among others. As international travel increases, pass options will expand even further.”

Visit Europe/SAS
$360/three coupon minimum. Additional coupons (to a maximum of eight) are $120 each. Travel limited to three months from the date of the first coupon flight. Backtracking is allowed. Destinations (not dates) must be chosen in advance. $50 fee per itinerary changes.

Visit Europe/Austrian, Delta, Sabena, Swissair or United
Fly with any of the five airlines listed above on your transatlantic flight. $130 per segment, $150 if you fly another carrier. Minimum/three; maximum/eight. Valid two months after the date of the first segment. First segment must be booked in advance; $50 per change. Other destinations and dates can be left open or changed without penalty.

France

La France Pass/Air France & Air Inter
$339/seven days of unlimited travel within a 30 day period. Travel dates do not have to be consecutive; valid for one year.

Italy

Visit Italy/Alitalia
$299 for a minimum of three cities/four segments. Additional segments $100 each/ten maximum. Validity determined by international ticket. Destinations must be chosen in advance. Backtracking allowed. $50 per routing change. Dates can remain open; no fee for date changes.

Japan

Welcome To Japan/JAL
Covers travel between 23 cities in Japan. Costs average about half the cost of full fare tickets. The coupons must be purchased before you travel to Japan and require a separate ticket from another country to Japan as a condition of purchase. Your ticket to Japan can be on the

Sets of handcuffs supplied to each Cathay Pacific crew: ten.

carrier of your choice. Coupon flights must be reserved at least 14 days in advance but you can change travel dates and your itinerary from the second coupon on, with no change fee. You have two months to complete coupon travel. Purchase in increments of two to five coupons, but there is no price advantage for purchasing more than two. The per-coupon cost averages about $104.

Latin America

Visit Argentina/ Aerolineas Argentinas or Austral
Qualify with an Aerolineas Argentinas flight and pay $450/four coupons. If you fly other carriers to Argentina the cost is $500. Additional coupons are $120 each ($130 if you flew with another carrier) with a maximum of eight. Travel to most cities in Argentina during a 30-day period. The first change of destination or date is free; additional changes/$50 each.

Avensa Airpass/Servivensa & Avensa
Your roundtrip flight from the U.S. must be on Servivensa and is included in the price and counts as two segments. Segments range from $40 (flights within Venezuela) to $180 (New York - Caracas). Minimum of four segments. Fly to most cities in Venezuela and Bogota, Lima, Mexico City and Quito. No limit on stopovers. 45 days maximum travel time. Destinations, dates and times must be chosen in advance. Dates and times may be changed without penalty. No re-routing is allowed.

Visit Bolivia/Lloyd Aero Boliviano
Pay $150 for travel to your choice of four cities including Cochabamba, La Paz, Santa Cruz, Sucre, Tarija and Trinidad. The pass is $225 if you fly another carrier to Bolivia. If you fly Lloyd, ask about a possible free stopover. Valid up to 30 days. $10 per change requiring ticket reissue.

Brazil Air/Varig Brazilian
Three passes allowing two connections and up to four additional stopovers at $100 each. Five cities/$490; four Central and Southern Brazil cities/$350; four Northeast cities/$290. Add $50 per base price for peak; stopovers remain the same. 21 maximum travel days. Dates and destinations must be chosen at time of purchase. One free change prior to departure. One $30 change after travel begins.

Brazilian Airpass/VASP
Pay $450 for five flights; each additional flight (up to a total maximum of nine) is $100.

Visit Chile/LAN Chile
Five separate itineraries including up to ten cities for $300 to $1,290 (depending on itinerary) with 21 days to travel. The Continental OnePass, for example, includes Santiago, Copiapo, Antofagasta, Calama, Iquique, Arica and return to Santiago for $300. The Pacifica Three pass has exact routing: Santiago, Copiapo, Calama, Antofagasta, Iquique, Arica, Santiago, Concepcion, Punta Arenas, Puerto Montt, Santiago, Easter Island and Santiago for $1,290.

Visit Colombia/Avianca
If you fly Avianca to Colombia pay $90 for a three segment pass. Pay $230 if you fly another carrier. Up to two additional segments can be purchased at $40 each. Fly Avianca and pay $170 for a five-segment pass; $389 if you fly another carrier. Valid for a maximum of 30 days. $30 per itinerary change.

Tumi Pass/Aeroperu
Purchase a minimum of two segments for $130; three for $189; four for $239; five for $285. Additional passes are $45 each with no quantity limit. Valid 30 days maximum. Destinations (not dates) must be chosen in advance. Change dates without penalty.

First airline to offer transatlantic ticketless travel: CityBird.

Mayan Airpass/
Aviateca, Lacsa and Taca
Central America multi-country pass for use between Cancun, Belize City, Flores, Guatemala City, La Cieba, Merida, Mexico City, Roatan, San Pedro Sula, San Salvador and Tegucigalpa. Requires arrival in any of those cities from Houston, Los Angeles, Miami, New Orleans, New York, Orlando, San Francisco or Washington. $360 for four coupons (minimum purchase). Some flights require two coupons. Minimum stay is three days; maximum is 60 days. Must be purchased at least three days prior to your international departure.

Mexipass/
Aeromexico & Mexicana Airlines
One pass issued in the U.S. (mention rule 1532); one issued in Mexico (rule 9675). The U.S. pass requires a flight into Mexico on Aeromexico or Mexicana. Three zones/$65-130 per coupon. Three-coupon minimum/no maximum. $20 per destination change plus fare difference. Valid up to 45 days. The Mexipass requires an international ticket on any carrier. Seven zones/$30-130 per coupon. Valid up to 90 days. Changes without fee. Non-refundable.

Visit Central America Program/
Aviateca, Copa, Lacsa, Nica or Taca
Prices vary by international departure city and cover travel to Belize City, Bluefields, Corn Island, Flores, Guatemala City, La Cieba, Managua, Puerto Cabezas, Panama City, Roatan, San Jose, San Pedro Sula, San Salvador and Tegucigalpa. Low season rates for Houston, Miami, New Orleans and Orlando at $499 (three flight minimum) and $1,059 (ten flight maximum). Low season rates for Los Angeles, New York, San Francisco or Washington are $699 (three flight minimum) and $1,259 (ten flight maximum).

South American/Aeroperu
Your flight from the U.S. is included in the price of the pass and counts as two segments. Four segments from the West Coast/$999; six/$1,499. Four segments from Miami/$799; six/$1,299. Add $200 for peak. Additional segments can be added (up to six segment passes) at $100 each. Travel throughout South America except French Guiana, Guyana, Suriname and Uruguay. Dates and destinations must be confirmed in advance. $25 per date change. Most flights connect through Lima. You are allowed to count a connection in South America (either leaving or returning to the U.S.) as one segment.

Sudamerica Pass/Aeroperu
Requires international roundtrip from the U.S. or Mexico to Lima. Allows travel to ten South American cities for $1,299 low season (from Cancun, Miami or Mexico City); $1,499 low season (from Los Angeles) for a maximum of 60 days. Destinations include Asuncion, Bogota, Buenos Aires, Caracas, Guayaquil, La Paz, Quito, Rio de Janeiro, Santiago and Sao Paulo.

Philippines

Philippine Airlines
Purchase a minimum of four coupons/$155; six/$182; ten/$198. Length of pass validity determined by your international ticket. Destinations (not dates of travel) must be chosen in advance.

Scandinavia

Finnair Holiday/Finnair
Fly Finnair to Helsinki to purchase this pass for $500 for ten coupons. Maximum of nine stopovers. Valid 30 days. First flight segment must be confirmed in advance. Remaining destinations and dates can be left open. $9 per itinerary change.

Japanese carrier scheduled to begin service in late 1998: Air Do.

Visit Norway/
Braathens SAFE/Passage Tours
Discount point-to-point fares with travel ranging from $85-170 per segment. No quantity limits or time restrictions. Destinations must be selected in advance but can be changed as you travel, without penalty.

Visit Scandinavia/SAS
$80 per segment covers Denmark, Finland, Norway and Sweden (except flights between Finland and Denmark). No minimum; six coupon maximum. Destinations must be chosen in advance; $50 per change. Dates and times can be changed without penalty. The *Visit Scandinavia* pass is valid for the length of your international ticket.

South Africa

African Explorer/
South African Airways
Up to 60 percent off point to point fares purchased before you depart the U.S. All destinations and the first flight date must be booked in advance. Other dates may be left open. Most connections are through Johannesburg and include points as far north as Nairobi.

Spain

Visit Spain/Iberia
Transatlantic travel on Iberia. Four coupons/$240, $260 peak or $299 and $349/peak to include travel to the Canary Islands. Additional coupons $50; maximum of eight. One route change allowed at no fee. Maximum travel time 30 days.

AROUND-THE-WORLD FARES

Around-the-world fares save money on international trips with extensive itineraries. You book your ticket on the host airline and are also permitted to fly its affiliates during a specific time frame, usually six to 12 months. They offer an incredible value, especially for Business and First Class travel. Your entire trip can cost about the same as one roundtrip.

Around-the-world fares start at about $2,500 for Coach, $3,600 for Business Class and $5,000 for First Class. Here is a sample itinerary: Chicago to Toronto and on to New York, London, Amsterdam, Frankfurt, Copenhagen, Stockholm, Athens, New Delhi, Bangkok, Hong Kong, Manila, Taipei, Seoul, Osaka, Tokyo, Guam, Honolulu, Seattle and back to Chicago.

The Star Alliance partnership provides a new opportunity for Around-The-World savings using Lufthansa, Air Canada, SAS, Thai Airways, United Airlines and Varig. Depart from the U.S. or Canada on an international routing that has a minimum of three stopovers and a maximum of 15. A seven-day advance is required. The minimum travel period is ten days; the maximum of one year. You must depart from and return to the same country on Star Alliance partner flights. Your price is determined by the number of miles in your itinerary. Pay 67 percent of the adult fare for a child's ticket; ten percent for an infant's ticket. There is no senior discount. Here is the basic fare structure.

First Class:
25,000 maximum miles/$6,199
32,000 maximum miles/$7,129
38,000 maximum miles/$7,749

Business Class:
25,000 maximum miles/$4,599
32,000 maximum miles/$5,289

Airline with ads featuring a penguin dressed in plaid: Icelandair (promoting service to Glasgow).

38,000 maximum miles/$5,749

Coach Class:
25,000 maximum miles/$2,499
32,000 maximum miles/$2,749
38,000 maximum miles/$2,999

If around-the-world fares interest you, take the time to gather route maps from the major airlines and plot a tentative itinerary. Most travel agents really can't provide the intensive time needed to plan an around-the-world-trip. Airlines offer special agents skilled in the complexities of around-the-world routing. *Best Fares* subscribers receive a four percent instant rebate when purchasing most round-the-world tickets through their International Air Travel Club. If your ticket is $5,000, for example, you get a $200 rebate.

OTHER WAYS TO SAVE INTERNATIONALLY

A discount-conscious travel agent can help you through changing variables of international airfares and help you save on every ticket. Factors affecting international fares include:

- **Travel days**: You usually have to meet the day of the week requirement on departure and return to get the applicable fare. Cheapest travel days are usually Monday through Thursday. Weekend travel adds $25 or more per direction to sale fares.
- **Travel season**: Examples of common international discount airfare seasons (excluding holiday travel):

  Asia: January and February

  Australia and New Zealand: April through August

  The Caribbean: May through December 15

  Europe: November through May

  South America: April through November
- **Length of stay**: A ticket allowing a stay of 30 days or less is generally the cheapest. Changing a return date may alter your fare and subject you to payment of the fare difference plus a change fee.
- **Travelers' ages**: Children under two generally pay ten percent of the adult ticket price; children two to 11 generally pay 50-75 percent of the adult fare. Some intra-Europe flights offer discount standby tickets for people ages 12-24, sometimes confirmed 72 hours before flight time.
- **Restrictions**: Plan to spend a little extra time on the phone when booking an international ticket. Lower priced tickets generally offer less flexibility and require higher fees for any changes. Some APEX fares are nonrefundable. Before you purchase an international ticket ask the agent to go through the major rules with you. After you purchase it, ask to have the rules printed out and enclosed with your ticket.

You can sometimes avoid paying a change fee when you want to return earlier than your ticketed return. If you show up at the airport and request a seat on an earlier flight with plenty of available space, there is a possibility you will get on the plane without having to pay the fee. This is at the gate agent's discretion, so having a good reason for your early return can be very helpful.

Free stopovers, also known as maximum permitted mileage, can sometimes be added to an international ticket at no extra cost. Sometimes you can even fly on anoth-

Inaugural year for the first airborne toilet: 1913 (on a Russian transport plane).

er airline. For example, a New York-Oslo ticket can be issued with a free stopover in London. In some cases, you can make multiple stops. You also accrue more frequent flyer miles. There are rules and limits to maximum permitted miles, so it's best to book them through a travel agent who is well versed in international routes.

Some European cities (including Paris, London and Amsterdam) have many travel agencies that sell discounted intra-Europe tickets. A good way to check prices before you travel is to head for your local library and check the classified ad sections of international papers. If you see fares that appeal to you, jot down the phone numbers and purchase your tickets in advance by credit card.

NOTES FOR BUSINESS TRAVELERS

Your flexibility helps determines the range of savings possibilities open to you. Non-stop flying is always convenient. Flying home right after finishing the Friday business day is desirable. If cost is a major factor, however, many of us will change travel dates, times and flights to save money. The changes are often easy to accommodate, and savings can be significant.

- **Be open to switching airlines** and you can often cut your fare in half.
- **Use connecting flights** and you can save as much as $1,000 per roundtrip.
- **Return in the evening**, rather than the afternoon, save $250 and increase your chances of a free upgrade.

Many surveys say business travelers care more about frequent flyer programs than value. The only possible logic in this is that the flyer gets to keep the miles and the employer foots the bill. If you are paying for the ticket, why not go for immediate savings so you can have the flexibility to buy a ticket (or two or three) with the money you save?

- **Placing price anywhere but number one on the priority scale** is a triumph of Madison Avenue over greater reality. You can have it all if you know how to play the game—from discounts that are just as available for Business Class as for Coach (and they are even more dramatic) to earning "free flights" that give you more flexibility than any frequent flyer award. If you must have miles, you can get them without sacrificing price.
- **You can often get miles while you're getting the best price** and when you can't, you're saving more than enough money to make up for the fraction of a "free" ticket that's dangling at the end of the frequent flyer carrot. When you limit yourself to one airline just to rack up miles, you've made it easy for your travel agent to earn commissions and easy for the airlines to charge their asking rates. The travel agent simply has to check one airline, then issue the ticket with no incentive to even look for a better price. The airline happily takes your money.

Use a travel expert or become one. The time you spend educating yourself to options and possibilities will pay off handsomely in annual savings.

- **Even small companies** benefit from assigning one person to oversee travel reservations.
- **If your client is paying for your travel**, retain control over choices whenever you can. Often you can take the money they've budgeted for your travel, save money and acquire upgrades by doing the booking yourself.

Largest U.S. airport without a rapid rail system to the city: Dallas/Fort Worth International.

Pick up extra time by knowing which flights to book and which flights to avoid. Travel agents and airline reservation agents have a number (from one to ten) next to each flight on their computer screens. The number rates the flight's on-time performance. One indicates the flight was on time ten percent of the time; nine means it was on time 90 percent of the time. Don't overestimate the importance of advertising claims regarding overall on-time statistics. Statistics average the records for all flights. Some flights—perhaps one you're considering—may be notoriously late. Airlines increase scheduled flight times trying to obscure reality. In some cases, the same routing on the same aircraft, flying at the same time, shows as much as 30 more minutes of flight time as compared to the year before. Jets aren't getting slower.

- **Choose flights that take off and land** outside of peak travel times. For most airports the busiest times are 9-11 a.m. and 4-8 p.m. on weekdays. Airports with a preponderance of leisure travel (such as Las Vegas and Fort Lauderdale) will have different peak periods.
- **Fly in and out of smaller airports**, when possible, to save money and avoid congestion: Burbank instead of LAX, Chicago Midway instead of O'Hare; Oakland instead of San Francisco; Dallas Love Field instead of Dallas-Fort Worth International.

Join all the major frequent flyer programs. Membership in all the major programs is free and new member bonuses are often awarded. Use tie-in programs to accumulate points and miles, but be careful not to develop a blind loyalty that keeps you from saving many times the dollar value of your award units. Qualify for elite level frequent flyer status to earn priority wait listing and baggage handling, preferred seating, special menu selections, liberal upgrade provisions and less limited blackout days for free travel. The requirement can be as little as 25,000 base miles per year.

> *"Business travelers who strategize and purchase bargain premium class tickets will be able to enjoy the benefits of high-dollar travel, without the cost. More than ever before, airlines are pulling every rabbit out of their hats in the attempt to engender business traveler loyalty. The gulf between Coach and Business/First Class service levels will become wider. All major airlines are developing sophisticated passenger tracking programs designed to let them know who their most loyal business travelers are. You'll see more special offers and more red carpet service. Enjoy it all, but never forget that your own bottom line is saving money."*

TOUR PACKAGES

FLY/DRIVES

Fly/Drives offer an under-used strategy that can save business travelers big bucks. You won't be able to use it every time you travel but, when you can use it, the savings will impress you. This strategy also provides a very substantial bonus for one of your best bargain travel allies: your travel agent. Fly/Drive packages are not subject to the same commission restrictions as airfares. Any savvy traveler knows that doing what you can to keep your travel agent happy pays off in better service, extra effort toward finding lower fares and overall customer appreciation.

You're never going to be quoted a Fly/Drive rate by regular airline reservation agents. You're not going to find them on any online booking engine. Each airline has its own special number to call. When you (or your travel agent) call the airlines' Fly/Drive divisions, you are linked to several immediate advantages:

- **The elimination of the Saturday night stay requirement**, resulting in big savings on weekday travel.
- **An advance purchase requirement of as little as three days**, useful even in cases where you do plan a Saturday night stay but have a brief advance booking window.
- **One rate that includes** roundtrip airfare and a rental car, often with a free one- or two- class rental car upgrade at no extra charge.
- **As a rule of thumb**, your roundtrip no Saturday stay airfare and your rental car can cost you about half what you would pay for airfare alone, if you didn't use this strategy.

Every strategy has its limitations, and Fly/Drive rates are no exception. Policies vary from airline to airline but, in general, here are the facts you need to know.

- **All Fly/Drive rates require a minimum stay** of two to four days, depending on the airline and the destination. You can't use them for a same day or one night trip.

Newest trend in package vacation themes: rock & roll nostalgia.

"Let's say I want to fly from Dallas/Fort Worth to San Francisco for meetings on Tuesday and Wednesday. Delta Air Lines quotes a roundtrip fare of $1,052. I look for a rental car and find a good bargain (of course!) that adds another $80 to my cost. I'm already out $1,132 before I even think about hotel costs. If I call Delta Vacations, I can get a Fly/Drive rate of only $539 including a compact car for the length of my stay. I've just saved $593 by calling one 800 number instead of another. Here's another example: While I'm in San Francisco, I do a couple of radio shows. The program director has to travel to Orlando to visit a sister station. He has to spend several days there, but he doesn't want to lose his weekend back home. American Airlines quotes $1,771 roundtrip for a Monday departure and Friday return. He knows I'm the guru of low-cost airfares so he's hoping I can shave a couple hundred bucks off his fare. My fare shaver is sharper than he imagines. By pointing him toward US Airways Vacations, he gets a $555 Fly/Drive rate with a rental car thrown in. He's just saved $1,216 plus the cost of his rental car. Is he buying dinner that night? You bet. Are we dining in style? Right again."

- **Some Fly/Drive plans are limited** to cities with a large amount of tourist travel. Fortunately, many of these cities are also hot business destinations. For example: Vancouver, New Orleans, Los Angeles, Denver, Florida cities Arizona cities, Reno and New York.
- **Solo travelers pay more** than the averaged cost of two travelers booking and traveling together (due to single supplements) but you still get a bargain.

Here are basic details, by airline, on Fly/Drive rate availability. TWA does not offer Fly/Drive deals but you may find that booking a vacation package (airfare/car rental/hotel) can also provide business travel advantages. In most cases, Fly/Drive rates are available for departure from any city served by that airline. Don't be thrown by the fact that you'll be calling the vacation division. That's just how this particular game is played. Keep the number close at hand because you may be calling them back soon to book a real vacation with the money you are saving on your business travel.

If you are flying on a frequent flyer ticket, check with the airline you're flying for possible bargains on/and packages that can include hotel and car rental. Often they can save you money on the land portion of your travel.

America West Vacations

800-356-6611

Destinations include: Las Vegas, Orange County, Orlando, Phoenix, Reno, Tampa and Vancouver.

Minimum stay: Two nights.

Minimum advance: Seven days (ask about a shorter advance window with payment of an additional fee).

Special Note: Las Vegas, Phoenix and Reno do not have a Saturday night stay requirement on any America West travel; a two-day minimum stay is required. You may find America West Vacations Fly/Drive rates most useful for situations with limited advance. They allow you to purchase (to select destinations) as late as the day before your departure.

The only state in the U.S. without legally incorporated cities: Hawaii.

American Airlines Vacations

800-321-2121

Destinations include: All cities served except those in Idaho, Minnesota, Nebraska, North Dakota, Oklahoma and South Dakota.

Minimum stay: Two nights.

Minimum advance: Four days.

Continental Vacations

800-634-5555

Destinations include: Honolulu, Las Vegas, Los Angeles, Miami, New Orleans, Orlando, San Diego and San Francisco.

Minimum stay: Three nights.

Minimum advance: Four to 14 days, varying by itinerary.

Special note: Continental requires a minimum of two passengers booking and traveling together.

Delta Vacations

800-872-7786

Destinations include: Albuquerque, Daytona, Denver, Fort Myers, Las Vegas, Melbourne, Miami, Oakland, Orange County, Orlando, Palm Springs, Pensacola, Phoenix, Reno, Salt Lake City, San Francisco and Sarasota.

Minimum stay: Two nights.

Minimum advance: Three days.

Special note: Travel to Florida cities requires a minimum of two people booking and traveling together.

United Vacations

800-328-6877

Destinations include: Denver, Las Vegas, Los Angeles, New Orleans, New York, Orlando, Phoenix, Reno and San Francisco.

Minimum stay: Two nights.

Minimum advance: Three days.

US Airways Vacations

800-455-0123

Destinations include: Fort Lauderdale, Key West, Las Vegas, Los Angeles, Miami, Orlando, Pensacola, San Diego, San Francisco and Sarasota.

Minimum stay: Four nights.

Minimum advance: Four days.

TOUR PACKAGES

Vacation packages come from two distinct sources: vacation divisions of the major airlines and packages offered by companies that utilize both charter and scheduled airlines. Each has a separate set of rules.

Airlines vacation divisions concentrate on tourist-popular destinations. You must call the vacation division directly because the 800 number you are accustomed to using will not let you access vacation package rates. Consumers are protected to the same degree as on the purchase of airline tickets, but specific policies can vary. Airline packages usually allow more flexibility than those offered by many tour companies. You can usually depart and return on the days you choose and stay as long as you like, as long as there is availability in the fare class the airline uses for its package travel. Get the lowest rates by traveling on off-peak days.

Number of people who visit Las Vegas on a typical weekend: 250,000.

Select Major Airline Vacation Divisions

Aeromexico Vacations 800-245-8585
Air Canada Vacations 800-774-8993
Air France Holidays 800-237-2623
Air New Zealand Vacations 800-722-4342
Alaska Airlines Vacations .800-468-2248
America West Vacations . .800-356-6611
American Airlines Vacations 800-321-2121
British Airways Holidays . .800-247-9297
Continental Airlines Vacations 800-634-5555
Delta Vacations 800-872-7786
El Al Tours 800-352-5786
Icelandair European Vacations 800-223-5500
LanChile Tours 800-995-4888
Mexicana MexSeaSun . . .800-531-9321
Midway Vacations 800-996-4392
Northwest World Vacations 800-727-1111
Qantas Vacations 800-641-8772
Reno Quick Escapes 800-736-6747
Sabena Holiday Desk 800-955-2000
SAS Tours 800-221-2350
Singapore Asian Affair Holidays 800-742-3133
Southwest Vacations 800-423-5683
Swissair Swisspak 800-688-7947
TWA Getaway Vacations . .800-438-2929
United Vacations 800-328-6877
US Airways Vacations . . .800-455-0123
Virgin Vacations 800-364-6466

Independent Vacation packages can be like the little girl with the curl in the middle of her forehead. When they're good, they're very, very good, and when they're bad, they're horrid enough to give the pleasures of travel a bad name. There are three irrevocable rules to follow when purchasing a vacation package from anyone other than a major airline vacation division:

- **Deal only with reputable, well-recommended companies**. The cost of your entire vacation is at stake. If you use a vacation division under the auspices of a major airline, you're protected. If you use a tour company not affiliated with an airline (and the fact that they book major airline travel does not mean they are affiliated), do some checking to make sure you're dealing with a reputable, well-established firm with a proven track record.
- **Always pay by credit or charge card.** Some tour companies may charge a small surcharge for the use of a particular card. If that's the only card you carry, pay the surcharge rather than risking payment by check. The protection credit card payment affords is well worth it.
- **Compare vacation package prices** against booking each component separately, using discount options. Vacation package companies often advertise savings of ten to 50 percent, but compare tour prices against two-for-ones, coupon deals, half-price hotels and other discount options. Don't compare them against rates consumers rarely pay such as non-discounted airfares and full rack rates at hotels.

Vacation tour companies come in a multitude of configurations. Some specialize in escorted tours. Some use only charter air; others use scheduled air; a few use both options. Major cities offer the

> *"One of my favorite uses of vacation package companies is last-minute travel bargains. As departure dates near, prices go down. During late 1997, for example, Adventure Tours USA offered roundtrip air from Dallas/Fort Worth to Crested Butte for select December dates at $199 total for two people as well as two-for-one travel to Grand Cayman; TransGlobal offered two-for-one airfares to Honolulu."*

greatest number of tour operators. You'll find that many of the major companies that do business in your hometown advertise in Sunday travel sections. A knowledgeable travel agent can also tell you which companies are your best bets. Some tour companies only book through travel agents; others allow consumers to book direct.

> *"Be particularly cautious with tour companies that offer very specialized packages, including those built around major sports events. Spring Break also gives rise to the scam artists masquerading as tour companies. There are good apples and rotten apples in this barrel. Check them out before you bite."*

Name recognition may be misleading. Certified Vacations, for example, is a company you've probably never heard of, yet they sell most American Express, American Automobile Association and Delta Air Lines vacation packages. Use companies that maintain membership in either of the two major trade organizations and establish their own escrow accounts. Federal law requires all tour companies to hold funds in escrow. If you have doubts, ask for specifics on escrow provisions. Tour company membership organizations:

- **U.S. Tour Operators Association,** which offers *The Smart Travelers Planning Kit*, a free brochure with information on choosing tour companies and vacations. Write to 211 E. 51st St., Suite 12B, New York, NY 10022; call **212-750-7371**.
- **The National Tour Association, 800-682-8886**.

Charter tour companies can offer the truest standby bargains. They count on filling all or most of their seats on every flight. As departure dates get closer, they bring down the price to attract more passengers. Often you can purchase airfare only, or opt for an air/hotel package. How low do the fares go? We've seen Dallas/Fort Worth-Honolulu roundtrips at $499 for two, three-night air-inclusive Las Vegas packages at $149 and $99 roundtrip airfares to resort cities in Mexico. The best place to find these deals is your Sunday newspaper travel section. Be prepared to act fast. If you can't book direct, check the bottom of the ad for agencies open on Sunday.

- **Charter flights fly under regulations that differ** from those of scheduled air. Most tour company flights are classified as public charters. Affinity charters are planes leased by a particular group or organization.
- **Charter flights can be cancelled** by the airline or the tour operator up to ten days before departure, but that rarely happens when you are dealing with a

Largest tourist groups visiting the U.S.: the Japanese and the British.

reputable firm.

- **Charter flights can be delayed** for up to 48 hours with no mandatory compensation to passengers. You will not be placed on an alternate carrier, for example, if your aircraft develops mechanical problems. The best tour companies rarely experience more than minimal delays.
- **Most charter tickets have no refund value.** If you're not able to take the flight, you lose the entire purchase price unless you've purchased cancellation insurance and fulfilled the terms for compensated cancellations. If you are buying a last-minute, $98 roundtrip, there's no reason to buy insurance. If you're investing $2,000 in a package tour, insurance should be purchased.
- **A missed departure may mean major trouble.** Tour companies are under no obligation to compensate you for any problems resulting from a flight you fail to make even if it means your holiday is half over before it begins. If you purchased insurance, you will be protected under terms outlined in your policy. If you miss the return flight, you may be forced to pay enormous one-way fares on scheduled air. The tour company may try to help you out, but they are under no obligation to provide alternate transportation.
- **Choose well-established tour companies** with fight schedules that increase the possibility that you can acquire an alternate seat within a reasonable time frame.

Traveling on weekdays usually gives you more for less. A four-night Sunday to Thursday trip may cost significantly less than a three-night Thursday to Sunday package with identical inclusions. Off-season travel can also offer substantial savings. Changing your travel dates by as little as a day or two can take you into off-peak rates and hundreds of dollars in savings. Always ask about date-specific last-minute deals.

Early booking discounts are usually offered on seasonal charters. For example, ski trips may be discounted when they are first put on sale in October. You also get to take advantage of a full selection of departure dates and accommodation choices.

Trip cancellation insurance is available from the larger tour operators and from private insurance companies (see *Travel Guide* for details). Provisions may include coverage for illness, injury, emergency medical evacuation, lost and damaged baggage, cancellation and defaults. Refund value in case of traveler cancellation decreases by increments the closer you get to departure. Cancellation is only covered for very specific medical reasons. Make sure the insurance fund is administered by an entity with financial separation from the tour or cruise operator. Otherwise, if the operator goes under, your insurance disappears too.

Read the most important part of any tour brochure, the terms and conditions. This small print explains the terms of the contract you are entering into with the tour company. It should clearly explain payment provisions, deposit and payment protection, cancellation and refund policies, insurance options, departure rules and provisions for flight time changes, baggage allowances and protection, rules on reconfirming flights, visa and passport information (when applicable), the guarantee that outlines the company's obligations and what they will do if those obligations are not met. The time you spend reading and understanding this fine print is well spent.

Cost of chartering the Air France Concorde: $80,000 per hour.

> *"A deposit will generally hold your vacation package until the final payment deadline. The stiffest cancellation penalties don't go into effect until final payment is made. Be sure you know how and when that final payment must be made. Tour companies and travel agents must advise you of these provisions, but they have no legal responsibility to remind you of deadlines as they near. If you miss your payment deadline, your deposit and your reservation most likely will be lost. If you are purchasing a deeply-discounted package for last-minute travel, you may have no financial recourse if you are unable to travel. Packages using scheduled charter air can bring you great deals, but be sure you understand all the fine points. If your charter company offers three flights a week to your destination and your Monday flight is cancelled, will you have to wait for Wednesday? What will they do to protect you in case of mechanical delays? If a delay takes eight hours out of a three day holiday, will you receive any compensation?"*

VACATION PACKAGE POINTERS

All-inclusive tours can ease budget planning, but be sure you know exactly what is included. Travelers who enjoy exploring on their own usually do best with more basic plans. Meals included in your package rate aren't a bargain unless you're willing to eat all your meals at the hotel or resort. Will you receive transfers from the airport to your hotel? In some cities, this can be a major added expense.

Escorted tours provide a more structured travel experience and more direct companionship, since you will be traveling with an intact group of people. Know the credentials of your tour leader, the size of the tour and the types of people who comprise the group.

Hotel ratings may be skewed to make a budget property sound more appealing. Check the hotels in an independent ratings guide to get a true picture. Remember that amenities matter only if they matter to you. If you just want a comfortable base, choose the economy package. If you're heading for Las Vegas, be aware that garden rooms at most hotels often translate to motel-type add-ons to the main building. If you want to be in the main part of the hotel, tower rooms are your best bet. If you're offered run-of-the-house, you get whatever is available when you arrive.

Ask for special coupon books often available as part of the most popular tour packages such as Disneyland, Walt Disney World and Las Vegas. Check for special deals on meals, attractions and car rentals.

Carry the necessary documents for international travel. Customs procedures do not relax when you travel with a tour group.

The United States Tour Operators Association has a consumer protection program that requires each active member to post a $1 million bond, letter of credit or certificate of deposit.

The following two pages list a number of major tour companies. For further information, go online **www.ustoa.com** or call **212-290-7355**.

World's busiest air routes: Tokyo-Sapporo, Tokyo-Fukuoka, Hong Kong-Taipei and London-Paris.

USTOA-AFFILIATED TOUR COMPANIES	
COMPANY	**DESTINATIONS**
Abercrombie & Kent Intl. 800-323-7308 www.abercrombiekent.com	Alaska, Western U.S., South and Central America, Galapagos Islands, Africa, Australia, South Pacific, Southeast Asia, China, India, Nepal, Egypt, Israel, Middle East, Antarctica, United Kingdom and Continental Europe.
All About Tours 800-274-8687 www.allabouthawaii.com/hawaii	Hawaii, Australia, New Zealand, Fiji, Tahiti, Reno, Las Vegas and Southern California.
Australian Pacific Tours 800-290-8687 www.atie.com.au/tours/auspac.html www.sightseeing.com	Australia, New Zealand, Fiji, United States and Canada.
Brendan Tours 800-421-8446 No web site available.	Australia, New Zealand, Fiji, Tahiti, Ireland, Britain, Europe, United States, Canada, South and Central America, Greece, Egypt and Africa.
Central Holidays 800-935-5000 www.centralh.com	Italy, Spain, Portugal, Morocco, Greece, Turkey and Israel. Ski packages to: Italy, Austria, Switzerland, France, United States and Canadian Rockies. Group travel throughout Europe and the Mediterranean.
Certified Vacations 800-233-7260 www.deltavacations.com	United States, Bahamas, Bermuda, Caribbean, Mexico, Britain, Belgium, Brazil, Canada, Central and Northern Europe, Eastern Europe, France, Ireland, Italy, Mediterranean, Portugal, Russia, Spain and Scandinavia.
CIE Tours International 201-292-3899 www.cietours.com	Ireland, England, Scotland and Wales.
Classic Custom Vacations 800-221-3949 No web site available.	Hawaii, North America, Western Canada, Greece and Turkey.
Collette Travel Service, Inc. 800-832-4656 www.collettetours.com	Continental United States, Alaska, Hawaii, Canada, South America, Europe, Australia and the Orient.
Contiki Holidays 714-740-0808 www.contiki.com	United Kingdom, Western Europe, Greece, Turkey, Egypt, Israel, certain United States, Alaska, Hawaii, South Africa, Zimbabwe, Namibia, Australia and New Zealand.
DER Travel Services, Inc. 800-782-2424 www.dertravel.com	Europe, Asia, Middle East, Africa and Central America.

Inaugural date of longest nonstop flight (United's 7,788 mile Chicago-Hong Kong): July 16, 1996.

USTOA-AFFILIATED TOUR COMPANIES	
COMPANY	**DESTINATIONS**
FreeGate Tourism, Inc. 800-223-0304 www.freegatetourism.com	Greece, Italy, Egypt, Turkey, Israel, South and Central America.
Friendly Holidays 800-221-9748 www.ten-io.com/friendly	Mexico, Hawaii, Caribbean, Costa Rica, Belize, Florida, Bahamas, Bermuda, Portugal, Spain and Las Vegas.
Gate 1 800-682-3333 www.nexaxs.com/people/gate1	Europe, Central Europe, Eastern Mediterranean, Asia, East and North Africa.
Globus & Cosmos 800-221-0090 www.globusandcosmos.com	Europe, Africa, Middle East, South Pacific, United States, Canada, Asia, Orient, South and Central America, Mexico and the Caribbean.
GoGo Worldwide Vacations 800-821-3731 No web site available.	Caribbean, Bahamas, Europe, Mexico, South and Central America, Middle East, North Africa, Canada and United States.
Homeric Tours, Inc. 800-223-5570 www.homerictours.com	Greece, Morocco, Portugal, Egypt, Cyprus, Italy, Turkey, Israel and Spain.
IST Cultural Tours 800-833-2111 No web site available.	Antarctica, Austria, Belgium, Brazil, Czech Republic, Egypt, France, Germany, Great Britain, Greece, Holland, India, Israel, Italy, New York City, Scandinavia and Turkey.
Japan & Orient Tours, Inc. 800-877-5223 www.jot.com	Orient includes: China, Japan, Hong Kong, Indochina, Singapore, Thailand, Korea, Nepal, India, Taiwan, Indonesia and Malaysia. South Pacific includes: Australia, New Zealand, Tahiti, Fiji, Tonga, Samoa, Vanuatu and Papua New Guinea.
Jetset Tours, Inc. (NA) 800-453-8738 www.jetsettours.com	Australia, New Zealand, South Pacific, United Kingdom, Ireland, Europe and Southeast Asia.

Airline that requires passengers to sit on the floor: Mongolian Airways.

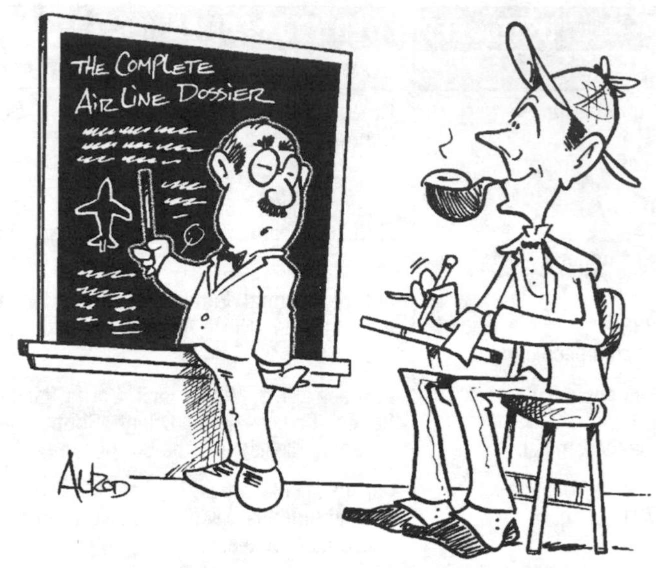

PRE-FLIGHT INTELLIGENCE REPORT

A REALITY CHECK ON AIRLINE POLICIES

Knowing your rights can help you financially; make it easier to deal effectively with airline personnel and increase comfort and amenities that help put some of the fun back in air travel. Knowing how airlines think and operate gives you the edge you need to be a savvy traveller.

What airline policies say and what they mean are not always the same. Sometimes what they *fail* to say is most important of all. Let's take a stroll down Reality Lane. The bold print contains statements most airlines would prefer you accept as fact. Our Reality Checks follow.

There is no price-fixing in the airline industry.

Reality Check: We have often seen airlines increase fares by exactly the same amount (to the penny) at exactly the same time. This is either a planned event, or all airline CEO's are psychic.

Airlines change fares often to remain competitive.

Reality Check: Airlines raise fares in markets where they have little competition and know they can get away with charging what the traffic will bear. They raise fares because they know their major airline competitors will raise their fares too. They lower fares when they're forced to, usually because a low-cost carrier has come to town and cut into the major airlines market share.

Airlines who cancel unredeemed frequent flyer miles are practicing good bookkeeping.

Reality Check: The few airlines that still cancel miles aren't thinking about bookkeeping; they want their miles back. Cancelling miles at the end of the year is well-timed to take advantage of the holiday season rush when air travellers may be too busy to worry about a few thousand (or 20,000) miles. Cancelling miles help the airlines bottom line. At the very least, they could give them to charity rather than forcing passengers to go through a maze of paper work or a ten-minute wait on the phone to do it themselves.

Call the airline for the best service and the best fare.

Reality Check: It's a wonder they don't all walk around with Pinocchio noses for this whopper. Calling the airlines and trusting that you will get the best fare almost guarantees that you won't. Good travel agents are your best allies; agents who do price comparisons and check low-cost airlines, including those not on major computer reservation systems. Call the airline when every travel agency is closed and a fare war is scheduled to end at midnight. Call the airline if you find an irresistible Snooze You Lose fare on *Best Fares* Online at 2 a.m. Call the airline when you need a fee waived or a special request granted and you know the travel agents' hands are tied. Otherwise, the best you can get from any airline is their best published fare. Do you really think they'll quote a competitor's better deal?

Flight delays are inevitable and aren't that big of a problem.

Reality Check: Twenty percent of all domestic flights arrive late (more than 15 minutes after scheduled arrival). You spend time on a stuffy airplane, stuck at the gate or on a runway, because airlines try to have too many flights coming and going during high demand periods. The schedules are so tight that inevitable mechanical or weather delays can play havoc with arrivals for hours. A departure is deemed to be on time if the aircraft pulls back from the gate on time—even one foot will do it. That's why you end up sweating and irritable during lengthy delays. If they let you back in to the gate area, they get a black mark on their on time record.

Most major airlines have similar policies.

Reality Check: Rules can vary from airline to airline, and from flight to flight. On one airline you can check a bicycle for free; on another, you pay $50. On almost every airline you must fight availability limits when you want to book a frequent flyer award ticket. (On Southwest, you get the last seat on the flight if you want it.) On most domestic flights, you are required to check-in a minimum of ten minutes prior to departure; on United you lose your seat assignment if you don't check in twenty minutes prior. You need 25,000 minimum frequent flyer miles to get a free ticket on all major airlines—except America West. We could go one for all the pages remaining in this book, but you get the idea. Knowing the rules on one airline does not make you conversant with other airline's rules.

If you can't get a fare war price, it's because you didn't act fast enough.

Reality Check: Pick an itinerary included in a newly announced fare war. Be the first person to get the airline on the phone and ask for a seat on a specific flight on that itinerary. "Sorry," you may be told, "there are no seats available." Where did

Aspect some low-cost European carriers use to keep costs down: direct booking only.

they go? A previous fare war may have already sold out the fare class set aside for the new fare war. Your best strategy when you run into this all-too-common event: try to be flexible on your travel times and put the best flight possible on hold (unless it's an instant purchase fare). Wait for the dust to settle and the other airlines to join the fare war, then call your travel agent. By then, another airline may have what you need.

CONDITIONS OF CONTRACT

Each time you purchase an airline ticket, you are agreeing to many terms of a contract you have probably never seen. Each airline's *Conditions of Contract* states policies that can have a significant effect on you. They are written in the airline's best interest. What protection do consumers get? Very little. Often, you don't even get to read the rules you are expected to follow. We find it interesting that airlines now offering quick reservations online, do not all offer complete Conditions of Contract by internet.

By law, each airline must make their full *Conditions of Contract* available on request at airport and city ticket offices and mail you a complete copy if you request one in writing. Last year we went out to the airport and tried to get a copy from each major airline. It was enough to make grown researchers cry. You would assume that, with over 550 million people passing through airports each year, gate agents could put their hands on their airline's *Conditions of Contract* without hesitation. The best we got was a brief summary from two out of the ten airlines we approached. Other responses:

"I don't know what you're talking about."

"The contract isn't readily available."

"You have to request it in writing from our legal department."

"The contract will take about two hours to duplicate."

This year, we called city ticket offices, hoping for a change for the better. The results mirrored those of last year. Southwest was the only airline that knew what we wanted and told us we could pick up a copy from any Southwest ticket agent, at our convenience.

Contract terms for international travel are even harder to acquire. They are in the form of published *Tariff Rules*, technically available at airports and city ticket offices. Try to get a copy of that document and you may as well be looking for the Dead Sea Scrolls.

Since *Conditions of Contract* are still difficult for passengers to acquire, we persevered, acquired copies of them all, and will tell you some very important details you probably never knew.

> *"The Department of Transportation is trying to make Conditions of Contract more accessible to passengers choosing e-ticket options. They now say that ticketless airlines must "give or make available" an abbreviated form of the Conditions of Contract by fax sent by the airline or travel agent, by hand delivery at check-in or through availability at airport gates, either in a box labeled "Consumer Check-In" or given to the passenger upon request. Forgive us if we are doubtful that the airlines will jump to full compliance."*

WHAT IT SAYS/WHAT IT MEANS

Here's a look at one airline's current *Conditions of Contract*. We chose a typical major airline, in line with most of its competitors. We'll call them Airline X. Its *Contract of Carriage* covers fare changes, *force majeure*, overbooking, delayed or cancelled flights, baggage, check-in requirements, acceptance of passengers, acceptance of children, refunds, ticket validity, claims and authority to change the contract. We'll hit the high spots, show you some of the loopholes the airlines add and let you know when they can work to your advantage.

What It Says: "All printed versions of the *Contract of Carriage*...are obsolete. Print as requested. Do not print advance copies."

What It Means: The rules can change so fast that "printed" (mass produced) publications would be out-of-date as soon as they roll off the press. Instead, they are printed one copy at a time on request via the printer attached to the airline's computer system. Will they actually print it when you ask? Rarely. Usually, you are put off; often you are told to request it in writing.

What It Says: "Air X may, in the event of a *force majeure* event, without notice, cancel, terminate, divert, postpone or delay any flight...without liability except to issue an involuntary refund. The involuntary refund will be made in the original form of payment in accordance with involuntary refund rules for any unused portion of the ticket." *Force majeure* is partially defined as "...any shortage of labor, fuel or facilities of Airline X or others, or any fact not reasonably foreseen, anticipated or predicted by Air X."

What It Means: Beware of documents with obscure terms! How many times does *force majeure* turn up in your daily conversation? We heard it once in a spy movie–the only time we've actually heard this obscure phrase being uttered. *Force majeure* usually refers to major events such as blizzards, wars and riots. If you run into the season's big snow storm, the airline will try to help, but per their contract, they don't have to do any more but offer what they call "involuntary compensation." If the airline cancels your flight, they are not even obligated to put you on the next flight out–even if they failed to give you any advance warning, and cancelled for reasons they obscure.

What It Says: "If a flight is oversold...you will be entitled to payment...unless..."

What It Means: You get nothing if they get you where you're going within an hour of your originally scheduled arrival, if you checked in late (according to an altered time limit you may never have been advised of), if a flight is cancelled or delayed or if a smaller aircraft (60 passengers or less) has been substituted.

What It Says: "Air X is responsible for transportation only on flight segments operated by Air X."

What It Means: If Air X wants to place you on another airline (because of overbooking, weather, etc.), they will use their interline agreement (contracts with other airlines) to reassign you. You are now under the other airline's *Contract of Carriage*. If that occurs, don't forget to "double dip." Mail your tickets and boarding passes to the original airline so you get frequent flyer miles on both your original and your reassigned flights.

What It Says: "Unless you have checked in, received your boarding pass and are at the boarding point ready to board the aircraft at least ten minutes before scheduled departure, your reservation is subject to cancellation. Such cancellation will apply to all segments in your itinerary, including those on other carriers."

What It Means: You can't show up, breathless, at the gate check-in counter ten minutes before your flight. You must have completed the check-in process. Custom dictates that just showing up is OK, but should the airlines decide to get picky, their legal verbiage allows them plenty of slack.

What It Says: "A ticket is invalid if...Airline X determines that the ticket has been purchased or used in a manner designed to circumvent applicable fare rules."

What It Means: This section goes on to specifically forbid back-to-back ticketing, throwaway ticketing and hidden city ticketing. Perhaps most amazing is the rule against throwaway ticketing which allows you to buy a cheaper, roundtrip ticket for one-way travel, throwing away the unused portion. To try to steer you to high-priced, one-way tickets, the airlines made a rule that says you can't fly half the distance on a purchased ticket, even though you've paid for it entirely. It's like buying a ticket for a double feature, trying to leave after the first movie and being told you can't. Some airlines aren't content to set prices. They also want to unfairly limit how you use your tickets once you've purchased them.

PASSENGER ALLIES

The Department of Transportation (DOT) is one of four agencies that accept complaints about airline performance and passenger service and otherwise attempt to keep the airline industry in line. The DOT only receives an average of 1,000 complaints from air passengers each month. Most people don't take the time to complain or may not know where to go with their complaints. The DOT also releases monthly statistics on airline performance and consumer complaints. The agency also helps deal with problems relating to baggage, flight delays and overbooking. You can record a complaint via voice mail by calling **202-366-2220**. To speak with a staff member, call **202-366-5957**. Address letters of complaint to Aviation Consumer Protection Division, DOT, C-75, Washington, DC 20590.

The Federal Aviation Administration (800-322-7873), deals with safety issues, airport security and carry-on baggage.

The Aviation Consumer Action Project (202-638-4000), is Ralph Nader's organization. They publish useful material and are also willing to advise passengers on their rights by phone. You're likely to get a voice mail recording. Leave a message and a representative will get back to you.

The International Airline Passengers Association (972-404-9980), publishes a bi-monthly newsletter on airline safety and other travel issues.

One of your most potent consumer aids is the ease with which you can now e-mail a message to your senator, representative or president. Since relatively few people take the time to do this, each communication is powerful. Many decisions made in Washington affect air travel and consumer rights. There are many sites you can use including Mr. Smith E-Mail Washington at **www.mrsmith.com**. The site also sends you to media e-mail links. Another site worth checking is Congressional E-Mail Addresses at **www.nyx.net/~anon3210**. It links you to e-mail addresses and to home pages of senators and representatives, as well as additional Congressional web pages.

The only person allowed to decide if it is safe to fly: the captain of each flight.

CODESHARE FLIGHTS

Codeshare agreements allow airlines to list one another's flights as their own, sell tickets for them and (of course) share the revenue. Consumers can benefit from better connections, advance seat assignments for all flight segments, easier baggage transfer and shared frequent flyer benefits.

You may think codeshare situations are one of the many details of travel you need not bother to stay on top of. There are actually good reasons for travelers to always ask if the reservation they are considering includes codeshare travel. Check on airport connections to make sure you will not have to travel to a distant gate or another terminal.

Some codeshare partners are not mileage partners. You may earn miles on the flight, but you may not be allowed to redeem them on that airline. Conversely, you may not earn miles at all on some codeshare flights. For example, American and Delta have codeshare agreements with Singapore Airlines but you can't earn AAdvantage or SkyMiles credit on Coach seats; only on Business and First Class.

The biggest consumer plus to codeshare agreements goes to passengers who can use them to accumulate miles on two or more airlines. Instead of a mileage account balance that allows you to do little more than purchase a magazine subscription, your cumulative miles can open up upgrade and award ticket possibilities. Of course, you also have more competition on popular award travel routes. Continental and Northwest are in the process of becoming total codeshare airlines. American and US Airways and United and Delta also have partnership agreements in process.

CODESHARE PARTNERSHIPS

AIRLINE	PARTNER
ALASKA	American Eagle, British Airways, Northwest and TWA
AMERICA WEST	Aeromexico, British Airways and Continental
AMERICAN	Alaska, British Midland, Canadian, China Eastern, Gulf Air, Hawaiian, LOT, Qantas, Singapore, South African and Transaero
CONTINENTAL	Air Canada, Air France, Alitalia, America West, CSA Czech and TransAvia
DELTA	Aer Lingus, Aeromexico, Austrian, Finnair, Korean Air, Malev, Sabena, Singapore, Swissair and TAP
NORTHWEST	Air UK, Alaska, America West, Asiana, Eurowings, Hawaiian, KLM, Pacific Island and US Airways
SOUTHWEST	Icelandair
TWA	Air Europa and Royal Jordanian
UNITED	Aeromar, Aeromexico, Air Canada, Air India, ALM, Aloha, Ansett, British Midland, Cayman Airways, Continental Connections, Emirates, Lufthansa, SAS, Saudia Arabian and Thai
US AIRWAYS	Deutsche BA

COMMUTER AIRLINES

Six of the Big Seven airlines have commuter, express and/or shuttle service. One of the more notable recent changes in this area is the creation of MetroJet, US Airway's airline-within-an-airline. US Airways formed MetroJet, in part, to deal with their relatively high passenger mile cost. They hope to bring in travel on the commuter affiliate at under 10-cents per passenger miles and they have chosen Baltimore as home base. Check this chart for a summary of commuter affiliates, accurate as we went to press. Check **www.bestfares.com** for updates.

COMMUTER AIRLINES		
MAJOR AIRLINE	**AFFILIATE**	**DETAILS**
AMERICAN	American Eagle	Consists of all aircraft containing less than 70 passenger seats.
CONTINENTAL	Continental Express	Serves regional markets around Continental's three hubs: Cleveland, Houston and Newark.
DELTA	Delta Express	A completely separate division patterned on the low-cost carrier mode.
	Delta Connection	Commuter service via airlines including ASA and Comair.
	Delta Shuttle	Single-class service with no reservations required.
NORTHWEST	Northwest AirLink	Commuter/feeder service on aircraft with less than 70 passenger seats. Some routes are served by both Northwest and Northwest AirLink. If you prefer to avoid smaller planes, have your travel agent check the airline code before you book.
UNITED	Shuttle by United	A 737 fleet that competes with Southwest in West Coast markets and participates in United's hub and spoke routing system.
	United Express	Operated by six regional carriers all of whom fly turboprops except Air Wisconsin (some jet service is available).
US AIRWAYS	MetroJet	A low-cost airline-within-an-airline, based in Baltimore and limited to flights under 1,000 miles.
	US Airways Express	Ten turboprops that serve as feeder flights to US Airways hubs.
	US Airways Shuttle	The descendant of Eastern Shuttle between Washington, New York and Boston.

Number of people in the air over the U.S. at any given hour: over 50,000.

THE REGIONAL AIRLINE JET REVOLUTION

Regional airlines are rushing toward the purchase of passenger jets, convinced by studies that show that up to 50 percent of all airline passengers avoid turboprop travel whenever possible. Several aircraft manufacturers have designed cost-effective jets with 50-100 passenger capacity. Some commuter airlines will phase out turboprop service completely; others will fly a mixed fleet. During this period of transition, passengers who want to avoid turboprop travel should ask if jet service is offered on a particular route. Increasingly, one or more flights each day utilize jet aircraft while other flights on the same route are still flown by turboprops.

REGIONAL AIRLINE JET UPDATE		
AIRLINE	JET FLEET	JET FOCUS MARKETS
Alaska/Horizon Air	15 F-28s (62-69 passengers)	Boise, Calgary, Portland (OR),Sacramento, San Jose, Seattle and Spokane
America West Express/ Mesa Air	Six Canadair 50-passenger CRJs	Phoenix
Continental Express	25 Embraer 50-passenger 145s	Cleveland, Houston and Newark
Delta Connection/ Atlantic Southeast	Five BAe 88-passenger 146-200s	Atlanta
	30 Canadair 50-passenger CRJs	Atlanta and Dallas/ Fort Worth
Delta Connection/ Comair	50 Canadair 50-passenger CRJs	Cincinnati and Orlando
Delta Connection/ SkyWest	Ten Canadair 50-passenger CRJs	Los Angeles and Salt Lake City
Mesa Airlines	Ten Canadair 50-passenger CRJs	Albuquerque
Northwest AirLink/ Mesaba	12 Avro 69-passenger RJ-85s	Detroit and Minneapolis/ St. Paul
United Express/ Air Wisconsin	15 BAe 86-100 passenger 146s	Chicago and Denver

“Many people are not aware that turboprops are actually powered by jet engines. The engines drive the propellers. On jet aircraft, the engines drive fans that are enclosed in the engine casing. The coming years won’t make turboprops obsolete, but we will see fewer and fewer of them each quarter, through the end of this century.”

AIRLINE TICKETS DE-MYSTIFIED

If you think airline tickets are printed in code you're right, but the code is easy to break.

- **The place of issue** is printed just above the main green bar.
- **The record locator** (PNR in airline lingo) is in the large, beige gap at the top of the main green bar. The first six letters and digits identify your reservation and should be used whenever you call regarding your ticket.
- **The rate type** is identified by a one-letter code at the second break in the main green bar. It shows if your ticket price came from the airlines, a travel agent or a negotiated corporate rate.
- **The class of service** is designated at the center of the main green bar. "P" or "F" indicates First Class and "C" or "J" indicates Business Class. "Y" or any other letter indicates Coach.
- **The ticket status** is marked on the green bar directly below the word "STATUS." It should read "OK." Anything else indicates that your flight is not confirmed, even though a ticket has been issued.
- **The computer and travel agent codes** are printed to the left of the third green bar on the boarding pass.
- **Form of payment** is indicated on the second line under the main green bar. If you used a credit card, the type of card and your number (minus the expiration date) will be printed.
- **Routing and fare information** are encoded on the third line under the main green bar, preceded by the two-letter airline code. It shows basic restrictions (by code) and the fare-per-segment.
- **Dates of travel** are most easily read on the fourth green bar on the boarding pass segment.
- **The ticket number** is printed at the lower bottom of the ticket against a white background. It validates the ticket and helps protect the airlines against fraud. Each ticket issuer must account for every ticket in each numbered sequence, even voided tickets.
- **The fare** is printed in the lower left corner. "USD" indicates the base fare. "US" indicates the federal tax. "XF" indicates the passenger facility charge, up to a total of $16 roundtrip. The total amount (printed on its own green bar) should be the exact amount you paid for your ticket.

TICKETING RULES & PROCEDURES

The Basics

Protect yourself each time you purchase a ticket by knowing the basic rules that govern airline ticketing.

- **Always ask the ticketing time limit** when making a reservation. Reservations for most domestic flights are only held 24 hours. A few airlines are experimenting with lengthening the limit to 72 hours. At press time, Midwest Express and American Trans Air were the only airlines offering this desirable service on all reservations.
- **Reservations for international flights** have ticketing time limits that vary considerably. The most important consideration on international tickets is to call and confirm your flight 72 hours before departure.

Percentage of airline passengers who purchase tickets by cash or check: 23 percent.

- **A guaranteed reservation does not guarantee a price.** As long as you observe the ticketing time limit, you'll get your ticket at the quoted price most of the time. Once in a while airlines raise rates in a manner that affects current reservations. You call to purchase your ticket only to be told that the price has gone up. That's why reservation people should always remind you that the price is not guaranteed until you purchase the ticket. Many times they don't, so be sure to keep this important fact in mind. You also want to make sure your reservation was actually entered. A fare quote and the recitation of flight times doesn't always mean a reservation was entered. You need the six-character record locator number.

- **Write down your record locator number**. It's the easiest way to reference your reservation. If any special provisions or promises have been made, or if you have special needs (wheelchair assistance, special meals, pets on board, etc.), be sure the agent notes the information in your record. After this is done, you should still contact the airline at least 48 hours in advance of your flight to be sure the proper information is in your record.

- **When you receive your tickets,** check them immediately. Make sure the destination, dates and times are correct. Make sure the dollar amount printed on the ticket is the same as the amount you were quoted. Check the status box to make sure it's been marked "OK." This is your assurance that your reservation is confirmed rather than placed on standby or a waiting list. Make sure it is to the right city and state. Portland, Oregon is 2,500 miles away from Portland, Maine.

- **Always reconfirm your reservation,** even when you are holding a confirmed ticket. International travel may require it and reconfirming domestic travel assures that you're aware of any change in schedule. Often departure times are changed by ten, 20 or more minutes. The airline will try to notify you or your travel agent, but if they fail to reach you, you could miss a critical factor in your travel plans. This is particularly vital for people who only allow themselves time for quick, last-minute check-ins. If you travel on a tight time limit, even a ten minute change in schedule can hurt.

Reissues And Downgrades

Many fares, including most excursion fares, are not refundable, but they can be exchanged.

You want to have your ticket reissued if the fare has gone down or if you have to change your travel plans. When an airfare goes down and you want to receive a refund for the difference, it's called a "downgrade" or "rollover."

A downgraded ticket is a good thing; the term can be confusing. It means that you are exchanging an existing ticket for one with a lower fare. One of the biggest mistakes consumers make is failing to check to see if a purchased fare has dropped. Imagine, for example, that you purchased a $448 Miami-Los Angeles ticket and **www.bestfares.com** Snooze You Lose deal offers it for $98. Even with the payment of a change fee, you could end up with big bucks in your pocket. An upstart airline, a fare war or a show of one-upmanship among airlines can lower a fare to the point where paying a change fee becomes a good deal.

- **All requirements** for the lower price ticket must be met, including advance purchase, minimum-stay requirements and availability in that fare class.

Increase in TWA First Class seats during 1997: 60 percent.

> *"Dedicated bargain hunters keep looking for value even after they have purchased tickets. Check fares on Tuesdays and Thursdays for the best shot at discovering a newly lowered fare. Be sure that sale seats are available for your flights. With many reissue fees now at $75 (see chart on the following page for details) downgrading has to be used more selectively than in the past. If you decide to downgrade and airline vouchers offer a better deal for the price difference, go for it. Just remember that vouchers lock you into a particular airline; a refund gives you booking (and comparison shopping) freedom."*

- **Some travel agencies** have computer systems that spotlight tickets available for reissuing at lower prices and they will call to give you that option. The airlines will never call and tell you about a lower fare.
- **If you're holding tickets** and a fare war hits, ask if you qualify for the lower rate.
- **Have tickets reissued** by your travel agent, at the airline's ticket office or at the airport. Some airlines require that certain changes be made only at the airline's ticket office or at the airport.

Generally, you have one year to have a ticket reissued, but some airlines allow two years and all allow you to apply for an extension. Some airlines allow you to travel up to two years after the original ticket date, but you have to make a reservation within a specified period of time. You can extend the life of almost any ticket by having it reissued. You cannot always change the name on a ticket without paying an additional fee.

Domestic downgrade or re-issue fees are detailed on the next page. American, Continental and Delta recently increased their fee to $75; Northwest, TWA, United and US Airways quickly followed. America West had previously increased their fee to $60. Southwest is the only major airline that charges no fee at all. Several airlines permit you to downgrade tickets to the lower fare with no change fee if you accept the difference between the original fare and the lower fare in vouchers to be used for future flights.

Special note on international tickets: Always ask about exchange policies on international tickets because they vary by carrier and circumstance. Currently American, Continental, Northwest, TWA, United and US Airways waive change fees on non-refundable tickets in certain compassion situations, but you must use your original ticket toward payment of a higher fare. If you want to change your return travel, you generally pay $150 and the change must fit the travel limits of the ticket you purchased. If you purchased a consolidator ticket (and many of the best international bargain fares come from consolidators) the rules may vary.

Be sure to check change penalties on sale tickets. There are some very good fare sales that save you money on your ticket price, but place a higher premium on any change in travel date or itinerary. Most consumers are certain of their travel plans when they purchase tickets, but unforeseen events often occur. It is best to make reissue policies part of your purchase decision for all but last-minute travel purchases.

Number of commercial airline pilots hired in 1997: 11,936.

RE-ISSUE FEES		
AIRLINE	FEE WITH AIRLINE VOUCHER	FEE WITH REFUND IN ORIGINAL PAYMENT FORM
ALASKA	None	$50
AMERICA WEST	$60	$60
AMERICAN	None	$75
CONTINENTAL	$75	$75
DELTA	None	$75
NORTHWEST	None	$75
SOUTHWEST	None	None
TWA	$50	$75
UNITED	$50	$75
US AIRWAYS	None	$75

LOST & STOLEN TICKETS

Airline tickets are like currency. Protect them as diligently as you protect your cash. Make a photocopy of each ticket and store it safely so you have the information you need in case you need to report a loss. You'll have the ticket number and proof that you purchased the ticket because your credit card number is printed on the ticket's face.

The procedure for reporting lost and stolen tickets is the same. Stolen ticket replacement or credit is hastened when you supply a police report or case number to authenticate your claim. The airline will attempt to stop anyone from flying on your stolen ticket. Report the loss directly to the airline. You can sometimes go through a travel agent, but the process takes longer. If your ticket is used while your refund is still pending, the airline may refuse to process the refund. They will certainly investigate your claim.

Most major airlines charge a $70 fee to process a lost or stolen ticket application. In almost every case, you will also have to purchase a replacement ticket at the current fare. If the fare is higher (through a fare increase or the lack of advance purchase requirement) you may have to pay the higher price. Exceptions to the need to purchase a replacement ticket include United (but only if you purchased directly from the airline) and TWA. You are always free to request special consideration.

> *"One of the best safeguards against lost or stolen tickets is to opt for e-tickets. Using e-tickets gives you one less piece of paper to keep track of. Because of the financial advantages e-ticketing provides to airlines, you also will often find bonus frequent flyer miles attached to an e-ticket option."*

Original name of British Airways: Imperial Airways, chartered in 1924.

PRE-PAID TICKETS

Pre-paid tickets allow you to pre-purchase an airline ticket and have it waiting at the airport of your choice. You can arrange pre-paid tickets through the airline or through a travel agency, allowing a minimum of one hour for the transaction to be completed. Positive identification will be required of the person picking up the ticket. If they are not carrying identification, the airline may allow you to select a code word, which can be used to access the ticket.

Pre-paid tickets are notorious for problems because of the speed in which the transactions are conducted and the need to guard against fraud. Always ask for the pre-paid ticket number and the confirmation number (record locator number), and always call the airline to confirm that the reservation has gone through its system. Make sure that the price charged to your credit card is accurate.

Avoid pre-paid ticket fees when you have at least an overnight before the passenger must travel. Purchase the ticket as usual and send it via overnight delivery with a guaranteed early morning arrival.

PRE-PAID FEES & E-TICKET POLICIES

AIRLINE	PRE-PAID FEE	E-TICKET POLICIES
ALASKA	$35	No advance is required. The ticket can be issued in the name of your choice.
AMERICA WEST	$40	Five-hour minimum advance. Ticket can be issued in the name of your choice.
AMERICAN	$75	No advance is required. The ticket can only be assigned to a passenger with the same last name as the purchaser.
CONTINENTAL	$40	Three hour minimum advance. The ticket can be issued in the name of your choice.
DELTA	$75	Seven-day advance required for purchase by phone. If there is less than a seven-day advance, you must go to a ticket office and show your credit card and identification. Tickets can be issued in the name of your choice.
NORTHWEST	$75	No advance. Ticket can be issued in name of choice.
SOUTHWEST	$25	One-hour minimum advance. The ticket can be issued in the name of your choice.
TWA	$40	Four-hour minimum advance. The ticket can be issued in the name of your choice.
UNITED	$75	The credit card holder must go to a ticket office and show both credit card and identification to have an e-ticket issued in another passenger's name.
US AIRWAYS	$40	Cardholders can only purchase e-tickets for themselves or passengers traveling with them on the same itinerary.

First Asian air carrier to operate jet aircraft: Pakistan International Airlines.

E-TICKETS

If you're among the breed of air traveler who still insists on a paper ticket in exchange for your big bucks purchase, you may want to consider joining the e-ticket revolution. Airlines love e-tickets because they cut the cost of ticket distribution dramatically. If all travelers used them, the total savings would reach about $1 billion per year. We're always suspicious when airlines love something so much because it usually means a big kick in the wallet for consumers. E-tickets are an exception. With an increasing number of travel agencies charging for ticket delivery (due, in large part, to the two major commission reductions) e-tickets can also save you a $10-15 fee.

The biggest advantage e-tickets provide is relief from the absurd problems and expense that arise when you lose a paper ticket or when your ticket is stolen. In the latter case, you could even be asked to supply a police report to authenticate your claim (there goes the better part of an afternoon). Airlines make very feeble attempts to stop people from traveling on lost or stolen tickets. Most charge a $70 fee to process a lost or stolen ticket application. In almost every case, you will also have to purchase a replacement ticket at the current fare. If the fare is higher (through a fare increase or the lack of advance purchase requirement) you will have to pay the higher price. Your refund could take months to arrive. Sometimes the replacement ticket requirement is waived, but usually only if you have purchased from the airline.

E-tickets often bring you frequent flyer bonus miles, usually contingent on booking through the airline's internet site. This isn't exactly an act of supreme generosity. For example, if an airline saves an eight percent travel agent's commission on a $400 ticket ($32) and gives you 500 bonus miles (worth about $10) they still come out ahead.

If you're purchasing a pre-paid ticket, you will pay a fee of at least $35 and as much as $75. By using e-tickets, you can often avoid paying this fee.

Most of the negatives of e-tickets can be easily dealt with if you follow a few simple procedures. Business travelers don't always get ticket receipts to attach to expense account reports. Check your company's policy and, if needed, suggest that they revise their policy to accommodate the increasing use of e-tickets.

Request an itinerary by fax. It isn't always automatic. Unless you're perfect at remembering or noting flight times and numbers, you need this piece of paper. It's also the easiest way to leave your schedule with your office and family.

Always write down the number on your e-ticket in those few minutes between the time you have it in your hand and when the gate agent rips the tab and takes the receipt. Because e-tickets are relatively new, errors can be made on the issuing end. Paying for one air ticket is bad enough. Don't let the cost of three of them burden your credit card balance until matters can be straightened out.

Airlines that have promoted e-ticketing most aggressively report that over 70 percent of passengers booking through the airlines opt for e-tickets. By contrast, only about 20 percent of passengers booking through travel agents use them, partly because of problems with availability on all major Computer Reservation Systems. Because of this limitation, one agency may be able to issue an e-ticket on a specific airline and a specific itinerary. The agency across the street may not.

Length of Southwest's commitment to pay travel agents ten percent commission: through 2000.

AVAILABILITY OF E-TICKETS	
AIRLINE	STATUS
AIRTRAN	Systemwide. (The airline is all ticketless.)
ALASKA	Systemwide for domestic tickets and tickets to Canada and Mexico.
AMERICA WEST	Systemwide for domestic tickets.
AMERICAN	Systemwide for domestic and transatlantic tickets originating in the U.S.
CONTINENTAL	Systemwide for domestic tickets and travel to San Juan. Some international destinations will be added this year.
DELTA	Systemwide for domestic tickets. Delta Shuttle and Delta Connection tickets will be systemwide this year.
NORTHWEST	Covering 95 percent of domestic destinations. U.S. to Europe and Japan scheduled for this year.
RENO	Systemwide.
SOUTHWEST	Systemwide.
TWA	Systemwide for domestic tickets. Also available for St. Louis-London Gatwick and St. Louis-Paris flights. More international destinations will be added this year.
UNITED	Systemwide for domestic tickets. Also available for flights from Chicago, Los Angeles, New York, Newark, San Francisco and Washington to London. Other international destinations will be added this year.
US AIRWAYS	Systemwide for domestic tickets and U.S.-Canada flights.

THE POWER OF GATE AGENTS

Never underestimate the importance of the gate agents. They have the authority to bend or break certain rules to your advantage. In almost every case, arrogance or anger on the part of the passenger is met with an iron-clad adherence to policy. Asking for their intercession is your best course. Calmly and firmly explain why you feel you are entitled to certain benefits and ask for their help rather than demanding it. Gate agents operate under policies that could be summarized in one sentence: "Give customers what they want to keep them happy, but don't give away any more than you have to." Some of the goodies they can select from:

- **Free upgrades**, usually reserved for elite-level frequent flyers.
- **Compensation for over-booking**, based on how many seats they need and how many passengers volunteer.
- **Preferred seating**, a change of seat assignment or blocking the middle seat in a row of three.
- **Waiving service and processing fees** on a case-by-case basis.
- **Providing free drink, headset and other vouchers** in the name of good customer relations.

First U.S. carrier to offer nonstop service to China: Northwest.

GETTING BUMPED

Things that go bump in the night are annoying. Passengers that get bumped by the airlines are either thrilled or disgruntled. Whether you want to be bumped or hate to be bumped, you need to know how the game is played. By law, airlines must first ask for volunteers on all over-booked flights but you lose any claim to compensation if:

- **You fail to meet the airline's minimum check-in requirement.** Deadlines vary, with ten minutes most common on domestic flights and 30 minutes for international flights. Some airlines require you to simply be at the airport ticket counter while others demand that you be in the boarding area. If you're picking up your tickets at the airline, a ten-minute deadline may be increased to 30 minutes. If the airline's rules are not printed on your ticket jacket, call the airline and have a reservation person document the information you've been given on your record. We've found that many reservation people don't know the correct answer. If there's an error, you want confirmation that the error was on the part of the airline. Minimum check-in times change. If you switch from one carrier to another, you may be under a different time limit.
- **You are rescheduled to a smaller plane.** Airlines aren't required to pay any compensation if they substitute a smaller aircraft.
- **If you are flying** on a plane that holds 60 passengers or less.
- **If you are switched to an alternate flight** that gets you to your destination within one hour of your scheduled arrival.

WHEN YOU WANT TO BE BUMPED

We're often asked which flights are best to book if you want to be bumped. It is not an exact science. Even if the flight is over-booked, a high no-show factor can mean that the plane takes off with plenty of available seats. High-demand business flights offer no guarantee since so many passengers are flying on unrestricted tickets without penalty for no-shows. We've been on flights that had 148 seats and 189 passengers booked, but it still took off with empty seats. We've been booked on flights few people would expect to be over-booked, yet the gate agents had to scramble to convince a couple dozen people to accept voluntary bumping.

Bumping can be unpredictable. Bad weather can force flight cancellations that load up later flights and effect flights throughout the airline's route system. Mechanical problems can send a planeload of people to already heavily booked flights. Bumping increases in summer and other peak travel periods due to heavier passenger loads. This summer we're looking at 75-80 percent load factors. Throw in higher temperatures that force planes to carry more fuel and allow less passenger weight, and you could be bumped even on a flight that takes off with empty seats.

Over-booked flights can be a golden opportunity. If you have a little time to spare and play your cards right, you could walk away with a free roundtrip ticket—not a bad return for an investment of a few hours time. Best of all, many free roundtrip certificates allow you to fly with no advance notice—the perfect insurance to tuck away for times when you might otherwise be forced into paying an exorbitant last-minute fare. Over 900,000 people received free or discounted travel last

Average passenger capacity of a 1981 aircraft: 185.

> *"I prefer roundtrip tickets as bumping compensation but say you have a short-haul family vacation coming up. A $250 voucher will just about cover four value-priced Dallas-Houston or Chicago-Detroit roundtrips. You don't have to pay tax on tickets you acquire by voucher, so when you use them, it's like getting an extra ten percent off the fare. A ticket that costs everyone else $88, for example, is yours for just $80 in airline bump vouchers. The only problem I have with vouchers is that using one for a flight that costs more than the voucher's value, makes me pull money out of my own pocket. It also makes me subject to the rules and restrictions of the purchased fare."*

year by volunteering to be bumped. The compensation is given to every member of your party who does not fly on the scheduled flight. A family of four, for example, can get four free roundtrips. In situations where quite a few people must be bumped, airlines love to be able to get these four-in-one deals. It makes their job quicker and easier.

Here are nine basic strategies for people who don't mind being bumped and want to get the best possible pay-off.

1. Call your travel agent within 24 hours of departure. Agents can review the seat charts and allocation of remaining seats. If the agent says there are no seats left to be assigned or if the airline says the seats are under airport control, it's a good indication that the flight is over-booked.
2. Arrive at the airport approximately 90 minutes before departure flight time.
3. Get to the gate even before it opens for your flight and make sure you are the first person in line.
4. Ask if the flight is oversold and if they are seeking volunteers. If they are, ask the gate agent what compensation you will get if you voluntarily give up your seat. If you like what's being offered, volunteer to be first on the list.
5. Be a savvy negotiator, but don't assume that the ante will be upped if you play a waiting game. If you hold off, you could be out of luck.
6. Ask the agent what flight you will be protected on. If they can't guarantee you a seat on their next flight out, ask them to protect you with a guaranteed seat on another carrier's flight, per their interline agreements.
7. Carry a flight schedule so you can tell the gate agent which alternate flight you want. You could find that after being bumped from a connecting flight, you can pocket a free roundtrip certificate, and get confirmed on a nonstop that gets you in a few minutes earlier than your original schedule.
8. If you are bumped and have more than a two-hour wait, ask for all the extras: a free long distance call (or five-minute calling card), a meal ticket, free admission to the airport club and free drink and headset coupons to use during your flight. It's important to be courteous and imperative to be presentable.
9. If you have been rebooked with the guarantee of a seat, and your next flight appears to be over-booked, go back to

Average passenger capacity of a 1996 aircraft: 197.

step one and observe the same strategies for your new flight. You could end up with another free ticket or airline voucher. You can be double bumped more frequently than you might imagine. It's great to come home from a trip with two free roundtrips as a bonus.

Remember that most airlines require that you check in at the gate at least ten minutes before a domestic flight. Standing at curbside to check your luggage or waiting in line at the ticket counter doesn't count. Being tenth in line at the gate doesn't count. If you don't meet this requirement, the airline is not obligated to give you a dime, even if the flight is over-booked with 100 extra passengers. Most airlines routinely use the ten-minute limit but they can change it on a whim. Always ask your travel agent or airline reservation agent for the current policy. If they don't know the answer, make them track it down.

WHEN YOU DON'T WANT TO BE BUMPED

If you don't want to be bumped there are some important facts and strategies to keep in mind.

- **By law, the airline must seek volunteers** before they deny boarding. If you get to the gate within the check-in limit and you're told the flight is full, remind the gate agent that they are obligated to board the aircraft and ask for volunteers before they deny you your seat. If they try to convince you that this can't be done because they want to keep the flight on time, remind them that *your* on-time arrival matters too, and most importantly, they have to follow the rules.
- **If there are not enough volunteers,** the airline must compensate passengers who are bumped involuntarily. The Department of Transportation (DOT) mandates that every passenger in this circumstance be given a written copy of the DOT policy on request.
- **If the delay causes you to reach your destination** between one and two hours after scheduled arrival (between one and four hours on international flights), the minimum compensation required is the face value of the current segment of your ticket (not the fare to your final destination) or $200, whichever is less. If the delay is more than two hours, domestically, or more than four hours, internationally, the compensation must be at least double the one-way fare or $400, whichever is greater. Most commuter flights carry a $100 minimum compensation.
- **Some airlines will offer a roundtrip ticket**, sometimes with blackout dates, requirements for last-minute reservations or even standby only. Ask specifically what limits your ticket carries,

> *"This past summer, United Airlines asked travelers holding advance seating assignments to arrive at the gate at least 20 minutes in advance, rather than the standard ten minutes. If you didn't, you risked losing your seat assignment. This is a trend to watch out for during any peak travel period. Alaska Airlines seems to have followed United's lead. American, Continental, Delta and Northwest seem to be quietly edging their way to a 15-minute minimum."*

and don't hesitate to ask for less limited terms.

- **Other airlines try to satisfy you with vouchers** for future travel. Ask if you are receiving less compensation than passengers who were voluntarily bumped. No law forces the airline to match the amount, but asking for more can have a worthwhile result.

International flights departing from the U.S. require the same compensation as domestic flights, but the airlines get a little more latitude. If they get you to your destination more than one hour and less than four hours later than your originally scheduled arrival, they must compensate you for the value of that segment of your ticket, up to $200. If you're delayed more than four hours, the compensation is two times the value of the segment, or $400. If you're bumped on a flight departing from abroad, you're subject to a web of rules that vary by country. Compensation in European Union countries, for example, ranges from approximately $50-200 USD, depending on the length of the delay and the length of your flight. Airlines flying from other countries can offer far less. Some offer nothing at all.

BASIC COMPENSATION FOR INVOLUNTARY DENIED BOARDING

AIRLINE	VOUCHER OR CASH COMPENSATION (USUALLY AT GATE AGENT'S DISCRETION)	WHO CAN USE VOUCHER/FREE RTS
AMERICA WEST	Cash or Silver Liner Pass valid for one free domestic roundtrip ticket.	Transferable.
AMERICAN	Cash, discount voucher or voucher for free Coach roundtrip travel within the 48 states.	Transferable until ticketed.
CONTINENTAL	Discount voucher or free Coach roundtrip travel within the 48 states.	Tickets can be issued in anyone's name at time of issuance. Vouchers are transferable.
DELTA	Cash or free roundtrip Coach travel within the 48 states or to the Caribbean and Canada.	Transferable to family members only.
NORTHWEST	Cash or free roundtrip Coach travel within the 48 states.	Transferable.
RENO	At gate agent's discretion.	Transferable.
SOUTHWEST	Vouchers for future travel.	Vouchers can be used to purchase a ticket for the passenger of your choice.
TWA	Cash or voucher. Compensation can include a free domestic or Puerto Rico roundtrip.	Non-transferable.
UNITED	Cash or voucher that can include free domestic Coach roundtrip travel.	Non-transferable.
US AIRWAYS	Voucher for free Coach roundtrip domestic travel.	Transferable.

DELAYED AND CANCELLED FLIGHTS

Delayed and cancelled flights don't routinely entitle you to compensation, particularly when the reasons are considered to be outside the airline's control. Airlines don't guarantee their schedules. The help you get is up to each airline's policy and the degree of their eagerness to maintain your goodwill. Unfortunately, we hear many stories of hardline attitudes from the airlines. Sometimes flights are cancelled with no reason given and no accommodation offered.

If the delay or cancellation is due to a factor not affecting other airlines, ask that your ticket be endorsed for use on an alternate carrier. You have to ask to be put on a competitor's flight; few airlines will offer it. They prefer that you wait for their own next scheduled flight. Be sure they give you a confirmed reservation with the alternate airline. If your original airline endorses your ticket and the new airline refuses to honor it, have that gate agent call the original airline's gate agent. Some discount tickets require an additional notation called a "Flight Interruption Manifest" (FIM).

If you're able to wait out the delay, ask for help with meals and lodging. Generally you'll get more help if the problem has come from mechanical delays or other factors the airline has some control over. It's less likely that you'll receive monetary compensation when, for example, a blizzard forces the cancellation of hundreds of flights. If the airline declines to arrange a reduced rate room, ask the hotel directly for a "distressed passenger" discount.

Most airlines will not offer accommodations if the bump is on the outbound (beginning) leg of your flight. If your plane is making a connection and your flight is cancelled, you should adamantly request a room, meal vouchers, phone call and transportation to and from the hotel, as necessary.

Delayed flight compensation policies are another airline secret. Discount vouchers tend to go to the people who complain the loudest, and sometimes just to those who take the time to write letters of complaint. Meals, overnight accommodations and even phone cards are at the disposal of airline airport personnel to use according to guidelines the public doesn't get to see.

If a delay means you may miss your connecting flight, make the gate agent or flight attendant aware of your situation. If enough passengers are involved, the connecting flight may be held. If not, alternative arrangements can be worked out while you're still in flight.

On close connections get the gate assignment of your connecting flight while you're still in the air, check the airport map in the in-flight magazine and map out your terminal route. As soon as you deplane, tell the customer service agent which flight you're trying for. They can either help with transportation by cart or call the departure gate and let them know you're on your way.

If a major weather problem is forecasted and you can change to any earlier departure to avoid it, ask the airline to confirm space on the flight with no change fee. It's to their advantage, as well as your own, to get you out before the bad weather hits.

If you think you are not being told the truth about a weather-related delay, check to see if the other airlines are affected or call your airline's 800 number to see what the phone version of the reason for the delay might be.

Year in which Robert Crandall came to American Airlines: 1973, as Chief Financial Officer.

On Board Basics

SEAT ASSIGNMENTS

You can make seat selections in advance during a range of time varying by airline. If you purchase your tickets before seat selection opens, make sure to call back on the first day seat assignments can be acquired. All advance seat assignments can be cancelled if you don't check in at least ten minutes before your flight. Usually airlines will wait until ten minutes before flight time, but you may find adherence to a 30-minute policy on heavily-booked flights. You'll maintain your reservation, but you might end up with a less desirable seat.

Unclaimed seats are released ten to 15 minutes before flight time. If your current seat assignment is unfavorable, ask to be put on a waiting list in case a better seat opens up. If you can't enjoy the comforts of Business or First Class, opt for the best seat you can get in Coach.

Exit row and bulkhead seats (the first row in Coach) provide the most legroom. Bulkhead seats have trays that fold out of a panel between seats rather than from the seat in front and no floor storage space. All carry-ons must go in the overhead bins. Exit row seats also guarantee you won't be next to small children or infants. They aren't allowed in exit rows. Some airlines don't release premium seating (such as bulkhead and exit row seats), until the day of the flight. Exit row seats can only be assigned to people 15 and over who are physically able to assist other passengers in emergency situations.

Airline named after a flightless bird: Kiwi International.

Seats in front of exit rows often have less reclining capability.

Seats in the emergency exit rows can be your very best bet. I have seen what seems to be double the leg room in exit rows, compared to First Class seating.

Best seating options for families vary by individual preference. Bulkhead seats provide additional leg room. Be aware that the arm dividing the seats does not lift up because it contains the fold-out meal tray. The rear of the plane, with its increased engine noise, seems to lull some infants to sleep. One point of agreement: children want window seats. When traveling in pairs, select window and aisle seats only, leaving the middle seat free. On all but the most crowded flights they'll remain unclaimed and give you extra room. Be sure to get advance seat assignments to assure that your family will not be split up on crowded flights.

TWA, Alaska, Kiwi and Midwest Express offer some of the most comfortable Coach seats in the skies. Midwest Express has all two-across seating with extra leg room and comfort comparable to Business Class on other airlines. TWA reconfigured seats on many of its jets to provide increased Coach leg room.

> *"When boarding rows are called, get in the back of the line that precedes your section. You'll be first in line when your section is called."*

Wide-bodies with two-five-two seating allow for extra comfort in Coach, providing that your seats are located in the outer, two-across sections rather than the five-seat across the middle area. Look for DC-10s, MD-11s and L1011s.

Never change seats without notifying the flight attendant. You'll usually have no problem getting permission to move within the same class of service but, particularly on direct flights, a passenger boarding at the intermediate city may be assigned to the seat you want to occupy.

Seat Selection Policies

All domestic airlines issue boarding passes a minimum of 30 days prior to your flight except Continental (34 days) and Northwest (35 days). You can request a specific seat much further in advance. International airlines vary widely on boarding pass dates of issue, from Air Canada's 29 days to Mexicana's 255 days. Check the list below to determine when you can reserve your seat selection on domestic and international flights.

Aeromexico . . . . 90 days in advance
Air Canada . . . . . .329 days in advance
Alaska . . . . .330 days in advance
America West . . . .340 days in advance
American . . . . .331 days in advance
British Airways . . .331 days in advance
Canadian . . . . .331 days in advance
Cathay Pacific . . . .180 days in advance
Delta . . . . .331 days in advance
Mexicana . . . . .331 days in advance
Midwest Express . .180 days in advance
Northwest . . . . .90 days in advance
Reno . . . . .60 days in advance
Sabena . . . . .120 days in advance
Tower . . . . 60 days in advance
TWA . . . . 60 days in advance
United . . . . 331 days in advance
US Airways . . . . . .130 days in advance
Virgin Atlantic . . . . .180 days in advance

Airline that offered Barbie-like flight attendant dolls for sale: JAL.

AIRLINE & AIRPORT SMOKING POLICIES

Smokers who found sanctuary in the few remaining United and American Airlines international flights that allowed smoking have lost their final options. Both carriers joined the majority of U.S. airlines voluntarily banning smoking on all international flights. U.S. airline flights to international destinations are now almost totally smoke-free. The only U.S. carrier flights that still permit smoking are: Continental Micronesia flights between Honolulu and Tokyo; Northwest flights to and from Japan; and all Tower Air international flights.

Airport smoking policies are changing rapidly with more and more U.S. airports banning smoking entirely. Almost one-third are completely smoke-free. Those that still allow smoking limit it to fewer areas. More than half of all airports have no direct control over smoking policies as they are mandated by city, state or county law. Most violations of airport smoking policies are handled by verbal warnings, though there have been cases of fines ranging from $10-125, levied when the warnings weren't heeded. Airports that don't allow smoking in their terminals usually do not restrict smoking outside though some (such as Boston and Miami) ask that you only smoke when standing away from terminal exits and entrances.

AIRLINE MEALS

Last year, the big news was that fewer airline meals were being served and airlines are spending less for each meal on domestic flights. You can now fly coast-to-coast on some connecting flights, and the sum total of nourishment provided can be two bags of peanuts and a couple of plastic cups of soda. This year, a couple of airlines (most notably United) have reversed the trend somewhat by making significant moves to beef up their Coach meal service. You will still find, however, the occasional mainland U.S.-Hawaii flight with a half-sandwich and a few condiments masquerading as a meal and other meal *faux pas* that might make packing a snack your best strategy. Overall, things are looking a little bit better. After all, United now offers larger servings of vegetables in Economy Class. The real improvements in meal service on most major airlines are in Business and First Class.

> *"United made a concerted effort to improve Coach meal service on coast-to-coast flights. Economy Class passengers now get a pre-arrival snack cart (in addition to regular meal service). Menu improvements are heavy on chicken entrees: Sunny South Beach Chicken, Lacquered Maple Syrup Chicken, Devilishly Good Roasted Chicken, Savannah Chicken, Savory Farmhouse Chicken and—our favorite—Rustic Tarragon Chicken in Repose."*

Midwest Express serves the best food overall on domestic airlines. Their one-class service provides for meals ranging from $10.32 and $10.65 per passenger depending on the meal cycle, double that of most competitors. You even get wine with your meal.

If you want to make sure you get your choice of the two standard menus offered on a flight, ask the flight attendant to take your request when you board the plane.

Cost of each of 18 wheels on 747 landing gear assemblies: $2,727.

SPECIAL MEALS

Special meals can be ordered on most airlines and most flights with six to 24 hours advance notice. They are usually better and fresher than the standard Coach fare. If a special meal is important to you, it's best to re-confirm, particularly if you ordered it far in advance of your flight. Not all meal choices are available on all flights.

Several airlines, including America West, Delta and American, hand out bagged lunches at the gate in lieu of some meal service. They jazz up the concept, if not the contents, with names like American Airlines *Bistro Service*. Northwest serves many meals a la carte, literally. Passengers choose what they want and how much from a selection of food that may include bagels, fruit, yogurt and other easy-to-serve items.

The easiest route to the best meal in the air is to book a flight that is the first domestic leg of an international flight. Meal service is markedly better.

If you're on a special diet, keep in mind that schedule changes can result in your requested meal not being available. Carry back-up food if necessary.

Infant and baby meals are generally only guaranteed on international flights.

Vegetarian meals can always be ordered and often include sub-varieties, including egg-free and ethnically oriented menus.

SPECIAL MEALS BY AIRLINE

AIRLINE	CHILDREN'S MEALS	SPECIALTY MEALS
AMERICA WEST	Strained Infant Food and Special Children's Meals including peanut butter & jelly sandwiches and chicken nuggets.	Asian Vegetarian, Bland, Diabetic, Fruit Meal, Gluten Free, High Fiber, Hindu, Kosher, Low Calorie, Low Fat & Cholesterol, Low Protein, Low Sodium or No Salt, Moslem, Non-Lactose, Oriental, Low Purin, Raw Vegetarian, Seafood, Vegetarian/Non-Dairy and Vegetarian/No Dairy or Eggs.
AMERICAN	Strained Infant Food, Junior Food, and Special Children's Meals including peanut butter & jelly sandwiches, hot dogs and hamburgers.	Asian Vegetarian, Bland, Diabetic, Fruit Meal, Gluten Free, High Fiber, Hindu, Kosher, Low Calorie, Low Fat & Cholesterol, Low Protein, Low Sodium or No Salt, Moslem, Non-Lactose, Oriental, Low Purin, Raw Vegetarian, Seafood, Vegetarian/Non-Dairy and Vegetarian/No Dairy or Eggs.
CONTINENTAL	Strained Infant Food and Special Children's Meals including peanut butter & jelly sandwiches, chicken fingers and sandwich with grapes, carrot sticks and celery.	Asian Vegetarian, Diabetic, Fruit Meal, Gluten Free, Hindu, Kosher, Low Fat & Cholesterol, Low Protein, Low Sodium or No Salt, Moslem, Non-Lactose, Oriental, Low Purin, Raw Vegetarian, Seafood, Vegetarian/Non-Dairy and Vegetarian/No Dairy or Eggs.

Amount of coffee served on Continental flights each month: 2,987,000 cups.

SPECIAL MEALS BY AIRLINE		
AIRLINE	**CHILDREN'S MEALS**	**SPECIALTY MEALS**
DELTA	Strained Infant Food, Toddler Meals and Special Children's Meals including peanut butter & jelly sandwiches and pizza.	Asian Vegetarian, Bland, Diabetic, Fruit Meal, Gluten Free, High Fiber, Hindu, Hot Seafood, Kosher, Low Calorie, Low Fat & Cholesterol, Low Protein, Low Sodium or No Salt, Moslem, Non-Lactose, Oriental, Low Purin, Raw Vegetarian, Seafood, Vegetarian/Non-Dairy and Vegetarian/No Dairy or Eggs.
NORTHWEST	Strained Infant Food and Special Children's Meals including peanut butter & jelly sandwiches, hot dogs and hamburgers.	Asian Vegetarian, Bland, Diabetic, Fruit Meal, Gluten Free, High Fiber, Hindu, Kosher, Low Fat & Cholesterol, Low Sodium or No Salt, Moslem, Oriental, Low Purin, Raw Vegetarian, Vegetarian /Non-Dairy and Vegetarian/No Dairy or Eggs.
TWA	Special Children's Meals including chicken nuggets, cheeseburgers and hot dogs.	Fruit Plate, Kosher, Low Calorie, Low Carbohydrate, Low Fat & Cholesterol, Low Sodium or No Salt, Seafood Platter and Vegetarian/Non-Dairy.
UNITED	Strained Infant Food, Refugee Meal, fruit and graham crackers and Children's Meals including McDonalds Happy Meals, peanut butter & jelly sandwiches and hot dogs.	Asian Vegetarian, Bland, Boneless Chicken, Chef Salad, Diabetic, Fruit Meal, Gluten Free, High Fiber, Hindu, Kosher, Low Calorie, Low Fat & Cholesterol, Low Protein, Low Sodium or No Salt, Moslem, Non-Lactose, Oriental, Low Purin, Raw Vegetarian, Seafood, Vegetarian/Non-Dairy and Vegetarian/No Dairy or Eggs.
US AIRWAYS	Strained Infant Food and Children's Meals including peanut butter & jelly sandwiches and macaroni and cheese.	Asian Vegetarian, Bland, Diabetic, Fruit Meal, Gluten Free, High Fiber, Hindu, Kosher, Low Calorie, Low Fat & Cholesterol, Low Protein, Low Sodium or No Salt, Moslem, Non-Lactose, Oriental, Low Purin, Raw Vegetarian, Seafood, Vegetarian/Non-Dairy and Vegetarian/No Dairy or Eggs.

Amount spent per year on food service by United Airlines: $650 million.

IN-FLIGHT COSTS

Beer, wine and mixed drinks are always free in First and Business Class on both domestic and international flights. They're also free in Coach on all international flights, except Continental's flights to and from Mexico, where the charge is the same as for domestic Coach drinks. Free drinks on international flights are only available during flight portions that occur over international waters. The following chart lists in-flight beverage costs on domestic flights plus the cost of headset rental when you fly in domestic Coach.

IN-FLIGHT AMMENITIES			
AIRLINE	HEADSET COST	DOMESTIC BEER & WINE	IMPORTED BEER & COCKTAILS
AMERICA WEST	$4	$3	$4
AMERICAN	$5	$3	$4
CONTINENTAL	$4	$3	$4
DELTA	$5	$3	$4
NORTHWEST	N/A	$3	$4
RENO	N/A	$4	$4
SOUTHWEST	N/A	$2	$4
TWA	$4	$2	$3
UNITED	$4	$3	$4
US AIRWAYS	$4	$3	$3 for margaritas/ $4 for others

IN-FLIGHT MAGAZINE DISCOUNTS

Even if you don't feel like reading, take the time to check the in-flight magazine for special offers and discount coupons. You'll find bonus miles offered for long distance service and airline credit cards. Sabena's *Passport* has offered coupons valid for discount on Avis car rentals in Europe. Southwest's *Spirit* frequently contains coupons for a $29.99 car rental in Las Vegas and an $11 souvenir t-shirt for $2.99. In-flight magazines can also contain special offers on in-flight calls, airline credit cards and frequent flyer bonuses attached to long distance service.

IN-FLIGHT TECHNO-TRENDS

The wave of the future is going to include technological bells and whistles that reflect the advances we are seeing on the ground. They include new antennae systems for aircraft, capable of pulling in live television transmissions. Until this innovation becomes standard technology, many travelers will still get pre-recorded material, but airlines are battling for a techno amenity edge as a customer lure. We will see many techno improvements implemented and many more announced. The chart on the following page provides an update and a preview.

Major airline that dropped most in-flight movies: Northwest.

TECHNO-TRENDS BY AIRLINE	
AIRLINE	**VIDEO PERKS**
AIR CANADA	Personal monitors in 747 and 767 First Class international. A340 First Class international has personal monitors and ten Nintendo games.
AIR FRANCE	Personal monitors with movie libraries in First and Business Class.
ALITALIA	Interactive touch-screen systems in Business Class.
BRITISH AIRWAYS	Testing interactive system with 24 movie choices, fax capability and gambling loss limits of approximately $,1112 in Economy and $225 in Business and First Class).
AMERICA WEST	FlightLink offers *USA Today* interactive news and other features on seatback screens.
AMERICAN	Portable video units in international Business Class. Armrest video monitors in transcontinental and international First Class.
CANADIAN	Individual monitors in Executive Business Class 747s and DC-10s; Sony Walkmans for Club Empress 767s.
CATHAY PACIFIC	Individual screens will be at every seat by the end of 1998.
CONTINENTAL	FlightLink on seatback screens with LiveTV being installed in Coach.
DELTA	LiveTV on select flights but viewing is limited to cabin monitors.
JAPAN AIRLINES	Armrest screens or larger folding-arm screens in Business and First Class on 747-400s and MD11s flown internationally. Sony Walkmans also available for Business and First Class.
KLM	Personal screens on Business Class in 747s.
LUFTHANSA	Armrest screens for Business and First Class on longhaul A-340, 747 and DC-10 routes.
NORTHWEST	Personal video systems in Business and First Class on A320s and 747-400s.
QANTAS	Armrest screens in Business and First Class with an interactive system under development.
SABENA	Armrest screens in Business and First Class A340-200s.
SINGAPORE	All 747 passengers have personal screen, 22-channel video systems; gambling feature being tested.
TWA	Personal monitors on transcontinental and transatlantic TransWorld One Class; interactive programming under development.
UNITED	Individual monitors in all classes on longhaul 767s and 777s; in Business and First Class on 747-200s.
US AIRWAYS	Seatback screens for Business Class 767 longhaul flights.
VIRGIN ATLANTIC	21-channel personal video, games, audio, flight mapping and video gambling (as allowed by law).

Year that marked the first commercial flight of the Boeing 747-100: 1970.

AIRPORT CLUBS

All major domestic carriers (except Southwest) and most large international carriers have membership only clubs. There are about 150 of them in the U.S. and internationally. Membership usually requires an initial membership fee plus annual dues. Couples can join at reduced rates. Some clubs charge for beverages and conference room use; some do not. They can be havens from airport crowds and discomfort but they can also get overcrowded during busy travel times.

Many airport clubs offer short-term memberships. United, Delta and American sell one-day passes for $25 or $30. The one-day fee includes your immediate family or two, unrelated guests. Continental sells a 30-day membership for $30. Diners Club and American Express also sponsor more than 50 clubs worldwide, with free admission to all cardholders but guests of cardholders may be charged a fee.

Advantages of any airport club membership include special check-in services; secure storage should you choose to leave your luggage behind while you move about the airport; business amenities including fax, copiers, computers and meeting rooms.

Join the club that has the best services at your home airport. The next consideration: airports you fly to most frequently or connecting city airports. Ask about policies regarding the requirement of a same-day ticket to access the airport club. Most clubs have it in their rules but only enforce it at crowded airports during peak travel times. Delta is reportedly the most stringent enforcer of this policy.

Many airlines are reacting to the increase in airline airport club memberships by expanding facilities at key airports and offering more amenities for business travelers.

Northwest Airlines recently introduced a two-tier system for airline airport club membership. You pay $225 per year for access to domestic airport clubs only; $395 for access to both domestic and international airport clubs. Previously, they charged $270 for access to all Northwest WorldClubs.

Find a chart on the following page to help you discover which airline club might best suit your needs. Please note that American Express Platinum cardholders are entitled to complimentary visits to Northwest WorldClubs and Continental Presidents Club each time they fly that airline.

The Priority Pass network could be your best choice if you fly multiple airlines. Membership allows access to 56 domestic clubs (including those sponsored by America West, Continental, Northwest and TWA) plus about 160 international locations. A bare bones Priority Pass standard membership is $79 per year plus a $21 fee each time you use an airport club. The money-saver is a $225 Priority Pass Prestige annual membership, allowing unlimited access to all member clubs for one year. If you are traveling with a non-member guest, you pay $21 for their admittance, per club entry. Call **800-352-2834**.

A dozen or so VIP airline clubs exist for preferred passengers. The only admission cost is the price of your First Class ticket. The best VIP lounges offer extraordinary amenities that may include candlelight dinners, caviar and premium champagne. Some VIP lounges offer little more than standard airport clubs, particularly those that share facilities with other airlines.

Total number of passengers who have flown on 747s: over one billion.

AIRLINE SPONSORED AIRPORT CLUBS

AIRLINE	ANNUAL FEES SINGLE/COUPLE	MEETING ROOM COSTS	COCKTAILS
AIR CANADA Maple Leaf Lounge 800-776-3000	By invitation only, based on frequent flyer status.	N/A	Free
ALASKA AIR Board Room 800-654-5669	$175/$245 per year	Two hours free	Free
AMERICA WEST Phoenix Club 602-693-2994	$150/$175 First Year $100/$125 Renewal	Two hours free then $20 per hour	$4
AMERICAN Admirals Club 800-237-7971	$350/$600 First Year $250 Renewal	$40 per hour	$4
ALOHA Executive Club 800-367-5250	$120 per year	N/A	Free
CANADIAN Empress Lounge 800-426-7000	195 CAD per person	Free	Free
CONTINENTAL Presidents Club 800-322-2640	$200/$275 First Year $150/$225 Renewal	$35 per hour	$4-5
DELTA Crown Room 800-323-2323	$200/$300 one year; $500/$750 three years	$35 per hour	Free
HAWAIIAN Premier Club 800-367-5320	$125/$180 First Year $105/$140 Renewal	N/A	Free
NORTHWEST WorldClubs 800-692-3788	$225/ Domestic $395/Domestic and International	$35 per hour	Varies
TWA Ambassadors Club 800-527-1468	$175/$250 First Year $150/$225 Renewal	$25	$2-3
UNITED Red Carpet Club 520-881-0500	$400 per year	$35-$50 per hour	$3.50-4.50
US AIRWAYS Airways Club 800-828-8522	$350 First Year $250 Renewal	$35	$4

First airline to show regularly scheduled in-flight movies: TWA, in 1961.

STAYING FIT IN-FLIGHT

Here are some tips to help make your time in the air more comfortable and easier on your state of health.

- **Pressure build-up** occurs in the ears during take-off and landing. Ease it by swallowing often and pinching your nostrils shut, then gently blowing against them. Chewing gum may also help.
- **Economy Class Syndrome** is a medically recognized complaint caused by cramped leg room and dehydration which inhibits symptoms inhibiting blood flow. Ask your doctor about taking one aspirin to thin your blood. Limit smoking before boarding and try to move and stretch as much as possible during the flight.
- **Dehydration is countered** by increasing your consumption of liquids before the flight. Drink at least eight ounces of water or juice per hour of flight time. Limit alcohol and caffeine consumption; both are diuretics. A small plastic atomizer of water will release a mist to replenish your skin.
- **Closed cabins and crowded situations** increase the number of germs in the air. Breathing through your nose rather than your mouth helps purify the air you take into your lungs.
- **Airline pillows and blankets** are guaranteed germ carriers. Airlines may only change them every 24 hours. If you need a pillow, consider carrying a small inflatable version. Try to keep warm with a coat or jacket rather than covering yourself with a blanket that may be a challenge to the best immune systems.
- **Slip off your shoes and elevate your feet.** Put a small pillow behind the small of your back. Buy a special inflatable pillow that cradles your neck and head.
- **If you experience severe cramps, gas-like pains or swelling** in the waist area, ask the flight attendant to check the cabin pressure. It sometimes requires an in-flight adjustment.
- **Tension and muscle tightness** resulting from sitting too long in one position will ease if you rotate your head, roll your shoulders in a modified shrugging motion and shake out your hands. Relax your legs by pointing and flexing your feet and spreading your toes.

Jet lag is your body's reaction to the disruption of its 24-hour cycle coupled with the demands placed on your body by lengthy flights. It's more common on eastbound flights. Every frequent international flyer has a cure to recommend. Some are rather unique—such as the wearing of battery-operated visors, said to send the proper, balancing light into the retina. Jet lag is like hangovers and common colds. There are no absolute cures, but there are some things you can do to ease the symptoms.

- **Set your watch** to your destination's time as soon as you take your seat. Adapt your flight behavior to the time of day you're scheduled to arrive.Try to relax and rest as much as you can so you wake up to a morning arrival. Try to stay awake if you will be arriving at night.
- **Deep breathing** can replace some of the oxygen deprivation that occurs from lowered cabin pressure.
- **The U.S. Department of Energy** will send you a free copy of their *Anti-Jet Lag Diet*. Send a stamped self-addressed envelope to Arizona

U.S. airline tickets issued in 1973: over 200,000, all handwritten.

Chemical, 9700 S. Cass Ave., Argonne, IL 60439. Following this diet requires the willingness to adopt a relatively strict eating regimen for four to five days prior to each flight.

- **Aromatherapy to ease jet lag?** Air New Zealand, British Airways and Delta think so. First and Business Class passengers are given kits with plant-based, fragrant oils to be inhaled, dabbed on pulse points or used in the bath or shower. Make your own kit by asking for help from a shop selling aromatherapy products. They can help you select the oils said to produce the effects you desire.

RIGHTS OF DISABLED TRAVELERS

Most disabilities can and must be accommodated under U.S. law. The Americans With Disabilities Act of 1990 and the Air Carrier Access Act of 1986 mandates full rights for all people with disabilities in airports and on all U.S.-based airlines. All carriers must accommodate you and give assistance as needed. Plan ahead and make use of services including by-request airline assistance in getting on/off the airplane, moving to and from rest rooms and retrieving baggage. Advise the carrier of the extent of your disability with regard to mobility, hearing, sight, etc.

You do not have to give notice of your disability unless you use a respirator hook-up, stretcher, on-board wheelchair or special battery pack for your wheelchair. Airlines can insist on attendants only for passengers who have severe mental illnesses, are on stretchers or are quadriplegic and unable to respond to safety instructions.

Airlines do not have a great record of practical compliance with the Americans With Disabilities Act. Complaints filed with the Department of Transportation have doubled. Most major airlines only offer their employees a brief computer training session on dealing with disabled passengers. Aisle chairs (necessary for restroom accessibility in-flight) aren't always available. Passengers who require lifting often receive that service from people who have not been trained. (We have even heard of one passenger being carried upside down.) Airport wheelchairs are often in short supply. If you encounter problems, we strongly recommend that you write the Department of Transportation and the airline involved.

Access Travel: A Guide To Accessibility Of Airport Terminals is available at no cost from the Consumers Information Center, Pueblo, CO 81009, **719-948- 3334**.

AIR TRAVEL SAFETY

You are far safer on a commercial jet than you are on your drive to the airport. On average more people in the U.S. are killed each day in car accidents than are killed each year in plane crashes. A statistical passenger would have to fly once a day for 26,000 years before encountering the odds of a fatal air crash.

International air travel safety is sometimes on a par with that in the U.S., but some countries are notorious for risky flying and poorly managed air traffic control systems. The FAA has begun publishing a list of countries considered to be lax in airline safety standards. Ask your travel agent to check out your destinations.

You can increase your safety in-flight by observing the following tips.

- **Use electronic equipment in-flight** only according to stated airline rules. Don't use laptops and CD players at all during takeoffs and landings.

Time it takes for deaths by car to equal all deaths in the history of U.S. commercial aviation: three months.

> *"Many commuter airlines are now held to the same safety standards as major airlines. Commuter airlines that feed passengers to the major airlines come under two categories: those carrying 30 or less passengers and those carrying 31 or more passengers. The smaller planes are still allowed looser safety standards. If you can't avoid a commuter flight, at least try to avoid the smallest planes. Your reservation agent can tell you the type of aircraft and the number of passengers it carries, but you must request that information."*

- **When told to put on your oxygen mask,** do so without delay. Apoxia, caused by a lack of oxygen, not only affects your thinking, it also affects eyesight in just a few seconds. If you're traveling with young children, put your mask on first, then help your children.
- **Wear natural fiber clothing** and avoid highly flammable synthetics. The worst thing you can wear on a plane is panty hose. If there is a fire they can melt against your skin.
- **Avoid the temptation to overload overhead bins** or place heavy objects inside.
- **Keep your seatbelt fastened at all times.** It may be a minor annoyance, but it can save you from injury in case of unanticipated turbulence or a sudden drop in altitude. More and more airlines will require that seatbelts remain fastened throughout domestic flights.
- **Don't carry sharp objects** in pockets or wear jewelry with sharp edges.
- **Carry a small, high beam flashlight** to provide light for situations that may extinguish the emergency back-up lights.
- **Pay attention to safety instructions** and review the information card in the pouch in front of your seat. Even frequent flyers can get confused.
- **Count the rows to the nearest exit** so you can get there by touch. Locate alternate exits.

> *"Since the first edition of Insider Travel Secrets, U.S. airlines agreed to waive the Warsaw Convention's liability limit for death and injury on international flights. U.S. citizens may obtain judgments under U.S. law, even when litigating in international courts."*

FEAR OF FLYING

Small fear levels can be managed by sitting in the front of plane or over the wing (where the ride is the smoothest), talking to your seat mate and not focusing on your fears. If you want every statistic on your side, sit in the back of the plane, the same place where the famous black box (which is actually bright orange) rides. Your ride will be a bit less smooth, but you will be in the area least likely to be destroyed in an accident. The second best option is over the wing where the aircraft structure is most stable.

The two major U.S. airlines that have never had fatal crashes: America West and Southwest.

> *"Thairapy, by aviation psychologist Glen Arnold, (**714-967-0772**), offers a $30 audio-cassette kit summarizing the teachings of his seminars. Three of his tips: plan a relaxing day before your flight; fight claustrophobic feelings by thinking of the cabin as protective, rather than confining; remember that turbulence is a natural quality of air and that airplanes are designed to accommodate it."*

Major problems that prohibit flying may require either psychological treatment or enrollment in one of the special programs that deal successfully with aerophobia. Costs start at about $300.

- **Northwest Airlines Wings Freedom to Fly** offers weekend seminars in Minneapolis and other cities served by Northwest. Call **612-726-7733**.
- **The Institute for Psychology of Air Travel** holds seminars including a flight for graduates. Call **617-437-1811**; go online at **www.ads-online.com/InsPsyAir/**.
- **The Pegasus Fear of Flying Association** provides an effective one-day program. Call **800-332-7668**.
- **US Airways Fearful Flyer Program** is offered in 11 cities and takes place over a five-week period. The cost is $325. Write to Box 100, Glenshaw, PA 15116 or call **412-366-8112** for details.
- **Flight To Freedom** is a two-day weekend seminar regularly conducted in Dallas, New York City, Chicago and Orange County, California, by a former American Airlines pilot. The cost is $350. Write to 2407 Crockett Court, Grapevine, TX 76051 or call **817-424-5108**.

IN-FLIGHT MEDICAL ASSISTANCE

The Federal Aviation Administration has minimal standards for medical emergencies in the air.

- **First aid instructions** plus an annual refresher course for all flight attendants.
- **A first aid kit** containing bandages, antiseptic and standard "small emergency" equipment.
- **A medical emergency kit** containing a stethoscope, syringes, needles and basic drugs that may only be used if an authorized medical person is aboard the flight as a passenger or flight attendant.
- **Contact by radio** with either airline staff physicians or a private firm offering 24-hour medical back-up.

Delta is the first U.S. carrier to commit to equipping its entire fleet with external heart defibrillators (with heart monitoring capabilities) and expanded emergency medical kits. Other major carriers are following suit. Flight attendants will be trained to use the defibrillators. The machines will be able to determine if patients require electrical shock and to deliver it appropriately. New medical kits with expanded contents mandated by the Federal Aviation Administration will help add to the safety of all travelers. The new kits will only be opened if a physician is on board. They contain special equipment and prescription medications of various types.

The Air Transport Association studied

Countries that spray arriving passengers with insecticide: Grenada, Kiribati and Madagascar.

in-flight medical events. They looked at 1996 data on over 580 million passengers from the nine U.S. carriers that account for 90 percent of all U.S. commercial airline travel. According to their study, 433 passengers reported chest pain, 141 passengers experienced heart attacks, 2,136 passengers reported significant dizziness or fainted and 438 passengers suffered from respiratory distress. The complete study results can be accessed at **www.airtransport.org**.

> *"If you need medical assistance at the airport, firefighters or paramedics will be called. Only six airports have medical staff available within their terminals: Denver, Honolulu, Philadelphia, St. Louis, San Francisco and Toronto."*

FLYING WITH PETS

There are three basic modes of air travel available for pets. Terminology and rules differ from carrier to carrier. Fees can also vary. United and Northwest initiated new policies on pets flying (in cargo) with ticketed passengers. Fees are now higher for larger dogs.

Carry-on travel is restricted to pets who fit comfortably in a 16" x 21"x 8" high carrier and are traveling with a human. Each airline has its own specific rules and policies regarding the size of the animal and

PETS PERMITTED BY AIRLINE			
AIRLINE	ALLOWED IN CABIN (IN ADDITION TO DOGS AND CATS)	MAXIMUM KENNEL SIZE	MAXIMUM PETS PER FLIGHT
AMERICAN	Birds	17x12x7.5	Seven
CONTINENTAL	Birds, rabbits and pot-bellied pigs	21x13x8	Three
DELTA	Birds, rabbits, hamsters, ferrets and guinea pigs	21x13x9	Three
NORTHWEST	None	21x15x6	Four
TWA	Birds	21x16x8	Four
UNITED	Birds	22x14x9	Varies by aircraft
US AIRWAYS	Birds	17x12x8	Two

Amount of money allocated by Congress to train bomb-sniffing dogs: $8.8 million.

how many are allowed on each flight. Always check 24 hours in advance to be sure your pet will be allowed on the plane. Some airlines allow small animals to travel in soft-sided pouches available from pet supply stores. Reservations are mandatory. All major airlines allow cats and dogs; some allow other friendly creatures. The fee (per direction) is $50 ($60 on Delta, but they are the only carrier that will let you travel with your ferret).

Cargo passage places your pet in a pressurized, climate-controlled cargo area. If you are traveling on the same flight, you pay $50 per direction for your pet (more on United if you have a large animal). Cargo passage for unaccompanied animals can either be priority (you specify the precise flight) or regular cargo (you can only specify the day of shipment).

Most pets dislike air travel and it can be very stressful for them. Make sure your reasons for taking your pet outweigh the risks and disadvantages. Never try to fly with an animal who is overly excitable or subject to motion sickness (as a rule, animals who are good car travelers will tolerate air travel). Don't subject your pets who are in heat, pregnant, under eight weeks old or elderly to air travel. Pug-nose dogs and cats should never travel as cargo; even passenger cabin air can inhibit their breathing due to the structure of their faces.

Select a nonstop flight whenever possible. Avoid peak travel periods. If you must use a connecting flight, be sure the size of each plane accommodates your pet carrier. Avoid the last connecting flight. You may arrive at your destination but your pet may not arrive until the following day, because cargo transfers were not completed.

Purchase an approved kennel from a discount pet store or, better yet, borrow one from a friend. Airlines sell them but you will pay a premium price. Be sure the kennel is large enough for your pet to stand up comfortably. Place a blanket and a favorite toy in the kennel and let your pet explore it before you go.

Get the required health certificate from your vet. This must be dated no more than ten days prior to your originating flight. It includes documentation of current immunizations (including rabies) and certifies that your animal is fit to travel. These papers will be affixed to the kennel by the airline. Make a copy to carry with you.

Exercise your pets before the flight so they are more relaxed and prone to sleep. Don't feed them for five to six hours prior to take-off and limit water two hours before the flight.

In-flight water is best provided by filling the carrier's plastic water container three-fourths full and freezing it before you

> *"Don't be too trusting when traveling with your pet. Airlines regard your beloved companion as cargo, with occasionally tragic consequences. Have the gate attendant call and confirm that your pet has been loaded before you board the plane. Make sure the pet has been placed in a pressurized, climate-controlled area. Make sure the pilot is aware that animals are on board. One quick sentence from you may save your animal's life in case of a lengthy ground delay. Lengthy flights only mandate that your animal be fed every 24 hours and watered every 12 hours. This includes transfers, layovers and ground delays. If you can avoid them, do so."*

leave home. The ice will melt slowly throughout the flight.

Tranquilizers are not desirable unless your vet believes your animal must have them. Travel-induced excitement is only a problem for animals who might harm themselves when excited.

Pets flying cargo should not wear collars and tags that can get hooked on metal grates. Identification will be attached to the carrier when you check in.

Never put a lock on your pet's kennel. Locks delay access if your pet needs emergency attention.

AIR TRAVELERS' DICTIONARY

Here's a quick reference to terms you'll hear most often when arranging air travel. If a reservation agent uses a term you don't understand, ask for a clarification. There is a great deal of industry jargon. The consumer should not be embarrassed about not being fluent in these terms.

APEX: Advanced Purchase Excursion Fare. One of the lowest-priced but most restricted ticket types.

ATB: Automated ticket and boarding pass, usually coded with a magnetic strip that allows machine processing.

Back-To-Back: Overlapping, roundtrip tickets used to fulfill Saturday stay requirements and lower costs.

Blackouts: Holiday, major event and seasonal dates when specific discount fares are not available.

Bucket Shops: A name originating in Britain to describe shops selling consolidator and wholesale airline tickets.

Bulkhead: The first row of seats in any commercial aircraft Coach cabin.

Bumping: The voluntary or involuntary removal of confirmed passengers from over-booked flights.

Cancellation Penalty: The dollar amount or percentage of your ticket price you lose if you request a refund.

Charters: Public charters fly regularly between specified cities, usually at rates lower than scheduled air. Private charters are usually used in conjunction with vacation packages.

City Codes: Three-letter designations used by airlines and air traffic control to identify specific airports. You should always check the city code the baggage handler or gate agent puts on your luggage to make sure it is being coded to the correct airport.

City Pair: The originating and destination cities of a flight.

City Ticket Office: An off-airport location that issues tickets for a specific airline.

Codesharing: Two or more airlines flying a route under one airline's name. One of the carriers may offer a lower service level or flights via commuter carriers. The Department of Transportation (DOT) mandates that passengers be informed when they are flying on codeshare flights.

Commuter Aircraft: Defined as 62 passengers or less. Commuters may be affiliated with major airlines but operate under separate rules and regulations.

Companion Fares: Pricing based on two people traveling together on an entire itinerary.

Connecting Flight: Requires one or more changes of plane.

Consolidator: A company that purchases bulk tickets from the airlines and sells

Time it takes to wash an aircraft exterior by hand: 11 hours; by machine, 4 hours.

them at a discount.

Cross-Border Ticketing: International tickets written to take advantage of lower fares or more favorable currency rates.

CRS: Computer reservation systems, interactively linked.

Deregulation: The 1978 law that phased out the Civil Aeronautics Board as well as some government regulation of routes and fares.

Direct Flight: Makes one or more stops and may even require a change of planes on codeshare flights.

Double Booking: Two reservations for the same person on the same route and date. If the airlines detect it, they'll cancel, without notification, the last reservation entered. Don't try to hold dual reservations on the same airline. Duplicate itineraries on more than one airline are rarely detected.

Excursion Fares: Roundtrip fares with minimum and maximum stay requirements and advance purchase requirements.

Gateway City: An airline's point of entry to a particular country.

Group Rate: A nominal discount usually offered to groups of ten or more people traveling together.

Hidden Cities: Flying (usually one-way) to a second city but deplaning in the stopover city to take advantage of a lower fare.

Hub & Spoke: A hub is a central connection airport for an airline. Passengers are further routed (spoked) to their final destination.

Interline Connection: A change of planes and airlines.

Narrowbody: An aircraft with one center aisle.

Nonstop Flight: Goes directly to the ticketed destination without a stop.

Open Jaw: Ticketing that allows travel to and a return from two separate cities with the fare based on 50 percent of each roundtrip.

Open Ticket: Good for transportation between specific points with no specific reservation needed.

PFC: Passenger facility charge, usually $3 per airport, added to the cost of most airline tickets.

Segment: A portion of an airline itinerary.

Split-Ticketing: Two low-priced tickets purchased to reach a high-price destination usually dominated by one nonstop carrier.

Standby: Waitlisted travel with no confirmed reservation. It normally requires pre-purchasing a ticket.

Waitlist: A holding-pattern for ticketed passengers without confirmed reservations. Tickets are confirmed as space becomes available.

Yield Management: Computerized tracking and adjustment of fares based on anticipated demand and closely monitored activity of competitors.

Amount of overall airline expense allocated for direct-use airport fees: five percent.

FREQUENT FLYER TWISTS AND TURNS

FACTS ON ONE OF OUR TASTIEST CARROTS

Frequent flyer programs were designed to create customer loyalty and they have worked (and continue to work) almost too well. Airline ledgers are swollen with billions of unredeemed miles. Some estimates indicate that only 15 percent of all earned miles are ever redeemed. According to Security and Exchange Commission figures, only 8.9 million frequent flyer awards were redeemed in 1996, a nine percent reduction from the previous year. Too many passengers go for miles rather than price and end up paying a pretty price for their "free" tickets. We believe that you can have it all—miles and low fares—if you keep track of specials, join multiple frequent flyer clubs and use every opportunity to maximize your miles.

There are so many frequent flyer miles on the debit side of the airlines' ledgers that they are coming up with merchandise, trips-for-bid and other enticements to try and lower the massive total. You can use them for magazine subscriptions (starting at 1,800 miles), bid for exotic trips and use them to purchase membership in airport clubs. More and more "reverse redemption" options are offered: you can earn miles, for example, for ordering flowers—and you can also redeem miles to pay for an order.

A frequent flyer mile is worth about two-cents. Some easy math will let you know if it's worth spending more on tickets just to get extra miles. If an airline gives you 1,000 miles for a flight but charges $50 more than competitors, you've just spent $50 to get $20 worth of value. If a car rental gives you 500 miles but the rate is $20 more than a competitor,

Number of people belonging to at least one frequent flyer program: over 40 million.

> *"Late in 1997, American AAdvantage members could actually earn miles for watching specific ABC television programs that ran during Fall premier week. This was the first time frequent flyers could earn miles for watching television, but definitely not the first television network-airline deal. Remember Western Pacific's Simpsons logo jet? Fox paid a million bucks for that flying advertisement. NBC pays United about $1 million per year for in-flight programming. Southwest ticket agents wear National Football League t-shirts on Sundays to promote Southwest sponsored Fox NFL broadcasts."*

you've spent $20 to get $10 in value.

Join as many frequent flyer clubs as possible but try to concentrate your miles on one or two airlines. There are no membership fees and you never know which card will give you the best advantage in a particular situation. You will also end up on desirable mailing lists that make you aware of special discounts.

Decide where to concentrate your mileage by examining what each program offers. If you fill out a membership form read it carefully. If you sign up by phone, ask that the program's specifics be mailed to you. Check the airline's web site for details on each program that interests you.

Frequent flyer programs change frequently, so don't rely on long term plans for spending or earning your miles. We have seen many airlines change the number of miles needed for a basic award jump 25 percent from 20,000-25,000 miles. Availability of award travel can be difficult. An airline can participate in a program one month and be out of it the next.

Never assume that you'll be earning miles for a partner car rental or hotel stay until you've been guaranteed that the rate you've been quoted and the location you're renting from provides bonus miles.

Read the inserts that come with your frequent flyer statements. You're likely to find some good discount deals plus periodic listings of travel routings that offer double or triple miles.

> *"One of the easiest ways to earn bonus miles involves keeping up with online booking bonus offers. Sometimes you even get bonus miles for answering surveys or accessing your frequent flyer account online. Your best source for these deals:* ***www.bestfares.com.****"*

The higher your level of membership the more benefits you get. Benefits may include priority upgrades, waitlisting and baggage handling; special contact numbers; access to Coach seats reserved for elite levels; limited blackout dates; and additional bonuses you earn after reaching a particular level. Learn what level of travel is required for elite membership and try to attain it on at least one airline. Then watch for offers from other airlines that may grant you reciprocal elite status.

Elite status is an accomplishment

Average number of frequent flyer memberships held per passenger: 3.7.

attained by less than ten percent of all travelers. Most airlines will not count miles earned by means other than flights. They don't usually count miles earned on flights on their partner airlines. Here are the miles you need to reach the first level of elite status.

5,000 miles:	TWA
15,000 miles:	Alaska Airlines
20,000 miles:	America West and Continental
25,000 miles:	American, Delta, Northwest and United
30,000 miles:	US Airways

Many of the newest bonus miles promotions require frequent flyer members to call an 800 number and pre-register. If you don't call first, you don't get the bonus. United experimented with this policy several years ago and US Airways brought it back for 1998. Now, many bonus miles offers from many airlines include this requirement.

Recent promotions indicate that companies trying to lure your patronage with miles are getting more creative than ever. Inter-Continental awarded a mile-a-minute on hotel stays. Thrifty's *Sweet 16* promotion awarded up to 2,000 AAdvantage miles per rental. Several major airlines offered 20,000-40,000 bonus miles with one premium class transatlantic roundtrip. American Hawaii Cruise Line offered 15,000 miles per booking. The Fort Worth Zoo awarded 5,000 Delta SkyMiles for a $35 zoo membership. Family memberships (at $65) awarded 5,000 miles per family member. American AAdvantage and Continental OnePass are testing miles for groceries programs in select Texas cities. *Best Fares* Magazine and *Best Fares* Online stay on top of these bonus mile offers with a special subscriber section that details promotions and changes to ongoing programs.

IT'S OK TO BUY MILES, IF...

Some airlines, including Continental and Air Canada, allow members who are a little short of the requisite miles for an award ticket to purchase miles. The Aeroplan Mileage Purchase Plan allows the purchase of up to ten percent of total required miles at three-cents (Canadian) per mile. Continental allows OnePass members to purchase up to 20 percent of the miles needed for an award ticket, providing the award ticket requires the redemption of at least 20,000 miles. You pay 25 percent more for your miles than charged in the business incentive program. Individual miles must be purchased in groups of 1,000 miles at a cost of $25.

Airlines have always had a problem with frequent flyer members selling miles but they have developed incentive mile purchase programs for corporations to use as customer and employee incentives. The structure is virtually the same for all airlines that have incentive miles purchase programs, except LatinPass which requires a whopping half-million-mile minimum purchase. The cost per mile doesn't vary. With new changes in the tax law, you'll pay a tax on all miles purchased. There are two areas to focus on when making a decision about which airline's miles you want to buy.

- **Which program provides the best incentive** to your market or your employees? Which airline offers the widest array of service from their home airport? Which airline do they prefer to fly?
- **What is the highest number of miles** you want to be able to award to one person each year? Continental and TWA are the only airlines that do not impose single recipient limits.

Air Canada promotion: scratch cards to determine miles awarded.

INCENTIVE MILES BY AIRLINE			
AIRLINE PROGRAM	MINIMUM PURCHASE	SERVICE CHARGE	MAXIMUM MILES PER RECIPIENT PER YEAR
AMERICAN 800-771-5000	$1,500 (75,000 miles)	$75	35,000
CONTINENTAL 800-340-9318	$1,000 (50,000 miles)	$60	None
DELTA 404-715-9426	$1,000 (50,000 miles)	$75	25,000
NORTHWEST 800-469-6453	$1,000 (50,000 miles)	$75	25,000
TWA 800-325-4815	$1,000 (50,000 miles)	$75	None
UNITED 800-742-5825	$1,200 (60,000 miles)	$75	20,000
US AIRWAYS 800-883-1019	$1,000 (50,000 miles)	$75	50,000

MILES FOR MORTGAGES

Five major airlines offer miles for mortgages programs. You can get these bonus miles for buying, selling or refinancing your home. Competition creates frequent changes and expansions in these programs.

Deciding which program is best for you requires some careful analysis. All programs require that you enroll before contacting your broker. Delta's HouseMiles program is the only program that covers all 50 states.

American, Continental, TWA and United do not offer miles for mortgages in Alaska, Idaho, Kansas, New Jersey, Oklahoma and Oregon. Additional exclusions:

- American: Kentucky, Louisiana and Mississippi
- Continental: Delaware, Kentucky, Louisiana, Maryland, Massachusetts, Michigan, Missouri, New York, Tennessee and Wyoming
- TWA: Connecticut, Delaware, District of Columbia, Kentucky, Louisiana, Maryland, Mississippi, Missouri, New Mexico, Tennessee and West Virginia
- United: Arizona, Mississippi, Missouri and Tennessee.

American AAdvantage Program For Mortgages/800-852-9744: Receive one mile per one dollar of interest paid on a mortgage held by a participating lender (an average of three per state to choose from). A $25 annual fee is required. Over the life of a 30-year mortgage, you will pay $750 in fees. You also receive 15,000 miles for every $100,000 of a sale or purchase price when you use a broker affiliated with PHH Real Estate Services or AFS Reality.

Continental/Prudential Referral Service/800-732-7391: Receive 12,500 miles for transactions of $50,000-99,999 with incremental increases (12,500 miles) for higher-priced transactions. A $100,000-149,999 transaction, for example, earns 25,000 miles; a $150,000-199,999 transaction earns 37,500 miles. The bonus mile ceiling is set at 125,000 miles for transactions of $500,000 or more.

Delta HouseMiles/800-759-0306: This collaboration with North American Mortgage Company gives SkyMiles

Motto of VLM Airlines frequent flyer program: "No Mileage, No Mail, No Nonsense."

members 1,000 miles for every $10,000 they borrow for home purchasing or refinancing. There is no limit on the number of miles you can earn, and all miles are awarded when your mortgage closes. You also receive 2,500 miles for taking out a home equity line of credit.

TWA/Better Homes And Gardens Real Estate Service/800-654-5409: Receive 20,000 to 40,000 miles for buying or selling a home through Better Homes and Gardens (1,500 offices nationwide).

United Airlines Residential Rewards/ 800-717-5330: Receive 3,000 to 120,000 miles for buying or selling a home; 1,000 miles per $10,000 on a refinanced loan; varying awards for as many as 50 different mortgage programs. Broker affiliations are North American and Country Wide.

EXPIRING MILES

Check the chart on the following page for expiring miles policies on each airline with whom you carry a frequent flyer account. Also see if you can buy more time by redeeming your miles for a flight certificate (usually valid for one year).

If you are unable to use your miles before they expire or want to engage in some seasonal charity, you can access donated miles programs. Some programs change quarterly.

- Alaska Airlines requires a minimum donation of 5,000 miles. Call **800-654-5669** or write Alaska Airlines Mileage Plan, P.O. Box 24948, Seattle, WA 98125-0948.
- American Airlines *Miles for Kids in Need* (**800-882-8880**) accepts donations toward flight needs of terminally ill children who are having their wishes granted; trips to Walt Disney World, for example. American will match your donation.
- Continental OnePass *Give the Extra Mile* accepts donations in any increment. Choose from five charities: Multiple Sclerosis, Disable Sports, Brass Ring, AmeriCares and CARE-FORCE. Call **713-952-1630** or write to Continental OnePass, P.O. Box 4365, Houston, TX 77210-4365.
- Delta *SkyWish* accepts donations for Make-A-Wish, CARE and The United Way in 5,000 mile increments. Delta will contribute one mile for every five donated. Call **800-323-2323**.
- Midwest Express *Miracle Miles* (**800-452-2022**) accepts donations in 1,000 mile increments. You can select the charity of your choice when you donate over 15,000 miles; otherwise, select a charity from the airline's list. Midwest Express will add one mile for every three miles on donations of over 5,000 miles. You can pool miles from more than one account to meet minimums.
- Northwest *Air Cares* selects a new charity each quarter. If you donated a travel certificate, you receive 500 bonus miles. Call **800-225-2525**.
- United accepts donations for a number of charities. They encourage the donation of travel certificates and money, as well as miles. Call **605-399-2400** or write Mileage Plus, Charity Department, P.O. Box 40, Rapid City, SD 57709.

> *"With new partnerships between major airlines, you may want to move your mileage account to the airline with the most favorable policy on expiring miles."*

MILEAGE PROGRAMS EXPIRATION POLICIES	
AIRLINE	POLICY
Alaska Airlines Mileage Plan	Miles do not expire. 800-654-5669
America West FlightFund 800-247-5691	Miles expire three years after your most recent flight.
American AAdvantage 800-882-8880	Miles expire three years from the first December 31 following your flight, except for Platinum Executive members.
Continental OnePass 800-621-7467	Miles do no expire. If you have not flown within 18 months, call to re-activate your account.
Delta SkyMiles 800-325-3999	Miles expire three years after your most recent flight. Miles earned before May 1995 currently do not have an expiration date.
Midwest Express Frequent Flyer 800-452-2022	Miles expire three years after your most recent flight.
Northwest WorldPerks 800-447-3757	Miles expire three years from the date they were earned.
Southwest Rapid Rewards 800-445-5764	Each credit expires one year from the date it was earned.
TWA Aviators 800-325-4815	Miles expire three years after they are earned.
United Mileage Plus 605-399-2400	Miles expire three years from the first January 1 following your flight. Miles earned before January 1997 expire December 31, 1998.
US Airways Frequent Traveler 800-872-4738	Miles do not expire.

REDEEMING MILES

Keep track of your mileage totals. There are no statistics on error rates, but logic will tell you that the odds of mistakes being made are astronomical, when billions of miles are swarming around in various data bases. Save all your boarding passes and the receipt portion of your ticket until you receive your frequent flyer statement and are sure all your miles have been credited. If they haven't been, send photocopies (never originals) to the frequent flyer program.

"If you want to redeem miles for upgrades, your odds are best on weekends when business travelers aren't vying for upgraded travel. The busiest day for business travel (and the day you most want to avoid) is Thursday."

The U.S. Congress is looking into frequent flyer programs, particularly the true number of award travel seats offered per-

> *"Here's a frequent flyer redemption offer that makes a lot of sense. United Airlines frequent flyers can redeem 30,000 miles for roundtrip travel for two on flights less than 750 miles per direction. It's like a 40 percent off sale on frequent flyer travel. Both passengers must book and travel together. All of the miles must be pulled from one account. American AAdvantage members usually get the opportunity to book award travel to and within Hawaii for 25 percent fewer miles during off-peak travel periods. Check Best Fares Online for updated information on special frequent flyer redemption programs."*

flight. Airlines have long fought to avoid revealing this information.

Redeem your miles for maximum value. Try to plan award travel three-12 months in advance.

- **You can book** as much as one year in advance, but that time period must include your return flight. Even if you can plan ahead, when you try to book popular destinations like Hawaii, you may not get the flights you request. This is one of the strangest ways of rewarding customer loyalty that we have ever witnessed.
- **Have alternate dates in mind whenever possible.** The best availability is usually for Tuesdays and Wednesdays. The best months are May and October.
- **Consider alternate cities.** This is particularly workable when you're trying to get tickets to Europe during heavy travel times. It can also help you out on domestic travel during peak season. For example, award travel availability to most Florida cities can almost be non-existent, but Jacksonville will almost always show availability.
- **Ask about mileage saver or mileage stretcher tickets** that fly during off-peak times and seasons at a lower mileage cost.
- **Ask to be waitlisted** for flights without frequent flyer seats available or call at one minute after midnight when newly available seats appear on computer screens.
- **Check with partner airlines.** They may have award seats available after the base airline has run out of inventory, especially where codeshare flights are included.
- **If you're a few thousand miles short** of what you need to earn an award, ask the program if you can buy enough miles to make up the difference.

AIRLINE CREDIT CARDS

One of the best ways to maximize miles are airline sponsored credit cards. They allow you to earn extra miles on all purchases charged to the card—generally one mile for every dollar spent. Annual fees and interest rates vary. Airlines that offer credit cards include:

- **Air Canada** CIBC from Visa, **800-465-2422.**
- **Alaska** Seafirst Bank Card from Visa and MasterCard, **800-552-7302.**
- **America West** FlightFund Card from Visa and MasterCard, **800-508-2933.**
- **American** Citibank AAdvantage

Standard and Gold MasterCard or Visa, **800-359-4444**.

- **British Airways** Chase Manhattan Visa, **800-242-7324**.
- **Canadian** Royal Direct Visa, **800-769-2511**.
- **Continental** OnePass MasterCard and Standard and Gold Visa, **800-850-3144**.
- **Delta** SkyMiles American Express Optima Card, **800-759-6453**
- **Midwest Express** Elan Standard and Gold MasterCard, **800-388-4044**.
- **Northwest WorldPerks** Standard, Gold and Classic Visa, **800-360-2900**.
- **Southwest** Rapid Rewards Visa, **800-792-8472**.
- **TWA** EAB Visa or MasterCard, **800-322-8921**.
- **United** Mileage Plus First Visa and MasterCard, **800-752-8888**.
- **US Airways** Dividend Miles Classic and Gold Visa, **800-732-9194**.

Airlines entice you to apply for their credit cards (and for upgraded versions of their cards) with promotions that vary in their aggressiveness. This can be one of the most confusing areas for consumers who would like an airline credit card, but don't want to settle for a few thousand bonus miles when next week's offer may include a free companion ticket.

Another area of confusion is target market mail-outs. If, for example, your neighbor receives a free companion ticket offer for upgrading to gold on a particular card, can you get the same deal? Sometimes you can sometimes you can't. We think that if the offer is good enough, it's certainly worth a phone call.

OTHER TRAVEL BENEFIT CARDS

There are other credit and charge cards that provide travel benefits. In some cases, they offer benefits that airline sponsored cards do not provide, but you can also lose some valuable benefits. Choose carefully. Check all the terms, conditions and benefits. Even after you have chosen the best card for you, remain vigilant because terms change often and are announced very quietly. Last year Bank One cut travel awards by two-thirds for all cardholders except those carrying a monthly balance. Some credit cards cut the standard 30-day payment limit to 28 days. American Express *Membership Rewards* got tough on cardmembers who do not pay their bills within 30 days of their statement closing date; don't pay on time and you forfeit *Membership Rewards* points. The 30-day period doesn't start when you receive your statement. The clock starts ticking on your account's monthly closing date. As soon as you receive your statement, check the closing date (printed toward the top of the statement) and act accordingly. Don't let them take away the rewards you've earned.

> *"You'll be seeing more credit cards that target special interest groups by offering travel benefits specifically tailored to the group's interest. For example, American Express launched an Optima credit card for golfers that lets you earn points for golf vacation packages at Marriott and Hilton. Call* ***800-297-4653****."*

CREDIT CARDS FOR TRAVELERS	
CREDIT CARD	**UNIQUE FEATURES & SPECIAL OFFERS**
Amalgamated Bank Of Chicago MasterCard Cardmiles 800-365-6464	Automatically receive airline dollar-off discount certificates: $25 at 5,000 miles; $50 at 10,000 miles; $75 at 15,000 miles; $100 at 20,000 miles; another $100 at 25,000 miles. Additional miles repeat the award cycle. Valid on the airline of your choice and can be redeemed individually or cumulatively up to $350 maximum per ticket.
American Express Membership Rewards 800-297-3276	Earn pooled miles on 12 airlines and with several hotel frequent guest programs. Miles can be redeemed for flights, hotel stays and car rentals.
American Express Platinum Card 800-525-3355 800-492-8468/corporate	The $300 annual fee provides excellent value for travelers. It includes free admission to Northwest's WorldClub and Continental's Presidents Club airport lounges (a $425 value); free enrollment in three premier car rental programs, Budget Express, Hertz #1 Club Gold and National's Emerald Club (a $125 value); and two-for-one premium class international RTs on 14 airlines; hotel added values and upgrades; travel emergency assistance and other benefits.
American Express Student Privileges 800-582-5823	Open to full- and part-time college and graduate students of any age. Five Continental Airlines discount certificates when you enroll; companions of any age travel at the same discount fare. Free MCI phone card valid for 30 minutes of domestic long distance each month of the program. $55 annual fee plus $25 if you choose to participate in Membership Miles.
Bank of America Travel Choices Visa 800-349-2632	One point per dollar charged. 25,000 points equal a RTs Coach ticket within the 48 states; 40,000 equal a RT to the Caribbean, Hawaii or Mexico; 50,000 equal an Economy RT to Europe. You do get some airline selection. Points expire five years after accrual. $25 annual fee.
Chase Bank Flight Rewards 800-581-7770	25,000 points earn a free ticket (48 states/valued at $500 or under) on the airline of your choice. You may opt to pay the difference for a more expensive ticket. The annual fee is $25 and there is a 1,000 mile enrollment bonus.
Diners Club Club Rewards 800-234-6377	Earn two points per $1 charged (two points = one airline mile). Earn pooled points on 20 airlines and with several hotel frequent guest programs. $80 annual fee.

Total 1997 revenue for Sabre Group online bookings: over $100 million.

CREDIT CARDS FOR TRAVELERS	
CREDIT CARD	**UNIQUE FEATURES & SPECIAL OFFERS**
First USA Platinum 800-955-9900	Value Miles program awards one mile per $1 charged; $3 for travel booked through their in-house program. 24,000 miles earn a free domestic RT ticket. Free the first year; $24 a year thereafter.
Hawaii Advantage Visa 800-342-2778	Up to one percent rebate accrued toward Hawaiian travel; free check cashing and ATM use in Hawaii; discounts on dining and attractions. First year's annual fee waived. Charge $2,500 minimum for waived fee each subsequent year.
MBNA/Visa TravelMax 800-858-0905	One point per $1 charged. Award tickets start at 12,000 points and are based on zone travel with no blackout dates.
MBNA Elton John AIDS Foundation Visa 800-523-5866	Point system that allows you to earn free airfare while using a card that benefits AIDS research. The award tickets carry no blackout dates and offer many major carrier options. The card is available in Standard and Platinum Plus and is no-fee but participation in the travel point system is $35 per year.
MBNA Platinum 800-739-5554	The *Plus Miles* program awards one mile per $1 spent with a 50 percent bonus of balances carried over the next month. 35,000 miles earns a free domestic RT ticket. $35 a year if you add the *Plus Miles* option.
PurchaseRewards MasterCard and Visa 800-850-8456	All miles are kept in a pooled account. The miles you earn are valid toward travel on any airline with no blackout dates or seating restrictions. You get 500 bonus miles the first time you use your card and awards start at 8,000 miles. You can ticket on the airline offering the lowest available fare or choose the airline of your choice with payment of a $25 fee. Annual fee: $40/Gold; $25/Classic.
Stop & Shop MasterCard SupeRewards 800-997-9116	Residents of Connecticut, Massachusetts, New York and Rhode Island earn double points on Stop & Shop purchases; no annual fee.
Visa FirstAir Classic Card 800-835-9373	5,000 bonus points when you charge your first purchase. You get your choice of airlines for award tickets and there are no blackout dates.
Wells Fargo MasterCard BusinessCard 800-359-3557	Small businesses can pool all employee and owner miles in one account for faster earning of award tickets, which can be issued in the name of any person.

DOMESTIC AIRLINES FREQUENT FLYER PROGRAMS

*Please note that bonus mile offers for new members change frequently and, in some cases, are only awarded after you take your first flight as a frequent flyer. Ask for complete clarification. Bonus offers for phone services and airline credit cards also change often. Visit **www.bestfares.com** for updates. Always check to see if pre-registration is required for bonus mile offers on specific flights.Program information listed in this section may apply to U.S.-based frequent flyers only.*

AirTran A-Plus Rewards

9955 AirTran Boulevard
Orlando, FL 32827
Reservations: **800-247-8726**
Service Center: **888-327-5878**
Online: **www.airtran.com**

Enrollment Bonus: None as we went to press.

Award Requirements: This program provides a unique option. You can earn free AirTran roundtrip travel after three Business Class roundtrips or six Coach roundtrips. You can also opt to earn free roundtrip travel on select routes of 16 other carriers: America West, American, Continental, Delta, Delta Express, Delta Shuttle, Eastwind, Midway, Midwest Express, Northwest, Reno, Southwest, TWA, United, US Airways and US Airways Shuttle. Award travel on these airlines requires six Business Class roundtrips or 12 Coach roundtrips.

Special Note: This program currently runs through December 31, 1998. Credits must be redeemed by March 31, 1999 for travel through December 21, 2000.

Alaska Airlines Mileage Plan

Customer Service Center
P.O. Box 24948
Seattle, WA 98124-0948
Reservations: **800-426-0333**
Service Center: **800-654-5669**
Online: **www.alaska-air.com**

Enrollment Bonus: None as we went to press.

Award Requirements: 20,000/Coach; 30,000/First Class, if all travel is on Alaska Airlines.

Minimum Miles: 500/Alaska, Northwest and Horizon; actual miles on other partners. Alaska First Class/50 percent bonus, including upgraded travel. British Airways, Northwest, Qantas and TWA First Class and Concorde/50 percent bonus; Business Class/25 percent.

Policies: Account may be cancelled if no mileage is credited during the first nine months of membership or if inactive for more than three years. Miles do not expire. Award certificates and tickets are valid for one year.

Redemption: Reservations can be made before award certificates are received, except on TWA flights. Complete the award request form on your statement and return it to the service center. Allow three weeks from date of receipt for delivery. Tickets are issued at any Alaska Airlines or Horizon Air ticket counter, except TWA awards, which are ticketed by TWA. Expedited award delivery (three-award limit) is $60, payable by major credit card. Instant award authorization is $75, and tickets will be express mailed the same day if your request was received by 1 p.m. (PST); the following business day if received after 1 p.m. Overnight service is not available for TWA awards.

Airlines/Miles & Redemption: Alaska

Airlines Commuter, British Airways, Horizon, Northwest, Qantas and TWA.

Airlines/Miles Only: LAB, Harbor and Trans States.

Airlines/Redemption: SAS.

Car Rentals: 500 miles per rental/participating Alamo, Avis, Budget and Hertz locations. No flight requirement except on Hertz.

Hotels: 500 miles per stay/participating Coast Hotels-Canada, Hilton, Holiday Inn, Hyatt, Kimpton, Preferred, Princess Tours Hotels, West Coast, Westin and Westmark. Most partners have no flight requirement.

Credit Cards: Alaska Airlines Seafirst VISA and MasterCard (**800-552-7302**)/1,000 mile sign-up bonus plus one mile per dollar charged. Diners Club converts Club Reward points to Mileage Plan miles/two points equal one mile.

Phone Service: AT&T and ALASCOM/one mile per dollar spent. Sprint/five miles per dollar spent on qualifying services.

Other Affiliations: The Flower Club/300 miles on minimum orders of $29.95 and an additional 100 miles for every $10 over $34.99. Alaska Airlines Vacations or Horizon Air Holidays leisure packages/500 bonus miles. Three miles per dollar spent at participating DineAir restaurants.

America West FlightFund

FlightFund Service Center
P. O. Box 20050
Phoenix, AZ 85036-0050
Reservations: **800-235-9292**
Service Center: **800-247-5691**
Online: **www.americawest.com**

Enrollment Bonus: 2,500 miles.

Minimum Award Miles: 20,000/Domestic Coach; 45,000/Hawaiian Coach; 60,000/European Coach; 20,000/Domestic upgrade.

Minimum Miles: 750/America West; 500/America West Express and Continental. 50 percent bonus/America West First Class or Full Fare Coach. Air New Zealand and British Airways Business Class/25 percent bonus, First Class/50 percent.

Policies: Account may be cancelled if no mileage is earned during the first 12 months of enrollment or with no activity for 24 months. Miles do not expire if you fly once within a three-year period. Award certificates valid three years from issue date.

Redemption: Receive four award certificates for every 20,000 miles accrued. Request tickets by mail or exchange certificates at ticket offices. If additional certificates are required for an award ticket and your account has available mileage, up to four individual 5,000 mile certificates may be requested by calling the service center. There is a $35 fee for this service, payable by credit card. Allow three to four weeks for delivery. Partner award certificates should be sent to the service center with a completed request form. Allow six weeks for mail delivery. Expedited deliveries are $35, payable by credit card or get tickets in two days at the airport ticket counter.

Airlines/Miles & Redemption: Air New Zealand, America West Express, British Airways and Continental.

Airlines/Redemption Only: Air France and Northwest.

Car Rentals: 500 miles/participating Alamo locations; 1,000 miles/participating Avis, in conjunction with qualifying flight, and Dollar locations; 1,500 miles/

Thrifty with special rates in conjunction with qualifying flight.

Hotels: 500 miles per stay/participating Hilton/Conrad International, Radisson and Westin. 65 miles per stay/participating Holiday Inn Express. 2.5 miles per dollar spent/participating Holiday Inns and Crowne Plazas. Some hotel partners require a flight within 24 hours of your stay.

Credit Cards: America West FlightFund Visa and MasterCard (**800-508-2933**)/sign-up bonus of 2,500 miles plus one mile per dollar charged. Diners Club converts Club Rewards points to miles/two points equal one mile.

Phone Service: Sprint/2,000 mile sign-up bonus plus five miles per dollar spent on qualifying services.

Other Affiliations: Skyway Vacations/500-2,500 bonus miles depending upon dollar amount spent. America West Vacation packages/500 bonus miles. Phoenix Club membership/2,500 sign-up miles. The Flower Club/300 miles on minimum orders of $29.95 plus 100 miles for each $10 spent over $29.99.

American Airlines AAdvantage

MD 5400, P.O. Box 619688
DFW Airport, TX 75261-9688
Reservations: **800-433-7300**
Service Center: **800-882-8880**
Fax: **817-963-7882**
Online: **www.aa.com**

Enrollment Bonus: None as we went to press.

Award Requirements: 25,000/Domestic Coach; 60,000/European Coach; 35,000/Hawaiian Coach; 20,000/Domestic upgrade.

Minimum Miles: American and all Domestic partners (except Hawaiian Airlines)/500 minimum miles. 50 percent bonus/First Class; 25 percent/Business Class. Canadian and Hawaiian Airlines Hawaii flights of one to 250 miles/250 minimum miles; flights of 251-500 miles/500 minimum miles. Flights within Canada at discounted Economy fares/50 percent of mileage flown. Hawaiian Airlines mainland flights/50 percent of miles flown on discounted fares, 100 percent of Y or V fares. Flights on International partners earn actual miles.

Policies: Three-year-old miles expire on January 1 of each year. Award tickets are valid one year from issue date.

Redemption: Request certificates by phone, mail or fax. Allow 21 days for delivery. Airline certificates can be exchanged for tickets at any ticketing location. Same-day expedited service (for airline tickets only) is $75, payable by credit card. Order at least two hours before the ticketing location closes. Overnight delivery of tickets and car and hotel certificates is $50, payable by credit card. Allow two business days for delivery when calling after 2 p.m. (CST) weekdays or anytime weekends and holidays. Quick Claim service for airline, car and hotel certificates is $50, payable by credit card. Call the service center by 2 p.m. (CST) weekdays. You should receive your award by 5 p.m. the following day. Four-business-day expedited service on airline, car and hotel certificates costs $40, payable by check. Send claim form and check payable to AA Expedite Service via overnight delivery to American Airlines Expedited Award Service, 4200 Amon Carter Blvd., Fort Worth, TX 76155-2604.

Airlines/Miles & Redemption: American Eagle, British Airways, British Midland, Canadian, Cathay Pacific, Hawaiian, JAL, Midway, Qantas, Reno Air, Singapore, South African Airways

Amount American saved per year by removing one olive per salad: $100,000.

and US Airways.

Car Rentals: Alamo, Avis, Dollar, Hertz, National and Thrifty rentals at participating locations/500 miles per qualifying rental in conjunction with any American Airlines or partner flight in the U.S., Canada and Puerto Rico. 250 bonus miles after parking three times at Thrifty Park. Rentals at participating International Alamo and Avis locations have no flight requirement.

Hotels: 500 miles per night/Inter-Continental Hotels; 250 per stay /Fiesta Inns and Best Western; 750 per stay/ITT Sheraton Tower or Suites; 1,000 per stay/Sandals; 500 per stay/Courtyard, Hyatt, Fairfield, Fairmont (Platinum or Gold members only), Fiesta Americana, Forte, Forum, Hilton/Conrad International, ITT Sheraton standard rooms, Le Meridien, Loews, Marriott, New Otani, Plaza, Radisson, Vista, Westin and Wyndham. 2.5 miles/dollar spent at Holiday Inn and Crowne Plaza.

Credit Cards: Citibank AAdvantage Standard and Gold MasterCard or VisaCard (**800-359-4444**) sign up bonus of 1,500 miles plus one mile/dollar charged with a 60,000 mile limit (waived for AAdvantage Platinum & Gold members). Diners Club converts Club Reward points to AAdvantage Miles/two points equal one mile.

Phone Service: MCI/2,000 mile sign-up bonus plus five miles per dollar spent. AT&T Wireless in-flight calling/five miles per dollar spent on qualifying services.

Other Affiliations: AAdvantage Dining members/ten miles per dollar spent. FTD Direct/300 miles for minimum order of $29.95 plus 100 miles for every additional $10 spent. AA Money Market Fund-Mileage/one mile per $10 invested. FlyAAway Vacations/500 bonus. Servicemaster/one mile per dollar spent. Miles for mortgage interest payments at participating financial institutions and one mile per dollar spent on real estate purchased from specific brokers. (Participants vary by location.) Numerous additional affiliations.

Continental OnePass

P. O. Box 4365
Houston, TX 77210-4365
Domestic Reservations: **800-525-0280**
International Reservations: **800-231-0856**
Service Center: **713-952-1630**
INFOPASS: **713-785-8999**
Award Travel: **800-344-1411**
Partner Awards: **800-344-3333**
Online: **www.flycontinental.com**

Enrollment Bonus: 2,500 miles on first flight.

Award Requirements: 25,000/Domestic Coach; 50,000/European Coach; 45,000/ Hawaiian Coach; 20,000/Domestic upgrade.

Minimum Miles: Continental and its partners give 500 minimum miles. 50 percent bonus/First Class; 25 percent/ Business and Business First. Air Canada discount fares/50 percent of actual miles within Canada.

Policies: Account may be cancelled if no mileage is deposited for 18 consecutive months, but you will receive a certificate for the highest eligible award. Miles do not expire as long as you have flown within the past three years. Award certificates are valid for one year from the issue date. There is a $35 fee for award redeposits, International changes, airport ticketing and expedited service. Stopover awards incur no fee.

Redemption: Request awards by calling the appropriate award desk. Allow two weeks. Expedited two-day delivery is $35/U.S., $40/Canada & Hawaii, $50/other locations. All fees are payable by credit card when ordered by phone.

Airlines/Miles & Redemption: Aerolineas Argentinas, Air Canada, Air France, Alitalia, America West, China, Colgan, CSA Czech, Gulfstream, Iberia, Frontier, LanChile, Malaysia, Northwest, Qantas and Skywest.

Car Rentals: Alamo, Avis, Dollar, Hertz, Thrifty and National. Hertz and Thrifty/500 miles; other agencies/750 miles at participating locations in conjunction with and within 24 hours of a Continental or partner flight.

Hotels: Aston Deluxe, Fiesta Inns, Forte, Hilton, Holiday Inn, ITT Sheraton, Marriott and Radisson/500 miles per stay. Camino Real Hotels, Fiesta Americana, Melia and Sol Hotels/1,000 miles per stay, all subject to eligible rates. Some hotel partners require a flight in conjunction with the stay.

Credit Cards: Continental OnePass Standard and Gold Visa and MasterCard (**800-850-3144**) give one mile per dollar charged. Diners Club converts Club Reward points to OnePass miles/two points equal one mile. American Express converts Membership Miles into OnePass miles on an equal basis.

Phone Service: MCI/500 mile sign up bonus plus five miles per dollar spent on qualifying services.

Other Affiliations: A $29.99 Flower Club order earns 300 miles plus 100 miles for each additional $10 spent.

Delta SkyMiles

Hartsfield International Airport, Dept. 745
P. O. Box 20532
Atlanta, GA 30320-2532
Domestic Reservations: **800-221-1212**
International Reservations: **800-241-4141**
Service Center: **800-323-2323**
Automated Service: **800-325-3999**
Online: **www.delta-air.com**

Enrollment Bonus: None as we went to press.

Award Requirements: 25,000/Domestic Coach; 50,000/European Coach; 30,000/ Hawaiian Coach; 10,000/Domestic upgrade.

Minimum Miles: 500 per qualifying Delta or Delta Connection flight. Actual flight mileage for airline partner flights except Singapore Airlines which does not credit Coach miles. Class of service bonuses with Delta and most partner airlines (except Aeromexico, Austrian and Finnair): 150 percent/First Class; 125 percent/Business Class. Some International airline partners only give miles on certain fares and offer reduced class of service bonuses.

Policies: Account may be cancelled with no activity within 12 months of enrollment. Miles do not expire providing you have flown within the past three years. Certificates must be ticketed for travel within one year from issue date. Award tickets are good for one year.

Redemption: Mail completed award request from your statement and allow two to three weeks. Tickets can be issued at ticket offices or airport ticket counters. Expedited delivery for flight certificates can be redeemed at ticket counters and city ticket offices for $60. There is no fee for expedited upgrades. Express mail expedited service is $35 per account transaction for general members; $20 for Medallion/Royal Medallion members—each payable by credit card. Awards are processed within 48 hours of receipt.

Airlines/Miles & Redemption: Aeromexico, Air New Zealand, ANA, Austrian

Worst year in the history of the airline industry: 1970, with losses totalling $150 million.

Airlines, Finnair, Malaysia, Sabena, Singapore, Swissair, TAP Air Portugal, United and Varig.

Car Rentals: Alamo, Avis, Hertz and National/500 miles per rental with a flight in conjunction with rental.

Hotels: 2.5 miles per dollar spent at Crowne Plaza and Holiday Inn; 65 miles per stay at Holiday Inn Express; 500 miles per night at Inter-Continental; 250-500 miles per stay at Forte Hotels. 500 miles per stay at Courtyard, Fairfield Inn, Forum, ITT Sheraton, Hilton/Conrad International, Hyatt, Le Meridien, Marriott, Preferred, Radisson, Renaissance and Swissotel. Conjunction flights not required.

Credit Cards: Delta SkyMiles American Optima Card Express (**800-759-6453**) gives one mile per dollar spent. American Express Membership Miles convert to SkyMiles on an equal basis.

Phone Service: MCI/2,000 mile sign up bonus plus five miles per dollar spent.

Other Affiliations: Special credits on Renaissance Cruise Lines promotional bookings. 300 miles for a $29.99 Flower Club order plus 100 miles for each additional $10. HouseMiles awards miles for mortgages.

Kiwi International Air Lines KiwiKlub

Hemisphere Center
570 US 1 and 9, Suite 624
Newark, NJ 07114
Reservations: **800-538-5494**
Online: **www.jetkiwi.com**

Award Requirements: 18 credits equal one free roundtrip.

Minimum Credits: The program operates on a credit system/one credit per one-way segment flown.

Policies: Credits expire within one year. Award certificates are valid for one year from the date of issue. Expiration dates will not be extended.

Redemption: An award certificate will automatically be mailed for every 18 segment credits earned during a consecutive 12-month period. A segment credit stamp is issued when the application is presented to a gate agent at check-in.

Car Rentals: Eligible rentals from Avis earn one credit.

Midwest Express Frequent Flyer

P. O. Box 37136
Milwaukee, WI 53237-0136
Reservations: **800-452-2022**
Service Center: **800-452-2022**
Fax: **414-570-0192**
Online: **www.midwestexpress.com**

Enrollment Bonus: None as we went to press.

Minimum Miles: 500/Midwest Express and Skyway Airlines. Other airline partners give actual miles.

Policies: Account may be cancelled if no mileage is credited during first 12 months after enrollment. Miles do not expire providing you have flown within the past three years. Certificates are valid for one year from issue date.

Redemption: Mail or fax award request form from statement to the service center. Qualifying miles from Midwest Express and Northwest can be combined for awards on Midwest Express or Northwest flights for $50. Allow two to three weeks for Midwest Express awards, six weeks for partner awards and four weeks for combined mileage awards. Tickets are issued at airport ticket counters or city ticket offices. Expedited service is $35, payable by credit card or check, with

Airline that provided financial backing for United's first employee takeover in 1989: British Airways.

delivery within three business days. Award requests are processed immediately upon arrival.

Airlines/Miles & Redemption: Northwest, Skyway Airlines, Swissair and Virgin Atlantic.

Car Rentals: Alamo, Avis, Hertz and National/500 miles at participating locations. Rentals must be within 24 hours of a Midwest Express or Skyway Airlines flight.

Hotels: Earn 500 miles per stay/participating The American Club, Grand Geneva Resort, Heidel House, Hilton, Loews, The Pfister, The Springs and Wyndham. Stays do not have to be in conjunction with flights.

Credit Cards: Midwest Express Standard and Gold MasterCard (**800-388-4044**), one mile per dollar charged on the plus a sign-up bonus of 1,000-2,500 miles, depending on the type of card you select. Double miles when you purchase Midwest Express and Skyway Airline tickets using your Midwest Express Elan card. Diners Club converts Club Reward points to miles/two points equal one mile.

Phone Service: MCI/500 mile enrollment bonus plus five miles per dollar spent on qualifying services.

Other Affiliations: 300 miles for minimum $29.99 order from Midwest Express Flower Club. 500 bonus miles for Midwest Vacations. Varying points awarded for Amtrak travel.

> *"Look for a big expansion in major airline online award miles redemption possibilities during the coming year. The actual process of redeeming miles should become easier than ever."*

Northwest WorldPerks

P. O. Box 11001
St. Paul, MN 55111-0001
Reservations: **800-225-2525**
Service Center/Award Reservations: **800-447-3757**
Fax: **612-727-4245**
Automated Service: **800-327-2881**
Online: **www.nwa.com**

Enrollment Bonus: None as we went to press.

Award Requirements: 25,000/Domestic Coach; 35,000/European Coach; 40,000/ Hawaiian Coach; 20,000/Domestic upgrade.

Minimum Miles: Northwest/Northwest AirLink/500 minimum miles. 50 percent bonus/First Class; 25 percent/Business Class. KLM flights between North America and Asia give 500 minimum miles; 25 percent/Business Class. KLM flights between Europe and the Pacific Region give actual mileage; 25 percent/World Business Class. All other KLM destinations give 500 minimum miles; 100 percent World Business Class. Aloha operated/Northwest designated flights give 250 minimum miles. Alaska Airlines gives actual miles.

Policies: Accounts with no activity for three consecutive years may be cancelled with miles forfeited. Certificates are good for one year from date of issue.

Redemption: Tickets are issued at city ticket offices or by the service center. International flights must be ticketed at the service center. Tickets are delivered via U.S. mail to the member's address. Expedited service (two-day minimum) requires a $50 fee payable by check, money order or credit card. Three-day service is $35 via Federal Express and same day service, $60.

Airlines/Miles & Redemption: Air New Zealand, Air UK, Alaska Airlines, America West, Asiana, Continental, Eurowings, Hawaiian, Horizon, Indonesia, KLM, Mahalo, Midwest Express, Northwest AirLink, Pacific Island Aviation and Trans States.

Car Rentals: Alamo, Avis, Hertz and National/500 miles per rental from participating locations. Rental must be in conjunction with Northwest, KLM, or partner airline flights and be booked within 24 hours of arrival.

Hotels: 2.5 miles per dollar spent at Crowne Plaza; 65 miles per stay at Holiday Inn Express; 250 miles per stay at Tulip; 500 miles per stay at Golden Tulip, Hilton, Holiday Inn, Hyatt, ITT Sheraton, Marriott, New Otani, Radisson, Shangri-La, Traders and Westin. All hotel partners except Holiday Inn and Radisson require a flight in conjunction with your stay.

Credit Cards: Northwest WorldPerks Standard, Gold and Classic Visa (**800-360-2900**) gives a 1,000-mile sign-up bonus plus one mile/$2 charged. Diners Club converts Club Reward points to WorldPerks miles/two points equal one mile.

Phone Service: MCI/five miles per dollar spent on qualifying services.

Other Affiliations: 500-2,500 miles for World Vacations packages. Three miles/dollar spent with Dining for Miles. 300 miles for Flower Club orders of $29.99 plus 100 miles for each additional $10 spent.

Reno Air QQuick Miles

Customer Relations
P.O. Box 30075
Reno, NV 30075
QQuick Miles Center & Reservations: **800-736-6501**
Online: **www.renoair.com**

Award Requirements: 15,000/Domestic roundtrip

Minimum Miles: 500 miles per flight; 50 percent bonus/First Class.

Policies: Miles expire after three years. Award travel is valid for one year from date of issue.

Redemption: Through QQuick Miles Customer Service Center.

Airlines/Miles and Redemption: American.

Car Rentals: 500 miles per qualifying Thrifty rental.

Hotels: Special offers at select properties that change monthly.

Phone Service: 500 miles for every $50 spent on long distance using an **800-PRE-PAID** calling card.

Other Affiliations: 250 miles for three uses of a Thrifty airport parking facility; 300 miles for a $29.99 minimum order from B&K Florists (**800-377-7080**); three miles per dollar spent on Delyse Gourmet French Food products (**800-441-NUTS**).

Southwest Rapid Rewards

P. O. Box 36657
Dallas, TX 75235-1657
Reservations: **800-435-9792**
Service Center: **800-445-5764**
Online: **www.southwest.com**

Enrollment Bonus: None as we went to press.

Award Requirements: 16 credits equal one free roundtrip.

Minimum Credits: The program is operated on a credit system/one credit per one-way segment flown.

Policies: Credits expire one year from the

date of your first flight. Award tickets are valid for one year from issue date.

Redemption: An actual ticket is automatically issued when 16 credits have been earned. You can reserve a specific roundtrip or use your award ticket for any available seat by presenting it at the ticket counter. Southwest does not limit seats available for award travel. Expedited mail service is $12 with a maximum 14-day processing time and one to two business days for express mail.

Car Rentals: Eligible rentals from Alamo, Budget and Hertz/one credit.

Credit Cards: Southwest Airlines Rapid Rewards Visa (**800-792-8472**) gives two point sign-up bonus plus one credit/$1,000 charged. Diners Club converts 2,000 Club Reward points to one Rapid Rewards credit. American Express Membership Miles converts 1,250 miles to one Rapid Rewards credit.

Phone Service: MCI/2,000 mile sign-up bonus and one credit for every $150 spent on qualifying services.

TWA Aviators

P.O. Box 800
Fairview Village, PA 19409
Domestic Reservations: **800-221-2000**
International Reservations: **800-892-4141**
Service Center: **800-325-4815**
Fax: **610-631-5280**
Online: **www.twa.com**

Enrollment Bonus: 3,000 miles after your first flight.

Award Requirements: 15,000/Domestic Coach shorthaul; 25,000/Domestic coach longhaul; 50,000/European Coach; 40,000/Hawaiian Coach; 20,000/ Domestic upgrade.

Minimum Miles: 750/TWA and TWExpress. Partners give actual miles. 50 percent bonus/First Class; 25 percent/ Business Class.

Policies: Three years, unless you fly the airline once in that time period. Award certificates must be redeemed within 12 months of issue date unless specifically exempted. Award tickets are valid for one year from issue date.

Redemption: Mail or fax the completed request form to the service center for TWA and partner awards. If the request is for the exact member or a family member with the same surname, it can be made by phone. Allow four weeks for processing. Certificates will be sent to the address on your account. If requested travel dates are not available you can exchange your certificate for a ticket at any TWA ticket office at the time of travel. Expedited service is $50, payable by credit card. Tickets for travel within seven days can be delivered next day if your request is called in before 2 p.m. (CST). Requests made after 2 p.m. or for travel within eight to 21 days will get two-day delivery. Airport pickup is available for U.S. members only for $100, payable by credit card. Allow two to three days for processing on airport pickups.

Airlines/Miles & Redemption: Aerolineas Argentinas, Air India, Alaska Airlines, Horizon Air, Ladeco, Philippine Airlines and TWExpress.

Car Rentals: Alamo, Avis, Dollar and Thrifty/500 miles per rental at participating locations. Some partners require a flight in conjunction with your rental. Thrifty/750 miles with a flight requirement. Rentals must be within 24 hours of a TWA or TWExpress flight and have specific rate requirements.

Hotels: 500 miles per night at Inter-Continental Hotels. 500 miles per stay at Adam's Mark, Conrad International, Forte, Hilton, Marriott and Radisson

Full-time meteorologists on American's payroll: 19.

Hotels. Flights in conjunction with your stay are not required by most properties but there may be rate requirements.

Credit Cards: TWA EAB Visa or MasterCard (**800-322-8921**) gives one mile/ dollar charged. Diners Club converts Club Reward points to Frequent Flight Bonus miles/two points equal one mile. The TWA Getaway card (an airline charge card good for air travel only) earns one mile for each dollar charged.

Phone Service: Sprint/2,000 mile enrollment bonus plus five miles per dollar spent on qualifying services. Members who reside outside the U.S. get a 1,000 mile sign-up bonus for the TWA/Sprint FONCARD plus five miles for every dollar spent. LDDS WorldCom/1,000 mile enrollment bonus plus five miles for every dollar spent.

Other Affiliations: A minimum $29.99 purchase from The Flower Club/500 miles plus 100 miles for each additional $10 spent. The TWA Ambassadors Club/5,000 miles with a one-year membership, 10,000 miles with a three-year membership and 15,000 miles with a lifetime membership. TWA Getaway Vacations/5,000 miles for each international vacation when your transatlantic flight is on TWA and 2,000 miles for other vacations when you fly TWA.

United Mileage Plus

P.O. Box 28870
Tucson, AZ 85726-8870
Domestic Reservations: **800-241-6522**
International Reservations: **800-538-2929**
Service Center: **605-399-2400**
Online: **www.ual.com**

Enrollment Bonus: None as we went to press.

Award Requirements: 25,000/Domestic Coach; 50,000/European Coach; 35,000/Hawaiian Coach; 20,000/Domestic upgrade.

Minimum Miles: 500/United and most partners. 50 percent bonus/First Class; 25 percent/Business Class. 250 miles on Aloha and National Airlines of Chile flights within Chile; actual miles on flights outside of Chile.

Policies: Miles are automatically converted into AwardCheques, which are valid for three years. All three-year-old miles expire on January 1 of each year. Award tickets must be used within one year of the date issued. Upgrades can be requested when reservations are made in full Coach or with any fare if you are a Premier member. Upgrades are confirmed 24-100 hours prior to departure, depending on your membership status.

Redemption: Certificates can be ordered by mail or at United ticket airport and city ticket locations. Awards can be express-mailed in two days or automatically transferred to a ticket counter in 24 hours for a $25 fee, payable by credit card.

Airlines: Aeromar, Air Canada, Air France, Air New Zealand, ALM Antillean Airlines, Aloha, Ansett, British Midland, Delta, Gulfstream, LAPA, Lufthansa, Mexicana, National Airlines of Chile, SAS, Saudi Arabian, Sunaire, Thai Airways, TransBrasil, United Express and Varig.

Car Rentals: 500 miles per rental at participating Alamo, Avis, Budget, Dollar, Hertz and National locations. Some agencies require rental within 24 hours of qualifying flights.

Hotel Affiliations: 500 miles per night at Inter-Continental hotels. 500 miles per eligible stay at Crowne Plaza, Hilton/Conrad International, Holiday Inn, Hyatt, ITT Sheraton, Libertel, Radisson, Shangri-La, Sol Melia, Vista and Westin.

Gifts offered by United on 1970 New York-Chicago flights: cigars & golf balls.

Hotel stays have to be in conjunction with a flight.

Credit Cards: United Mileage Plus First Visa and MasterCard (**800-752-8888**) gives one mile per dollar charged plus a variable enrollment bonus. There's a 10,000 mile maximum in a billing period and a 50,000 mile maximum per year (both waived for premium level members).

Phone Service: AT&T/five miles per dollar spent on qualifying service in excess of $25 per month. One AT&T True Rewards point converts to five Mileage Plus miles. Mileage Plus Pre-Paid Phone Card gives 1,000 miles for $50 worth of airtime.

Other Affiliations: 800-FLOWERS gives 300 miles with a minimum $29.99 order. Special cruise promotions award miles from Crystal, Norwegian and Renaissance. Elite level frequent flyers earn ten miles per dollar spent at participating restaurants.

US Airways Dividend Miles

P.O. Box 5
Winston-Salem, NC 27102-0005
Reservations: **800-428-4322**
Service Center: **800-872-4738**
Online: **www.usairways.com**

Enrollment Bonus: 2,000 miles after your first flight.

Award Requirements: 25,000/Domestic Coach; 40,000/European Coach.

Minimum Miles: 500/US Airways, US Airways Express and US Airways Shuttle. Partner airlines give actual miles. 50 percent bonus/First Class; 25 percent/ Business Class.

Policies: Miles do not expire. Award certificates and tickets must be redeemed within one year of the date issued.

Redemption: Call Service Center or mail completed award request on statement or request the form by mail. Allow four weeks from receipt of request for processing. Reservations must be made within 30 days. Tickets are issued at city or airport ticket offices or through tickets by mail. Hotel and car rental certificates must be exchanged at check-in. Expedited service is $40 for domestic members and $50 for international members, payable by credit card. Allow four business days for delivery.

Airlines: Air France, Alitalia, American, ANA, British Airways, LatinPass, Northwest, Qantas, Sabena, Swissair, US Airways Express and US Airways Shuttle.

Car Rentals: Alamo, Avis, Hertz and National/500 miles per rental at participating locations. Rentals must be made within 24 hours of a qualifying flight.

Hotels: Earn 500 miles per stay at participating Hilton/Conrad International, Hyatt, ITT Sheraton, Marriott, Radisson, Renaissance and Westin. Some partners require stays within 24 hours of qualifying flight and have specific rate requirements.

Credit Cards: US Airways Dividend Miles Classic and Gold Visa (**800-441-0130**) gives one mile per dollar charged. American Express converts to US Airways miles on an equal basis. Diners Club converts Club Reward miles to Frequent Traveler miles/two points equal one mile.

Phone Service: AT&T/five miles per dollar spent on residential long distance on monthly bills $25 and over; ten miles/per dollar spent on monthly bills over $75. One AT&T True Rewards Point/five Dividend Miles.

Other Affiliations: The Flower Club gives 300 miles for a minimum $29.99

purchase plus 100 miles for every additional $10.

Vanguard Airlines Frequent Flyer

7000 Squibb Road-Second Floor
Mission, KS 66202
Service Center: **913-789-1795**
Reservations: **800-826-4827**
Online: **www.flyvanguard.com**

Award Requirements: 16 credits equal one free roundtrip

Minimum Credits: The program operates on a credit system/one credit per one-way segment flown.

Policies: Credits expire within one year. Award travel is valid for one year from date of issue. Award travel is transferable.

Redemption: Mail completed frequent flyer application with 16 credits and a credit file will be established. Allow two weeks for processing before calling for reservations.

INTERNATIONAL AIRLINE FREQUENT FLYER PROGRAMS

Some very interesting alliances are taking place and they will have a positive impact on frequent flyer programs. The Star Alliance, for example, is composed of Air Canada, Lufthansa, SAS, Thai Airways and United with Varig also slated to come on board. The goal is for all six airlines' frequent flyer programs to be integrated. Look for the seventh partner to be South African Airways, already a partner of Lufthansa, Thai Airways and United. The Atlantic Excellence Alliance is composed of Austrian Airlines, Delta, Sabena and Swissair.

Aer Lingus TAB

122 East 42nd Street
New York, NY 10068-0016
Reservations: **800-223-6537**
Service Center: **800-223-6876**
Online: **www.aerlingus.ie**

Enrollment Bonus: U.S. members earn 400 points; United Kingdom and Ireland members earn 200 points on first flight.

Minimum Points: Varies by destination. 100 percent bonus/Business Class.

Policies: Membership is renewed every two years. Points are valid for three years.

Redemption: A 14-day advance is required. Tickets are available for pick up at local ticket offices or at ticket counters.

Car Rental Affiliations: 50 points/Avis, Europcar and Hertz, only in conjunction with an Aer Lingus flight.

Hotel Affiliations: The Jury Hotel Group, with some rates not allowing miles.

Credit Card Affiliations: Aer Lingus/AIB Visa Business Card earns one point per ten pounds charged.

Aeromexico Club Premier

P.O. Box 922016
Houston, TX 77292-2016
Reservations: **800-237-6639**
Service Center: **800-247-3737**
Fax: **713-939-7242**
Online: **www.wotw.com/aeromexico**

Enrollment Bonus: 4,000 kilometers

Minimum Kilometers: 1,000 on most Aeromexico and partner airline flights; 25 percent bonus/First Class within Mexico;

50 percent/international First Class and for America West First Class or full fare Coach.

Policies: One flight per year required to keep account active. Kilometers expire two years from date of accrual. Award tickets are valid for one year from the date issued. Air credits are in kilometers; other credits are in miles.

Redemption: Request by phone, fax or mail. When requesting by fax or mail, include signature, account number, and PIN. Awards are sent within ten business days. Express award delivery is available in the U.S. for $25 handling plus a courier fee, payable by credit card only.

Airlines/Kilometers & Redemption: Aeroperu, Air France, America West, British Airways, Delta, Japan Airlines and Mexicana.

Airlines/Kilometers Only: Aerolitoral and Aeromar.

Car Rentals: Avis and Budget/625 kilometers at participating locations in Mexico; 500 kilometers at participating locations outside Mexico. Avis miles can also be used in conjunction with America West flights. Rentals must be within 24 hours of an Aeromexico or selected partner flight.

Hotels: 500 miles per night at Inter-Continental Hotels. 500 miles for stays outside Mexico or 1,000 for stays within Mexico at Crowne Plaza, Fiesta Americana, Fiesta Inn, Holiday Inn and Radisson. Your hotel stay must be within 24 hours of an Aeromexico or selected partner flight.

Credit Cards: American Express Membership Rewards converts their miles into Aeromexico kilometers on an equal basis.

Phone Service: Globe One/eight kilometers per dollar spent on qualifying services.

Air Canada Aeroplan

P.O. Box 16000
Station Airport
Dorval Canada H4Y1H6
Reservations: **800-776-3000**
Service Center: **800-361-8253**
Fax: **514-395-2496**
Online: **www.aircanada.ca**

Enrollment Bonus: None as we went to press.

Minimum Miles: Within Canada, discount fares earn 50 percent of regular miles; all other flights earn 500 minimum miles. 50 percent bonus/First Class; 25 percent/Executive First and Business Class.

Award Requirements: 25,000/Domestic Coach; 40,000/Hawaii Coach; 60,000/ European Coach

Policies: Account may be cancelled if no mileage is earned the first 12 months after enrollment or is inactive for three years. Some airline partners require Canadian residency for mileage accrual. By law, all Canadian frequent flyer programs must have an end-date but the mileage expiration date has always been extended annually. Award certificates are valid for one year from the date issued, unless otherwise stated.

Redemption: Award certificate requests by mail or fax require three to four weeks processing. Requests may also be made by telephone. Award certificates must be redeemed at ticketing offices or authorized travel agencies within 21 days of issue date. Requests made four to 14 business days prior to departure can receive expedited service for $35, payable by credit card. AeroRush service for Air Canada and Air Canada Connector tickets

Price of a litre of jet fuel in Nairobi: 85 cents.

is available via airport and ticket offices in four days or less for $50. Requests made within 36 hours of departure cannot be guaranteed.

Airlines/Miles & Redemption: Air Canada Connectors, Air Creebec, Austrian Airlines, Bearskin Airlines, Cathay Pacific, Continental, Finnair, First Air, Interprovincial, Lufthansa, Swissair and United.

Airlines/Miles Only: British Midland

Car Rentals: Avis and Budget/500 miles when you rent from participating locations. Rentals do not have to be in conjunction with flights. Not valid on certain discounted rates. Hertz/500 miles when you rent from participating locations. Rentals must be in conjunction with qualifying flight.

Hotels: 250 miles at Holiday Inn Express; 500 miles per stay at The Charlottetown, Crowne Plaza, Hilton/ Conrad Inter-national, Holiday Inn, Hotel Des Gouverneurs, Marriott, Ocean Pointe Resort, Radisson, Regina Inn, Vista and Westin. Your stay does not have to be in conjunction with a flight. Not valid on certain discounted rates.

Credit Cards: Diners Club/en Route and CIBC Visa (**800-465-2422**/ Canadian residents only) earn one mile per Canadian dollar charged. Diners Club converts Club Reward points for U.S. residents only/two points equal one Aeroplan mile.

Phone Service: AT&T Canada/five miles per Canadian dollar spent on qualifying services. Sign-up bonuses are offered frequently, for a variety of AT&T Canada services.

Other Affiliations: 2,500 miles on Air Canada Vacations. 250 miles when you use Park 'N' Fly.

Air France Frequence Plus

40 Ramland Road South, Suite 2
Orangeburg, NY 10962
Reservations: **800-237-2747**
Service Center: **800-375-8723**
Fax: **805-295-1464**
Online: **www.airfrance.fr/**

Enrollment Bonus: 3,000 miles on first flight.

Minimum Miles: 1,000/First Class and 150 percent bonus miles/Concorde; 100 percent bonus miles/Business Class.

Policies: Mileage expires two calendar years from date of travel. Active membership retained through one flight every three years.

Redemption: Complete award request application and return to an Air France agent or mail to the service center. Tickets are mailed to the member or can be picked up at an Air France office within three weeks. No expedited service available.

Airlines: Aeromexico, Air Canada, Air Inter, Continental, Delta, Eurowings and Japan Airlines.

Car Rentals: Avis and Hertz give 100-400 miles depending on rental rate. Rentals must be in conjunction with Air France flights.

Hotels: Concorde, Forte Grand, Hotel Ritz-Paris, ITT Sheraton and Le Meridien. A free-night voucher is given after five stays at partner hotels/ L'Invitation or Carte Noire–or exchanged for 4,000 miles.

Credit Cards: European residents with American Express cards can convert Membership Miles into Frequence Plus miles. Diners Club converts Club rewards points to Air France miles.

Other Affiliations: Varying miles awarded for Euro Disney ticket purchases and with GlobalOne.

ANA Mileage Club

2050 West 190th Street, Suite 100
Torrance, CA 90504
Reservations: **800-235-9262**
Service Center: **800-262-4653**
Fax: **310-782-3185**
Online: **www.ana.co.jp**

Enrollment Bonus: 2,500 miles.

Minimum Miles: Actual miles in Economy Class; 50 percent of miles/ discount Economy Class; 50 percent bonus/First Class; 25 percent/Business Class.

Asiana Bonus Club

3530 Wilshire Boulevard, Suite 145
Los Angeles, CA 90010
Reservations: **800-227-4262**
Service Center: **888-222-4359**

Minimum Miles: 500; 25 percent bonus/Business Class; 50 percent/First Class.

Policies: Account cancelled if no mileage is accrued in one year. Miles do not expire. Award tickets are valid three months from date of issue.

Airlines/Miles & Redemption: Northwest.

Car Rentals: Hertz Korea and National/Nippon give 500 miles per qualifying rental. National/Nippon requires a qualifying flight in conjunction with rental.

Hotels: 500 miles per stay at participating Holiday Inns, Radissons and Westin Chosun Seoul.

Phone Service: 500 mile enrollment bonus with MCI.

British Airways Executive Club USA

P.O. Box 1757
Minneapolis, MN 55440-1757
Reservations: **800-452-1201**
Service Center: **800-955-2748**
Online: **www.british-airways.com**

Minimum Miles: Actual miles on long-haul flights and all Qantas and Alaska flights. A minimum 500 miles on short-haul flights and US Airways, TAT European Airlines and Deutsche BA flights. British Airways First Class and Concorde earn a 50 percent bonus; Club World and Club Europe, 25 percent. Qantas, Alaska/Horizon and US Airways First Class/50 percent bonus; Qantas and US Airways Business Class/25 percent bonus.

Policies: Must reside in the U.S., Bahamas, Bermuda, or Puerto Rico. Accounts inactive for five years expire. Award certificates and tickets are valid one year from date issued.

Redemption: Order by phone or mail. British Airways tickets require two weeks. Other award tickets require three to four weeks. Tickets are sent to the member's address. Seven to ten-day service is available for $50, payable by credit card.

Airlines/Miles & Redemption: American, Alaska, ANA, Braathes, Cathay Pacific, Malaysia, Qantas, Singapore and US Airways.

Airlines/Miles Only: America West, Canadian, Deutsche BA and TAT European Airlines.

Car Rentals: Alamo and Hertz/500 miles per eligible rental at participating locations. Avis/250-500 miles depending upon participating location. Rental must occur within 24 hours of a British Airways flight.

Hotels: 500 miles per stay at Concorde,

Percentage of bags mislaid on U.S. airline domestic flights: .5 percent.

Hilton/Conrad International, Hyatt, Inter-Continental, Mandarin Oriental, Marriott, Radisson/Edwardian, Ritz-Carlton, The Savoy Group, Southern Sun and Taj Hotels. Not all rates are eligible. Stays do not need to be in conjunction with a flight to earn miles.

Credit Cards: BA/Chase Visa (**800-242-7324**) sign up bonus of 4,000 miles plus one mile per dollar charged and an additional 1,000 miles for first $1,000 charged. Diners Club converts club Reward points to Executive Club miles.

Phone Service: One AT&T True Rewards point/five miles.

Other Affiliations: 30-750 miles at Travelex Foreign Currency Exchanges (depending on amount exchanged). 300 miles for minimum $29.99 order with the Flower Club plus 100 miles per additional $10 spent. 200 miles per booking at Camelot Chauffeur Drive. Miles are also awarded for some transactions with Abercrombie & Kent International, Cunard Cruise Line, Hewlett-Packard and Venice Simplon-Orient Express.

Canadian Plus

P.O. Box 7737
STN MAIN
Vancouver, BC, Canada V6BSW9
Reservations/Service Center:
800-426-7007
Fax: **604-270-5476**
Online: **www.cdnair.ca**

Enrollment Bonus: None as we went to press.

Minimum Miles: Miles are tabulated as points. 250 minimum on Canadian and most domestic partners; 50 percent bonus/First Class; 25 percent/Business Class; a 500 minimum on American/American Eagle and Aloha. Actual points on Air Labrador or 500 points on full fare tickets.

Policies: Account will be cancelled after three years of inactivity. National law requires an expiration date each year, which is traditionally extended. Award certificates and tickets are valid one year from date issued.

Redemption: Requests by mail will be responded to within three to seven business days. Tickets can be picked up at travel agencies or ticket offices. American Airlines and Canadian Holidays awards tickets must be issued directly by Canadian. Two to five-day service on tickets and award certificates is $35, payable by credit card. Less than three business day delivery service is $50, payable by credit card.

Airlines/Miles & Redemption: Air Alma, Air Atlantic, Air Labrador, Air New Zealand, Air Schefferville, Aloha/Island Air, American/American Eagle, British Airways, Calm Air, Canadian Regional Airlines, Canadian North, Lufthansa, Mandarin Airlines, North-Wright Air, Pem-Air, Pacific Costal and Qantas.

Car Rentals: 500 points/participating Alamo, Europcar, National/Tilden and Thrifty locations. Rentals do not have to be in conjunction with a flight.

Hotels: 500 points per night at Inter-Continental Hotels. 500 points per stay at Albatross/Gander, Best Western, Cambridge Suites, Canadian Pacific, Coast Hotels, Delta Hotels, The Evaz Group, Explorer, Forum Hotels, Gateway, Howard Johnson, Inter-Canadian, ITT Sheraton, Loews, Ramada, Shangri-La, West Coast, Westmark and Wyndham Hotels. Stays don't have to be in conjunction with a flight.

Credit Cards: Royal Direct Visa (**800-434-7587**) awards 2,500 point sign-up bonus plus one point per dollar charged. American Express (AMEX Bank of Canada) converts Membership Rewards points into Canadian Plus points on an equal basis.

Phone Service: Long distance points varying by plan with BCTel, Bell Canada, Island Tel, MT&T, MTS, NBTel, NewTel, SaskTel and TELUS.

Other Affiliations: 250 points per one-way ticket with Brewster Transportation & Tours and for each Park & Jet, Aeropark and YVR Park usage. One point per Canadian dollar spent with AMJ Campbell/Atlas Van Lines. 300 points for $30 Canadian order with Flowers 24 Hours; 100 additional points per $10 spent. 1,500 points for air inclusive or air only packages for Canadian Vacations.

El Al Matmid

Frequent Traveler Club
120 W. 45th Street
New York, NY 10036
Reservations: **800-223-6700**
Matmid Service Center: **212-852-0604**
Fax: **212-852-0632**
Online: **www.elal.co.il**

Enrollment Bonus: None as we went to press.

Award Requirements: 1,400 points/ Domestic Coach; 1,800 points/California Coach; 800 points/London Coach

Minimum Miles: Based on a point system. 200 points one-way Coach for U.S. (excluding California) to Israel; 250 points one-way Coach for California to Israel. 300 points one-way Business Class for U.S. (excluding California) to Israel; 375 points one-way Business Class for California to Israel. 400 points one-way First Class for U.S. (excluding California) to Israel; 500 points one-way First Class for California to Israel.

Policies: Points are valid for one year. One time membership fee is $35 and registration is on an individual basis. Points are available for purchase (a dollar per point) to be combined with points earned for bonus travel ticket. No more than half of required bonus points can be purchased.

Redemption: Bonus voucher request forms are located on the back of Member Statements. To request a form, call the service center and enter option 4. The completed voucher request form must be

> *"Since El Al's Matmid frequent flyer points expire in one year, many families received no benefit from the points they earned. Each individual family member could not accumulate enough miles for award travel. An alternate frequent flyer program solves this problem, albeit with a couple of small prices to pay. The Loyal Traveler Club requires a one-time membership fee of $25 per person and requires 50 percent more points per award ticket. The advantage is that two family members (12 and above) who share the same address can pool points and the points remain valid for three years. Children's award tickets can be acquired for fewer points than adult tickets. The airline also allows you to purchase up to 50 percent of the required award ticket points, if you do not have enough banked points. Enrolling (or acquiring more information) involves a small investment in patience. You can either fax to* ***212-852-0632*** *(include your mailing address, phone and fax numbers) or call* ***800-223-6700*** *and record a request for more information via voice mail."*

faxed or mailed to the frequent traveler center. Allow two weeks to process voucher. There is an unlimited use of bonus tickets with no blackout dates.

Hotels: One point/$20 spent at Holiday Inn Worldwide. Points can also be earned at Isrotel's Royal Beach Hotel, King Solomon Hotel, Sport Hotel, Laguna Hotel, Laromme Hotels, the Riviera Hotel and the Ramon Hotel.

Car Rentals: Ten points per rental at Avis and Hertz.

Credit Cards: American Express Membership Rewards converts their points to Matmid points. Matmid membership can also be obtained through American Express Membership Rewards (**800-297-3276**) for $15.

Finnair Plus

228 East 45th Street
New York, NY 10017
Reservations: **800-950-5000**
Service Center: **800-950-3387**
Fax: **212-499-9036**
Online: **www.us.finnair.com**

Enrollment Bonus: None as we went to press.

Minimum Miles: Operates on point system; 750 points for first flight. Double points/Business Class; Triple points/First Class on Lufthansa.

Policies: Points are valid for five years and are awarded according to origin and destination.

Redemption: Book through service center 14 days in advance. Award tickets will be mailed to the name on account. Expedited service is available for departures less than 14 days in advance for 250 FIM.

Airlines/Miles & Redemption: Aer Lingus, Austrian, Lufthansa and Swissair.

Airlines/Miles Only: Braathens, Delta, Sabena and Transwede.

Car Rentals: Avis, Europcar and Hertz/500 points per rental at participating locations. Rentals must be in conjunction with flights.

Hotels: 500 points per night at Arctia Hotels, Holiday Inn, Inter-Continental, Hotel Savoy/Moscow and Hotel Scandic KNA.

Other Affiliations: Tax-Free Plus, earn one point per one FIM spent worth 100 FIM ($18.40 USD). Helsinki Airport Congress Centre, 250 points/reservation of meeting room. Fly Inn Restaurant, Intermezzo Cafe, Mar Lodge, Pronto earn one point/one FIM spent worth 100 FIM ($18.40 USD).

JAL Mileage Bank Americas

300 Continental Boulevard, Suite 401
El Segunda, CA 90245
Reservations: **800-525-3663**
Service Center: **800-525-6453**
Fax: **310-414-0149**
Online: **www.jal.co.jp/english**

Enrollment Bonus: 5,000 miles on first flight.

Minimum Miles: 500. Actual miles in full fare Economy; 70 percent/Discount Economy; fifty percent bonus/First Class; 25 percent/Business Class.

Policies: Mileage expires at the end of the second calendar year. Award certificates are valid for three months from the date issued (travel must be completed within six months). Positive-space upgrade certificates are valid three months from date of issue, space-available upgrades one year and hotel awards six months.

Redemption: Order by phone, mail or fax at least three weeks prior to departure date. Tickets can be issued at any JAL

Airport that closed for one day due to clouds of volcanic ash: New Zealand's Auckland Airport.

ticket office. Expedited service is not available.

Airlines/Miles & Redemption: Air France and American.

Airlines/Redemption Only: Aeromexico and Aeroperu.

Hotels: Nikko Hotels/1,000 miles. Hotel New Otani Tokyo /500 miles.

Korean Air Skypass

FTBS Mileage Dividend Program
Passenger Marketing Department
1813 Wilshire Boulevard
Los Angeles, CA 90057
Reservations: **800-438-5000**
Service Center: **800-525-4480**
Fax: **213-484-5790**
Online: **www.koreanair.com**

Enrollment Bonus: None as we went to press.

Minimum Miles: 500 miles; 50 percent/ First Class bonus; 25 percent/Business Class.

Policies: Miles do not expire. Award tickets must be used within six months of issue date, and three 90-day extensions may be requested for a particular award. The first extension is free and can be validated at the ticket counter. Each subsequent deducts 5,000 miles from the member's account. Requests must be made through the service center and made two weeks in advance of the current expiration date.

Redemption: Tickets are issued at the local office, or by mail. If the award request is made at a Korean Air office it will take one week to process; two weeks if mailed. Car rental and hotel awards must accompany a request for a flight award and be used in conjunction. Expedited service is not available.

Airlines: Delta

Car Rentals: 100 miles per rental day for a maximum of seven consecutive days at participating Korean Rent A Car locations. Rentals do not have to be in conjunction with a flight.

Hotels: 300 miles per night at KAL Hotels, the Los Angeles Hilton, ITT Sheraton Anchorage and Waikiki Resorts in Honolulu. Maximum of 14 consecutive nights. Stays do not have to be in conjunction with a flight.

Credit Cards: American Express Membership Miles give one point per dollar charged; points convert to Skypass miles.

Other Affiliations: Hanjin Duty-Free Shop gives 100 miles/$100 spent.

LatinPass

1600 NW LeJeune Road
Miami, FL 33166
Service Center: **800-445-2846**
Online: **www.latinpass.com**

Enrollment Bonus: None as we went to press.

Minimum Miles: 500/international flights; actual miles/domestic. 50 percent bonus/First Class; 25 percent bonus/ Business Class.

Redemption: Miles expire after three years of accrual date. Miles can be redeemed by mail request or by phone. Allow three weeks for delivery of mail request; two weeks for delivery of phone request. Expedited delivery is available for a domestic fee of $25; an international fee of $50. Award tickets are valid one year from date of issue.

Airlines: Aces, APA, Avianca, Aviateca, Copa, Faucett, KLM, Lacsa, LanChile, Mexicana, NICA, SAETA, TACA and US Airways.

Car Rentals: 500/Avis or Hertz in Latin

Airline that proudly prints "We Overbook" on its ticket jackets: Southwest.

America, North America and the Caribbean.

Hotels: 500 miles per stay at Radisson. 2.5 miles per dollar spent at Holiday Inns. 65 miles per night at Holiday Inn Express.

Credit Cards: Diners Club Club Rewards (two points/one mile) and American Express Membership Miles (one point/one mile) convert to LatinPass miles.

Phone Service: AT&T/five miles per dollar spent on qualifying services.

> *"LatinPass miles no longer expire providing you take at least one flight within a three year period."*

Lufthansa Miles & More

P.O. Box 243
East Meadow, NY 11554-1096
Reservations: **800-645-3880**
Service Center: **800-581-6400**
Fax: **516-296-9474**
Online: **www.lufthansa.com**

Enrollment Bonus: None as we went to press.

Minimum Miles: Lufthansa and most European partners give 500-1,000 minimum/Coach; double miles/Business Class. 200 percent bonus/First Class; 100 percent bonus/Business Class. Canadian gives 500 miles minimum on shorthauls; 1,000/longhauls. United gives 1,000 minimum on Domestic U.S. flights. Varig gives actual miles. 200 percent bonus/First Class; 100 percent bonus/Business Class.

Policies: Miles expire two years from date accrued. Certificates for flights and upgrades are valid six months from date issued. Certificates issued for non-airline partners are valid for 12 months. Award tickets are valid for one year.

Redemption: Redeem by mail or phone. Make your requests at least 14 days in advance. If an award ticket is not issued within 21 days of your reservation, the reservation is cancelled. Tickets are mailed to the member's address. Award certificates can be exchanged for tickets at ticket offices or airport ticket counters. Phone orders are sent by mail. Expedited service is available for a fee.

Airlines/Miles & Redemption: Adria Airways, Air Canada, Air Dolomiti, Business Air, Finnair, Lauda Air, ModiLuft, SAS, Thai International, Tyrolean, United/United Express and Varig.

Car Rentals: 500 miles at participating Avis, Budget, Hertz and Sixt locations. Rentals do not have to be in conjunction with a flight.

Hotels: 500 miles per qualifying stay at Forum, Hilton/Conrad International, Holiday Inn, ITT Sheraton, Inter-Continental, Kempinski, Luxury Collection, Marriott, Radisson, Ramada International, Renaissance, Shangri-La, Traders and Vista USA. Stays do not have to be in conjunction with a flight.

> *"In 1997, Lufthansa lowered award levels for U.S.-based frequent flyers. The lower levels are also available on partner airline, United."*

Mexicana Frecuenta

3201 Cherry Ridge Drive, Suite 200
San Antonio, TX 78230
Reservations: **800-531-7921**
Service Center: **800-531-7901**

Fax: **210-525-0712**
Online: **www.mexicana.com**

Enrollment Bonus: 6,400 kilometers.

Minimum Kilometers: 1,000 per flight. Y Fare International earns a 50 percent bonus. LatinPass earns 50 percent/First Class; 25 percent/Business Class.

Airlines/Kilometers & Redemption: Aerolitoral, Aeromar, Aeromexico, Aeroperu, LatinPass, Mexicana Inter and United.

Car Rentals: 1,000 kilometers per rental at participating Avis and Executive Car Rental locations in conjunction with qualifying flight.

Hotels: 1,000 kilometers per stay at Camino Real, El Cid Mega Resorts, Fiesta Americana, Fiesta Inns, Hilton/Conrad International, Maeva, Presidente Inter-Continental and Radisson.

Credit Cards: American Express Membership Rewards converts to Frecuenta kilometers. Diners Club converts 2,000 Club Reward points to 1,600 Frecuenta kilometers.

Qantas Frequent Flyer

2801 East Elvira Road, Building B
Tucson, AZ 85706
Reservations: **800-227-4500**
Service Center: **800-227-4220**
FAX: **520-741-5331**
Online: **www.qantas.com**

Enrollment Bonus: None as we went to press.

Minimum Points: Full Coach/one point per mile; discount fares/70 percent of actual mileage. 50 percent bonus/First Class; 25 percent bonus/Business Class.

Policies: Points are valid for five years. Award tickets are valid for one year.

Redemption: Redeem at local reservations offices or by mail. Allow two weeks minimum for delivery. Expedited service is available for a fee.

Airlines/Points & Redemption: Air Pacific, American, British Airways, Canadian, SAS and US Airways.

Car Rentals: Eight points per one dollar Australian spent in Australia; 1,000 points for International rentals with participating Australia and Thrifty locations. Rentals must be in conjunction with a flight.

Hotels: Five points per Australian dollar spent for stays within Australia at Centra, Hilton International, Holiday Inn, Hotel Sofitel, Hyatt, ITT Sheraton, Ibis, Mariott, Novotel, Qantas Island Resorts, Radisson, Rydges and Stamford. 250-3,500 points per stay outside of Australia at Carlton, Comfort Inn, Forum, Hilton, Holiday Inn, Hotel Sofitel, Ibis, Inter-Continental, ITT Sheraton, Mandarin Oriental, Mariott, Millennium, Quality, Radisson, Rydges, Shangri-La, Thistle and Westin. Stays must be in conjunction with Qantas flights.

Credit Cards: American Express Membership Rewards convert to points on an equal basis.

Phone Service: Telecom Australia calling cards/four points per dollar spent. MAN Phone Rentals/two points per dollar spent.

Sabena Frequent Flyer Programme

C.S. 8910
41 Pinelawn Road
Mellville, NY 11747
Reservations: **800-955-2000**
Service Center: **800-221-8125**
Online: **www.sabena.com**

Enrollment Bonus: None as we went to press.

Minimum Miles: Miles accrue as points/500 minimum per flight. 250 minimum for flights within Switzerland and Austria. 200 percent bonus/First Class; 100 percent/Business Class.

Airlines/Miles & Redemption: Austrian and Swissair.

Airlines/Miles Only: Air Canada, Air One, ANA, Ansett, Austrian Airtransport, Cathay Pacific, Crossair, Delta, Finnair, Malaysia, Singapore and Tyrolean.

Car Rentals: 200-400 points from participating Avis, Europcar and Hertz locations.

Hotels: 250 points per night with ANA, Hilton/Conrad International, Holiday Inn, Inter-Continental, Radisson, Sabena, Swissotel and Vista Hotels.

Credit Cards: 3,000 point enrollment bonus for residents of Belgium and Luxembourg with the Diners Club/Sabena card plus ten points/1,000 BEF spent. American Express Membership Rewards convert to miles for European members.

Other Affiliations: Transair/Jet packages/ten points for every 1,000 BEF spent.

SAS EuroBonus

9 Polito Avenue
Lyndhurst, NJ 07071
Reservations: **800-221-2350**
Service Center: **800-437-5807**
Fax: **201-896-3725**
Online: **www.sas.se**

Enrollment Bonus: 2,500 points.

Minimum Points: Points are awarded for various routes. EuroClass/double points.

Policies: Membership may be cancelled with no activity in three years. Points expire December 31, four years after accrual. Awards are valid for one year from date issued.

Redemption: A minimum seven-day advance. Allow three weeks for delivery. Open vouchers are issued for car rental awards. Make reservations directly with any Radisson SAS Hotel. Make reservations through the service center for other partner hotels. Expedited service is not available.

Airlines/Points & Redemption: Air Baltic, Air Canada, Air New Zealand, British Midland, Continental, Icelandair, Lufthansa, Qantas, Skyways, Spanair, South African, Thai and United.

Car Rentals: 500 points/qualifying rentals with Avis and Hertz.

Hotels: 300-500 points per night at Forum, Hilton, Inter-Continental, SAS International Hotels and Swissotel. 500 points per qualifying stay at Radisson.

Credit Cards: Diners Club enrollment earns 2,500 points for residents of Denmark, Finland, Iceland, Norway, Sweden and the U.K.

Phone Service: Tele2/500 point sign up bonus plus 500 points per $200 spent.

Swissair Qualiflyer

41 Pinelawn Road
Melville, NY 11747-8910
Reservations: **800-221-4750**
Service Center: **800-221-8125**
Online: **www.swissair.com**

Enrollment Bonus: None as we went to press

Award Requirements: 5,000/upgrade; 15,000/companion ticket; 20,000/roundtrip ticket.

Minimum Miles: Coach Class accrues actual mileage. Business Class earns an additional 50 percent mileage bonus; First Class earns an additional 100 percent mileage bonus.

Policies: Miles are valid for three years. Award travel is valid for one year from

Lifespan of carbon brakes on commercial jets: up to 2,500 landings.

date of issue. A $35 fee will apply for dates changed on award travel.

Redemption: Exchange miles for reward travel by calling the service center or your local Swissair, Sabena or Austrian Airlines office. "Experience Awards" are also available instead of air travel. For example, luxury hotel stays can be redeemed for 60,000 miles.

Airlines/Miles & Redemption: Austrian, Delta, Sabena and Swissair

Airlines/Miles Only: Air Canada, Air One, ANA, Ansett Australia Austrian Airtransport, Cathay Pacific, Crossair, Finnair, Lauda Air, Malaysia Airlines, Singapore Airlines and Tyrolean Airways.

Hotels: 500 miles per night at Swissotel; 500 miles per stay at Holiday Inn Worldwide; 250 miles per stay at Hilton, Inter-Continental and Radisson. Additional hotels include: Sabena, ANA Hotel International and Shangri-La Hotels & Resorts.

Car Rentals: 500 miles/Europcar Interrent; 250 miles/Avis and Hertz.

Credit Cards: American Express, Diners Club and Eurocard/MasterCard.

Phone Service: Global One and Swiss Telecom

Other Affiliations: Tax-free shops

Virgin Freeway

747 Belden Avenue
Norwalk, CT 06850
Reservations: **800-862-8621**
Service Center: **800-365-9500**
Online: **www.fly.virgin.com**

Enrollment Bonus: 2,000 miles plus 25,000 miles with first Upper Class roundtrip.

Minimum Miles: Actual miles for premium Economy and Mid-Class fares. Double miles/Business and Upper Class. Actual miles for Economy if you fly one Upper Class or Premium roundtrip or three Economy roundtrips in a one-year period. Actual miles on full fare Air New Zealand and SAS; 500 minimum on British Midland; minimum 1,000 on SAS flights within Europe; 150 percent bonus/ SAS EuroClass to Europe or Asia; 200 percent bonus/Air New Zealand First Class, 150 percent/Business Class, 25 percent/Economy Class. 150 percent bonus/ Austrian Business or Grand Class; 100 percent/Malaysia; 150 percent/Business Class, 200 percent/First Class.

Policies: Miles expire three years after accrual date.

Airlines/Miles & Redemption: Air New Zealand, Austrian, British Midland, Malaysia and SAS.

Airlines/Redemption Only: Delta

Car Rentals: 500-1,000/Avis and Budget.

Hotels: Ten miles per pound spent at Blakes and Virgin Hotels. 250 miles per stay at Holiday Inn Express. 500 miles per stay at Westin. 1,000-6,000 per qualifying stay at Asia Pacific, Doyle Hotels, Forte, Holiday Inn, Inter-Continental, Le Manoir aux Quat'Saison, Mandarin Oriental, Marco Polo, Omni Hotels, Radisson/SAS and Summit International Hotels.

Phone Service: 2,500 sign up bonus with Sprint plus five miles per dollar spent.

Credit Cards: One mile/dollar charged on Diners Club.

Other Redemption Only Affiliations: Eurostar and Radisson/SAS London.

Other Affiliations: Ten miles/one pound spent on Virgin Duty-Free shopping. One mile per dollar spent on PerryGolf packages.

Airline offering in-flight magic shows: Asiana.

SOLVING THE HOTEL MYSTERY: 'INN'-SIDER TRADING

The lodging industry isn't the stock market; sharing *inn-sider* secrets is perfectly legal. When I am on the road, I do live radio shows from my hotel room, so I need two phone lines. I don't even consider staying at a hotel that collects telephone surcharges. When I'm too busy to head for a restaurant, I want room service at a fair price without hidden charges. I get what I need for half the going rate—or less. This chapter will show you how it's done, beginning with five methods that produce maximum savings:

Limited-time promotions you may have to request by name.

Consolidator discounts of 20 to 72 percent. High volume allows them to offer volume discounts single travelers may not be able to negotiate.

Discount hotel directories offering savings of up to 50 percent on rooms many travelers book at twice the price.

Booking direct and negotiating rates that toll-free reservation agents may not know about or cannot authorize.

City discount promotions that lower hotel rates and often throw in discounts on dining, entertainment and shopping.

The hotel industry has fooled a lot of people with nominal discounts that satisfy too many travelers' search for bargains. I don't blame hotel owners. If I owned a chain of hotels, I'd probably do the same thing. Understanding how hotels play the game does not, however, prevent me from countering with my own bargain strategies. Some cities make life harder for travelers by increasing hotel taxes to finance sports facilities. Every time you travel to Fort Lauderdale, for example, you pay a two percent tax for the Florida Panthers hockey stadium. Travelers coming to Dallas will help pay for a new sports complex. Some costs are unavoidable and some are not, but you have to take control of your lodging costs or risk paying much more than necessary.

You gain control by understanding hotel strategies, knowing *all* discount possibilities and using those that save you the most. A Ritz-Carlton room will always cost more than one at Travelodge, but every room can cost you less.

- You can stay at higher-amenity hotels with discounts that place them well within your price range.
- Business travelers can save enough nightly to cover the cost of three good restaurant meals.
- Families can get a room for five near Walt Disney World for $59.95, including meals for the kids, attraction tickets and a coupon book with up to $300 in discounts.
- You can book just one night at a budget hotel and get $75 off your next airline ticket.

Clues To The Best Bargains explains how to use my five favorite lodging discount tips.

Other Ways To Save describes creative discount opportunities, including discounts by internet, off-season discounts and ways to save internationally.

Standard Discounts & Benefits shows you which programs are offered and helps you optimize them.

Inn-sider Info provides key information that can make or break any stay. It explores hidden costs, deciphers lodging lingo, updates you on business amenities, new technologies and much more.

Hotel Highlights looks at major chains' distinguishing characteristics, on-going and recurring rate breaks, senior discounts and frequent guest programs. It details economy properties that have added a level of business features and extended-stay properties that charge about $50 per night less than many competitors.

Other Lodging Options tells you about alternative lodging. You'll find new and expanded ways to save while adding to your vacation experience.

After you read this chapter you will realize how much *you* control the price you pay for each night's stay.

Clues To The Best Bargains

Limited Time Promotions

Hundreds of promotions go unnoticed each month. Sometimes they are in your local paper or hidden among the many pages of your billing statements. Sometimes they're loaded into the computer reservation systems of hard working travel agents who barely have time to answer the phone, much less scan their computers for hot deals. Most often, they come and go without being noticed by most travelers. They discount rates, add upgrades and amenities and offer free added nights.

You can find more of these promotions, if you know where to look.

- **Monthly statements** from credit card companies, automobile clubs, frequent flyer programs and other sources should be scanned carefully.
- **Newspapers**, particularly Sunday travel sections, include limited-time promotions. Check your hometown paper but don't stop there. For example, if you are traveling to Los Angeles, check the Los Angeles, San Diego and San Francisco papers; if you are traveling to New York check the Boston and Washington papers. Many hotel ads are designed to attract people looking for nearby getaways. Business travelers who know about them can use these deals too.
- **Access out-of-town papers** at newsstands or libraries. For leisure travel, start early and check weekly until you find an ad that fits your needs.
- **Business travelers** can scan ads when they travel, particularly in cities they return to regularly.
- *Best Fares* and *Best Fares* Online details the best discounts and promotions from the above sources and from many industry sources. We uncover deals including:

  A $99 Coach or First Class companion airfare worldwide when you join a $100-per-year frequent guest program.

  A free compact car for the length of your stay in Hawaii.

  $20 rates at top Las Vegas hotels plus free breakfast, $10 off dinner and a book of discount coupons.

  Up to 50 percent off 25 Seattle hotels, plus added discounts.

  A free triple room upgrade plus a car rental upgrade.

  Free and discounted weekend nights plus upgrades and bonus awards.

  1995 rates for 1998 stays at hotels in the United Kingdom.

  Up to 60 percent off rates in 14 major cities in Asia.

U.S. city with the most hotel rooms: Las Vegas, over 100,000.

CONSOLIDATORS

Consolidators provide discounts ranging from 20 to 72 percent. Most consolidators specialize. Some cover a specific area; others offer discounts in many major cities. Good ones know the markets they serve, keep up with new hotels, monitor quality and may even be able to find you rooms during special events when availability seems non-existent. Some only offer discounts when projected occupancy is under 80 percent.

Some consolidators offer two-tier discounts. The more substantial discount is a non-refundable rate. Ask for the cancellation policy in detail. When you book through a consolidator, you are subject to *their* rules, not the policy of the hotel.

Hotel Reservations Network (800-964-6835), a no-fee consolidator, serves Anaheim, Boston, Chicago, Las Vegas, London, Los Angeles, Miami, New Orleans, New York, Orlando, Paris, San Diego, San Francisco and Washington. They work with independent hotels and chains, including Best Western, Doubletree, Hilton, Hyatt, Inter-Continental, ITT Sheraton, Nikko, Ramada and Westin. Here are some of the deals they recently negotiated:

- **$139.95 at the Belvedere Hotel in New York**, about $100 less than rates at comparable hotels.
- **$99.95 at San Francisco's Cartwright Hotel**, 60 percent off rack rate for a Fodor's "Most Highly Recommended" property.
- **$109.95-149.95 at Chicago's Drake Hotel**, as much as 72 percent off rack rate for a Windy City classic.
- **$59.95 at the Days Inn Suites in Kissimmee** for a one bedroom suite accommodating up to six people comfortably, plus free meals for kids.
- **$79.95 at the four-star Crowne Plaza** in Washington, DC.
- **$39.95 at The Sahara** in Las Vegas.
- **$69.95 at Miami's Red Sands**, a brand-new Art Deco oceanfront hotel.
- **$79.95 at the New Orleans Pallas Hotel** on Canal Street including breakfast and a welcome drink.
- **$99.95 at the three-star Bel Air** in Paris.
- **$149.95 at London's four-star Oki Kensington Hotel**, including full breakfast.

DISCOUNT DIRECTORIES

Discount hotel directories include hundreds (sometimes thousands) of name-brand hotels you can book at discounts of up to 50 percent. Membership ranges from $19.95 to $99.95 and usually lasts a year (except for Entertainment Publications, which may last as long as 18 months, depending on when you enroll). Some annual fees drop after the first year. Travel agents don't book rates these books offer, because they are not commissionable. You request rooms by phone or fax, giving your membership number and dates needed. If they have availability on the night(s) you need, the discount is yours. Simply show your membership card when you check in. Discounts are usually limited to times when projected occupancy is under 80 percent.

Choose your program(s) by evaluating the number of hotels included, the areas they cover, the membership fee and the credit cards accepted. Some programs include airfare and car rental discount

Three most expensive U.S. hotel cities: New York City, Washington, DC and Boston.

coupons in addition to other discount offers attractive to travelers. Credit card acceptance on the following chart is indicated by A/American Express, DS/Discover, DC/Diners Club, M/MasterCard and V/Visa.

DISCOUNT HOTEL PROGRAMS		
PROGRAM	FEE AND CREDIT CARDS	COVERAGE
America At 50% Discount 800-248-2783	$19.95 M/V/DS	Over 1,200 budget properties in the U.S. and Europe.
Carte Royale 800-847-7002	$49.95 M/V	Over 350 first class and deluxe hotels worldwide.
Encore Preferred Travelers Club 800-444-9800	$49.95 A/DC/DS/M/V	Discounts at over 4,000 hotels worldwide plus second night free offers.
Entertainment Publications 800-445-4137	$27.95-69.95 M/V	Over 1,800 U.S. hotels in the cheapest editions. A wide variety of editions are offered.
Great American Traveler 800-548-2812	$49.95 A/DS/M/V	Over 2,200 first class hotels in the U.S., Canada, Mexico and Europe.
Impulse 800-730-2457	$53 M/V	Over 500 hotels in the U.S., Canada, Mexico and the Bahamas.
International Travel Card 800-987-6216	$49 A/DC/M/V	3,800 hotels worldwide. Good Asia/ South Pacific coverage.
Privilege Card International 800-236-9732	$79.95 M/V	Over 7,500 hotels in 50 countries.
Quest 800-638-9819	$99 A/DS/M/V	Over 2,100 hotels in the U.S., Canada, Mexico, Europe and Asia.

BOOKING DIRECT & NEGOTIATING RATES

Booking direct will almost always lower your rate. On-site reservation agents know about site-specific promotions and often have the authority to lower rates when you want to negotiate. They also offer more complete information and will accept very specific requests that 800 reservation lines may not be able to handle. Call the 800 number for general information, their best rate and the number of the hotel that interests you. Call the hotel directly during times when long distance rates are favorable or late afternoons when business typically slows down. The discount you get is likely to be far more than the cost of the call.

Never pay rack rate unless you are trying to book the last room in town for Super Bowl Sunday. Paying rack rate is like paying the asking price at a used car lot. The average hotel occupancy rate hovers around 69 percent. They need to fill empty rooms. You have room to negotiate and you should. It requires persis-

Increase in the 1996 average per night hotel rate in Hawaii: 7.3%.

tence and an awareness of what you can get, if you don't settle for the first offer.

- **Make your needs clear.** If you want specific features, make it known at the beginning of your call. If you are eligible for any standard discount, tell the agent. Ask which rooms are most popular. You may discover important information, such as rooms with exceptional views at no extra charge.
- **Ask for the lowest rate, then ask for one that's even lower.** Ask about rate breaks, promotional rates and frequent guest rates (membership is often free and you can sign-up instantly). If you will be celebrating a special event, tell the agent. You may be given a special room or an upgrade. Ask for an introductory rate if you have never stayed at the hotel before. This is particularly effective at independent and boutique hotels. If you travel to the city frequently, let them know that you could be a steady customer. Ask if the hotel is undergoing any substantial renovation. Fifteen percent of all hotels are, at any given point in time. You want to book a room away from the sounds of construction and you want a discount.
- **If you're booking multiple nights**, check on day-to-day rate variations. If you get a rate of $79 for the first night, $139 for the second and $89 for the third, ask for the $79 rate for each night of your stay in exchange for streamlined daily maid service.
- **When you get a rate you like**, ask for an upgrade, free breakfast or another added value. When you finalize the deal note the rate code, confirmation number and agent's name in case you are charged a different rate when you arrive.

> *"Challenge the reservation agent to find you the lowest possible rate in the quickest possible time. Agents are trained to offer the highest rates first, so ask for the lowest rate—then ask again."*

CITY DISCOUNT PROMOTIONS

City discount promotions are sponsored by tourism offices, sometimes in conjunction with a credit card company, or built around specific events. You may be issued a card that entitles you to discounts or given a brochure listing hotels that offer special rates. Promotions may be oriented toward seniors or families, but most are for general use. They are designed to promote leisure travel, but business travelers can use them too.

Call the tourism office in the city you plan to visit (see *Know Who To Contact*) and ask what promotions are available. Some will fax information to you or make reservations for you. As a bonus, you may get discounts on meals and attractions. You can get these deals in U.S. cities and many international cities.

> *"If you can't find a room in New York, call **800-846-7666** (The New York Convention & Visitors Bureau Peak Season Hotline); in Boston call **800-777-6001** (The Boston Special Event Hotel Hotline); in Chicago call **800-511-5740** (Hotel Reservations Network). They can help you find availability when it may seem all but impossible."*

Hotel in which Tennessee Williams wrote part of A Streetcar Named Desire: the Boston Ritz-Carlton.

OTHER WAYS TO SAVE

DISCOUNTS BY INTERNET

The internet can give you a close-up preview of hotels and an inside track to discount opportunities. You will find details on amenities, travel distances from the airport and much more. Best of all, you will find rate reductions, particularly for last-minute travel.

Many major chains now offer discounts by internet. The best sites have discounts updated weekly and offer booking capability with secured web browser features. Most allow the same discounts for booking by phone, but you may need to request a specific code. Hilton, Radisson, Inter-Continental and Renaissance are among the first hotel chains to use the internet aggressively.

Hotel chains that participate in weekly discounts by internet become more numerous each month. Here is a select list. Each Wednesday, **www.bestfares.com** publishes two comprehensive charts listing all of these weekly discounts by city. One chart covers U.S. destinations; the other chart covers international travel. Many cover discounts for the coming weekend (often in conjunction with airline internet fares). Others include travel dates as much as a month in the future.

- **Delta Hotels & Resorts** (**800-268-1133**), in conjunction with Air Canada WebSavers. **800-268-1133**.
- **Fiesta Americana** (**www.fiestamexico.com**), in conjunction with American International internet fares. Online booking is required.
- **Hilton Value Rates** (**800-774-1500** and **www.hilton.com**). Domestic and international discounts in conjunction with airline internet specials (American, Continental and TWA) and other discounts available to the general public.
- **Holiday Inn** (**888-764-5775**), available to the general public. Can include domestic and international locations.
- **Hyatt Special Rates** (**800-233-1234**). Domestic discounts for Friday, Saturday, Sunday and Monday nights. Sunday night stays includes continental breakfast. Available to the general public.

Percentage of Americans who check to make sure hotel bed sheets are clean: 59%.

- **Inter-Continental Click It! Rates (www.interconti.com/clickit.html).** Domestic and international discounts that require online booking and are available to the general public. Includes Inter-Continental, Forum & Global hotels.
- **Radisson (www.radisson.com).** Domestic and international discounts. Some are in conjunction with Air Canada, Continental & Northwest internet specials. Radisson Hot Deals are offered to the general public. They include week night and weekend days. Online booking is required.
- **Wyndham (800-996-3426** and **www.wyndham.com)**, in conjunction with American International internet fares.

> *"The Hotel Discount web site at **www.80096hotel.com** combines discounts and discoveries. The site offers discounts, on-line booking, extensive information and full graphics—and it includes a wide variety of hotels representing many chains plus unique independent hotels. Specials are updated regularly."*

Bonus frequent flyer miles (usually 500) are sometimes offered for bookings by internet. Before you take the $10 worth of value, make sure the rate you select is the best available. Sometimes, these bonuses apply only to higher rates.

The Promus Group found a new way to win favor with hotel guests. The Route Planner option on three of their sites lets you customize road trips using scenic or direct routing, toll or no-toll highways and other specifications. Miles and driving time are calculated. Route Planner is available at **www.embassy-suites.com**, **www.hampton-inn.com** and **www.homewood-suites.com**. Look for more traveler-friendly features to appear as internet competition increases.

PLANNING AHEAD

Booking seven- to 30-days in advance can result in discounts of up to 50 percent. You'll often find this benefit at premium business hotels. The Boston Marriott, for example, has a $189 corporate rate that you can beat with a 21-day advance rate of $139. Some advance rates require prepayment for your first night's stay and may be non-refundable. Advance booking rates can require a credit card guarantee.

CREDIT CARD PROMOTIONS

Charge card promotions offer discounts and added values when you reserve and pay for your room with their card. Find these offers included with your billing statement, as part of newspaper and magazine ads for hotels and enclosed with your frequent flyer statement *Best Fares* and *Best Fares* Online keeps up on these offers. Before you make any reservation, ask if you can get an extra discount by paying with a specific credit card.

DAY RATES

Day Rates, long popular in Europe, are now available at many U.S. hotels. The charge is usually about half the rack rate. Hours of availability vary but usually fall between 7 a.m. and 5 p.m. They're useful for business meetings, leisure travelers who prefer night driving and international travelers dealing with lengthy layovers. You can sometimes get corporate and senior discounts on day rates. And yes—you are allowed to sleep on the bed.

Washington hotel that hosted presidents Franklin Pierce through John Kennedy: the Willard Inter-Continental.

OFF SEASON SAVINGS

It's always off-season somewhere, and if you travel regularly, you're likely to run into seasonal rate breaks. Business travelers locked into the corporate rate mentality miss these seasonal rates (often lower than corporate rates). The Knickerbocker in Chicago, for example, discounts all rooms in January, February, July and August. If you make a business trip to Chicago each month and pay the same corporate rate each time, you'll miss four months of savings. All discount seasons exclude holiday bookings.

U.S. discount seasons include:

- **Arizona**—Summer, when temperatures rise above 100. Book a room at an ultra-luxury resort with plenty of air conditioned amenities at a discount of up to 75 percent.
- **Boston**—Mid-November through March.
- **Chicago**—January through March.
- **Florida**—In general, look for lower rates from Easter through mid-December. September and October are generally rainy months, so rates can drop accordingly. Florida Panhandle rates drop after Labor Day and stay low through early March. Orlando rates drop from January 7 to February 15, from mid-April to early June and from early September to mid-December.
- **Hawaii**—September and October offer the best rates with slightly higher rates for November and early December. This past year brought an expanded discount season, due to a small decrease in peak season tourism.
- **Las Vegas**—Late November through December 20, unless there are major convention bookings.
- **New Orleans**—Memorial Day through Labor Day.
- **New York City**—January through March, July, August and mid- to late December.
- **The Northeast Coast**—Columbus Day through Memorial Day. Resorts that stay open for the winter offer very favorable rates.
- **The Pacific Northwest**—November through early April. Coastal hotels offer Storm Watcher discounts.
- **Palm Springs**—June through September, with rates as low as $29.
- **San Francisco**—November through March.
- **Washington, DC**—January, February, July and August.

> *"Peak travel periods also offer bargains as hotels and resorts compete for bookings. Discounts are most available at the beginning and end of peak seasons. Skiers, for example, can save 25-30 percent in early December, late March and early April, as well as Sunday through Thursday all season long. Las Vegas rates are almost always lower for Sunday through Thursday stays."*

International discount seasons include:

- **Australia & New Zealand**—Fall and winter.
- **Brazil**—April through November.
- **The Canadian Rockies**—October

Average room rate in Las Vegas: $54, lowest among the top 33 cities in the U.S.

through April.

- **The Caribbean**—Mid-April through October. Rooms are often half-price, but the climate is similar to peak season climate except for hurricane season, which runs from August through October.
- **Greece**—November through March.
- **Jamaica**—May through mid-December.
- **London**—November through March, with cheapest rates in January, February, July and August.
- **Mexico**—May through October, with rooms at luxury resorts starting at $50.
- **Paris**—November through March.
- **Rome**—July through August.

HOLIDAY DISCOUNTS

Holiday rates go up at resort hotels, but they go down at big city hotels that are oriented toward business travelers. Book a room during these down times and you can enjoy some of the finest hotels in the country at rates comparable to what you usually pay for moderately priced hotels. These properties must remain open and well-staffed, even though bookings plummet. To avoid a five-to-one staff-guest ratio, they offer discounts and package promotions designed to fill their rooms with leisure travelers.

STOCKHOLDER DISCOUNTS

Check your portfolio. Even minor players in the market may hold shares in umbrella companies that list hotel chains among their assets. We live in the age of mergers, so check annual reports to see if you currently hold stock in a company with a lodging subsidiary. If you own Disney stock, for example, you get preferred rates and VIP treatment at all Disney hotels. You don't have to be a major stockholder to get these discounts. As little as one share may qualify.

MORE BUSINESS & LEISURE STRATEGIES

Use your dollars wisely. If you value amenities, you are generally better off with a lower-priced room in a deluxe hotel, rather than a top-of-the-line room in a moderate hotel. General amenities and service levels come with all rooms. Take advantage of amenities that lower your overall travel expenses. Use hotel shuttles, free breakfasts and concierge-floor food and beverages. If you just want a restful night's sleep, stay away from hotels with rates that cover amenities you are not apt use.

When you book at the last minute, you could have an extra edge if rooms are still available. At that point, management is eager to do what they can to fill up their empty rooms. Particularly for arrivals after 6 p.m., managers authorize deals that can give you a substantial rate break while keeping another room from sitting empty for the night. Always ask for a special rate—preferably less than half of rack rate.

Be loyal—but only to a point. If a particular chain makes you feel most welcome, you've found a valuable travel asset. If you belong to a frequent guest club, enjoy the benefits your loyalty earned. Continue to monitor competitors, however. When you find a great promotion, use it. You may be very happy with the bargain and you may even find a new hotel chain favorite.

Avoid high city center rates when a central location is not crucial. Business travel-

Anti-jet lag service offered by the Charles de Gaulle Airport Hilton: a Turkish bath and sauna.

ers can choose hotels near the location of their business call. When you are meeting suburban clients off-site, don't make the mistake of obligating them to travel to the city center. The right location can bring a lower rate, eliminate the expense of a rental car and save time on local travel.

> *"Shop around, particularly in major metropolitan areas, where rooms can range from $30 to several hundred dollars per night. With a little investment in time, you'll develop low cost lodging sources in cities you visit frequently. Remember to be a smart consumer and use hotel directories, consolidators and promotions to get your best hotel options for less."*

Avoid being overcharged. Surveys have shown a 20 to 40 percent error rate in hotel bills. Errors are quickly corrected—but you must point them out. Simplify the process by making sure all your optional charge totals end with the same digit. For example, add tip amounts to make restaurant and bar bills end with a five. When you review the bill, you can quickly spot unauthorized charges, simply by looking at the last number in each charged amount.

SAVING INTERNATIONALLY

Most consolidators and hotel discount directories cover international as well as domestic locations. You may want to collect several directories to optimize your range of choices. See *More Dollars & Cents* for details.

Most well-known international hotel chains offer standard discounts and special promotions similar to those offered domestically. U. S. based budget chains with a significant international presence include Budgetel, Choice, Courtyard by Marriott, Econo Lodge, Hojo Inns, Holiday Inn Express, La Quinta, Motel 6, Red Roof Inns, Super 8 and Travelodge.

Pre-paid voucher programs are prevalent, but don't always provide maximum value. If you buy them at standard rate, you have purchased rack rate, international style. A guaranteed rate will lock in your price without necessarily requiring that you pay for your entire stay in advance.

Stay away from city centers. Use usually excellent rail travel options to link you to the city and to enable you to enjoy the charm and discounts of smaller towns and outlying areas.

Utilize tourist information centers. Ibis Europe marks down open inventory each evening and offers travelers age 26 and under. Many city tourist offices will list similar deals. Tourist offices tend to be located in airports, train stations and in city centers. Ask for a free map with the location of the hotel they recommend clearly marked.

Never judge international hotels by their lobbies. Ask to see a room. Often, you'll be pleasantly surprised. It's common for hotels in other countries to focus their money on room amenities, rather than first impressions.

If you enjoyed your prior night's lodging, ask the hotel manager to recommend a place in the next town you're visiting.

Beat high rates in expensive lodging areas by checking little-known sources and being flexible in the type of accommodations you will accept. If you are using a request-by-mail source, be sure to

Anti-jet lag service offered by London's Gatwick Hilton: aromatherapy.

request information well in advance of your travel dates.

- **Climat de France**, **800-332-5332**, costs $50 ($20 for seniors) and allows you to access ten to 30 percent discounts at hotels in several price categories. The card can be purchased in France from tourism offices.
- **Inexpensive rooms in Japan** are offered by the Welcome Inn Reservation Center. They offer 500 hotels, pensions and inns with maximum prices of $80 per night. Fax them (in Tokyo) at 33211-9009. The Japan National Tourist Office offers rooms for two at about $124 per night, including two meals. Call **212-757-5641**. Fax to **212-307-6754**.
- **Economy lodging in the United Kingdom** is available at Granada Inns and Little Chief Lodges. They're located along major motorways and are similar to our Motel 6 chain. Central London Accommodations, **44-171-602-9668**, has nightly offerings for as little as $22.
- **The Italian Government Travel Office** will help you locate information on inexpensive lodging throughout Italy. Write to the Italian Government Travel Office, 12400 Wilshire Boulevard, Suite 5500, Los Angeles, CA 90025.
- **Explore discount options in New Zealand** with *Where To Stay*, a free 720-page guide which includes information on and hundreds of color photographs of one- to five-star lodging options. Call the New Zealand Tourism Board at **800-388-5494**.
- **Save in Austria** with the *Salzburg Plus Card*, a debit card covering hotels, meals, city transportation, attractions and a cultural event. Various versions of the card are available for stays of two or more nights with accommodations in three-five star hotels. You can customize a package that fits your needs and your budget. Call **212-229-1768**.
- **Formule 1 Hotels** offer budget lodging in France, Australia, Belgium, Great Britain, the Netherlands, South Africa, Spain and Switzerland. Write for a Formule 1 and ETAP directory; Formule 1 Hotels, 31 Rue du Colonel-Pierre-Avia, 75904 Paris Cedex 15, France.
- **Best Western's *Travel Guide and Road Atlas*** offers budget options in the Americas (the Caribbean, Central America, Latin America, North America and South America), Europe (including Africa, Asia and the Mediterranean) and Australia/New Zealand. Request the free guide(s) of your choice by calling **800-528-1234**.

New York hotel located on a private island: the Sagamore, Lake George.

STANDARD DISCOUNTS FOR THE ASKING

WHEN TO USE THEM

Standard discounts are for times when better discounts and special promotions aren't available**.** Many groups of people qualify for various discounts. Your job is to find the one that gives you the best rate. Consider corporate, government, senior, frequent guest and automobile club discounts as well as special rates offered to frequent flyers.

CORPORATE RATES

Corporate Rates reflect ten to 20 percent discounts. Basic corporate rates are usually extended to any guest who can show a business card at check in. Major corporations negotiate rates that can sometimes double the discount in exchange for the guarantee of a certain number of bookings per year. If you are with IBM, your corporate discount may be the backbone of your hotel booking strategy. If you're with ABC Window Washing, you will probably do better with other discount plans.

- **If you are making a business call on a large corporation**, ask the hotel about *their* discount. You may be allowed to use it.
- **Don't assume corporate rates are lower** than standard rates. Some hotels charge more to cover added business amenities.
- **Some corporate contracts cover standard rooms** and require a $15-20 surcharge for business-class

Best customer of Holiday Inn Worldwide: the U.S. government & military at 2.4 million room nights per year.

upgrades, usually including business amenities, breakfast, free local calls and a daily newspaper.

WEEKEND RATES

Weekend rates usually apply for Friday through Sunday stays. Some hotels discount rooms on a per night basis; others require a two-night minimum. A Sunday discount almost always requires a stay on the previous Saturday. A few programs offer "weekend rates" seven days a week, subject to availability. Many weekend rates include extras such as breakfast, champagne or dinner.

One chain may offer several different weekend rates, varying by location. If you are looking for a weekend rate with a particular chain, ask the agent to check all the properties within the city. *Hotel Highlights* includes many ongoing and recurring weekend rate specials that you can ask for by name.

SENIOR DISCOUNTS

Senior discounts are offered by most hotel chains and many independent hotels. Some require membership in the chain's senior club (free or nominal cost) and/or advance booking. Some require membership in the American Association of Retired Persons (AARP), available to people 50 and above. AARP has official arrangements with about 25 hotel chains, but many others honor their card. See *Senior Travel* for enrollment details and information on other senior membership organizations.

Seniors may also get discounts on hotel dining, particularly at Omni, Hilton, Doubletree, Marriott, Holiday Inn and Radisson. Many hotels also allow you to book second rooms at senior rates.

Age limits and availability vary. See *Hotel Highlights* for chain-by-chain specifics.

STANDARD RATE COMPARISONS

This chart gives a general indication of how standard discounts compare. Check all discounts you qualify for. Promotional rates, consolidators and discount clubs often beat standard discounts hands down.

STANDARD RATE COMPARISONS

HOTEL	RACK	CORPORATE	WEEKEND	SENIOR
Crowne Plaza/Los Angeles	$140	$120	$140	$140
Doubletree/Fort Lauderdale	$189	$109	N/A	$139
Inter-Continental/Chicago	$159-179	$169	$139	N/A
Hilton/New York	$179-305	$179-305	$174-189	N/A
Holiday Inn/San Francisco	$108-118	$102	$103	$97
Le Meridian/Dallas	$139	$129	$89	$109
Marriott Pavilion/St. Louis	$99-154	$129	$109	$125
Ramada Downtown/Seattle	$150-175	$89	$69	$127
ITT Sheraton/Denver	$95-115	$114	$69-89	$97

Number of Holiday Inn room nights booked by the U.S. government since 1987: over 15 million.

FREQUENT GUEST PROGRAMS

Frequent guest programs provide discounts and added values including preferred reservations, upgrades and free meals. Many hotels dropped or watered down frequent guest programs, awarding bonus air miles instead. Some programs, however, expanded. This chart lists basic award policies of the largest programs. A program that provides ten points per dollar spent is not necessarily better than one that awards one point per dollar spent. Redemption value counts. Also check for variations for elite level membership. Some of these programs are free. Holiday Inn Priority Club charges $10 per year if you choose points over miles; Inter-Continental is $100 for the first year and $25 for subsequent years; Sheraton Gold level is free after four stays or you can purchase it for $50 for the first year and $25 for subsequent years.

BASIC AWARD POLICIES OF THE LARGEST HOTEL POINT PROGRAMS

PROGRAM	BASIC POINT POLICY & SAMPLE REDEMPTIONS
Best Western Gold Crown Club International 800-237-8483	One point per dollar spent on regular room rates; 100 points per partner car rental. Sample redemption—600 points equals $25 off a night's stay.
Crowne Plaza Preferred 800-277-4567	One point per dollar spent on qualifying rates; 50 points per qualifying Hertz rental. Sample redemption—1,250 points equals a free weeknight stay.
Hilton HHonors Worldwide (Basic, Silver and Gold) 800-552-0852	Miles plus ten points per dollar spent on business rates and eligible charges at U.S. Hiltons and Conrad International; 500 points per stay at resorts or on discount rates; 250 points for partner airline flights or partner car rentals in conjunction with hotel stays; two to three points per dollar charged on Hilton Optima card. Sample redemption—20,000 points equals one free stay at an airport location.
Holiday Inn Priority Club and Priority Plus 800-272-9273	One point per dollar spent on most business and leisure rates; 50 points per qualifying Hertz rental; varying points for flights in conjunction with hotel stays. Sample redemption—750 to 2,500 points equals one weeknight stay depending on class of hotel chosen.
Hyatt Passport (Gold, Platinum and Diamond) 800-544-9288	Five points per eligible dollar charged to room; 300 bonus points with special promotions; 500 points per night on Hyatt Vacation Packages. Sample redemption—8,000 to 13,000 points equal a free weekend stay during specific seasons.
Intercontinental Six Continents Club (Basic and Executive) 800-466-6890	This program does not award points but offers excellent travel benefits. See information on the following page.

Number of hotel guests who go to bed earlier when traveling: 54%.

BASIC AWARD POLICIES OF THE LARGEST HOTEL POINT PROGRAMS	
PROGRAM	**BASIC POINT POLICY/SAMPLE REDEMPTION**
ITT Sheraton Club International (Basic & Gold) 800-247-2582	Two ClubMiles per dollar spent on eligible room charges; three ClubMiles per dollar spent for SCI Gold; one ClubMile per dollar charged on ClubMiles card. Club Gold members traditionally receive certificates valid for free airline upgrades. 500 miles for partner car rental in conjunction with your stay; varying ClubMiles for partner flights in conjunction with your stay. Sample redemption—3,000 to 7,000 points equal one free weeknight stay depending on class of property chosen.
Marriott Rewards (Basic, Gold, Black & Platinum) 801-468-4000	Ten points per dollar charged to room; 25 percent bonus for stays in conjunction with partner airline flights; one to three points per dollar charged on Marriott First Card Visa. Sample redemption—20,000 points equals one free weekend stay.
Ramada Business Card 800-672-6232	Ten points per dollar spent; 25 percent bonus points with partner car rental in conjunction with your stay; three points per dollar charged with RBC MasterCard. Sample redemption—20,000 points equals one free weeknight stay.
Renaissance Club Express 800-824-3571	One point per dollar spent; 20 bonus points each way with a US Airways flight; 20 bonus points for partner car rental in conjunction with your stay. Sample redemption—2,000 points equals one free weeknight stay.
Westin Premier (General, Burgundy & Gold) 800-228-3000	1,000 points per night plus 500 frequent flyer miles. Sample redemption—20,000 to 30,000 points equal one free weeknight stay depending on class of property chosen.

Programs that work hard to reward your loyalty include:

- **Hilton HHonors Worldwide (800-445-8667)**, now including U.S. and international hotels plus Conrad International and Vista. Earn hotel points *and* airline miles on qualifying rates.
- **Inter-Continental Six Continents Club (800-327-0200)** does not award points but is a standout in terms of standard benefits and special quarterly offers that have frequently included a free or $99 companion roundtrip airfare.
- **ITT Sheraton Club International Gold (800-247-2582)** offers standard benefits, including a 50 percent bonus on ClubMile awards. Their new member welcome packet recently included two coupons valid for free one-way air travel upgrades, a coupon for one free health club visit and a two-for-one dinner coupon.

The average per-stay value of standard frequent guest benefits is $10. If you can beat the rate by more than $10, you are better off using another chain.

Some programs that award points only allow one year for redemption. Others require at least one hotel stay per year to keep your account active. Know terms and policies and keep up with changes.

BONUS MILES

Never base your hotel choice on miles unless you like miles more than money. Most hotels offer 500 to 1,000 miles per stay. Inter-Continental offers 500 miles on a per-night basis. They also kicked off 1998 with a limited-time promotion offering a frequent flyer mile for each minute of your stay. Offers like these are worth emphasizing. On the other hand, use programs offering 500 miles per stay, and you have to stay 50 nights to earn a free airline ticket. Saving just $10 per night by not being locked-in to miles gives you $500 to buy your own ticket, without the restrictions frequent flyer tickets carry. Business travelers may opt for miles over low rates because they get to keep the miles while their companies pay the bill.

> *"Get miles for discount rates when you book through Hotel Reservations Network,* ***800-964-6835****. They award 500 miles on your choice of four major airlines when you book three nights during one phone call."*

Some programs require a flight in conjunction with your stay to qualify for bonus miles. Most award miles for qualifying rates only. Ask if your rate qualifies. Special promotions offer bonus miles for consecutive or cumulative stays during a stated period. Hotel miles promotions are detailed in *Best Fares* magazine and on *Best Fares* Online at **www.bestfares.com**.

FAMILY DISCOUNTS

Family discounts come in several different forms including second rooms at 50 percent off, second rooms for free, added values and no extra charge for children under a certain age (usually 17-18) staying in the same room as parents or grandparents. International hotels frequently have lower maximum ages for kids stay free programs—often 12 or 14 years of age.

One of the best rate breaks for families are kids eat free programs offered by many locations of Days Inn, Doubletree, Holiday Inn, Ramada and other chains. Usually children 12 and under dining at the hotel restaurant with parents or grandparents eat free from special children's menus. Sometimes the offer extends to room service meals. Some hotels limit the offer to one free children's meal per each adult meal ordered.

GROUP & ORGANIZATION DISCOUNTS

Group Discounts are available when you book a specific number of rooms, sometimes as few as five. Some group discount programs require the same form of payment on all reservations. Unless you are booking a large number of rooms through a group reservations desk, negotiate for the lowest single room rate first, then ask for an additional discount for your multiple room booking.

Organizations offering hotel discounts include the American Automobile Association and other automobile clubs. Special interest clubs (pet care clubs, for example) have begun to offer nominal hotel discounts. Other organizations offer free or reduced membership in hotel discount directory programs. Nominal discounts are often accorded to government employees and retired or active members of the military and their dependents.

'INN'-SIDER INFO

HIDDEN COSTS

The worst hidden cost occurs when you are charged for a room you never use. Hotels have become bolder in billing for unused room nights.

- **Don't use a guaranteed reservation rate unless** your plans are reasonably firm. If you cancel (even with a great deal of advance), you can still be charged. If you have booked multiple nights, you may be charged for one night or even for your entire stay.
- **Observe check-in deadlines**. If you don't, you can be charged for one night's lodging, and you may not even find the room available when you finally arrive.
- **Observe cancellation policies.** Some hotels require that you cancel by noon or 24 to 72 hours in advance. A few require as much as seven days. When you cancel, record the cancellation number, the date and time you called and the name of the person you spoke with as protection against an unwarranted charge.
- **Be on the alert for early check-out penalties.** Select Hiltons charge $50 if you are part of a meeting or convention group. Hyatt charges $25 at some locations; Inter-Continental, Loews, Renaissance and Wyndham charge $50. Westin charges $25 at urban locations; $50 at resorts.
- **If you are dissatisfied with your room and check out**, your credit card may still be charged. Get confirmation from the manager on duty, stating that your stay will not be charged to your credit card and get it in writing. If the charge does appear on your bill, dispute it immediately, using a copy of your written back-up.

Hotel guests who use mini-bars: 30%.

> "You are not completely home free, even after you have paid the hotel charges on your credit card statement. Periodic billing audits can result in incidental charges appearing on your credit card weeks or months after your stay. Hotels are authorized to do this within a reasonable period of time. Compare these late charges with your original receipt to make sure you are not paying twice."

Pay now, stay later policies can decrease your credit card spending limit as soon as you make your reservation. Some hotels bill your card for the entire cost of your stay as soon as they guarantee your reservation. If you'd rather not pay until you've been served, register your protest by selecting another hotel.

Other hidden costs can cause shockwaves at check-out time unless you ask the right questions before you check-in or before you use a service that can entail an out-of-line hidden charge.

- **Taxes and surcharges**—We expect our hotel bills to jump when taxes and surcharges are added, but the jumps have been getting higher. In some U.S. cities they add 15 percent to your bill. Many cities have added new hotel taxes to finance sports facilities (we all know how cash-strapped most pro sports team owners are). Staying at suburban locations can keep you from having to pay big city taxes. If you are planning a convention, ask about the tax rate as well as the room rate. Sometimes you can avoid high city taxes by booking in a suburban location. Internationally, hotel taxes can add as much as 25 percent to your bill, so special consideration is required.
- **Surcharges for payment by credit card** is a relatively rare problem that is prohibited by all credit card companies. Report any hotel or resort attempting to add a credit card surcharge to your bill.
- **Telephone surcharges**—This potential nightmare is covered in depth in *Calling From The Road*. There is a new twist of the price-gouging knife this year: $5 per day "communication fees" charged by some hotels, purportedly to cover local calls—but what if you never pick up the phone? Fax fees as high as $15 per *page* at some international hotels can provide major economic shock at check-out time.
- **Parking**—Ask to have parking included in your rate. Avoid mandatory valet parking that increases basic fees. Consider using shuttles, taxis and mass transit when staying at hotels that charge high fees for parking.

> "If you've tried in-room coffeemakers in the past and been dissatisfied with weak, inferior-grade coffee, give this money-saving option another try. Chains including Budgetel, Country Inn, Crowne Plaza, Hilton, Hyatt, ITT Sheraton and Wingate supply in-room coffeemakers and many locations are adding premium brand coffee. If you don't want to risk encountering brand-X, pack a few ounces of your favorite blend. It beats paying $15 a pot—and there is no waiting."

Most commonly stocked mini-bar items: bottled water, candy and beer.

> *"You can avoid many extra charges by joining frequent guest programs. They often waive fees for upgrades, health club use, rollaway beds and cribs, faxes, late check-out and extra-person charges. Hilton HHonors members, for example, have health club fees waived at many locations. Even if you pay a nominal membership fee, you are buying value worth many times the annual cost."*

- **Room service**—Room service minimums and service fees above and beyond the gratuity can give you indigestion even when the food is excellent. Some hotels bill you for a base or minimum charge even if you only order coffee. We have found mandatory service charges as high as 20 percent at some hotels—and that does *not* include the tip. The money goes to the hotel, not the server.
- **Laundry charges**—Minimize them with an extra shirt or blouse in your overnight bag. You can pay as much as $10 for laundering that costs $2 at your hometown cleaners.
- **Mini-bars**—Their best use is free refrigeration for items you buy outside the hotel and carry in. If you use already stocked items, you pay a premium price.
- **Bellman fees**—This service, usually yours for a discretionary tip, can appear as an added fee on group bookings.
- **Energy fees**—Some resorts, particularly in the Caribbean, should be given masters degrees in extra fee inventiveness. Energy fees cover that "extra" expense of electricity. There isn't a lot of money at stake, but shouldn't we be able to expect electricity to be included in the basic rate?

DECIPHERING LODGING LINGO

Read and interpret hotel rates and specials correctly by understanding the language that is used.

Terms for payment requirements:

Advance Deposit—A partial payment to secure your room, often required if you don't reserve with a major credit card; also pertains to credit card deposits.

Late Charges—Credit card billing additions added after you check out. They can include last minute room service, mini-bar purchases or telephone and fax charges. They can also include mistakes. Record any legitimate last-minute charges so you can verify them at check out. Hold on to your hotel receipt and your credit card statements for at least three months.

Terms that concern reservations:

Confirmed Reservation—Your room is guaranteed until a specified time—usually 4 or 6 p.m. in the time zone the hotel is located in. Be sure to verify the time.

Overbooking—There are no laws to protect you if you arrive and find that there is no room at the inn. You must rely on diplomatic insistence and the hotel's commitment to customer satisfaction. You want a comparable room in a nearby hotel (request that you get it at no

Most popular New York Novotel Hotel mini-bar item: for men, beer; for women, Evian water.

charge), taxi fare, a long distance call to advise your family and/or office where you will be and a discount or upgrade for a future stay. Make sure the switchboard is told to refer your calls.

Sold-Out—A changeable state. Hotels can be sold out one day and have rooms available the next. Hotels that *are* sold-out may accommodate you at a discount in the living-room of suites booked as single rooms.

Walk-in—A guest arriving without a reservation.

Rate descriptions:

Single Supplement—An additional charge for a single person occupying a double room.

Extended Stay—Five nights or longer at reduced rates. Some hotels offer an additional rate break at 30 days.

Soft Opening Rates—Discounts offered by new hotels or hotels near the end of major refurbishment.

Rate inclusions:

All-Inclusive—Meals, drinks and most activities are included. Policies vary so ask for full details. Can you order premium brand drinks? Are meals ordered from the full menu or are they buffet-style? Is tipping additional? All-inclusives do not include taxes. Some super-inclusives include tips and some taxes.

Continental Plan—Includes a light breakfast ranging from coffee and donuts to cereal, fruit and pastries. Ask for specifics.

European Plan—Meals are not included.

Full American Plan—Includes three meals from the hotel restaurant menu.

Modified American Plan—Includes three meals a day with some menu restrictions.

Room descriptions:

Connecting—Room-to-room access without going into public corridors. If you're booking multiple rooms and want them to connect, make your desire clear to avoid getting rooms separated by other rooms, across a hallway or even several floors apart.

Club or Concierge—Extra amenities at a higher rate. Specifics vary and can include food, beverages, business services and special access lounges. If you can live without a guaranteed upgrade, take a small gamble. Book at the lower rate, then request a free upgrade when you arrive. A frequent guest membership card is a big plus when requesting a courtesy upgrade.

Twin—Two single beds.

Double—Two single beds, one double bed, two double beds or a king-size bed in the U.S. (you have to ask); usually one double bed in Europe.

Junior Suite/Parlour Suite—Sleeping and sitting areas separated by a half-wall or partition.

One bedroom suite—Include junior suites and accommodations with separate living rooms, bedrooms and apartment-style

Number of guests who locked themselves out of New York Novotel Hotel rooms in 1996: 210.

kitchens.

Room locations:

Garden view—Usually the least scenic/least expensive option, often without a garden (or a flower) in sight.

Mountain view—Panoramic views or a few small hills beyond the parking lot.

Oceanfront—Facing the water but possibly with a four-lane highway or another hotel between you and the view.

Ocean view—A splendid view of the water or a speck of blue visible only to contortionists.

Types of hotels:

Boutique—Intimate and usually expensive with exemplary service, though moderately-prized boutique hotels are becoming more numerous.

Full Service—24-hour room service, fine restaurants, business centers and other amenities (some hotels use this term loosely).

Tourist Class—In the U.S., standardized, economy rooms with small bars of soap; in Europe, simple, comfortable rooms and the likelihood of a shared bath.

> *"You have the right to review your room before you check-in. If the room does not meet your standards or fails to fulfill any promise made when you made your reservation, let the front desk know immediately."*

HOTEL RATINGS

Accurate hotel ratings can be accessed by travel agents in the *Official Hotel Guide*, updated quarterly. Other guides are useful only if they offer subjective ratings with clearly stated criteria and are updated regularly. You will find systems utilizing stars, diamonds, suns and other designations but you may be left in the dark as to standards employed. Dependable consumer guides also include those offered by the American Automobile Association and Mobil.

Some international hotels are rated by their governments. These ratings tend to be based on basic statistics like room size and percentage of rooms with private baths.

BUSINESS AMENITIES

Business amenities are increasing. They include modem ports, in-room fax machines, two incoming phone lines and loaner computers. Business centers often offer access to printers, copy facilities, business supplies, on-site secretaries and translation services. Guests are usually charged by the hour for business center usage; some services are available with no extra charge. Premium business rates can include all business services. Rooms equipped with business features generally go for $15-20 above standard rates. Highly equipped rooms may cost $35-50 more. Many hotels offered by consolidators and discount hotel directories provide business amenity convenience as well as significant savings on room rates.

The true two-phone-line room is getting a little easier to find, to the relief of many business travelers. When you are making a reservation, be sure you are getting two separate lines, rather than two phones on the same line. Reservation agents aren't

Locked out guests who were in various stages of undress: 43 percent.

used to this question and can give confusing information. If you want a separate modem line be sure that's what you get.

AVAILABILITY OF POPULAR BUSINESS AMENITIES

AMENITY	PERCENTAGE OF HOTELS
Fax service	85.4%
Free fax	16.2%
800 Access Without Surcharge	64.8%
Free local calls	48.0%
In-room data ports	47.4%
Secretarial services	25.1%
Voice mail	21.6%
Teleconferencing	15.7%
Two-line phones	13.7%
In-room computers	2.2%

NEW TECHNOLOGIES

The techno-age is not being ignored. Many innovations are being tested. If any of these services are important to you, a word to the manager (to compliment their presence or ask that they be included) will carry maximum impact. This area is exploding with change and you can help it go in the directions you prefer. Recent innovations include:

- **Internet access**—Holiday Inn and Hilton took the lead in test-marketing guest internet access. Fourteen rooms at the Renaissance in Washington offer access. The Royal Garden in London offers Megastream links for guests' laptops and loans pre-loaded laptops to guests who need them. The wave of the future may be internet access through smart-TV.
- **Interactive television**—Pioneering hotels are bringing new technologies to guests by in-room television: internet options, electronic shopping services and information on local restaurants and attractions.
- **Telecommunications**—Hilton is investing over $35 million in a three-year program that will provide features including a toll-free number that will follow frequent guests around the world when they stay at Hilton hotels. Callers will be able to leave voice, fax or e-mail messages.
- **Cyberbooths**—Chains not willing or able to make major investments in in-room internet access are installing Cyberbooths (similar to those in airports) in lobbies, business centers or other public areas. Guests can surf the net and receive and send e-mail. Several California locations of Holiday Inn, Hilton, Countryside Suites, Embassy Suites and Crowne Plaza have opted for cyberbooths.
- **Entertainment, comfort and luxury options**—Holiday Inn's E-Space program debuted Cafe Connection (internet access and cybergames by the hour) and CyberArcades (eight computer playstations) at select properties. The Comfort Inn on the Philadelphia waterfront has a motion sensor that adjusts the temperature when you walk in the room. The Century Plaza in Los Angeles offers a $2,000 per night Cyber Suite with a voice-activated environmental system that will draw your bath on command.
- **Business options**—Select Hilton hotels offer TeleSuites for virtual reality teleconferencing that projects the images of all participants on a virtual reality screen. Promus (incorporating Embassy Suites, Hampton Inn

Average per day use for in-room fax machines: one minute.

and Homewood) lets you reserve rooms from General Motors rental cars equipped with OnStar navigation systems.

EXPRESS OPTIONS

Express check-in and check-out options are designed to attract guests and reduce overhead for the hotels.

Express check-in methods include:

- **Hand-held computers** operated by roving employees who check you in before you reach the front desk.
- **Pre-issued check-in folios** that are ready when you arrive. In some cases, you call for your room assignment and complete the check-in procedure by phone.
- **ATM-like machines** that issue your key after you respond to a few simple prompts.
- **Streamlined front desk procedures,** including guest profiles on file, designed to cut check-in time to a minute or less.

Express check-out methods include:

- **Bills slipped under your door** the night before departure.
- **Bills accessible for review via in-room television**. A few hotels let you print your own bill on your in-room printer.
- **Breakfast check-out** that delivers your bill to your hotel restaurant table.
- **Check-out by computer.** Unfortunately, if you find an error on your bill you end up at the back of the line you are trying to avoid.

THE CONCIERGE

The concierge is employed to assist guests with dinner reservations, travel plans, car rentals, theater and event tickets, childcare and countless other wants and needs. Mid-range hotels offer more limited concierge services. Luxury hotels provide concierges who have encyclopedic knowledge of the city and effective contacts who can sometimes make the seemingly impossible occur. If you appreciate the services a concierge provides, tip accordingly and let the management know. Some hotels are limiting concierge hours or doing away with them entirely as a means to reduce overhead. Others are expanding concierge options. Ask if the concierge is a hotel employee. Those who are not may try to steer you in the direction of the company that sponsors them. While this isn't necessarily a negative, it is a piece of information you deserve to know.

Don't be intimidated by what some guests see as an imposing concierge presence. Many have developed an air of authority as away to help assure guests that they are dealing with a man or woman with encyclopedic knowledge of their city. They are always there to help you and the best are unfailing gracious, even in the face of very challenging requests.

SMOKING POLICIES

If you smoke, or if you don't, the hotel industry is interested in giving you what you want. Most hotels set aside 20 to 50 percent of their rooms as non-smoking inventory. Many U.S. hotels are subject to municipal anti-smoking regulations. Boulder, Colorado and some California cities, for example, must ban smoking in all public areas. Hotels with a high percentage of international clientele and international locations set aside a lower percentage of non-smoking rooms and have more relaxed smoking policies in restaurants and other public areas.

It costs about $600 to effectively change a room from smoking to non-smoking. When occupancy is high, hotels are tempted to remove the ashtrays from rooms and call them non-smoking. If you are presented with a non-smoking room that bears the scent of cigarette smoke, request a new room, particularly if you are highly sensitive to smoke. Green Rooms are the best choice for people with severe smoke allergies or other sensitivities. They include air and water filters, hypo-allergenic toiletries and chemical-free carpeting. You will find them in some upper-end hotels, including Inter-Continental. The penalty for smoking in a non-smoking room? At worst, mild censure from the front desk.

> *"If you plan to conduct business meetings in your room or suite, take your colleague's smoking preferences into account."*

HOTEL SAFETY

Never leave your luggage unattended. If the front desk or bellman suggest you go to your room in advance of your luggage, ask for a receipt. Make sure all luggage is accounted for when you leave the taxi or shuttle and when you check-out.

The safest rooms are on preferred guest floors. On standard floors, a room near the elevator minimizes walks down deserted hallways.

If the desk clerk announces your room number at a volume that can be heard by anyone other than you, ask that it be changed. Women are free to register by using a first name initial, rather than a gender-identifying first name.

Valuables belong in the hotel safe or, better yet, at home. Liability for in-room theft is very limited. Liability for items in hotel safes varies by state and may be as low as $500. International liability limits tend to be higher. Homeowners insurance may cover items kept in hotel safes, but verify your coverage before you entrust your valuables. If you stash cash and valuables in your room, don't put them all in the same place. If a burglar strikes, he may find one item, then leave. Don't leave hidden items behind when you check out. Special locks for dresser drawers have become somewhat popular, but they are really like arrows pointing out where the good stuff is hidden.

Inspect the safety features of your room as soon as you check in. Read the safety notice posted on the door. Check patio doors, connecting doors and all locks. Plan a fire exit route. Although stairways in international hotels are not always fire-protected, they are safer options than elevators which should be avoided completely if there is any indication of smoke or fire. This is true even if you only need to travel one or two floors.

Lock in your safety by engaging locks when you are inside your room. A chain lock won't keep a determined person out, but it will slow him down and let him know the room is occupied. Leaving the "Do Not Disturb" sign on your door provides a little added security. Choose hotels with electronic card key locks with codes that change with every guest. Don't accept two keys unless there are two people using your room. Notify the desk immediately if your key is lost or stolen, even if your travel partner still has a key. Never lay your key on a restaurant table or leave

Most common bedtime for business travelers: 11 to 11:59 p.m.

it unattended in any public area.

Leave the television and one light on when you leave your room. The television can fool thieves into thinking your room is occupied; the light provides a measure of safety when you return.

Confirm identities before opening your door. If you haven't requested hotel staff, call the desk even if the person at the door is in a recognizable uniform. Don't invite strangers to your room. Their presence in the hotel guarantees nothing—not even that they are guests.

Unattended pool areas and workout rooms should be used with caution. They are only supposed to be used by registered guests, but security is often lax. Due to their relative isolation, workout rooms can be target areas for criminals.

Memorize the direct number to hotel security in case you need to reach them in an urgent situation. Contact security if you see anything suspicious. They're trained in discretion.

> *"Many hotels have installed small armies of security cameras. The Hyatt Regency Atlanta, for example, uses 50 cameras to survey public areas. The Crowne Plaza Miami installed video surveillance equipment and completely eliminated robbery and theft in the months following their installation."*

Use the main hotel entrance during low traffic periods, even if it means a longer route to your room.

Sleep with your room key and travel flashlight on the nightstand so you can find them immediately. Add any items you would want to take with you if you had to evacuate quickly.

Don't fall asleep wearing headphones or with the television or radio on. They can prevent you from hearing alarms and warning sounds. If soothing sounds help you fall asleep, place a small tape player next to your bed or program the radio to turn itself off in 30 minutes.

If you smell smoke and your room door feels hot, don't open it. Turn the air conditioner or heater off and put a wet towel at the base of the door. If the phone system is working, let the desk know you need assistance or call 911 and give them your room number.

HOTEL COMPLAINTS

Try to resolve all disputes while you are still at the hotel. There is always a manager on duty, anytime of the day or night. If you can't resolve your complaint with the first person you talk with, ask to speak with the manager on duty. If possible, wait for business hours when the most powerful management staff is available.

If you cannot get satisfaction from the hotel management your next step is the hotel chain's corporate office. The American Hotel & Motel Association represents the U.S. lodging industry and will mediate disputes that aren't resolved to your satisfaction. Write to 1201 New York Avenue NW, Washington, DC 20005-3931 or fax to 202-289-3199. You can reach them by phone at **202-289-3100**, but you will still be asked to send a written complaint.

Recent room service requests at New York's St. Regis: a pound of watermelon seeds and pizza in a blender.

HOTEL HIGHLIGHTS

Major changes transform the hotel industry year to year. Renaissance absorbed Stouffer and Marriott bought Renaissance. Doubletree purchased Red Lion. Hilton did its best to acquire ITT Sheraton (which began managing hotels in China). Hilton and Hilton International formed a powerful global alliance, bringing crossover benefits to travelers who travel to domestic and international locations. Choice created MainStay Suites; Marriott created Fairfield Suites; Wingate Inns made its debut.

The more you know about hotel chains, the better your decision-making capability. Most chains operate under the directives of the corporate office. Franchise hotels (Best Western, for example) exhibit more variance. Confirm all policies that are important to you before you make your reservations. This section looks at what the most prominent chains are doing to attract your business. Confirm any policy important to you before you place your reservation.

- **Basic daily room rates** are indicated as follows:

  $/$50 or less

  $$/$51-100

  $$$/$101-199

  $$$$/$200 and above

- **Rate breaks** include on-going offers and recurring promotions.
- **Senior** age minimums are listed in parentheses.
- **Frequent guest** programs are free, except where noted.

Note: Rate breaks, seniors and frequent guest categories have been omitted from individual listings when no official programs are offered.

- **GX** designates the standard guaranteed reservation deadline (all times are p.m.).
- **K** designates the age maximum for kids staying free in parents or grandparents rooms.
- **V** designates a wide degree of variance within a category.

ADAMS MARK (800-444-2326), 18 locations ($$$) plus two Florida resorts. **GX**/4; **K**/17.

- **Seniors**—(50 & AARP) discounts vary.
- **Frequent guests**—*Gold Mark* awards the 11th stay free; complimentary health club use, early check-in and late check-out and other benefits.

AMERISUITES (800-833-1516), 40 all-suite locations ($$). *Taking Care of Business* suites offer executive desks, speaker phones with dual lines and basic office supplies. Free continental breakfast, local transportation and local calls. **GX**/6; **K**/17.

- **Rate breaks**—AmeriStay discounts for seven-night or longer stays; SuiteEnds weekend bed and breakfast rates; two-for-one promotions.
- **Seniors**—(50 & AARP) ten to 33 percent.
- **Frequent guests**—*AmeriClub* awards a free night after 12 stays and offers discounts, added amenities and car rental discounts. *AmeriFun!* offers a free weekend stay after five paid weekend nights in one year.

ASTON (800-922-7866), 30 locations ($-$$$) on four Hawaiian islands: Oahu, Kauai, Maui and the Big Island. **GX**/None. Minimum one-night deposit required; **K**/17.

- **Rate breaks**—Discounts of 20 to 30 percent for seven-night or longer stays; *Astonishing Deals* coupon book presented at check-in; discount dining coupons; ten to 20 percent off car rentals; *Triple Great Rates* offer nightly discounts and free added nights; *ASTONishing Deals* vary by season and location.
- **Seniors**—(50) 50+/20 to 25 percent, seventh night free and discounted car rentals.
- **Frequent guests**—Aston Corporate Travel Club offers preferred rates, guaranteed reservations without deposit and 24-hour cancellation courtesy, with no penalty.

BEST WESTERN INTERNATIONAL (800-528-1234), 3,400 locations ($). Over 1,000 European locations, and 360 in Asia and the South Pacific. North American locations have on-premise food service or are within 500 feet of a restaurant. **GX**/6; **K**/V.

- **Rate breaks**—Added-value benefits that vary by location (for example, Honolulu Zoo passes in Waikiki, a two-for-one meal and other discounts); trucker discounts; *Best Rates* and *Breakaway Weekend Escapes* packages; Guestcheque vouchers for North and South America and the Caribbean; Euro-Guestcheques for over 900 hotels in seven price categories.
- **Seniors**— (50) Best Western Seniority offers 15 percent plus points redeemable for awards and gifts; Mature Benefits (55) ten percent.
- **Frequent guests**—Gold Crown Club International awards points redeemable for travel benefits. Young Travelers

Number of Gideon Bibles distributed annually: 43 million in 76 languages.

Club for children 16 and under awards points redeemable for games, CDs and other gifts.

BUDGET HOST INNS (800-283-4678), 180 locations ($) in 38 states and Canada. Calls to the toll-free number are directed to the inn you select. Free continental breakfast. **GX**/V; **K**/V.

- **Seniors**—(50) ten percent at most locations.

BUDGETEL INNS (800-428-3438), 135 U.S. locations ($). Business Plan rooms include fax machines, printers and modem jacks. Free continental breakfast. **GX**/6; **K**/18.

- **Rate breaks**—*Double Discounts* offer reduced rates plus frequent guest credits.
- **Seniors**—(55 & AARP) ten percent.
- **Frequent guests**—Roadrunner Club awards a free night after 12 stays.

CANADIAN PACIFIC (800-441-1414), 25 locations ($$$). Largest owner-operated hotel company in Canada. Chateau-style architecture and complete health clubs. Many rates provide data ports, portable phones and printers by request. Children get their own check-in counter and welcome gifts. **GX**/V; **K**/18.

- **Rate breaks**—AAA discounts up to 50 percent.
- **Seniors**—(65) ten to 30 percent.
- **Frequent guests**—Canadian Pacific Club provides late check-out, health club privileges and discounts at hotel shops. Reservations Plus Premium offers added benefits for business travelers.

CHOICE HOTELS, 3,147 locations with 861 under development.

Clarion (800-252-7466), 93 locations ($$) and 28 under development in the U.S. and 18 countries. Business Rooms include two-line speaker phones with data port, basic office supplies and in-room refrigerators. Biznet Centers offer personal computers, printers, fax and photocopiers. Food courts offer a variety of quick-dining options. **GX**/6; **K**/None.

Comfort (800-228-5150), 1,482 locations ($-$$) (84 suite locations) and 274 under development in the U.S. and 22 countries. Free continental breakfast and morning paper. Total money-back guarantee. Compact refrigerator and partitioned living/bedroom suites. **GX**/V; **K**/None.

Econo Lodge (800-553-2666), 681 locations ($) and 114 under development in the U.S. and Canada. Seniors (50) get 30 percent off with advance booking; 10 percent without. Econo Lodge and Rodeway Inns offer Senior Rooms with bright lighting, large-button phones, grab bars in baths and lever handles on doors and faucets. *Tips For Travelers Over 50* free by request at check-in. **GX**/V; **K**/18.

MainStay Suites (800-660-6246), 3 locations ($$) with 167 in development. Fully-equipped kitchens, complimentary continental breakfast, work space with data port and voice mail. **GX**/V; **K**/None.

Quality Inns, Hotels & Suites (800-228-5151), 592 locations ($$) and 113 under development in the U.S. and 26 countries. Executive Rooms with speaker phones, data ports, over-size desks and fax modems. Quality Suite rates include daily continental breakfast and evening manager's reception. **GX**/V; **K**/18.

Rodeway Inns (800-228-2000), 187

Hotels that place The Teachings of Buddha in their rooms: 1.9%.

locations ($-$$) and 36 under development in the U.S. and Canada. Free continental breakfast, newspaper and local phone calls. **GX**/V; **K**/18.

Sleep Inn (800-753-3746), 113 locations ($-$$) and 132 under development in the U.S., Canada and the Cayman Islands. Data ports, morning coffee and doughnuts and over-size showers rather than baths. **GX**/V; **K**/18.

CLUBHOUSE INNS (800-258-2466), 17 locations ($) in nine states. Rooms and suites. Free breakfast buffet, evening cocktails, local calls and long distance access. **GX**/6; **K**/16.

- **Rate breaks**—*Kickback Weekends* (November to March) include the third weekend night free; *Big Splash Weekends* (April to October) offer weekend discounts; *Double Play Weekends* offer double rates at single prices.
- **Seniors**—(AARP) ten to 25 percent.
- **Frequent guests**—Best Guest awards a free night after 12 stays.

COUNTRY INNS & SUITES (800-456-4000), 80 locations ($$) in the U.S., Canada and Mauritius. *Did You Forget* provides a dozen personal care items by request. *Kids Stuff* provides a fun package at check-in. Free continental breakfast, cookies and fruit throughout the day, local calls and long distance access. **GX**/6; **K**:/18.

- **Seniors**—(55 & AARP) ten percent.

DAYS INN (800-325-2525), 1,700 locations ($) in the U.S., Canada, Colombia, India, Israel, Mexico, the Netherlands, the Philippines and Puerto Rico with franchise agreements under way in 13 additional countries. **GX**/V; **K**/V.

- **Rate breaks**—*Sunbelievable* packages include admission to local attractions and events; *Simple Super Saver* offers $29-69 guaranteed rates at most properties with 29-days advance and pre-payment.
- **Seniors**—(49) *September Days* offers 15 to 50 percent off plus car rental and attraction discounts. Grandchildren eat free at many locations. $15 annual fee/$25 for two years; $33.50 for three years; $50 for five years.
- **Frequent guests**—Inn-Credible Club Card provides discounts, car rental bonuses and other benefits at $4.99 per year.

DELTA HOTELS (800-877-1133), 21 locations ($-$$$) in Canada and Orlando. A toll-free 24-hour concierge line is available for frequent guests even when they are not staying at the hotel. Overall service is exceptional. **GX**/6; **K**/18.

- **Seniors**—(55) discounts vary.
- **Frequent guests**—Delta Privilege members get free local calls, no long distance access charges, express check-out, upgrades and check-cashing privileges.

DOUBLETREE (800-222-8733), 216 locations ($$) in 37 states, the District of Columbia and Mexico. Includes Red Lion and Club Hotels. *Meetings by Fax* allows meeting planners to preview details of any property 24-hours a day. Signature chocolate chip cookies at check-in. **GX**/4; **K**/18.

- **Rate breaks**—*Dream Deals* offer two-for-one rooms and free breakfast; *DoubleTreat Weekends* discounts rates and offers added values, including 6 p.m. Sunday check-out; kids under 12 eat free.
- **Seniors**—(60 & AARP) ten to 30 percent.

Hotels that place the Book of Mormon in their rooms: 5.2% (mainly Mormon-owned Marriotts).

- **Club Hotels** target business travelers. There are 20 locations with 80 under development.

DRURY INNS (800-325-8300), 88 Midwest and Southern U.S. locations ($-$$). Free Quick Start breakfast, courtesy van and shuttle. **GX**/6; **K**/18.

- **Seniors**—(50) ten percent.
- **Frequent guests**—Preferred Customer membership provides the 11th night free and other benefits.

ECONOMY INNS OF AMERICA (800-826-0778), 22 locations ($-$$) in California, Florida and South Carolina. Free breakfast and local calls. **GX**/V; **K**/V.

- **Seniors**—(55) ten percent.

EMBASSY SUITES (800-362-2779), 140 locations ($$) in the U.S., Canada, Thailand and Colombia, recently incorporating Crown Sterling Suites. Vacation resorts in Florida and Hawaii. Your bill is waived if you are dissatisfied in any way and the problem is not immediately corrected. Any hotel employee (housekeeping to manager) can approve the guarantee. Seventy-five percent of inventory is non-smoking. Free cooked-to-order breakfast and evening manager's reception. **GX**/V; **K**/13.

- **Seniors**—(55) ten percent minimum.
- **Frequent guests**—Diplomat Club offers various discounts and added values.

EXEL INN (800-356-8013), 26 locations ($) primarily in the Midwest, South Dakota and Texas. Living Rooms include kitchens, extra-long beds, expanded closet space and shower massage. Deluxe King Rooms include in-room coffee makers and shower massage. Free continental breakfast, local calls and microfridges on request. **GX**/V; **K**/17.

- **Seniors**—(55) ten percent.
- **Frequent guests**—The Insiders Card awards a free night after 12 stays.

EXTENDED STAY AMERICA (800-398-7829), 60 locations ($-$$) in 20 states with rapid development scheduled. Weekly rates average $189-299. Free local calls. **GX**/V

FAIRMONT HOTELS (800-522-3437), seven U.S. locations ($$$) with deluxe amenities. **GX**/V; **K**/V.

- **Rate breaks**—honeymoon/anniversary promotions; Sale Savers with rates as low as $69; recent promotion offered a $99 American Airlines companion certificate with each stay.
- **Seniors**—(AARP) discounts vary.
- **Frequent guests**—The President's Club awards points redeemable for miles, upgrades and car rental and suite upgrades at nominal cost.

FIESTA AMERICANA (800-343-7821), 40 locations ($$-$$$) in Mexico. **GX**/V; **K**/12.

- **Seniors**—(55) discounts vary.
- **Frequent guests**—Guest Awards program at some locations provides added-values.

FORTE, GRAND & LE MERIDIEN (800-225-5843), 250 locations ($$$) in the U.S., Europe and the Middle East. Includes London's Hyde Park and The Watergate in Washington. **GX**/V; **K**/V.

- **Rate breaks**—*Summer and Winter Passport* programs offer discounts of 30 to 50 percent; the Forte 30 program offers 30 percent off at 200 hotels in 23 countries with 30-day advance and credit card confirmation.
- **Frequent guests**—Forte's Corporate Privilege program guarantees room

Asking price for an 87-room Days Inn in Alabama: $2.6 million.

availability with added benefits, including ten percent off meals at all U.K. hotels.

FOUR SEASONS AND REGENT (800-332-3442), 43 locations ($$$-$$$$) in the U.S., Canada, Europe, Asia, Australia and the South Pacific. Fourteen properties are AAA five-diamond award winners. Ultimate amenities include European-style full-service concierges, twice-daily maid service, check-in as early as you like providing rooms are available and complimentary airport shuttle via limousine. **GX**/6; **K**/18.

- **Rate breaks**—*Kids for All Seasons* resort programs.

GOLDEN TULIP WORLDWIDE HOTELS (800-344-1212), 300 locations ($$$-$$$$) in the Americas, Africa, Asia, Europe and the Far East. **GX**/V; **K**/V.

- **Seniors**—(60) ten percent at some locations.

GRAND HERITAGE (800-437-4824), 46 locations ($-$$$) in the U.S. and Europe. **GX**/V; **K**/V.

- **Seniors**—(55) discounts vary.
- **Frequent guests**—Heritage Rewards provides upgrades to Executive Level rooms. U.S. locations award points redeemable for Tiffany gifts.

HAMPTON INNS (800-426-7866), 14 locations ($) concentrated in the Eastern U.S. Free local calls. **GX**/6; **K**/17.

- **Seniors**—(50) Lifestyle 50 offers benefits including up to four guests per room at the single rate.

HAWTHORN SUITES (800-527-1133), 19 locations ($$) primarily in the Southern U.S. Newer locations have mini-convenience marts in the lobby. Free breakfast and evening reception. **GX**/V; **K**/18.

- **Rate breaks**—Hot 'N Suite offers bonus tickets to area attractions.
- **Seniors**—(AARP) discounts vary.

HILTON (800-445-8667), 403 locations worldwide ($$) including Hilton, Hilton International, Conrad International and Vista. Extensive business amenities. Most hotels have dual line phones and have dropped phone access fees. Hilton Garden Inns mark the chain's entry into the budget/suburban market. SmartDesk rooms include full-size desk, Intel-486 computer with all major business programs, fax modem, and laser printer/copier with parallel cable for laptop printing. Vacation Station provides amenities and services for families, including welcome gifts and free use of toys, games and Sega video systems. Available at 80 properties Memorial Day through Labor Day and at 30 properties year-round. Sleep-Tight rooms have special noise- and light-proofing features. **GX**/6; **K**/18.

- **Rate breaks**—*BounceBack Weekend* rates start at $79 including continental breakfast; *Summer World of Savings* at international hotels offers discounts of up to 30 percent plus Hertz upgrades; special promotions offer discounts of up to 40 percent to Eurail ticket holders; Day Break rates in Europe and at select U.S. airport locations are half the usual rate and come with a toiletry kit, t-shirt and slippers.
- **Seniors**—(60) Senior HHonors offers 20 to 25 percent off, 20 percent off many restaurant meals and discounts on Hertz car rentals. Membership is $50 per year; $265 lifetime.
- **Frequent guests**—HHonors Worldwide awards points and miles, priority reservations and express service. Double-dipping allows great flexibility in changing points to miles and miles to

Asking price for a 30-room Super 8 in California: $875,000.

points. Members can purchase five advance upgrade certificates for $100; $75 for Gold VIP members.

HOLIDAY INN (800-465-4329), the world's largest single hotel brand, with 2,200 locations ($-$$$) in 60 countries. Ninety are company owned; the remainder are franchises. Kids under 12 eat free from a special children's menu at over 1,100 hotels. **GX/6**; **K/19**.

- **Rate breaks**—*Best Breaks* weekend packages and *Great Rates*, provide up to 50 percent off; *Family Great Rates* offering discounts plus free meals for children; *Weekender Plus* offers bed and breakfast rates in Europe, the Middle East and Africa; *Europe For Less* offers $99 and $129 guaranteed rates in 120 European locations; second night free offers are promoted through newspaper and magazine ads.
- **Seniors**—The Alumni Club (60) offers 20 percent off to seniors, complimentary continental breakfast, a ten percent meal discount (even if you're not a guest) and two-for one birthday dinners. The $10 annual membership fee is waived the first year.
- **Frequent guests**—The Priority Club frequent guest program includes all Holiday Inn divisions except Holiday Inn Express. Benefits include room upgrades and extended check-out. There is a $10 annual fee.

Designations within Holiday Inn include:

- **Crowne Plaza**—Designed for business travelers desiring a high level of amenities.
- **Holiday Inn**—Full-service hotels in city-centers, small towns, airport and highway locations.
- **Holiday Inn Express**—Upper economy with free local calls and breakfast.
- **Crowne Plaza & SunSpree Resorts**—Leisure destinations. Crowne Plaza is high-end; SunSpree is moderately priced.
- **Holiday Inn Garden Court**—Three-star properties in small European towns and cities.
- **Holiday Inn Select**—Urban and suburban hotels oriented to business travelers.
- **Holiday Inn Hotel & Suites**—Ninety-percent guest rooms/ten percent two-room suites for extended stay travelers.

HOMEWOOD SUITES (800-225-5466), 37 U.S. locations ($$) built around hospitality centers that include a convenience store, exercise center, laundry, meeting space and business center. Free breakfast, evening reception and local calls. **GX/6**; **K/V**.

- **Rate breaks**—Discounts for six or more consecutive nights.
- **Seniors**—(50) discounts vary.

HOTEL SOFITEL (800-221-4542), over 100 locations ($$$) in the U.S., Asia, Africa, Europe, the Caribbean, the Middle East and South America. **GX/V**; **K/V**.

- **Rate breaks**—*Summer Sale* discounts of as much as 57 percent plus 50 percent off the reduced rate for second-night stays at some locations; voucher program covers bed and breakfast at 40 city-center hotels in 11 countries; one child under 12 stays free with an adult; *Invitation Enfants* provides a second room at 50 percent off at 45 European hotels; *Weekend Escapes* discounts North American weekend nights and adds free amenities; *Best Of France Invitations* offers added values for one and two night stays in eight French cities.
- **Seniors**—(60) discounts vary.

Annual savings from Inter-Continental's North American eco-conscious toiletries program: over $300,000.

- **Frequent guests**—The Exclusive Card ($68/leisure traveler; $125/business traveler) offers North American guests 15 percent off weeknight rates and 50 percent off weekend rates, free nights, car rental and meal discounts, welcome gifts and other added values.

HOWARD JOHNSON (800-446-4656), 600 locations ($-$$) including Howard Johnson Plazas, Park Square Inns, Lodges and HoJo Inns. **GX**/6; **K**/17.

- **Rate breaks**—Fall Sale, Winter Sale, Spring Sale and Summer Sale; special promotions often offer a discount coupon for Continental Airlines with just one stay.
- **Seniors**—(60 or AARP) Golden Years Travel Club offers 15 to 50 percent off plus discounts on car rentals, airfares and insurance. Lifetime membership is $29.95/couples or singles.
- **Frequent guests**—Business Traveler Club offers awards including airfare discounts, auto club membership and cellular phones. Current new member bonus includes a Continental Airlines discount of up to $75.

HYATT (800-233-1234), approximately 155 hotels ($$$) in 33 countries. BusinessPlan rooms offer in-room fax, printer, copier and express breakfast. Camp Hyatt for kids offers special rates and supervised activities for ages three to 12 at about 100 locations. Costs vary by property and average $7 per hour. Some promotional specials include Camp Hyatt days. Some programs are seasonal. **GX**/6; **K**/18.

- **Rate breaks**—Hyatt Vacations packages include hotel stays, airfare and car rentals; *Free Fall Nights* offers free added nights at U.S. and Caribbean resorts; families get 50 percent off second rooms.
- **Seniors**—(62) 25 percent at most hotels and meal discounts at many locations.
- **Frequent guests**—Gold Passport awards points redeemable for travel benefits.

INTER-CONTINENTAL (800-327-0200), 182 worldwide locations ($$$), including Forum and other global partners. **GX**/V; **K**/14.

- **Rate breaks**—*Leisure Options* gives you your choice of a food and beverage credit, suite upgrade, free parking, second room at half-off or double miles; *Global Business Options* provides similar benefits internationally; Winter Spectacular offers discounts as high as 60 percent in Europe, Africa and the Middle East.
- **Frequent guests**—Six Continents Club requires a $100 enrollment fee and $25 per-year membership renewal, waived for Executive card holders each year they qualify. Members receive exceptional promotional discounts, including occasional free companion airfares, guaranteed room upgrades, double occupancy at single rates and other added values. Thirty stays in a 12 month period earns the Executive Card with upgrades to executive rooms and suites.

ITT SHERATON (800-325-3535), 416 locations ($$-$$$), including 50 Luxury Collection hotels and mid-range Four Points hotels. Business Rooms may include computers, laser printers and fax machines. **GX**/4; **K**/17.

- **Rate breaks**—*SureSaver* discounts of five to 40 percent; *Endless Weekend* rates including breakfast and late check-out (maximum discounts usually require 14-days advance); free added nights at resort locations; *Freedom of*

Europe promotions offer up to 30 percent off with no minimum stay requirement.

- **Seniors**—(60 & AARP) 25 percent; grandchildren stay free in the same room.
- **Frequent guests**—Club International basic membership is free and offers special rates and two-for-one promotions. Upgrade to Gold ($25 per year) and earn points at an accelerated rate, automatic upgrades when available, guaranteed 4 p.m. check-out and free airline upgrades. Members also may check in as early as 9 a.m. and check-out as late as 5 p.m. at 72 participating U.S. and Canadian locations.

KEMPINSKI (800-426-3135), 20 locations ($$$$) in the Americas, Asia and Europe. **GX**/48-hr; **K**/16.

- **Rate breaks**—Winter discounts bring rates as low as $110-150.
- **Seniors**—(65) discounts vary.

KNIGHTS INNS (800-843-5644), 210 franchise locations in 19 states ($). **GX**/V; **K**/17.

- **Seniors**—(50) ten percent.
- **Frequent guests**—The Royalty Club provides discounts and added values.

LA QUINTA (800-531-5900), 240 locations ($-$$) primarily in the Sunbelt. Gold Medal Rooms include desks, 25-inch televisions with smart cards and dataports on all phones. Free breakfast, local calls and airport shuttle at most locations. La Quinta Inn & Suites ($$) offer apartment-style ambiance with extra amenities. **GX**/6; **K**/18.

- **Seniors**—(65 & AARP) ten to 15 percent.
- **Frequent guests**—Returns Club provides the 12th night free, express service options and a room rate below the standard corporate rate. You can enroll after three stays.

LOEWS (800-223-0888), 14 locations ($$$) in the U.S., Canada and Monaco. Business-class rooms include computer work stations, printers and dataports. Star Service lets you access most hotel services at one central number. **GX**/V; **K**/17.

- **Rate breaks**—Summer Sale; American Express promotions with second rooms at half-price; Visa promotions offer discounts and added miles.
- **Seniors**—(65) discounts vary.
- **Frequent guests**—Loews First provides upgrades, guaranteed room availability with 48-hours notice, welcome amenities, complimentary fitness center use and other benefits.

MARRIOTT subdivides into several divisions including 1,144 properties in the 50 states and 28 countries. They recently acquired 158 Renaissance hotels in 38 countries (see separate Renaissance listing). Rate breaks, varying by division, include *Two For Breakfast* with discount rates, complimentary breakfast and bonuses that may include free meals for two children ten and under with each adult entree purchased and 25 percent off adult dinners.

Courtyard by Marriott (800-321-2211), 285 locations ($$) in the U.S. and ten in the U.K. King-beds in 70 percent of inventory. Dataports and separate seating areas. Two-phone-line rooms coming soon. Seniors who are AARP members get discounts of 15 percent. Non-member seniors can request the discount. The Courtyard Club ($10 annually) offers one night free after 12 paid nights, $20 in Courtyard Cash when joining or

Hotel amenity that has all but disappeared due to lack of guest use: electric blankets.

renewing and other benefits. **GX**/6; **K**/18.

Fairfield Inn and Fairfield Suites (800-228-2800), 283 U.S. locations ($-$$). Free continental breakfast. Seniors (62) get a ten percent discount; AARP members get 15 percent. INNsiders Club offers a free night after 12 paid and other benefits. **GX**/6; **K**/17.

Marriott Hotels, Resorts & Suites (800-228-9290), 252 U.S. locations ($$-$$$), Extensive business amenities. Rate breaks include *Two for Breakfast* weekend promotions with discounts of up to 40 percent, breakfast, dinner discounts, late Sunday check-out and car rental upgrades. Senior discounts vary. AARP members generally get ten percent off; some locations offer as much as 50 percent off with 21-day advance. Frequent guests get their choice of Honored Guest Awards with bonus points for frequent stays or Marriott Miles. **GX**/6; **K**/18.

Residence Inns (800-331-3131), 195 locations ($$) in 42 states. Complimentary visitor's suites for the use of families of extended stay guests. Complimentary breakfast and weekly barbecues. Seniors (62 & AARP) receive discounts of 15 to 40 percent. **GX**/6; **K**/18.

MICROTEL (888-771-7171), 75 U.S. franchise locations ($) with over 100 under development. **GX**/4 or 6; **K**/16.

MOTEL 6 (800-466-8356), 770 locations ($), primarily in the West and Southwest. Small pets (under 20 pounds) accepted at all locations. New locations include elevators, interior corridors, modem hook-ups, free local calls and fax and free HBO and ESPN. **GX**/6; **K**/17.

- **Seniors**—(55) ten percent.

NATIONAL 9 INNS (800-524-9999), 100 locations ($) in Western states. **GX**/4; **K**/V.

- **Seniors**—(50 & AARP) ten percent.

NIKKO HOTELS INTERNATIONAL (800-645-5687), 43 locations ($$$$) in Asia, the Pacific and the U.S. **GX**/V; **K**/V.

- **Seniors**—(AARP) 25 percent.

OMNI HOTELS (800-843-6664), 35 locations ($$$) in the East and Southeast. **GX**/V; **K**/V.

- **Rate breaks**—*Supersavers* and *Emotional Rescue* promotions offer discounts of up to 50 percent.
- **Seniors**—(AARP) up to 50 percent with advance reservations.
- **Frequent guests**—Select Guest offers discounts and added values.

OUTRIGGER HOTELS (800-462-6262), 30 Hawaiian locations ($-$$$). **GX**/pre-payment or deposit required; **K**/17.

- **Rate breaks**—Free breakfast; first night free and free rental car promotions.
- **Seniors**—(50) 20 percent; AARP/25 percent.

PAN PACIFIC (800-327-8585), 14 locations ($$$-$$$$) in Bangladesh, Bangkok, China, Japan, Hawaii, Hong Kong, Indonesia, San Francisco, Singapore and Vancouver. **GX**/V; **K**/V.

- **Rate breaks**—*Pacific Plus* discount promotions.
- **Frequent guests**—Pacific Club International offers discounts, late check-outs and upgrades.

Radisson location that was formerly a territorial prison: Stillwater, Minnesota.

PREFERRED HOTELS (800-323-7500), 110 U.S. and 23 international locations ($$$-$$$). Some locations allow guests to check-in and out at the time of their choice as long as a 24-cycle is observed. **GX/V**; **K/V**.

- **Seniors**—Age and discounts vary by location.

RADISSON (800-333-3333), 305 locations ($$-$$$) in 39 countries range from budget Radisson Inns to high-end Radisson Plazas. Radisson Business Class (available in over 200 hotels in 23 countries) provides full breakfast, dataport, free phone calls, movies, fax service, computer hookup and coffee. **GX/6**; **K/V**.

- **Rate breaks**—*Shades of Summer* from May to September offers 30 to 50 percent off plus free breakfast; *Great Fall Rates* from September to December; *Shades of Winter Bed and Breakfast Breakaways* at 290 hotels include weekend discounts and breakfast.
- **Seniors**—(50) ten to 30 percent on rooms, food and beverages.

RAMADA (800-272-6232), 700 locations ($-$$$) ranging from budget Ramada Limiteds to high-end Ramada Plazas. **GX/4**; **K/17**.

- **Rate breaks**—*Super Saver Weekend* rates offer discounts of up to 50 percent; *Bed & Breakfast Weekend* promotions offer the same discount plus breakfast for two; kids 12 and under eat free at participating locations.
- **Seniors**—(60) Best Years Club offers discounts of 25 percent and award points. Lifetime membership/$15.
- **Frequent guests**—The Ramada Business Card awards points redeemable toward travel expenses and merchandise, preferred rates and other benefits.

RED ROOF INNS (800-843-7663), 242 locations ($) primarily in the Eastern U.S. **GX/6**; **K/18**.

- **Seniors**—(60) The Senior RediCard offers ten percent off room rates, $15 in discount coupons and other added values. Lifetime membership/$10; $12/couples.
- **Frequent guests**—RediCard at $10 per year provides three $5 discount coupons issued three times annually.

RENAISSANCE (800-228-9898), 150 locations ($$$) in 38 countries. **GX/V**; **K/V**.

- **Rate breaks**—*Breakation* summer rates start at $69.
- **Seniors**—(60) receive standard discounts up to 25 percent and special discounts of up to 50 percent at some properties.
- **Frequent guests**—Club Express (the Americas and Europe) awards points for every dollar spent—even restaurant meals when you are not a current guest. The Prestige Card offers benefits and discounts in the Asia Pacific region.

RITZ-CARLTON (800-241-3333), 29 locations ($$$-$$$$) in the U.S., Australia, Hong Kong, Indonesia, Korea, Mexico, Singapore, Spain and the U.S. Virgin Islands. Club Rooms ($50-100 above standard rates) include five complimentary food and beverage services daily, in-room VCRs and fax machines. All properties offer 24-hour babysitting services; resorts offer programs for ages four-13. many locations are very pet - friendly. **GX/V**; **K/17**

- **Rate breaks**—Summer rate discounts; American Express promotions.
- **Seniors**—(AARP) discounts vary.

Time it took the Atlanta Ritz-Carlton to knock down a wall to enlarge a room for a waiting guest: six hours.

SHILO INNS (800-222-2244), 46 locations ($-$$) in Western states. **GX**/V; **K**/12.

- **Seniors**—(60) ten percent.

SHONEY INNS (800-222-2222), 79 locations ($) in 19 states, primarily in the Southeast and Midwest. Free local calls, newspaper and breakfast at some locations. **GX**/6; **K**/18.

- **Seniors**—(55) ten percent; (AARP) 15 percent discount.
- **Frequent guests**—The Sho-Business Club provides discounts and added values.

SIGNATURE INNS (800-822-5252), 23 locations ($$) in Iowa, Illinois, Indiana, Ohio, Kentucky and Tennessee. Signature rooms offer work centers including modem ports. Free Guest office use, continental breakfast and local calls. **GX**/6; **K**/17.

- **Rate breaks**—Discounts at area restaurants when you show your room key; Saver Rates offer seasonal discounts on weekend stays; Family Plan offers two rooms at single room rates.
- **Seniors**—(AARP) ten percent.
- **Frequent guests**—Signature Club offers discounts and added values.

SUPER 8 (800-800-8000), 1,500 locations ($) in the 48 states and Canada. Most locations offer free coffee, local calls and fax service. **GX**/V; **K**/12.

- **Seniors**—(50) average ten percent.
- **Frequent guests**—VIP Club provides discounts of ten percent and 15 percent off Alamo car rentals. $3.50 one-time fee. Corporate memberships are also available.

SUSSE CHALET (800-524-2538), 36 locations ($) in New England and Mid-Atlantic states. Data ports in 30 percent of inventory. **GX**6 ; **V**/18.

- **Rate Breaks**—Recently offered eight to 14 days free parking and free airport shuttle to guests spending one night at several airport locations.
- **Seniors**—(60) ten percent at most locations.
- **Frequent Guests**—VIP membership gives free nights after six to eight paid nights.

SWISSOTEL (800-637-9477), 13 locations ($$$) in the U.S., Europe, the Middle East and Asia. Swissotel is owned by Swissair. **GX**/6; **K**/11.

- **Rate breaks**—Show your Swissair flight coupon for a free room upgrade; families get second rooms at discounts varying by location; weekend rates vary by location; hotel business centers are free for the first two hours.
- **Seniors**—(AARP, NAARP, 60) Retired guests present proof-of-age at check-in for discounts varying by location.
- **Frequent guests**—Club Swiss offers discounted rates, free upgrades, no phone access fees for 800 and credit card calls, continental breakfast, 25 percent off business center services and other benefits.

THISTLE HOTELS (800-847-4358), 100 locations ($$$) in the U.K. Many contain awarding-winning restaurants. **GX**/6; **K**/None.

- **Rate breaks**—*Pound for Dollar* discounts rooms by up to $100 per night with a two-night minimum
- **Seniors**—(55/United Silver Wings members only) discounts vary.

THRIFTLODGE (800-525-9055), 40 locations ($) in the U.S. and Canada.

Winner of the 1996-97 "Loo of the Year" award: The Tower Thistle Hotel in London.

GX/V; **K**/17.

- **Rate breaks**—*Travel Break Rates* offer discounts of ten to 20 percent.
- **Seniors**—(50) ten percent; (AARP) 15 percent.
- **Frequent guests**—Gold Guest Rewards provides the 11th night free and other benefits.

TRAVELERS INN (800-633-8300) 34 Western locations ($). **GX/**6; **K/**11.

- **Seniors**—(50) discounts vary.

TRAVELODGE (800-578-7878), 450 locations ($) in the U.S., Canada, Mexico, Puerto Rico, Europe & Australia. **GX/**6; **K/**17.

- **Rate breaks**—Sixth night free; *TravelBreak* promotions offer discounts of ten to 60 percent.
- **Seniors**—(50) The Classic Travel Club/15 percent.
- **Frequent guests**—Guest Rewards in the U.S. and Canada provides free nights, upgrades and car rental discounts and upgrades. Earn Silver status after ten stays; Gold after 20.

VAGABOND INNS (800-522-1555), 48 locations ($) in the Western U.S. Free continental breakfast and airport shuttle at some locations. **GX/**4; **K/**18.

- **Seniors**—(55) Club 55/minimum ten percent.
- **Frequent guests**—Your tenth stay is free. Business Club offers a more rapidly earned free stay benefits plus added values.

WALT DISNEY WORLD HOTELS include 13 properties under various management entities. We strongly suggest you confer with your travel agent rather than attempting to research all rate, discount and amenity possibilities. Some information is available online, via the main Disney site. Most properties include rooms and suites and offer special Disney benefits.

- **Buena Vista Palace & Spa**—1,014 rooms on 27 acres ($$$).
- **Courtyard By Marriott**—323 rooms in Hotel Plaza near Disney Village ($$).
- **Doubletree Guest Suites Resort**—229 suites each sleep six. The only all-suite hotel within Disney Village ($$$).
- **Grosvenor Resort**—629 rooms in Disney Village ($$$).
- **Hilton Resort**—814 rooms a short walk from Disney Village Marketplace and Pleasure Island ($$$).
- **Hotel Royal Plaza**—394 rooms with private balconies or terraces, facing Walt Disney Village ($$$).
- **Polynesian Resort**—853-rooms; South Sea island motif; monorail service to the Magic Kingdom ($$$$).
- **Port Orleans Resort**—French Quarter ambiance with water theme park ($$$).
- **The Villas At Disney Institute**—585 villas; packaged Disney Institute programs (three days/$499).
- **Walt Disney World Dolphin**—1,509-rooms surrounded by Epcot, Disney-MGM Studios and Disney's Boardwalk ($$$$).
- **Walt Disney World Swan**—758-room Westin hotel allowing park admission one hour before the general public ($$$$).
- **Wilderness Lodge**—728 rooms with national park ambiance ($$$).
- **Yacht And Beach Club Resorts**—630- and 583-room New England

Amount budgeted by Westin to launch an ad campaign to appeal to "hip" travelers: $145 million.

1800's theme resorts within walking distance of Epcot and the Boardwalk ($$$$).

WESTIN (800-228-3000), 99 locations ($$$) in 22 countries. Travel Light provides toothbrush, toothpaste, razor, hair dryer and alarm clock. Guest Office rooms include laser printers, copy and fax machines, direct fax lines, speaker phones with dataports and no surcharge on local, toll-free, credit card calls and incoming and outgoing faxes. Children get gift packs, planned activities and movies. Request a Safety Kit with night light, outlet covers and children's ID bracelets. **GX**/6; **K**/18.

- **Rate breaks**—Free meals for children 12 and under dining with parents; *Worldwide Weekend Values* offer discounts and added amenities; Visa promotions offer triple miles and 50 percent off future stays.
- **Seniors**—(V) discounts vary. United Silver Wings members get additional discount offers.
- **Frequent guests**—Westin Premier offers daily credit toward breakfast, check-cashing privileges, discounts and award points. Burgundy and Gold levels increase benefits.

WINGATE INNS (800-228-1000), 10 U.S. locations ($$) and 290 in development. In-room cordless phones, two-line desk phones with dataport, portable phones for use within the hotel, free local calls and no long distance surcharges. **GX**/V; **K**/17.

- **Senior**—(60) 15 percent at some locations.

WYNDHAM (800-996-3426), 69 locations ($$-$$$) in the U.S., Bermuda and the Caribbean. Phones with dataports. Free long distance phone access, voice mail and daily newspaper. **GX**/V; **K**/V.

- **Rate breaks**—Weekend packages can include tickets to area attractions and meals; *Third Weekend Night Free* promotions; holiday promotions at select hotels; triple upgrades for American Airlines frequent flyers on flights, hotel stays and car rentals.
- **Seniors**—(AARP) minimum ten percent; as much as 50 percent at Caribbean resorts.
- **Frequent guests**—Wyn Club provides upgrades, complimentary breakfast and other benefits.

Length of time it took the Stratosphere/Las Vegas to record its millionth visitor: three months.

OTHER LODGING OPTIONS

BED & BREAKFASTS

Bed & Breakfasts offer rooms in home-like settings, usually including at least one meal. Before choosing a bed & breakfast, determine the answers to the following questions:

- Is there a private bath?
- Is there a phone and/or television in the room?
- Are there pets in the house?
- Is smoking permitted?
- Do guests have kitchen privileges?
- Are children permitted and welcomed?
- Which meals are included and when are they served?
- Are there locks on guest room doors?
- What forms of payment are accepted?
- What are the cancellation policies?

Find bed & breakfasts by checking newspaper travel sections or through a specialized bed & breakfast service. Don't rely on any guidebook over a year old.

The Thrifty Family Bed and Breakfast Club, 800-599-3730, provides lodging worldwide at about $10 per night for a family of four. You may sleep on the floor in sleeping bags or you may have a private room. An annual $50 membership gives you the information you need to arrange stays directly with host families.

American Historic Inns offers a free second night at any of 1,600 locations when you purchase *Bed & Breakfasts and Country Inns*, an extensive guidebook by Deborah Sakach, for $19.20. Call **714-499-8070**.

HOSTELS

Hostels are available worldwide. Some are basic. Others have pools, coffee bars, bike rentals, scuba lessons and other amenities. Most offer accommodations ranging from dormitories to private rooms.

Make sure a particular hostel meets your needs:

- Are men and women housed in separate dorms?
- Are family rooms or private rooms available?
- Are there set times when you must be up and about and when you must be back in your room?
- Are there kitchen facilities and/or communal meals?
- Should you bring your own towel and soap or bedding?
- Is a membership card required? Will you receive a discount if you join?
- Is there a limit on the length of stay?

Sources for information on hostels include:

- **Hostelling International**, listing over 5,000 member hostels. Annual membership is $10 for individuals under 18; $15 for individuals age 54 and above; $25 for other adults. Family memberships are $35. When you join, request a copy of the

Number of heart-shaped bathtubs at resorts in the Poconos: 888.

Hostelling Guide (separate editions for North America and other location). You also get discounts on lodging and discounts on some attractions, dining option and transportation sources. Call **202-783-6161**; write to HI-AYH, P.O. Box 377613, Washington, DC 20013. If you aren't ready to join HI-AYH but would like a copy of any of their guides, you can purchase them separately. The North America guide, for example, is $2 and includes location, amenities, rates and hours for approximately 225 locations.

- **A more extensive guide to North America hostels** lists over 600 options (including HI-AYH hostels). It is available for $4. Call **212-926-7030**. Order by mail (checks must be made out to compiler Jim Williams): 722 St. Nicholas Avenue, New York, NY 10031.
- **Surf the Web** for hostel locations at **www.hostels.com**.
- **ElderHostel**, **617-426-7788**, offers packages combining lodging, meals and activities. Accommodations range from university dormitories to deluxe hotels. Prices for the U.S. and Canada can be great deals. European prices are usually close to the price of standard package tours but offer special features.

> *"Best Fares spotlights new and unique hostels, including a near-Disney World lake-front hostel at $13-16 per night, a 70-bed, fully-restored Victorian hostel in Sacramento at $13-15 per night and private bungalows in Hollywood at $45 per night."*

UNIVERSITIES

University and College rooms usually go for $15-30 per day. They are most available in summer, but some are offered year-round. Some institutions offer deluxe lodging in faculty homes and apartments.

700 U.S. and international schools offering accommodations are available by sending $12.95 for *U.S. and Worldwide Travel Accommodations Guide*, Campus Travel Service, Box 5483, Fullerton, CA 92636. It also lists YMCA's, YWCA's, bed and breakfasts, farms, cottages and home exchange programs.

A free listing of 60 British universities offering private rooms and family lodging can be acquired by writing to the General Secretary, British University Accommodations, Box 1165, University Park, Nottingham NG72RD England, or by calling **011-44-115-950-45-71**.

> *"Most university libraries have a wealth of university accommodation guides. Copy the pages that interest you and take them home for further study and contact."*

YMCA'S AND YWCA'S

YMCA's and YWCA's are available in the U.S. and in Europe. International travelers are big fans of Y's in the U.S. You might be too. Get domestic YMCA information by calling **312-977-0031** or by writing to 101 N. Wacker Dr., Chicago, IL 60606. For YWCA's: **212-273-7800** or Empire State Building, 350 Fifth Avenue, Suite 301, New York, NY 10118. Call **212-308-2899** for international locations and rates.

RETREATS

Ashrams, monasteries and retreats offer inexpensive, peaceful lodging options. Some require you to contribute a bit of work. Others accept you on a guest-only basis. Tourism Offices in specific countries (including Spain and Italy) have free listings of monasteries and abbeys that take guests. *U.S. and Worldwide Guide to Retreat Center Guest Houses* ($17.95 postpaid) lists many options. Write to CTS Publications, Box 8355, Newport Beach, CA 92660. Call **714-720-3729**. Options at $15-40 per night include:

- **The Trappist Monastery in Hong Kong, 852-2987-6292**—includes three meals. Lights out at 10 p.m.
- **The Retreat House in Big Sur, 408-667-2456**—500 acres with views of the Pacific.
- **Sabbathday Lake Shaker Community, 800-533-9595** — a Maine retreat that is part of the only remaining Shaker community in the world accepting guests.

RANCHES/ FARM STAYS

Ranches and farm stays include hands-on experiences and good vacation values for families.

Farm Stay information can be acquired from state tourism bureaus, 4H headquarters and agriculture-extension offices. Sources include:

- **Pennsylvania Dutch Farm Stays, 800-723-8824, ext. 2475**.
- **Swiss Farm Stays**—The Swiss National Tourist Office, **212-757-5944** (per person cost can be as little as $10-20).

Ranch options (inexpensive to J. R. Ewing-style) are detailed in a free brochure available from the Dude Ranchers Association, P.O. Box F471, LaPorte, CO 80535. Call **970-223-8440**. American Wilderness Experience offers free brochures on Old West Dude Ranch Vacations or Back Country Adventures. Write to 2820-A Wilderness Place, Boulder, CO 80301-5454. Call **800-444-0099**.

UNIQUE OPTIONS

Specific parts of the planet offer economical lodging options unique to their locale. State and national tourist offices provide good leads. Options include:

- **Greece**—The Government Tourist Organization's Traditional Settlements program offers accommodations in eight regions. Call the office nearest you: **212-421-5777**/NYC; **312-782-1084**/Chicago; **213-626-6696**/LA.
- **Israel**—Over 2,200 rooms are available at kibbutz locations throughout Israel. Nightly rates average $45/single, $54/double and including a hearty breakfast. Bonus pass programs provide discounts of 25 percent on multiple stays. Call **888-542-2889** or **800-552-0141**.
- **U.S. National Parks**—Rates of $12-130 for accommodations ranging from tent camps to majestic lodges. Options include:
- **Cedar Pass Lodge/Badlands National Park, South Dakota**—24 pine cabins with full baths sleep four to six. Open year round. Call **605-433-5460**.
- **Haleakala National Park/Hawaii**—Three cabins so popular that they are awarded by lottery. Write to P.O. Box 369, Makawao, HI 96768.

Hotel located in a converted 19th century armory: the Regency in Portland, Maine.

- **Appalachian Mountain Club System**—11 cabins sleep 36 to 90 people. Meals are included. Three cabins are open year-round; 8 are open late spring through mid-fall. Call **603-466-2727**.

RENTALS AND SUBLETS

This chart offers a selection of prime rental contacts. Some require a nominal membership fee, often applied to your first rental. Others are free and do not require membership.

Rentals and sublets can be arranged for stays as short as one week. Rentals are easiest to find in tourist-attractive cities. They range from studio apartments to mansions. Prime rentals often are booked six months to a year in advance. Begin your search with plenty of lead time.

RENTALS AND SUBLETS		
SOURCE	**PHONE**	**COVERAGE**
At Home Abroad	212-421-9165	Caribbean, Europe & Mexico
Barclay International	800-845-6636	Major cities worldwide; emphasis on Europe
Caribbean Destinations	800-888-0897	Caribbean
Condominium Travel Associates	800-492-6636	Australia, Caribbean, Europe, Mexico & U.S.
Creative Leisure International	800-426-6367	Caribbean, England, Hawaii & Mexico
Europa Let	800-462-4486	Caribbean, Europe, Hawaii, Mexico & Pacific Islands
Florida Vacation Rental Managers	407-382-2276	Florida
Hideaways International	800-843-4433	Caribbean, Europe, Mexico & U.S.
Homes Away	800-374-6637	France & Italy
In The English Manor	800-422-0799	U.K.
Interhome	201-882-6864	Europe
Paris Connection	954-475-0615	Paris
Rent A Home International	206-789-9377	Australia, Canada, Caribbean, Europe, Mexico & U.S.
Vacation Rental Managers Association	408-458-3573	U.S.
VHR Worldwide	800-633-3284	Worldwide
Villas International	800-221-2260	Caribbean, Europe & Mexico
Worldwide Home Rentals	800-299-9886	Worldwide

Sign in an Istanbul hotel: "To call room service, open the door and call 'Room Service'."

- **Contact a broker.** If you are unfamiliar with rentals, using a reputable broker affords you some protection.
- **Good newspaper sources** include the *International Herald Tribune* and the Sunday *New York Times*.
- **Many international organizations list rentals.** Inquire at the U.S. office of the tourism bureau representing the country that interests you. Options include:

  England—Landmark Trust, 802-254-6868 and The Royal Oak Foundation, 212-966-6565

  France—The French Experience, 212-986-1115

  Italy—Grand Luxe International, 201-327-2333

  Scandinavia—ScanAm World Tours, 800-545-2204

  Sweden—Swedish Tourism & Travel Council, 212-949-2333

> *"A free guide to rentals and sublets is offered by The Barclay International Group,* ***800-845-6636****. Request The Savvy Consumers' Guide To Short-Term Apartment Rentals. Mail a stamped, self-addressed, business-size envelope to 150 E. 52nd St., New York, NY 10022."*

HOME EXCHANGES

Home Exchanges list and reference-check people willing to exchange stays in their homes for stays in another location. You may need about a year's advance to accomplish an effective exchange. Correspond with the people with whom you'll be trading. Don't rely solely on the agency's information and reference checks. You want full information, including photographs or videos. Check the contract thoroughly and check your homeowner's insurance to make sure you're completely covered.

Listing sources:

Home Exchange Network, 407-862-7211 or **www.homeexchange.com**

Intervac USA, 800-756-4663

Teacher Swap, 516-244-2845

Trading Homes International, 800-877-8723

Vacation Exchange Club, 800-638-3841

HOME STAYS

Home stays are all-inclusive programs that place you with a host couple or family. They're typically two weeks in length. International home stays usually provide English-speaking hosts. You generally get a private room and bath, all meals and hosts who enjoy welcoming you into their homes.

- **American International Home Stays, 800-876-2048**, covers Eastern Europe, Russia and China.
- **Friendship Force**, **404-522-9490**, covers Europe and other select worldwide locations.
- **Servas**, **212-267-0252**, covers the U.S. and 80 other countries.

Location of the Lizzie Borden Bed and Breakfast/Museum: Fall River, Massachusetts.

CAR RENTALS THAT DON'T EXHAUST YOUR SAVINGS

The last thing you want after a long flight is confusion at the car rental counter— particularly when it can double the price you pay. Renting a car shouldn't be like haggling over the price of a straw hat in Montego Bay, where the going rate is whatever you're willing to pay. All too often, it is.

To add to the confusion, the expansion of express rental programs eliminates human contact. I find myself sitting in a different new car almost every time I rent, with no idea of where the ignition switch is, how to lower the windows or whether a particular button will lower my seatback or turn on the windshield wipers. My helpful hint of the year to car rental companies is a suggestion that they place a simple hang tag in each car explaining these great mysteries.

When I travel, I check the current issue of my magazine and our internet site (I can't remember *every* deal) to see if I can use any special/limited time offers. I look for deeply discounted rates, free upgrades or free added days. If I don't find a deal that fits my travel needs, I pull five more cards out of my savings deck.

Internet only discounts that can save you up to 67 percent.

Frequent flyer discounts that take three to 50 percent off quoted rates. We'll tell you how to get closer to the high end of that range.

Negotiated discounts arranged by automobile clubs and other organizations (*Best Fares* subscribers have their own discount rates with five major companies).

Sunday newspaper travel section ads that offer special deals, usually limited to bookings within seven days of publication.

Fly/Drive packages offering discount airfare and car rental packages.

Counter-hopping at the airport with a competitor's best rate in hand.

The price of vehicle acquisition has gone up by almost 30 percent a year since 1992—far more than rental rates have risen. Car rental companies are looking for ways to fill in their revenue shortfall. They want to get the highest dollar amount possible on every rental; you want the lowest possible rate. To get what you want, you have to know how the game. You also want to put loyalty factors engendered by bonus frequent flyer miles offers in perspective. Most rental agents try to be helpful; a small percentage subject you to incomplete information or attempt to sell you options you don't need. The situation is complicated by the fact that many car rental locations are franchises. The name is familiar but the policies can vary from location to location. Rates aren't just dependent on which rental company you choose. They're also determined by factors including the day of the week, the length of the rental, the type of car, the driver's age, insurance options, airport fees, affinity memberships, special offers and last but not least, your negotiating skills.

This chapter begins with *Clues To The Best Bargains*, explaining my six favorite discount methods and how to use them to *your* best advantage. It goes on to show you more ways to save: corporate and senior discounts, weekly and weekend rates, holiday discounts, special offers, one-way rentals, advance reservations, cost effective refueling options and more. You'll find out how standard discounts that may be your car rental staples, are actually taking money out of your pocket. If you don't use creative discounting methods, you are paying rates that subsidize everyone who does.

Play Their Game And Win gives you the knowledge you need to be a savvy renter. It covers driving record checks, financial requirements, waivers and insurance, additional drivers, express options, ways to avoid common rental headaches and other basics.

International Counter Intelligence teaches you the language of savings for international rentals. It gives you strategies, rental requirements, car selection tips, short-term leasing options, country specific information and other matters that can help you feel more comfortable while arranging to get behind the wheel in any country.

This chapter could make you more knowledgeable than many people who work in the car rental business. That's a good position to be in when negotiating a deal. You always want to stay one step ahead of the latest marketing ploys. If you want to save money every time you rent a car, read on. It's easier than you think. Once you know the rules of the rental road, you're the one in the driver's seat.

CLUES TO THE BEST BARGAINS

Magnify your savings by using one of our car rental maximizers. You'll find that they bring you the best consistent savings in cases where a special, limited-time promotion is not in effect for the market you need.

INTERNET ONLY DISCOUNTS

The past year has brought an increase in discounts by internet, now that most major companies are firmly online. Car rental discounts are proving to be one of the most dynamic aspects of travel discounts by internet. Some sites change offers frequently; others are still a little slow with updates. Always check expiration dates before you get too excited about a deal. Some car rental sites are not great about deleting expired deals. Some sites offers weekend discounts you can book several weeks in advance. Alamo discounts 21-day-advance rentals covering a wide range of locations and car classes. Several sites use print-your-own-coupon deals, including a free one-class upgrade coupons and dollars-off rentals at particular locations. Thrifty, for example, offers added-days coupons. National offers free upgrades.

Many car rental companies participate in weekly airline internet discount offers. Most car rental discounts are released on Wednesday and cover travel the following weekend. Special rates are primarily for economy class cars. Hertz and other companies often add discounts for full-size cars (in select markets). Avis adds four-wheel drives and minivans in select markets.

- **Alamo (800-462-5266** and **www.goalamo.com**) offers weekend rentals in conjunction with American international internet fares and American and TWA domestic internet fares.
- **Avis (800-331-1212** and **www.avis.com**) offers weekend rentals in conjunction with Air Canada internet fares.
- **Hertz (800-654-3131** and **www.hertz.com**) offers weekend discounts to the general public and in conjunction with Air Canada internet fares.
- **National (800-227-7368** and **www.nationalcar.com/index.html**) offers weekend discounts in conjunction with Continental and Northwest internet fares and in conjunction with weekly Radisson Hot Deals.

***Best Fares* Online (www.bestfares.com)** publishes special internet deals daily. They are growing in number and variety, as more and more care rental companies use the internet as a primary marketing tool. In addition to the sites listed above, you may want to check out:

- **Auto Europe** at **www.autoeurope.com**
- **Budget** at **www.budgetrentacar.com**
- **Dollar** at **www.dollarcar.com**
- **Kemwel** at **www.kemwel.com**
- **Thrifty at www.thrifty.com**

Most expensive car rental cities in the U.S.: New York City, Newark and Hartford.

FREQUENT FLYER DISCOUNTS

If you ignore frequent flyer discounts, you can end up paying as much as 50 percent more than you have to pay. On the other hand, rely on them too heavily and you could miss a much more favorable discount. All major airlines have negotiated agreements with major car rental agencies (except Enterprise and National, which follow a strategy of lower base and promotional rates). Daily rental discounts range from three to 30 percent, but they can go up to 50 percent on weekly rentals. In both cases, you are also likely to get bonus miles, though you do want to watch for changes during the next few years.

It pays to enroll in all major airline frequent flyer programs, even if you rarely book flights on the specific airlines. In some cases, you get a frequent flyer discount from car rental agencies without the requirement of flying in on a partner airline. Since frequent flyer discounts vary, you want to use the one that gives you the best discount percentage. Ask the reservation agent or your travel agent to check the discount available with each airline partner frequent flyer membership. If the agent asks which airline you are flying, say that you haven't decided yet, and the car rental discount could be a determining factor.

When you pick up your car, you will be asked to show your frequent flyer membership card and (when necessary) your airline ticket. If you don't have the card, your rate can be bumped up to the standard rate.

We spot-checked daily rental rates in three major cities, with and without frequent flyer discounts. Keep in mind that these are samples only. The standard rate is listed first, followed by the best frequent flyer rate available.

CHICAGO

Avis—$61.99/$51.87
You save $10.12

LOS ANGELES

Alamo—$38.99/$29.24
You save $9.75

NEW YORK CITY

National—$69.99/$56.24
You save $13.75

> *"Be sure and check rates at alternate airports. Newark, for example, can be cheaper than La Guardia; Baltimore can be less than Reagan National or Dulles; Midway can be cheaper than O'Hare."*

You can also get deals and discounts from hotel/car rental partnerships. Members of Best Western International's frequent guest program, for example, earn 100 points for each qualifying rental. Accrued points can be redeemed for free rental days from Budget. Members of Hyatt's Gold Passport frequent guest program get special promotional discounts at various times during the year.

The chart on the next page details current car rental/airline affiliations. Be sure to ask if a flight in conjunction with your rental is required. Airlines listed in italics usually do not require conjunction flights, but always re-confirm this policy. These affiliations change frequently. Some allow car rental discounts; others simply award bonus miles. Check *Best Fares* Online at **www.bestfares.com** for updates.

Typical price airlines pay for bonus miles: 1.5 cents per mile.

CAR RENTAL AIRLINE AFFILIATIONS	
COMPANY	**AIRLINE PARTNERS**
ALAMO 800-462-5266	Alaska, America West, *American*, British Airways, Canadian, Continental, *Delta*, Midwest Express, Northwest, *Southwest*, TWA, United & US Airways
AVIS 800-331-1212	Aer Lingus, Aerolinas Argentinas, Aeromexico, *Air Canada*, Air France, Alaska, *America West*, *American*, Ansett, Austrian, Avianca, Braathens, British Airways, British Midland, Cathay Pacific, Continental, CSA Czech, *Delta*, El Al, Eva, Finnair, Iberia, KLM, *LatinPass*, LOT, Lufthansa, Malaysian, Midwest Express,Sabena, SAS, Saudi, Singapore, South African, Swissair, TAP Air Portugal, Thai, United, Varig, Viasa & Virgin Atlantic
BUDGET 800-527-0700	Aeromexico, *Air Canada*, Air New Zealand, Alaska, Lufthansa, Southwest & United
DOLLAR 800-800-4000	*Aloha, America West*, American, Continental, Delta, TWA & *United*
HERTZ 800-654-3131	Aer Lingus, Air Canada, Air France, Air New Zealand, Alaska, Alitalia, American, British Airways, Cathay Pacific, China, Continental, Delta, El Al, Finnair, Iberia, Icelandair, KLM, Lauda, LOT, Lufthansa, Malaysia, Qantas, SAS, Singapore, Swissair, United & US Airways
NATIONAL 800-328-4567	*America West*, *American*, Canadian, Continental, Delta, Finnair, Midwest Express, Northwest, Swissair, United & *US Airways.*
THRIFTY 800-367-2277	Air New Zealand, *America West*, American, *Canadian*, *Continental*, Qantas & *TWA*

NEGOTIATED DISCOUNTS

Negotiated discounts of ten percent or more come from membership in organizations including *Best Fares* (we also give you free express service memberships), the American Automobile Association (AAA) and other auto clubs, the American Association of Retired Persons (AARP), the Small Business Association, the American Red Cross, Sam's Warehouse Club, COSTCO, The National Association of the Self Employed and other groups. AAA discounts tend to be extremely favorable and, in some cases, offer a better deal than frequent flyer discounts.

SUNDAY TRAVEL SECTIONS

The Sunday travel sections of major newspapers provide discount information on car rentals, fly/drive packages and other specials that can lower your car rental rate. Scan them carefully. A hotel or airline ad may also contain a car rental discount offer. Note the rate code for each special, and ask for it by name or number.

Here is an example of deals we found in one recent Sunday paper. All rates were available for bookings made within seven days of publication but you could use them, in most

Average daily rental cost in 1997: $47.

> *"If you live in a small city, pick up a major city paper, such as the New York Times or Chicago Tribune. The larger circulation papers tend to get the greatest number of travel ads. If you don't want to purchase the paper, visit your local library and check the travel section of the Sunday paper. There are generally no coupons required. All you have to do is note the code and copy other pertinent details."*

cases, for reservations many months in advance.

- **Avis**—an $85 three-day weekend rate nationwide with no refueling charge and a $179 weekly rate in California and Florida.
- **Budget**—a $25 full-size weekend daily rate nationwide, except New York City, Phoenix, Colorado, Florida, Hawaii, Nevada & New Mexico and a $104 weekly rate on an economy car in the U.K.
- **Dollar**—a $35 weekday mini-van rate in Florida.
- **Hertz**—a $23 weekend day rate for AAA members ($25 for non-members) nationwide, except New York City, Florida and Hawaii.

FLY/ DRIVE PACKAGES

Fly/Drive packages (and car rental/hotel packages, new to the U.S. this year) can provide excellent savings for leisure and business travelers. Your car rental discount comes from the volume business the air carrier or charter company provides the car rental company. Airfares are often discounted too. Savings vary dramatically and can be particularly favorable when your trip does not include a Saturday stay because your airfare is not based on a high-priced class of ticket.

- **America West Vacations**, for example, offered a $149 Phoenix package from select cities, including roundtrip air and car rental. It substantially beat their best discount airfare with no Saturday stay—$640. Renting a car would have added $54 per day ($162 total for a three-day rental) making the total cost $802. The package had no Saturday stay requirement and included a rental car. Since most Fly/Drive packages are based on double occupancy, there was also a $35 single supplement, making the total airfare and car rental cost $184. The savings—$618. It's like a four-trips-for-the-price-of-one offer. Even business travelers with savvy travel agents are frequently amazed by this trick.

You have to call each airline's vacation division directly or book through your travel agent. You can't get these deals from regular reservation numbers. The numbers for major airline tour divisions are included in *Know Who To Contact*, under Airline Reservations. Generally, you have complete flexibility on departure and return dates, as long as seats are open in the fly/drive fare category.

Some charter companies also offer Fly/Drive packages. Check the Sunday travel section for cities served from your hometown. These packages focus on popular vacation destinations and may have limited flight dates.

Increase in some Orlando car rental prices during the week after Christmas: 3 times early December rates.

> *"Each spring, Avis repositions its fleet to get ready for the summer travel market. Leisure travelers can participate in great packages from Preferred Holidays, Avis' package subsidiary. You get one-way airfare for two, an Avis car for seven days and seven night's accommodations. You fly to your destination, pick up the car and take as long as a week to return it to your home town. Your total cost for two people can be as low as $598. Call* ***800-508-5454****. Also look for one-way specials out of Florida on Autumn. As many as four rental companies offer them and rates can be as low as $6.95 per day."*

AutoNet's new car/hotel packages for leisure travelers offers deals like seven-nights accommodations for a party of four plus a rental car with unlimited mileage at rates beginning at $430. The program was launched in Europe, but is now offered in select U.S. cities. You pre-book all the hotels, or book the first night and select your hotel (from a list of approved choices) as you go. Many participating hotels include free breakfast. The program is offered in Atlanta, Denver, Las Vegas, New Orleans, Phoenix, Tucson and statewide in California and Florida. Expansion is likely, both in terms of areas served and hotel choices offered. Book through your travel agent or call **800-221-3465**.

Autonet's European car/hotel package lets you rent a car for three or more days and get free hotel nights in Europe. You purchase an optional $15 Flexibreaks Discover Europe kit which includes vouchers valid for free hotel nights at almost 800 hotels in Andorra, Belgium, France, Italy, Luxembourg, the Netherlands, Portugal, Spain, Switzerland and the U.K. The free nights are contingent on the purchase of breakfast and dinner in the hotels for each night of your stay. Since a range of hotels is offered, you can opt for economy to luxury lodging and meals.

COUNTER HOPPING

If you can't find a great deal in advance, shopping around when you arrive at the airport can often get you some of the best discounts or perks available. Be sure to reserve your best rate in advance as a back-up, then hop from counter-to-counter and check for a better deal. You are likely to end up with a lower rate, a larger car, or both. This system can also introduce you to regional and local rental agencies offering bargain rates, made possible by lower advertising costs.

> *"If a car rental location has cars sitting on the lot, they lose revenue. The best yield management forecasters can't absolutely predict demand. Most lots have, on average, ten percent more vehicles than they need. National recently invested $410 million in a new yield management system to try to solve that problem. In the meantime, when you arrive at the airport, the rental agency manager could be in the mood to make a deal."*

Growing trend in car rentals: vehicles in which smoking is prohibited.

OTHER WAYS TO SAVE

Here is your rundown on standard discount possibilities and other ways to save every time you rent a vehicle.

CORPORATE RATES

Car rental companies (as well as airlines and hotels) count on getting maximum revenue from business travelers. Many corporate travelers unwittingly subsidize these industries. Regarding car rentals, they obligate themselves to a particular company through guaranteed annual usage in return for a corporate rate—or they simply head for a familiar name. A corporate rate should be an option—not an obligation—unless the discount is remarkable.

Corporate rates are available to all business clients. You apply as a company. Budget, Dollar and Enterprise encourage even the smallest companies to apply. Larger companies rate qualifications on estimated annual car rental expenditures and usually require minimums of $12,000-25,000. The higher end of the standard ten to 35 percent discount range goes to high volume corporate users. *Know Who To Contact* lists phone numbers for major car rental company corporate account applications. The process can take three to four weeks. Benefits that can be negotiated include:

- **Guaranteed lowest rates** that provide a five to ten percent discount on promotional rates if they are lower than your corporate rate. This assures that you won't have to choose between lowest possible rates and corporate rate protection.
- **Reduced liability**, even if the optional insurance is declined. Typically, your liability ceiling for loss or damage is set at $3,000.
- **Protection against liability** from injured parties. Large corporations can

Amount Hertz spent on bonus miles in 1997: over $30 million.

often negotiate $1 million-plus in coverage.

- **Waived surcharges and fees** for under-age or additional drivers and waived safe driver checks.
- **Free upgrades,** rental days and amenities (including car phones) and free membership in preferred-service clubs.
- **Availability guarantees** to assure that cars are available when you need them, even during peak periods.
- **Discount refueling** charges that help keep your overall rental expenses in check.

> *"When you negotiate corporate accounts, hold out for deals that let you use coupons and special offers without sacrificing your corporate rate. Alamo is the only company we are aware of that traditionally allows that privilege."*

SENIOR DISCOUNTS

One of the best routes to a senior discount can be membership in a senior organization such as the American Association of Retired Persons. You can join the AARP at age 50 and begin enjoying senior savings before you reach some programs age minimums. It could mean an extra five to 12 years of discounts.

You rarely get senior discounts on promotional rates, so be sure not to settle for five to ten percent off when greater discounts are available. If you're a senior and a member of the American Automobile Association (AAA), you will almost always do better with your AAA discount. Senior discounts can vary by market, type of car rented and availability, and some require advance reservations. General policies include:

- **Alamo**—five to ten percent at age 50; no membership required.
- **Avis**—five to ten percent at age 50; no membership required.
- **Budget**—five percent at age 62; age 50 with an AARP card.
- **Dollar**—amount varies by market; must be an AARP member.
- **Enterprise**—no senior discount available.
- **Hertz**—amount varies by market and membership organization.
- **National**—generally ten percent; must be an AARP member.
- **Thrifty**—ten percent for age 55 and above; no membership required.

WEEKLY RATES

You'll get considerable savings with a weekly rate, available for rentals of five days or longer. In fact, the deals can be so good that there are significant penalties for early returns. If you return the car early, you could be asked to pay a high daily rate for the entire rental period; if you return it late, you'll pay a high rate for the added day. Ask for specific policies when you rent. For extra protection, get a written or faxed copy of the policy.

> *"Let's say your weekly rate is $179—a little under $26 a day. If you return your car late, you could be billed at a rate as high as $59 a day. Multiply it by seven and your bill is $413—more than double what you were quoted."*

WEEKEND RATES

Weekend rates can be as low as one-third the standard weekday rates. In select resort cities and major cities where many people don't own cars, weekend rates can be higher, due to high demand, but these markets are exceptions. In a market where peak daily rates for compact cars range from $28-83, weekend rates can drop to $20-30 per day. A mid-size rental that costs $62 per day at 11 a.m. Thursday can drop to $23 one hour later since noon Thursday generally marks the point at which weekend rates begin.

- **Weekend rates are generally in effect** from Thursday noon to Monday noon, but there is usually a two-tier pricing system. Keeping your car over Saturday night often qualifies you for the cheapest rates. Be sure to define the policy when you make your reservation.
- **Some companies offer one-day rentals** at weekend rates; others require two- or three-day minimums. Policies vary by market and rental car company.
- **Some companies cancel your weekend rate** if you return the car late and raise the rate of each day on your rental contract to the premium weekday rate. Just as with weekly rentals, determine the policy in advance and do your best to abide by it.

> *"Business travelers can save by scheduling flights to arrive early Thursday afternoon. Your daily rate will be based on the weekend schedule and you will arrive in time to have Thursday afternoon and all day Friday to get your business done."*

This chart illustrates typical rate variances for weekday and weekend day mid-size car rentals in various markets. The weekday rate is listed first, followed by the weekend daily rate. It's a supply and demand game. More than anything, this chart illustrates the importance of comparison shopping. You will see some very apparent exceptions to the standard "rule" of weekend daily rates being less expensive than weekday rates.

DAILY MID-SIZE RENTAL RATES (Weekday/Weekend)

COMPANY	BOSTON	HOUSTON	SAN FRANCISCO
ALAMO	$57.99/$43.99	$59.99/$27.90	$38.99/$22.99
AVIS	$63.99/$49.99	$64.99/$22.99	$58.99/$31.99
BUDGET	$61.99/$47.99	$61.99/$22.99	$55.99/$31.99
DOLLAR	$38.82/$34.90	$37.95/$20.95	$45.99/$29.99
ENTERPRISE	$41.95/$43.95	$45.95/$25.95	$37.95/$35.95
HERTZ	$63.99/$63.99	$64.99/$30.99	$58.99/$31.99
NATIONAL	$62.99/$46.98	$59.99/$22.90	$56.99/$30.99
THRIFTY	$41.82/$41.82	$37.90/$21.90	$27.92/$27.92

Domestic market share controlled by Thrifty: three percent.

HOLIDAY DISCOUNTS

Holiday discounts are similar to weekend rates, but are a little harder to pin down. Coordinating holiday schedules around holiday rental parameters can provide significant savings. It's worth taking the time to find out what is being offered. Sometimes a change of one day in your arrival time will dramatically affect your entire rate.

Holiday discounts are generally in effect in major cities for any holiday that substantially decreases the number of business renters. New York City and Boston are often notable exceptions since a small percentage of residents own cars and rentals are in hot demand for holiday and three-day weekend trips. You'll also find that rates remain stable in some popular resort areas.

Thanksgiving discounts are easy to keep track of, since the holiday always falls on Thursday. Holiday rates typically apply from 12 noon Wednesday through 11:59 p.m. Monday. Wednesday pick-ups may require a four-day minimum rental. Pick-ups on other days usually follow standard weekend rules. Christmas 1997 fell on Thursday so holiday rates extended from Christmas week through the first business day after New Year's. Hertz daily rates were as low as $19.

SPECIAL OFFERS & ADDED VALUES

Special offers for discounts and added values can be found in frequent flyer statements, credit card inserts, in-flight magazines and newspaper ads. You have to keep your eyes open and resist the temptation to throw away all your statement inserts without scanning them first. Travel agents are supplied with coupons by car rental agency sales representatives, but sometimes you have to ask if they are available. They are usually reserved for preferred customers, but you'll rarely be turned down if you take the trouble to inquire.

***Best Fares* magazine and internet site** keep track of these offers on a regular basis. We also include promotional books offered by rental companies that often include discounts on hotels, attractions and restaurants for the area in which you are renting. For example:

- **Budget offered the third rental day free** in California and Arizona—but you had to know the promotional code.
- **Hertz Savings Certificates** feature coupon discounts in Florida, California and Hawaii.
- **Avis' *Florida Discount Guide*** includes coupons for everything from discounted car rentals to free orange juice.

> *"Friends or family visiting the U.S. from abroad can often get significant discounts by booking their car rental from their home country and requesting a U.S. visitor's promotional rate. This discount is designed to promote tourism and can cut 30 to 60 percent off standard rates. Alamo offers this discount regularly under code ZF."*

ONE-WAY RENTALS

Drop-off fees and one-way rates are usually set high enough to discourage the removal of cars from their markets. Avis, Budget, Hertz and National charge higher rates but do not charge drop-off fees, Alamo, Dollar, Payless and Thrifty charge regular rates but add a drop-off fee of up to $300.

- **Comparison shop.** Your cost will be determined, in part, by the company's local surplus of cars and the need for them at your destination—factors that can change daily. You'll only get the information you need by calling each car company direct at their individual location. The local number of the location can be obtained by calling the main reservation number of the car company. Ask about weekly one-way rental rates if you need the car for five or more days.

Get a great deal on one-way rentals with special promotions. National's Great Florida Drive Out, for example, offers special rates from 15 Florida cities to 45 locations in 16 states during spring. You rent by the day or by the week (two week maximum), get unlimited mileage and do not pay a drop-off fee. In 1996, they even included premium and luxury cars in this promotion. Mid-size or full-size cars went for $19.99 a day/$89.99 a week; premium for $29.99 a day/$129.99 a week; minivans for $49.99 a day/$199.99 a week; luxury cars for $59.99 a day/$239.99 a week. In fall, the deals repeat for travel *to* Florida. Competition can bring daily rates down to only $6.95 per day.

***Deadheading* opportunities** exist when a rental company has a need to move cars to another city. You're most likely to find this situation between nearby cities. For example, Austin, San Antonio, Houston, and Dallas/Fort Worth; between Chicago and Milwaukee; Detroit, Dayton, Cincinnati, Columbus and Cleveland; San Francisco, San Jose, Sacramento and Los Angeles.

Drive-away companies transport their customers' automobiles for a fee. Finding the right connection means you can fulfill their contract and get the transportation you need for only the cost of your gas. You must be at least 21 years of age, have a good driving record and put up a fully refundable deposit of about $250-350. The use of these cars is limited to transportation from your city to the destination city. Once you arrive, discretionary driving is not allowed. They usually advertise in newspaper classifieds and can often be found in telephone directories under Automobile Transporters or Drive-away Services. Two of the largest companies: Auto Driveaway (U.S. and Canada)—**800-346-2277** and Advantage Auto Transports—**800-233-4875**.

RESERVE IN ADVANCE

Reserve in advance whenever possible, for price breaks and to lock in promotional rates. Many companies guarantee rates on reservations as much as a year in the future. Promotional rates often have a one to three month window. Even if you like to go from counter-to-counter looking for on-the-spot deals, you'll have a guaranteed reservation as a fall-back. Always tell the rental agent you are arriving by air. Some agencies increase rates for local renters.

Once you've confirmed your best rate, keep checking back with the car company (or your travel agent) for a better rate and watch the papers for any new discounts offered.

Always get a confirmation number and reconfirm your rate prior to arrival. The most savvy travelers call back within 24-hours of making a reservation to make sure the rate on their record matches their quote. If your arriving rate isn't the same as the rate on your reservation, give the local office your confirmation number and have them call the main reservation number on the spot.

Purchase price HFS paid for Avis: $800 million.

FREQUENT RENTER PROGRAMS

Frequent renter programs operate separately from express and added-service programs. Frequent renter programs give upgrades and rental days for points earned through paid rentals. You also get frequent flyer miles on partner airlines—generally 500 miles (Thrifty rentals in conjunction with a TWA flight earn 750 miles or one flight credit on Aloha or Southwest). Special promotions often up the ante. Alamo, Avis and Thrifty also have hotel partners: Alamo—Hilton, Hyatt and Ramada; Avis—Best Western, Hilton, Hyatt, ITT Sheraton and Renaissance; Thrifty—Hilton.

Get free brochures that detail frequent renter programs, point and mileage awards and redemption policies by calling each car rental company. Basic policies are detailed in the following chart:

FREQUENT RENTER PROGRAMS	
COMPANY & PROGRAM	**POLICIES & TYPICAL BENEFITS**
ADVANTAGE Frequent Rental Club 800-777-1374	Every renter is automatically enrolled. Four rentals earn one free day. Other benefits include guaranteed rates.
ALAMO True Blue 800-422-0000	Now limited to priority and express programs only. Point awards ended April 30, 1998. They can be used through December 31, 1999.
AVIS RentSavers 800-331-1212	Being tested in Arizona and select California cities. Three rentals earn one free day.
BUDGET PerfectDrive 800-621-2844	Two rentals earn one upgrade; four earn a free day; 16 earn a free week. Other benefits include double credit promotions.
HERTZ Business Account 800-654-3131	Limited to corporate accounts and includes free Gold Club membership. Five qualifying rentals earn one free day.
PAYLESS Championship Club 800-729-5377	Three rentals earn a free upgrade; four earn a free weekend day. Other benefits include a $25 pre-paid gas card after ten rentals and a $75 Marriott gift certificate after 25 rentals.

DON'T BE A FOOL WHEN IT COMES TO FUEL

You have three refueling options. Choose the wrong one and you will lose every penny you saved by finding the best rental rate.

- **Accept the pre-pay option** offered by the rental company. If you choose this option, be sure you return the car with needle as close to empty as possible. If you return the car with a half-tank of gas, for example, a $1.30 per gallon charge becomes $2.60 per gallon. Any gas left in the tank is like a gift to the rental agency.

Purchase price Republic paid for Alamo: $625 million.

- **Return the car with an empty tank without having chosen a pre-pay option.** This is your worst choice. You will be billed for refueling at prices as much as three times gas station rates. An 18-gallon tank of gas can easily be billed at over $50.
- **Re-fill the tank before returning the car.** Unless you are really on a tight schedule and willing to sacrifice money for convenience, this is the way to go. Gas up several miles from the airport to avoid paying premium rates at near-airport stations.

> *"Don't let the pump go until the automatic shutoff activates. Most tanks read full about a gallon before the tank's limit is reached. Most rental agencies allow you to drive up to ten miles after filling up, providing you can show a receipt (on request) that includes the gas station's address."*

ALTERNATE AIRPORTS

Flying into an alternate airport can save you money in two ways; lower airfare and lower car rental cost. Many car rentals in Newark are as much as 30 percent less than rentals at New York JFK or LaGuardia. Colorado Springs rates often beat Denver International. Check our Alternate Airports chart in the first chapter of this book for other possibilities.

CHOOSING THE RIGHT CAR RENTAL CATEGORY

The class of car you choose to rent will almost always affect your price. If you want certain features—such as a navigation system—you are limited to renting from among the top rental categories. If you are looking for an advertised rate, chances are the boldly advertised dollar figure is for a compact or sub-compact car. If you want a larger vehicle, don't get overly excited about the deal until you see how much the rate jumps.

You generally have six basic categories to choose from plus specialty categories including convertibles, four-wheel drives and mini-vans. Standard rate variances depend on market, availability and the company you are renting from. Typically, you can expect the following daily rate jumps when you move up to the next category:

FROM/TO	ADD
Sub-Compact/Compact	$1-2
Compact/Mid-Size	$5-10
Mid-Size/Full-Size	$1-5
Full-Size/Premium	$6-10
Premium/Luxury	$3-10

Your needs and driving preferences (as well as cost) will help determine your choice. Remember that the smaller the car, the less expense you have for fuel. If you are using the car for business travel that includes transporting clients, consider their comfort. Will a luxury car impress them? That depends. Some people in business are impressed by luxury; others value economy.

Some car models cross categories. National, for example, lists Pontiac Sunfire as both a sub-compact and compact rental. Typical cars in each class include:

- **Sub-Compact**—Dodge Colt, Geo Metro and Ford Aspire
- **Compact**—Dodge Neon, Ford

Escort, Honda Civic, Mercury Tracer and Nissan Sentra

- **Mid-Size**—Buick Skylark, Chrysler Cirrus, Honda Accord, Mazda Protege and Nissan Altima
- **Full-Size**—Buick Regal, Chevrolet Monte Carlo, Dodge Intrepid and Pontiac Grand Am
- **Premium**—Buick LeSabre, Ford Thunderbird, Mercury Sable and Pontiac Bonneville
- **Luxury**—Cadillac DeVille, Chrysler LHS and Lincoln Town Car

RENTAL CYCLES & SURCHARGES

Car rental companies base their rates on 24-hour cycles. If you use the car for eight hours, you generally still pay for the full 24 hours. If you return the car late (beyond the basic one-hour latitude), you will usually be charged an added hourly fee for up to four hours; a full day's fee if you are four or more hours late. As with all car rental policies, ask for the terms before you rent. If you are a member of an airport club, take your car back in time to meet the deadline, and wait for your flight in the comfort of the club. Paying a late fee (or paying for an extra day) is something savvy travelers definitely try to avoid.

Use off-airport rental locations and don't rent for your entire trip if you only need the car part of the time. Use free hotel shuttles to and from the airport to save one or more days in rental cost, plus parking fees. When you're ready for your car, rent from an in-hotel or nearby location or call Enterprise, the only major car rental company that will deliver your car to you or pick you up and take you to their nearest office. Enterprise's rates are usually less than most daily rates at airport or off-airport locations. No matter which agency you use, you'll also save by avoiding airport surcharges, which most on-airport rental locations add to your bill. We've found that, on average, you can save $10-20 per day by renting from an off-airport location.

Travelers who rent cars are unwittingly subsidizing many new sports facilities in cities nationwide. The total number of cities hitting travelers with these fees will soon reach 20 if local voters (who are spared paying for these facilities themselves) say yes to a few more proposals coming up for vote. You can be hit with an airport surcharge, a city tax, a county tax, a state tax *and* an additional surcharge.

The total of all taxes on the average car rental is $8.24. It can jump to as high as 20 percent in cities including Denver, New Orleans, Phoenix and Orlando. You pay a three percent tax in Atlanta, earmarked for a new home for the Atlanta

> *"We've seen a lot of recent deals on sports utility vehicles—one of the fastest growing rental demand vehicle types. They typically rent for $60-80 per day, but limited time promotions bring them down to $45—or even lower. They used to be limited to seasonal, ski area rentals. Now they are available year-round, nationwide. Hertz, for example, offers them at 70 U.S. locations; National doubled the number of sports utility vehicles in their fleet in one year. Seven percent of Enterprise's fleet is sports utility vehicles, up from 3 percent two years ago."*

Number of rental vehicles available in 1989: 900,000; in 1997, 1.6 million.

Hawks basketball team; two percent in Washington state to help cover the Seattle Mariners' new baseball stadium; a whopping $2.50 per rental in Tucson to keep up Corbett Stadium (spring training headquarters for the Colorado Rockies). These traveler taxes usually pass local vote easily, as the cities get improved multi-million dollar facilities without any cost borne by local residents. Some travelers utilize sports facilities; most don't. Is this new way of taxing fair? Of course not. Is it here to stay? Unfortunately, yes.

This trend isn't going to change any time soon. The business traveler is a captive taxpayer at the car rental counter. Leisure travelers aren't likely to avoid a planned destination because of a small additional tax. City governments know this and despite protests from their tourist bureaus, move ahead with sports facility tax plans.

EXTRA SAVINGS TIPS

Remember that most advertised rates are just the base-point. They usually apply to sub-compact or compact cars. A higher car category, insurance, taxes, surcharges, airport fees and other hidden fees can double the rate you expect. Ask for the complete cost when you reserve and confirm it when you pick up your car. Read all the important fine print at the end of every ad, for special restrictions, date specifics and booking deadlines.

Sometimes limited mileage is your best bet. Car rental companies tried to bring back metered mileage, but consumers put a quick end to it. Unlimited mileage is the norm again, but you will find limited mileage options on many rentals, particularly from local and regional companies. If you plan to drive less than 100-150 miles per day, the limited mileage rate might be more economical.

When you begin shopping for your rental, ask your travel agent to fax you a copy of computer rates for the date and location you need. All major and some secondary car rental companies will be covered and some (but not all) of their discounts. You can then opt to do additional research or plug in added discounts you've gathered from sources, including *Best Fares*. As a courtesy to your travel agent, be sure to book your rental through the travel agency to compensate them for their assistance.

Watch out for cancellation fees, now being test marketed by several major car rental companies.

PLAY THEIR GAME AND WIN

This section will give you a sound base of knowledge on many of the variables you need to know to choose car rental companies and make your way through the many choices that comprise every rental decision.

CHOOSE YOUR BEST SOURCES

Over 2,000 separate rental businesses exist: regional companies, independent locations, dealerships, franchises and national chains (eight of them dominate the market).

- **National companies built around substantial airport presence.** Hertz leads the pack (with over 5,400 locations), followed by Avis, National, Thrifty and Budget (1,000 to 4,800 locations). Alamo is the small fry of this category, with about 220 locations.

> *“If you're looking for a unique rental, Budget has some interesting options and even Harley Davidson rentals in select locations. Rates range from $75-130 per weekday; $99-150 per weekend day. You get 200 free miles, then pay 30-cents per additional mile. You must have a valid motorcycle license. Special promotions have offered your second consecutive day at half-price or a half-day rate of $39.99 on weekdays.”*

> *"In some ways, Enterprise is to the car rental industry what Southwest is to the airline industry. They are both major innovators who charge low prices and focus on customer service. Enterprise's off-airport locations usually mean lower daily rates and they'll either deliver the car to you or take you to their nearest location. They celebrated their 40th anniversary by sending five classic cars on a U.S. tour. Art school students created designs for all the cars and additional design elements were added in all 53 cities on the tour. When the tour ended, the cars were given away in a drawing."*

- **National companies with minimal or no airport presence.** Time spent shuttling to an off-airport facility may not be much longer than the time it takes to get to airport rental sites at larger airports—and rates are substantially lower.
- **Regional companies**, such as Payless, that grew around vacation destinations.
- **Smaller national companies,** like Rent-A-Wreck and Ugly Duckling, that once served niche markets have grown to a national presence. (Their cars, are in far better condition than the company names imply.)
- **Local rental agencies** can be cost-effective choices if you can work within their limited hours and locations.

Ownership of many car rental companies has changed or is changing. HFS purchased Avis (previously employee owned). Republic purchased Alamo in 1996 and National in 1997.

Which car rental company is currently the biggest? Let's look at the top three companies in three different categories. In terms of revenue, Hertz leads, followed by Avis and Budget. In terms of the number of U.S. locations, Enterprise leads, followed by Hertz and Avis. In terms of the number of cars in U.S. fleets, Hertz leads, followed by Enterprise and Avis. This picture will change with the entry of Hertz into local markets.

WHEN DRIVING RECORDS MATTER

Rental agencies began checking driving records in 1992, in reaction to high liability judgments. Many agencies check computerized driving records to a greater or lesser extent, according to accessibility of your home state's record by computer and their willingness to pay $4 or more per check.

You're most vulnerable to a record check if you show up at the rental counter without a reservation or if you hold a driver's license from the District of Columbia or one of the following states: Alabama, Arizona, California, Connecticut, Florida, Idaho, Kansas, Kentucky, Louisiana, Maryland, Massachusetts, Michigan, Minnesota, Nebraska, New Jersey, New York, North Carolina, Ohio, Pennsylvania, South Carolina, Virginia, Washington and West Virginia. That's a total of 23 states. By the time the next edition of *Insider Travel Secrets* comes out, it will probably be easier to list the excluded states, rather than those that are included.

Average age of a rental car in Dollar's fleet: 5 months.

As additional states put their driving records online, they're apt to be included in rental agency record checks. International applicants aren't checked because agencies do not have access to data from other countries.

The other variables in record checks are where you rent and whom you rent from. Hertz, for example, checks when you rent at most U.S. locations; Budget and National check when you rent in any of 20-25 states; Avis and Dollar check in 5-10 states; Enterprise checks only in New York.

> *"The most common reason for declining a prospective renter is lack of a valid driving license. Amazingly, thousands of people each year try to rent cars without one. Rental agents will notice if your license has expired."*

Check your own driving record in advance by calling TML Information Services, **800-388-9099**. They provide 80 percent of the checks for the car rental industry. They will check your eligibility against the standards of your choice of three or four companies for a $10.95 fee ($8.95 for AAA members). In about a minute, you will know if you qualify. You can also get a copy of your record from the State Department of Motor Vehicles and do your own basic comparison.

The rate of denials due to record checks was almost four percent in the first year of the program. Now it's under one percent, due to increased applicant awareness and modification of the reasons used to deny. You are no longer automatically denied for involvement in an accident causing death or serious injury, because some states list them on your record even when you are not at fault. The trend is to focus on convictions for serious offenses, rather than cumulative totals of relatively minor tickets. Without this refinement, renters are disqualified for three moving violations in three years, no matter if they were ticketed for going ten miles over the speed limit or clocked at 95 miles per hour in a school zone. Reasons that may trigger rejection:

- **Suspended**, revoked, invalid, surrendered or expired license.
- **Conviction** for reckless disregard for life and property.
- **Conviction** for driving while intoxicated or alcohol impaired or any other alcohol or substance abuse conviction.
- **Failure** to report an accident or leaving the scene of an accident.
- **Possession** of a stolen vehicle or use of a vehicle to commit a crime.

If you are denied a rental on the basis of your driving record, you will have no immediate appeal and no recourse other than to try to rent from a company that doesn't check records. Those options are decreasing in number. In many cities, you would be forced to use a local company. You can appeal to your state's Department of Motor Vehicles if you believe the information on your record is in error, but it won't produce immediate results. You can also appeal to the rental company that denied you by writing to the address they give you when the denial occurs. If you have reason to doubt your ability to pass a driving record check, look into the situation before you reach the car rental counter. The check will not be done until you arrive to pick up your rental.

FINANCIAL REQUIREMENTS

A major credit or charge card is required by all major and most local companies. Persuasiveness and an amiable rental agency manager in a small-to-medium city will sometimes get you around the credit card requirement, but the odds are stacked against you. Drivers age 24 years and under are unlikely to ever have the credit card requirement waived—unless they have been included in a corporate rate agreement.

Debit cards and secured credit cards are not accepted by many rental locations. If you prefer a debit card, confirm the corporate policy when you make your reservation, but be prepared with a regular credit card as back up when you pick up your car. Most agencies require that you reserve your car with a credit or charge card. Most allow you to switch payment to a debit card when you return your car. At press time, Avis, Hertz and National did not allow reservations held by debit cards. Budget accepted them.

Cash rentals (when they are allowed) require a refundable deposit which can be as little as $100 (in smaller cities) and as much as $500 or more. Screening is likely to be more rigorous and may include employment and credit checks which could hinder renting on weekend rentals due to inaccessibility of information. Hertz takes up to two weeks to authorize a customer's first cash rental; National takes about two days per rental.

Local rentals in high-crime areas may be difficult to get in general, and invoke more stringent credit card requirements. To help guard against renting cars for use in the commission of crimes, drivers may be screened more thoroughly, charged more, and, in some cases, flatly denied.

> *"The final bill you agree to when you return your car may not be the final word. Rental agencies have the legal right to bill you later for damage, refueling and other "final audit" charges. They cannot increase your bill if they miscalculated a rental rate. That comes under the category of deceptive business practices."*

AGE REQUIREMENTS

Drivers 25 and over meet the age requirements of all car rental companies. There is no age maximum in the U.S. If you have a valid license and meet other renter requirements, you can get a car.

Drivers 21-24 may be denied rentals and almost always pay a per day add-on cost unless they rent under the corporate plan of an employer who has negotiated lifting the young driver fees. Some companies demand proof of personal car insurance. Policies are likely to be more liberal for renters with premium credit cards, and at the higher end of the 21-24 age spectrum. An impeccable driving record, a major credit card in your own name, and your willingness to pay a daily surcharge ranging from $5-25 may gain you acceptance. Location managers may have discretion in these areas, but those who will make exceptions are getting harder to find..

Drivers 18-20 are forced to find the few locally based agencies willing to rent to them, usually for higher daily rates. For drivers under 21, car rental prospects in the U.S. are limited to select local operators. Even then, the provisions for rental will be stringent.

Payless Car Rental's growth plan: triple U.S. locations by the end of 1998.

"New York state's highest court ruled, in the spring of 1996, that car rental companies cannot refuse to rent to drivers solely because they are under 25. The car rental industry cited young driver accident rates to support their position, but they rent to drivers 70 and above, who statistically pose a greater risk of accident. The lawsuit was based, in part, on current high-speed consumer access to driving records now enjoyed by car rental companies. It moves to force car rental companies to stop refusing rentals to anyone over 18 "solely on the basis of age, provided that insurance coverage for persons of such age is available." Hertz was the first company to state that they will comply with the ruling in New York state. An unfortunate side effect is that many weekly specials now exclude Long Island and the New York City metro area"

WHAT THEY'RE TRYING TO SELL

"Persistent" is the diplomatic word for some car rental company attempts to induce you to purchase Collision Damage Waiver (CDW) and Loss Damage Waiver (LDW) coverage. It's rarely mentioned when you make your reservation and it's usually in the fine print of advertised rates. It can almost double your daily rental cost at rates from $7-30 per day. If you decline coverage and do not have alternate coverage, you can be liable if your rental is wrecked or stolen—up to the full replacement value of the car.

Under common law, you are only liable for damage to a rental car caused by your own negligence. When you sign a rental contract—something you can't avoid—you waive this right and accept liability for damage caused by any factor. Then the rental company offers CDW/LDW coverage which, if you take it, waives their right to collect from you. CDW coverage pays for damage to the rental car only. LDW covers personal injury.

Six states limit some insurance charges by law, by regulating their use, capping the amount car rental agencies can charge and limiting your liability.

- **California**—LDW is capped at $9 a day; if you decline LDW, you have no liability for theft (unless you leave your keys in the car or are at fault in some other way) and a maximum $500 liability for damage.
- **Illinois**—The sale of LDW is prohibited. Renters are responsible for $200 in damage.
- **Indiana**—LDW is capped at $5 a day.

"If you blindly accept CDW/LDW options, you increase your daily rate by 46 percent on average, and as much as 93 percent, according to the U.S. Public Interest Research Group. Car rental companies all say they don't instruct counter agents to push optional CDW/LDW, but some agents receive compensation that's partially based on the dollar amount of options they sell. It's hard for some people to offer objective information when there's profit in slating it."

- **Nevada**—LDW is capped at $10 a day.
- **New York**—Sale of LDW is prohibited. Renters are responsible for $100 in damage.
- **Texas**—LDW is capped at $8.50 a day.

The Chicago office of the Federal Trade Commission (FTC) has asked for repeal of the Illinois CDW/LDW ban, claiming the law actually increases rental rates. We compared rental rates for Chicago and other major cities and found no pattern that would bear out the claim.

Most rental companies have changed their liability coverage to secondary coverage. Primary coverage is the first source of payment on any claim. With this change, the bulk of liability still falls on your personal policy. Secondary coverage is usually limited to the deductible on your private insurance policy.

If you plan to take your rental out of the state in which you are picking it up, tell the reservation agent. Some rentals limit the range of travel permitted. Breaking the rules cancels any CDW/LDW you purchased or also leaves you vulnerable if you need emergency service.

COVERAGE OPTIONS

Purchasing CDW/LDW coverage from the car rental agency is not the only option you have. In many cases, it can be your worst option.

Personal car insurance policies can provide more effective CDW coverage at a lower annual cost, if you rent frequently. Private insurance usually meets all leisure rental needs. If you want coverage for business rentals, you may require a rider. Business coverage once was standard, but several companies now omit it from new policies and drop it when current policyholders renew. Be sure to get specifics from your agent. Your rental coverage is generally subject to the same deductible you've chosen for your personal vehicle. It may also limit liability to the replacement cost of your personal car—a potential problem if you drive more expensive rentals.

Named non-owner policies are available from insurance companies. They cover people who do not carry insurance on their personal car (or don't have one) but want liability coverage for rentals. The cost is about $300-600 per year.

Corporate insurance allows companies to insure all employee car rentals for far less than rental agency CDW/LDW. An increasing number of companies are electing to insure employees driving on company business with a rider that includes full coverage. Ask for a copy of the policies of your corporate insurance coverage terms so you can be aware of variables that can negate coverage, such as retaining the car for personal use and driving record considerations.

Credit Card Coverage usually requires you to pay any claim and then reimburses you, but premium coverage may pay for damages directly. Terms of coverage vary widely, generally improving dramatically with premium cards. Diners Club and MasterCard BusinessCard are among the few cards that provide full primary coverage and handle claims without notifying your private insurer. Some cards provide optional coverage at a nominal annual fee (about $10) and a per-rental charge of about $7. It's a better deal than the rental agencies offer but more expensive than adding a rider to your personal car insurance.

- **Each rental must be paid for with the applicable card.** Using an alter-

Car rental industry loss in 1995: over $150 million.

nate card (even for partial payment) negates your coverage.

- **You must decline the optional CDW/LDW coverage** from the rental agency. Accepting it negates your credit card coverage.
- **You must be listed as primary renter** on the rental contract.
- **Damage to other vehicles is not included.**
- **Claims can be denied** when alcohol or drug impairment are factors or if, on the date of your claim, you are in arrears for two monthly payments.

Check all cards you use for travel. You're likely to find one preferred card for car rental needs. Call the customer service department of your credit card issuer, or the issuing bank and determine the answers to the following questions:

- **Do you pay for damages and get reimbursed** or will damages be paid directly to the car rental agency?
- **What duration of a consecutive rental period is covered?** The basic rule is 15 days on domestic rentals; 15-30 on rentals abroad. Diners Club excels with 30 consecutive days of protection worldwide.
- **Are additional drivers covered?**
- **How does domestic and international coverage differ?**
- **Which vehicles types are excluded?** Common exclusions include luxury cars, mini-vans, trucks and sports utility vehicles.
- **What are the limitations** on driving on specific types of roads?

International rentals often require special insurance needs that may make the rental agency CDW/LDW a good deal. It's mandatory in Italy and New Zealand and you want to have it in high-risk rental areas. (Italy's astronomical car theft rate makes Theft Protection coverage a good bet.) Check your other forms of coverage to see what they include. If you are covered, carry your insurance card and a statement from your insurer itemizing foreign coverage provisions.

> *"Your credit card may have effective CDW coverage, but it generally won't cover personal injury or personal liability for your passengers or the driver and passengers in another vehicle. Coverage sold on a per-rental basis is sky high. You can purchase a liability policy from an insurance agent for about $200 per year, providing up to $1 million in coverage."*

- **If you rely on personal insurance or credit card coverage,** you must settle all damage charges directly with the rental company before you leave the country you are renting in. Then you have to file for reimbursement from the provider of your coverage—a process that entails a police report, a lot of paperwork and a lot of time.
- **If you decline CDW coverage,** ask what dollar amount will be blocked on your credit card. Up to $2,500 is not an uncommon amount.
- **Some companies offer "inclusive" rates** which provide CDW at a presumed discount. Check the deductible. At times it is so high that the coverage is virtually useless.

Car rental industry profit in 1996: about $5 million.

You can reject car rental agency CDW/LDW if you are adequately protected by any other means (including personal assets). You are not obligated to state or substantiate the reason for your rejection.

You should consider car rental agency CDW/LDW if you are not renting via a premium credit card or a card with secondary coverage that satisfies you; if you do not carry private insurance or if it is inadequate for rental coverage; or if you are renting internationally.

> *"Car rental agencies also sell personal accident insurance (U.S. and international) and theft protection insurance (international only). If you think you need it, get it from a less expensive source."*

ADDITIONAL DRIVERS

Extra driver charges apply when multiple drivers use a rental vehicle. Fees range from $3.50 to $25 per day, per additional driver. All major companies (except Alamo) waive the extra driver fee for spouses, employees and employers of primary drivers. There are no extra driver charges in California. Hertz waives some additional driver charges for AAA members. Some corporate rate plans allow additional drivers at reduced (or waived) fees.

Avoid the temptation to falsify any part of your rental agreement. It's usually done to try to save a few dollars but you're risking a lot more. Not listing additional drivers invalidates your contract and leaves you unprotected in case of an accident. You can lose many times what you tried to save. Driving out of the authorized area does the same thing.

> *"It doesn't cost the car rental agency a penny more to authorize an additional driver for your rental. It makes sense that they want information on all drivers to be part of the insurance contract, but the additional fee is one of the more apparent "up-the-revenue" tactics agencies use."*

CANCELLED RESERVATIONS

There are two areas of risk regarding cancelled reservations. If you need to cancel, you want to protect yourself against cancellation penalties charged by the rental agency. If the rental agency cancels a reservation you need (usually done through human or computer error), you need to know what to do to get your reservation reinstated.

You can be charged a penalty for cancelled reservations on some peak period rentals, one-way rentals and pre-paid rates to vacation destinations like Florida, California and Hawaii. The standard fee is $25. If you fail to appear without cancelling by phone, you will be billed the entire rental amount. Never reserve a car with a cancellation fee provision unless the deal is extraordinary enough (and your plans stable enough) to merit the risk. If you do have to cancel, note the cancellation number, the name of the person you spoke with, their location and the time of your call.

If your reservation is cancelled in error and you arrive at the counter with no car waiting, be prepared to substantiate your

General Motors vehicles purchased by car rental companies in 1997: 600,000.

case. Your first job (fair or not) is to show the agent that you actually did have a reservation. Some people claim they do when they don't.

- **Know when the reservation was made**, the confirmation number and the rate code. If you rely on someone else to make your car rental reservations, be sure you get this information from them before you leave for your trip.
- **If you are met with resistance**, call the toll-free reservation number and have them look up your reservation. Sometimes their information doesn't make it through to the on-site computer.
- **Don't accept an offer to enter a new reservation** unless it is at the same rate you were quoted. If you are told no car is available, insist on one of the following options:
- **A commitment to the next car available** with a 50 percent rate reduction to compensate you for the inconvenience. If you need your car immediately, ask the manager to arrange for a rental from another company. They don't like having to do this because of the extra expense, but it is a reasonable request if you are on a tight schedule and the company you made your reservation with cannot honor it.
- **If cars will not be available for several hours**, you want transportation to your hotel and delivery of the rental car as soon as possible.

Each car rental company has a different policy on how long reservations will be held. If you arrive later, you may get a car, but the company does not have to honor the quoted rate. You may also be subject to individual franchise policies and high-demand times that decrease your window of flexibility. Always call to let the agency know you will be delayed and update them on your time of arrival.

> *"If a cancellation penalty is charged to your credit card and you were not warned of it in advance, dispute the charge with your credit card company. Cancellation fees legally require sufficient notice. Since car rental companies are testing the waters with these fees, they should be very responsive to agreeing to wipe out these charges until they become commonplace."*

Standard grace periods (but don't bet your rental on them) include:

- **Alamo**—Until midnight.
- **Avis**—Up to 15 hours.
- **Dollar** and **Hertz**—Until midnight or closing time.
- **National**—As long as cars are available.
- **Payless**—One hour, unless your flight has been delayed.

EXPRESS SERVICE

When time is money you may save overall by renting from a company with major convenience features like express check-in options, frequency of courtesy buses and use of personal profile databases (offered by all major programs) that keep your basic information and preferences on file. These services can account for about 15 percent of your rental dollar.

Ford vehicles purchased by car rental companies in 1997: 450,000.

EXPRESS SERVICE CLUBS		
PROGRAM	**ANNUAL FEE**	**EXPRESS SERVICES**
ALAMO Quicksilver 800-882-5266	None	Express counter, self-service computer check-in and roving attendants.
AVIS Preferred Renters 800-831-8000	None	Express check-in counter, roving attendants and curbside valets at about 20 airports.
BUDGET FastBreak 800-866-6317	None	Express counter, roving attendants and drop-box return.
HERTZ #1 Club Gold 800-654-3131	$50	Express check-in counter, roving attendants, self-service computer check-in, drop-box return and curbside valets at about 11 airports.
NATIONAL Emerald Club 800-962-7070	$50/ free renewal for active rentals	Self-service computer check-in, roving attendants and drop-box return.
THRIFTY Blue Chip 888-400-8877	None	Assigned personnel greet renters and escort them through a rental process that should take a minute or less.

SPECIAL EQUIPMENT

Give at least 24 hours notice (longer for smaller companies) if you want a particular model of car, hand controls, a car equipped with a navigation system, a child safety seat, a smoke-free car, a cellular phone, a ski or luggage rack or any option not included in standard rentals. Tell the rental agent your rental is conditional on your request(s) being met. (Details on rental vehicles for handicapped travels are included in *Accessible Travel*.)

Navigation systems are becoming more prevalent, but they are still mostly confined to premium cars. The technology can be quirky, but it is improving rapidly. Voice-recognition systems are particularly apt to confuse you *and* the computer.

- **Hertz has almost 8,000 cars** in 35 major cities equipped with Rockwell navigation system s. You pay $6 more per day and can choose from mid-size or premium cars. Locations offering *NeverLost* include Atlanta, Baltimore, Boston, Burbank, Chicago, Dallas, Denver, Detroit, Fort Lauderdale, Fort Worth, Houston, Los Angeles, Miami, New York, Newark, Oakland, Ontario (CA), Orange County, Orlando, Palm Springs, Philadelphia, Phoenix, Sacramento, San Diego, San Jose, San Francisco, Santa Barbara, Seattle and Washington.
- **Avis has about 1,000 Oldsmobile Ciera Cutlasses and 88s available**, also using a Rockwell system. You can *request* one (confirmation of inclusion is not yet offered) in Atlanta, Boston, California, Denver, Florida, Houston, New York, Philadelphia, Washington (DC) and a few Midwest locations. You'll pay $5

Chrysler vehicles purchased by car rental companies in 1997: 222,000.

more per day.

- **Budget is test-marketing** a dozen voice-navigation equipped cars in Boston, Chicago and Los Angeles.

If you prefer economy rentals but find a little basic navigational aid helpful, there are options:

- **The AAA Trip Planner** is a CD-ROM program that retails for about $60. Create your own maps with mileage and time projections and access data on over 30,000 AAA-rated hotels and restaurants. Call **800-222-5357**.

> *"Premium cars may include cellular phones at no additional cost. If you add a cellular phone option to other car categories, expect to pay about $5 per day plus about $1.25 per call and $1.95 per minute."*

- **The Road Whiz Plus** ($60) looks like a small calculator and can direct you to the nearest gas station, rest stop, hotel or tourist attraction. Its database includes 45,000 facilities in 50 states. You get basic driving instructions and a mileage estimate. Major office supply stores and travel superstores carry it. Write to Laser Data Technology, 9375 Dielman Industrial Dr., St. Louis, MO 63132 for a location near you.

HOW TO AVOID RENTING A LEMON

Rental agencies try to give you cars in good condition. They don't want your ill will or the expense involved in emergency road service. Since companies are keeping vehicles in their fleet longer, there may be a few more lemons on the lot. Here are some tips that will help you avoid them:

- **Get a low mileage car** by asking the rental agent at the check-in counter to check the computer. Every listing contains the total number of miles each car has been driven. Select cars with low mileage, but not brand new cars that may have yet-to-be-revealed glitches.
- **Check safety features and basic running condition** before you leave the lot. Five extra minutes spent checking the basics could save you hours of breakdown time.
- **Check for damage to the car's body.** If the damage will not interfere with performance (and if it doesn't indicate some serious past problems) make sure it is noted on the rental contract so you can't be held liable when you return the car. If it's dark outside, find a well-lit spot on the lot and proceed with your check. This is also the time to make sure the gas tank has been filled.

> *"Rental agency employees assigned to check returned cars have to look at a lot of them every day. They're going to miss some damage. You don't want to be stuck with a bill for damage caused by the person who drove the car before you. Take the time to do your check. It could be the most important five minutes of your day."*

Toyota vehicles purchased by car rental companies in 1997: 84,500.

EMERGENCY SERVICE

All major companies tow, repair and replace according to roughly the same standards. Smaller companies try to match them, but the actual service you get can be more limited due to fewer locations and contracts with tow and repair services.

Smaller companies and independents tend to have older cars and more limited emergency road service provisions. Ask for specifics before you rent. Some limit towing and replacement vehicle services to business hours and simply authorize repair after hours. This policy could leave you without a vehicle for a significant period of time. Some even ask you to pay for approved repairs and reimburse you when you return the car.

Automobile club membership can be invaluable. You get car rental discounts and have an emergency road service to call if you're in an area where the rental agency's emergency service seems to be coming by way of Guam.

SAFETY CHECK YOUR RENTAL

Don't rent cars easily identified as rentals either by license plate stickers or special letter and number sequences. They make it easier for carjackers to prey on people unfamiliar with their surroundings. When you call to make your reservation, ask if the company has taken steps to make their cars less obvious. Most locations have after realizing that crooks and carjackers had easy access to rental car license plate sequences.

Avoid luxury rentals unless you are willing to assume a higher risk. Not only are they more desirable to car thieves, they also attract the attention of smash-and-grab crooks who assume higher-priced cars contain more items worth stealing.

Look through the safety tips you should be given when you rent your car (if they are not offered, ask for them). If you need help with driving instructions, ask. Take special note of directions out of the airport. Most rental car accidents take place between the lot and the airport exit.

If you rented a car model that's new to you, take a few minutes to familiarize yourself with its basic features and check the glove compartment to make sure the owner's manual is available.

Safety check your car before you leave the lot. Make sure the locks, horn, emergency flashers and restraint devices work and that the tire pressure is correct. Also check that a spare tire and a jack are in the trunk and you have what you need for current weather conditions.

Make a copy of your rental car key to use if you accidentally lock the keys in the car. Carry it in your wallet. You won't get stranded or incur the expense of a locksmith if you accidentally lock your keys inside the car.

Where many Avis rental cars go when they're retired: AutoNation used-car lots, also owned by HFS.

INTERNATIONAL 'COUNTER' INTELLIGENCE

RENTAL SAVINGS BASICS

You can keep the accent on savings when renting internationally. Rent by prepaid voucher, pre-pay a portion of the rental amount to lock in the dollar rate or pay after you use the car, just as you do in the U.S. Get a rental car as part of a fly/drive package. Get weekend rates to use in conjunction with low weekend airfares; weekly rates for rentals of five days or longer (this year, we have seen weekly rates in Belgium, Germany and the U.K. as low as $89—including double frequent flyer miles or credits). If you need a car for longer than two weeks, a lease may be your best option.

Some rentals must be paid for when you pick up your car; others require payment when you return it. If you hold prepaid vouchers, you must present a major charge or credit card when you pick up your car or pay a substantial cash deposit. The vouchers simply show that you have paid for all normally anticipated costs. If you opt to pay for your rental in cash, exchange funds first at a bank exchange rate or withdraw funds directly from a local ATM.

The best rental rates normally require a 14-day advance (three to seven days on some promotional rates). Save the most money (up to 50 percent) by booking in advance and pre-paying. Rates can vary by season, but per-day, walk-up rates are generally prohibitive regardless of the time of year. If you book a weekly rental at Charles de Gaulle Airport in Paris, you

Hertz international locations that are corporate owned: 33%.

> *"You may not need a rental car in Europe, and that could be the biggest savings of all. Rail systems are excellent. See Travel By Rail & Road to see what a wide extent of ticket and pass options you can use. Having a rental car may seem essential because you are used to driving in the U.S. Believe it or not, many European residents get by very nicely without cars, and you can too. Car rental fees, higher fuel costs (as much as $5 per gallon), parking fees and tolls all add to your expense. City driving in Europe can also present special challenges that interfere with your enjoyment. Business travelers may find that a rail and taxi combination saves them time and money."*

will pay a base rate of about $311-377. If you call in advance and book using an 800 number (or through your travel agent) you'll pay $249-265, plus you may find out about specials that will save you even more.

Ask about additional charges and restrictions. You can take a car rented in the U.K. to Ireland, for example, but you cannot do the reverse. Restrictions on taking any rental car to Italy, Greece or Eastern Europe are common. CDW rates are generally higher (as much as $25 per day for the average rental).

If you are visiting multiple countries, consider flying into the country that offers the best combination of airfare and car rental rates. Take Value Added Tax and airport surcharges into account. In Austria, for example, the VAT is 21.44 percent; in Switzerland it's 6.5 percent.

Students can get across-the-board discount privileges from the Council on International Educational Exchange, **212-822-2700**.

One-way rental policies can be more liberal than those in the U.S., depending on when and where you travel. There are many one-way rentals with minimal or no drop-off charges. Hertz for example, offers the Rent-It-Here, Leave-It-There program. Rent at one of 200 locations in eight countries and drop your car off at another. The drop-off fee is $50. You may even be given free upgrades on one-way rentals that fit into the company's car relocation needs.

Fly/drive packages are offered by all major airlines serving international destinations, and by internationally-based carriers. You always get a deal and, during special promotions, you can get a *great* deal. Recent offers have included:

- **El Al and Hertz**—a $7 weekly rental when you fly El Al to Israel.
- **Delta and Kemwel**—a free rental when two passengers flew roundtrip to Europe. A solo passenger paid a surcharge of just $50.
- **Virgin Atlantic and Avis**—up to seven free rental days in the United Kingdom.

SHORT TERM LEASES

Leasing is available in Europe as a means to provide a way for locals to avoid hefty taxes when purchasing new cars. Visitors lease them for a minimum of 17 days to three weeks (depending on the company) and "sell" them back to the dealer. In some cases, you can get extensions for up to one year. Because they now

Estimated amount frequent flyer promotions cost car rental companies per year: $100 million.

qualify as used cars, the eventual purchaser saves considerably on taxes. This perfectly legal loophole was created in France by Renault EuroDrive. Some leases still require that you pick up your car in France, but you are free to drive it (and drop it off) in countries including Belgium, Germany, Italy, the Netherlands, Portugal, Spain and the U.K. The minimum age is often just 18 or 19, a bonanza for young drivers. There is rarely an age maximum.

You will be driving a brand new vehicle with availability ranging from sub-compact to full-size. The type of cars most available are the types of cars Europeans prefer to own. If you are particular about air conditioning or automatic transmission, lease with an added amount of lead-time to increase your odds of getting what you want. Rates include all government taxes (they can go over 20 percent, in some cases), airport delivery fees, unlimited mileage, liability insurance, non-deductible collision, theft coverage, personal accident coverage and 24-hour emergency assistance.

Rates vary considerably by season, type of car and length of rental. A 30-day, air-conditioned mid-size will run about $1,300. Rent for 90 days and the price is about $2,100. A six-month sub-compact rental is about $2,800 –a little more than $100 per week.

Leasing sources include:

Auto Europe—800-223-5555

Auto France—800-572-9655

Bon Voyage By Car—800-272-3299

Europe by Car—800-223-1516

Kemwel—800-678-0678

Renault EuroDrive—800-221-1052

RENTAL REQUIREMENTS

A U.S. driver's license is usually sufficient for international driving, but an international driver's permit, printed in nine languages, can be helpful, particularly in Asia, Austria, Eastern Europe, Germany, Greece, Italy, Portugal, Spain and Russia. The permit is invalid without your original license. Permits are sold at AAA offices for $10. Take two passport-size photos and your driver's license when you apply. Allow four to six weeks. You do not have to be an AAA member to secure an international license. Call **800-222-4357**.

Other requirements vary. Some countries require that you have held a license for at least one year. Always mention your age when reserving your car so you don't run into difficulty when you arrive. The chart on page 231 lists age requirements in Europe (where no age maximum is listed, none is in effect), along with Value Added Tax percentages and surcharges for airport pick-ups.

GLOBAL RENTAL SOURCES

Choose from among rental companies based in the U.S. and companies based internationally. North American-based companies often offer a higher percentage of larger vehicles and a wider area availability outside of Europe. Several internationally based companies (including Auto Europe and Kemwel) offer to meet or beat any comparable quoted rate. Here are the numbers to call for the major players, with some details to help familiarize you with what they offer:

- **Alamo—800-522-9696**—locations in 12 countries, one-third being on-airport sites.

First rental company to test market shuttle bus flight monitors: Hertz, at Atlanta Hartsfield.

> *"Avis recently expanded their Before You Go program. Customers can call* ***800-297-4447*** *any time prior to departure, and get up-to-date, country-specific information. They'll tell you the current cost of gas, speed limits, major holidays, locations of U.S. embassies and consulates and much more. Before You Go covers Austria, Belarus, Belgium, Britain, Bulgaria, Croatia, Cyprus, the Czech Republic, Denmark, Estonia, Finland, France, Germany, Gibraltar, Greece. Holland, Hungary, Ireland, Italy, Latvia, Lithuania, Luxembourg, Malta, Norway, Poland, Portugal, Romania, Spain, Switzerland and Turkey. As international travel increases, we will see more expansion in destination information offered by all major car rental companies."*

- **Auto Europe—800-223-5555**—An international giant. They are tour operators and wholesalers with access to 4,000 locations in Europe, the Middle East, Africa, the Caribbean, Latin America, the Pacific and Canada. They have no cancellation or no-show fees until the time of departure, allow some rentals with cash deposits in lieu of credit cards, provide 24-hour road service and cars equipped for handicapped drivers.

> *"Auto Europe offers a free week of cellular phone use with many rentals through 1998. The deal is limited to premium car classes, chauffeur service or SkyDrive air, car and hotel packages. If staying in touch is important to you, this deal is worth checking."*

- **Avis—800-331-1084**—Locations in 140 countries. They also offer rail and drive passes, cellular phones, rapid check-in and return options, plus 24-hour international road assistance. Fly/drive packages are available at **800-508-5454**.
- **Budget—800-472-3325**—Locations in 118 countries and territories, including Moscow, Croatia and Zimbabwe. Signature cars at some international locations include Jaguars and Mercedes. They rent Harley Davidsons in Germany, Jeeps in Israel and Latin America, and camper vans and 4-wheel drives in New Zealand. WorldClass Drive programs with easy-to-follow itineraries for individual tours are available in the U.K., Australia and Western Canada.
- **DER Tours** operates in 17 countries but accepts reservations only from travel agents. Have your agent obtain a quote for you. Their rates are very competitive.
- **EuroDollar—800-800-6000**—Locations in 35 countries. They offer 24-hour rate information and general conditions of rental by fax, **800-329-6000**. When you are mailed your confirmation voucher, you also receive information on mileage, language and other country specifics. Dollar offers *Europe On Wheels* and *Road Map Europe* (trip planning, car selection, local traffic laws and more). Call **800-800-6000**.

Car rental company still owned by the family that began it: Enterprise.

- **Hertz—800-654-3001**—Locations in 170 countries. They offer 24-hour international road service and expedited service at over 590 locations in 21 countries. Computerized driving directions are available at 40 locations in your choice of Danish, Dutch, English, French, German, Italian, Norwegian, Spanish and Swedish.
- **Holiday Autos—800-422-7737**—Locations in 50 countries. They specialize in leisure tours and their agents are very knowledgeable in country-specific information.
- **I.T.S.—800-521-0643**—A company representing European-based car rental companies in 15 countries.
- **Kemwel—800-678-0678**—Extensive international coverage. Their CarPass Plan allows you to purchase vouchers with U.S. dollars and choose your rental dates as you travel at savings from 20 to 50 percent. Unused passes are fully refundable. They also offer short-term leases under the European Car Vacation Plan. *To Help You Plan Your Trip* from Kemwel covers travelers tips on European cars and travel. Call **800-678-0678**.
- **National Interrent—800-227-3876**—An international presence composed of Interrent, Tilden (Canada), Europcar and Nippon Interrent (Japan).
- **Payless—800-729-5377**—22 international locations.
- **Thrifty—800-367-2277**—159 Canadian locations and 463 locations in North, Central and South America, Australia, Europe, the Middle East, the Caribbean, Asia and the Pacific.

OTHER CONSIDERATIONS

Unless you know a Tipo from a Vauxhall Cavalier, you will want to ask questions to familiarize yourself with car models available for international rentals. Check statistics that will help you make reasonable comparisons: trunk space in cubic feet, size of engine, length, body type and miles per gallon. Always tell the rental agent how many people need to be comfortably accommodated and what your luggage requirements will be.

- **The least expensive rentals** are likely to be appreciably smaller than American sub-compacts.
- **Cars with automatic transmissions** are not plentiful in all locations and will generally cost more.
- **Air conditioning** very often is not a standard feature. If it's important to you, be prepared to rent at least a mid-size car and even then, verify that air conditioning is included.
- **Locking trunks** don't exist in hatchbacks, which are prevalent in international rentals.

Airport rental agency counters, except in major gateway cities, don't have 24-hour service. Off-airport locations often send drivers with handheld signs to wait for you at the passenger exit. Many in-city rental offices have restricted weekend hours and some southern European offices close for lunch. When you return the car, take business hours into account to avoid being charged for the time that may elapse between your arrival and the time an employee reappears.

Emergency road service is prevalent, but not always as readily available as in the U.S. Get emergency contact numbers

How Enterprise got its name: owner Jack Taylor served on the U.S.S. Enterprise in WWII.

from your rental agency and ask if there are special procedures for late nights or remote areas. Membership in an international auto club is often offered to members of major U.S. auto clubs for a very low rate. Arrange for this coverage in advance as a back-up for emergency situations.

When you pick up your car, check out its unique features. The gas and brake pedals, for example, may be closer together than on U.S. rental vehicles. Many international rentals have electronic anti-theft systems. Make sure you know how to override the system to start the car. If you have any doubt about the roadworthiness of your car, insist on a short test drive.

All rental agencies should provide you with written safety guides that include the most commonly used road signs. The European Community, for example, has standardized signs and signs particular to each country. A car within a circle means cars can't enter; an exclamation point within a triangle means danger; a red-rimmed triangle with an X in the center indicates an upcoming intersection.

Seat belts are often mandatory, sometimes in both front and back seats. Children may not be allowed to travel in front seats at all until they reach a minimum age (usually between seven and 14).

Orientate your mind to basic differences; driving on the left-hand side of the road, for example. Don't be timid when driving on expressways and super-roads. Drive competently and aggressively to fit in with the traffic flow. On super-roads, slow traffic stays to the right. Be prepared to be passed by other vehicles and don't rely on no-passing signs, because they are routinely ignored. Cars manufactured for use in other countries tend to have more power because of the lack of emission control standards, and drivers tend to use it.

Fuel is often charged by the liter. One gallon equals 3.79 liters. Become familiar with local terms for grades of gas. In the U.K., for example, gasoline is called *petrol* or *benzine*; diesel is called *gasoil*; and *essence* is another name for regular gasoline. Be prepared for hefty per-liter prices.

> *"The easiest way to convert kilometers to miles is to divide kilometers in half and add ten percent. Another method—divide kilometers by ten and multiply by six. Sixty kilometers per hour, for example, is roughly 35 miles per hour. Your speedometer will guide you but keep in mind that there is a big difference in a 50 kph and a 50 mph speed."*

LOCATION-SPECIFIC TIPS

Here are three particularly challenging rental areas with some advice on how to make vehicle rentals less of a hassle when you visit. We've also added some tips on renting in Canada, our northern next-door neighbor.

Asia

Asia presents a unique set of challenges. Traditionally, travelers have been leery of driving in Asian countries because of the combination of intense traffic and street signs in unknown characters. Most international car rental companies do not rent vehicles in Asia. U.S. rental chains are aggressively entering the market, in part to acquire business from North American and European visitors; in part to establish

Company that offered up to 2,000 miles per promotional rental: Thrifty.

a local presence that will encourage Asian renters to use their agencies when they travel in other countries.

Chauffeur Drives are offered by some companies (including Hertz) to provide you with a car and driver for the rental period. Rates are quite economical and they may provide the best choice for most renters.

Independent renters should carry their passport, driver's license, an international driver's license, a major credit card and their return airline ticket with them at all times. You may get a right-side-driver car in countries where you drive on the left side of the road. Age minimums range from 18 to 35; Some countries have age maximums of 65 to 80. If you choose an Asian rental, be sure to ask the company to send you any information they have available on driving in the applicable country. Don't take the availability of any add-ons (child-seats, cellular phones, etc.) for granted.

To save you time on checking out this relatively new rental territory, here is a list (current at time of publication) of major U.S. rental companies serving the Pacific/Asia area, and the countries they serve (all companies listed also offer rentals in Australia, Japan, Malaysia, New Zealand, Singapore and Thailand):

- **Avis**—American Samoa, Cook Islands, Fiji, French Polynesia, Guam. Hong Kong, Indonesia, Korea, Macao, Nepal, New Caledonia, Pakistan, Papua New Guinea, Philippines, Solomon Islands, Sri Lanka, Tonga, Vanuatu, Vietnam and Western Samoa.
- **Budget**—Cook Islands, Fiji, Guam, India, New Caledonia, Niue, Papua New Guinea, Solomon Islands, Sri Lanka, Tonga and Vanuatu.
- **Hertz**—India, Indonesia, Korea and Philippines.
- **National**—Guam, Indonesia, Korea, Philippines, Saipan and Taiwan.

Eastern Europe

Taking rental cars to Eastern Europe is permitted by an increasing number of companies. Avis will allow certain types of cars rented in Germany and Austria to be driven within Eastern Europe with a minimum seven-day rental. Hertz permits driving in select Eastern European countries from locations including Austria, Denmark, Finland, Norway and Spain. National Car Rentals' corporate account members can drive to Eastern Europe. Auto Europe lets you rent in your choice of 14 Western European countries and drive in Bulgaria, the Czech Republic, Estonia, Lithuania, Macedonia, Poland, Romania, Russia, Serbia, Slovakia, Slovenia and the Ukraine. Rates can be surprisingly low—$140 per week, for example, with unlimited mileage. In all cases, cars must be returned in the West. You can rent cars in Eastern Europe, but be prepared to compromise on selection, service and price.

Mexico

Mexico may provide the ultimate challenge in car rentals. If you rent in the U.S., be sure you meet the provisions for taking the car into Mexico. If you rent in Mexico, you may avoid some extra paperwork, but you will pay premium rates. If your driving is confined to within 15 miles of the border or in Baja, California, and parts of the Mexican State of Sonora, you escape much of the red tape.

- **Your private car insurance will not cover driving in Mexico**, so you must buy insurance, whether renting or driving your own car. Border-area

Fine for honking your car horn too often in Egypt from midnight to 6 a.m.: about $150.

> *"The Green Angels have patrolled 20,000 miles of Mexican roads since 1960. From 8 a.m. to 8 p.m., they repair simple breakdowns at no charge, guide lost motorists and report on safety and road conditions. Reach them toll-free within Mexico at **91-800-90-3-92** or, in Mexico City, **250-8221**. English-speaking assistance is available. Traveling to Mexico by Car is available from Mexican tourism offices. There is no charge. The number for the New York office is **212-755-7261**."*

insurance offices have sprung up to fulfill the demand. You may choose independent agencies, rental agency insurance or AAA insurance sold at border offices.

- **If your credit or charge card covers collision damage** in Mexico (a big if), it will automatically become your primary coverage.
- **All insurance paperwork can be done at the border.** Driving into Mexico requires proof of citizenship and a Mexican Tourist Card for stays over 72 hours. Get no-cost tourist cards at Mexican consulates or tourism border offices.

Canada

Canada requires all drivers to carry liability insurance, with minimum coverage of $160,000 (USD) except in Quebec where the limit is $40,000. The law applies to rentals also. Your personal insurance is likely to provide collision and damage coverage that extends to Canada. Be sure to ask your insurer for a Canadian Non-Resident Inter-Provincial Motor Vehicle Liability Insurance Card. Car rental companies should provide you with a copy of their own insurance card when you rent. Credit card CDW coverage usually extends to Canada but may not meet specific liability requirements. If you are driving your own car, carry a copy of the vehicle registration. If you are driving someone else's, carry a signed letter of permission.

> *"Check Travel By Rail & Road for additional tips on driving in international countries—hard facts and details like time-of-day vehicle restrictions in Manila and where bicycles have the absolute right of way. You can have a great time exploring a new country by car if you spend the time it takes to orient yourself before you go."*

EUROPEAN CAR RENTAL FACTS			
COUNTRY	AGE MIN/MAX	VALUE ADDED TAX	SURCHARGE
Austria	21	21.44%	9%
Belgium	23	20.5%	9%
Bulgaria	21	18%	N/A
Croatia	21	10%	N/A
Cyprus	23	8%	N/A
Czech Republic	21	22%	6%
Denmark	21	25%	50 DKK
Estonia	21	18%	N/A
Finland	21	22%	N/A
France	21	20.6%	$11
Germany	21	15%	13 DEM
Greece	21	18%	6%
Holland	21/69	17.5%	40 NLG
Hungary	21	25%	7%
Ireland	21/70	12.5%	N/A
Israel	21	N/A	20 USD
Italy	21	19%	10%
Luxembourg	21	15%	6%
Malta	21	N/A	N/A
Norway	21	23%	N/A
Poland	21	22%	N/A
Portugal	21	17%	1,800 PTE
Romania	21	18%	2%
Russia	21/60	21.5%	5%
Slovenia	21	5%	N/A
Spain	21	16%	1,500 ESP
Sweden	20	25%	80 SEK
Switzerland	21	6.5%	11%
Turkey	21	15%	N/A
United Kingdom	21/75	17.5%	10%

Percentage of all General Motors new car sales made to rental agencies in the early '90s: 33%.

DON'T LET YOUR CRUISE DOLLARS MELT AWAY

This decade will see $9 billion in new ships making their debuts, offering more on board variety than ever before. Innovative promotions have made cruise vacations more affordable as cruise lines vie for repeat passengers and set out to attract new passengers from the 93 percent of North Americans who have yet to enjoy cruise travel. Good deals abound but we want you to get a *great* deal.

The internet has opened up new bargain opportunities in almost every area of travel. Cruise discounts are the primary exception. You can certainly get a much wider range of information and there are some special pricings. We have yet to see widespread weekly discounts such as are offered by airlines, hotels and car rental companies.

This chapter shows you how to set your course toward the best possible price on any cruise. Three maximizers help your ship come in at a price you can easily afford:

Cruise discount agencies—large, specialized companies with the volume of sales and industry connections that allow them to negotiate the lowest prices.

Sunday newspaper travel sections with excellent limited-time offers. We'll tell you where to look and how to evaluate the deals.

Early booking (at least six to eight weeks in advance—longer on some lines) providing deep discounts and the widest choices of ship, itinerary and cabin category.

Selecting a cruise is like planning a temporary move to a floating city. The choices you make are key to the success and enjoyment of your holiday. You don't have to follow the standard route, go to routine destinations and pay more than you should. Opt for elegance just a cashmere thread away from top hat and tails or a budget cruise where comfort is the only dress code. Sleep in the splendor of a suite or make your base of operations an inside cabin that still affords you the run of a $400 million ship. Take a three-night cruise on a floating casino or a three-month voyage around the globe. Cruise the oceans or sail the rivers of the world. Select a cruise line with an international flavor or go all-American.

A major part of the selection process is finding ways to save that will help you afford a cruise that fits your budget *and* your personality. Use the clues in the first section of this chapter to book a cruise vacation that can cost far less than a comparable hotel stay—and give you a long list of added benefits. Learn how our maximizers work, how to calculate the true cost of often confusing promotions and which standard discounts are usually available. Get free or low cost upgrades, beat the high cost of solo cruise travel and learn other creative discount methods many experienced cruise passengers have yet to discover.

Why Cruise Now? puts you in the best position to take advantage of rate breaks brought about by the tremendous growth in the cruise industry. It explains the bargain of all-inclusive pricing and lets you know what to expect in the way of additional expenses.

Cruise Control helps you choose your ship, itinerary, cruise season, cabin (one of the biggest determining factors in your price) and shore excursions. It tells you about cruise insurance (a form of travel insurance we *always* recommend), safety and health considerations and tips to help you optimize your cruise experience.

Cruise Line Profiles gives you a keen overview of standard features and special attributes of major cruise lines and provides clues to their personalities. It covers itineraries, special promotions, children's programs and past passenger discounts.

Charting Your Course gives you significant facts at a glance: the capacity of each ship and the number of crew members it carries, when it was built and when it was last refurbished, dining room smoking policies and price category. The essential facts and significant details in this section can lift you out of a confusing ocean of possibilities.

Off The Beaten Wave increases your options with sections on masted ships, North American riverboat cruises, North American ocean cruises, unique cruise options, cruises to nowhere and freighter travel.

Clues To The Best Bargains

Cruise travel provides all-inclusive vacation value. The savvy saver will want to look at all possibilities but if you want a specific itinerary or ship, you can still save. Last year many cruise lines offered two-for-one deals on a total of over 200 different departures. We saw deals that allowed second, third and fourth passengers to cruise for free or for as little as $99-129 per person on three to seven night cruises. Most of us are familiar with the frustration that occurs when we discover that the passenger sitting next to us on an airplane paid less than we did. Cruise prices are no different. Passengers on the same ship (and in the same class of cabin) can pay widely varying prices. Begin your savings search by checking out these bargain maximizers.

CRUISE DISCOUNTERS

Cruise discounters emphasize price and generally limit their services to cruise travel only. Smaller, general purpose travel agencies have a lot of ground and air to cover. Even with the best intentions it's difficult for them to keep up with cruise deals or generate the sales volume that allows them to negotiate for the best discounts. Large cruise discount agencies usually provide the best option for travel on most major cruise lines. Choose an agency that offers specialization, attention to matching you to the right cruise *and* major discounts.

Almost 99 percent of all cruise bookings are made through travel agencies. Most of them provide good service; some are great. A few have invested little more than the cost of some business cards and a listing in the yellow pages. Ask questions and make sure the answers indicate that the agency will help you wade through the deep waters of pricing and get to the best discount.

The Cruise Line, Inc. (800-777-0707) is one of the largest cruise agencies in the world and the only cruise discount agency that maintains membership in the National Tour Association. They take the time to match you to an appropriate cruise and offer considerable discounts on most cruises; dramatic discounts on many specific cruises. They also provide top-notch service. Volume sales enable them to offer individuals low rates that are usually only offered for large group bookings. Recent specials illustrate their effectiveness:

- **A discount of almost $1,000 per person on Norwegian Cruise Line's *Norwegian Crown*.** Their price on a seven-night Caribbean cruise with ports-of-call including Grand Cayman, Cozumel, Key West and a private island was $399—a savings of over $1,000 per person.
- **Two-for-one prices on Holland America plus an additional $175 off per person** on seven-night Caribbean cruises. Their two-for-one deal brought rates down to as little as $549.
- **Better than two-for-one rates on**

Top market shares in the U.S. cruise industry: Carnival, 26.9% and Royal Caribbean, 16.1%.

Carnival's *Inspiration* with per person rates for a seven-night Southern Caribbean itinerary starting at $349—a $1,060 savings.

- **A discount of $2,524 per person on a 12-night Princess Cruise's Alaska hosted cruise-tour** on board the *Star Princess*. Their $2,014 price covered a seven-night cruise, two nights in Fairbanks, one night at the Denali Princess Lodge and one night in Anchorage.
- **Two-for-one prices on Orient Line** 19-night cruise tours from Cape Town, South Africa to Argentina. This special covered the popular Christmas cruise season and slashed prices from $5,995 to $2,997
- **Two-for-one prices on Windstar Cruises** through the French and Italian Riviera.

SUNDAY NEWSPAPERS

Sunday newspaper travel sections showcase some of the biggest sales cruise lines offer. Any travel section will have some special offers. Big city papers and papers in or near port cities offer extra deals. Find discounts for New Orleans embarkations, for example, in New Orleans, Houston and Dallas papers. You can purchase a short term subscription to a few major city papers—well worth the price if you find a great deal—or you can check out the ads in big city newspapers carried by most major libraries. Keep in mind that prices in these ads are minimum rates applying to a limited number of cabins and select sailings and cabin categories.

- **Some promotions are limited** to specific regions, but a good cruise agency may be able to override the geographic qualification
- **Check on consecutive Sundays** to acquire a base of knowledge, useful in evaluating other deals offered by cruise agents.
- **Each ad is designed to make you believe** that the offer it contains is the best deal available. Don't forget comparison shopping, but remember that many advertised offers have quick expiration dates.
- **Don't automatically call agencies listed at the bottom of the ad.** They're listed simply because they've paid a small fee to be included. Call a cruise specialist—preferably an agent you know and trust.

BOOK EARLY

Some of the deepest discounts go to passengers who book many weeks or months in advance. You get a combination of choice of sailings and cabin type, plus a significant discount. Some cruise lines guarantee to refund any difference if the price falls below what you paid. Be sure to ask about specific requirements for these rate guarantees. Don't assume that they exist for your particular booking.

Early booking discounts come in two forms:

- **Capacity controlled rates**, which expire when a pre-determined number of cabins are sold.
- **Fixed expiration date discounts**, which are available until a specified booking deadline.

Get early booking discounts through a cruise discount agency for double savings. You get the reduction offered by the cruise line program, and you also get a volume-seller discount from the agency.

Number of different itineraries offered by Royal Caribbean: 73.

AN OCEAN OF SAVINGS POSSIBILITIES

This section describes many ways to save on cruise travel. Check *Cruise Profiles* for more information on promotions popular with specific cruise lines.

RATE REDUCTIONS

Free or reduced rates for third and fourth passengers (also applying to children) are offered by many cruise lines, sometimes as part of a special promotion; sometimes as a standard discount. They are usually offered for three-, four-, and seven-night sailings. Airfare is not included. Fifty to 80 percent off third and fourth passenger rates really amount to 25 to 40 percent off per person. When you are offered a price with variations for multiple passengers, divide the total cost by the number of passengers to get the true rate per passenger.

Two-for-one deals can be money savers, but they can also be marketing ploys based on inflated prices for the first passenger. It's math time again. Divide the brochure price (excluding air allowance, port charges and fees, if included) by two, then compare it to other discount rates to determine the real value of the offer.

Flat rate specials offer two fixed rates (usually one rate for inside cabins and a higher rate for oceanview). You get the best available cabin or suite when you book by a specific date. The earlier you book, the better your accommodations. Run-of-ship rates are similar, but your specific cabin is not usually confirmed until two weeks before departure.

Senior citizen discounts were once relatively common but are now giving way to a wider range of promotions available to all age groups. Senior rate eligibility (when such deals exist), usually requires that one person per cabin is at least 55 years old.

Group discounts are available for multiple bookings on a specific cruise. A formal connection (family relationship, club membership, etc.) is not required, but you must book as a group. Your discount is contingent on the number of people traveling; eight people/four cabins is usually the minimum requirement for extra amenities or upgrades. If you have 15 passengers, based on double occupancy, you may be able to get one free berth.

SPECIAL PROMOTIONS

Affinity promotions save you money when you use a cruise line and its promotion partner. The partner is often a credit or charge card company offering free upgrades, discounts or shipboard credits. Visa Gold, for example, has offered bonuses on 22 major cruise lines. Credit and charge card promotions require that you reserve and pay with the co-promoting card.

Added value promotions give free night, land package add-ons, free shore excursions and free or discounted pre- or post-cruise hotel rooms.

Past passenger specials provide discounts to people who have sailed on a specific cruise line in the past. Most lines enroll you automatically, but be sure to inquire. Most programs also offer added amenities and other benefits.

CREATIVE WAYS TO SAVE

Repositioning cruises combine value and variety. They're available twice a year when ships are moved from one itinerary to another. Common repositionings include the Caribbean to Europe or Alaska, and back again. An Alaska repositioning cruise may include highlights from Eastern, Western and Southern Caribbean sailings, as well as the Panama Canal and the Mexican Riviera—all in just ten to 17 days. Caribbean to Europe repositioning cruises can include stops in Portugal, Tangier and Morocco. Most lines feature repositioning cruises in their brochures.

Most around-the-world cruises allow you to book a segment of the itinerary at a per-night cost. Arrange your own discount airfare to meet the ship at the port you choose. You also get the ambiance of a different type of ship with a more varied passenger profile and ports-of-call standard cruises don't offer.

Back-to-back specials offer discounts for two or more consecutive cruise segments on the same ship. For example, buy one week and get the second week free, or get a significant discount on both weeks. Look for some variation in itinerary unless return visits to favorite ports-of-call appeal to you.

Stand-by rates can be as much as 60 percent below standard rates. You rank your preferred sailings and cabin preferences, pay a nominal deposit at the time of booking and wait to be confirmed until 30 or more days before departure. If you're not confirmed, you get a full refund. If you are offered your first choice and decline, your deposit is not refunded.

Special event discounts or added values may be yours for the asking. Newlyweds, couples celebrating their wedding anniversaries and people enjoying other special events should let their cruise agent know. You could save a few hundred dollars, get a free upgrade or find flowers and chocolates waiting in your stateroom.

The last year in which more people crossed the North Atlantic by sea than by air: 1958.

Cut port spending. The average passenger on a seven-night cruise spends about $400 in port. If you limit purchases and extra-cost shore excursions you may be able to book a higher category cruise, upgrade your cabin or go home with a healthier bank account. On some cruises, $400 is enough to cover the cost of third and fourth passengers in your stateroom. Ports-of-call are interesting on their own. Planned shore excursions can be wonderful, but they are not essential to the enjoyment of your cruise. Shopping can also be enjoyed without ruining your cruise budget. Look for indigenous crafts and small keepsake items. Don't rely on cruise ship personnel to steer you to the best bargains. Many lines are given financial consideration for their recommendations. They may not be your most helpful source for true bargains and they may divert you from discovering your own hidden bargain shops.

Discounts by internet are not yet widely available. Most cruise lines are apt to stick to travel agents and specialty, high-volume agencies to offer their best deals. Most cruise travelers will remain comfortable booking cruises only with a human on the other end of the deal, ready to answer all necessary questions. *Best Fares* internet site at **www.bestfares.com** includes cruise discounts for subscribers and summarizes special sale fares offered to the general public.

UPGRADES

Free or low-cost upgrades give you added comfort with little or no additional expense. There are three basic possibilities:

- **Upgrade authority given to large cruise agencies** to promote passenger bookings. The Cruise Line, Inc., for example, offers two-category upgrades on Carnival, Royal Caribbean and other cruise lines.
- **"Guaranteed" upgrades**, available on some cruises when the cabin category you want is sold out. You pay the rate for the category you would have selected and get an upgraded cabin unless a cancellation opens up a cabin in your original category.
- **Paid Upgrades** can cost as little as $10 per person, per category on some sailings.

BOOKING FOR ONE

Singles can save on cruise travel even though they're typically asked to pay a single supplement of 50 to 200 percent above the per person/double occupancy fare. Check the chart on the following page and ask your cruise consultant to focus on lines that calculate single supplements most favorably or offer alternate plans and promotions.

Guaranteed single rates charge prices slightly higher than per person/double occupancy rates. They give you the benefit of private accommodations and assign your cabin prior to sailing. Choose a slow season to increase your odds of getting an outside cabin. Cruise lines that don't routinely offer this program may extend it upon request.

Match-up plans called Single Share Guarantees usually charge close to the standard per person double occupancy rate. They try to place you with a cabin partner of the same gender and smoking preference. If they fail, you get a private room at no extra charge. If you don't adapt easily to new people, this plan is not for you. If you are adaptable and would enjoy a cruise companion, it can provide an attractive option. Ask your cruise consultant to fill you in on specific match-up policies and procedures. Some cruise lines pride themselves on thoughtful match-ups; others are haphazard.

Year in which the first Blue Ribbon was awarded for fastest Transatlantic crossing by ship: 1900.

SINGLE TRAVELER POLICIES

This chart gives a broad overview of single traveler policies. The second column indicates the number of single cabins available per ship; the third shows availability of match-up plans; the fourth shows the single supplement range, which can vary by ship, cabin class and itinerary.

CRUISE LINE'S SINGLES POLICIES

CRUISE LINES	SINGLE CABIN AVAILABILITY	SINGLE MATCH-UP PLANS	SINGLE SUPPLEMENT
American Hawaii	19	Yes	160-200%
Carnival	0-14	Yes	160-200%
Celebrity	None	Yes	150-200%
Commodore	2	No	135-200%
Costa	None	No	150-200%
Crystal	None	No	Starts at 115%
Cunard	0-110	Yes	115-200%
Dolphin	0-2	Yes	150%
Holland America	0-36	Yes	135-190%
Norwegian	0-20	Yes	Guaranteed Single Rates
Orient	None	Yes	125% sometimes waived
Princess	0-2	Yes	150-200%
Radisson Seven Seas	None	No	Starts at 125%
Royal Caribbean	None	Yes	150%
Seabourn	None	No	110-150%
Seawind	6	No	0-200%

AIR TRAVEL OPTIONS

Air/Cruise packages have been the norm since the 1980s. They protect you from variables on independently booked flights that could cause you to miss embarkation. Cruise lines including Carnival and Royal Caribbean recently began unbundling their brochure prices, offering cruise only rates with air add-ons optional.

If you choose to book air travel as part of your cruise package, here are some key points to keep in mind.

- **Cruise lines reserve blocks of seats** about a year in advance. If demand is higher than anticipated, you may be assigned less convenient flights. If you want a specific

Countries that dominated travel by sea in the 1930s: Great Britain, France, Germany and the U.S.

flight or airline, you must request it at the time the reservation is made. There is no guarantee that you'll get what you want (and there may be a deviation charge of $35-50), but the cruise line agent will try to accommodate your request.

- **Reduced rate air is sometimes available.** An air rate of $299 from Chicago to Miami, for example, may be reduced to $149 or $99. Norwegian recently offered free roundtrip air travel from select cities to Houston, to promote Port of Houston departures of the *Norwegian Star.*
- **When your flight is confirmed** (usually three to five weeks before departure) call the airline to register your frequent flyer number and request seat assignments.

Alternate air travel options may save you money, particularly with increased availability of low fares to Florida. You may also want to use your frequent flyer miles.

- **Think twice about independent air travel in winter** if you are departing from or connecting in a cold-weather city. Consider purchasing extra cruise insurance coverage for delayed flights.
- **Factor in the cost of airport to seaport travel.** Cruise lines include all transfers only if they arrange your air travel.
- **Plan to arrive early.** You may want to fly in the night before. You can often get bargain rates on overnight accommodations at hotels in cruise embarkation cities.
- **Plan your return flight** to allow for a two to three hour disembarkation process. Let the purser know that you have independent flight arrangements so you can be among the first passengers to disembark.

*"The Greater Fort Lauderdale Convention & Visitors Bureau doesn't want cruise travelers to simply pass through their city. They have put together two-night packages at 16 hotels, under the A Shore Thing moniker. Package rates start at $86 per person (two nights, based on double occupancy) for the Seabonay Beach Resort (Hillsboro Beach). Each package includes admission to a local attraction (options include Butterfly World, the Water Taxi, Everglades Holiday Park airboat rides and many others), a $20 dining credit (per person) and discount coupon booklet. For more details, call **800-227-8669.**"*

WHY CRUISE NOW?

THE BROADENING APPEAL OF CRUISES

The cruise industry will have to attract eight million people annually by the turn of the century to make their multi-billion dollar new ship investments pay off. The new ships have been designed to attract a wider variety of passengers and aggressive discount promotions are meant to catch their attention.

Modern cruise options appeal to all tastes and personalities. Some people still believe that cruises are for more mature and upper income travelers. In fact, the cruise industry has planned for baby boomers, young singles, families, budget watchers, active travelers, intellectuals, fun-lovers and just about any personality type you can imagine. The size of the new mega-ships allows for a diversity of activities and public areas designed to keep many different types of people happy.

> *"Older ships are being retired to avoid improvements mandated by amendments to the Safety of Life at Sea Treaty. These amendments began to go into effect in 1997. It can cost $20-40 million to bring one ship up to standard. But new ships continue to be arrive, keeping supply high and rates low."*

Today's ships and the itineraries they sail can contain more adventure and variety than land-only vacations. While you're enjoying the ship's amenities you are also getting closer to interesting ports-of-call. Each time you disembark, you are in the midst of a new environment and culture—possibly even a different country.

As the stress level of modern life increases, so does the appeal of cruise vacations. The floating island of a cruise ship provides one of the best environments for relaxation—an opportunity those of us who have learned to co-exist with stress can appreciate. Remember fresh air? You'll be surrounded by it. Pack away your troubles, your pager and your cell phone, take a deep breath and truly relax.

NEW & UPCOMING SHIPS

This is a new era of options in cruise ship ambiance, cabin choice, recreation and entertainment. A significant percentage of today's cruise passengers definitely think bigger is better. New mega-ships carry between 1,740 and 2,642 passengers. (Five years ago the standard was 300 to 900.) Consider Royal Caribbean's 130,000-ton ships (costing over $500 million each), set for delivery in 1999 and 2000. Each ship will accommodate 3,100 passengers. When they are completed, they will increase overall Royal Caribbean capacity by over 26 percent.

Each of the three largest cruise lines (Carnival, Princess and Royal Caribbean) and seven other lines are contributing to the new ship growth spurt. Disney Cruise Lines enters the market in 1998 with two ships that are already heavily booked. Each new ship has its own personality. The traditional "floating city" has become an architectural wonder. New ship features include:

- **High-tech entertainment options**, including virtual reality theaters, cyber game centers and computer kiosks with internet access. More costly cabins have in-room computers. Some lines let you borrow a laptop to use during your cruise.
- **Grand-scale public areas** towering as high as nine decks with sweeping staircases, sculpture, caviar bars and (on some ships), glass-domed ceilings that showcase the skies.
- **Themed restaurants** offering nightly options to the main dining room. Some are informal; others offer gourmet presentation of Italian, Asian and specialty cuisine. There is also increased main dining room availability of tables for two or four.
- **Spas and fitness facilities** to a degree previously available only on a handful of luxury ships. You may find your hometown health club lacking by comparison.

HIGHLIGHTS OF THE NEWEST SHIPS

Carnival's *Destiny* is the industry's first 100,000-ton ship. Her sister ship, the *Grand Princess*, soon joined her in this honor. The *Destiny*, at her highest point, is 55 feet taller than the Statue of Liberty. Her central atrium rises nine decks in height and is hung with Venetian glass chandeliers. Over 1,150 cabins accommodate 2,600 passengers; more than half have unobstructed floor-to-ceiling views. Passengers dine in their choice of two-tiered restaurants. She sails Eastern and Western Caribbean itineraries from Miami as she is too wide to pass through the Panama Canal.

Celebrity's *Mercury* is the largest ship to transit the Panama Canal and to sail to

Two of over 100 exotic drinks offered by Carnival: the Queen Bee and the Blue Neon.

"Here are some numbers on the Destiny's provisions for an average week: 2,800 pounds of prime rib; 6,000 pounds of chicken; 22,000 shrimp; 2,300 pounds of pasta; 600 pounds of salmon; 1,800 pounds of coffee; 4,100 bottles of wine; and 815 liters of Scotch."

Alaska. The 1,870-passenger wonder offers the largest penthouse suites in the industry, private verandas, high-tech Sony entertainment options (including a 40-feet-tall video wall in the Grand Foyer and a Cyberspace room), an observation lounge with telescopes. an extensive collection of avant garde art, a luxurious spa (9,340 square feet) and gourmet cuisine from Michelin chef Michel Roux. She sails the Western Caribbean October through April, the Panama Canal in April and October, and Alaska from May through September.

Costa Cruises' *Costa Victoria* accommodates 1,928 passengers in 964 cabins. She is entered through a seven-deck, glass-domed atrium. A four-deck observation lounge at the front of the ship provides floor-to-ceiling views. She has paddle tennis courts that are about two-thirds the size of a regulation tennis court. Her indoor pool is lined by Roman columns and a mosaic wall that accent's Costa's Italian theme. She is the first Costa ship to include an indoor pool, twin dining rooms and refrigerators in each cabin. She sails Eastern and Western Caribbean itineraries in winter; European sailings from Venice in the summer.

Holland America's *Veendam* expresses her elegance with Venetian glass sculpture in her four-deck atrium and a $2 million art and antique collection. She carries 1,266 passengers in 633 cabins designed to enhance relaxation with peach and blue color schemes and comfortable sofas. She sails Eastern and Western Caribbean itineraries, except during summer, when she sails a unique New York-Montreal itinerary.

Royal Caribbean's *Grandeur of the Seas* carries 1,950 passengers in 975 cabins. Her seven-deck atrium rises above a champagne and caviar bar and is centered with a grand piano. Many cabins are as much as 23 percent larger than earlier Royal Caribbean ships and all have ocean-view picture windows (the porthole is becoming an artifact of the past). Verandas and sliding glass doors are featured in 25 percent of the cabins. An enlarged spa and fitness center spans two decks and is adjacent to a sunning deck with two pools and six whirlpools. She sails a year-round Eastern Caribbean itinerary.

UPCOMING SHIPS

The chart on the next page lists new ships scheduled to arrive through 2001. In addition to the ships listed, three new boutique ships will also debut: The 320-passenger *Paul Gauguin* from Radisson Seven Seas Cruises and two 396-passenger ships from Silver Sea Cruises. New ships include:

- **Disney Cruise Line's *Disney Magic* and *Disney Wonder*** catering to adults, families and seniors, with special activities for each group. Three- or four-night cruises are packaged with three- or four-night hotel stays at Walt Disney World. Both ships are styled on a classic ocean liner

Feature of Carnival's Destiny: glass balconies adjacent to over 370 outside cabins.

SHIPS COMING ON-LINE THROUGH 2001		
CRUISE LINE/SHIP	YEAR	PAX
Carnival Cruise Lines *Paradise*	1998	2,040
Carnival Cruise Lines *Triumph*	1999	2,642
Carnival Cruise Lines *Victory*	2000	2,642
Disney Cruise Lines *Disney Magic*	1998	2,400
Disney Cruise Lines *Disney Wonder*	1999	2,400
Holland America/*Volendam*	1999	1,440
Holland America/*Zaandam*	1999	1,440
Norwegian Cruise Line/*Norwegian Sky*	1999	2,100
Princess Cruise Lines *Sea Princess*	1999	1,950
Princess Cruise Lines *Ocean Princess*	1999	1,950
Princess Cruise Lines/Unnamed	2001	2,600
Princess Cruise Lines/Unnamed	2001	2,600
Royal Caribbean International's *Vision of the Seas*	1998	2,050
Royal Caribbean International/Unnamed	1999	3,100
Royal Caribbean International/Unnamed	2000	3,000

theme. Almost 75 percent of the cabins have ocean views. There will be 24-hour room service and self-service launderettes. Families can dine in their choice of three themed restaurants; an alternative restaurant is limited to adults. Over 15,000 square feet on each ship is dedicated to activities for three to 12 year olds and both ships will have the largest number of children's counselors of any ship at sea. Adult entertainment options include an interactive sports club and a comedy showcase—but no casinos. The first Disney ship (the *Disney Magic*) should be sailing in summer of 1998, after two delays. The *Disney Wonder* and the *Disney Magic* are both heavily booked in advance of their arrival.

- **Princess Cruises' *Grand Princess*** will join the ranks of advanced technology mega-ships at 109,000 tons. Her 15th-deck nightclub, suspended 144 feet above the water, will be accessed via a moving walkway called the travelator. She will have a virtual reality theater, a blue screen room where you can step into virtual reality and be filmed into your choice of blockbuster movies, three theaters, a wedding chapel, a 24-hour food court, a golf driving range and an upper pool area enclosed by a retractable glass dome (a popular new ship feature).
- **Princess Cruise Line will grow by over 200,000 tons** with the placement of orders for two more sister ships to the *Grand Princess*. Delivery dates are the spring and fall of 2001. These additions, plus the three other

ships already under construction, will double Princess' capacity to 13 ships and 22,500 berths. The two new sister ships will cruise the Caribbean year-round. Price tag for each ship: about $425 million.

ALL-INCLUSIVE PRICING

What Your Cruise Includes

Cruises typically offer some of the best vacation values and allow you to plot your vacation expenses almost to the dollar. Even though some added costs have gone up, you can cut down on them or (if you choose) eliminate most of them entirely. You also buy a consistent level of quality with no worry that your accommodations might be great one night and inferior the next. You don't have to pick a local restaurant and hope for the best. You are purchasing a package of consistent quality.

Cruises typically include:

- **Roundtrip airfare**, but remember that many advertised specials do not include airfare. Read the small print and clarify this important inclusion with your cruise consultant. Ask for a cruise-only and an air-inclusive rate to see if you can save money by booking airfare independently. Using **www.bestfares.com** Snooze You Lose fares, for example, could bring you tremendous savings.
- **Ground transportation** between the airport and your ship, when you purchase an air inclusive cruise. You'll be met by a ship's representative on arrival and transported to port. A motorcoach will take you to the airport after your cruise. You may prefer to arrange your own airport-embarkation port transportation by taxi (at your own expense) to avoid extra waiting time.
- **Accommodations** in the stateroom category you select.
- **Shipboard amenities** including pools, whirlpools, spas, health clubs, games, aerobics, yoga, skeet shooting, volleyball, contests, bridge tournaments, paddle tennis, basketball, card rooms, libraries (book and video), and deck space for sunbathing and conversation. Many ships have playrooms, teen discos, video arcades, computer rooms, jogging tracks, extensive health spas and gyms. Some have paddle tennis and basketball courts and miniature golf courses or driving ranges.
- **Entertainment** in the main lounge (home to Las Vegas-style reviews and other types of performances), cabarets, films, theme dance clubs, discos and piano bars. Often, there are also seminars, lessons, cooking classes and other features varying by cruise line and departure date.
- **Visits to ports of call,** typically three or four stops on a seven-night cruise, sometimes including a stop at a private island.
- **Food, food and more food** – up to eight meals and snacks per day. Start with three meals a day, the equivalent of fine restaurant dining and sometimes outdoing most restaurants. You will also find daytime and late night buffets so extensive that passengers who can't summon a single hunger pain pose for pictures in front of them. Many ships add specialty restaurants, 24-hour buffets, pizzerias, poolside grills, coffee bars, theme restaurants and ice cream and yogurt parlors.

Mode of travel Grace Kelly used when she went to Monaco to marry Prince Rainier: cruise ship.

> *"Take advantage of the options modern cruise travel provides. Most special diet requests can be honored, but be sure to make them known in advance. There is an overall trend towards more healthful menu choices without sacrificing lavish variety. Night owls usually prefer late dinner seating, and the earlier seating can be perfect for early risers; you have a long evening to enjoy after finishing your dinner. If you don't enjoy your assigned dinner companions, discretely ask the maitre d' to re-assign you. Some people choose to offer a $10-20 tip when they make their request."*

ADDED CHARGES

Port charges, government taxes and fees ($125 average on seven-night Caribbean cruises) used to be excluded from advertised prices. Six cruise lines, under prodding from the Florida Attorney General's office, agreed to change that policy and paid a total of $250,000 in fines. Look for all cruise lines to follow this new policy (many already have) or, at the least, bring port charges up from fine print to a major part of advertised materials.

Other expenses not included—Optional tours in ports-of-call; ship-to-shore phone calls and faxes; casino gambling; most alcoholic beverages; soft drinks and juices not served with meals; personal expenses such as massage, hair care and boutique purchases; cruise insurance (five to six percent of the cost of your cruise—see *Cruise Control* for details) and gratuities (except on the few lines that discourage it). Super all-inclusive fares include certain shore excursions, gratuities and alcoholic beverages and are mostly limited to five- and six-star cruise lines such as Silversea and Seabourn.

If you don't watch discretionary expenses you can end up incurring a large on board bill. Here is a sample of extra cost items and typical charges.

- Ship-to-shore phone calls: $9.50 to $19.50 per minute
- Cocktails: $2.95 to $4.50
- Half-hour massage: $35
- Manicure: $20
- Laundering one shirt: $2

Tipping guidelines are supplied on each cruise. Suggested amounts average $60 per person for a seven-night Caribbean cruise, usually paid in cash on the last night and covering your cabin steward, waiter and bus boy. Set aside an appropriate amount of cash to avoid lining up at the cashier's desk on your last day at sea. You may want to tip your head waiter at time of service if he performs a special service. Some cruise lines advertise no-tipping policies. Ultra-luxury lines usually mean what they say. Others may state that tipping is included, but most passengers still leave nominal gratuities, relied upon by cruise line employees as a significant part of their income.

Some ships offer cash-free systems. You are given a plastic card to present with each purchase. Your bill is payable on the last night of your cruise. If you prefer, you can establish credit when you board the ship by presenting a major credit card at the check-in desk or the purser's office.

Function of a ship's Chief Radio Officer: all ship-to-shore communication.

CRUISE CONTROL

CHOOSE YOUR PRICE RANGE

Pick a price range you can live with, then collect brochures from lines that meet your needs. Take into account the fact that savvy travelers rarely pay brochure rates. Read the small print terms and conditions on the back of each brochure to understand factors that can affect your cruise purchase, then call a cruise discounter for a great deal.

Be flexible. If you cruise during peak and holiday periods, you are going to pay more. Caribbean rates are typically lowest from Labor Day to mid-December, except for Thanksgiving sailings. You'll find bargains on early-spring economy cruises, but you may share the ship with high-energy college students. Alaska cruises are best buys from May to early June and in September. European rates are lowest for spring and fall travel.

Here is a thumbnail sketch of cruise lines categorized by cost.

- **Budget**—Commodore and Premier
- **Moderate**—American Hawaii, Carnival, Costa, First European, Norwegian, Orient, Renaissance and Royal Olympic
- **Deluxe**—Celebrity, Disney, Holland America, Princess, Royal Caribbean and Windstar
- **Ultra-Deluxe**—Crystal, Cunard, Radisson Seven Seas, Seabourn and Silversea
- **Boutique cruises** overlap the ultra-deluxe category but include the smaller, all-suite ships of Seabourn and Silversea and the sailing ships of Windstar and Star Clipper.
- **Adventure and expedition cruises** are available in moderate to deluxe price ranges.

The first profit-making pleasure yacht: P&O Line's 2,376-ton Ceylon, in 1881.

CHOOSE YOUR ITINERARY

Water covers over 78 percent of our planet and there is a cruise line ready to take you through most of it. Choose from over 180 ports on seven continents. Some routes are seasonal; others, year-round.

The Caribbean remains the most popular cruise choice. Some cruise lines add variety to ports-of-call by obtaining exclusive landing rights on private islands.

- **The Eastern Caribbean** includes Nassau, St. John, St. Maarten, St. Croix, St. Thomas and San Juan.
- **The Western Caribbean** includes Grand Cayman, Jamaica and Playa del Carmen/Cozumel.
- **The Southern or Deep Caribbean** is sailed by ships based in San Juan, allowing visits to islands including Antigua, Barbados, Caracas, Curacao, Grenada, Guadeloupe, Martinique, St. Barts, St. Kitts, St. Lucia, St. Maarten, St. Thomas, Trinidad and Tobago.

Alaska itineraries primarily depart from Anchorage or Vancouver with ports-of-call including College Fjord, Glacier Bay, Juneau, Ketchikan, Seward, Sitka and Skagway. Itineraries include roundtrip Vancouver (Inside Passage) and one-way itineraries—Vancouver to Anchorage, for example, and the reverse.

This chart shows peak cruise seasons by itinerary. The chart on the following page summarizes current itineraries by cruise line.

POPULAR CRUISE SEASONS

ITINERARY	PEAK SEASONS
Africa	Year-round; May-October emphasis for North Africa; November-April for Eastern and Southern Africa
Alaska	May-September
Asia & The Orient	October-March
Baltic	May-October
Bermuda	May-October
Canada	May-October
Caribbean & Mexico	Year-round
Hawaii	Year-round
India & Southeast Asia	Year-round; November-April emphasis
Mediterranean	Year-round
New England	May-October
Panama Canal	September-May
South America	Year-round, North Coast; September-April, other areas
South Pacific	Year-round; November-April emphasis

The first cruise from England to the Mediterranean: Orient's Chimborazo, in 1889.

SELECT CRUISE LINE ITINERARIES

CRUISE LINE	ALASKA	BERMUDA	BAHAMAS	CARIBBEAN	MEDITERRANEAN	HAWAII	PANAMA CANAL	OTHER ITINERARIES
American Hawaii						X		
Carnival	X		X	X		X	X	West Coast/Mexican Riviera
Celebrity	X	X	X	X		X	X	
Commodore				X				Central America
Costa			X	X	X			Baltic, Black Sea, Greece, Orient, South America, Southeast Asia & Transatlantic
Crystal	X		X	X	X	X	X	China, Mexico, Orient & Asia
Cunard	X	X		X	X	X	X	Canada, Orient, around-the-world, South America, South Pacific & Transatlantic
Disney			X					
Holland America	X		X	X	X	X	X	New England, Southeast Asia, Transatlantic & world cruise
Norwegian	X	X	X	X	X	X	X	
Orient Lines					X			Africa, Antarctica, Australia/ New Zealand, India, Indian Ocean South America & Southeast Asia
Premier			X	X	X			Canada, New England & South America
Princess	X		X	X	X	X	X	Africa, Amazon, Australia/South Pacific, Baltic, Canada, Mexico, Pacific, Orient, Southeast Asia & Tahiti
Radisson Seven Seas				X	X		X	Arctic, Antarctica, Galapagos, Greenland, Iceland, Norway, South America, Southeast Asia & Transcanal
Renaissance					X			Asia & Africa
Royal Caribbean	X	X	X	X	X	X	X	Far East & Mexico
Royal Olympic					X			South America
Seabourn	X			X	X	X	X	Asia, Australia, Baltic, Canada, Norway, South America, South Pacific & Transcanal

First cruise line to offer millennium cruise itineraries: Cunard.

DO A COMPATIBILITY CHECK

An astronomer who unwittingly books a Wheel of Fortune theme cruise is probably not going to have a great time. Personal taste is a prime consideration in choosing a cruise. Do a compatibility check to match your personality with the ship and sailing you are considering. You are choosing a total environment that will surround you for the duration of your vacation. Your ship will be your hotel, entertainment, outdoor playground, restaurant and meeting place. Go back to your brochures and look at the photographs. Do you see children? Are the models younger or older? How are they dressed? Is the tone festive or refined? Talk to friends who are cruise veterans and have tastes like yours. (*Cruise Line Profiles* contains many clues.) One of your best allies is a cruise consultant willing to be honest about each ship's personality. Don't rely on cruise line information. In most cases they will tell you that every ship they sail is perfect for everyone.

Consider the following factors and share your preferences with your cruise consultant:

- **Are you excited by the mega-ships** or would you feel more comfortable on a smaller ship? For the peak of relaxation, consider a smaller ship with fewer ports-of-call. Your ship can be your best destination.
- **New ship or older ship?** The new ships are most impressive from the outside, offer more deck space, larger public areas and improved cabins and bathrooms. They will almost certainly be the choice of anyone who appreciates the latest innovations. Older ships have been re-built, refurbished and updated. They provide a more classic cruise experience and can offer considerable savings.
- **Are you looking for optimum tranquility or a lot of activity?** Some ships offer dozens of planned activities each day and an energy level that appeals to many people. Other ships provide a backdrop conducive to relaxation.
- **Do you like to be among people in your own age group** or is a wide age mix more interesting? Ships with a good passenger age mix are best for families and groups with members of different generations. If you want a vacation from *your* kids, don't book a ship full of other people's children.
- **What children's programs are offered?** Families should consider the needs and likes of all children in the family. Some ships offer many activities for teenagers and less for young children; others are the opposite. If you need childcare while you

"Candyce Staphen, noted family travel columnist, has written Cruise Vacations With Kids (440-pages/$14.95/Prima Publishing) to help you make intelligent choices when planning family cruise travel. Separate attention is paid to children in four age groups: under two, two to four, five to eleven and pre-teens/teens. The age-wise approach continues with an intensive look at ports-of-call. Best Bet activities are listed for each of three age ranges and for adults. You will even learn where to go to buy reasonably priced food with kid-appeal."

Cruise ship that offers 24-hour childcare services: The Big Red Boat.

enjoy nighttime activities, ask about availability, cost and qualifications of childcare workers.

- **How important is the dining experience?** All successful cruise lines serve plentiful arrays of food. It would be hard to find a ship that did not offer above average meals, but beyond that given, there are distinct levels of excellence, from lavish offerings of very good food to extraordinary presentations of gourmet cuisine.
- **How important is the casino?** If you love Las Vegas, make sure the ship you book has a casino large enough to challenge you with an ample number of games and tables.
- **What is the smoking policy?** You can request smoke-free cabins on many lines. All ships have non-smoking areas and most have major smoke-free zones. Ask about policies for casinos, lounges and showrooms. Rules will be more relaxed on lines that attract a significant percentage of international travelers. Smoking is becoming increasingly restricted (or banned entirely) in dining rooms. Check *Charting Your Course* for guidelines.

The Unofficial Guide To Cruises by Kay Showker with Bob Sehlinger, offers 798 pages of cruise travel information, including extensive looks at the individual ships of all major cruise lines. The book is published by Macmillan Travel and retails for $18. If your bookstore doesn't stock it, request a special order under ISBN #02-860495-4. Libraries also carry it.

Preview almost any cruise with promotional videos that cost about $15 each. Call Vacations on Video, **602-483-1551** or fax to **602-483-0785**.

CHOOSE YOUR CABIN

Your cabin category is a big factor in the cost of your cruise. There are two schools of thought: choose an inexpensive category, because you spend little time in your cabin; choose a higher category, because size, amenities, views and placement on the ship matter greatly.

- **Inside or outside**—Inside cabins offer the most economical options. Outside (oceanview) provides a window to the world, but choose carefully to make sure your view isn't limited to traffic on a busy deck or bright orange lifeboats.
- **Placement**—The higher above the water line, the more expensive the cabin. On older ships, cabins midship are most stable and free of noise and vibration.
- **Beds**—What's worse than sharing a double bed when you'd rather not? Sleeping in twin beds when you want to be together. Most new ships solved this problem with twin beds that join to create a king-size bed.
- **Bath or shower**—Most cabins have showers only. On some ships you will have to book a suite to get both a bath and shower.

Get an idea of how much cabin choice affects your price by checking these low season brochure prices on Princess Cruise Line's *Crown Princess* seven-night Alaska itineraries. Brochure rates range from $1,499 to $4,199, cruise-only, based on double occupancy—a $3,700 variance. Prices within a given range vary by cabin location.

- $1,499-1,799—Inside with two lower beds
- $1,799—Outside economy with

Wind speed described as calm: 2-6 mph; as light wind, 7-10 mph; as light breeze, 11-15 mph.

queen bed

- $1,849—Outside with one lower bed and one upper berth
- $1,899—Outside economy with two lower beds
- $1,949-1,999—Outside with two lower beds (some obstructed views)
- $2,089-2,629—Outside with two lower beds
- $2,699-2,999—Outside with two lower beds/private balcony
- $3,449—Outside mini-suite with private balcony
- $4,199—Outside suite with private balcony

CONSIDER YOUR SHORE EXCURSIONS

Most shore excursions cost extra, except for adventure and expedition cruises and cruises in China's waters, per government mandate. Most lines do not allow you to book in advance, but you may receive a pamphlet detailing them with your cruise documents. Previews are often given on board your ship the day before you arrive at each port or you may be asked to select your shore excursions during the first day of your cruise. Many popular excursions sell out quickly so plan on signing up as soon as possible.

The price of shore excursions varies. Caribbean and Mexico shore excursions (city or island tours, snorkeling and glass bottom boat rides, for example) can range from $25-50 per person. Special excursions have higher per person rates of about $40-90 for golf, $40-55 for scuba diving, $65 for seaplane or helicopter rides, $50 for submarine rides or horseback riding and $30-45 for sailboat rides. Extended tours, such as an all-day Tulum Mayan Ruins tour from Playa del Carmen can be bargains at about $55-75 per person. As a general guideline, plan on spending $11-13 per tour hour. European shore excursions tend to be all-day events and average $135-175.

Independent tours are yours for the taking. You are free to do as you like until it's time to re-board your ship. In many Caribbean ports you will find taxi drivers who give private island tours for less than the group tour price offered on board your ship.

Alaskan shore excursions are extremely popular. Pre-purchase when possible. Options include salmon bakes, two hour motorcoach tours and 90 minute flights over Glacier Bay.

ALASKA CRUISE-TOURS

Alaska cruise-tours give you an overview of Alaska that you can't get in brief port visits. Some are hosted; others allow for independent activities. Here is an example from Princess Cruise Line's 14-night hosted cruise-tour.:

- **Days one through seven**—Depart from Vancouver for a cruise through the Inside Passage and ports-of-call at Ketchikan, Juneau, Skagway, Glacier Bay and College Fjord.
- **Day eight**—Arrive in Seward and take a scenic motorcoach ride to the Kenai Peninsula. Spend the night at the Kenai Princess Lodge. (If you miss Kenai, you've missed Alaska.)
- **Day nine**—Enjoy Kenai on your own or add an optional adventure tour.
- **Day ten**—Travel to Anchorage for an overnight stay.
- **Day 11**—Board the Midnight Sun Express Ultra Dome train and travel to an overnight stay at the Denali

Cost of Carnival's 1998 new ship orders: $1.8 billion.

Princess Lodge.

- **Day 12**—Tour Denali National Park in the morning, then re-board the Midnight Sun Express for travel to Fairbanks.
- **Day 13**—Tour Fairbanks, see a working gold mine, enjoy a riverboat cruise on board the *Discovery* and enjoy the evening at your hotel or exploring Fairbanks' nightlife before your morning departure by air.

CRUISE INSURANCE

Because you are investing a considerable sum of money, cruise insurance is almost always worth purchasing. You can purchase insurance from the cruise line, your booking agent or directly from the insurance company. Your cost will range from five to six percent of the total cost of your cruise. Unless you are purchasing a cruise for very last-minute travel, insurance is almost mandatory, in terms of your peace of mind.

The most important component of Trip Cancellation Insurance is coverage for trip interruption. Policies also usually include medical and luggage coverage. Trip cancellation protects you from losing the entire cost of your cruise should you need to cancel. Policies differ greatly. If you have any questions about terms, terminology or areas of coverage, ask for complete clarification and be sure you are satisfied with the answers.

- **Ask to have the terms and conditions faxed** to you so that you can review them carefully.
- **Understand the difference between a waiver and insurance.** A waiver is *not* insurance. It is a for-fee option in which the company waives its own penalties if you cancel your cruise for any reason, usually up to 72 hours before sailing. It provides no protection against operator default and is usually full of clauses that limit the acceptable conditions under which you may cancel without penalty.
- **Emergency medical evacuation** and other medical coverage also varies and may not apply to pre-existing conditions. Remember that Medicare, Medicaid and many private health insurance policies do not cover health care outside the U.S.
- **Extra luggage coverage** is rarely necessary since cruise ships only handle your luggage while it is on board. Without insurance their liability is usually limited to $100 per bag; with insurance it is $500-1,000. Your biggest risk occurs when you are asked to leave your bags outside your cabin door the night before you disembark. Be sure to lock all luggage. Air segments are covered by the airline's standard baggage liability limits.

Sources for cruise insurance include Access America Cruise Policy, **800-284-8300**; CFA, **800-234-0375**; Travelex, **800-228-9792** and Worldwide Assistance, **800-821-2828**. Your cruise agent should also be able to refer you to reputable companies.

> *"Insurance terms are always worth reading, no matter how boring. Even if it's a struggle to read the fine print, make an effort. If you don't, you could be missing a term or provision that cancels or greatly effects your coverage. For example, in winter if a storm delays your arrival in the port city, you may not be covered at all."*

HEALTH ISSUES

Is there a doctor on board? Always. A cruise ship infirmary is not the Mayo Clinic, but it should be able to handle minor to moderate problems and stabilize seriously ill patients. The degree of sophistication of each infirmary varies from ship to ship. Royal Caribbean's smaller ships, for example, carry a doctor, a nurse anesthesiologist and a registered nurse. Mega-ships carry two doctors, a nurse anesthesiologist, an emergency room nurse and an operating room nurse. Celebrity's *Galaxy* began a unique program in 1997, offering complete physical examinations on board (including electrocardiograms, chest x-rays, blood profiles and stress tests) at $150-250.

- **If you have a chronic condition,** be sure to carry basic medical records with you and communicate your situation to the ship's doctor. Carry enough medication to last through the duration of the cruise.
- **If you require medical treatment** on board, get a copy of your records before you leave the ship, so you can update your primary physician.
- **In the rare event that full hospital services are required,** you will be evacuated by helicopter or treated in a port city. The ship's doctor is aware of the quality of care available at all ports.

Motion sickness is usually easily managed. If you're prone to motion sickness, consider a cruise that travels where waters generally remain calm: Alaska's Inland Passage, for example, or a river voyage.

- **Over-the-counter aids** for motion sickness include Dramamine, Marazine and Bonine.
- **If you use medication** to avoid or ease motion sickness, ask your doctor about possible interaction with other medications.
- **The "patch"** contains medication—usually Scopolamine—that releases through the skin. The patch is worn behind the ear or on the wrist. It was unavailable for a while, due to manufacturing difficulties, but it is widely available. Purchase at pharmacies and travel stores or order from Travel Accessories, **216-248-8432**.
- **Holistic options** include bands positioned to touch an accupressure point on the wrist, and ginger, chewed to relieve nausea.

> *"Don't take oral medication and also wear the patch. You would be over-medicated and apt to suffer negative effects. If you were once prone to motion sickness but haven't been on a cruise ship for awhile, time may have solved the problem. Older people are much less likely to experience motion sickness."*

Accessible cruise travel is available but, most ships have a limited number of cabins for passengers in wheelchairs. Ask for accommodations that meet your total needs. Determine if accessibility extends to the pool, boutiques, casinos and other public areas. Do automatic door sensors have beams low enough to register people in wheelchairs? The non-profit Society for the Advancement of Travel for the Handicapped is a trustworthy source of information. Call **212-447-0027**; write to 347 5th Avenue, Suite 610, New York, NY 10016.

Popular purchases on Bermuda shore excursions: British-made china, crystal and porcelain.

PASSPORTS & VISAS

Passport and visa requirements specific to your cruise will be detailed in the information packet sent with your cruise documents. Take your passport, even for travel to destinations where it is not technically required. (in these cases, an expired passport will suffice as proof of citizenship.) Some countries require that your passport expiration date is at least six months later than your cruise travel dates. Double check visa requirements against current State Department policies. Most countries permit the cruise line to dock under a blanket visa.

SEAWORTHY TIPS

Ask your cruise agent for packing tips that specifically address the cruise you've chosen. Most cruise lines offer at least one formal night with a less formal atmosphere the rest of the time. Most lines prohibit shorts in dining rooms at dinner seating. The ports you visit help determine what you need to take. The essential item: rubber-soled walking shoes for on-deck safety and comfort. You will also find them comfortable for shore excursions.

Call tourism offices for information to enhance your enjoyment of ports-of-call. Check *Know Who To Contact* for numbers. *Cruise Ports Rated* ($5.95 from Vacation Publications, 1502 Augusta Drive, Suite 415, Houston, TX 77057) covers almost 200 ports in the Caribbean, Alaska, the Mediterranean, South America and the Far East.

Pack an overnight bag with an eye toward possible lost luggage. It will also come in handy on the last night of your cruise when checked luggage must be left outside your cabin door.

Cruise documents may not arrive until two weeks before departure. Your agent may even arrange for you to pick them up at the pier. Have proof of citizenship handy when you check in and be sure you have filled out all pre-cruise documents completely prior to your arrival.

Shipboard photographers and videographers are omnipresent at meet-the-Captain receptions and other events. The photographs are printed and posted so that passengers can place orders. An economical alternative: your own camera.

Consider being last to disembark, rather than first. You can enjoy a leisurely breakfast and avoid lengthy lines.

If you are dissatisfied with any aspect of your cruise, register your complaints and concerns immediately. Cruise lines count on repeat bookings and are very attentive to problem resolution.

A quick course in cruise terminology:

- **Add-on**—A charge added to the basic cruise fare, usually for airfare or land tours.
- **Aft**—Near or at the rear of the ship.
- **Bow**—Front or forward portion of the ship.
- **Knot**—A rate of travel equal to one nautical mile (6,080.2 feet).
- **Leeward**—In the direction of the side of the ship that is opposite the direction from which the wind is blowing.
- **Open seating**—Main dining room seating that is not pre-assigned.
- **Purser**—The ship's senior manager.
- **Upper berth**—A single bed (similar to a bunk bed) that usually folds into the wall or ceiling.
- **Windward**—Toward the direction from which the wind is blowing.

Popular purchases on St. Thomas shore excursions: liquor, jewelry and linens.

Cruise Line Profiles

These profiles give style and savings sleuths essential facts and small details that offer bargain-hunting clues and cruise line personality tips. We've included some fanciful passengers to give you an idea of the type of people apt to enjoy each cruise line. Phone numbers and internet sites are in *Know Who To Contact.* Keep in mind that your best booking source is often a mega-volume cruise discount agency.

AMERICAN HAWAII CRUISES travels among the Hawaiian Islands. They attract families during the summer and a wide mix the rest of the year. Three- to four-night sampler cruises and longer itineraries are available. Culture buffs, sunworshipers (and many other types of travelers) will be at home on American Hawaii's *Independence*. The ship was built in 1951 but has been completely refurbished. She is the only American flagged ocean liner still in operation.

- **The ambiance is strongly Hawaiian** from flower lei greetings to Polynesian cuisine. Dress is so casual that men will wear ties just once—at the captain's party. Shore excursion options are extensive. Theme cruises include Blue Hawaii and whale watching January through March.
- **Promotions include** free upgrades for cruises booked with deposit at least six months in advance, free nights on various islands, discount hotel nights in Waikiki and $100 single supplements on some deluxe cabins. Airfare specials are also offered once or twice a year.

The first indoor pool on a cruise ship: White Star's Olympic, sister ship of the Titanic, in 1910.

CARNIVAL CRUISE LINES, the most booked cruise line in the world, offers mega-ships and traditional ships with larger than average cabins for their price category. They pride themselves on extensive recreation and entertainment options. When Carnival tells you their cruises appeal to all ages, you can believe them. This is the cruise line for people who love people. Picture Kathy Lee Gifford (of course) with a ship full of people who love Disney World, Mardi Gras in New Orleans and Times Square on New Year's Eve. Carnival is a big favorite of families but denies booking to guests under 21 unless sharing a cabin with someone 25 or older or sailing with parents or grandparents.

- **Itineraries include** Bahamas, Caribbean, Baja Mexico, Mexican Riviera, Panama Canal, Hawaii and Alaska. Departures are from Miami, Cape Canaveral, San Juan, Tampa, New Orleans, Los Angeles and Vancouver.
- **Promotions include** $400-600 off per cabin for advance Super Saver bookings on three- to four-night cruises and up to $1,200 on seven-night cruises.
- **Camp Carnival** is offered year-round with programs for toddlers to teenagers.
- **You won't forget that you're on a Carnival ship**. The underlying theme is always fun, but each ship has its own flavor. A popular feature is the Lido Restaurant (on all ships), allowing casual dining options for breakfast, lunch and dinner.

CELEBRITY CRUISES offers stylish ships with exceptional five-star Berlitz rated cuisine. Many seasoned cruise travelers view Celebrity as an underpriced value, providing very good return for the money. Fans of Julia Child and all passengers who enjoy fine cuisine and high calibre service should enjoy this line. Each ship has a special passenger service manager who grants daily wishes and presides over high tea on the last day of every cruise. Celebrity offers the best cruise ship access to Bermuda.

- **Itineraries include** Alaska, Bahamas, Caribbean, Bermuda and Panama Canal.
- **Promotions include** Five Star advance booking discounts of up to 50 percent off and discounts on combined Eastern and Western Caribbean itineraries.
- **The *Century, Galaxy* and *Mercury*** have state-of-the-art access to the information superhighway, interactive guest service networks, video bars, computer kiosks and conference centers with multi-media presentation systems.
- **Past passengers** are offered lifetime membership in The Captain's Club for $35 per family. It provides discounts, upgrades and amenities.

COMMODORE CRUISE LINES embarks from New Orleans, opening up interesting opportunities for inexpensive flights (or driving) to port from some parts of the country. Roseanne would have dreamed of a Commodore Cruise before she won the lottery. Commodore is a solid value for travelers on budgets, first-time passengers who want to try cruise travel without making a major investment and people who like Southerners (it's in the neighborhood).

- **Itineraries include** Western Caribbean and Central America; elaborate theme nights are offered.

Languages Costa uses for all onboard announcements: English, French, German, Italian & Spanish.

- **Promotions include** $150 off per cabin with deposits made at least 90 days in advance of departure.
- **Past passengers** can book two cabins at discount rates. Special discounts are offered four times a year to members from specific regions of the U.S.

COSTA CRUISES has an Italian flair (though it is now a subsidiary of Carnival) with an average of 80 percent North American passengers on its Caribbean itineraries; 80 percent European passengers on its Europe itineraries. It is #1 in the rapidly-growing European market. Ships combine classic qualities with new design features. Many of their ships have been re-routed from the U.S. to European itineraries.

- **Itineraries include** the Caribbean in winter and the Baltic, Black Sea, Europe, Greece, the Orient, and transatlantic in summer.
- **Promotions include** Andiamo discounts of 10 to 25 percent for bookings made 90 days in advance.
- **Costa Kids** provides activities for children five through 12 and for teenagers. European cruises also have a club for children three through six and free childcare.
- **Past passengers** are offered special discounts by mail.

CRYSTAL CRUISES is simply one of the finest lines in existence. Their casino is operated by Caesar's Palace. Gourmet Italian and Japanese cuisine restaurants compliment main dining room choices. Celebrity guest speakers are often on board and itineraries generally include more nights at sea—because why would you ever want to leave? Service is so impeccable that not even Martha Stewart could find fault.

- **Itineraries include** South America, Europe, Mexico, Alaska/Canada, Panama Canal/Caribbean and Orient/South Pacific.
- **Promotions include** advance purchase discounts from 10 to 50 percent that can be combined with promotional rates and past passenger discounts.
- **Extra amenities** include gentleman hosts, full business centers with secretarial and translation services, laptop computers and an exceptional crew/passenger ratio.
- **Past passengers** have an extensive Crystal Society rewards program, including discounts of as much as 50 percent for the second passenger and five percent discounts that can be combined with other discount offers. Ten sailings per year are designed primarily as members-only discount cruises.

CUNARD LINE is so diverse that it could appear to be several separate cruise lines united by a subtle British tone. Its five ships range from two 116-passenger vessels to the 1,850-passenger, 13-story *QE2*. Prices vary dramatically, even within the *QE2* with three classes of service available.

- **Itineraries** are worldwide.
- **Promotions include** early booking discounts of 20 percent.
- **The *QE2* is still unique**, despite the appearance of the amazing mega-liners. She has gold-plated fixtures in penthouse suites, a croquet court, walk-in closets, a 40-car garage, a kennel and a tuxedo rental office. She is also a floating Maritime Museum, with an on board Heritage Trail tour that tracks 150 years of Cunard Line history.

Amenities for dogs who sail the QE2: 16 air-conditioned kennels and a British lamp post.

- **Past passengers** receive exclusive promotional fares and special events on board. The World Club also provides Cruise Miles, similar to airline frequent flyer programs. The Skald Club provides separate discounts for past passengers on five Cunard ships. The Samuel Cunard Key Club (for members who have sailed at least 50 nights on *QE2* world cruises) provides benefits including $2,000 per couple on board credit.

DISNEY CRUISE LINE will offer the *Disney Magic* and the *Disney Wonder,* both combining three- to four-night cruises with three- to four-night Walt Disney World Vacations.

DELTA QUEEN offers paddle wheel cruises along the mighty Mississippi from New Orleans to St. Paul. Many theme cruises are offered.

- **The cruise line with a drawl** is the only line with two cruises built around war themes. Take your choice of World War II in Music and Speakers, or the Civil War. Other themes include Big Band, The Old South, Fall Foliage and The Kentucky Derby.
- **The *Delta Queen* is a National Historic Landmark** but both the *Mississippi Queen* and the *American Queen* offer the wonderful modern-day comfort of air conditioning.

HOLLAND AMERICA LINE was voted best overall cruise value three years in a row by *Ocean and Cruise News*. Beautifully maintained ships combine tradition with new ship amenities. Ambiance is sophisticated but not suffocatingly elegant. Picture your accountant enjoying this line, additionally pleased because of Holland America's unique no-tipping policy.

- **Itineraries include the** Caribbean and Panama Canal; Alaska, Europe, New England and Transatlantic in summer; Hawaii and Asia spring and fall; world cruises in winter. Departures are from Fort Lauderdale, New Orleans (all featuring a salute to jazz), Tampa and Vancouver.
- **Promotions include** early booking discounts of up to 45 percent, a Membership Miles program with American Express and low third/fourth passenger rates.
- **A wide array of shore excursions** include 175 choices at 30 Caribbean ports (including 20 environmental and culture-conscious choices) and extensive Alaska excursions befitting their lead in the Alaska cruise marketplace.
- **Past passengers** receive special discount offers five times a year through the Mariners Club, upgrades on select sailings and added amenities.

NORWEGIAN CRUISE LINE is owned by a family that has been in the shipping business since 1906. If the mainstream was an actual place, Norwegian ships sail down the center of it. Half of the fleet's unusually spacious cabins are non-smoking and they are grouped together so corridors remain smoke-free too. Theme cruise options are extensive. There is a Chocaholic Buffet, strolling musicians at dinner seatings and fruit baskets to welcome all guests. Picture '90s versions of the Cleavers, the Brady Brunch and their extended families.

- **Itineraries include** Australia/New Zealand, the Bahamas and the Caribbean year-round; Bermuda, Europe and Alaska spring through fall; Panama Canal in May and

The first cruise line to offer a private island port-of-call: Norwegian Cruise Line.

September; South America in winter.

- **Promotions include** early booking discounts of 20 to 30 percent, LeaderShip fares with two basic prices (inside and outside cabin) and upgrades beginning at $15 per person/per category.
- **Children's programs** are offered year-round on the *Norway* and *Seaward*; seasonally on other ships.
- **Western Caribbean cruises** embark from Houston and Miami with ports-of-call including Cozumel, Mexico and the Bay Islands.
- **Past passengers** receive Latitudes member-only discounts and added amenities. Free membership provides the Transmedia/Latitudes card with dining rebates of up to 25 percent at over 7,000 restaurants worldwide.

ORIENT LINES sails one mid-size, luxury oceanliner on light adventure cruises. Passengers are almost exclusively adult, though children are welcome. Picture W.C. Fields after a couple years on a StairMaster.

- **Itineraries include** Africa, Antarctica, Asia, Australia, India, Indian Ocean, New Zealand and the Mediterranean.
- **Promotions include** discounts for booking 120 days in advance, discounts on consecutive cruises and waived single supplements on select cruises.

PREMIER CRUISES includes the Big Red Boat and five additional ships offering a variety of cruise experiences. Check with your cruise travel agent for updates on current itineraries and promotions for Premier. This line is going through some major changes. Here is information on their hottest product.

- **The *Big Red Boat*** with your hosts—the Looney Tunes characters, (Bugs Bunny, Tweety Bird and Yosemite Sam) is geared to family travel. There is a casino for adult entertainment, a fact that may give this ship an edge in the family market when the big new Disney ships arrive. Their prices are also much lower.
- **Itineraries include** three- to four-night cruises coupled with three- to four-day visits to Walt Disney World.
- **Promotions include** discounts for specific cabin categories booked three months in advance (about $400 for a family of four), family reunion discounts and 10 to 15 percent off for passengers 60 and above and one companion.
- **Twenty-four-hour child care is provided** with planned activities from 9 a.m. to 10 p.m. for ages two through 12. Add a deluxe Looney Tunes tuck-in at $40 for one child/$75 for two, including a Looney Tunes pillowcase, a stuffed toy and a photo.
- **Past passengers** receive Captain's Club discounts by mail and on-board amenities.

PRINCESS CRUISES gained fame as the Love Boats, but times have changed. One of the stars of the *Love Boat* went to Congress and Princess Cruises expanded itineraries to a wealth of new destinations and became a major player in the Alaska cruise market. There is even a British touch: the line is British-owned and half her crew members come from the U.K. Picture Fergie, enjoying a post-divorce holiday.

- **Itineraries include** Africa, South America, Australia/South Pacific, the Caribbean, Hawaii/Tahiti, Mexico, the Panama Canal, Orient and

Southeast Asia in winter; Alaska, Baltic, Canada, Europe, New England and the Mediterranean in summer.

- **Promotions include** Love Boat Saver discounts of 10 to 25 percent for advance bookings; 50 percent for second passengers and frequent two-for-one sales.
- **Shore excursion information** is excellent and a wide array of options are offered. Three ships offer Exotic Adventures to the Orient, South Pacific, South Asia & India and Africa.
- ***Love at First Sea*** offers honeymooners champagne and souvenir glasses, a private cocktail party with the captain, cabin flowers and chocolate-dipped strawberries, a keepsake photo and other gifts for $150 per couple.
- **Past passengers** receive Captain's Circle discount coupons, on-board cocktail parties and other amenities.

RADISSON SEVEN SEAS is owned by Diamond Cruises and managed by Radisson Hotels International. The *Radisson Diamond* features catamaran-style construction that merges small ship style with big ship amenities. All cabins are oceanview and amenities and service levels are exemplary. Picture Maya Angelou (or any prosperous poet) enjoying superb service (no tipping allowed) on the poetically named *Song of Flower*, one of three Radisson ships.

- **Itineraries include** Antarctica, Asia, the Caribbean, Panama Canal, Galapagos Islands and South America in winter; Arctic, Greenland, Iceland, Mediterranean, Northern Europe and Norway in summer.
- **Promotions include** early booking discounts and seasonal offers.
- **Past passengers** receive Seven Seas Society special sailings with added values and discount prices plus gifts based on the number of days travelled.

ROYAL CARIBBEAN INTERNATIONAL provides a consistent level of quality that maintains its high customer satisfaction rating. An extraordinary array of activities are offered. Royal Caribbean offers some of the finest suites in their price category. Their cruise style is indicated by the superlatives used to name their fleet: *Grandeur*, *Majesty* and *Splendour*. Picture the cast of *Friends* and a week's worth of winners on *The Price Is Right*, all having a fine time. A popular feature is a seven-night soda fountain card at $15 per person–a bargain for families traveling with children.

- **Itineraries include** Bahamas, Caribbean and Mexico year-round; Alaska, Bermuda, Europe, Panama Canal and Hawaii seasonally.
- **Promotions include** Breakthrough Rates with the highest discounts usually available for the earliest bookings, 10 to 20 percent off other advance bookings and frequent third/fourth person discounts.
- **Adventure Oceans** offers programs for children three through 17 with special daily newsletters on board. Kids Galley menus provide grilled cheese sandwiches, alphabet soup and other favorites.
- **This line loves golfers.** The *Legend of the Seas* and the *Splendour of the Seas*, provide 18-hole miniature golf courses under retractable glass domes. They were designed to be as challenging as traditional golf. Each

Main function of a ship's Chief Purser: financial and business matters for passengers and crew.

hole replicates a hole on a different world-renowned course. The longest hole is 32 yards long. Royal Caribbean is the official cruise line of the PGA. Golf Ahoy arranges tee times at over 25 courses around the Bahamas, Bermuda, the Caribbean, Mexico and Miami.

- **Past passengers** are offered four levels of Crown and Anchor Society membership with discounts on special sailings and on board parties. The higher your status level, the more discounts and added amenities you are offered.

SEABOURN CRUISE LINE sails six-star ships that are the Rolls Royces of the cruise industry. You will feel as if you are on a private yacht. Ships feature underwater viewing rooms and foldout water sports marinas. Service is without parallel. Lavish buffets feature stewards who carry passengers' plates and anticipate every need. Picture Secretary of State Albright comparing notes with Warren Christopher.

- **Itineraries include** Asia, Australia, the Caribbean, South America, South Pacific and Panama Canal in winter; the Mediterranean and South Asia in spring; Alaska, Baltic, British Isles, Canada, Europe and Norway in the summer and fall; Hawaii seasonally.
- **Promotions include** Worldfare advance purchase discounts on 45- and 120-night itineraries and third person discounts of 25 percent.
- **Past passengers** receive a 25 percent discount after 20 nights of sailing—typically two Seabourn cruises—and free trip cancellation, accident and medical insurance.

SILVERSEA CRUISES sails two 296-passenger all-inclusive, ultra-luxury ships. They are a unique cruise line, voted not only number one cruise line, but number one vacation in the world by readers of *Conde Nast Traveler*—the first time that a cruise line earned that distinction. Silversea's pricing includes airfare, transfers, all port fees and taxes, insurance, most wines and alcoholic drinks, a shoreside event, gratuities and pre-cruise luxury hotel accommodations. Itineraries vary. Promotions can include special rates on premium class air travel and other offers geared to passengers who are accustomed to first-class travel amenities.

- **Itineraries include** Africa, Canada/New England, the Caribbean, the Mediterranean, the Orient and Southeast Asia.
- **Promotions include** a 15 percent discount when you pay in full 6 months prior to sailing. Get reduced rate upgrades to Business Class air.

WINDSTAR offers cruise travel with the ambiance of a large, private yacht. Itineraries change often and usually include ports-of-call most cruise lines seldom offer. Picture any political candidate, seeking escape after the rigors of election.

> *"On the following five pages, we get down to the facts and figures on ships currently comprising major cruise line fleets. The amount of change (as compared to the first edition of this book) reflects the dynamic activity in the cruise industry."*

Value of dishes broken in a typical Norwegian Cruise Line's Maasdam cruise: $1,800.

CHARTING YOUR COURSE

- Passenger capacity (PAX);
- Crew members (CREW) to give you an idea of the level of service you can expect;
- When each ship was built and when it was last refurbished (BUILT/REF);
- Main dining room smoking policies (D/R SMOK) with Des. indicating that smoking allowed in designated areas;
- Price Categories: B/Budget, M/Moderate, D/Deluxe, U/Ultra-Deluxe and U*/Ultra-Luxury smaller/boutique ships and V/Variable.

SHIPSHAPE INFORMATION

CRUISE LINE/SHIP	PAX	CREW	BUILT/REF	D/R SMOKING	PRICE CATEGORY
AMERICAN HAWAII					
Independence	1,020	315	1950/1997	No	M
CARNIVAL CRUISE LINE					
Celebration	1,486	670	1987	No	M
Destiny	2,642	1,100	1996	No	M
Ecstasy	2,040	920	1991	No	M
Elation	2,632	920	1998	Des.	M
Fantasy	2,044	920	1990	No	M
Fascination	2,040	920	1994	No	M
Holiday	1,452	660	1985/1994	No	M
Imagination	2,040	920	1995	No	M
Inspiration	2,040	920	1996	No	M
Jubilee	1,486	670	1986	No	M
Sensation	2,040	920	1993	No	M
Tropicale	1,022	550	1981/1989	No	M
CELEBRITY CRUISES					
Century	1,750	843	1995	Des.	M
Galaxy	1,870	909	1996	Des.	M
Horizon	1,354	650	1990	Des.	M
Mercury	1,888	909	1997	No	M
Zenith	1,386	650	1992	Des.	M

Most common points for cruise ship registration: the Bahamas, Italy and Liberia.

SHIPSHAPE INFORMATION *continued*					
CRUISE LINE/SHIP	**PAX**	**CREW**	**BUILT/REF**	**D/R SMOKING**	**PRICE CATEGORY**
COMMODORE CRUISE LINE					
Enchanted Isle	850	350	1958/1997	No	B
COSTA CRUISE LINE					
CostaAllegra	800	450	1970/1992	Des.	M
CostaClassica	1,300	650	1991	Des.	M
CostaMarina	770	385	1969/1990	Des.	M
CostaRiviera	974	500	1963/1996	Des.	M
CostaRomantica	1,350	650	1993	Des.	M
CostaVictoria	1,950	800	1996	Des.	M
CRYSTAL CRUISES					
Crystal Harmony	940	545	1990	Des.	U
Crystal Symphony	940	545	1995	Des.	U
CUNARD					
Cunard Royal Viking Sun	758	460	1988/1993	Des.	V
QE2	1,496	1,015	1969/1994	Des.	V
Sea Goddess I	116	89	1984	Des.	V
Sea Goddess II	116	89	1985	Des.	V
Vistafjord	675	380	1973/1994	Des.	V
DELTA QUEEN					
American Queen	436	3,707	1995	No	M
Delta Queen	174	3,360	1927/1992	No	M
Mississippi Queen	414	3,364	1976/1994	No	M
FIRST EUROPEAN					
Azur	800	330	1971/1996	Des.	M
Bolero	900	350	1968/1995	Des.	M
Flamenc	900	350	1972/1997	Des.	M
HOLLAND AMERICA LINE					
Maasdam	1,266	602	1994	Des.	D
Nieuw Amsterdam	1,214	542	1983	Des.	D
Noordam	1,214	542	1984	Des.	D

Projected annual economic impact of Houston's new cruise port facilities: $40 million.

SHIPSHAPE INFORMATION *continued*					
CRUISE LINE/SHIP	PAX	CREW	BUILT/REF	D/R SMOKING	PRICE CATEGORY
HOLLAND AMERICA LINE					
Rotterdam VI	1,316	602	1997	Des.	D
Ryndam	1,266	602	1994	Des.	D
Statendam	1,266	602	1993	Des.	D
Veendam	1,266	571	1996	Des.	D
Westerdam	1,494	642	1986/1990	Des.	D
NORWEGIAN CRUISE LINE					
Leeward	950	400	1992/1995	No	M
Norway	2,032	900	1960/1993	No	M
Norwegian Dream	1,754	650	1992/1997	No	M
Norwegian Dynasty	800	320	1993	No	M
Norwegian Majesty	920	400	1993	No	M
Norwegian Sea	1,502	630	1988	No	M
Norwegian Star	793	380	1973/1997	No	M
Norwegian Crown	1,052	470	1973/1997	No	M
Norwegian Wind	1,758	630	1993/1997	No	M
ORIENT LINES					
Marco Polo	800	350	1965/1993	No	M
PREMIER CRUISE LINE					
Big Red Boat	1,800	565	1965/1997	Des.	M
Islandbreeze	1,146	612	1961/1997	Des.	M
Oceanbreeze	776	400	1955/1997	Des.	M
Rembrandt	1,250	420	1959/1997	Des.	M
Seabreeze	840	400	1958/1997	Des.	M
Seawind Crown	768	365	1961/1997	Des.	M
PRINCESS CRUISES					
Crown Princess	1,590	696	1990	No	D
Dawn Princess	1,950	900	1997	No	D
Grand Princess	1,950	900	1998	No	D
Island Princess	640	350	1971/1992	No	D

Usual minimum age for admission to cruise ship lounge shows: 13.

SHIPSHAPE INFORMATION *continued*					
CRUISE LINE/SHIP	**PAX**	**CREW**	**BUILT/REF**	**D/R SMOKING**	**PRICE CATEGORY**
PRINCESS CRUISES CONT.					
Pacific Princess	640	350	1972/1993	No	D
Regal Princess	1,590	696	1991	No	D
Royal Princess	1,200	520	1984/1994	No	D
Sky Princess	1,200	535	1984/1992	No	D
Sun Princess	1,950	900	1995	No	D
RADISSON SEVEN SEAS					
Bremon	164	80	1990/1993	Des.	U
Hanseatic	188	125	1993	Des.	U
Paul Gauguin	350	90	1997	Des.	U
Radisson Diamond	350	192	1992	Des.	U
Song of Flower	180	144	1986/1990	Des.	U
RENAISSANCE					
R6	114	73	1991	Des.	M
R7	114	73	1992	Des.	M
R8	114	73	1992	Des.	M
ROYAL CARIBBEAN INTERNATIONAL					
Enchantment of the Seas	2,446	760	1997	Des.	D
Grandeur of the Seas	1,950	760	1996	Des.	D
Legend of the Seas	1,808	720	1995	Des.	D
Majesty of the Seas	2,355	822	1992	Des.	D
Monarch of the Seas	2,354	825	1991	Des.	D
Nordic Empress	1,606	671	1990	Des.	D
Rhapsody of the Seas	2,435	765	1997	Des.	D
Song of America	1,402	535	1982	Des.	D
Sovereign of the Seas	2,276	840	1988	Des.	D
Splendour of the Seas	1,804	720	1996	Des.	D
Viking Serenade	1,512	612	1982	Des.	D
Vision of the Seas	2,000	800	1998	Des.	D

Usual minimum age for admission to cruise ship casinos: 18.

SHIPSHAPE INFORMATION *continued*					
CRUISE LINE/SHIP	**PAX**	**CREW**	**BUILT/REF**	**D/R SMOKING**	**PRICE CATEGORY**
ROYAL OLYMPIC					
Odyseuss	400	200	1962/1995	Des.	D
Olympic Countess	840	350	1976/1996	Des.	D
Orpheus	280	110	1952/1996	Des.	D
Stella Oceanis	300	150	1965/1996	Des.	D
Stella Solaris	620	320	1973/1997	Des.	D
Triton	620	315	1991/1996	Des.	D
World Renaissance	455	235	1996	Des.	D
SEABOURN CRUISE LINE					
Seabourn Legend	212	140	1993	Des.	U*
Seabourn Pride	212	140	1988	No	U*
Seabourn Spirit	212	140	1989	No	U*
SILVERSEA CRUISES					
Silver Cloud	296	185	1994	Des.	U*
Silver Wind	296	185	1994	Des.	U*
WINDSTAR					
Wind Star	148		1986/1996	Des.	M
Wind Spirit	148	91	1986/1996	Des.	M
Wind Surf	312	163	1990/1998	Des.	D
Wind Song	148	91	1986/1997	Des.	M

Shore excursion options on Premier's Island Breeze: ostrich encounters and canoe safaris.

OFF THE BEATEN WAVE

Some off the beaten wave cruises offer sheer luxury; others offer an original experience at affordable prices or a small taste of cruise travel. Before booking any of these ships, check with a large cruise discount agency such as The Cruise Line Inc. at **800-685-6518**, to see if they can offer you an appreciable discount.

MASTED SHIPS

Masted ships put the sail back in sailing. A wide range of prices provide the perfect masted ship cruise for almost any budget. Be sure to check on the activity level expected of passengers. Some ships involve you greatly; others offer more relaxed journeys.

Star Clippers offer two 172-passenger replicas of nineteenth century sailing ships with traditional cruise comfort. They provide the mid-range choice. Itineraries include Caribbean, Mediterranean and Transatlantic sailings April through October. Booking 120 days in advance provides a ten percent discount. Single fares without large supplements added are available. Call **800-442-0551**.

Windjammer Barefoot Cruises provides a relatively economical option with many cruises involving passengers as sailors. Itineraries concentrate on the Caribbean and the New England coast. Five-night and longer itineraries are sailed on 200-passengers or smaller vessels. After three cruises at full fare, you pay $99 to become a Sudden Sailor, eligible for savings of up to 51 percent on stand-by fares confirmed 14 days before departure. Call **800-327-2601**.

Windstar Cruises (owned by Holland America) offers three 148-passenger, four-masted sailing ships with five-star amenities. It fills the high-end of this category. Itineraries include the Caribbean and Costa Rica in winter, the Mediterranean in late spring through early fall, transatlantic April and October. Each ship has 74 outside suites with queen beds, VCR, CD

Caribbean island where all beaches are public: Barbados.

player and mini-bar. They recently purchased the 312-passenger *Windsurf,* which will sail the Mediterranean from May to September; the Caribbean, the balance of the year. Call **800-258-7245**.

Dirigo Cruises has a fleet of 16 small sailing ships that cover Europe, British Isles, Newfoundland, the Caribbean, Galapagos, New Zealand and South Seas Islands. Call **203-669-7068**.

Maine Windjammers offers three- to seven-night cruises embarking from Rockland, Maine and traveling the New England coast. Call **800-807-9463**.

Special Expeditions sails the 60-passenger *Sea Cloud* in the Eastern Caribbean in the winter and other waters during the rest of the year. Call **800-762-0003**.

NORTH AMERICAN RIVERBOAT CRUISES

Delta Queen Steamboat Company offers paddlewheel steamships that cruise the Mississippi River. Some cabins feature brass beds and tiffany windows. Promotions include early booking discounts of up to 15 percent on select cruises and select sailings that allow one child 16 or under to cruise free in certain cabins. Call **800-543-1949**.

The America West Steamboat Company offers *Queen of the West*, a 165-passenger paddlewheeler built in 1995. Two- to seven-night cruises depart from Portland (OR) and cruise the Columbia, Snake and Willamette Rivers. Call **800-434-1232**.

St. Lawrence Cruise Lines sails the *Canadian Empress* from Kingston, Montreal, Ottawa and Quebec City on four- and five- night trips along Canada's St. Lawrence, Ottawa and Saguenay Rivers. Call **800-267-7868**.

NORTH AMERICAN OCEAN CRUISES

North American waters offer unique experiences for cruising, American style.

World Explorer Cruises offers Alaska cruises on the 50-passenger *Universe.* Her 12,000 volume library hints at the line's cultural orientation. She bypasses cabaret revues for on board lectures, casual attire and increased port time. Biking - Cruise packages are offered three times a year and biking excursions are offered on many cruises in eight ports-of-call. Promotions include early booking incentives on select sailings, including free pre- or post-cruise hotel stays in Vancouver or Seattle. Call **800-854-3835**.

American Canadian Caribbean offers cruises on 76- to 90-passenger ships with itineraries that include Rhode Island to Florida and New Orleans to Chicago. Call **800-556-7450**.

OTHER CRUISE OPTIONS

Renaissance Cruises offers four deluxe 50- to 114-passenger Italian-built ships with two new 600-passenger ships under construction. The line specializes in unique itineraries, such as a ten-night cruise of the Seychelles Islands coupled with a four-night Kenya Safari. Call **800-525-5350**.

Norwegian Coastal Cruises explore the intricate coast of Norway from late May through fall. Options include cruise ships, freighter-passenger ships and cruise ferries (many carrying well over 1,000 passengers). Call Bergen Line at **800-323-7436** or EuroCruises at **800-688-3876**.

Captain Cook Cruises sails the 168-passenger *Reef Endeavor* on two- to seven-night Great Barrier Reef and Australian Island itineraries. Air inclusive packages

Films commonly shown on Delta Queen riverboats: Showboat and Gone With the Wind.

are available from Qantas Vacations, **310-535-1070**.

Book a stateroom on a yacht from Preferred Yacht Holidays, **800-535-7289** Itineraries include the Caribbean and the South Pacific.

Uniworld offers cruises through Russian waterways with itineraries including Moscow to St. Petersburg or the Amur River through the Russian Far East. Call **800-868-7892**.

Galapagos Cruises depart from Ecuador for three- to seven-night cruises of the Galapagos Islands. Call **800-527-2500**.

Temptress Cruises explore Costa Rica and Belize on 62 to 99 passenger adventure cruises that offer special children's programs. Call **800-336-8423**.

Quark Expeditions sails seven 38- to 106-passenger Russian-built ships with Russian crews on Antarctica itineraries. Itineraries include the Falkland Islands to Antarctica and a Canadian Arctic expedition from Resolute to Greenland and Ellesmere and Baffin Islands. Call **800-356-5699**.

INTERNATIONAL RIVER CRUISES

River and barge cruises travel the major rivers of the world, including the Amazon, Danube, Nile, Rhine, Seine, Volga and Yangtze. European cruises generally operate April through October, docking in the heart of key European cities where you can set off on your own walking tour. Early season discounts are often available.

Abercrombie & Kent books boat and barge travel on European and Amazon itineraries. Call **800-323-7308**.

Amazon Tours and Cruises offers two- to six-night trips on 16- to 44-passenger boats that travel South America's Amazon River. Call **800-423-2791**.

Cunard EuropAmerica River Cruises offers a wide array of European river cruises. Call **800-348-8287**.

Europe Cruise Line sails the 148-passenger *Blue Danube* between Nuremburg, Germany and Budapest. It departs every other Saturday from May through September. Call **800-688-3876**.

European Waterways offers river barge cruises from spring through fall and centrally heated barges that cruise the south of France and Scotland well into the winter. *Le Boat* and *La Reine Pedauque* (12-passenger barge) have special facilities for accessible travel. Other options include self-driven boats on canals in five European countries. Call **800-922-0291**.

KD River Cruises of Europe sails the length of the Danube, Elbe, Moselle, Rhine and Seine; the new canal that links the North and Black Seas; and the Volga between St. Petersburg and Russia. Call **800-786-5311**.

CRUISES TO NOWHERE

Cruises to Nowhere sail out of many port cities in the U.S. and abroad. They often feature themes, gambling and dinner and dancing. They can be wonderful discoveries for people who want to try out the cruise experience without making a major investment in time and money. It isn't quite fair to compare the amenities of a mega-ship accommodating 2,000 passengers with a smaller Cruise to Nowhere ship, but if you have never been on a cruise ship and would like to get a taste of onboard life before investing in a cruise, one of these mini-cruises might introduce you to a new way to travel.

- ***Discovery Cruises*** offers overnight trips from Fort Lauderdale and Miami

International cruise port with no port taxes: New Zealand.

> *"Be sure to thoroughly check out any cruise line offering brief ocean cruises. Be particularly careful about pricing. Some operators have been around long enough to establish very good track records. Others have been notorious in advertising very low prices, then sticking inflated port charges on to the final bill. In some cases, the port charges and fees are greater than the price of the cruise. The state of Florida has made this practice illegal, but it's going to take some time for full enforcement to be achieved. Also, be very leery of cruise scams that can come to you by phone, fax, e-mail or U.S. mail. Often they bundle a cruise in with port city hotel stays. They make it seem as if you are getting a top-of-the-line cruise when, in fact, you could end up with an inexpensive day cruise and a string of over-priced hotel nights that you may never use. One clue to scam cruise offers: the claim that you were "specially selected" for the offer."*

with an overnight in Freeport. The price is about $150 per person, including hotel. Day trips are also available. Call **800-866-8687**.

- **Explore islands off Washington's coast** with Victoria Clipper, offering an assortment of narrated day cruises, departing from Seattle's Pier 69 year-round. The Seattle-Friday Harbor roundtrip itinerary gives you over ten hours of travel experiences for only $59/adult, $54/senior and $23.50-29.50 per child. Purchase at least 14-days in advance and your adult ticket cost comes down to $47, reflecting a $12 discount. Other itineraries include Victoria (Vancouver Island) and other San Juan Islands, including Roche Harbor. Add-ons includes an $18-25 Whale & Sealife Search from Friday Harbor on board a touring vessel and hotel stays in Seattle, the San Juans, Victoria and Vancouver. Call **800-888-2535**. Go online at **www.victoriaclipper.com**.
- **Manhattan Cruises** offers overnight itineraries onboard *The Edinburgh Castle*. The seven-night-a-week schedule (departing from Pier 88) offers fine dining, live entertainment and a full range of shipboard activities. Once beyond the three-mile limit, casino gambling is also offered. Weekends cruises also feature showroom entertainment. The 32,753-ton line ship has 510 cabins, can accommodate 1,000 passengers, and will be New York City's largest locally-based cruise ship. Passenger boarding starts at 4:00 p.m. and the ship departs at seven in the evening. Sunday through Thursday night departures return at 8:00 a.m. the following morning. Friday and Saturday night departures return at 3:00 p.m. the following afternoon. Tickets prices include cabin, meals, entertainment and all onboard activities. Weekday cruises are $99 per person; weekend cruises are $199. Call **888-611-2784**.

Dinner cruises can even be found in cities you think of as being land-locked. Here's a selection to get you started.

- **Cleveland**—The *Nautica Queen* travels the Cuyahoga River and the Lake Erie waterfront. Brunch, lunch and dinner cruises are buffet-style and live music is provided. Rates range from

$20.95-42.95 for adults; $10.95-19.95 for children 12 and under. Call **800-837-0604**.

- **Dallas**—The *Texas Queen* is a riverboat berthed on Lake Ray Hubbard in Rockwall, about 20 minutes east of downtown Dallas. Wednesday through Sunday 7:30 p.m. cruises are bring-your-own-bottle with down home cooking. Theme cruises (blues, jazz, casino) are often offered. Prices range from $35.50-50. Call **972-771-0039**.
- **New Orleans**—The *Natchez* departs from the French Quarter on two-hour Southern-style dinner cruises. The steam sternwheeler also features Dixieland bands. Dinner cruises are $42.50; lunch cruises are $20.70. Call **800-233-2628**.
- **New Orleans**—The *Creole Queen* departs from Riverwalk Marketplace at 7 p.m. each night for a dinner cruise along the Mississippi. Jazz clarinetist Otis Bazoon and his band provide music on the promenade deck. Adults pay $39; children under 12 pay $18. Call **504-524-0814**.
- **Orlando**—*Rivership Grand Romance* offers a three-hour lunch cruise at $31.00 per person; a Moonlight Magic dinner dance cruise is $45.10. Purchase your tickets at the Orlando Visitor Information Center and get as much as $5 off per person. Call **407-363-5872**.
- **Portland**—The *Portland Spirit* is a three-level yacht, complete with baby grand piano, that cruises the Willamette River. There are lunch, dinner and Sunday brunch cruises, all featuring gourmet Pacific Northwest cuisine. Adults pay $24-46; children four to 12 pay $16-41; children under three eat free. Call **800-224-3901**.
- **St. Louis**—Gateway Riverboat Cruises offers the *Tom Sawyer* and the *Becky Thatcher*, replicas of 19th century sternwheel paddleboats. Dinner cruises along the Mississippi are accompanied by a Dixieland band. The price is $32.50. Call **800-878-7411**.
- **Tampa**—The *Starlight Princess* departs from Garrison Seaport Center on a three-hour inland waterway paddlewheel cruise past the Davis Islands and Harbor Island. Sit-down dinner provides a choice of seven entrees and there is dancing to live music afterward. Cruise-only prices are $12.50-15; dinner is $8.95-17.95. Call **800-444-4814**.
- **Waikiki**—Paradise Cruises offers a two-hour cruise on the 320-passenger *Starlet*. The $47 price includes a three-course steak and fish dinner, cocktails and a Polynesian revue. Call **800-334-6191**.
- **Waikiki**—Have an early dinner at Gordon Biersch at Aloha Tower Marketplace, then depart on the *Navatek I* for a two-hour cruise along the Honolulu coast (8:15-10:15 p.m.). Onboard desert and cocktails are included and a jazz band plays for your listening and dancing pleasure. Transportation between the restaurant and the oceanfront is included. Call **800-852-4183** and request the *Dazzling Duo* package.

FREIGHTER CRUISES

Freighter Cruises can be ideal for people who like being at sea for long periods of time and enjoy the companionship of a small and interesting group of travelers looking for unusual experiences and seldom-visited ports-of-call. The passenger mix is eclectic, usually comprised of mul-

Cost of wedding vow renewal ceremony on Holland America: $95, including reception.

tiple nationalities and an extensive range of ages and backgrounds. You could meet some of the most interesting people of your life on just about any freighter cruise. Start planning six to twelve months in advance and expect some itinerary changes, as these ships must alter itineraries to meet the needs of their primary business: shipping freight. A ten to 20 percent deposit is usually required with final payment due 45 to 60 days prior to sailing.

Many freighters accept a maximum of 12 passengers, the point after which, per maritime law, a medic has to be aboard. A few lines (notably Ivaran) carry about 88 passengers. Most lines do not allow children under 12 or adults over 80 and may require proof of good health from passengers 65 and above.

Freighter itineraries stretch from 30-100 nights and allow you to choose the segment you prefer to book. You embark and disembark at pre-determined ports. Several carriers offer fly/sail options that help you book half-length or segments of voyages. Stopover time in port cities may be several hours or several days. Some quick stops do not allow time for passengers to disembark.

Freighter cabins tend to be more roomy than many cruise ship cabins. Food is good and plentiful, but don't expect ice-carvings and midnight buffets.

The average per night cost ranges from $70-100. More luxurious lines may cost up to $160. Discounted freighter cruises are available for off-season travel. For example, fares to Australia, New Zealand and South America are often lower during North America's summer.

There is often no single surcharge for freighter travel. When it does exist, it's usually only 10 to 20 percent.

Ivaran Lines' *Americana* exemplifies the upper end of freighter travel with plenty of deck space, a swimming pool and jacuzzi, an indoor lounge, a library and game room, a fully-equipped gym, a sauna with masseuse and a small casino. It can be a great transition cruise line for travelers curious about freighter travel, but accustomed to major cruise line amenities. Call **800-451-1639**.

Ford's Freighter Travel Guide, published twice a year, lists freighter itineraries. Check your local library or subscribe ($23 per year) by calling **818-701-7414**.

Booking sources for freighter cruises include:

- Freighter World Cruises, **800-531-7774**
- TravLtips, **800-872-8584**

Cruise passengers embarking from Miami in 1997: 3.2 million.

TRAVEL BY RAIL & ROAD

After the first edition of *Insider Travel Secrets* was released, we received several requests to expand our coverage of rail travel. I always pay attention to my readers, so we went to work to give you what you want. This chapter is packed with information on travel from a ground level perspective. It gives you the latest news, ways to save and ways to make your trip more enjoyable—even ways to have a very unique time using very standard forms of transportation.

U.S. Rail Travel focuses on one of the most under-used forms of travel—Amtrak. We think Amtrak may be under-used partly because most travelers don't realize the range of options it provides. There are definitely travel situations where time is of the essence, but there are also times for more leisurely travel, particularly in cases in which it saves money and adds the ability to really experience the land between here and there. For people traveling with children, Amtrak can be like a rolling lesson in geography and history, with no need to keep active children sitting still in one spot for hours. For couples, there is a romance to rail travel and the invitation to remember what leisurely travel really is.

Amtrak has had some struggles in recent years, but it will triumph if travelers understand how important Amtrak is to the U.S. travel scene. This chapter will hopefully introduce many of you to possibilities never even considered. One of the best new travel deals in existence is offered by Amtrak and VIA Rail Canada. You can purchase a 30 day pass allowing virtually unlimited travel on 27,000 miles of roadway (to 900 destinations) for $645 (US) or $895 (Canadian). You can visit many of the places you've always wanted to see without incurring a high single destination ticket cost.

We continue with *International Rail Travel,* offering basics, ways to save, travel tips and prime sources for rail travel in Europe. It also takes a look at rail travel in other countries. Because most countries have learned to value their railroads, you will find (for the most part) amazingly efficient trains with routing and schedules that get you just about anywhere you want to go on scenic itineraries.

Travel By Car offers helpful highway tips, whether you are using a rental car or a family vehicle. We'll offer advice on how preparation can ease your travel, show you how to play it safe on the roads and highways of the U.S. and Europe and give you some interesting itinerary ideas to get you started on a unique roadtrip.

Travel By Recreational Vehicle takes a look at a form of travel more and more people prefer. RVs let you take your "hotel room" with you on the road. If you are considering purchasing an RV, check out our ideas on how you can try this form of travel on for size before you commit to a major purchase. We'll tell you how to join special clubs that focus on RV travel and where to rent RVs internationally.

Travel By Motorcoach gives you the basics on domestic and international bus systems and motorcoach tours. If you haven't taken the bus in years, you may be in for a few surprises. It has become one of the favorite forms of travel for seniors, with a wide variety of theme packages offered year-round. And, if you've never considered international travel by bus, you could be missing out on an enjoyable and economical option.

Two-Wheel Travel offers tips and ideas for cyclists who can take advantage of one of the least-expensive (and most interesting) ways to see the world.

Walking & Hiking gives you some interesting leads on source for planned itineraries in the United States and in other countries.

By wheel or by foot, travel by rail and road, pathway and byway, could show you a whole new world of travel.

U.S. Rail Travel

WHY TRAVEL BY RAIL?

The U.S. Congress has given Amtrak a mandate to operate without subsidy by 2002. Toward that end, Amtrak is keeping a very close eye on which routes are profitable and which are not. They are cutting service in low service areas and adding and enhancing service on profitable routes, including the East and West Coasts. When Congress gave Amtrak a $225 million cash infusion, Amtrak was kept alive in many of the 42 cities and towns that would have suffered from the elimination of rail service. Some states stepped up to the plate, also. Vermont decided it would subsidize rail travel and saw an almost immediate pay-off in increased tourism.

The future of U.S. rail travel is bright if you live in parts of the country where Amtrak ridership is significant or if you live in a state blessed by legislators who understand the need for rail travel and are not unduly influenced by lobbyists working for competing factions. Amtrak would like a half-cent of the federal gasoline tax. Lobbyists with an interest in travel by road disagree. We have traditionally lagged far behind European countries that have developed rail travel to state-of-the-art. We face many of the same problems—over-crowded highways, air pollution and rising fuel costs. During the next several years, we will decide how important viable rail travel is.

If you have a strong opinion on supporting Amtrak, now is the time to make your voice heard, particularly if you live in parts of the country threatened with the elimination of passenger rail service. All it takes is a phone call, a letter or an e-mail to your congressperson and your opinion will count. One of the easiest ways to e-mail: **www.mrsmith.com**.

Amtrak continues to look to the future, testing the Danish-built, high-tech Flexiliner passenger train, which may become the train of Amtrak's future on short-to-medium runs. The *American Flyer*, Amtrak's version of the bullet train may arrive on the New York-Boston route in 1999, traveling at 110-150 miles per hour. Other innovations include bi-level Superliner cars and Viewliner Sleeping Cars on New York-Miami and New Orleans-Chicago routes. Florida has committed $70 million over 40 years to high-speed rail; Michigan and Illinois are collaborating on a high-speed rail system to link Detroit and Chicago.

Here are some fast facts about Amtrak:

- **Number of stations**—530 in 45 states, excluding Alaska, Hawaii, Maine, Oklahoma and South Dakota.
- **Number of passengers annually**—54 million, including commuter routes.
- **Number of trains per day**—208, including 101 Northeast Corridor trains, 91 Intercity and West Coast trains and 16 long distance trains.
- **1996 revenue**—$1.5 billion with $2.2 billion in expenses.

Rail travel gives you time to relax, mobility while en route, transportation from city center to city center and (even in Coach), seats that remain comfortable on long journeys. It can be one of the best

Average speed of Amtrak's Metroliner trains: 80 mph.

forms of family travel. (Children are wonderful, but being confined to a small space does not bring out the best in them.) Don't forget the ecological advantages, a factor which becomes more important with each passing year.. The typical train uses one-sixth the fuel used to travel the same distance by car.

WHEN RAIL TRAVEL IS A DEAL

Consumers are often shocked to discover that they won't always save a bundle when going by rail. Sometimes the cost of rail travel is greater than the price of an airline ticket, particularly if the lowest-priced Amtrak fares are sold out. A solo traveler booking a sleeping berth will definitely pay more. Rail travel bargains consist of special promotions, unique travel considerations and the purchase of a more leisurely travel mode. Families can save by using rail travel since, unlike most domestic air travel, children receive discounted fares. It's difficult to provide hard and fast fare comparisons because of all the variables involved but, to give you an idea of how prices for rail and air travel compare, check the following charts. They use the lowest non-promotional Amtrak fare and typical (non-fare war) advance Coach airfares . The first chart compares costs for a solo traveler.

In all of our sample cases, a solo traveler saves on rail over air, if purchasing the lowest available Amtrak fare. Sleeper travel would only be a wise choice if you are willing to pay more for the experience, the relaxation and the privacy your accommodations will provide. Fare war prices can lower your airfare and Amtrak specials can lower your rail fare. You have to get your quotes and compare prices on your specific itinerary, before you make your decision.

RAIL/AIR COMPARISONS

RT ITINERARY SOLO TRAVELER	AMTRAK COACH	AMTRAK SLEEPER	21-DAY ADVANCE COACH AIRFARE	RT AMTRAK TIME/AIR TIME
Dallas-Chicago	$182	$488	$399	44 hrs./4 hrs.
New York City-Miami	$146	$614	$220	54 hrs./6 hrs.
St. Louis-Los Angeles	$264	$924	$389	78 hrs./8 hrs.

Now let's look at the same itineraries, using a family of four to compare fares: two parents and two children under 15 (both receiving standard discounts). You'll see that Amtrak Coach travel comes through with shining colors and sleeper travel gets an edge on the Dallas-Chicago route.

FAMILY RAIL/AIR COMPARISONS

RT ITINERARY FAMILY OF FOUR	AMTRAK COACH	AMTRAK SLEEPER	21-DAY ADVANCE COACH AIRFARE
Dallas-Chicago	$504	$1,280	$1,598
New York City-Miami	$438	N/A—Maximum of 3 people	$ 880
St. Louis-Los Angeles	$792	$1,932	$1,556

Biggest impediment to high-speed Amtrak travel: inferior roadbeds.

AMTRAK FARE CLASSES

Standard Coach (generally unreserved seating) is the least expensive option, outside of promotional specials. Upgraded Custom Class (reserved seats) is available on some trains.

First Class is comprised of passengers with club and sleeping car tickets. It includes the use of private Metropolitan Lounges at stations in New York City, Chicago, Philadelphia and Washington, DC (comfortable seating areas, desks, phone, fax and complimentary beverages). Club service usually includes one meal served at your seat.

Metroliner service is available in the Northeast. It designates travel on trains with few or no intermediate stops. Metroliner service can cost as much as double other trains on the same routes but is extremely popular with commuters whose time is at a premium.

Sleeping car service is available at $60-600 per night above the cost of individual Coach tickets. Only one sleeping car charge is added per compartment, no matter how many people occupy the room. There usually is a two- to three-person minimum, with the other travelers paying regular fare. Meals are included with most tickets. Options include:

- **Roomette**—Accommodates one person with an arm chair and pullout bed. The toilet and sink are in the same area. You won't be able to use them when the bed is folded down.
- **Bedroom**—Either two chairs or one sofa, two folding beds and a separate bathroom.
- **Deluxe Bedroom**—A sofa and two chairs, two beds, toilet and shower.
- **Family Bedroom**—Accommodates a family of four comfortably.

Reservations are required for long distance overnight Coach; some short distance trains; Custom Class; Club Service; First Class sleeping cars; Metroliner service; some NortheastDirect trains; and some EmpireService trains. They can be made up to 11 months in advance. Reservations can be helpful on most trains to assure the lowest fare and availability on the dates you want.

Most tickets are fully refundable as long as no portion has been used. Passengers holding tickets for sleeping accommodations must cancel at least 48 hours in advance to avoid substantial cancellation penalties. Club Service ticket holders must cancel at least one hour in advance or be assessed a penalty equal to 50 percent of the fare. Lost or stolen tickets are generally not refunded.

AMTRAK DISCOUNTS

Amtrak has become more aggressive in fare promotions and also offers several standard discounts. Try to book as far in advance as possible since the least expensive fares sell out first. Standard discounts include:

- **Children two to 15**—50 percent off when traveling with a full fare passenger. You can use this discount on *Explore America* fares also. Children two and under travel free with a full fare passenger but separate seating is not guaranteed. Children eight and above are allowed to travel alone on some trains and under certain restrictions. They must pay full fare.
- **Students 16 and above**—The Amtrak *Student Advantage* card offers 15 percent off most fares plus discounts at hotels, restaurants and campus-area retailers. The annual fee is $22.50.

Fastest Amtrak longhaul route: the Southwest Chief between Chicago and Los Angeles at an average 55 mph.

> *"Fantasy Flyer offers Amtrak tickets, transfers and Disneyland admission as a package. For example, choose a one-day Passport to Disneyland or a five-day Flex Passport offering five consecutive days of admission for the price of two and get 25 percent off Amtrak California's San Diegan (serving Anaheim from over 500 cities nationwide) and San Joaquin trains. Other deals are offered as special, limited time promotions."*

Call **800-962-6872**.

- **Seniors 62 and above**—15 percent off Coach fares Monday through Thursday and *Explore America* fares. The discount does not apply to sleeper cars, auto trains, Metroliners, Club Service or Custom Class passengers.
- **AAA discounts**—Show your American Automobile Association card when you pick up your tickets and ten percent will be deducted on the spot. This offer applies to most tickets, except Auto Trains (trains that transport passengers with cars).
- **Discounts by internet**—Two Amtrak sites offer discounts (and information) on U.S. rail travel. Visit **www.amtrak.com** for systemwide information; **www.amtrakwest.com** for western U.S. routes. Special offers change regularly and can include free companion travel.
- **Group and family rates**—Ask about group and family rates if you have as few as four people traveling together. What constitutes a group varies by train, routing and season.
- **One-way travel for half the price of roundtrip**—In most cases, you pay a premium for one-way travel. Amtrak altered one-way ticket pricing policies on California, Oregon and Washington routes to make one-ways half the price of roundtrips.
- **Rail/hotel packages**—Amtrak Travel Packages offer discounts for train and hotel packages. A free *Travel Planner* is published twice a year and details special offers.
- **Rail/air packages**—Amtrak and United Airlines offer rail/air packages between 86 cities. Air Rail Vacations allow up to three stopovers on the rail portion of your trip. You can book hotel accommodations and tour packages as part of your package. You get frequent flyer miles on your return flight and up to 1,000 airmiles for your train travel. Call **800-440-8202**.
- **USA Rail Passes**—These are similar to Eurailpasses. They are only available to residents of countries other than the U.S. and must be purchased in the traveler's home country.
- **Executive Privileges**—Amtrak's new frequent rider program is available for *Metroliner* service between New York and Washington (DC), and *Empire* service within New York state. Awards include free Amtrak tickets and hotel and dining discounts.

Examples of seasonal and promotional discounts (many recurring each year) include:

- **Free Companion Tickets**—This past winter Amtrak offered a two-for-one

> "*For details on Amtrak discounts and promotions, call* **800-872-7245**. *For vacation packages, call* **800-321-8684**. *Go online at* **www.amtrak.com.** *Ticket through Amtrak or through your travel agent. Amtrak offers several free travel guides. The Amtrak Travel Planner is a 100-page guide full of travel trips and suggestions for particularly scenic routings. The Amtrak Vacations Sampler details vacation packages. Call to request your copy. Easy Tips For Easy Travel is a quick overview of Amtrak that usually includes coupons valid for car rental and attraction discounts. Pick up a copy at any staffed Amtrak station.*"

promotion on routes covering three Midwest states (great timing for travelers who did not want to drive on winter roads) and a separate promotion offering two-for-one within California (available even for one-way travel, including trips to Disneyland/Anaheim).

- ***Explore America*** **fares** usually become available for booking in early spring and can be used for travel in spring and peak summer periods. You pay one fare that allows roundtrip travel with stops in three locations. Take up to 30 days to complete your trip. This promotion divides the 48 states into three regions—Eastern, Central and Western. Based on 1997 rates, pay $168 for travel within one region; $198 for two regions; $278 for travel anywhere in the continental U.S. Last year, these prices covered travel through early May. For just $50 more, travel was available through August 17. Discounts for children and seniors can be used.
- ***All Aboard America*** **fares**, usually offered for about 30 days in summer and 30 days in winter (including some holiday travel) are similar to *Explore America* fares. They are a little higher priced but offer fewer restrictions.
- **Visa cardholders often get five percent off** sleeping car accommodations.
- ***Amtrak Meets You More Than Half Way*** tends to appear regularly. You get discounts of up to 55 percent on tickets priced at $75 and above.

> "*Amtrak recently printed a half-price companion fare coupon on eleven million cereal boxes. Look for more innovative marketing ideas in the future (and look for Best Fares to announce them).*"

AMTRAK POLICIES & STRATEGIES

Most trains allow three pieces of checked luggage not exceeding 75 pounds each or 150 pounds total. Carry-ons are limited to two per Coach passenger. Sleeping car passengers can carry on as much as their rooms can reasonably accommodate. Take along a small pillow and light blanket for lengthy trips when you are traveling Coach. Some trains offer pillows and blankets for small fees, but supplies often run out.

Smoking is allowed in designated cars

only on trips with more than four-and-a-half hours running time between stops. Smoking is also allowed in some sleeping cars.

Trains providing meal service offer dining car service for dinner ($8-14); lunch ($5-7); and breakfast ($4-6). Trains without dining cars offer a limited selection of microwave cuisine.

Laptop computer users should plan to run on batteries or bring an extension cord and a two- and three-prong adapter plug. Trains frequently enter areas that temporarily wipe out electrical power sources. As a matter of courtesy to other passengers, headphones are required for radios, tape and CD players.

On board phone service is available on some trains including Metroliners, New England Express trains, San Diegans, San Joaquins and Capitols. Calls are billed to your credit card.

Ask for a free route guide before you board the train. The counter staff and conductors should have copies. They detail the schedule and spotlight points of interest viewable from the train.

SPECIAL AMTRAK OPTIONS

Ski Amtrak with rail travel only, rail and air packages or complete package options that include rail fare, transfers, accommodations and lift tickets.

- **From Los Angeles**, the *Southwest Chief* takes you to Lamy, New Mexico to access Santa Fe and Taos ski areas. You're looking at an hour or two of driving once you reach Lamy, but the drive takes you through some of the most incredible scenery in the Southwest. The *Pioneer* heads for Jackson Hole. The *Empire Builder* will take you to Montana, Idaho and Washington.
- **From Chicago or San Francisco**, board the *California Zephyr* to access Denver and Salt Lake City area resorts.
- **From Chicago and New York/Washington, DC**, the *Broadway Limited* and *Capitol Limited* travels to budget resorts with great skiing in Pennsylvania and Maryland. The *Cardinal* will take you near West Virginia's Snowshoe, Winterplace and Silver Creek ski areas.
- **From Washington, DC and Montreal** you can access several Northeast resorts including Woodstock, Killington, Stowe Smuggler's Notch and Sugarbush.

Taking a trip by train can make getting there as exciting as being there. Amtrak's most scenic routes include:

- ***The California Zephyr***—Oakland to Chicago with a scenic route that takes you through the Sierra and Rocky Mountains, the Glenwood Canyon and the six-mile Moffat Tunnel that runs beneath the Continental Divide.
- ***The Coach Starlight***—between Los Angeles and Seattle, along the Pacific shore and through the foothills of the Cascade Mountains.

Fall foliage routes attract riders from September through mid-November. Popular routes (and their usual peak viewing times) include:

- **Midwest (September 1-20)**—*The Empire Builder* from Chicago to Seattle and *The California Zephyr* from Chicago through the Rockies.
- **Northeast (October 1-15)**—*The Northeast Direct* between New Haven and Boston, *The Empire* from New

Year in which Amtrak was founded: 1971.

York to Boston, *The Adirondack* from Lake Champlain to Montreal, *The Maple Leaf* from Buffalo to Toronto and *The Vermonter* from Washington (DC) to St. Albans (VT).

- **Southeast (September 15 to November 25)**—*The Crescent* from the Virginia foothills to northern Alabama, *The Silver Star* and *The Silver Meteor* through Virginia and the Carolinas and *The Piedmont* from Raleigh to Charlotte.

OTHER U.S. RAIL OPTIONS

Several unique rail options offer day trips to long-range itineraries:

- **Travel on the Alaska Railroad**, ferries and motorcoaches in Alaska and parts of Canada. The *AlaskaPass* can be purchased for eight to 30 consecutive days of travel or a specified number of days of travel within a three week to 45-day period. There are off-peak rates (September 15 to May 15) and peak rates. Senior discounts are available for off-peak travel times; children's discounts (ages three to 11) are available year-round. Call **800-544-0552**; go online at **www.alaska pass.com.**
- **The American *Orient Express*,** now in its third season, is in the upscale tradition of Europe's *Orient Express*, including twin club cars with baby grand pianos. Several six- to nine-day itineraries are available at prices beginning at $1,790, including most meals, excursions at stops along the way, special presentations and added amenities. Call **800-727-7477**.
- **The Grand Canyon Railway** offers vintage 1920s cars that travel between Williams, Arizona and the Grand Canyon National Park. The 130-mile roundtrip is punctuated by 3.5 hours at the National Park or an optional overnight stay. Rates begin at $49.50 ($19.50 for children) plus $4-6 for park admission. Family packages are available. Call **800-843-8724**.
- **The *Montana Daylight*** is a new, deluxe railroad offering two-day trips between Livingston, Montana and Sandpoint, Idaho, with an optional transfer to Spokane. The 455-mile route is covered during daylight hours to optimize passenger views on this scenic route. It offers three classes of service beginning at $399, including meals. Call **800-519-7245**.
- **The Napa Valley Wine Train** offers a 36-mile roundtrip vintage railroad journey past two dozen Napa Valley vineyards. Rates begin at $56.50, including brunch. Call **800-427-4124**.

> *"The Florida Fun Train travels between Fort Lauderdale and Orlando. Universal Studios Florida is a partner in the new enterprise. Passengers are encouraged to board up to 90 minutes early and begin enjoying the train. It has glass-domed passenger cars and four entertainment cars, including Kid Zone for younger children and a car full of electronic games for older kids. Roundtrip tickets are $139 for adults; $99 for children under 12. Special promotions are offered frequently. Call* ***954-920-0606***.*"*

INTERNATIONAL RAIL TRAVEL

EUROPE

Rail, Rental Car Or Air?

Several factors help determine if rail travel within Europe is a better option than rental car or airfare. It doesn't have to be an either/or choice. Rail/car passes give you a specified number of rail days and a specified number of car rental days; rail/air passes combine rail and air. France offers rail/car/air options, allowing you to sample three modes of travel. Points to consider:

- **Number of people traveling**—Solo travelers and couples usually save by taking the train. Three or more travelers should compare car rental deals against the cost of rail, keeping in mind that surcharges, parking fees, high fuel costs and toll roads multiply the daily cost of any car rental.
- **Itinerary**—Rail routes are so extensive that you can reach just about any destination you could desire. You're not limited by less extensive air routes. Check scheduling if you want to focus on villages and rural areas. Chances are, you'll do fine. If your travel plans focus on major cities, you'll have no problem getting a train when you want one.
- **Length of travel**—If you need less than five days of transportation, opt for the train. Car rental rates for shorter time periods are generally astronomical, particularly if you haven't reserved in advance.

Passes Or Individual Tickets?

Passes provide financial advantages for most travel. The major exception would be minimal miles traveled in any particular country. When traveling by pass, you often must make a reservation, particularly during busy travel times. Reservations sometimes require a small fee over and above the one-time cost of the pass.

Major Flexipass options include Eurail, Euro, French, German and Scandinavian.

Eurailpass lets you travel in Austria, Belgium, Denmark, Finland, France, Germany, Greece, Holland, Hungary, Ireland, Italy, Luxembourg, Norway, Portugal, Spain, Sweden and Switzerland. A First Class Saverpass is now available for two to five people traveling together. Current prices for a ten-day flexipass are $444 Second Class, $540 First Class Saverpass and $634 First Class. Children under four travel free. There are no companion discounts.

Europass is less expensive and a bit more restrictive. It covers France, Germany, Italy, Spain and Switzerland. An even less expensive option for travel within three of the five countries was offered, but prices are now based solely on the number of travel days you select. You can add travel to Austria, Belgium, Greece, Hungary, Luxembourg, the Netherlands or Portugal at added zone charges. Current price for a five-day basic pass is $326. One companion receives a 40 percent discount. Children four-11 get 50 percent off.

Peak speed of Europe and Japan's high-speed trains: 150 mph.

Regional passes cover several nearby countries. They include:

- **Balkan Flexipass**—Bulgaria, Greece, Macedonia, Montenegro, Romania, Serbia and Turkey.
- **Benelux Pass**—Belgium, the Netherlands and Luxembourg; discounted Junior Passes are offered for students under 26.
- **Central Europe Pass**—The Czech Republic, Germany, Poland, and Slovakia; children four to 11 pay half-price.
- **European East Pass**—Austria, the Czech Republic, Hungary, Poland and Slovakia; children four to 11 pay half-price.
- **Scanrail Pass**—Denmark, Finland, Norway and Sweden. Children four to 11 pay half-price.
- **United Kingdom**—BritPass, Brit-Germany Pass, BritIreland Pass, and BritFrance; travel in Wales and Scotland is included; some passes include ferry travel.

National passes cover one country only. They include:

- **Austrian Railpass**—Also covers lake ferries and steamers. Children seven to 15 receive discounts; children up to six years of age travel free.
- **Bulgaria Railpass**—Children four to 12 pay half-price.
- **Czech Flexipass**—Children four to 13 pay half-price.
- **Finland Railpass**—Children six to 17 pay half-price; children under six travel free.
- **GermanRail Pass**—Flexipass options, TwinPass discounts for two or more adults traveling together, Junior Fares (ages 12 to 26) and half-price fares for children four to 11.
- **Greek Railpass**—Children four to 11 pay half-price.
- **Hungarian Flexipass**—Children five to 14 pay half-price.
- **Irish Rover Pass**—Covers the Republic of Ireland and Northern Ireland; the Irish Explorer Pass covers the Republic of Ireland only.
- **Italian Railpass**—Flexipass options; children four to 11 pay half-price.
- **Norway Railpass**—Standard and flexipass versions with discounted prices for low season, October through April.
- **PolRail Pass**—Children under ten pay half-price; ages ten to 26 receive discounts; buffet car on all overnight journeys.
- **Portuguese Flexipass**—Children four to 11 pay half-price.
- **Romanian Flexipass**—Is the newest addition, with three days of First Class travel (in a 15 day period) priced at $60.
- **Spain Railpass**—Children four to 11 pay half-price.
- **Sweden Pass**—Two children (up to age 15) travel free with each pass-holding adult.
- **Swiss Travel System**—The Swiss Pass and Swiss Flexipass covers the Swiss Federal Railway routes plus many private railways, lake steamers, motorcoaches, cable cars and municipal buses; children ages 16 and under travel free with an accompanying adult.

Get the best price by purchasing your passes before you leave the U.S. Many

Cities with mass transit systems called DART: Dublin and Dallas Area Mass Transit.

passes must be purchased in your home country or a country apart from those you will travel in. Discount prices are designed for visitors rather than locals. In the few cases where you can purchase abroad, you will almost always pay a minimum of 20 percent above the advance purchase price. The exception: rail travel in Eastern Europe. Purchasing in the U.S. will cost you quite a bit more.

More Options To Consider

Categories of service—First Class is the only class available for Eurail and Europasses unless you are 26 or younger. For other passes (and tickets), you will pay about 50 percent more for First Class. Second Class satisfies most travelers and is usually available with youth and student discounts. Eurail and Europass Second Class purchase is limited to travelers 25 and younger. Most country passes allow travelers of any age to purchase their choice of First or Second class travel.

Days of travel—A full-time pass lets you travel as often as you like during the validity of the pass. A flexipass lets you travel a prescribed number of days within the period of validity—for example, five days of travel within a two-month period. If you like to spend a couple of days at each destination, a Flexipass will be your best bet.

Passenger categories are one of the strongest rate-determining factors.

- **Companion passes** lower rates for two people traveling together. Group passes lower rates for three to five travelers. You must travel together at all times since only one pass is issued.
- **Youth passes** are offered to travelers under 26 years of age. The German Youth Pass and the Holland Junior Rail Pass cover travel in one country.

There are eight passes that offer travel in multiple countries.

- **Balkan Junior Flexipass**: Bulgaria, Greece, Macedonia, Romania, Turkey and Yugoslavia (Serbia and Montenegro)
- **Benelux Junior Tourrail Pass**: Belgium, Luxembourg and the Netherlands
- **BritRail Youthpass and BritRail Flexipass Youth**: United Kingdom
- **Eurail Youthpass and Eurail Youth Flexipass**: Austria, Belgium, Denmark, Finland, France, Germany, Greece, Holland, Hungary, Italy, Luxembourg, Norway, Portugal, Republic of Ireland, Spain, Sweden and Switzerland
- **Europass Youth**: France, Germany, Italy, Spain and Switzerland
- **Scanrail Youth Pass**: Denmark, Finland, Norway and Sweden

> *“Don't forget special city passes for local or regional trains. The Paris Viste card, for example, provides unlimited travel on the Metro and public buses and rail lines within Paris and as far outside of Paris as EuroDisney, Versailles and both major airports. The cost for a two-day pass is $40. It must be purchased in conjunction with a Rail Europe pass. Tourism agencies can fill you in on more options. Check More Dollars & Cents for other city rail savings options.”*

- **Students 12 through 25** get varying discounts when showing an International Student ID.
- **Children's discounts** are available with varying age minimums and discount percentages. Some passes allow children up to age six to travel free.
- **Seniors discounts**, available with age confirming identification, are offered in Finland (minimum age, 65), Luxembourg (60), Norway (67) and Portugal (60). Other countries require an official senior ID issued by the railroad and valid for one year. You must supply a passport-type photo, so it's a good idea to carry a few extras to save the on-the-spot expense. The following chart addresses some countries that require railroad-issued senior IDs.

SENIOR RAIL DISCOUNTS		
COUNTRY	FEE & DISCOUNT	AGE MINIMUM
Austria	$30 fee; 50% discount	60/women; 65/men
France	$26-48 fee, depending on length of validity; discounts up to 50%	60
Germany	$132/First Class fee; $66/Second Class fee	60
Greece	$24/First Class fee; $16/Second Class fee; your first five trips are included at no charge; subsequent trips are discounted at 50%	60
Sweden	$7 fee; 25% discount for off-peak travel only	67

Sleeping accommodations on European trains can be great bargains, compared to hotel stays. Of course, you can sleep in your seat with no added charge. You can also purchase a couchette (bunk-style sleepers) for $20-29 additional. Couchettes are co-ed and you can expect up to five people sharing your compartment. Pay $40-100 extra for a sleeper, offering more privacy and comfort. Sleeper compartments usually accommodate two or three travelers.

Most unused passes are refundable at 85 percent of the purchased price, but you must return them within six to 12 months of your purchase date (varying by type of pass purchased) and refunds take six to eight weeks. Lost or stolen passes are non-refundable, but you can purchase insurance for approximately $10 per pass.

Rail travel in Eastern Europe falls outside of the guidelines for most European rail travel. Point-to-point tickets are very inexpensive. For example, travel between the Baltic capitals for about $15. The only advantage in purchasing passes may be less currency conversion difficulty.

Knowledgeable Sources

The chart on the following page lists major sources for European rail passes. You can also purchase passes from your travel agent. Telephone numbers are listed first, followed by fax numbers and internet addresses (when applicable).

EUROPEAN RAIL PASS SOURCES	
SOURCE	**PASSES AVAILABLE**
BritRail Travel 888-274-8724 www.britrail.com	Britain
CIE Tours International 800-243-8687 800-338-3964	Ireland
CIT Rail 800-223-7987	Eurail plus Britain, Germany & Italy
DER Travel Services 800-421-2929 800-282-7474 www.dertravel.com	Eurail, Balkan, Benelux & Scanrail plus Austria, Britain, Czech Republic, Denmark, Germany, Greece, Italy, the Netherlands, Norway, Spain & Sweden
Europe Through The Back Door 206-771-8303 206-771-0833 www.ricksteves.com	Eurail, Europass, Benelux, European East & Scanrail plus Austria, Czech Republic, Finland, France, Germany, Italy, Norway, Portugal, Spain, Sweden, Switzerland & the U.K.; also offers a free 64-page guide to Europe, including extensive rail information
Forsyth Travel Library 800-367-7984 816-942-6969 www.forsyth.com	All passes; bonus American AAdvantage miles with some purchases
Orbis Polish Travel Bureau 800-223-6037 212-682-4715 www.orbis-usa.com	Poland
Rail Europe 800-438-7245 800-432-1329 www.raileurope.com	Eurail, Balkan, Benelux, European East & Scanrail plus Austria, Bulgaria, Czech Republic, Finland, France, Germany, Hungary, Italy, Norway, Portugal, Romania, Spain, Sweden & Switzerland
Rail Pass Express 800-722-7151 614-764-0711 www.eurail.com	Eurail, Balkan, Benelux & Scanrail plus Austria, Britain, Denmark, Germany, Greece, Italy, the Netherlands, Norway, Spain & Sweden
Scandinavian American 800-545-2203 201-835-3030 www.travelfile.com/get/scnm.html	Scanrail plus Finland, Norway & Sweden
Scantours 800-223-7226 310-390-0493	Eurail, Balkan, Benelux, European East & Scanrail plus Austria, Bulgaria, Czech Republic, Finland, France, Germany, Hungary, Italy, Norway, Portugal, Romania, Spain, Sweden & Switzerland

Number of routes in New York City's subway system: 238; in London's Underground, 255.

Special Savings

Special limited-time promotions add bonus savings to rail travel in Europe. *Best Fares* magazine and *Best Fares* Online has offered deals including:

- **Fly, drive & ride the train through France for less**—Special offers from Rail Europe that allow you to customize your European travel forms to your taste, with one discount rate.
- **A free day on Swiss Rail**—To celebrate its 150th anniversary, Swiss Rail offered a free day's travel with the purchase of an eight-, 15- or 30-day pass.
- **Free Chunnel Train roundtrips**—Virgin Atlantic offered a free Chunnel roundtrip London to Paris with the purchase of a 21-day advance APEX roundtrip airfare to London from the U.S.
- **The BritRail** ***Party Pass***—This pass offered 50 percent off to third and fourth passengers.

Unique European Rail Journeys

Get a unique taste of European rail travel by booking a specialty trip. They often use refurbished, historic trains and offer itineraries so unique that you'll have little trouble trying to decide something to write on those postcards home. The classic *Orient Express* is the most famous example. It includes a luxury train that travels between London and Venice and *The Eastern Orient Express*, which travels between Singapore and Bangkok. It also includes *The British Pullman* steam train (restored 1920s and '30s carriages) offering day-long trips from London to castles and cathedrals. *British Pullman* fares start at $160. Call **800-524-2420**. Other options are available from tourism offices in most European countries

WORLDWIDE RAIL

Rail Australia markets five state railroads and offers rail pass travel options perfect for covering the wide scope of the country. Single trips vary from a 90-minute ride through the Queensland rain forest on the Kuranda Scenic Railway to a 64-hour journey between Sydney to Perth. There are three pass categories, all available in two classes and varying lengths of validity: the Australia Flexipass ($319 for an Economy pass covering eight days of travel within six months); the Austrail Pass ($386 Economy for two weeks of unlimited travel); the East Coast Discovery Pass, designed to provide low cost Economy travel, primarily for backpackers. *Great Rail Journeys of Australia* details 16 rail trips and is free, by request. Call **800-423-2880**.

Canada's VIA Rail offers high-speed trains between Montreal and Toronto and

> *"The Real Ale Rail Trail in Pembrokshire, Wales gives you a great excuse to enjoy the local product. Stop by the tourist office to get a Real Ale Rail Trail brochure. It lists 16 family-owned pubs along three rural rail lines. Buy a $7 ticket, stop at your choice of eight participating pubs (and have the barkeep sign your brochure each time) and you're eligible to win a free South Wales and West Railway ticket. The season runs from April through early December. Luckily, you do not have to say Real Ale Rail Trail out loud each time you have your brochure signed."*

an extensive network of leisure trains. The Toronto-Vancouver and Jasper-Prince Rupert routes are among the most scenic. The Canrailpass allows unlimited Coach travel for 12 days within a 30 day period. Prices in Canadian dollars start at about $275/adult; $250 for people 24 and younger and seniors 60 and above. Prices are higher during peak season and pass travel may be blacked out during holiday periods. The VIA Preference frequent rider program awards 1,000 bonus miles on enrollment, and one point per dollar spent. Free trips start at 1,500 points. Call **416-236-2029** to enroll. Call **800-561-3949** for VIA Rail reservations.

Indrail of India offers passes covering one- to 90-day periods. There are three categories of service: Air-conditioned First Class, First Class and Second Class. Rail travel in India has a better on-time record and is generally safer than the country's domestic airlines, but opt for one of the two First Class categories. Call **212-957-3000**. *The Palace on Wheels* is an ultra-luxury train from New Delhi to northwestern India (including Jaipur, Jodhpur and Agra). Its amenities are on a five-star hotel level. Call **213-380-8855**.

The Japan Railway specializes in high-speed trains, including the bullet train from Tokyo to Osaka. A seven-day pass usually costs less than one roundtrip ticket. Green Class (the equivalent of First Class) and Ordinary (Second Class) categories are available. An Ordinary, seven-day pass costs $280. Children six to 11 pay half-price. Some bus and ferry travel is included in some passes. Call **800-223-0266**.

The Russian Flexipass covers travel between major cities. A Second Class pass providing four days of travel in a 15-day period is $210; add about $100 for First Class. Call **800-848-7245**.

Tips For Worldwide Rail Travel

It's hard to generalize in a world of travel as varied as Second Class India Rail and black-tie dinners on the *Orient Express*, but these tips can help you through almost any rail itinerary:

- **Many major cities have two or three rail stations**—Paris has six. Be sure you're at the right one and that your connections allow travel time between stations, if needed.
- **You are generally not required to stay in your reserved seat** unless the train is unusually full. If an open seat is more to your liking, you're free to use it.
- **Smoking is more apt to be allowed** than disallowed.
- **Know the local spelling and pronunciation of your destination.** Both may differ from the Americanized versions.
- **Make sure you're in a rail car** that is going all the way to your destination. Sometimes cars are detached at intermediate stations.
- **Ask if food and beverages will be available** on lengthier train trips and plan accordingly.

> *"Kemwel's Premier Selections offer attractive prices on 15 luxury trains in Asia, Canada, Europe, Mexico, South Africa and the U.S. Options include a two-day trip from Vancouver to Banff and a six-day trip through the Scottish Highlands. Call* ***800-234-4000*** *to request a free brochure."*

Railroad that offers free welcome aboard champagne on longhaul routes: VIA Rail of Canada.

TRAVEL BY CAR

BEFORE YOU GO

Automobile club memberships cost $22-60—an amount of money that could be one of your best travel investments. You're protected all year at home, and you get travel benefits for every road trip—emergency road service, trip planning with up-to-date details no atlas can provide, insurance options and travel discounts. Most clubs cover the primary member and a spouse. If you have a larger family of drivers, choose a plan that includes them all at the lowest added cost. Exxon's Travel Club, **800-833-9966**, offers the best emergency service due to the number of service affiliates they can utilize. The American Automobile Association, **800-222-4357**, offers the most extensive discounts for hotels and car rentals and superior trip-planning services.

Give your car a thorough maintenance check that takes into consideration special climate and geographical demands you may experience during your trip. Check tires for proper inflation; recommended tire pressure changes with the climate. Decide if you need anti-freeze or snow tires. Consider renting if you have any doubt that your car can make the trip without problems. If you're driving through a colder climate, pack warm clothes and blankets in accessible areas and add flares and food for emergency situations.

Visa and Historic Hotels of America offer six free booklets on driving tours, each containing discounts and added-values. Choose Southern California, Northern California & Oregon, Colorado, Florida, Vermont & New Hampshire or the Mississippi River Delta. Send a stamped self-addressed business-size envelope (one for each booklet requested) to Historic Hotels of America, ATTN: Visa, 1785 Massachusetts Avenue NW, Washington, DC 20036.

Traveler Discount Guides focus on discounts for hotels and attractions along specific highways. They are updated every three months and cover Alabama, California, the District of Columbia, Florida, Kentucky, Louisiana, Maryland, Mississippi, North Carolina, South Carolina, Tennessee, Virginia, Interstate 95 from Maine to Florida and Interstate 10 from Texas to Florida. Pick them up for free at truck stops and other businesses along the interstates or order specific guides by calling **800-222-3948**. Third class mail delivery is $2 for the first guide and $1 for each additional guide; First class mail delivery is $3, plus $1 for each additional guide.

SAFETY ON THE ROAD

Stay alert—Take a small break every two hours or 100 miles. Breaks don't have to last more than a few minutes to be effective. Time zone travel and changes in sleep patterns can create drowsiness that many studies show to be responsible for almost 50 percent of highway accidents. Keep cool by lowering the air conditioner or rolling down the windows. Scan the road; don't hypnotize yourself by staring at a fixed point. Rotate driving duties and choose driving times that match the time of day when each driver feels most alert.

Observe speed limits. Miles per hour times 1.5 equals the number of feet you

The only state with no speed limit on U.S. highways: Montana.

travel per second. Allow yourself a safety margin by maintaining posted speeds.

Be aware of changes in traffic laws as you travel. In Oklahoma, you can't be cited for not wearing a seat belt unless you have been stopped for a separate violation. Drive across the border to Texas (or head to 12 other states) and you can be stopped and ticketed solely for not wearing a seat belt. You can wear tape player and radio headsets in Michigan (it's still a bad idea, even though it's legal) but you can't in neighboring Ohio and 14 other states. Mount a radar detector on your dashboard with impunity—except in Virginia and Washington, DC where they are banned by law.

Headlights increase your visibility to other drivers. Turn them on whenever you use your wipers and always use them when driving during twilight and dawn.

Pay attention to the weather. Tune-in local radio talk shows to get the forecast. If you are caught in a blizzard, stay in your car and wait for help. If you keep your motor running for heat, keep a window rolled down several inches to avoid carbon monoxide poisoning. Better yet—turn the motor off and use blankets to keep warm. Don't turn on high beams in fog; reflections can be blinding. Use low beams and slow down. When you're driving through hot climates, be aware of the extra strain on your vehicle's engine.

Beware of destination-specific road hazards you may never encounter at home—mud and rock slide areas, ice, snow, fog near large bodies of water and quick-flooding areas where the depth of the water is hard to determine. Dial *HP or 911 on your car phone to report accidents or hazardous driving conditions.

> *"Disaster Driving is a free pamphlet of tips available from Aetna Insurance. Call **203-273-2843.**"*

CRIME PREVENTION

Guard against ploys used by criminals to get travelers to stop their cars. They include pretending to need assistance and bumping your car from behind. If another driver tries to force you off the road, don't stop even if it means damage to your car. Use evasive action and head for a well-lit and well-populated area. Don't pick up hitchhikers. If someone seems to need assistance, send help to them, rather than transporting them in your car.

When you are stopped at intersections, keep doors locked and windows raised high enough to prevent someone from reaching in. Keep the car in gear. If someone tries to get in, hit the horn then step on the gas. Keep anything of obvious value

> *"Some drivers think they can ignore tickets for speeding and other infractions when they're out of state. They can't. Even if the law is different from the law in your home state, you're still obligated to know it and follow it. Many travelers get tickets for right turns on red, for example. They're used to doing it at home, but when they run into a state that doesn't allow it, they get nabbed. AAA offers a Digest of Motor Laws, updated annually. The $8.95 cost is cheaper than a ticket. You can purchase it at any AAA office."*

> *"Play It Safe is a free safety brochure available from AAA. Get a copy at any of their 1,000-plus locations—even if you are not a member. If you travel alone and feel vulnerable, consider the $99 inflatable Safe T Man. Make him look more authentic by sticking a hat on his head and only use him at night—he won't fool anyone during the daytime. Call* ***800-999-3030*** *for ordering information."*

locked in the trunk to help avoid becoming an attractive target.

Park in well-lit areas. When you approach your vehicle, make sure your keys are already in your hand. Check inside and underneath your vehicle before entering the car.

Maintain an adequate gas supply. Be particularly alert when driving a car with radically different gas mileage than the vehicle you are accustomed to driving. If your car breaks down, evaluate your surroundings before deciding whether to go for help or wait in your vehicle. If you decide to wait, request that anyone offering assistance notify the police or highway patrol for you.

SCENIC ROUTES

If you've had your fill of interstates, head for the blue highways—named for the color that marks them in most atlases. You won't make good time, but you'll *have* a good time along the way. As a bonus, the businesses that have been able to remain open on these secondary roads tend to offer lower prices, provide great service and are willing to share information about the area. Two particularly interesting blue highway routes:

- **Northern New Mexico**—Head north on U.S. 64 from Taos into the Sangre de Christo Mountains and through the Carson National Forest. Continue on, using a route locals call the Enchanted Loop, to Bobcat Pass (at 9,820 feet), Eagle Nest and Wheeler's Peak (13,161 feet) before returning to Taos. It's an 84-mile drive you'll never forget. Call **800-545-2070** for more information.
- **Southern Utah**—State Highway 24 will start you out on a 300-mile drive through red rock canyons, mountains, deserts, Capitol Reef National Park, Zion National Park, Bryce Canyon and a national forest. Call **800-200-1160**.

DRIVING IN EUROPE

Cars own the road in America, but even the most proficient U.S. driver needs to know the terms of driving in various international countries where the car is not king. In all European countries (except Cyprus, Ireland, Malta and the United Kingdom) traffic travels on the right side of the road, just as it does in the U.S. Seat belts are mandatory in front *and* back seats except in Malta (which doesn't require them at all) and Bulgaria, Denmark, Ireland, Romania, Russia, Slovenia and Spain (which require them in front seats but not in back seats).

Different countries have different driving personalities. Many German drivers enjoy high-speed travel and drive aggressively. Driving in Mediterranean countries can seem like participating in a car horn concerto.

Popular bus route for tourists in Vienna: the #1 or #2, traveling the Ringstrasse which circles the city.

This chart provides some of the basics: speed limits (in kilometers) for city-country-motorway travel in Europe, approximate price per gallon of gas and some interesting facts to know before you go. Don't be confused about kilometers. We'll give you basic conversions following this chart.

INTERNATIONAL DRIVING BASICS			
COUNTRY	**SPEED LIMITS**	**GAS**	**KNOW BEFORE YOU GO**
AUSTRIA	50-100-130	$4.20	Be prepared to pay tolls on some roads that go through mountain passes.
BELGIUM	50-70-120	$4.45	No toll roads in the entire country.
BULGARIA	50-80-120	$1.50	Many require vouchers to purchase fuel.
CROATIA	60-90-130	$2.50	Motorways in and out of Zagreb are toll roads.
CYPRUS	60-80-100	$3.50	Child seats are mandatory up to age five.
CZECH REPUBLIC	60-90-110	$3.95	Trams have the absolute right of way.
DENMARK	60-90-100	$4.30	Headlights must be on whenever your vehicle is in motion, day or night.
ESTONIA	50-90-100	$1.60	Unleaded gas is called benslin 95E; diesel fuel is called diisel.
FINLAND	50-100-120	$4.60	Pass only on the left, except when in multi-lane traffic.
FRANCE	50-90-130	$5.25	Trams have the right of way and may only be passed on the right.
GERMANY	50-100-130 *	$4.65	Pedestrians have priority at zebra striped crossings.
GREECE	50-80-120	$3.80	Cars may not be taken on ferries.
HOLLAND	50-80-100	$4.65	Headlights must be on whenever your vehicle is in motion, day or night.
HUNGARY	50-80-120	$3.25	Flashing green lights mean the same as flashing ambers in the West.
IRELAND	50-65-95	$3.75	Low car rental rates and some of the most beautiful terrain.
ISRAEL	60-70-90	$2.60	Headlights must be kept on at all times during winter months.
ITALY	50-90-130	$4.50	Cars parked in green zones are towed.
LUXEMBOURG	50-90-120	$3.25	Unleaded gas is called essence sans plomb; diesel is called gasoil.
MALTA	50-80-N/A	$2.75	All gasoline stations signs are in English.
NORWAY	50-80-90	$5.25	Toll roads exist around most major cities.

City that straddles two continents: Istanbul.

INTERNATIONAL CAR			
COUNTRY	SPEED LIMITS	GAS	KNOW BEFORE YOU GO
POLAND	60-90-110	$2.10	Unleaded gas is called benzyna bezolowiowa; diesel is called olej napedowy.
PORTUGAL	50-90-120	$4.00	A high prevalence of toll roads.
ROMANIA	60-80-90	$1.25	Unleaded gas is called benzina fara plumb; diesel is called motorina.
RUSSIA	60-90-110	$2.65	Non-waivable damage responsibility on rental cars is $300-700.
SLOVENIA	60-80-120	$2.00	Unleaded gas is called nrosvincen bencin; diesel is called dizel.
SPAIN	50-100-120	$3.50	Coastal roads have lower speed limits than comparable inland roads.
SWEDEN	50-90-110	$4.35	Pedestrians have priority at all crosswalks.
SWITZERLAND	50-80-120	$4.00	Ascending traffic on mountain roads gets the right of way.
TURKEY	50-80-120	$2.50	At unmarked intersections, traffic from the right has priority.
UNITED KINGDOM	50-80-110	$4.25	Vehicles on roundabouts (traffic circles) have priority over merging vehicles.

*130KM is the suggested maximum speed on Autobahn but is not mandatory

KILOMETERS TO MILES PER HOUR			
KPH	MPH	KPH	MPH
30	19	90	56
40	25	100	63
50	31	110	69
60	38	120	75
70	44	130	81
80	50		

In many countries, fines and tickets are payable on the spot. If you are driving a rental, you may be ticketed and fined even after you return your rental. Radar/photography systems record infractions and obtain your credit card information from the car rental company. Many other countries have less tolerance for drinking and driving than in the U.S. The consumption of even one drink can land you in jail.

Bikes, motorbikes, pedestrians and other relatively slow forms of transport are in abundance in many countries. Drive accordingly.

The highway fatality rate in most European countries exceeds that of the U.S. We average 1.1 fatalities per 620,000 miles. Only Sweden and the U.K. have better statistics. At the high end: Egypt, 44.1; Turkey, 20; Portugal, 7.5; Spain, 4.2; the Czech Republic, 3.9; and Belgium, 3.3. Use extra caution any time you drive on unfamiliar roads.

Proper way to point in Indonesia: right thumb extending from a closed fist.

TRAVEL BY RECREATIONAL VEHICLE

THE BASICS

RV rentals give groups and families vacation options with transportation and accommodations provided at one daily rate. It's possible to save as much as one-half the cost of an airfare/car rental/hotel vacation. Average daily rental cost is $150 per day plus mileage, add-on insurance and drop-off fees when applicable. There will either be prohibitions against travel on rough terrain or extra insurance requirements. Be aware of the height of your RV in reference to tunnel, overpass and bridge heights. RV's that carry compressed gas aren't allowed to use some ferries, tunnels and long bridges.

Cruise America is the largest renter of recreational vehicles. Discount coupons are usually available in Entertainment Passbooks (see *More Dollars and Cents* for information on how to order). Reach Cruise America at **800-327-7799**.

The Recreation Vehicle Industry Association offers a free guide with RV, campground and trip-planning information for RV owners and renters. It includes new ski resort area campgrounds with free shuttles to the slopes and ski resorts with parking areas for RVs. Call **888-467-8464** or **703-620-6003**.

The Recreation Vehicle Rental Association sells a $5 membership directory with complete information on where to rent, requirements for rental and what types of vehicles are available. Call **703-591-7130**.

All KOA Campgrounds offer a free directory that details facilities at their sites, nationwide. If you prefer, order by mailing a $3 handling fee to KOA, Box 30162, Billings, MT 59107. Call **406-248-7444**.

The most mountainous country in the Caribbean: Haiti.

The Good Sam Club is an international organization of over one million members who enjoy travel in recreational vehicles. The introductory membership fee of $12 per family provides ten percent off campground fees and propane; trip routing, telephone messages, emergency road service options and a directory of campgrounds. It also includes events hosted by its 2,200 local chapters. Call **800-234-3450**.

RENTING RVS IN EUROPE

RVs are commonly called motorhomes in Europe. Several agencies (including Global Motorhome Travel at **800-468-3876**) offer rentals from base points including Amsterdam, Copenhagen, Frankfurt, London, Madrid, Milan, Paris and Zurich. You will find rental options that sleep two to six people. Choose from six or seven size and amenity categories. Rates include unlimited mileage, all taxes and insurance. Often rates are based on calendar days, rather than 24-hour cycles. Bedding and kitchen equipment, cleaning fees and propane charges are usually covered by a one time fee of about $70 per person.

Rates for off season and peak season travel will vary. When your planning your budget, be sure to allow for high fuel consumption. Renting a motorhome to drive through France, for example, may not be a good bet because fuel charges are about $5.25 a gallon. Renting in Spain (where gas is about $3.50 a gallon) will save considerable amounts of money unless your daily rental cost is significantly higher. Rentals are not available in all categories in all countries.

The following chart looks at Global's daily rates for a Minimum (sleeping two), an Economy (sleeping four), a Compact (sleeping five) and a Premium (sleeping six). Off-peak rates are listed first, followed by peak rates. Off-peak travel includes all periods except June 9 to September 3.

SAMPLE RV RENTAL RATES IN EUROPE

RENTAL CITY	MINIMUM	ECONOMY	COMPACT	PREMIUM
Amsterdam	$139/$149	N/A	$159/$199	N/A
Copenhagen	N/A	$169/$239	$169/$239	$199/$319
Frankfurt	N/A	$139/$169	$149/$179	$189/$209
London	$149/$179	$159/$209	$179/$219	$189/$239
Madrid	$119/$149	$179/$239	N/A	$259/$349
Milan	N/A	$139/$169	$149/$179	$189/$219
Paris	N/A	$159/$219	N/A	$199/$259
Zurich	$129/$149	$149/$189	$159/$199	$199/$239

Campground and parking facilities are not quite as extensive as they are in the U.S. and hook-ups may be closer together, but options are increasing every year. KOA campgrounds has extended its network to include Germany, France and Switzerland, as well as Mexico. Call **406-248-7444**.

Location of Timbuktu: Mali, West Africa.

TRAVEL BY MOTORCOACH

GREYHOUND

Greyhound is the biggest name in U.S. motorcoach travel. Ticket prices are based on 21-day advance purchase and walk-up rates. Children under two travel free; children two through 11 pay half-price on walk-up fares. Seniors 55 and above get 15 percent off walk-up fares, making advance-purchase fares a better bargain, even without the availability of a senior discount. Here are examples of standard fares in effect as we went to press. Call **800-231-2222** for current fare quotes.

SAMPLE GREYHOUND ROUNDTRIP FARES				
RT ITINERARY	21-DAY ADVANCE	WALK-UP	AGES 2-11	55 & ABOVE
New York City-Dallas	$118	$159	$79.50	$135.10
Los Angeles-Chicago	$118	$169	$84.50	$143.65

***See America* fares** are generally offered in spring and summer (1997's ran from April 9 through July 29). You pay one price and receive a pass good for unlimited travel for the duration of the pass. Choose from seven-day ($179), 15-day ($289), 30-day ($399) or 60-day ($599). Standard discounts for children and seniors apply.

Other limited-time promotions (*Best Fares* includes them both in the magazine and on our internet site) tend to recur and have included:

- ***Friends Ride Free,*** allowing two people to travel for the price of one ticket on select fares.

Most popular activities for U.S. motorcoach tour travelers: shows, sightseeing and gambling.

> *"There are a couple of reliable discount bus options, mostly used by people who stay in hostels or backpack. They include East Coast Explorer (**800-610-2680**) connecting New York City, Boston and Washington, DC. It takes backroads and offers some door-to-door service. Go online at **www.pipeline.com/nyguide/ece/**. Green Tortoise (**415-956-7500**) does cross-country and West Coast trips between Seattle, Portland, San Francisco and Los Angeles, as well as within Mexico and Central America."*

- **$59 one-way tickets** to any of 2,400 destinations with a 21-day advance purchase; $79 with a 14-day advance.
- **Free travel giveaways.** A 1997 standout was Greyhound's *Wizard Of Oz* Promotion. Their Yellow Brick Road Bus Tour traveled the country, making stops in major cities. Everyone attending received a coupon for a free return trip with the purchase of a qualifying one-way ticket. Those who purchased a $19.95 *Wizard of Oz* video also received a coupon valid for a free Greyhound companion ticket.

Greyhound went international this past year by extending its network across the southern border of the U.S. with service between Los Angeles and several cities in Mexico. This extension of service, under an operating agreement with Crucero (the "Greyhound of Mexico") means that passengers will no longer need to change bus lines at the border. Buses feature on-board videos and bi-lingual drivers. Sample fares include $18/one-way or $30 roundtrip between Los Angeles and Tijuana.

MOTORCOACH TOURS

Motorcoach tour travel is a particular favorite of senior travelers and offer special event options to all travelers. Some tour companies regularly head for major league or college sports games and include hard-to-get event tickets in the package price. Motorcoach tours go to Branson and the Ozarks; on fall foliage tours in the North and Northeast; to the Mall of America in Minneapolis. Solo travelers may opt for travel by motorcoach because of the built-in companionship of fellow travelers.

National and regional companies package motorcoach tours. Be sure any package you book comes from a company that is a member of the United States Tour Operators Association (USTOA) or the National Tour Association (NTA)—organizations that provide some consumer protection. USTOA members operate under a $1 million bond; the NTA has $250,000 in coverage. The rule holds true whether you are purchasing one ticket or arranging a charter for a church or club group. Check cancellation and trip interruption policies carefully.

Determine if your tour will have a guide to provide information and assistance as you travel; an escort to provide a smaller range of services such as head-counts and baggage checks; a step-on guide (usually used on longer tours), who joins you at a specific location; or if it's just you and the driver.

Make sure you're being given the total cost without hidden charges. If you're booking a tour from a vacation destination, find out where you have to go to board the bus. Ask if tipping is expected

Top 5 states for motorcoach tours: Missouri, Tennessee, Florida, Virginia & Massachusetts.

(it often is). Get clarification on which meals and activities are included. If accommodations are included and the names are not familiar to you, check them out through an independent source.

The Department of Transportation (DOT) monitors the safety records of motorcoach lines and rates companies satisfactory, conditional or unsatisfactory. Your travel agent can access these ratings or you can call the DOT's Safety Hotline at **703-280-1749**.

INTERNATIONAL MOTORCOACH TRAVEL

Mexico offers an array of motorcoach options. Mexico City alone has four bus terminals—North, South, East and West. You'll probably be happiest sticking to *primera clase* (first class) travel. Seats are assigned. Sandwiches and beverages are offered for sale at many stops. For information, call the Mexico Tourism Bureau at **800-446-3942**.

Greyhound of Canada, operating separately from Greyhound U.S., diversified in 1996 and added a low cost airline, also named Greyhound. You can read about it in our Airline chapter. Greyhound of Canada (ground level) offers ten percent off most fares for seniors and half-price companion fares on most fares (use them for travel with children). The Canada Pass offers one price for unlimited travel during time periods ranging from seven to 60 days. Call **403-260-0877**.

Eurobus, in its second year of operation, connects 25 European cities and will pick you up and drop you off at your door or campsite, in most cases. You travel by pass, with purchase price based on zone travel. There are three zones. Travel through one zone for $225; through two zones for $500; through three zones for $525. Travelers under 26 pay $210, $350 and $470, respectively. You have to follow the prescribed route, but you can choose your travel dates (there is a small penalty for cancelled reservations) and take up to four months to complete your trip. Call STA Travel at **213-934-8722**, Council Travel at **210-208-3551** or University and Student Travel Service at **714-824-4237**.

- **Northern Zone**—Paris-Reims-Brussels-Amsterdam-Berlin-Prague-Vienna-Salzburg-Munich-Basel-Switzerland-Paris.
- **Central Zone**—Basel-Munich-Kirchdorf (Austria)-Venice-Rome-Florence-Nice-Lucerne-Zurich-Basel.
- **Southern Zone**—Paris-Basel-Geneva-Nice-Avignon-Carcassonne (France)-Barcelona-Madrid-Bordeaux-Paris.

EuropaBus also connects Europe by motorcoach. Some rail/bus options are offered. Call DER Tours, **800-937-1234**.

> *"Destination Europe, a division of Auto Europe, offers eight to 32 day escorted motorcoach tours ranging from $675 to $3,599 per person, double occupancy (air not included). Packages offered include exotic options such as the 16-day Turkish Delights and the 15-day Highlights of Eastern Europe, as well as more traditional tours. Motorcoach travel, accommodations, admissions to attractions, daily breakfast (and some dinners) and the services of an English-speaking tour manager are included. For a free brochure call* ***800-223-5555****."*

TWO-WHEEL TRAVEL

BICYCLES

The cheapest way to see the U.S. by bicycle is to load up your bikes and set out on a car trip that puts you in close proximity to a great biking itinerary. You save bike rental costs and, if you carry lightweight camping gear, your overall expenses can be cut to a minimum. If you are relatively new to travel by bicycle, plan short day trips but be sure to route them so you can get back to your hotel before you tire. If you are on a really tight budget, you can even stick close to home and see off-the-beaten-track parts of the region you live in, possibly for the first time.

Take your bicycles with you on international airline flights and chances are you won't have to pay extra to have them transported—unlike most U.S. airline polices. Be sure you have arranged for a rental or roof rack that will hold your bikes safely.

The internet offers a wide array of resources for information on cycling.

- **America By Bicycle** offers long distance tours and annual events that tend to attract many of the same people year after year. Their trips are graded by degree of difficulty so you know exactly what you are committing to. Options range from tours along the great rivers of the U.S. to a People's Republic of China Cycling Tour. Go online at **www.abbike.com**; call **603-382-1662**.

Number of people who toured by bicycle in 1996: over 7 million, a 30 percent increase in 2 years.

- **The GORP (Great Outdoor Recreation Pages)** internet site at **www.gorp.com/gorp/trips/actbike.htm** offers Alaskan Bicycle Adventures, New Mexico Mountain Bike Adventures, biking tours for seniors and international expeditions.
- **A stand-out internet site** with a wealth of information on two-wheel travel can be found at the rather lengthy address of compiler George Farnsworth, **www.nicom.com/%7Egeorgef/access**. He covers airline rules for shipping bikes, U.S. and international travel, rental information and more. A great feature is click-on box where you can enter your e-mail address and be notified when anything significant is added to the site.
- **Another good site** (with another long address) is the Travel-by-Cycle Organized Tours site with extensive options and information for cyclists. It even includes a Dutch language option. More accessible aspects include information on bicycle tours (described as environmentally friendly and economically responsible) in Africa, Asia, North America and Europe. This site doesn't sponsor tours; it organizes information on tours from a wide variety of sources, including companies and individuals. Go online at **http://ourworld.compuserve.com/homepages/Raph_de_Rooij.htm**.

Other good sources for special excursions for cyclists are listed below. Some encourage you to bring your own equipment; others include rentals in package rates or offer them as options.

- **Backroads** offers packages including a six-day California microbreweries tour. Camp along the way, or pay a higher rate for lodging at inns between Mendocino and San Francisco. Call **800-462-2848**.
- **Bicycle Adventures** offers packages including a six-day tour of Hilo and Kona with snorkeling thrown in for variety. Call **800-443-6060**.
- **Bike Riders Inc.** offers a variety of tours in the U.S. and Europe, covering a range of price categories. Call **800-473-7040**.
- **Butterfield & Robinson** offers mid-range to upscale international tours, Call **800-678-1147**.
- **Chateaux Bike Tours** is an upscale option with packages including a tour of France with dining at Michelin-rated restaurants. Call **800-678-2453**.
- **Gerhard's Bicycle Odysseys** is owned by the energetic Gerhard Meng who personally leads seven tours each year in Europe (he's been doing this since 1973). Call **503-223-2402**.
- **Michigan Bicycle Touring** offers packages including five-day trips through the Amish country of northern Indiana and southern Michigan. Call **616-263-5885**.
- **REI Adventures** offers packages including the Loire Valley tour, which made *Bicycling's* magazine's list of highly recommended tours. All rates include bike rentals. Call **800-622-2236**.

> *"The Bike Card Visa (no annual fee) provides merchant discounts and added-values for cyclists. Call* ***215-786-5147****; go online at* ***www.corestates.com****."*

MOTORCYCLES

Motorcycles are a favored mode of travel for Southwest CEO Herb Kelleher, Jay Leno and other people who wear suits and ties when they're not putting on leather and hopping on their Harleys. The range of people who enjoy motorcycle travel is vast. some prefer lightweight mopeds; some ride BMW's or Harleys. They all know that motorcycles can take you on roads cars can't travel and, what you may sacrifice in quiet, you gain in the amount of ground you can cover and the excitement of doing it by motorcycle.

Most motorcycle touring is geared both to people who own their own bikes and to people who rent them specifically for tours. Many motorcycle owners rent so they can join a tour at a distant departure point. A good starting point is Moto Directory at **www.mshopper.eurografix.com/links/touring.htm**. From there you can branch off to sites as varied as American Spirit Motorcycle Tours and Rentals in Santa Fe, Costa Rica Harley Tours, *Moto Evasion* of Quebec, Motorcycle Routes In The U.K., The Official Great Road List and a couple dozen motorcycle rental sites, many offering both independent travel and tours.

Motorcycle rentals generally include helmets, helmet locks, rain gear and motorcycle locks. You must have a valid motorcycle license. Some rental sources require a minimum of two-years motorcycle driving experience. Rentals are most plentiful in scenic vacation areas including Florida, Hawaii, and mountain states including Colorado, New Mexico and West Virginia. Rates vary by location and the type of bike you prefer. American Spirit in Santa Fe, for example, charges $160 for 24 hours with 200 free miles (25-cents a mile thereafter). A $1,000 open credit card deposit is needed. Reduced rates are available for rentals of four days or longer. Parkway Motorcycle Rentals in Ashville (NC) offers BMWs at rates starting at $120 a day/$600 a week.

> *"If you plan on driving your own motorcycle or borrowing one from a generous friend, be sure to have it checked out mechanically before you leave. If you think some highway repair shops prey on tourists in cars, multiply the problem for motorcycles. A limited number of people are qualified to repair them. Some take advantage of that fact and try to charge exorbitant rates to people who break down on the road."*

Adventure Cycle Tours at **www.winternet.com/~act** organizes tours in the Midwest and in Canada designed for people who want a great deal of back-up on their tour. A chase vehicle follows the tour, carries extra luggage and can help with any mechanical problems along the way. Hotel accommodations are prearranged and two meals a day and a tour guide are included. A seven-day tour costs about $1,425 per person ($2,220 per couple using the same motorcycle) if you provide your own bike. Add a rental for about $500 for a BMW or Goldwing; $995 for a Harley. Call **612-449-4908**; fax **612-449-4908**; write to 15820 16th Place, Plymouth, MN 55447.

Beach's Motorcycle Adventures has been conducting Alpine motorcycle tours for 26 years. They also offer European tours and tours of New Zealand. Call **716-773-4960**; fax **716-773-5227**; e-mail to **bma@buffnet.net**; write to 2763 West River Parkway, Grand Island, NY 14072.

Best motorcycle route from Santa Cruz to Saratoga, CA: Route 9.

Walking & Hiking

Start out with a city walking tour to get a little experience before committing to a major hike. Many cities offer interesting itineraries. The Victorian Home Walk in San Francisco, for example, leaves the Westin St. Francis Hotel at 11 a.m. every morning for a 2.5 hour walking tour, punctuated with a trolley ride. The cost is $20. Call **415-252-9485**; e-mail to **jay@victorianwalk.com**.

Increase your hiking proficiency by enjoying a stay at a scenic resort with extensive hiking possibilities. Here's a perfect example. Wit's End Guest Ranch and Resort in the Colorado Rockies is surrounded by the San Juan National Forest. Organized mountain hikes and overnight pack trips are offered, along with other resort activities. Call **800-236-9483**; e-mail to **weranch@aol.com**. National Parks provide excellent opportunities for low-cost hiking tours.

When you're ready to make the commitment to serious walking and hiking, a whole new universe opens up. You may wonder why you should pay anyone for a hiking tour, but check these samples and we think you'll understand why organized hikes can be good investments.

- **High Sierra Goat Packing**—Guided tours are $120 per day and include meals and beverages. The goats carry the heavy items. Call **209-536-9576**; e-mail to **goatpack@mlode.com**.
- **Alta-Can Tours**—15-day Canadian Rocky itineraries including accommodations, meals, guides and horses and equipment for packhorse hiking run about $1,400. Call **403-452-5187**; fax **403-452-5180**; e-mail to **jlouw@planet.eon.net**.
- **Europeds**—A wide variety of walking tours graded by skill level. Get full itineraries by calling **800-321-9552**; e-mail to **europeds@aol.com**.
- **European Walking Tours**—If you're still a little leery of getting around on your own foot power, their description of "gentle walks" will put your mind at ease. Go online at **www.walkingtours.com** to request a free brochure or call **217-398-0058**.
- **Hiking In China**—Two-week itineraries designed for people who can easily cover about ten kilometers a day. The Great Wall Trip starts in Beijing and goes to the China Sea. Overnight stays are in comfortable hotels. Call **416-605-7479**; e-mail to **info@china-hiking.com**.

> *"You'll probably be amazed at the wealth of travel information you can get from bike and hiking companies and internet sites. Most people who organize bike tours are enthusiasts who decided to try to make a living out of what they love doing. Many sites contain tips and experiences from cyclists and hikers. What other travel source do you know of that will tell you where to get the best catfish sandwich in Illinois? (It's reportedly the Barefoot Inn in Hardin on the Great River Road)."*

Popular three-day hiking trek in Peru: The Inca Trail between Cuzco and Machu Picchu.

More Dollars and Cents!

Welcome to travel math, *Insider Travel Secrets* style. Travel costs add up quickly but we'll show you how to subtract significant amounts from your travel budget while multiplying your enjoyment. It can be like pennies from heaven.

We've covered five major areas of travel expense—air travel, lodging, car rentals, cruises and travel by rail and road—but we have only begun to save you money. *More Dollars & Cents* is packed with ideas, strategies and phone numbers that will help you save money at every turn—not just at the usual travel crossroads. We'll help you spend your dollars in ways that make the most sense and show you how much value you can receive by having access to this information.

Something For Nothing & More For Less provides thousands of dollars in discounts for the asking. It's so valuable that you could use one offer and save many times the cost of this book. Most of the offers are absolutely free. They are the kinds of deals we showcase each month in *Best Fares' Something For Nothing* column and on **www.bestfares.com**.

You'll learn how one phone call can get you hundreds of dollars in savings and how to pay less for dining, shopping, entertainment and all the activities that can make any travel budget fall apart. Some offers require a small investment but you receive an immediate return on your dollar and multiply your travel savings. Listings are grouped by U.S. destinations, international destinations and student benefits.

Dining & Entertainment Discounts details special programs that save you as much as 25 percent on restaurant bills at participating restaurants worldwide. Many include discounts on hotels, attractions and airlines. Other programs offer bonus frequent flyer miles when you dine at participating restaurants.

Save By How You Pay helps you decide when and how to use plastic, cash and other forms of payment. It tells you how to get the best international exchange rates, which credit and charge cards are best for travel-related purchases and steers you toward saving money on travel taxes.

Tips on Tips simplifies one of the most confusing travel expenses with a basic guide to gratuities that will see you through most tipping situations worldwide.

Travel Insurance helps explain one of the more misunderstood aspects of travel. Too many people have horror stories of lost vacations, sometimes costing thousands of dollars. Some of them even thought they were protected by purchasing optional insurance—but they were not. We'll tell you how to get some automatic coverage, your best and worst sources for optional insurance, how to evaluate coverage and the kinds of travel insurance you should never buy.

Calling From The Road unravels the tangled phone cord of calling options. For many travelers, the telephone is a lifeline. Getting the service and features you need for the least amount of money is important. We'll tell you how to hack your way through the long distance jungle, the advantages offered by some pre-paid phone cards and some creative ways to save.

I am sure you are getting the message that my concept of discount travel is to get the most value from every single dollar. Read on for simple strategies that can save you money every step of the way.

SOMETHING FOR NOTHING AND MORE FOR LESS

YOU REALLY CAN GET A FREE LUNCH

You can get a free lunch—or dinner or dozens of added values, two-for-one deals and discounts on dining, shopping, attractions and many other travel-related expenses. *Best Fares* researchers spend hundreds of hours each month keeping up with the latest offers for discounts, guides, coupon books and bonus deals. We do it because our subscribers tell us that these offers consistently save them money and provide information that makes their trips easier to plan and more enjoyable. Credit card companies, tourism bureaus and other organizations offer billions of dollars in discounts annually to lure you to a particular destination or business with the promise of saving you money once you arrive. We try to find them all.

Some programs are seasonal and some are updated annually and given new names. If an offer you request is not available, ask if an alternate promotion is in effect.

Most of these offers are free for the asking. If a price is noted, the offers provide a great return for a nominal investment. Most can be ordered by phone. Please allow time for items requested to make it through the postal system. Two to three weeks is standard; popular offers may take even longer. Some deals can be picked up in person when you arrive at your destination.

Many programs have expiration dates and restrictions that could effect your travel plans. Ask what time period each deal covers. When you receive the material, review the fine print on each offer you plan to use.

Restaurant with a robot maitre d': The Encounter at the LAX Airport Theme Building.

U.S. DEALS & DISCOUNTS

Alaska

Statewide—The *AlaskaPass* discounts travel on rail, ferry and bus lines throughout Alaska and into Canada. Early season travel (winter through May) receives an additional discount. Various options cover the travel period of your choice. Call **800-248-7598**.

Inside Passage—Southeast Alaska Tourism Council offers a free guide to Alaska's Inside Passage. It includes descriptions of Inside Passage communities, calendars of events and accommodation and attraction information. Call **800-423-0568**; go online at **www.alaskainfo.org**.

Arkansas

Statewide—Get discount offers in a tour guide that includes a 72-page calendar of events and a 46-page booklet on state parks. Call **800-628-8725**.

Statewide—Request a *Heart of Arkansas* tourism package and get special package rates plus free guide services. Call **800-844-4781** or **501-370-3209**.

Statewide—*Vacation Packaging Guide* details discount packages, including lodging, meals and attractions. Call **800-628-8725**.

California

Statewide—*The California Visitors Guide* includes a $3 Universal Studios discount coupon, valid for up to six people. Call **800-862-2543**.

Anaheim—Residents of California zip codes 90000-93599 can purchase up to eight Resident Salute Disneyland day passes at $26 each, valid for residents and their guests. The offer generally is available from late January through mid-May. Purchase at the Disneyland ticket office.

Anaheim—The Disneyland Flex Passport offers five days admission for the price of two. You also get admission to the park 90 minutes before the general public is admitted on one of your five days. Generally, this offer requires that you book accommodations at a Disneyland hotel and purchase the Flex Passport at the hotel when you check in. The cost—$47 for children three-11 and $63 for ages 12 and above. Call **800-524-8700** for a brochure on the Flex Passport and Disneyland Travel Packages.

Catalina Island—The *Catalina Island Discount Card* offers ten percent off cruises, gift shops, discovery tours, Pavilion Lodge and campgrounds and is valid year-round. Call **800-228-2546** or **800-538-4554**.

Los Angeles—*L.A. "Free-Ways" And Other Ways To Save* offers savings of up to $400 on area attractions including Universal Studios, Six Flags, Magic Mountain, Sea World, the Los Angeles Children's Museum, The Hollywood Wax Museum, the Guiness World of Records and Ripley's Believe It Or Not Museum. Hotel, shopping and car rental discounts are often included. Most attraction coupons are good for up to six people. Write to Coupon Book, Los Angeles Convention & Visitors Bureau, 633 W. Sixth St., Los Angeles, CA 90071.

Los Angeles—The University City Hilton and Towers offers an annual Total Entertainment Package. Pay $195 for one night's accommodations (a deluxe room suitable for a family of four) and two adult tickets to Universal Studios Hollywood. Call **800-445-8667**.

Palm Springs—Free R & R Club membership entitles you to reduced rates at

San Francisco restaurant with famous inmate placemats: the Alcatraz Bar & Grill.

select Palm Springs resorts and restaurants and other special offers, valid from April through December. Call **800-417-3529**; go online at **www.desert-resorts.com**.

San Diego—The Convention & Visitors Bureau offers a discount coupon book for Sea World and Universal Studios plus other attractions, including the zoo, the beachfront roller coaster and a microbrewery tour. A separate book, *Star Spangled Values*, includes over 100 discounts on hotels, dining and attractions. Call **800-892-8258** or **619-236-1212**.

San Francisco—The San Francisco *City Pass* includes a Bay Area cruise and tickets to the Exploratorium Science and Art Museum, the San Francisco Museum of Modern Art and other attractions. The cost is 29.95/adults; $19.95/seniors 65+; $17.95/children 12-17. Purchase at participating attractions or call **415-974-6900**.

San Francisco—Purchase same-day, half-price theater tickets at STBS, 251 Stockton in Union Square, Tuesday through Thursday from 11 a.m. to 6 p.m. and Friday and Saturday from 11 a.m. to 7 p.m.

Sonoma County—The *Sonoma Wine Country Passport* can be ordered online at **www.visitsonoma.com**; call **800-326-7666**. It offers discounts of up to 35 percent at several wineries and discounts of up to 50 percent on accommodations. You also receive a 46-page visitors guide.

Colorado

Statewide—The Colorado Dude and Guest Ranch Association's directory is a full-color guide including photos, special rates and full descriptions of each property. Call **970-887-3128**.

Statewide—The Colorado Agency for Campgrounds, Cabins & Lodges offers *The Colorado Directory*, listing over 325 economical lodging options plus information on outdoor activities. The cost is $6.50, including shipping and handling. Call **888-222-4641**.

Aspen—The $10 Aspen Classic Pass lets you ski for as little as $19 a day at any of Aspen's mountains during early and late ski season. You also get peak season discounts and discounts from area merchants. Call **800-787-2886**.

Denver—The Children's Museum of Denver is an interactive facility offering hands-on activities including working in a television broadcasting studio, an artificial snow hill for skiing and in-line skating lessons. Admission is $5 for children and adults; $3 for people 60 and above. Call **303-433-7444**.

Denver—Purchase same day, half-price theater tickets at The Ticket Bus at 16th and Curtis (downtown) from noon to 6 p.m. weekdays and Saturday from 11 a.m. to 3 p.m.

Denver—The *City Connection* pass provides unlimited rapid transit travel for one day plus discounts on shopping and major attractions. The cost is $10/adults; $7/seniors (65+) and children. Get it at RTD stations, local travel agencies, some car rental companies and Denver Visitor Centers.

Telluride—The $105 Telluride Card takes $13 off the regular $49 daily rate lift ticket rate during early and late season. Call **970-728-6900**.

Vail—Vail Resorts Peaks Loyalty Program offers points redeemable for lift tickets, lodging and meals at Beaver Creek, Breckenridge, Keystone and Vail. You can earn the points one season and use them next, if you prefer. Sign up at **www.snow.com**.

The top two tourist destinations in 1997: France (61.5 million) and the U.S. (44.7 million).

Connecticut

Statewide—The *Connecticut Vacation Kit* contains statewide information on family oriented attractions and hotel discount coupons. Call **800-282-6863**. Call the same number 24 hours a day for information and reservations on child-friendly lodging.

District of Columbia

Congressional Tours—Reserve a free space on Tuesday through Saturday VIP tours by contacting your home state's senator or representative. Call **202-224-3121** or mail your request to the House or Senate Office Building, Washington, DC 20510.

Kennedy Center—Half-price, day-of-performance Kennedy Center tickets are available at the Old Post Office Pavilion, Pennsylvania Avenue at 12th Street. Call **800-444-1324**.

Seniors—Travelers 60+ get restaurant, accommodation and shopping discounts in the *Gold Mine Directory*, free at many Washington hotels or the Visitor Information Center.

Smithsonian—*Star Wars: The Magic of Myth* is at the Smithsonian's National Air and Space Museum through October 1998. Admission is free, but tickets are required. Pick them up at the museum beginning at 9:45 a.m. each day (maximum of four tickets per person). If you want to be sure to get a ticket for a particular day, you can opt to order in advance from ProTix (**800-529-2440**) but there is a $2.25 fee per ticket and a $1 handling fee per order (maximum of ten tickets per order).

Theater Tickets—Purchase same-day, half-price theater tickets at the Ticket Place, Listener Auditorium Main Lobby/George Washington University, Tuesday through Friday from noon to 4 p.m. and Saturday from 11 a.m. to 5 p.m.

Tourism Information—America Online subscribers can have specific tourism questions answered on the oddly named Tacky Tourist site (they say it's a friendly description) using keywords **Visit DC**. Get immediate response from 7-10 p.m. EST; response within 12 hours during other time periods.

Florida

Statewide—The $20 Family Entrance Permit allows unlimited 15-day access to most state parks, covering up to eight people in one vehicle. The $25 Family Recreational Permit allows unlimited access for up to four people and includes special privileges such as after-hours fishing and boat ramp use. Call **904-488-9872** or purchase at any state park.

Statewide—The *Florida Traveler Discount Guide* contains maps and discount coupons and is issued quarterly. Pick up a free copy at entry stations and tourism bureaus statewide. Order an advance copy of the newest edition for a $3 postage and handling fee. Call **352-371-3948**. Write to Exit Info Guide, Department US 797, 4205 NW 6th Street, Gainesville, FL 32609.

Statewide—*Econoguide '98: Walt Disney World, Universal Studios, Epcot and other Major Florida Attractions* includes over $2,500 in coupons valid for hotel and attraction discounts of up to 50 percent. The cost is $13.95. It's available at major book stores, including Barnes & Noble.

Statewide—The *Official Florida Vacation Guide* includes accommodation information, tourist information by region, internet resources and maps. Call **888-735-2872**; write to Visit Florida, P.O.

Top states in tourism spending for fiscal 1996-1997: Illinois ($32.8 million) and Hawaii ($25.3 million).

Box 1100, Tallahassee, FL 32302-1100; go online at **www.flausa.com**. Pick up a copy at any of five Official Florida Welcome Centers. Be sure to also request a copy of the latest discount coupon booklet, such as the *Spring Value Guide*.

Cocoa Beach—The Chamber of Commerce offers a discount coupon book that is revised four times a year. Call **407-452-4390** or **407-459-2200.**

Destin/Fort Walton Beach—The Destin/Fort Walton Beach Savings Card includes free long distance minutes and up to 20 percent off at restaurants, attractions and specialty shops. Call **800-322-3319**.

Florida Keys—Get a total of over $2,500 in discount coupons for dive trips, excursions, attractions, dining, hotels and shops in two discount coupon books. The Key Largo edition has over $1,500 in discounts; the Islamorada edition, $1,000. For Key Largo call **800-822-1088**; for Islamorada, **800-322-5397**. They're both updated in January and available year round.

Kissimmee/St. Cloud—*The Kissimmee/St. Cloud Vacation Guide* provides 80 pages of information, event listings and discounts. Call **800-327-9159**. The Great Fall-Winter Getaway promotion offers seasonal discounts including up to 50 percent off at nearly 100 hotels and attractions. Call **800-362-5477**.

Lake Country—The Lake Country Plus Vacation Card offers Orlando-area discounts at campgrounds, golf courses and local attractions. The card is valid year-round and also entitles you to special amenities at participating hotels and inns. Call **800-798-1071**.

Miami—*The Miami Visitors Guide* includes discounts on area attractions and restaurants and extensive tourist information. Call **800-933-8448**.

Orlando—The Orlando Magicard provides savings on accommodations, attractions, dining, transportation and shopping—some valid for up to six people. Discounts include $200 off at Mercado shops, 15 percent off at Medieval Times, $26.95-36.95 rates at Best Western Kissimmee (including a free Water Mania ticket), up to ten percent off car rentals and much more. Call **800-646-2092**.

Orlando—Purchase discount tickets for all major attractions at the Orlando Convention & Visitors Bureau, open every day except December 25. Attractions include Walt Disney World, Busch Gardens, Cypress Gardens, Pleasure Island and Water Mania. Call **407-363-5872**.

Orlando—*Disneygram*, an unofficial newsletter of Walt Disney World, keeps up with the latest attractions, reviews rides, offers tips and throws in discount dining coupons. A subscription is $9.95 per year, but you can get a free sample issue by writing to 241 Winn St., Burlington, MA 01803.

Orlando—Get a free sample issue of a magazine offering Walt Disney World information by sending a stamped, self-addressed envelope to *Mousetales*, Box 383, Columbus, OH 43216.

Orlando—The Vacation Value Pass provides unlimited visits for seven days to Universal Studios, Sea World, Wet 'n Wild and Busch Gardens. Children three-11 pay $96.95; ages ten and above pay $119.95. Get the pass at any of the four participating parks.

Orlando—Florida residents get special Walt Disney World discounts from mid-January to mid-February. An all-day, one-park ticket ($30) provides admission to the Magic Kingdom, Epcot or Disney-MGM Studios. Proof of residency is required for adults, but if you are visiting Florida relatives, their ID should allow them to purchase discount tickets, even for visiting children. Call **407-939-6397**.

Orlando/Tampa—Cypress Gardens offers free admission to children through age 17. Attractions include Island in the Sky, *Hot Nouveau Ice*; The Florida Historical Outdoor Railway Garden; Wings of Wonderful Butterflies Conservatory, with over 1,000 butterflies flying free in a tropical rain forest setting; bird and reptile shows and a bird aviary starring lories and lorikeets who eat from your hand; exotic animal habitats and their famous water skiing shows. The park is mid-way between Tampa and Orlando. Adult admission is $29.95; seniors (55+) pay $24.95. Each paying adult is entitled to free admission for one child. If your group includes more children than adults, you pay $19.95 for each child (six-17) who doesn't fall under the free admission offer. Children under six are admitted free. Call **800-282-2123**; go online at **www.cypressgardens.com**.

Orlando Area—The Kennedy Space Center offers free admission and two new features: the International Space Station Center and the Launch Complex 39 Observation Gantry. The Kennedy Space Center is 45 minutes east of Orlando and is open to visitors daily, except December 25 and certain launch days. Hours are 9 a.m. to dusk. Admission and parking are free. You can opt to add a bus tour and IMAX film at a cost of $19 per adult; $15 per child (three-11). Call **407-452-2121**; go online at **www.kennedyspacecenter.com**.

Sarasota—*The Sarasota Vacation Guide Book* and Sand Dollar Savings Card bring you special values and discounts at over 140 area restaurants and retail shops. The card is good for the neighboring Gulf Coast areas of Longboat Key, Lido Key, Siesta Key, Casey Key, Venice, Manasota Key, Englewood and North Port. Savings are valid during off-season periods. Call **800-522-9799**.

Tampa—*Tampa, What A Great Idea* includes $250 in discount coupons. Call **800-448-2672**.

West Palm Beach—*$500 Worth of the Palm Beaches Free* offers discounts on scuba diving, tennis and golf, museums, art galleries, theater tickets, sail-planes, shopping and more. Also included are coupons for complimentary cocktails, two-for-one dinners and vacation packages. The coupons cover an area from Jupiter to Boca Raton. New coupon books come out every April. Call **800-554-7256**.

Georgia

Atlanta—The Atlanta/DeKalb Guest Card comes with coupons valid for up to $500 in discounts at hotels, attractions and restaurants in the greater Atlanta area. Call **800-999-6055**.

Atlanta—The *Atlanta Dream Pass* and the *Atlanta Culture Card* offer discounted weekend packages, discounted Marriott rates, $5-10 off tickets at Six Flags Over Georgia, free admission for parents at American Adventures, up to $18 off at White Water, and discounts at over 80 cultural attractions. Call **800-285-2682** or **404-521-6601**. Write to 233 Peachtree St. NE, Atlanta, GA 30303; go online at **www.acvb.com**; e-mail to **acvb@atlanta.com**.

Jekyll Island—A 90-minute $3 guided walking tour explores the nature of this unique area through the experience of an expert guide. Call **800-841-6586**.

Hawaii

Statewide—*Driving & Discovering*

Most visited warm weather internet sites: Queensland, Orlando, Phoenix, Hawaii and Cancun.

Oahu, named the Best Hawaii Guidebook in a competition sponsored by the Hawaii Visitors Bureau and American Airlines, retails for $16.95 and is currently sold out. Ask for it at any participating Budget Rent A Car location on Oahu, however, and you'll find it in stock at a bargain $5.99 price. Also available: *Driving and Discovering Maui and Molokai*, which Budget also offers at a discount. Go online at **www.discoveringhawaii.com**.

Kauai—The Kauai Discovery Club helps you learn about the culture and people of Kauai. The free membership comes with a quarterly newsletter for upcoming cultural events, a certificate of membership, a poster of the island and an annual gift. Call **800-262-1400 ext. 896**. Visit **www.hshawaii.com/kvp** for extensive online information on the island.

Maui—Get meal and attraction bargains usually only offered to locals by checking the ads in free copies of *Maui Gold* or *This Week In Maui*, available at any BC Convenience Stores.

Oahu—Physically challenged guests of the New Otani Kaimana Beach Hotel/Honolulu can arrange for free use of an all-terrain wheelchair that can roll across sand and be safely taken into shallow water. Call **800-356-8264**.

Oahu—Hilo Hattie retail stores provide free shuttles to the Dole pineapple cannery with pick-ups at 12 Waikiki locations. The shuttle leaves every half-hour between 8:30 a.m. and 3:45 p.m. and provides a narrated tour of the island. Also available: two-for-one coupons (with purchase) for area restaurants.

Illinois

Chicago—The annual WinterBreak Festival (held in early February) offers hotel specials, airline discounts and The WinterBreak Value Passport (available at three city visitor information booths) with savings on museum admissions and other attractions. Free trolleys offer transportation to many activities. It often ties in with a Winter Blues Festival. Call **312-567-8500**.

Chicago—Purchase same-day, half-price theater tickets at HOT TIX, 24 South Street on the Loop, 1616 Sherman Avenue in Evanston or the Park Square Atrium in Oak Park. Hours are Tuesday through Saturday from 10 a.m. to 3 p.m. The Loop location is open until 6 p.m.

Indiana

Statewide—Get a selection of winter coupons in *Cold Cash*, containing hundreds of discounts on lodging, attractions and restaurants. Get a 92-page *Play Money* book with hundreds of discount coupons covering summer season lodging, attractions and restaurants. Call **800-289-6646**.

Iowa

Statewide—*The Iowa Travel Guide*, published each December, includes about 80 money-saving coupons for lodging, casinos, and restaurants. Call **800-345-4692**.

Kansas

Wichita—Fans of fans have their own museum. The Museum of American Fan Collectors has over 350 models on display in the lobby of Vornado Air Circulation Systems (415 E. 13th Street). The exhibit can be viewed weekdays from 8:00 a.m. to 5 p.m. Call **316-733-0035**.

Kentucky

Statewide—Get a 24-page brochure full of coupons for lodging and attraction discounts. Call **800-225-8747**.

Louisville—The Kentucky Derby

Most visited cold weather internet sites: Aspen, Austria, Sun Valley, Lake Tahoe and Calgary.

Museum includes films, interactive displays and *Time Machine* footage going back to the 1920s (a must for any big Run for the Roses fan). Admission is $6/adults; $5/seniors (55+) and $2/children. Call **800-273-3729**.

Louisiana

Statewide—*The Louisiana Tour Guide* covers the entire state with tourist information and discount coupons. Call **800-753-2860**.

Statewide—*Louisiana Music Trails* offers 38-pages of information on jazz clubs, music festivals, music museums and historic sights and other points of interest for fans of all forms of music indigenous to Louisiana. Request it from the Louisiana Office of Tourism, **800-685-0654**.

New Orleans—*The New Orleans Good Times Guide* provides over $2,000 in shopping and entertainment discounts. Call **800-632-3116**.

Massachusetts

The Berkshires—American Express Ski, Stay and Save packages include lodging, breakfast, two days of skiing at your choice of six ski areas and vouchers valid for 15 percent off at participating restaurants, attractions and shops. Call **800-237-5747**.

Boston—*Travel Planner* and *Family Value Pass* include attraction, hotel and dining discounts in Boston. Call **888-738-2678**; write to BGCVB, 2 Copley Plaza, Suite 105, Boston, MA 02116. Pick up a copy at the Convention & Visitors Bureau.

Boston—Purchase same-day, half-price theater tickets at BOSTIX at the Faneuil Hall Market, Congress and State Streets Tuesday through Sunday from 11 a.m. to 5 p.m.

Michigan

Statewide—*Michigan Free* details free activities and tours, concerts, plays, museums, national parks and forests, wineries, festivals and more. The book costs $16.95 plus $3.50 for shipping and is available from University of Michigan Press, 839 Green Street, Ann Arbor, MI 48106. Call **313-764-4388**.

Statewide—The White Gold Card at $149 provides $500 in savings for Michigan skiers. Get one day's free skiing at each of 21 resorts and a free ski tune-up. The card runs through each ski season with blackout dates of January 1-5. Call **810-625-0070**.

Bridgeman—The American Electric Power Plant offers printed material on free tours of their lakefront power plant. Tours feature the *Energy Update 2001* show, energy experiments and a sculpture garden overlooking Lake Michigan, composed of parts from energy generation systems. Call **800-548-2555**.

Detroit—*The Detroit Hometown Tourist Book* is offered by the Metropolitan Detroit Convention & Visitors Bureau. It offers discounts at over 100 stores, restaurants, hotels and popular attractions and is updated annually. Call **800-338-7648**.

Mississippi

Bay St. Louis—Take a 90-minute pontoon boat tour departing from Bay St. Louis and winding through the bayous and swamps of Mississippi. Adults pay $15, seniors pay $14 and children under 12 pay $7. Call **601-466-4824**.

Tupelo—The Convention & Visitors Bureau offers *Preferred Guest Coupons* with discounts on dining, shopping, entertainment and attractions. Call **800-533-0611**.

Missouri

Statewide—*Missouri Fun Money* contains lodging discounts, attraction coupons and 16-pages of discounts on Branson hotels and shows. Call **800-877-1234**.

Branson—$250 worth of savings are available in a 272-page guidebook also containing trip planning tips, maps, and detailed information on restaurants, accommodations, theaters and shows. The discounts cover hotels, restaurants, shops and attractions. *The Branson Guidebook* costs $16 plus shipping and handling. Call Fodor's Travel Publications, **800-533-6478**.

Kansas City—The Kansas City Jazz Museum offers a great look at a famed jazz scene. Admission is $6/adults and $2.50/children 12 and under. It's open Tuesday through Thursday from 9 a.m. to 6 p.m.; Friday and Saturday from 9 a.m. to 9 p.m.; and Sunday from noon to 6 p.m. Call **816-474-8463**.

Nebraska

Omaha—The *Omaha* visitors guide includes a pack of coupons discounting travel services and local purchases. Also available, the Aha! discount card, issued at the end of each January. Call **800-332-1819**.

Nevada

Statewide—The *Discover Nevada* bonus book covers far more than Las Vegas. This 58-page publication has 132 discount coupons (including a coupon you can redeem for a "bag full of coupons" at the Carson Valley Chamber of Commerce) and information on many state attractions. The coupons have a total value of up to $1,500 and include free roller coaster rides, discounts on gaming, rooms, meals, tours, rental cars and much more. Call **800-638-2328**.

Las Vegas—Las Vegas is full of Fun Book offers and all of them are packed with two-for-one and other discount deals. At least four hotels offer Fun Books for the asking: Aladdin, Riviera, Sahara and Vacation Village. You don't even need to show an out-of-state I.D., a requirement for some Fun Book offers.

Las Vegas—Palace Station will give you a value book with food, entertainment and gaming specials. Go to the property promotion center and present a room key from another Las Vegas hotel and your out-of-state driver's license.

Las Vegas—Sam's Town on Flamingo Road offers Sunset Stampede, a free laser and water show at 2, 6, 8 and 10 p.m. daily at their Mystic Falls Park.

Las Vegas—*Experience Las Vegas* is a 584-page sourcebook by Bruce Brown, selling for $12.95 (plus $3 shipping). Call **800-881-7456** or write to P.O. Box 35050, Las Vegas, NV 89133.

Las Vegas—*The Las Vegas Advisor,* a monthly newsletter, covers deals at hotels, casinos, restaurants and attractions. Annual U.S. subscriptions are $50 and include a coupon package valued at over $700. A sample issue (without the bonuses) is $5. Write to 3687 South Procyon Avenue, Las Vegas, NV 89103 or call **800-244-2224**.

Las Vegas—*Comp City: A Guide To Free Las Vegas Vacations* ($33.95) shows you how to get complimentary stays at Las Vegas hotels that can also include free drinks, meals, shows, and airfares. It also tells you how to meet each casino's qualifications. *The Las Vegas Advisor Guide To Slot Clubs* ($6) details freebies and discounts for slot play activity. Shipping charges per book are $3/book rate postage or $6/UPS. Call **800-244-2224**.

Cities that send the most gamblers to Las Vegas: New York, Philadelphia, Los Angeles & Memphis.

Las Vegas—*Bargain City: Booking And Beating The New Las Vegas* ($11.95) is a comprehensive guide to deals and freebies—from where to find $2 steak dinners to how to get free hotel rooms. Call **800-244-2224**.

Las Vegas—*The Cheapskate's Guide to Las Vegas* includes tips on locating freebies and discounts. It's $9.95 at bookstores; order by phone at **201-866-0490**.

Las Vegas—The *Las Vegas Visitors Guide* includes 128 pages of information about hotels, casinos, shopping, transportation, events, cultural events and even wedding chapels. It also contains a basic guide to casino games and information on Boulder City, Henderson, Jean, Laughlin, Mesquite and North Las Vegas. Call **702-892-7576**; write to Las Vegas Visitors Information Center, 3150 Paradise Road, Las Vegas, NV 89109.

New Jersey

Statewide—*The New Jersey Travel Guide* is published by the Division of Travel and Tourism at the beginning of every year. It divides the state into six regions and includes a listing of special events, transportation information, tourist information centers, and a New Jersey highway map. Over 120 coupons offer up to $2,500 in savings at various hotels, bed and breakfasts, restaurants, shops and attractions. Call **800-537-7397**; order online at **www.state.nj.us** .

New Mexico

Statewide—*The New Mexico Vacation Guide* is a 200-page book spanning the state's attractions and offering discounts on lodging, skiing, galleries and attractions. Call **800-545-2040**.

Statewide—Travelers with physical disabilities can enjoy travel even more with a free 87-page *Access New Mexico* guide, published by the Governor's Committee on Concerns of the Handicapped. Request by mail: Governor's Committee on Concerns of the Handicapped, Lamy Building, Room 117, Old Santa Fe Trail, Santa Fe, NM 87503; by voice Mail at **505-827-6465**; by TDD/TTY at **505-827-6329**; by e-mail at **103203.400@compuserve.com**.

New York

The Catskills—Get a free vacation planning video from Golden Acres Family Farm & Dude Ranch in Gilboa. Call **800-252-7787** or write to Golden Acres Farm & Ranch, Gilboa, NY 12076.

New York City—Request free tickets to Manhattan television tapings by calling with as much advance time as possible. Be sure to check minimum age limits. Most tapings do not allow small children. *Late Night With Conan O'Brien, Saturday Night Live* and most other NBC shows/**212-664-4444**; *The Late Show With David Letterman*/**212-975-1003**; *Rosie O'Donnell*/**212-664-3056**; *Ricki Lake*/**212-889-8167**; *Live With Regis & Kathie Lee*/**212-456-7777**; and *Sally Jessy Raphael*/**212-582-1722**.

New York City—Spend a free day at the Sony Wonder Technological Lab enjoying new techno-wonders including sound wave manipulation, robotics, the newest video games and digital recording. You even get a diploma with your photograph on it. The lab is located at 550 Madison Ave. Call **212-833-8100**.

New York City—Travel on a free downtown bus that follows a lower Manhattan loop. Buses run every five to ten minutes and give you access to stops including the Hoboken Ferry, Ellis Island Ferry and the World Financial Center. Call **800-533-3779**.

New York City—*Larry's Opinionated*

Areas that lost the most convention business since 1993: San Francisco, Washington and Dallas/Fort Worth.

Guide to New York City ($3.95) includes information on low cost lodging, dining, sightseeing and airport transportation; reduced-rate tickets for Broadway; and museums that offer free admission on specific days or during specific hours. The author is the owner of East Coast Explorer, a bus service that provides low cost transportation between New York City, Boston and Washington, DC. Write to Larry Lustig, 210 Congress St., Brooklyn, NY 11201.

New York City—Heritage Trails Maps are available at visitor centers and hotels throughout Manhattan. Four walking tours synchronized with brightly colored dots on tour streets and sidewalks help you discover famous landmarks and lesser-known points of interest.

New York City—The *FUNPASS MetroCard* provides over $2,500 in discounts on dining, shopping, entertainment and sightseeing, plus special hotel package deals. Pick up your card at Visitors Bureau locations, including Two Columbus Circle, Grand Central and Penn Stations, 229 W. 42nd Street (Times Square), Two World Trade Center or 59th and Broadway. Order it by phone as part of the Big Apple Visitors Kit at a cost of $4.95. Call **800-692-8474**.

New York City—The Free Fax Service from the New York City Convention & Visitors Bureau offers a list of *42 Things To Do In New York For $10 Or Less*, Call **800-692-8474** and choose program #300. Go online at **www.nycvisit.com**.

New York City—Purchase same-day, half-price theater tickets at TKTS Times Square from 10 a.m. to noon and 3 to 5 p.m. and at World Trade Center Building Two, Tuesday through Friday from 11 a.m. to 5:30 p.m. and 11 a.m. to 3:30 p.m. Saturday.

New York City—Citywalks two-hour tours of Greenwich Village, downtown and the Lower East side year-round, except January and February. Prices start at $12 per person. Call **212-989-2456**.

New York City—The Municipal Art Society sponsors various architectural and historical walking and motorcoach tours that include Immigrant New York, Irish New York, Skyscraper Evolution, Central Park and more. Prices start at $8 per person. A few tours (including Grand Central Terminal) are free. Call **212-439-1049**.

New York City—Continental Airlines and *The New York Times* co-sponsor The Broadway Line, a toll-free information service providing show information, ticket prices and booking options. You can opt to be patched to Ticketmaster for ticket purchases. Call **888-411-2929**; call **212-302-4111** from within the New York City metro area.

New York City Area—Get updated information on country weekends, historic vacations, water vacations, family weekends, romantic weekends, city weekends and adventure trips. Call **800-456-8369**.

Ohio

Statewide—*The Ohio Getaway* packet includes up to $500 in savings. Call **800-282-5393**; go online at **www.ohiotourism.com**.

Pennsylvania

Statewide—*The Pennsylvania Visitors Guide* offers over $2,500 in discounts and 228-page guide that details year-round events and attractions. Call **800-847-4872**.

Statewide—The *Senior Discount Booklet* (ages 50+) offers savings on tours, restaurants, shopping and accommodations. Call **800-537-7676**; go online at **www.libertynet.org**.

Number of states offering Native American-run gambling in 1982: zero; in 1997, 24.

Pennsylvania Dutch Country—*The Visitors Guide To Pennsylvania Dutch Country* lists attractions, events and savings available in the Lancaster County area. The 36-page guide features savings on meals, lodging, shopping and admission to many area attractions. Call **800-723-8824**.

Pittsburgh—The Pittsburgh Passport provides admission to your choice of three attractions, plus two local transportation options. Attractions include the Andy Warhol Museum, the National Aviary, the Carnegie Museum, Phipps Conservatory, Pepsi Plaza Ethnic Festivals, the Pittsburgh Zoo, Photo Antiquities, the Carnegie Science Center and the Frick Art & Historical Center. The cost—$10 for individuals; $35 for four people. Call **800-359-0758** or **412-281-7711**.

The Poconos—*The Poconos Coupon Booklet* contains over $250 in discounts on hotels, restaurants, shops and attractions. They include 15 percent discounts at Adventure Sports Canoe & Raft Trips, ten percent off at Foxmoor Village Outlet Center, $4 off at the Mountain Creek Riding Stable and ten percent off at the Mountain Laurel Resort. Call **800-762-6667**.

Tennessee

Statewide—*This Is The Year To See Tennessee* comes with a separate guide to Nashville and a discount coupon for Best Western. Call **800-836-6200**.

Nashville—Get coupons worth up to $300 in *Nashville's Vacation Guide*. It includes discounts at Opryland Theme Park and Willie Nelson & Friends Museum & Gift Emporium. Call **615-259-4700**.

Texas

Statewide—The free 274-page *Texas State Travel Guide,* available at **800-452-9292**, includes a brochure on the Texas Passport—a $19.95 membership card that gives you discounts of ten to 50 percent at over 1,500 attractions, hotels, campgrounds, restaurants and car rental locations in over 200 Texas cities and towns. Major attractions include Six Flags Over Texas and Hurricane Harbor in Arlington, SeaWorld in San Antonio and The Palace of Wax/Ripley's Believe It Or Not in Grand Prairie. Passports are valid from January 1 through December 31 of each year. Call **800-687-6264** to order the Passport directly or get it at no cost with a one year subscription to *Texas Highways* magazine ($12.50) by calling **800-839-4997**.

Statewide—*Mountain Biking State Parks* provides details on 42 state parks with mountain bike trails. Call **800-792-1112**.

Statewide—The Texas Parks & Wildlife Discovery Passport provides benefits including collector patches and camping discounts. You get every sixth camping night free. The passport is valid through February 28, 2000. Purchase for $1 at any State Park; call **800-792-1112, ext. 3**; go online at **www.tpwd.state.tx.us**.

Amarillo—The Amarillo Convention & Visitors Council includes a packet of hotel and attraction discount coupons with their visitor's brochure. Call **800-692-1338**.

Dallas/Fort Worth—*The Big Bucks Coupon Book* contains up to $1,500 in discounts and information on attractions, shopping, and other entertainment options in Dallas, Fort Worth, Irving, Arlington, Addison and Grand Prairie. Call **800-452-9292** or pick up a copy at tourist information centers.

Houston—*The Greater Houston Passport Book* is offered annually by the Greater Houston Convention & Visitors Bureau and features discounts at hotels,

Location of the world's largest K-Mart: Guam (duty free).

restaurants, shops and attractions including AstroWorld. Call **800-446-8786**.

New Braunfels—This small German-settled town in central Texas, offers an accommodations guide with discount coupons. Call **800-572-2626**.

San Antonio—The *San Antonio Vacation Experience* booklet includes discount coupons. A new version is issued in March and coupons are valid year-round. It often contains a discount coupon for Southwest Airlines travel to San Antonio. This year's version requires payment by American Express. Call **800-447-3372**.

San Antonio—*San Antonio, Something To Remember* is a free vacation kit that includes discount coupons. Call **800-843-2526**.

Vermont

Statewide—The 160-page *Vermont Traveler's Guidebook* contains a coupon valid for two free Ben & Jerry's ice cream cones when you stay in Waterbury. Call **800-837-6668**.

Stratton Mountain—The $79 Stratton Express Card provides 25-50 percent off lift tickets, VIP lift access and discounts from area merchants. Call **800-787-2886**.

Virginia

Virginia Beach—*The Virginia Beach Guide* offers $200 in discount coupons for restaurants, attractions, jet-ski, sailing and bike rentals, dive trips and more. The coupons cover a 12-month period, from May to May of each year. Call **800-446-8038**.

Williamsburg—The Williamsburg Convention & Visitors Bureau offers seasonal brochures with coupons valid for discounts at hotels, shops and restaurants. The *Holiday Brochure* covers December and early January, the *Early Bird Brochure* covers January through March, and the *Fall Brochure* covers September through November. Call **800-368-6511**.

Washington

Seattle—Seattle Super Savers discounts winter rates at over 20 downtown hotels and provides discount coupons for dining, shopping and sightseeing. Call **800-535-7071**.

Seattle—The Seattle *CityPass* reduces your admission to six popular attractions by 50 percent. It's valid for seven days from the first date of use and includes the Museum of Flight, Pacific Science Center, Seattle Aquarium, Seattle Art Museum, the Space Needle and the Woodland Park Zoo. Adults pay $23.75; seniors 65+/$19.25; children six to 13/$15. It's available at Seattle hotels including Howard Johnson, Ramada and the downtown Westin.

Wyoming

Jackson Hole—The $50 Express Pass/Trailblazer Card for $50 entitles you to 128 days of skiing at discount rates (averaging $9 off per day). Call **800-443-6931**.

Nationwide

Bed & Breakfasts—*Bed & Breakfasts and Country Inns* ($21.95) contains a buy-one-night-get-one-free coupon valid at any of the inns and B&Bs listed in the book. The coupon is a $50 to $350 value. The book contains detailed descriptions of over 1,600 lodging options, over 500 illustrations, state maps and a section that spotlights particularly unique inns and B&Bs. It covers the 50 states, Canada and U.S. territories. *Best Fares* subscribers receive a $5 discount. Send $21.95 or $16.95 plus $2.25 shipping and handling to American Historic Inns, P.O. Box 669, Dana Point, CA 92629; call **714-499-8070**.

Main culinary influences in Australia's new cuisine: Greek, Italian and Asian.

Camping—The U.S. Bureau of Land Management offers a detailed map listing public-use camping and recreation areas, historic and scenic trails. Call **202-452-5125**.

Family Travel—The National Parenting Center at **www.tnpc.com** offers information on resorts and cruise lines that have earned their Seal Of Approval for family vacations. Parenting Resource Center at **www.parentsplace.com** offers trip planning tips and submissions from parents offering feedback on major family vacations.

Free Bike Use—At least eight cities offer free bicycles for the use of locals and tourists. Look for distinctly marked bikes (or inquire at tourism offices) in Austin, Boulder, Charleston, Denver, Madison, Missoula, Orlando and Portland (OR).

Gambling—The 1998 edition of the *American Casino Guide* is $15.95 (*Best Fares* subscribers receive a $3 discount). It includes over $500 in discount coupons. The 244-page book covers casinos in 30 states. Call **800-741-1596**. Find it in bookstores under ISBN 1883768071.

National Parks—The *Golden Eagle Pass*, available to any U.S. citizen, offers one year's unlimited admission to U.S. National Parks. It can be purchased for $50 at any National Park that charges an entry fee by mail. Call **202-619-7289**. Seniors, age 62 and up, can buy a Golden Age Pass, valid for a lifetime, for $10. Call **202-208-4747**.

Skiing—The American Skiing Company offers The Edge, a reward point program that operates in a similar fashion to frequent flyer programs. Get 400 points for each midweek ski day, 150 points for Saturday, 250 points for Sunday and 200 points for any holiday. A total of 2,000 points earns a free day of skiing at participating resorts. Enrollment is free at participating New England resorts including Attitash Bear Peak, Killington, Mount Snow-Haystack, Pico, Sugarbush, Sugarloaf and Sunday River. Call **800-668-7669**.

Skiing—The *World Ski Card* from The World Ski Association costs $9.95-19.95 per year depending on which point during ski season you purchase it. You can get a discount by purchasing online at **www.worldski.com**. It discounts lessons, rentals, lift tickets, hotels and restaurants at over 1,000 ski areas in North America and Europe. Call **303-629-7669** or write to P.O. Box 480825, Denver, CO 80248.

Skiing—The $30 Ski Card Passport allows lift, dining and accommodation discounts at 250 U.S. and Canada ski areas. Call **800-333-2754**.

Skiing—Deaf skiers can check a regularly updated list of discount lift tickets and snowboarding with daily rates as low as $5. Visit **www.teleport.com/~eingham/usdsa/discount.htm**.

Skiing—Mountain Resorts Database at **www.mtnresorts.com** offers an impressive and comprehensive array of ski resort information and discounts. It covers North America and over 30 other countries worldwide, from Andorra to Turkey.

INTERNATIONAL DEALS & DISCOUNTS

Prices vary by exchange rate.

General Information

Languages—Web sites can teach you basic international travelers' phrases. Martin's Foreign Languages for Travelers at **www.travlang.com/** provides basic phrases in 32 languages. The Human Languages Page, **www.june29.com/HLP**

Annual amount France spends to attract tourists: $72.9 million.

has several offerings on less-common languages and dialects. Traveler's Japanese With Voice, **www.nt.co.jp/japan/japanese** lets you hear the phrases you're trying to master. The Berlitz site, **www.berlitz.com/**, offers mini-lessons.

Passports—Avoid the per-minute fee now charged for information on U.S. passports by downloading information from **http://travel.state.gov/passport_services.html**. The site allows you to print forms to apply for or modify a passport or report a lost or stolen passport.

Travel Guides—Rough Guides offer a good selection of travel tips and destinations through the Hot Wired internet site. Go to **www.hotwired.com/rough** to access information on Canada, Mexico, Europe, India, Australia, Hong Kong and the United States.

Travel Books—Get ten percent off over 6,000 travel books offered by Have Book, Will Travel. Give the company your destination or special interests and they will send you a list of applicable titles. Call **203-761-0604**.

Antarctica

Antarctica—Marine Expeditions offers a free 13-minute Antarctic cruise video. Call **800-263-9147**.

Australia

Countrywide—The Australian Tourist Commission offers an 80-page guide to ethnic and gourmet restaurants, bed and breakfasts, wineries and wine and food festivals. Request *Enjoy Good Living...Australia* by calling the Aussie Help Line, **847-296-4900**.

Countrywide—The 50-page *Backpacker Accommodation Ratings Guide* lists hostels in Australia for backpackers and other budget travelers. Get a free copy at any Australian hostel or tourist information office.

Countrywide—A new program simplifies travel to Australia. An Electronic Travel Authority (ETA) takes the place of the standard visa. When you book an airline ticket your travel agent enters your passport number and other information into the computer reservation system. In most cases, an ETA is issued automatically, eliminating the need to apply through the Australian Consulate. Your travel agent can give you a printout of the ETA. You can currently use the system for travel on Qantas and Air New Zealand. It is being tested by United Airlines. Call the Aussie Help Line, **847-296-4900**, for more information.

Countrywide—The ATS SprintAustralia Fax-On-Demand service offers a variety of information for travelers. Call **800-423-2880**, select voice mail option #5 and follow the easy directions to the prompt that calls for your selections. Options include: Australian Farmhost Holidays/ Countrywide (503), Daintree Eco Lodge/ Queensland (517), Skyrail Cableway/ Queensland (677), Rail Australia/ Countrywide (512), Queensland Rail/ Queensland (659), Kangaroo Island Fast Ferries/South Australia (548), Outback Ballooning/ Northern Territory (534) and Sidney Pass (522). Request tourism information by region: Canberra (608), Hunter Region/New South Wales (609), New South Wales (622), Northern Territory (641), Queensland (654), South Australia (680), Tasmania (684), Victoria (686), Victoria's Shipwreck Coast (689), Western Australia (692) and Yarra Valley & Dandenong Ranges/Victoria (585).

Sydney—The Sydney Transit Pass, available at local tourism offices, covers airport buses, some tour buses and all State Transit ferries and buses. It's valid from 9:30 a.m. to 9 p.m. daily and costs

Average cost of a mixed drink in Japan: $13.90; Germany, $8.24; South Africa, $3.03.

$30/three-days; $39/five-days; $65/seven-days.

Sydney—Purchase same-day, half-price theater tickets at Martin Place/City Center. Monday through Friday from noon to 5:30 p.m. and Saturday from noon to 5 p.m.

Austria

Salzburg—The Salzburg Card offers free admission to many attractions plus free public transportation. The 24-hour card is $18; 48-hour/$25; 72-hour/$34. Groups may purchase in bulk at a $4-7 discount per card. The Salzburg Plus Card gives you one debit card covering hotel, meals, city transportation, attractions and a cultural event. The card is available for stays of two or more nights and includes accommodations in your choice of a three-, four- or five-star hotel. Prices vary by options chosen. Call **212-229-1768**.

Vienna—*Young Vienna Scene* covers accommodations, dining, transportation, nightlife and cultural events from the point of view of the younger traveler. Write to the Austrian National Tourist Office, PO Box 1142, Times Square Station, New York, NY 10108-1142; call **310-478-8306**.

Vienna—The *Vienna Card* ($17) discounts transportation by bus, tram and underground train and provides discounts at specified restaurants, shops, museums, attractions and concert halls. The card is valid for four days. It's available at most hotels and tourist offices in Vienna.

Belgium

Brussels—The *Brussels Visitors Passport* entitles you to numerous discounts at popular attractions and is also good for free 24-hour city transportation. It's free, if ordered in advance; $6 if purchased in Brussels. Call **212-758-8130**.

Canada

Niagara Falls—*The Niagara Falls Ontario Vacation Guide* is updated and available each May. It contains information on the Falls, accommodations and dining and over $300 in coupons for area attractions, hotels and restaurants. Call **800-668-2746** or **800-563-2557**.

Toronto—Purchase same-day, half-price theater tickets at Five Star Tickets at the Royal Ontario Museum and outside Eaton Centre from Monday through Saturday, noon to 6 p.m. and Sunday, 11 a.m. to 2 p.m.

The Caribbean

Multiple Islands—*Caribbean Jewelry and Gemstones* ($3) is a 47-page guide that gives you the tools you need to evaluate carat, cut, color and clarity. Many visitors to the Caribbean purchase gemstones; few know how to tell a bargain from a rip-off. Learn what you need to know before you go. Write to Caribbean Jewelry and Gemstones, 1100 Sixth Avenue, Suite 30, Naples, FL 33940.

Multiple Islands—The *Caribbean Classic Card* ($10) offers discounts ranging from five to 50 percent at restaurants, supermarkets, car rental agencies, tour companies, nightclubs, duty-free shops and pharmacies. Over 1,000 merchants participate. The card covers Anguilla, Antigua, Aruba, the Bahamas, Barbados, Curacao, Grenada, Jamaica, Puerto Rico, St. Croix, St. John, St. Kitts, St. Lucia, St. Thomas, Tortola, Virgin Gorda, Trinidad, Tobago and Miami. It's issued annually each August. Call **246-427-5046**.

The Bahamas Tourist Office— The *People-to-People* program matches locals with visitors who want to see more than Bay Street and the Straw Market. Your

Location of the world's first ski-through McDonald's: Sweden's Lindvallen Resort.

local guide provides about a two-hour tour that shows you the aspects of Nassau he or she most appreciates. Most volunteers devote two or three afternoons a month to *People-to-People* activities. For information, call **800-422-4262**. Sign up for *People-to-People* at **242-322-7500**.

Cayman Islands—Request a free 45-page guide to the Cayman Islands by calling **800-346-3313**. *1998 Rates & Facts Guide to the Cayman Islands* includes information on lodging, car rentals, dive companies and more.

Curacao—*Discover Curacao Now* is a discount card that provides savings on attractions, dining and shops. Pick it up at participating hotels or call **800-270-3350**.

Margarita—*Viva Margarita Visa* is available by e-mail request to **dsagredo @visa.com**. It offers discounts through October 1, 1998.

Czech Republic

Prague Welcomes Visa offers discounts through August 31, 1998. It's available at the tourist information office in Prague.

Denmark

Copenhagen—The *Copenhagen Card* allows entry to over 50 museums and attractions (including Tivoli Gardens, normally a $9 ticket), public transportation and a guidebook. A 24-hour pass is $22; 48-hour/$36; 72-hour/$46. It's available at tourist offices, train stations and hotels.

Copenhagen—Get free use of a bicycle with a 20-Kroner ($4) deposit, refunded when you return the bike. About 120 bicycle racks are placed around the city.

Europe/Multiple Countries

Also see individual country listings.

Tax Free Shopping—Get a free copy of *Tax Free Shopping in Europe* (covering taxes and recovery methods) by writing to ETS, 233 S. Wacker Dr., Suite 9700, Chicago, IL 60606.

Travel Guide—Rick Steves, author of *Europe Through The Back Door,* offers a free copy of his 64-page newsletter and a free guide to rail travel in Europe. To request either or both call **425-771-8303**; order online at **www.ricksteves.com**; e-mail to **europe@ricksteves.com**.

Travel Guide—Get a free 68-page *European Planner* covering 26 countries. Call **800-816-7535**.

Finland

Helsinki—The *Helsinki Card* provides admission to over 50 museums and galleries and more. A 24-hour pass is $24; 48-hour/$31; 72-hour/$38. Purchase at tourist centers and train stations or order from the Scandinavian Tourist Board, **212-949-2333**.

France

Countrywide—The *Club France Card* has a high initial price but provides substantial discounts and is good for a year from the date of purchase. Benefits include free hotel upgrades, seasonal discounts at over 500 hotels and inns, car rental discounts, three-day admission to 65 museums in Paris and more. Members have access to a toll free information line (the regular 900 tourism line charges 95 cents a minute). The annual fee is $65; $35 additional for each family member. Call **800-678-5000**.

Countrywide—The *France Discovery Guide* is a combined offering of the French Government Tourist Office, Air France and American Express. The guide offers guaranteed hotel rates and packages. The AT&T *France Fun Book* features over 100 discount coupons.

Request either or both from Air France, **800-237-2747**.

Countrywide—The *Museums and Monuments Pass* offers free entrance to 65 monuments and museums. A one-day pass is $14; three-day/$28; five-day/$40. Purchase at any participating museum or call **900-990-0040** (a toll call billed at 50-cents per minute).

Countrywide—Purchase a three-day pass for any of ten cities in France, covering admission to multiple museums, monuments and attractions. You also get an audio tour tape. Available cities include Besancon, Dijon, Lille, Lyon, Metz, Nancy, Nimes, Orleans, St. Etienne and Toulon. Purchase at each city's tourism office at $10-19, depending on location. Call **212-529-8484**.

Germany

Berlin & Brandenburg—The *Welcome Card* ($22) offers free entry into many museums and tours plus discounts of up to 50 percent on other museums and tours. You also get unlimited access to public transportation for three days. The card is valid for one adult and up to three accompanying children, ages 13 and under. Cards may be purchased at many area hotels. Call **310-575-9799** or **212-661-7200**.

Hamburg—The *Super Hamburg Card* and The *Multiple Day Card* are valid, respectively, for one and two days free admission to 11 museums, free use of public transport and discounts of up to 30 percent on sightseeing tours. The card is available at Hamburg subway ticket counters. The one-day version costs $9 per adult; $19 per family. The two-day version costs $19 per adult; $32 per family. Purchase at subway ticket counters or call **212-967-3110**.

Hungary

Budapest—The *Budapest Card* provides admittance to museums, caves, the zoo and an entertainment park, plus free public transportation and other benefits. A three-day card is $18 for adults and $13 for children. Purchase at Tourinform offices or call **212-355-0240**.

Ireland

Dublin—The *Dublin Cultural Connection Pass* ($21.50) offers discounts averaging 30 percent on admission to museums, castles and more. Call the Irish Tourist Board, **212-418-0800**.

Japan

Countrywide—Beat astronomical costs in Japan with creative options from the Japan National Tourist Office. 260 *minshukus* (bed and breakfasts, Japanese style) offer rooms for two at $124 per night, including two meals. For information or a list of availabilities call **212-757-5641** or write to One Rockefeller Plaza, Suite 1250, New York, NY 10020. You can also request a directory published by Welcome Inn that lists over 500 lodging options from $38-76 per night, single occupancy.

Countrywide—*Goodwill Guide Groups In Japan* provides contacts for free tour guides in 35 cities and districts. Call **212-757-5640**; fax to **212-307-6754**; e-mail to **jnto.nyc@interport.net**; go online at **www.jnto.go.jp**.

Monaco

Monaco—*Le Club Diamant Rouge De Monaco*, issued by the Monaco Government Tourist Office costs $75 but special promotions can bring the price lower. You get VIP treatment, including hotel upgrades with champagne and flowers/fruit baskets on arrival, admission to

Country in which tourist safety is virtually assured: Japan.

all museums, rental car upgrades, shopping discounts, casino admission and helicopter transport to and from the airport. The card is valid for one year. Purchase in conjunction with a stay at participating hotels in Monaco. Call **800-753-9696**.

The Netherlands

Amsterdam—The *Amsterdam Culture and Leisure Pass* ($20) provides one year's free access to museums, 25 percent discounts on boat tours and attraction and dining discounts. Purchase at tourist offices in Amsterdam. Call **312-819-0300** for information.

Norway

Oslo—The *Oslo Card* provides free and discounted admission to attractions and free use of trains, subways, buses, streetcars and public boats. A one-day pass is $19; two-day/$30; three-day/$38. Purchase at tourist centers, hotels and train stations.

Russia

Moscow—Moscow's first U.S. tourist office has opened. Call **888-966-7269**; fax to **973-884-1711**; write to 300 Lanidex Plaza, Parsippany, NJ 07054.

Scandinavia

Also see individual country listings.

All Countries—Scandinavian Travel Cards provide city specific discounts in Copenhagen, Odense and Aalborg, Denmark; Helsinki, Finland; Reykjavik, Iceland; Oslo, Norway; and Stockholm and Gothenburg, Sweden. Features and cost vary. Call **212-949-2333** for more information.

Singapore

Singapore—*The Singapore Plus Card*, distributed by the Singapore Tourist Promotion Board, provides discounts at over 150 shops, restaurants and attractions. Cards are issued annually and are valid through December of each year. Call **212-302-4861** from the Eastern U.S.; **213-852-1901** from the Western U.S.

Singapore—Free two-hour tours depart from Changi Airport. Nine tour groups leave the airport on the hour, beginning at 10 a.m. Sign up at the transit lounge.

Switzerland

Countrywide—The *Swiss Museum Passport* provides admission to approximately 180 museums. A one-month pass is $30; $25/seniors (62+ for women/65+ for men); $25/children six to 16. A family pass that covers one adult and up to five children is $35. Purchase at participating museums and Swiss Tourist Offices. Call **212-757-5944**; fax to **212-262-6116**; go online at **www.switzerlandtourism.com**.

Zurich—Use a free bicycle in Zurich with payment of a refundable $17 deposit and the showing of your passport. Bicycles are available at the Werdemuhplatz, Theatreplatz and Tessinerplatz rail stations.

Turkey

Countrywide—*Turkey Youth Travel Guide Book* offers museums and lodging discounts. Call **212-687-2194**.

United Kingdom

The U.K.—The *Great British Heritage Pass* allows admission to over 500 castles, manor homes, gardens and other historic properties in England, Scotland and Wales. The pass costs $42/seven days, $64/15 days and $90/one month. Call **800-677-8585** or **800-86908184**.

The U.K.—Get information on the royal palaces (Kensington, Kew and Hampton Court) and other attractions including the Tower of London and the Banqueting House in Whitehall. Call **800-806-7187**.

Architectural features of Amsterdam homes: narrowness and tallness.

London—*Travelcards* discount transportation including BritRail travel within London, the Underground and public buses. The Gatwick train and Heathrow Airbus are not included. A one-day pass is $4.50, covering Central London; $6 covering expanded London. The pass is valid from 9:30 a.m. weekdays and all day weekends and holidays. It's sold at Underground stations.

London—The *London Arts Card*, available from the London Arts Information Center is valid for discounts and special offers at over 100 restaurants and art and cultural venues. The card is a valid for three or seven days at $10-15. A $35 family pass, valid for two adults and up to four children ages 16 and under, is valid for seven days. Call **212-529-9069**.

London—The *London For Less Card* ($19.95) discounts over 200 London attractions, shows, concerts, tours, hotels, shops, and restaurants. You'll also receive a map and guidebook. One card is good for up to five people for four consecutive days. Similar cards are offered for Bath, Edinburgh and York. Call **800-244-2361**.

London—A network of 80 kiosks in and around London (shopping areas, tourist sites, travel centers and hotels) offers free information and services relating to entertainment and events. Go online to access the information you need. Then print it out or book by kiosk phone. Discount rates are offered for select shows and concerts. A nominal fee is charged for print-outs.

London—The *London Countdown Card* ($12) offers 50 percent off at select restaurants and shops in London and ten percent off at thousands of shops, nightclubs and services displaying the Countdown sign. The card is valid for three months. Purchase at Countdown Place, 88-92 Earls Court Road, Kensington, London W8 6EH; call **0171-938-1041**.

London—The *London Museum White Card* is a three- or seven-day pass allowing admittance to a dozen popular museums. The three-day pass is $36; the seven-day is $64. Family passes covering two adults plus two children under 17 are $50-92. Purchase in London at participating museums, galleries and hotels and at major tube stations. Order in advance through Edwards & Edwards, **800-223-6108**.

London—The *London Visitor Travel Card* provides unlimited bus and underground travel for your choice of three, four or seven days. All cards come with discount vouchers for attractions and restaurants. Cards cannot be purchased in England. Call the British Tourist Authority, **800-462-2748**. Rates vary by length of validity.

London—Harrods of London offers an annual January Sale with bargains to attract the attention of any devoted shopper. Stay at The Athenaeum Hotel & Apartments and receive early access to the sale usually only accorded to Harrods account holders. The hotel will provide assistance in reclaiming your Value Added Tax and with packing and shipping. Call **800-335-3300** and request the January Sale at Harrods promotion.

London—One call to the British Tourist Authority gets you a wealth of free information, including a copy of *London Accommodations for Budget Travelers*, a guide to London, and information on how to acquire discount museum cards and transit passes. Call **800-462-2748**. Find the same information online at **www.visitbritain.com** and select and print what interests you.

London—Purchase same-day, half-price theater tickets at Leicester Square, Monday through Saturday from 2 to 6:30 p.m. Be wary of other unauthorized ticket vendors.

Typical English breakfast: eggs, toast and bangers (sausages).

> *"Only purchase discount theater tickets from legitimate vendors. Many scam offices have been operating out of storefronts in London (and other cities). They appear to be very legitimate but they are not. Travelers have been duped into purchasing either worthless pieces of paper or very poor seats misrepresented as premium seats. If you have any doubts about the authenticity of any discount vendor, check with the tourism bureau or the concierge at your hotel. The concierge, or the local tourism bureau, can direct you to legitimate discount sources."*

STUDENT & YOUTH DEALS

Students 26 & Under—Full-time students 26 and under who enjoy travel can turn twenty dollars into a year full of discounts. The *1998 International Student Identity Card* has been around for 30 years and each year it gets better. Currently, you can use it for travel savings and free or reduced admissions to attraction in over 90 countries. The card is sponsored by the International Student Travel Confederation, a non-profit group that works all year to improve the deals offered. They negotiate with airlines, other businesses and governments to get the kind of deals most useful to student travelers. Purchase for $20 from Council Travel at **310-208-3551**.

Europe—The *Euro 26 Card* discounts over 200,000 shops and services in 24 European countries. It's available to anyone age 26 and under and can be purchased at most Youth Hostel Association (YHA) locations. Countries included in the discount program are Andorra, Belgium, the Czech Republic, Cyprus, England, Finland, Ireland, Italy, Liechtenstein, Luxembourg, Malta, the Netherlands, Norway, Portugal, San Marino, Scotland, the Slovak Republic, Switzerland and Wales. Discounts are offered on a wide array of purchases. The phone number for YHA's National Office in London is **01727-855215**; fax to **01727-844126**.

Foreign Study—The Educational Foundation For Foreign Study arranges foreign language study combined with stays in an international host family's home. Stays for several months are common; shorter stays can sometimes be arranged, particularly for summer stays. Call **800-447-4273**.

International Travel—The Council on International Educational Exchange, a non-profit agency, offers a free magazine oriented toward independent, adventuresome student travelers. If you can't find an office on your campus, write to CIEE, 205 E. 42nd St., New York, NY 10017-5706.

International Travel—*Student Tips* costs just $1 and is filled with information on youth fares, rail passes, hotels, hostels, budget travel, work/study opportunities, customs, visas, trip planning, packing and discount car rentals. Call **213-463-0655** or write to *Student Tips*, Council Travel, 10904 Lindbrook Drive, Los Angeles, CA 90024.

International Travel—The **Go 25 Card** is issued by the Federation of International Youth Travel Organization

Percentage of Western European college students who visit the U.S.: 37 percent.

(FIYTO) and is available to people 25 and under with no academic requirement. It provides discounts at over 11,000 businesses worldwide. The card can be purchased from FIYTO tour operators and travel agents or write to FIYTO, Bredgade 25 H, DK-1260, Copenhagen K, Denmark. The best source for information by phone is Top Deck in London at **0171-244-8641**.

Ireland—The Irish Student Travel Service offers economical lodging options, (including one-bedroom apartments for as little as $36 per day and even lower priced rooms and dorms) available from June through mid-September. Call **0110353-1-269-7111**.

United Kingdom—*UK The Guide*, oriented to teenage and young adult travelers, is a free magazine published by the British Tourist Authority. It explains cost-cutting options available to students and details many free or low cost activities in London and other areas of the U.K. Get a free copy by calling **800-462-2748**; write to the British Tourist Authority, 625 N. Michigan Avenue, Suite 1510, Chicago, IL 60611.

United Kingdom—The *National Express Discount Coachcard* takes 30 percent off adult fares on Britain's National Express Railway and Scottish Citylink Coaches. The card is available to full-time students of any age and to all travelers 16 to 25. The cost is $15. The card can be purchased in the U.K. from Eurolines at Victoria Station.

"Most of these discount deals are designed to increase tourism and to attract tourists to particular attractions and business. They represent the investment of a significant percentage of many tourism budgets. Stopping by the tourism office at your destination can help you discover other special offers and give you information to make your trip more enjoyable. Also check in-flight magazines and welcome magazines provided in most hotel rooms. They will help orient you to your destination and they often contain special offers too. Another discount source in the United States: telephone directories with discount coupon pages, offering special restaurant and attraction discounts."

DINING ¢ ENTERTAINMENT DISCOUNTS

YOUR MAP TO A GOLDMINE OF SAVINGS

Even if you're not the type to clip coupons, it's worth using the big discount books with coupons that give, in some cases, up to $100 off a single travel purchase. A 50-cent off grocery coupon may not be worth clipping, but when you get 200 times the value, get out the scissors.

Most of these programs are issued annually. Many are sold by schools and non-profit organizations as part of their fund-raising activities. We'll tell you how to buy them direct. Most are in coupon format; some supply a membership card with a directory of participating vendors. They may focus on hotels or restaurants, but also include dozens of attraction discounts and even airline discount coupons. Having several of these books in your deck of discount cards is a good idea. Having at least one is mandatory if you want to save on travel and related expenses.

There is no limit to the number of directories you may purchase. Some savvy travelers purchase an edition to cover each major city they visit frequently. At a cost of under $50, and with deals like two-for-one restaurant meals, it doesn't take long for them to pay for themselves.

Publication dates are staggered so be sure and ask when the directory or directories that interest you are first released each year. That way you can get them in time to enjoy maximum benefit for all the time-sensitive coupons. If the airline coupons are important to you, ask specifically which coupons are included and the travel period they cover.

Most expensive U.S. restaurant cities: New York City, Washington and Chicago.

Entertainment Publications offers so many discount directory options (over 165) that you might have to set aside a bookshelf to hold the ones you want. Each provides hundreds of discounts. Call **800-445-4137** to order any of the selections we highlight or to receive a complete list of available directories. You can also write to Entertainment Publications, 2125 Butterfield Road, Troy, MI 48084. Most books include discount coupons for Continental Airlines. In many cases, they are each valid for up to four people booking and traveling together and will be accepted by Delta, Northwest and US Airways on competing routes.

- **Entertainment's *Hotel & Dining Directory*** ($42.95) includes discounts of up to 20 percent at over 2,500 restaurants in the U.S. and Canada, 50 percent at over 3,600 hotels, car rental discounts, Continental Airlines discounts and discounts for theme parks, movies, museums, theaters and other attractions.
- **Entertainment's *Hotel & Travel Ultimate Savings Directory*** ($62.95) contains dining, hotel and attraction discounts, plus two coupons good for discounts on Continental Airlines.
- **Entertainment Regional Editions** ($38-48) come in 140 varieties, each covering a specific metropolitan area. You get dining, hotel and attraction discounts plus coupons for up to $2,700 off on Continental Airlines discounts. Select a directory (or directories) that cover your choice of major metropolitan areas in Arizona, Arkansas, California, Colorado, Connecticut, Delaware, the District of Columbia, Florida, Georgia, Hawaii, Idaho, Illinois, Indiana, Iowa, Kansas, Kentucky, Louisiana, Maryland, Massachusetts, Michigan, Minnesota, Missouri, Nebraska, Nevada, New Jersey. New Mexico, New York, North Carolina, Ohio, Oklahoma, Oregon, Pennsylvania, Rhode Island, Tennessee, Texas, Utah, Vermont, Virginia, Washington and Wisconsin. Get the directory that covers your hometown to take advantage of local bargains.
- **Entertainment's San Juan Edition** ($45) covers dining, hotel and attraction discounts and includes airline coupons.
- **Entertainment's Mexico Edition**, printed in Spanish ($38 USD) includes two-for-one and 50 percent off restaurant coupons, hotel and attraction discounts and two coupons good for up to $700 in discounts on Continental flights originating in Mexico to anywhere in the contiguous U.S., Canada or within Mexico.
- **Entertainment's Canadian editions** ($43-54 USD) include dining and attraction coupons and are available in separate editions covering Calgary and Edmonton (Alberta); Oknagan Valley, Vancouver Island and Vancouver North Central (British Columbia); Winnipeg (Manitoba); Hamilton/ Burlington/ Oakville, Ottawa, Toronto Central and Toronto West Central (Ontario); and three Montreal (Quebec) editions. Each includes airfare discount coupons valid for up to $600 in discounts on Canadian Airlines and up to $1,400 in discounts on American Airlines.
- **Entertainment's Australia editions** ($35) include dining, attraction and hotel discounts, plus airline coupons. Three separate editions cover Brisbane, Melbourne and Sydney.
- **Entertainment's *London*** ($48) offers hundreds of money-saving coupons,

including over 800 dining discounts, airline coupons valid for discounts of 20 to 40 percent on roundtrip travel from Europe to the U.S., discounts on Club Med and car rental discounts and upgrades. Hotel discounts of up to 50 percent cover over 900 international properties. Attraction discounts include 25 percent off performances including *Miss Saigon* and *Oliver*. Other European editions are available.

MEMBERSHIP CLUBS

Choose the best dining membership club for you by examining the factors most important to you. Do you want a wide array of restaurants or a maximum discount with fewer dining choices? Are you better off with a free program with more nominal discounts? Does the program allow you to visit your favorite restaurants multiple times each year?

Watch for special promotions that offer free membership in some dining programs. *Best Fares* has publicized recent deals offering from three months to one year's free membership.

DINING PROGRAM OPTIONS

PROGRAM	ANNUAL COST	NUMBER OF RESTAURANTS & LOCATIONS	MAJOR BENEFITS
Diners Club LeCard 800-234-6377	Free to Diners Club cardholders; $80 to others	1,700 in 26 states and the District of Columbia	20% off, including alcohol, tax and tip
Dining à la Card 800-253-5379	$49.95; free 60-day offer	Over 6,000 in 43 states and the District of Columbia	20% off, including alcohol, tax and tip
Dinner On Us 800-346-3241	$49	Almost 15,000 in 47 states and the District of Columbia	10-25% off, excluding tip and two-for-one offers
In Good Taste 800-444-8872	First six months free, then $25	1,600 in 20 states and the District of Columbia	25% off, including alcohol
Premier Dining 001-44-171-387-5757	$75 (May vary by exchange rate)	400 in England, Scotland & Wales	25% off, including alcohol and tax
Transmedia 800-422-5090	$50	6,000 in 28 states and the District of Columbia	25% off, including alcohol
Transmedia Basic 800-422-5090	Free	6,000 in 28 states and the District of Columbia	20% off, including alcohol

Average cost of lodging and three meals in Chicago: $239.

MILES FOR MEALS

The best miles for meals programs award ten airline miles per dollar spent—the equivalent of a 20 percent discount. Separate programs are sponsored by seven major airlines. Some of them are operated by the dining programs in the previous chart or an *Entertainment* program. The following chart indicates those tie-ins in parentheses. Continental, United and US Airways also offer separate Transmedia Cards at $9.95 a year that give you ten miles per dollar charged on food-only portions of your tab. The mileage accrues in a separate account until you request that it be transferred to the airline (in 500 mile increments). If you don't dine out frequently, this limited program could be your best bet.

MILES FOR MEALS			
PROGRAM	**ANNUAL COST**	**WHO CAN JOIN**	**BENEFITS**
Alaska DineAir 800-207-8232	Free	All frequent flyers	3 miles per dollar spent, including alcohol; 300 restaurants in Alaska, Arizona, California, Idaho,Nevada, Oregon & Washington
American AAdvantage Dining (Entertainment) 800-267-260	Free	All frequent flyers	10 miles per dollar spent, including alcohol and tax
Continental OnePass Dining (Dining a la card) 800-677-4848	$49.95	All frequent flyers	10 miles per dollar spent on your total tab; maximum miles per visit, 6,000
Delta SkyMiles Dining (Entertainment) 800-346-3341	Free	All frequent flyers	3 miles per dollar spent, including alcohol and tax
Northwest WorldPerks Dining (Dining a la Card) 800-289-6902	Free	All frequent flyers	3 miles per dollar spent, including alcohol and tax
TWA Miles For Dining (Dining a la Card) 800-804-7109	$49.95	All frequent flyers	10 miles per dollar spent on your total tab; maximum miles per visit, 6,000
United Mileage Plus Dining (Dining a la Card) 800-555-5116	Free	All frequent flyers	10 miles per dollar spent on your total tab; maximum miles per visit, 6,000

Most popular pizza topping in Japan: squid.

SAVE BY HOW YOU PAY

CREDIT CARDS

Save money by how you spend it. Using the wrong payment form can add over ten percent to your domestic trip; up to 20 percent on foreign travel. Often your most intelligent payment form is credit or charge card because of buyer-protection features. You will find that more and more travel vendors require a credit card (to hold your hotel reservation, for example). If you are among the rare breed of consumer that does not like to use credit, a debit card can be advantageous for many travel purchases.

Credit and charge card buyer protection-features can be your cheapest forms of insurance. An annual fee may be easily justified by the consumer protection you receive. If the tour operator who sold you a package vacation goes under, your fastest and often best protection is disputing the charge with your credit card company. Many also offer cash-advance features that can save you time and inconvenience when traveling.

> *"When you travel internationally, cash advances by debit card are subject to the exchange rate at the time of transaction. Credit card cash advance rates aren't set until the point at which the debit is reported to the bank—usually one to three days."*

CHOOSING THE BEST CARD FOR YOU

Your best-bet credit card choice depends on your lifestyle, your travel patterns and the special features you value most. From a traveler's perspective, Diners Club and American Express (particularly AmEx Platinum) offer excep-

Airline passengers who purchase tickets by cash or check: 23%.

tional value. If you can pay your total balance each month, give these cards serious consideration. (American Express offers extended pay options for air travel only.) They give you the best overall travel benefits. The American Express Platinum Card has a $300 annual fee, but you get two-for-one tickets on 14 international airlines (Business or First Class), access to Continental and Northwest's airport clubs, enrollment in your choice of premier service programs from Avis, Hertz and National and many more valuable perks.

Consider the following factors before making any decision on which credit card to use:

- **Corporate cards and Gold and Platinum** cards offer better travel protection features and extend more promotional offers than standard cards. Special services may include trip planning, worldwide legal referral, message delivery, emergency transportation, medical assistance and extra lost luggage benefits.
- **If you tend to carry a balance,** stay away from no-fee cards that usually charge higher interest rates. If you pay in full each month, the interest rate won't be a major factor.
- **Cards that offer perks** in the form of frequent flyer miles or another award point system usually require annual fees and higher interest rates. Make sure new benefits don't come at the expense of favorable basics.
- **Note when your introductory interest rate expires**. The cardholder will notify you in a very understated way. If the rate jumps too high, switch cards as soon as possible.
- **Cards that offer sign-up bonuses** may be worth applying for, even if you never actually use the card. Usually the annual fee is waived as part of the offer and you can get perks like free companion tickets worldwide.
- **Determine how interest is charged.** Some cards, for example, charge interest on cash advances from the date of the advance rather than the billing cycle's due date. Some cards compound interest. You pay on the principal plus the current interest and raise your real interest rate by two percentage points.
- **Look at the whole picture** before changing cards. It costs issuing banks almost $100 to attract a new cardholder. Their rules are not carved in stone. You can attempt to negotiate, particularly if your requested change is a return to a term or condition that existed when you first acquired your card.
- **Compare benefit levels on services you'll actually use.** You can eliminate half the confusion of comparisons if you eliminate features that don't apply to your needs.

> *"If you're asked to fax a copy of your credit card when purchasing travel over the phone, state the limit of the authorization, in writing. Are you approving a single purchase or will you allow your travel agent to use the authorization for a longer period? Keep in mind that many airlines and travel agencies mail tickets only to your billing address. If your credit card statement goes to a post office box, you may not be able to get overnight delivery on your tickets."*

TRAVEL BENEFITS

Travel benefits vary according to the card you carry and the issuing bank. You and your neighbor may have the same card at the same level but, if they come from different issuing banks, the benefits may differ. Benefits change in reaction to monitored costs and market competition. Call to request precise policies in writing. You only get travel benefits from your card when you use it for each specific travel expense. Features may include:

- **Buyer protection coverage**, either in the form of an actual program or through your ability to dispute charges for defective merchandise and services. Be aware of notable exclusions. Many basic credit cards, for example, will not reimburse you for the cost of defective items purchased internationally.
- **Travel accident coverage** is standard on premium cards. Diners Club coverage excels because it includes trips taken on free and frequent flier tickets.
- **Car rental collision and damage waiver coverage** has been reduced in recent years. Diners Club and some corporate cards like Visa's Business Card still offer primary coverage; most other cards provide secondary coverage. Some cards exempt trucks, campers, vans, jeeps and other vehicles from any coverage or exclude travel on certain types of roads.
- **Car rental coverage abroad** is subject to the card's provisions and the willingness of the rental agency to accept it. Some foreign rental companies decline acceptance of credit card insurance benefits and place a hold on your entire credit limit if you decline their CDW coverage. Agencies in Italy, New Zealand and Mexico tend not to accept credit coverage at all.
- **Special billing itemization**, calling card links, improved express cash terms, more liberal travel insurance coverage and special discount offers are built into corporate cards. Even if you own a small business, look into them to see if the benefits they provide offer real advantages to you.

Check the exact travel benefits your card provides by calling the appropriate customer service number:

- **American Express—800-528-4800**; Gold—**800-327-2177**; Platinum—**800-525-3355**
- **Diners Club—800-346-3779**
- **MasterCard**—Contact the issuing bank for Standard cards; for Gold Cards call **800-622-7747**
- **Visa**—Contact the issuing bank for Standard cards; for Gold Cards call **800-847-2911**

MARKETING TACTICS

Credit card companies are full of bright individuals who constantly come up with innovations to the credit card issuers' advantage. Here are some marketing pitfalls to avoid:

- **If the bank doesn't quote a firm interest rate**, don't apply. They're protecting their right to charge higher interest to bigger credit risks. If you apply for too many cards, your credit rating can be negatively affected.
- **Ask if the introductory interest rate** applies to new purchases or only to balances you transfer from another card.
- **Beware of lowered minimum payment percentages.** Some cards ask for

Year in which travel is projected to be the largest percentage of credit card spending: 2000.

just two percent of your total balance. If you give in to the minimum payment temptation, you'll end up paying exorbitant amounts of interest.

DISPUTING A CHARGE

Dispute any charge you deem unwarranted, including situations where the company you purchased from fails to deliver as promised. If a tour operator defaults, for example, disputing the charge with your credit card company is likely to get your money back in your hands faster than any other means.

The Fair Credit Billing Act allows you to dispute charges or withhold payment while a charge is investigated under the following three circumstances:

- **The charge is in error**, or was not made by you or someone authorized to use your card;
- **The charge is for goods or services** you rejected on reasonable grounds;
- **The charge is for goods or services** not delivered as agreed.

Charges can be removed from your bill immediately or it can takc months. The difference is the immediate clarity of the situation, the vendor's willingness to acknowledge that your request is justified and your ability to insist on prompt action. If the vendor disputes your right to a chargeback you'll be asked to provide complete documentation. Interest may not be charged on disputed amounts, but the amounts will remain on your bill until the dispute is settled.

Dispute deadlines vary by card and issuing bank. At minimum, you have 60 days to notify the credit card company. You can do it by phone, but always follow up with a letter. Your dispute must be acknowledged within 30 days. Resolution must be achieved within 90 days.

If your credit card company denies the chargeback, appeal to the appropriate regulatory entity. Visa and MasterCard are regulated by agencies covering the bank that issues their cards. Call and ask for the name and number you need. American Express appeals go to the Federal Trade Commission, **202-326-2222**. You can also contact the Better Business Bureau in the city where the vendor is based.

The General Services Administration offers *Using Credit and Charge Cards Overseas.* Send 50 cents in check or money order to the Superintendent of Documents, Consumer Information Center, Dept. 365 D, Pueblo, CO 81009.

AFFINITY CARDS

Affinity cards in co-branded and rebate varieties are available in ever-expanding variety. Co-branded cards are based on a marketing alliance between a retailer and a bank. Rebate cards operate on cash-back or point systems. They both provide unique benefits, but you're unlikely to get the most favorable interest rates and likely to have to pay annual fees without getting extra travel protection. Airline cards usually offer better deals than hotel or cruise line cards. We detail them in this book's Frequent Flyer section.

- **Interest rates and annual fees** tend to increase after introductory offers expire. Evaluate the interest rate, the annual fee and how much you have to charge to get real benefits.
- **Be sure you'll use the points, miles or premiums you earn.** These cards can be like the Green Stamps of the '90s. Many affinity award credits expire before they're ever used.
- **Many rebate cards encourage high revolving balances** by offering special

Cost of a recent five day strike by workers at the Eiffel Tower: $500,000.

awards for minimum balances. A few cards actually add a monthly service charge if you pay your full balance.

- **Know how the sponsoring bank computes** the balance subject to interest. The adjusted balance system is best but is rarely offered by bonus cards. The average daily balance is next in preference. Avoid two-cycle average daily balance systems that compute interest based on two billing cycles. Look for optimum grace periods between purchase and posting.
- **Get the best of both worlds** by charging regular monthly purchases on bonus cards to rack up points. Pay the bill in full each month. Use your basic, lower-interest card on large purchases where balances may be carried over.

CREDIT CARD PROMOTIONS

Promotions to attract new cardholders change as often as freshman senators change their position on issues. *Best Fares* magazine and **www.bestfares.com** detail these offers, so those who are interested in a new card can apply when introductory offers are most beneficial. You also want to check your mail for credit card and frequent flyer billing inserts that offer bonuses for upgrading your current card or applying for a new card. We recently revealed credit card promotions including:

- **Free companion tickets on American** for new Citibank charge card applicants or upgrades to Gold.
- **Free roundtrip travel on Northwest** for using selected Midwest banking services.
- **A free companion ticket anywhere Delta flies** when you are approved for the Delta SkyMiles corporate card.

BLOCKED FUNDS

Your ability to use your credit can be hampered when car rental agencies and hotels block your available funds against ultimate charge contingencies. This can tie up a good portion of needed funds when you are on a trip or even render your card unusable. Ask if funds will be blocked when you make your reservation. If the amount is reasonable, mentally deduct it from your available limit or use an alternate credit card for day-to-day expenses.

Demand that any block be removed as soon as your transaction is completed. It's a brief procedure that many vendors tend to do in batches, depriving you of your total card limit for as long as several days.

LOST OR STOLEN CREDIT CARDS

Know Who To Contact **lists numbers to call** if your card is lost or stolen. Don't delay making your report. You must do so in a timely fashion to avoid liability for unauthorized purchases. Different companies have various parameters for replacing cards.

- **American Express** takes one to two days to replace cards lost while you are in the U.S. Cards lost abroad can take two to four days to be replaced, but you can often get an almost instant replacement by visiting an AmEx international office.
- **Diners Club** replaces cards in the U.S. within 24 hours; abroad, in one to three days.
- **Discover** replaces cards in the U.S. overnight; abroad, in two days.
- **MasterCard** replaces standard cards in the U.S. within two business days;

Gold cards, the next day. Standard cards are replaced abroad according to the policy of the issuing bank—usually a minimum of two days. Gold cards are replaced the next day.

- **Visa** replaces standard cards in the U.S. in one business day and tries to replace Gold cards within 24 hours. Abroad, standard cards require three days; Gold, one business day.

> *"If you want to stop pre-approved credit cards from being mailed to you, call the following two agencies and state your request: Experian at **800-353-0809** and Trans Union at **800-680-7293**."*

ATM CARDS

General Use

Travelers benefit from the prevalence of Automatic Teller Machines (ATMs). You don't have to carry large amounts of cash, because ATMs let you tap into your funds from almost anywhere on the globe.

- **Check your daily withdrawal limit** before you leave. You'll probably want to access unusual amounts of cash. There can be different daily limits for domestic use and for international use.
- **Get a number to call in case your card is lost or stolen**. Report lost or stolen cards as soon as possible. Policies vary bank by bank, but your liability is usually determined by the length of time you wait until reporting the card missing. In a 48-hour period, your liability can increase ten-fold.
- **ATM withdrawals can cost less than credit card cash advances**, which usually incur interest from the date of transaction and charge fees up to three percent. ATM cash advance fees are usually two percent, with a minimum charge of $2.50 and a maximum charge of $20. You must also pay the standard transaction fee.

International ATM Use

Using ATMs internationally is relatively easy and extremely smart. You get foreign currency at wholesale rates—the same rates banks pay when transferring in excess of $1 million. There is no cheaper way to get cash abroad.

- **Money is issued at wholesale exchange rates** that range from three to five percent lower than standard bank rates, as much as 40 percent lower than airport exchange counters and as much as 55 percent lower than some hotel currency exchanges. You usually get a better deal by using an ATM than you would get at a bank counter.

> *"In 1996, ATM access fees of $2-4 above transaction fees began to appear in the South and West and have now gone national. They tend to be charged by airport ATMs and ATMs in other areas frequented by travelers. As many as 25 percent of Plus and Cirrus machines now charge extra. By law, a surcharge warning must flash on the screen, but if you blink, you might miss it. Your best defense is to head for an ATM with an identifying bank logo.New mega-mergers are also apt to increase ATM fees."*

> *"During the past year several banks began marketing ATM cards that also serve as Visa or MasterCards. These cards carry several distinct disadvantages. If they are stolen, the crooks have access to your total checking account and you could be liable if you don't report the theft almost immediately. You don't get any kind of credit float, as you do with zero-balance credit cards. And you are at a great disadvantage if you dispute a charge since the bank already has your money."*

- **Transaction fees are technically the same** as in the U.S., but in rare instances you'll encounter higher fees, because you're dealing with multiple banks. Minimize transaction fees by withdrawing an adequate amount of cash and keeping the bulk of it in your hotel safe.
- **Countries with two-tier monetary systems**, whether official or tolerated, provide the exception to the ATM rule. Use tourist exchange facilities rather than banks or ATMs.

You can get ATM location information before you leave home.

- **If your card is part of the Cirrus network** call **800-424-7787** for locations in 66 countries; go online at **www.mastercard.com/atm**.
- **If you're part of the Plus network,** call **800-491-1145** for locations in 75 countries; go online at **www.visa.com/cgi-bin/vee/pd/atml/main.html?2+0**.
- **Your bank should have ATM directories**, but few people request them, so ask a bank officer if you're told directories are not available. Consider photocopying and enlarging the pages you need to get around tiny type size and avoid having to carry the entire directory.

You will need to make a few modifications to your usual ATM procedure.

- **Convert your PIN to four numbers.** Some international machines won't accept a longer number and some don't have alpha-numeric keypads.
- **Instructions are usually multi-lingual,** but basic foreign language skills can come in handy if you try to use one of the three percent that are programmed in one language.
- **24-hour ATMs are not the rule** in suburban and outlying areas. You won't always have the same degree of accessibility you have at home.
- **If the machine says "No Foreign Cards,"** heed the notice or it may consume your card without warning.

TRAVELERS CHECKS

Some people still prefer travelers checks for the loss and theft protection they provide. They usually cost a one percent service fee but are free for American Automobile Association (AAA) members and preferred bank customers—a status you can usually attain by request and by carrying a nominal minimum balance in a savings or checking account.

- **Avoid losing ten to 20 percent value** when cashing travelers checks internationally by buying foreign denomination checks before you leave. American Express Travelers Checks can be exchanged at low fees (sometimes for free at American Express international offices), but the exchange rate may not be as favorable as bank rates. Try to closely approximate the amount you need to avoid the expense of converting unused checks back to U.S. dollars.

> *"American Express and Visa offer dual signature travelers checks that allow use with either of two approved signatures. They're great for two people traveling together but not always choosing the same activities."*

- **Purchase travelers checks through your travel agent**, bank, credit union or a currency exchange service.
- **As soon as you receive your travelers checks,** make copies of the numbers and record the telephone number to call if they are lost or stolen.

Services that sell international travelers checks include Ruesch International—foreign denomination travelers checks only. There is a $2 fee per currency transaction if you purchase in person (see your telephone directory for the closest office); $10 if you purchase by mail. Call **800-424-2923**.

CARRYING CASH

Carry a reasonable amount of cash to handle tips and incidental expenses. Too much cash makes you vulnerable to theft and loss; too little forces you to complicate inexpensive transactions by using payment forms that require more time and may not even be accepted.

Use cash when you have reason to suspect that your credit card number might be used for unauthorized reasons. When traveling, your credit card company may not be able to reach you to question unusual activity.

Don't rush to exchange currency before you leave on an international trip. You may be tempted by momentarily favorable exchange rates, but rates rarely fluctuate enough to make more than a few dollars difference.

Don't count on cashing personal checks with the airline you're flying or at your hotel. The credit card age has made that traditional courtesy subject to your persuasiveness and their interpretation of risk.

> *"Diners Club cardholders can exchange up to $1,000 in currency per week at 65 Inter-Continental hotels worldwide. You pay bank rate, less a four percent service charge—a vastly improved deal as compared to usual hotel exchange rates."*

EMERGENCY CASH OPTIONS

The best way to deal with emergency cash situations is to pre-plan and try to avoid having the need arise.

- **Know your credit card and ATM limits** before you leave. If you're going to be charging expenses outside your usual charge pattern, notify the bank to avoid being questioned on individual purchases. If you're traveling internationally, have sufficient funds in your main checking account as it is the only account many overseas ATMs will access.
- **Unanticipated expenses** can make the difference between easy going and

financial strain. Make sure you've allowed the means to cover anticipated expenses, and a little extra for unforeseen expenses. Parking rates in some cities hit $40 per day. Hotel taxes add ten to 20 percent to the quoted rate. The $10 gin and tonic and $5 cola are not uncommon. Do a little research into prices at any new destination and adjust your budget accordingly.

When emergency funds are needed, you have several options.

- **Bank transfers** are safe and cost effective, providing your bank has a branch in the city or country you are in. The cost of international transfers ranges from $25-45. You can pick up your funds in local currency.
- **Overnight services** from Federal Express, Airborne and the post office can get a cashiers check or money order to you by 10:30 the next morning. If you have a business account that provides a volume-user discount, the cost can be as low as $4.50. Have the funds sent in a form that is easy to cash in the country you are in.
- **Have money wired** via Western Union, **800-325-4176**, at fees calculated by the dollar amount sent. If you use a credit card, an additional fee is charged. American Express Money Grams, **800-926-9400**, offers lower rates, but you must make the transfer in person at an affiliated outlet. You can pay for the transfers with cash, Visa, MasterCard or Discover Card.
- **The U.S. Department of State, 202-647-5225,** in conjunction with Western Union will send emergency cash internationally for the Western Union charge plus a $15 consulate fee. Funds arrive quickly and can be picked up in local currency.

VALUE ADDED TAXES

North American travelers unnecessarily leave over $50 million in Europc each year by not applying for Value Added Tax (VAT) refunds. VAT refunds are available on purchases that are taken out of the country. You cannot get them for goods and services used while in the country. In some countries, the VAT adds as much as 20 percent to the final price of many items. There are five ways you can avoid contributing to this multi-million dollar drain.

- **Exit refunds**—Show your passport when you make your purchases and request the appropriate paperwork. Add about two hours to your check-in time at the airport. Take purchases in their original containers to the airport as carry-on luggage. Customs will inspect your purchases, stamp your form and send you to another line to get a check or charge card credit.
- **Direct export**—Have purchases shipped directly to the U.S. You pay the shipping costs and items may be subject to U.S. duty. Use this method if shipping and handling is less expensive than the VAT.
- **Refunds by mail**—Use forms available at larger shops and at U.S. Customs checkpoints. Read the instructions carefully and observe filing deadlines.
- **European Tax-Free Shopping sites**—There are over 60,000 member shops, usually identified with a blue and silver ETS sign. They simplify VAT refunds in exchange for 20 percent of your refund value. The shop fills out the paperwork, seals your packages and issues a refund check on the spot. Checks are cashed at an ETS desk after you've passed through

U.S. cities with the highest travel-related taxes: Chicago, Seattle, Houston, New York & Dallas.

departure customs, with payment in charge card credit, U.S. or local currency. For more information call **203-965-5145**.

- **VAT refund processors**—After you return home you can utilize a service skilled in untangling red tape. There is no up-front charge. The fee is a percentage of the refund they expedite. Most require a minimum refund amount of $190-200 per quarter. Sources include:

  Euro VAT Refund—310-204-0805

  International Sales Tax Refund—716-284-6287

  International VAT Consulting Group—703-478-2220

  Meridian VAT—212-554-6600

  Universal VAT Services—800-627-1002

  VAT America—609-924-3646

VAT rates can vary by item as well as by country. Belgium, for example, charges 11 percent on electrical appliances and 25 percent on luxury clothing and jewelry. This chart shows the variance you can expect by country plus the minimum purchase requirement for applying for a VAT refund.

GENERAL VAT RATES		
COUNTRY	VAT RATE	MINIMUM PURCHASE FOR MOST REFUND APPLICATIONS
AUSTRIA	16.7%	$ 90
AUSTRALIA	20%	$ 90
BELGIUM	17%	$215
BRITAIN	7.5%	None, unless required by merchant
DENMARK	20%	$ 50
FRANCE	18.6%	$250
GERMANY	15%	None, unless required by merchant
ITALY	19%	$200
THE NETHERLANDS	17.5%	$185
SPAIN	6%	$ 95
SWEDEN	20%	$ 13
SWITZERLAND	6.5%	$340

Number of separate taxes that can be incurred by tourists worldwide: 40.

SAVING TAXES IN CANADA

Travelers to Canada can obtain refunds on national Goods and Services Tax (GST) and Provincial Sales Tax (PST), charged in most provinces.

- **GST refunds** are available on purchases taken out of Canada and on hotel room charges. Refunds are not applicable for tax paid on meals, car rentals and gas. Forms are available at most hotels and large stores and must be mailed in with original receipts. If you're claiming less than $500 Canadian, you can file your claim at the border. Call the Canadian Consulate, **404-532-2000** or the Visitors Rebate Program, **613-991-3346** for details.
- **PST refunds** on tax rates ranging from six to 12 percent are obtained by filing by mail directly to the provincial refund office. Hotels and stores have the forms which must be completed and in the applicable office within 30 days of purchase or use of service.

MORE WAYS TO SAVE INTERNATIONALLY

There are many other ways to save money on international travel. Here are a few additional tips. Check the internet for location specific information or consider travel chat rooms for in-person reports.

- **Be a savvy shopper.** Americans are accustomed to inflated prices at airport shops, but European airport shopping offers some bargains and, in some cases, VATs lower than what you'll find in city shops. Learn when and how to bargain. The simplest strategy: make your initial offer half the asking price and let the negotiations begin. In some cultures walking away is an expected part of the process and necessary to getting the lowest price.
- **Simplify currency exchange.** Posted foreign exchange rates are affected by small-print fees, charges and commissions. Don't try to figure out all the variables. Ask a simple question: "If I give you X dollars, how much local cash will you give me in return?"
- **Familiarize yourself with local currency.** Program yourself for systems that make cost comprehension difficult for Americans. For example, a meal that costs $10 U.S. may cost 12 Australian dollars or 71 Hong Kong dollars. A small travel computer will translate for you, but you may not need one. A free Foreign Currency Guide is available from Ruesch International, 700 11th St. NW, Suite 400, Washington, DC 20001. Call **800-424-2923** or **202-408-1200**. Off the beaten path, local currency may be the only form of money that counts. Your second best alternative—using travelers checks in the local currency.
- **Guarantee hotel and car rental rates** by pre-paying and locking them in at the current exchange rate.
- **Check menu prices posted in many restaurant windows.** Rely on them for cost estimates rather than making snap judgments based on neighborhoods and outward appearances.
- **Don't incur extra taxi fees** by carrying luggage in the trunk. Some countries charge extra for any luggage not stowed in the passenger section.
- **Develop a panhandler policy.** You've learned to deal with the homegrown variety, but panhandlers appear in unexpected places and forms when you travel.

Cost of 100 aspirins in Mexico City: $1.16; in Tokyo, $35.93.

TIPS ON TIPS

ESTABLISH YOUR TIPPING PERSONALITY

The common explanation for the word tips is that it is an acronym for "To Insure Prompt Service." Curiously enough, most tips are given after the service is performed. Tips are never mandatory but are usually factored into pay rates. As long as that practice remains standard, it's best to accept tipping for decent service as a reality of modern life.

Many people would like to see the end of the custom of tipping, but many people in service professions are not given the type of hourly wage that makes this possible. Until these pay scales change, tipping is here to stay. Some people "comment" on poor restaurant service by leaving a few pennies as a tip. You'll have a better effect if you let the management know the service is bad before you finish your meal.

Try to carry coins and currency that allow you to tip without negotiating change. Hand deliver tips when you're uncertain they'll get to your intended recipients.

We'll give you some tipping guidelines to assist you in unfamiliar situations, but guidelines can be broken. The tip you decide to render is ultimately up to you.

- **Under-tipping** can express your displeasure with poor service, but be sure you are sending the message to the right person. Don't hold anyone liable for what they can't control. For instance, don't under-tip the waiter because of an unorganized kitchen staff.
- **Standard tipping** expresses your satisfaction and fulfills your obligation.
- **Over-tipping** should be a considered response to an extra level of service.

Top sources of U.S. tourism dollars: Japan, 22 percent; the U.K., 10 percent; Canada, 9 percent.

TIPPING ON THE MOVE

Airport shuttle drivers—$1 per bag only if direct assistance is provided.

Skycaps—$1 per bag, minimum. This is an up front tip that almost always pays off.

Taxi drivers—15 percent or $1, whichever is greater.

Train porters and attendants—tip as service is rendered; $1 usually is fine. Tipping for meal service follows the same standards as regular restaurant dining. Sleeping-car attendants are tipped at the end of the trip at a suggested $5 per night.

Tipping on escorted tours is done on the last day at $2-5 per person per day for lengthy tours, and half that for shorter tours. A guide leading a side-tour that lasts several hours is tipped according to the number of people in the group; the larger the group, the smaller each traveler's contribution. A guide with exceptional skills, such as a safari guide, should be tipped at or above the $5 per day rate.

TIPPING ON CRUISES

Most cruise tipping is easily handled near the end of the cruise. Envelopes and suggested amounts are provided by the cruise ship staff. Some lines publish tipping guidelines in their brochures or you can get advance notice of standards on the cruise line you choose from your cruise consultant. On the last full day of your cruise, your cabin steward will leave tip envelopes and tip suggestions. Some ultra-luxury lines include tipping in their prices.

Suggested tips for most cruise lines:

- **Cabin stewards and waiters**—$3-5 each, per day.
- **Busboys**—$2 per day.
- **Other service staff**—Bartenders, wine stewards, masseurs and hairdressers are tipped as services are rendered. You may tip childcare workers, but it is not required or expected unless you use their services outside of normal operating hours. There is no need to tip people staffing standard cruise ship children's programs.
- **Captains and ships officers**—Never tip. The best way to acknowledge them is a thank you letter, copied to the cruise line's corporate office.

TIPPING AT HOTELS

Hotel tipping is strictly for services performed. In some cases, you tip as you go; in others, a cumulative tip is sufficient.

- **Doormen**—The customary tip is $1, but not every time you enter or leave the hotel. You should tip if the doorman provides special assistance, such as helping you with luggage or hailing a cab.
- **Front desk staff**—Rarely tipped. If you're given a great upgrade, you might consider a tip but it won't be expected.
- **Bellmen**—Tipped according to the amount of luggage they transport at 50 cents to $1 per bag.
- **Housekeeping staff**—Tipping optional, but $1-2 on the pillow each morning is considerate and probably well-spent, especially for extended stays.
- **Room service**—Follows the standard 15 percent restaurant rule. Tipping in cash gives the waiter immediate use of the gratuity. Adding it to your credit card charge can delay it by days. Some hotels charge service fees and delivery fees. Usually the server doesn't get a penny of it.

Most expensive international cities for travel: Hong Kong, $624 per day; Tokyo, $599; Monte Carlo, $579.

- **The concierge**—Tips are not required for brief general information, but should be extended for special services. Tickets to a sold-out play or reservations at a hot new restaurant, for example, could merit a $10 tip or more if the concierge was able to acquire a benefit you could not have attained on your own.
- **Extended stay hotels**—Make note of which day(s) of the week you received maid service and leave a tip for the maid each week. The amount depends on, more than anything, the amount of work she will have to do. If you are neat as a pin, a few dollars in a clearly marked envelope is fine; if you are at the opposite extreme, $10 is not excessive.

> *“The Seaport Hotel in Boston is considering a no-tipping policy with revenue to cover higher wages built into the daily room rate. The only non-resort property already doing that (to our knowledge) is the Union Square in San Francisco —a 30-room innovator.”*

TIPPING ON THE TOWN

- **Valet parking attendants**—Tip when you claim your car. $1-2 is fine for most vehicles. You might want to tip more if you drive a super luxury car.
- **Coatroom attendants**—In establishments where tips don't go to the management (always ask) tip $1 or more, depending on what you check and the tone of the establishment.
- **Bartenders**—15 percent or $1, whichever is greater. If the bartender has provided lengthy conservation (at your behest) a larger tip is considerate.
- **Musicians**—At least $1 for any special request and $5-10 for something remarkable (believe it or not, most bands don't enjoy amateur guest vocalists).
- **Restaurants**—15 percent for good service; 20 percent for excellent service. A good way to figure an average tip is to double the tax amount. In most U.S. cities that will come close to 15 percent.
- **Fine dining**—Tip the *maitre'd* according to the status of the restaurant. You have wide discretion. Wine stewards are tipped $2-5 per bottle or ten percent of the cost of the wine, whichever is greater.
- **Buffet dining**—$1 tip per person if drinks and other services are provided.

TIPPING INTERNATIONALLY

Service charges are automatically added to restaurant bills in many countries. Be sure to ask and be sure to use that specific term. In some places a tip is considered an extra gratuity over and above the service charge, but the existence of a fixed service charge can cancel your tipping obligation.

Tip in local money whenever possible. Residents of some countries appreciate tips in U.S. currency, but don't do it unless you're sure it is desirable. Tipping customs vary by country, but standard at establishments frequented by travelers often override local customs. Tipping can be deemed an insult in China, for example, and inappropriate in Tahiti. Your tip may be refused in Australia or New Zealand, or gratefully accepted. The chart on the following page can serve as a basic guide.

TIPPING INTERNATIONALLY		
COUNTRY	RESTAURANT	TAXI
AUSTRIA	5-7%	10%
BELGIUM	Included	Included
BELIZE	5-15% optional	Included
CYPRESS	5%	Included
DENMARK	Included	Not required
FINLAND	Included	Not required
FRANCE	Round up to the nearest franc	10%
GERMANY	Round up to the nearest mark	One or two marks
GREECE	10%	10%
GUATEMALA	10%	Not required
HUNGARY	10%	10%
ICELAND	Included	Included
ISRAEL	10%	Not required
ITALY	Included	5-10%
JAPAN	Not required	Not required
KOREA	Not required	Not required
THE MIDDLE EAST (except Israel)	10-15%	10-15%
NORWAY	Included	Included
PORTUGAL	Included	10%
ROMANIA	10% if not included	10%
SPAIN	5-10%	5-10% if metered; not required for set fares
SWEDEN	Included	10%
TRINIDAD	10-15%	Not required
THE UNITED KINGDOM	10-15% if not included	10-15%
VIRGIN ISLANDS	10-15%	15%

Typical time when dinner is served in Madrid: 10 p.m.

Travel Insurance

Travel insurance is sold by a number of sources. It is as important to choose the right source as it is to choose the right coverage.

- **Retail sources** include major insurance companies, sometimes operating under special travel insurance names. You'll pay about $6 for every $100 of coverage. Custom policies let you select your inclusions; bundled policies combine the most popular forms of coverage. Sources include:

  Access America International 800-284-8300

  American Express–800-756-2639

  Berkeley Carefree–800-323-3149

  Global Emergency Medical Services 800-249-2533

  Health Care Abroad–800-237-6615

  Travel Guard—800-826-1300

  Travel Insurance Service 800-937-1387

  Travelers–800-243-3174

  Worldwide Assistance–800-821-2828

- **Wholesale policies** are sold by cruise and tour operators. They are similar to retail policies but don't usually cover one of your biggest risks—the default of the cruise or tour company. They are less expensive, usually averaging $4-5 per $100 in coverage. Companies that offer flat rates ($49 for a four-day trip or $59 for a seven-night cruise, for example) can be even cheaper. They may be the right choice if you have confidence in the vendor and they have a good track record. If you don't know, ask your travel agent.

Annual number of tourists who visit Florida: 42 million.

> *"Don't overlook your most basic form of protection—paying by credit card that affords effective buyer-protection features. Before you purchase additional insurance, check your credit card coverage, your general insurance policies and coverage that may be included with association or automobile club memberships. In many cases, you can add travel-related coverage to your existing policies at an annual cost lower than separate per-trip coverage."*

- **Cancellation waivers** offer your cheapest form of coverage, but they are also the least effective. All they do is waive trip cancellation penalties under certain conditions. The closer you get to your departure date, the less coverage you have. Most waivers rescind coverage a stated number of days prior to departure.

TRIP CANCELLATION INSURANCE

Trip Cancellation Insurance (TCI) costs from four to eight percent of your trip cost and protects you against four variables that may cause cancellation of your trip. Benefits are limited to your actual loss. TCI's usually pay the non-refundable portion of what you've paid for your trip minus any refund paid directly to you by vendors. If you have to postpone your departure or leave a tour midway for covered reasons, they can pay for alternate transportation, but check these provisions carefully. General coverage includes:

- **Serious illness or death** of the traveler or, in some cases, a family member or business colleague. Pre-existing conditions are exempt for specified time periods and injuries that occur during active sports are usually precluded.
- **Home-based contingencies** that prevent you from traveling, such as fire, flood, car wreck, jury duty or weather catastrophe.
- **Destination disasters** including earthquakes, quarantines, terrorist activity or general strikes.
- **Operator failure**—but be aware that most coverage is contingent on the vendor officially filing bankruptcy. Most failed companies never do. Most policies won't cover default by the company that sold the package to you, but they do cover failure by airlines, tour operators and cruise lines contracted for your trip.

> *"If you have to cancel your trip, even the most well-crafted letter detailing heart-wrenching, unforeseen circumstances will not obligate a cruise line or vacation package vendor to refund your money. It may not even give you any special consideration. Making even one exception to the rule could obligate the vendor to honor other requests by setting a precedent. It isn't apt to occur. That's why TCI is a good choice for travelers who have invested a significant amount of money in their vacation."*

MEDICAL INSURANCE

Emergency Medical Evacuation insurance (EME) pays for air ambulances and other emergency transportation needs, as well as expenses not always covered by standard health insurance, health maintenance organizations and Medicare. It fills in the gaps on policies that limit coverage outside the U.S. and may be particularly desirable for seniors. Medicare covers very limited medical needs internationally, unless you have a top-of-the-line supplemental policy. EME coverage can be a wise purchase for travelers at relatively high risk for an illness that could intensify during travel.

EME offers TCI options, but exclusions on cancellation provisions are extensive. If you want both EME and TCI, buy TCI-based coverage with an EME add-on. If medical emergencies are your primary concern, choose an EME policy.

Evaluate coverage by checking which benefits are included and where they affect your scale of possibilities. The cost will range from $6-9 per $1,000 in trip cost. Windows for pre-existing conditions are usually 60-90 days. Frequent inclusions and range of coverage:

- **Medical expenses** with coverage usually ranging from $3,000-10,000.
- **Emergency medical evacuation** ranging from $10,000-50,000.
- **Accident benefits** ranging from $10,000-100,000.

WHEN YOU HONESTLY DON'T NEED A POLICY

Peace of mind is important, but buying a smidgeon of it at a high price isn't necessary unless you really have to cover every base in order to feel secure. Here are two forms of insurance you may never need:

- **Theft protection**—A good homeowner's or renter's policy insures your belongings when you travel. If not, you can probably add a floater to your existing policy for less than the cost of theft insurance for a one to two week trip. You'll be covered for an entire year.
- **Airline flight insurance**—Your money would be better spent on insurance to protect you from a lethal bee sting. The odds that you'll need it are greater than the odds that you will die in a plane crash.

> *"Make a photo-copy of important provisions of your health insurance policy and take it with you when you travel. If you happen to need its coverage, you want to be clear on every detail."*

CALLING FROM THE ROAD

THE LONG DISTANCE JUNGLE

Ma Bell now has second cousins, kissing cousins and distant relatives. You have to shop your way through the calling card maze. Your best choice depends on where you travel, calling patterns, savings versus convenience and multiple service discounts. Choose the card with the best rates on the options you'll use the most. The most important rule with any calling card or long distance service is to monitor your bills. Rates change often. The great deal that caused you to choose a particular company may disappear a few months after you sign up. Unless you're a thorough reader of every bit of fine print that comes your way, you won't know about the changes without checking the per-minute cost of each bill.

CHOOSING A CARRIER

The Big 3 or the ever-increasing 300? AT&T, MCI and Sprint offer the widest array of services. Some small companies charge exorbitant amounts for access to their systems; others provide rates comparable to or even below those of the Big 3. Cut through the hype and compare facts. Disregard introductory rates, unless you are willing to change carriers when they expire.

Special services vary from company to company and change often due to competition. Common inclusions:

- **Message delivery** that lets you record a one minute message and attempts to resend it until your party answers.
- **Enhanced fax options** for multiple sends and retries.

City on which the game of Monopoly is based: Atlantic City, New Jersey.

- **500 numbers** that give your callers a number that will reach you anywhere within the continental U.S.
- **800 voice mail** with message retrieval service from any touchtone phone.
- **Accounting codes** to simplify multiple client billing.
- **Interpreter services** in as many as 140 languages.
- **Radio/telephone service** to connect you to cruise ships and seafaring vessels.
- **Travel services** that include destination-specific calling info, three-way speed calling and weather information.

CALLING CARDS

Be clever when choosing a calling card to use while traveling. If you choose the wrong card (even from one of the large phone companies), you are likely to get a shock when your phone bill arrives. You can end up paying a high surcharge on every call in addition to the per-minute rate. Choose cost-effective calling cards for ease and security, staying away from cards that charge a per-call surcharge. You pay the surcharge whether your call lasts an hour or a minute. Also check the per-minute rate. You will find that some cards will charge as much as 60 cents a minute; other cards charge as little as nine cents.

Check all restrictions, such as calling area (international or domestic) and expiration dates, to be sure the card you purchase suits your needs. There should always be toll-free access and customer service numbers on the card.

Determine the rate plan. Some cards charge more for peak calling times. Some round off your calling time to the nearest minute, while others bill in six-second increments.

Look for a card from a company you recognize. If you do have problems, you have somewhere to turn. Some fly-by-night companies sell pre-paid cards with 800 access numbers that have been disconnected or constantly are busy, making the card worthless. If you buy a card from an irresponsible seller, you may wind up with a card that has only ten minutes left on it when it advertises a full hour. You can't tell by looking. Don't buy a large quantity of cards at a time, particularly if you are not completely familiar with the company. Besides, better deals can also appear.

Airline-issued calling cards may entice you because of the bonus miles offered (generally around 500). When making a mileage influenced purchase, remember miles have a value of two cents, so your bonus miles are worth $10. When combined with a high per-minute rate, the cards are no bargain. Some better bargains have begun to appear. United's prepaid card, for example, offers 1,000 bonus miles per $50 of calling time. Spend $1,250 and you have a free roundtrip.

Phone companies have begun to safeguard themselves against calling card theft. If they notice a sudden change in your calling habits (traveling almost always causes a change), they may freeze your account until they can verify the charges with you. Most of the time this works to everyone's benefit, but the occasional glitch does occur when the phone company freezes an account that has not been stolen. A pre-paid calling card can be good for travelers. If it falls into the wrong hands, only a small amount of money is lost, instead of possibly hundreds of dollars charged to your account. If your calling card is stolen, the phone company will not necessarily hold you responsible, if you report the loss as soon as possible.

Cost of a ten-minute operated-assisted call to Chicago from a room at the London Hilton: $95.

INTERNATIONAL DEBIT CARDS

International debit cards have been used since the early '70s. Common points of sale are post offices and newsstands. Japan sells them from vending machines and local calls cost the equivalent of a dime. They are routinely used by locals, so ask for tips on where to buy them, how to use them and where to get the best values. Unlike U.S. debit cards, international cards cannot be used from hotel rooms. They're great for public phone use, because you avoid the hassle of mastering and carrying foreign coins. They work for local, inter-country and long distance calls and are available in over 170 countries. Each card can be used only in the country of issue.

> *"Get free bonus debit cards during special promotions by car rental agencies and other travel-related vendors. Best Fares magazine and **www.bestfares.com** keeps track of these offers."*

PAY PHONE PARANOIA

Pay phone paranoia is a requirement of budget-wise living, unless you want to pay as much as ten times standard rates. Under deregulation, the only long distance rates subject to federal restriction are AT&T's. The theory was that operator service providers (OSP's) would lower rates through competition. In practice, many privately owned pay phones automatically connect you to their high-dollar carriers and additional fee services. A recorded announcement must precede all long distance calls and tell you which carrier you're on. Switch to the carrier of your choice by using your access number or enter "00" and demand to be connected. New rate caps are underway but in the meantime, don't trust the label on the pay phone.

Domestic credit card access numbers:

AT&T—800-225-5288

GTE—800-225-5483

MCI—800-888-8000

Sprint—800-366-2255

Complaints about telecommunications price gouging should be addressed to the Federal Communications Commission Enforcement Division, Common Carrier Bureau, 1919 M St. NW, Suite 500, Washington, DC 20554. Call them at **202-418-0700** or **202-418-1500**. You can also contact your state's consumer protection agency. If you really want to be effective, don't stop there; copy your complaint to your state legislators.

AVOIDING HOTEL ACCESS FEES

Hotels are reducing or eliminating phone access fees, usually number one in guest complaints. Resistance comes from the almost $1.8 billion in annual revenue that will be lost. Some chains allow member hotels to individually opt out of the move to eliminate fees. Beware of chains advertising the elimination of these charges when they only do so in high-dollar rooms used by five percent of the traveling public. Marriott has all but eliminated access fees. ITT Sheraton has almost phased them out.

Ask about access fees before you make your reservation. They can be free or cost as much as $1.25 per call. Let the reservation agent know this is a high priority item for you. Asking at check-in

Cost of the same call using MCI's Worldphone service: $16.27.

gives you the information but takes away your choice. Calling card calls are cheaper than direct-dial even at hotels charging the highest fees. Direct-dial calls billed to your room carry up to a 40 percent surcharge. Rates are comparable to operator-assisted calls, even though no operator intervention is required.

> *"Every hotel should clearly state its telephone rate and surcharge policy in printed material in every guest room. The front desk should, at minimum, provide you with a copy on request. Since phone policies are rarely the same at all properties within a chain, it pays to check this material out as soon as you check in."*

Access charges for 800 numbers have been cropping up since hotels realized customers were using AT&T, MCI and Sprint 800 access numbers to avoid hotel access fees. Get around the 800 fee by entering a five-digit code before you enter your carrier's 800 access number:

AT&T—10-288-0

MCI—10-222-0

Sprint—10-333-0

> *"Minimize access fees by grouping calls and hitting the pound sign between each call. This should allow you multiple calls at a single call rate. If your hotel charges for local calls, make a deal with the front desk for a flat rate, particularly if you plan on doing a lot of local calling."*

Blocking specific long distance carriers to keep you locked in to the hotel's preferred carrier is illegal. If you get a persistent busy signal after you enter an access number, you may have been blocked. Call the desk and demand to be given an access route and make sure you're not charged for it.

Normal discount times—nights and weekends—aren't usually discounted when you make a direct-dial call from your room. Hotels reap the savings and keep them for themselves. Always use access numbers to get around these surcharges.

Head for pay phones to avoid per-call fees, but check to avoid inflated rates. All rates must be posted by each phone. If they're not, ask the desk for a copy, available to you by law.

> *"Always complain about outrageous telephone charges. Hotel guests are frequently charged for incomplete calls, for example. You'll get most charges removed and, at the same time, discourage price gouging. Malfunctions and limitations in computerized billing systems result in overcharges about 40 percent of the time."*

INTERNATIONAL TIPS

Callback Programs are another of technology's gifts to travelers. You are assigned a U.S. number and you specify an international callback number, which you can change as you change locations. Use it with any touchtone phone by entering the 800 number you have been assigned and hanging up after one ring. You get an immediate call back with a dial tone. Place as many calls as you like, by using the # sign between them. Your calls are billed at bulk time, discount rates.

- **Callback programs claim savings of 20-60 percent**. You can use them to call the U.S. or other foreign countries.
- **Membership programs** may have start up fees, monthly minimums and per-call charges. You must pay for the dial-in call if you are in a country that doesn't allow access to toll-free numbers, but you will still save overall.

Check out details from:

America Tele-fone –800-321-5817

Globate –770-449-1295

International Telephone –800-638-5558

Prime Call–800-698-1232

TeleGroup –800-338-0225.

Renting a cellular phone for international use may be considered a necessity by some. U.S. cellular phones will not work overseas. Specialized rental companies provide the equipment and assign you a number that is good for the duration of your trip—even for visits to multiple countries. The basic weekly rental rate is about $60-80; daily rates start at $10. Delivery charges may be waived if you rent for two weeks or more. Sources include:

Destination Europe—800-223-5555

Global Cellular Rental—800-999-3636

The Parker Company—800-280-2811

Worldwide Cellular—888-967-5323

Taxiphones are pay phones that calculate your cost based on call length and distance covered. Many countries have pay phones that charge by this method, even for local and regional calls. You will usually do better financially using your own calling card.

International telephone and telegraph offices are found in most major cities and offer competitive rates for infrequent callers. You give the number you wish to call to the clerk who places the call for you and shows you to a private booth. You pay on completion of your call.

Access English-speaking operators from 110 international destinations via programs available from AT&T, MCI and Sprint. You get a wallet-size plastic card with all access information. Call the following numbers to enroll:

AT&T's USADirect—800-331-1140

MCI's Call USA—800-444-3333

Sprint Express—800-877-7746

"Most international telephone directories have a page written in English with numbers for multilingual operators. Calling U.S. directory assistance from abroad averages over $3 per call. Carry frequently called numbers with you."

IN-FLIGHT PHONES

There are variances in the percentage of planes in major airline fleets equipped for phone and fax capabilities. American and United lead the way with 100 percent; Southwest is at 97 percent and America West is at 95 percent; Alaska Airlines is at 90 percent; Delta and Northwest are at 80 percent; TWA is at 60 percent; Continental is at 33 percent; US Airways declines to release a percentage, but is in the process of dramatically increasing availability.

GTE's Home & Office program provides 25 percent off your two most frequently called numbers. Calls to the two numbers you select will be billed at $11.25 per call, regardless of how long you talk. Enrollment is free at **800-247-3663**.

Special promotions cut the cost of in-flight calls. Always check the seat pocket for cards that promote deals like all-you-can-call promotions that offer a flat rate for the entire flight. GTE Airfone recently cut the cost of evening in-flight calls by 50 percent in a limited-time promotion we're likely to see repeated. The reduced rate was available on domestic calls placed from 7 p.m. to 7 a.m. MCI FlightLink recently offered unlimited airtime for $29 (plus tax) per flight for domestic calls.

CREATIVE WAYS TO SAVE

Renting cellular phones in the U.S. from car rental agencies and hotels seems attractive, particularly when the rental is free. Even a $5 per day charge (plus $1.75-2.50 per minute) may tempt you. Unfortunately, your liability for a lost or stolen cellular rental averages $500-800—much higher than the cost of replacing most cellular phones. Ask about special add-on insurance options when you rent. With high roaming fees disappearing, carrying your own cellular phone may turn out to be your best choice.

Some companies offer debit cellular calls, allowing you to pre-pay calling time in blocks of $20-100. If, for example, you have a college student traveling over the summer, this option can protect you against large bills while still affording basic safety and convenience features. Call American Cellular Rental at **800-381-0888** or Mitsubishi at **800-726-2777**.

Personal and business toll-free incoming numbers save money on frequent calls by sidestepping many of the fees inherent in calling from the road. The basic charge is about $15 per month and the per-minute fee averages 12 cents. You could also save a hefty access fee every time you call from phones with surcharges. You don't have to change your current long distance carrier to get toll-free service from a competitor, so shop around for the best deal. You can even get a marketing bonus on business numbers by choosing one that translates to an easy to remember word or phrase. Trying to find an available 800 number of this sort was difficult, but with the addition of the new 888 toll-free prefix, many new possibilities have opened up.

> *"Cellular phones are high on criminals' wish lists. You know you need to protect them from outright theft, but did you realize that your number can be picked up in slow-moving traffic by scanner? These thieves are tied into networks that can rack up enormous charges within hours. Protect yourself by turning your unit off when traffic slows to a crawl or ask your vendor about special line protection features. Consider a nationwide page to cut down on cellular phone costs. You can get a simple numeric pager or an alpha-numeric version that can relay about a paragraph of content. If you choose the second option, you'll need to join an answering or paging service that can transmit the text or purchase an office unit for about $250-300. Alpha-numeric pagers can eliminate as many as half the long distance calls you usually make from the road by providing you with on-the-spot information you previously had to call to get."*

TRAVEL GUIDE

Travel planning is easier and trips become more enjoyable when you know the answers to common problems and can prepare for them in advance. The first part of this chapter contains information that will help all travelers find a direct route through a maze of options. The second part offers information for special groups of travelers.

A Consumer's Guide To Travel Agents tells you how to find your most effective allies in travel. Today's travelers deserve specialists. The travel world has become too big and too changeable for one person or agency to master. We will explain how our specialist concept works, tell you how to make sure you are dealing with creative agents who explore discount options and show you how to help them get the deepest discounts for all your travel needs.

Solving Problems shows you how to eliminate trouble before it happens and how to get quick action on any travel-related complaint.

Scam Stoppers shows you how to prevent contributing to the estimated twelve billion dollars travel scammers will pocket this year. We have always hated travel scams. This year we are devoting a great deal of time and effort to stopping them in their tracks, including a special Scam Watch section at **www.bestfares.com** that stays on top of the latest ploys and the latest ways to stop scammers cold. We are going to do our best to plug the holes scammers try to poke in your pockets.

Luggage Logic details checked luggage and carry-on policies, how to deal with lost luggage, what to ask for when you're buying new luggage and tips developed by those of us who have learned how to pack effectively by trial and error.

Healthy Travel helps you to decide when medical circumstances could affect your travel plans, helps you to prepare for low stress travel and suggests methods to help your body adapt to the demands of travel.

Special Categories of Travel provides tips on seven areas of travel. Be sure to also check tips and strategies for special categories of travelers in our other chapters. Matters pertaining to air travel, for example, will be found in the *Airlines* section

- *Business Travel* provides some of the newest tips, techniques and tools that can make life on the road more pleasant and productive.
- *Solo Travel* can be one of the best ways to go if you accentuate the positive and learn trip-enhancing strategies. For those who would like travel companions, there are ideas on where to start your search.
- *Senior Travel* reminds seniors of their consumer clout, outlines standard senior savings not covered in our other chapters and looks at some unique opportunities for exceptional trips.
- *Children & Travel* can be a perfect match if you are creative and prepare yourself *and* your children. This section will give you ideas on how to make every trip more enjoyable for every family member.
- *Accessible Travel* shows you how to book with you particular needs in mind and how to make sure you are given the consideration you deserve. It also offers ideas on trips designed to accommodate travelers with various disabilities.
- *International Travel* has nuts and bolts data on passports, visas and customs. I'll also tell you how to help make language barriers disappear, how to get better deals on international trips, where to go to get shopping bargains and some general information to help you feel more in control in all cultures.
- *Travel With Animals* lets you know when you can, if you should and how to do it in ways that cause the least stress on your pet and on yourself.

A Consumer's Guide To Travel Agents

UNDERSTAND YOUR OPTIONS

Consumers are faced with new options and prices that change in the blink of a marketing department's eye. Gone are the simple days of basic fare structures and limited choices. To get the best deals today, you have to know your options.

Booking directly with vendors (airlines, hotels, cruise lines, car rental agencies and other travel suppliers) almost always costs you more money. Often they quote prices that don't reflect the best they have to offer and they very rarely tell you about a competitor's better deal. The vendors' main goal is to maximize profit. Yours should be to maximize savings. People who routinely bargain shop for other purchases too often tend to accept vendor quotes as if they were etched in stone. They're not. Accepting the first price a vendor gives you is like paying income tax without taking any deductions.

Online booking services offer a wealth of information and arrows to point you in money-saving directions, but their best use is for checking fares, special offers and shorthaul tickets that are rarely discounted. Online booking does not allow the use of discount coupons. It doesn't check alternate airports or travel dates. Using online booking will rarely result in maximum savings on ticket purchases, unless you are booking a special deal available for online booking only.

We list hundreds of deals each week on **www.bestfares.com.** We believe the best current use of the internet for travel bargains is offering consumers hundreds of deals they can book in the manner they prefer. We never underestimate the impor-

Standard commission paid to travel agents by airlines in the 1970s: 5 percent.

> *"Good travel agents are worth their weight in gold cards. When you find agents who understand what you want and are willing to work to help you get it, you've found allies who can save you hundreds or thousands of dollars every year. Treat them accordingly. For example, rather than booking a flight directly with the airline, place your reservation on hold and let your travel agent ticket for you. Letting an agent get a quick commission is a kindness that can help get you better service on more time-intensive bookings. Agents have suffered big blows from most major airlines, including a 25 percent cut in commissions. Treat the good ones right, so they can continue serving you."*

tance of a good travel agent and frequently remind online guests and subscribers to build a good working relationship with a great agent.

TRAVEL SPECIALISTS

Travel agencies come in many forms, from full service agencies to agencies that specialize in a particular form of travel or a target travel group. Many agents who rely on revenue from airline ticket sales feel as if they are being squeezed out by changes in airline policies, commission structures that favor volume sellers, the increased popularity of niche carriers and online booking. More and more full service agencies are moving to niche marketing—corporate accounts, tours or other revenue enhancers.

You deserve travel specialists because of the expansion of travel possibilities. Fifty years ago a general practitioner knew all there was to know about medicine. Now you'd never consider having an orthopedist do an organ transplant or a neurologist perform heart surgery. This theory carries through to travel. Travel specialists have intensive knowledge of their segment of the industry. Specialization allows for the knowledge and the clout which combine to offer maximum discount opportunities. Some larger agencies have created specialty areas within their companies, but that doesn't guarantee the best deal if they are still geared towards selling computer-listed or rack rates.

FULL SERVICE VS. DISCOUNT AGENCIES

Full service agencies will book all your travel needs. If price is not your primary consideration and if you require a great deal of time spent planning your trips, they provide a reasonable alternative. They are generally not the people to call to book a new low cost carrier ticket or to get the best consolidator deal on an international ticket. Weigh special services against savings. Ticket delivery is convenient, but not if it costs you creativity in ticketing and the hundreds of dollars you could save by using a discount agent. It's nice to have your customer profile information kept on file so you don't have to repeat it each time you make a purchase, but is saving three minutes worth paying more? If you opt for high service agencies, do so only after knowing the real price you'll pay for the extras.

Discount agencies focus on getting you the lowest possible rate. The lower the ticket price, the less commission they make on the sale, so they often require that you have a reasonably firm idea of what you want and are ready to book if the

Amount Marriott pays annually in travel agent commissions: over $99 million.

> *"Travel agents are expected to be the Jacks and Jills of all travel-selling trades and have knowledge of all travel needs, whether clients are heading for Tulsa or Timbuktu. Most of us have trouble remembering which gas station offers the lowest per-gallon price, but we expect travel agents to have photographic memories and instantly recall a two-for-one airfare to an alternate city or a 50 percent off car rental deal available to people who arrive on Tuesday. Dealing with specialists doesn't solve all your problems, but it does provide you with agents you can reasonably expect to have pervasive knowledge in their particular area."*

price is right. They are usually unable to hold reservations or provide a full line of services. They are not the people to ask about hotels in New Guinea or the availability of red convertibles at Atlanta car rental agencies. They concentrate on knowing the cheapest way to *get to* New Guinea, Atlanta or anywhere else on the globe. Some discount agencies (including *Best Fares* subscriber-only Travel Clubs) can ticket most reservations made with the airlines and give you a rebate. They reward your search for the lowest fare by sending you a check that reflects part of their commission. They will also check to see if they can get you a deal that is far better than the one the airline is holding for you.

CHOOSING AGENTS

You need to think creatively and so do your travel agents. Finding the right agent is as important as finding the right agency. The quality of agents within a company can vary. You want an agent able to work the system, backed by an agency that encourages them to do so.

- **You want agents who know about** alternate cities, hidden cities, back-to-backs and low cost and niche carriers; who keep up on basic promotions and scan industry publications to monitor changes and trends. You don't want agents who can't see beyond their computer screens. Many niche and low cost carriers cannot be booked on any travel agent's computer reservation system. If they do a check for the lowest available fare, these options won't even show up.
- **You want agents who sidestep "fixed" prices** in favor of the many legitimate ways to get around them—agents who *enjoy* the challenge of finding the best bargains and are given the time and training to do it.
- **You want strong agents** who either wield enough clout or have enough belief in consumers' rights to look out for your interest as well as their own. Some airlines try to intimidate agencies. Stepping out of arbitrary boundaries can cause an agency to lose its right to ticket on the offended airline. Look for agents who understand how to bend the rules while staying completely within the boundaries of legitimacy.
- **Experience counts** but creativity counts more. Fifteen years experience means little to the consumer if the agent has never learned the knack of creative ticketing or opts for the easiest booking route.
- **Let agents tell you if they can help** on a particular aspect of travel. Corporate agencies may welcome the

Top three revenue sources for travel agencies: airline tickets, 55%; tour sales, 19%; cruises, 14%.

opportunity to refer you to another source for your cruise travel, for example. Discount agencies may not want to book car rentals. Smart agencies know when their needs and yours are compatible.

MAKE YOUR NEEDS & WANTS CLEAR

Emphasize price if that is your primary consideration. Believe it or not, you can't assume any agent works from that perspective. Some travelers place price second or third on their priority list. If you have very specific needs (nonstop flights, for example, or hotel rooms with business amenities) be upfront. You can get discounts on the most luxurious modes of travel. If price matters most, tell the agent what you're willing to do to bring the price down. Will you take a connecting flight if it saves you $100? What if it saves you $300 or more? Do you favor your preferred carrier enough to pay 20 percent or even double what a competitor is offering?

> *"A recent audit indicated that corporate travel agents who favor specific airlines for their clients cost them, on average, an additional $130 per ticket."*

Let travel agents know you want value. If the standard rate for a flight is $900, tell the agent you want it for $300. You want the $200-a-night hotel for $60; the $189-a-week car rental for $89; the $2,000 cruise for half that price. Your agent may not always meet your expectations, but he or she deserves to know the type of discount that will make you happy. Good agents are motivated by the challenge inherent in locating the best deal. Do your part by identifying yourself as a value-conscious client. Share any tips or special offers you are aware of.

Ask agents how they will help you find the best deal. Will they simply check the computer for the lowest published fare? What if your best option is a niche airline, a companion ticket or a charter? Ask about creative ticketing. Will they book low cost and niche airlines, back-to-back tickets, hidden city tickets, fly/drive packages, alternate airports and so forth?

Will they check promotional offers? It isn't fair to expect an agent to know about them all. About one billion travel savings coupons are issued annually. You do want agents who are aware of major promotions and you certainly want agents who are willing to go to a little extra effort to use them. If you have an airfare discount coupon, for example, it will take the agent a few more minutes to issue your ticket and they lose commission equal to a percentage of the discount your coupon provides. On the other hand, you save $25 to $100—or possibly even the cost of a companion ticket, depending on the coupon you are using.

Don't be fooled by jargon about limited seating. Special offer and fare war seats *are* limited, but if at first you don't succeed, try, try again. There is more than one airline in most markets, and inventory can change in a moment's notice. With persistence, you can generally get the rate you want on the date you need. Many fare sale tickets are placed on hold but never purchased. Once the reservation deadline expires, the seats go back into the open availability category.

Ask about procedures on ticket prices that go down. Some agencies have computer systems or procedures to scan ticketed itineraries during fare wars and alert clients to lower prices. You will have to pay a change fee on most economy tickets, but the savings can often be many times the fee. If your agent doesn't have an automated system, don't wait to be called. The minute you hear about a fare war, call and check to see if you qualify for the lower fare.

WHAT AGENTS NEED FROM YOU

Give agents everything they need to find the deal that's best for you.

- **Encourage them to offer options** that may require some flexibility on your part. You can decide how flexible you are willing to be based on the potential savings.
- **Be clear and specific** about your travel plans including travel dates and departure and destination cities. Don't waste your time or the agent's time by asking for the lowest fare to London without specifying that you need to travel during the peak summer season. If you want your agent to be a savings sleuth, you must provide all the clues possible.
- **Relate the number of people traveling** and any eligibility you have for special fares such as senior or government rates. If you have two people traveling and request a companion fare, be aware that in almost every case you will need to book and travel together on all segments of your itinerary.
- **Fax your travel requests**, if possible. It saves time on both ends and eliminates any confusion on your travel requirements. Many agencies have forms they can supply so you can be sure you are transmitting all the information they need to begin their search for the best deal.
- **Listen carefully** when your agent recaps your travel plans. The time to catch errors is before the tickets have been issued.

CHECKING AN AGENT'S SAVVY

There are two easy ways to check an agent's savvy on ticketing options that are invisible to those who use the computer as a crutch.

- **Pick a pair of cities serviced by a low-cost or niche carrier.** Call the airline to get the lowest possible rate between those cities. Usually, picking dates less than a week in advance or dates without a Saturday stay will show the most dramatic savings over major carriers. Then call the agent and simply ask for the best fare between the two cities you've chosen. See if they offer you a low cost or niche carrier option or if they merely quote the lowest available major carrier price.
- **Check the Sunday travel section for charter flights.** MLT Tours, for example, is based in Minneapolis and offers deeply discounted last-minute fares to about 20 U.S. cities. The one-way fare to Dallas/Fort Worth can be as low as $120. We called ten agents in the Dallas area and asked for the lowest one-way fare to Minneapolis. MLT was offered only once. In our test case, using that option would have saved as much as $700 roundtrip for last minute travel.

Get bids on all your travel needs. Call several agencies and tell them what you need. Make sure to give each agent the same specifics so your rate comparisons are apples-to-apples. You'll soon see a pattern develop that will help you determine which agencies work the best for your needs.

Year in which research on the SABER travel agent reservation system began: 1953.

Check the reputation of travel agents locally. Ask friends and colleagues for recommendations. You can check with the Better Business Bureau and travel agency organizations to weed out really bad agencies. Keep in mind that bad news can travel slowly, and never completely rely on clean bills of health from these organizations.

WHAT AGENCIES CANNOT DO FOR YOU

Agents do not have the power to alter or waive airline rules. Just like you, they have to ask for special exemptions to standard policies. Avoid potential problems by listening carefully to terms and conditions. If your agent does not tell you about refund policies, ticketing deadlines and other pertinent facts, be sure to ask. Travel agencies do not set airline policies. Each airline has its own restrictions and rules. Surprisingly, an airline is generally more apt to extend special favors when asked directly by a passenger than if the travel agent tries to intercede on a passenger's behalf.

Travel agents aren't mind readers. Give them your feedback, both positive and negative. If they fail to find the lowest price, let them know. Don't hold agents liable for failing to find the lowest rates unless you are sure that is where the fault actually lies.

Some agencies extend special courtesies to favored customers. The 24-hour ticketing deadline, for example, can be stretched to the agency's weekly ticket reporting deadline. These sorts of favors are technically violations of their agreements with the airlines so they should never be demanded or expected as routine.

SERVICE FEES

Many travel agency services are free. When the airlines capped commissions, many of the over 35,000 U.S. travel agencies began discussing when and if they should charge service fees on high-effort, low-commission services. Last year domestic airlines saved $630 million through limiting commission on a single domestic ticket to $50, rather than the approximate ten percent that was customary. Then, most major airlines cut commissions from ten to eight percent. For many agencies, that 25 percent represented their profit. As a result, many agencies are focusing on vacation packages and cruises, where commissions have not been capped. A great many others have turned to fees, usually starting at $10 per ticket, and varying by the type of service provided. It has reached the point where we cannot fault agencies for charging service fees, providing they come up with deals. *Best Fares* Air Travel Clubs, with negotiated deals and very high volume, do not charge service fees. We plan to continue offering that perk to our subscribers as long as *Best Fares* exists.

COMMISSION OVERRIDES & VENDOR PREFERENCE

Commission overrides encourage some agencies to steer you to a particular vendor. They occur when a vendor agrees to increase the commission percentage paid to an agency if a certain dollar amount is sold within a given period of time, or if the past sales record is good. It can be very tempting for an agency to try to steer clients to that vendor. They may even imply that their preferred carrier's price is the lowest when, in fact, it is identical to (maybe even higher than) competitors. Every agency wants to maximize

Why the reservation system SABER became SABRE: an executive liked a Buick LeSabre ad.

its profit, but, in this case, it's at your expense. A commission override works to your advantage only if you're getting the best deal or if some of the increased commissions are passed on to you.

Vendors also offer incentive programs to agencies. They are usually limited to specific time periods and may provide an increased commission percentage, a bonus point system with points redeemable for gifts or a lowered travel agent cost (book ten clients with one car rental company, for example, and get a $10-day rate the next time the agent rents). Most good agents will not sacrifice your money for a small reward. Your continued business is more important to them. If you sense that an agent is really steering you toward a particular vendor, ask why and make sure you are satisfied with the reasons given.

Agents may tell you about one company's special offer and neglect to mention competitors because they've just been visited by a sales rep and a particular deal is foremost in their minds. Always ask if competitors are offering equal or better deals. Most vendors are very good at playing follow the leader.

PROBLEMS WITH AGENTS

Even the best agents and agencies can sometimes have you reaching for the aspirin bottle. (It's a two way street, many agents would claim.) Agents and agencies who care about professionalism and the results they provide to clients are always willing to explain any confusion and to rectify a situation if they are clearly at fault.

Do your part by understanding the rules. If, for example, you ask an agent to hold a reservation for 24-hours and the airline raises the fare, there is nothing the agent can do. The promise was made in good faith. Usually reserved fares are not increased. When it happens, most travelers feel anger toward the agent who had no control over the situation. On the other hand, if an agent tells you a fare will be good for several days and you call back the next day to find out that it has increased, you have a legitimate complaint. Wise agents never guarantee a fare until it is booked.

If you have a complaint, talk to the agent and try to resolve the problem. If you are not satisfied, go to the owner or manager. Give them a chance to explain and correct the situation. Be clear that your repeat business is contingent on the satisfaction they provide.

If you're still not satisfied, contact the airline or vendor the agent used. They are usually very willing to try to straighten out problems that involve their companies.

If you still need help, the Better Business Bureau or a consumer affair's office may serve as your advocate. You can also contact the office of the travel association the agency in question is affiliated with.

- **American Society of Travel Agents**, 1101 Kings Street, #200, Alexandria, VA 22314. Call **703-739-2782**.
- **Association of Retail Travel Agents**, 501 Darby Creek Road, Suite 47, Lexington, KY 40509. Call **717-545-9548**.
- **International Airlines Travel Agent Network**, 300 Garden City Plaza, Suite 342, Garden City, NJ 11530; call **516-747-4716**.
- **Institute of Certified Travel Agents**, P. O. Box 081059, Wellesley, MA 02181-0012. Call **617-237-0280**.

Money TWA spent to develop its first reservation system (nicknamed "George"): $75 million.

TRAVEL-AGENTS-IN-A-BOX

> *"These fraudulent card mills have begun to target corporate travelers with a pyramid scheme version of the standard card mill scam. They promise lower corporate travel costs in exchange for purchasing instant certification and continuing to sign-up new members."*

There is no such thing as an instant travel agent. Scam artists sell instant "certification" for $495. The bait is the offer of discounted travel, an amount just under the $500 figure that would subject them to greater fraud penalties. Some require a minimum amount of bookings to maintain travel agent status. That spells trouble not only for the person who falls for the deal but also for consumers who try to book travel through untrained people. Others don't care if you ever book. They simply want your $495. No matter how attractive the offer, never pay for "instant certification." If you are doing so in hopes of accessing travel agent discounts, be aware that vendors have set up additional requirements that you are not likely to be able to meet. For more details, check the *Scam Stoppers* section of this chapter.

OUTSIDE AGENTS

It's important to differentiate between travel-agents-in-a-box and legitimate outside agents. If you respond to an ad or visit a new agency, how can you tell the difference?

- **Reputable outside agents** are usually affiliated with local travel agencies. They work under a shared commission arrangement.
- **Ask if the agent or agency does its own ticketing.** Agencies that issue tickets must be bonded. If the tickets come from a secondary source, ask who will be issuing them and where they are located. If it is anywhere other than in your hometown, your suspicions should be aroused. This rule applies to major airline tickets only. Consolidator and tour tickets routinely come from out-of-state sources.
- **Ask the outside agent why** he or she prefers to work outside of an agency structure. Some people thrive on the independence and the commission-based structure (most agents who work for agencies receive salaries or an hourly wage). If you are not satisfied with the answer you get, go elsewhere. You could be encountering a gem of an agent for package travel or you could end up with a travel-agent-in-a-box who is simply trying to meet a sales quota with no real consideration for the service being rendered.
- **Some independent agents** offer very personalized service on tours and cruises—big buck items for which they may receive premium commissions. Unless they are affiliated with a mega-agency that can negotiate great deals, they are not able to wheel and deal on prices. You may find that one of the best uses of an independent agent is booking last minute tour company specials that hit newspaper travel sections on Sunday morning. Many of these packages can only be booked through travel agents. The independent agent that remains open on weekends can book your sale package on Sunday, before most agencies open.

Then-TWA executive who pulled the plug on the development of "George": Robert Crandall.

SOLVING PROBLEMS

WHEN & HOW TO COMPLAIN

You know it is time to complain when you have been treated with excessive rudeness, lost money or did not receive what you were promised.

Isolate your complaint. What did you expect and what were you given instead? Mentioning unrelated details can confuse the situation and make your cause less sympathetic. Stay calm and in control.

Complain when the problem occurs. The situation may be resolved on the spot. Airline customer service representatives, for example, have authority to arrange meals and accommodations for stranded passengers, endorse tickets to other carriers, approve vouchers for bumped passengers, arrange for the repair of airline-damaged luggage, and issue taxi, meal and drink vouchers as they deem reasonable.

Set a goal. Do you want reimbursement or credit against future travel? (A credit for future travel is worthless if the service was so bad that you never want to use the vendor again.) Do you want a rude person censured or an ignorant person educated? Do you think a major policy change is in order?

Find out if you have legal rights or if resolution relies on the good will of the supplier. Clear legal violations allow for adamant behavior. Negotiable situations call for charm and the reiteration of your value to the vendor.

Go to a person who has the power to help. Don't jump too high in the chain of command unless it becomes necessary. Try to make the person with whom you are dealing see the reasonableness of your complaint. If you don't get results, go to the next level and keep going until you reach someone who satisfies your complaint.

Phone complaints can be effective, particularly with simple complaints to smaller companies. Many large companies and most governmental regulatory agencies insist that complaints be made in written form. Many companies that accept complaints by phone, often end up asking you to submit the details in writing. If it is worth complaining about, it is worth the time it takes to write a letter.

LETTERS OF COMPLAINT

The most effective letters of complaint follow this format:

- **Letters should be typewritten,** contain your daytime phone number and be as close to one-page in length as possible. Include clear copies of any pertinent documentation. Do not send originals.
- **Begin with the positive** to establish that you are viewing the situation in perspective.
- **Describe what happened** and suggest a remedy. If additional travelers were involved, note the number of people affected by the problem.
- **Include any possible indication** of your worth to the company such as your frequent flyer number, preferred guest number or the times per year you use the vendor.
- **Address your letter appropriately.** Decide if you want to send it to the customer service department or a company executive. It is usually worth a phone call to get the information you need.

If you get a form letter or an unsatisfactory response in return, send a follow-up letter by certified mail. Set a response deadline. If the issue involves a great deal of money, you may want to copy the letter and the initial response to an appropriate consumer organization or draft a letter for your attorney to send on his or her letterhead. The fee is usually nominal.

UNRESOLVED COMPLAINTS

Some situations demand persistence. If your letter(s) of complaint did not provide resolution, you are left with several options.

- **Accept the situation as a learning experience.** This only makes sense when the damage done is small enough to make you consider that spending any more time on the matter would be pointless.
- **Small claims courts** can give you a favorable judgment, but you have to make sure your case falls within the court's jurisdiction and monetary guidelines. You cannot file in small claims court against a company located in another area. If your claim is accepted, realize that judgments can be difficult to enforce.
- **The effectiveness of the Better Business Bureau (BBB)** varies greatly. Some people say it's a paper tiger and others predicate their consumer choices on BBB advisories. Its power is usually limited to the negative report it can relay to future consumers who call for information. It rarely helps you acquire monetary compensation. It is most effective on complaints directed at local businesses that rely heavily on a steady flow of new customers. They are the companies most likely to be

affected by a negative BBB report.

- **Parent organizations, governmental agencies and consumer groups** are three of the most effective second-level complaint avenues. If the company with which you have a complaint is a subsidiary of a larger corporation, the corporation is likely to have more refined complaint-resolving skills. Governmental and consumer agencies can take advocacy positions for consumers. A query on the letterhead of your state's attorney general will attract the attention of even the most complaint-resistant company.
- **Contact the advertiser** who led you to the vendor or the special offer. Even though they have no liability, they will pay attention to a complaint pattern and may deny future advertising rights.

WHERE TO COMPLAIN

Complaints about air carriers, hotels and car rental services should be made to the appropriate consumer affairs office of that carrier, chain or company. A complete listing can be found in *Know Who To Contact.*

If you have not received satisfaction by direct complaint to the company with whom you did business, check the consumer allies listed at the end of *Scam Stoppers*. The contact information is valid for service complaints as well as claims of fraud and other injury. Other contacts include:

- **Air safety issues**—The Federal Aviation Administration, 800 Independence Ave. SW, Washington, DC 20591; call **800-322-7873**.
- **Canadian air travel issues**—The National Transportation Agency, 15 Eddy St., Hull, Quebec K1AON9; call **819-953-9151**.
- **Amtrak**—Customer Relations, 60 Massachusetts Ave. NE, Washington, DC 20002; call **800-872-7245**..
- **Cruise health conditions**—The Center for Disease Control, 1015 N. American Way, Room 107, Miami, FL 33132.
- **Cruise safety**—For serious problems during a cruise, go to the U.S. Coast Guard office in the first port city. For general complaints, write to the U. S. Coast Guard, 2100 W. 2nd St. SW, Washington, DC 20593.

Consumers Resource Handbooks are available from most county and state governments. Check the blue pages of your telephone directory. Also check *Know Who To Contact* for helpful numbers.

The Consumer Federation of America, 202-387-6121, offers *How to Resolve Your Consumer Complaint*. Send a stamped, self-addressed envelope to: Consumer Complaint Brochure, P. O. Box 12099, Washington, DC 20005.

PREVENTING PROBLEMS

Tickets should be guarded as carefully as you guard your cash. If you lose your ticket, you will, at the least, be inconvenienced. You may also have to purchase a replacement and wait weeks or months for compensation for your lost ticket. Ticketless travel, now being offered by almost every airline, is a great safety measure for consumers. If you choose a paper ticket always observe the following procedures.

- **Have your tickets delivered** to a secure location, preferably where someone can sign for their delivery. Tickets left in a mailbox all day may never reach your hands. Ask when to expect your tickets and call immediately if they don't arrive as scheduled.

- **Photocopy tickets immediately** or record the ticket numbers in a safe place.
- **If your tickets are stolen**, make a police report to strengthen your case when you file a lost ticket form.
- **Report any ticket loss or theft** immediately to the company that issued the tickets. Airlines, for example, have increased their ability to alert gate agents to watch for stolen tickets. You want to do all within your power to assure that the stolen ticket is not used since reimbursement may depend on it or be contingent on establishing that you did not authorize its illicit use.
- **Policies on lost or stolen tickets** vary. You usually must fill out a lost ticket application. If, for example, an airline believes it can effectively block use of your original ticket (international tickets are most secure) it may issue a replacement ticket for a nominal fee. Policies, detailed by airline, are in the first chapter of this book.

SOLVING HOTEL PROBLEMS ON THE SPOT

When your hotel room isn't up to par, you have several options.

- **If the room doesn't meet your specifications** but is generally acceptable (queen bed instead of king, for example), advise the front desk that you will accept the room if you are compensated with a discount or a perk, such as a free massage at the hotel's health club.
- **If the problem is easily remedied**, such as a room that has not been given good turnover service, demand that the problem be remedied within a time frame that's acceptable and request a free drink or meal while you wait. A little charm mixed in with your demand won't hurt.
- **If the problem is major**, demand another room. Malfunctioning heat or air conditioning that cannot be quickly remedied, a room next to a convention's hospitality suite or other serious defects should be resolved by a transfer to an acceptable room. With luck, the alternate room may be an upgrade provided to you at standard room rate.
- **Some hotels guarantee satisfaction,** or your stay is free. They advertise their policies as a means to assure you of their emphasis on guest satisfaction. Most hotels try to make you happy without surrendering all revenue from your stay. We think the refund should fit the circumstance, no matter what the official policy is.

SCAM STOPPERS

THE $12 BILLION INDUSTRY

Travel fraud puts $12 billion in criminals' pockets each year. Because so much money is at stake, scammers put a lot of time and effort into perfecting their pitches and producing legitimate-appearing certificates, advertising and other documents. Some scams are relatively transparent; others are sophisticated. All types of people can be scammed. This section will help you avoid being one of them.

As new laws are enacted to fight travel fraud, the incidence of travel scams continues to increase. In Florida, for example, there was a 54 percent jump in consumer complaints from 1995 to 1996, and the numbers are still rising. This type of negative growth means that we must be more vigilant than ever. Don't let your guard down. Support new legislation by reporting any suspected incident of travel fraud. If you are asked to testify in a travel fraud case, take the time to do it. We have to drive home the message that these new laws have teeth and the bite will go deep.

HOW SCAMMERS STRIKE

Marketing research isn't the sole province of legitimate salespeople. Crooks do market research too. Many scams start out on a hit or miss basis, with mass telemarketing, faxes or mailouts. If and when you respond, they play to your

Laptop computers stolen each year in the U.S.: over 200,000.

vulnerabilities as they try to reel you in.

- **Scammers want to make you feel special.** They say you won a prize, then attach a hefty handling charge. They pretend to offer you a special price or reduce the first quote, sometimes even following a script in which they pretend to ask their supervisor for a special favor.
- **Scammers want you to decide immediately.** They want to rob you of the time you might spend researching their deal or thinking over its terms. They say their offer is only available for a brief period when it is actually available until the police come knocking on their door.
- **Scammers obscure the truth.** They tell you their offer is free or quote a ridiculously low price for a hotel stay, contingent on your purchasing expensive airfare. When you are asked to pay a processing fee, watch out. Scammers use them to jack-up their low quotes to the price they have intended you to pay all along—full price or worse.
- **Scammers hide essential facts.** They offer two-for-one-deals that are based on grossly inflated rates for the first traveler. They refuse to reveal significant details, often requiring you to come to their office for a special presentation or send money for mail-out material.

TIP-OFFS TO SCAMS

Here are some signs that should tip you off to a potential scam, whether it arrives by phone, fax, mail or internet.

- **If a deal sounds too good to be true,** it probably is. There are real bargains out there, but they rarely come your way by unsolicited marketing.
- **If you are asked to name several acceptable travel dates**, beware. It makes the deal sound as if it is in high demand. It actually means the con is buying time. If you do get any of your choices (an unlikely prospect), a long list of surcharges and extra fees will suddenly apply or you will have booked far enough in the future to give the scammer time to get out of town.
- **You are asked to pay a lot of money** to purchase "bargain" vacations for a five or ten year period. You have no assurance the company will be around for a month—much less several years. Legitimate travel suppliers do not generally guarantee rates more than 12 to 18 months in advance.
- **You are offered membership in a high-fee travel club** that supposedly will give you access to unbelievable deals. Many people pay thousands of dollars each only to find out that the discounts are not as advertised. *Best Fares* subscribers get free membership in five discount travel clubs and we

> *"Many scams are not obvious at first. A trusted friend or relative may unwittingly refer you to a scam artist. They think they are passing along a great deal. When either of you actually try to take your trip, the rip-off becomes apparent. Word-of-mouth referral can be one of the most reliable recommendations there is—but be sure the person who referred you isn't just repeating the attractive bait they swallowed."*

> *"A Dallas man sent several mass fax transmissions to businesses claiming that he had two weeks to sell packages of three airline deals. For $4.70 you would allegedly receive a certificate valid for a free roundtrip ticket on a major (unnamed) airline, plus two airfare discount certificates. He always claimed to have a very limited number of these certificate packages but the number changed frequently. Sometimes it went up; sometimes it went down. In reality, the number of fake certificates he could offer was only limited by the number of sheets of paper in his copy machine. If you responded, you were given travel dates six months in advance plenty of time for this guy to disappear. The scam was stopped and he went to prison, but no one recovered a penny of the money they sent him."*

will lay you odds that our prices are better than any offered by these high-dollar membership clubs.

- **You are asked to pay by cash or check**. Scammers can take your money and run without worrying about a possible chargeback from your credit card company when your travel deal falls through.
- **The travel vendors are not named.** Any legitimate offer will clearly spell out the name of the airlines, hotels and other travel suppliers who will deliver on the deal. If you call the vendors, they will verify their participation.
- **You are given a list of "satisfied customers"** who will verify the authenticity of the deal. Scammers hire people to answer these phones and tell you whatever you want to hear. These 'plants' are adept at making the deal sound irresistible.

SCAMS BY PHONE

Scam artists who work by phone are as friendly as talk show hosts and as sincere as bogus used car salespeople. They ask about your health, chat about the weather and try to keep you on the line long enough to make their pitch.

The Telemarketing Sales Rule was passed in reaction to the profile ration of scams by phone. It enacted federal legislation that includes the following provisions:

- **Telemarketers may only call** between 8 a.m. and 9 p.m. If you ask them never to call again, they must comply.
- **They must provide, in writing,** all details concerning any direct withdrawal from your bank accounts. We advise that you decline any direct withdrawal option, even with the most carefully worded assurances, unless you know the company you are dealing with.
- **They may not ask you for payment** in any form unless they have told you the total cost of the goods or services in advance.
- **They may not misrepresent or mislead you** in any way concerning the offer they are making.
- **They must offer** the name of the company for which they are calling.
- **If a prize is offered,** it must be stated that there is no purchase necessary to claim it.

> *"My mother once received a call asking her to participate in a survey. She asked what type of survey she was being asked to take. The caller responded by asking if my mother was between the ages of 60 and 80. My mother replied, "Oh, the scam age." The caller quickly hung up. Seniors are a major target market for travel scams. They often have a higher percentage of disposable income and the free time needed for travel. Often telemarketers will call repeatedly in an attempt to make the person feel as if they have a friend who would not possibly cheat them. Be a smart cookie, like my mother, and save yourself a lot of time and a lot of money."*

SCAMS BY INTERNET

Every innovation opens the door to good *and* bad. The internet is no exception. Some scams are high-tech recyclings of scams that have been in operation for years. Others are new ways to take your money with the speed of a mouse click. Online scams will snowball as more and more people become regular internet users—unless we all exercise vigilance, follow some common-sense rules and share the news of any scam that crosses our screens. Use the same precautions you use when making purchases through more traditional means, and follow these tips.

- **Transmit your credit card number** only if you are using a secure service. Never disclose passwords or credit card account information on any interactive site unless you know where the information is going.
- **If you are unfamiliar with the company**, do some background checking before you invest any money with them.
- **Don't trust the references** a site gives you. They could lead to partners in crime eager to give you whatever false assurances you require. Verify the authenticity of deals by going to the vendor. If you're being offered a deal on Continental Airlines, for example, the promoter should be able to give you a coupon code that you can verify directly with the airline.
- **Don't rely on chat-room testimonials.** Scammers will place paid plants in chat-rooms as a source of advertising.
- **Beware of disguised advertising** formatted to resemble an information site.
- **If you suspect an internet scam,** report it to all appropriate agencies and to your internet provider.
- **Order *Online Scams*** from the Consumer Information Center, Department 377C, Pueblo, CO 81009. Request info by e-mail with the message "send info" to **cic.info@pueblo.gas.gov**.

BASIC SCAM STOPPERS

Before you make any travel purchase from an unknown company, you should know the following information.

- **The company's full name**, street address (not P.O. Box) and phone number other than an 800 number.
- **The bank** that holds the company's escrow account.
- **Policies on changes** and cancellations, in writing.

State that staffs its visitor information lines with prison inmates: North Carolina.

- **Which vendor** (airline, hotel, etc.) you are booking. If you have any doubt, call them directly (acquire the number on your own) and confirm all details.
- **What is included** in the price you are quoted. Does it include all taxes, port charges and handling fees?

Write your own scam insurance policy by paying attention to all the clues these crooks provide. Refuse to give your credit card number over the phone unless you have placed the call to a business you know to be legitimate. Never agree to overnight a check. You could stop payment but why go through the bother and the expense? There is usually no good reason to pay for travel with anything other than a major credit or charge card. Comparison shop. If you are quoted a tempting price, call a travel agent or call the vendors direct. Any good deal will stand up to comparison shopping.

CALLBACK NUMBER SCAMS

Nine hundred numbers are not toll-free. A postcard claims you have won a prize and instructs you to call a 900 number to claim it. Your next phone bill contains charges of $3.99 per minute. If the spiel was good enough to keep you on the line for ten minutes (and it usually is) you end up paying $40 for something that is usually worth a couple of dollars.

> *“If you get a message to call an 800 number to claim a prize, ignore that too. Often you are switched to a 900 line without your knowledge and end up paying through the nose.”*

A cross-border scam growing in popularity sends you a page or an urgent phone message. You call the number back and end up being hit with a hefty phone charge for the “privilege” of listening to the scammer's spiel. You may even remain connected after you hang up. The scammer uses the open connection to place high-dollar long distance calls. The phone company might forgive the charges if your teenager called a 900 number without your knowledge, but so far they have not been very cooperative in waiving these international phone scam fees.

Here is a list of area codes from Canada and the Caribbean that have often been used in this scam. We've listed them in numerical order for ease in pinpointing the location of the area code you have been given.

204 Manitoba
242 Bahamas
245 Cayman Islands
246 Barbados
264 Anguilla
268 Antigua and Barbuda
284 British Virgin Islands
306 Saskatchewan
403 Alberta
416 Toronto
418 Quebec
441 Bermuda
473 Grenada
506 New Brunswick
514 Montreal
604 British Columbia
613 Ottawa
664 Montserrat

Two of the over 400 species of birds in Trinidad: purple honeycreepers and white-bellied antbirds.

706 Ontario

709 Newfoundland

758 St. Lucia

767 Dominica

784 St. Vincent and the Grenadines

809 The Dominican Republic

819 Quebec

868 Trinidad and Tobago

869 St. Kitts and Nevis

876 Jamaica

902 Nova Scotia

SPECIAL EVENT PACKAGES

It happened during the Olympic Games in Atlanta. It happened at the Rose Bowl, Super Bowl and at so many sports events that you might as well be purchasing a trip to the Scam Bowl. Most package vacations are legitimate, but high-demand events provide exactly what a scammer needs to score—travelers who want the "impossible" deal. People who wouldn't think of booking a trip to Las Vegas or Cancun with an unknown company will take chances when they are dying to see their favorite team play in the big game. Scammers may imply that their packages include event tickets when they do not.

The Department of Transportation (DOT) adopted new rules on December 7, 1994, applying to any tour or charter package that includes tickets to any special event. Bowl games are included, as are other sporting events and cultural, educational, religious, social or political events of specific duration and requiring admission tickets.

- **A special event tour may not be advertised unless** the company has sufficient tickets in hand or on order to meet the needs of a substantial number of purchasers.
- **Packages may not be sold until** the tickets are in hand or under contract to guarantee one to the purchaser.
- **If you purchase a package** and the promised event ticket is not delivered, you have the right to a full refund (without penalty) unless you specifically agree to allow the operator to retain your money until more tickets can be purchased.
- **If the package price increases** more than ten percent after you book, you may cancel and receive a full refund (without penalty). The price may not increase within ten- days of departure.

There are legitimate specialty agencies that arrange and book special event packages. You may be able to purchase better tickets and cheaper travel independently. A good travel agency is an invaluable asset. They can check out separate deals. They can also tell you if a package company has been in existence for a decent length of time and has provided satisfactory service.

Get all details on any tour operator in writing, including information on escrow accounts and financial accountability. Don't be lulled into a false sense of security just because you are purchasing your package through a school or sports organization. Several years ago the University of Wisconsin's trip to the Rose Bowl was marred because of fraudulent travel packages. The University of Wisconsin has high academic standards, but they are not in the travel business and were as vulnerable to a smooth-talker as any member of the general public.

Average number of days per year when the sun shines in Tampa: 361.

TIME-SHARE SCAMS

There are legitimate time-share offers but the field is also full of false promises. After sitting through a tedious seminar on the joys of owning a time-share you were never even interested in, you get your hotel vouchers and discover that you are staying at the Pit O'Hell Motel three dusty miles from the beachfront you were hoping to enjoy.

You may get a postcard offering a great deal on a trip while failing to even mention the fact that a time-share pitch is involved.

STOLEN TICKET SCAMS

A former American Airlines ticket agent was convicted of selling stolen airline tickets. The warning signs of stolen ticket scams are obvious in the way he operated:

- **He sold vastly under-priced tickets.** No legitimate ticket-seller can get you a First Class, 2,000-mile roundtrip for $250.
- **He sold tickets for cash.** The sale of airline tickets is highly regulated. Anyone who is afraid of leaving a paper trail probably has something to hide.
- **He sold tickets out of a local sports bar** to customers, including members of the Dallas Cowboys. Legitimate tickets are sold from legitimate offices.

If you are tempted to try to make your multi-million dollar (or far more modest) salary stretch by purchasing stolen tickets, keep in mind that knowingly receiving stolen property can be a felony. If you try to fly on a stolen ticket you could be stopped at the gate and put in the precarious position of proving your innocence.

MISLEADING ADS

"Free" vacation certificates are sometimes offered in promotions sponsored by reputable stores. For example: a jewelry store offers a "free airfare" honeymoon certificate to engaged couples purchasing wedding rings. They believe they are giving their customers something special, but they are actually exposing them to a bait & switch tactic. Maybe the airfare is contingent on purchasing an overpriced hotel package. Maybe the available dates on the airfare are so limited that high "surcharges" come into play. Reputable companies do give travel discounts away with many types of purchases, but you should always recognize the name of the vendor and confirm details before you buy.

Travel Rebaters often deliver your rebate only after you have jumped through a hoop of requirements. They know that a high percentage of travelers will never see the process through. Most common is the request that you mail your boarding pass and a copy of your receipt. Banking on the fact that most of us are not as organized as Felix Unger, they know that this task might get put off until the rebate deadline expires. Check all requirements of any rebate offer (and get them in writing) before putting any part of your nest egg in a rebate club's basket.

> *"Best Fares subscribers belong to an Instant Rebate Club set up with these frustrations in mind. Our subscribers receive an instant rebate check with their travel documents. In many cases, it is equal to four percent of the pre-tax price. In some special promotions, the rebate can go up to seven percent."*

Number of high-tech pay toilets installed on the streets of San Francisco 19.

Other forms of misleading advertising include airlines advertising one-way rates available only if you purchase a roundtrip ticket, hotels that advertise double rooms using a per person rate (a $69 room is really $138) and tour operators who advertise packages as cheaper than air alone, but base their comparisons on ticket prices that are rarely used by savvy travelers.

SCAMS FOR THE PLASTIC AGE

We love their convenience. Credit cards, ATM cards and other forms of abstract money have made life more convenient for us—and also for crooks.

- **When traveling, carry only as many credit cards as necessary.** Some people travel with eight or more cards. The more you have, the more you have to lose.
- **Be very discrete** when you enter your ATM or phone card Personal Identification Number (PIN) in public places. Crooks who steal these numbers are so plentiful that they have their own name—shoulder surfers.
- **Safeguard all receipts** that have your account number on them. This includes airline ticket stubs. If they fall into the wrong hands, they could be used to make fraudulent cards or to order purchases over the phone.
- **Report loss or theft of cards immediately.** If your card has been stolen, you may be required to file a police report (which can usually be done over the phone). Record credit card account numbers and the phone numbers to call if your cards are lost or stolen.
- **Check your monthly statements** as soon as they arrive for charges you did not make. Thieves do not need a card in hand to make the most of your money.

> *"Travelers on lengthy trips should arrange to have someone trustworthy check their bank and credit card statements monthly. Anyone who knows you will be gone for awhile can manipulate your accounts, since most banks have a 90-day limit on disputing withdrawals and checks. Credit card dispute limits vary by issuing bank."*

- **Never write your credit card number on checks.** In most states it is unlawful for businesses to require it as a condition of check acceptance.
- **Do not answer requests for personal information** over the phone (your Social Security Number or your mother's maiden name, for example). Crooks can use the information to apply for credit in your name or steal your identity by obtaining and using your birth certificate.

SCAMMERS WITH AN ACCENT

Currency Conversion Scams include slight-of-hand-held-calculator tricks. You are asked how much money you would like converted. The clerk reaches for a calculator and deftly pre-programs a fraudulent amount (one that sounds plausible but is lower than the amount you should be receiving) in the memory function. The calculator is placed on the counter and the clerk proceeds with a calculation you observe. You think the clerk is doing the

Increase in the average per acre price of nearby land when Disney World opened: times 65.

math properly but instead of hitting the "=" button he hits the memory button, bringing up the pre-entered amount. The buttons may be so worn that you have no way of knowing he made the switch. If you question the number, the clerk may let you use the calculator to do the equation, but tell you the memory button is the "=" button. To avoid falling for this scam, check two different quantities of money. If the calculator comes up with the same answer for both equations you'll know it has been rigged.

Renegade cabbies are a problem in many countries. If you arrive without a hotel reservation a "helpful" cabbie can offer to find a reasonably priced room. He takes you to a series of hotels, ducks inside and comes out each time reporting that the hotel is full. The meter is ticking all the while. You may actually end up with an inexpensive room, but if you add in the high taxi meter fare, you probably could have stayed at the Ritz for the total amount you paid.

People offering help to travelers are sometimes just hoping to help themselves to your property. If you use a locker to store your luggage during a layover, be cautious of anyone who offers to help you. A thief can switch keys and hand you one that is useless, making off with the key to the goods. Thieves like a long getaway window. Your layover provides the perfect opportunity. When you use a locker, secure your belongings yourself.

Self proclaimed travelers' helpers frequent tourist spots and offer deals that are hard to resist. They ask for up-front payment and never return with the promised goods. Scams include claiming they can get a low hotel rate available only to citizens of their country. You wait in the cafe while they purportedly book and pay for the room. They never return.

Not all attractions come with admission prices, but enterprising scammers count on your unfamiliarity with an area to make you think otherwise. Head for Egypt to view the pyramids, for example, and you may encounter scammers collecting fees (there are no fees charged to view the pyramids). Similar scams are run in countries where local economies facilitate black and gray market activities. Check out internet information on destination cities or stop by a bookstore or library and check out guidebooks that give practical tourist information.

CONSUMER ADVOCATES

Three states enacted "Seller of Travel" laws during the last three months of 1996. In all cases the annual fee paid by the travel seller ($100-325) goes to fighting travel scams. The new legislation only protects state residents. It's a step in the right direction, but we need to go further.

California—Anyone selling air or sea transportation must register. The law is in effect until January 1, 1999.

Oregon—Anyone selling air, sea or land transportation for more than $50 must register and maintain a $10,000 bond.

Washington—Any direct seller of travel must register and deposit all client money in a trust account.

States vary in their overall consumer protection laws. California has been in the forefront of consumer activism, but other states are catching up. We have recently seen great efforts from states including Florida, Illinois, Pennsylvania and Texas. The Federal Trade Commission is becoming more aggressive in fighting travel scams. If you suspect a travel scam or have been victimized by one, contact the attorney general in your home state and in the state from which the scam operates.

U.S. towns with names the same as presidential surnames: Clinton (25) & Madison (18).

OTHER CONSUMER ALLIES		
ORGANIZATION & ADDRESS	**PHONE/FAX/NET**	**SERVICES OFFERED**
The Department of Transportation Office of Consumer Affairs 400 7th St. SW, Room 4107 Washington, DC 20590	202-366-2220 www.dot.gov.	Monitors fraudulent advertising regarding air travel.
The Aviation Consumer Action Project P.O. Box 19029 Washington, DC 20036	202-638-4000 Fax: 202-638-0746	All consumer airline issues and lobbying efforts.
The American Hotel and Motel Association 1201 New York Ave. NW, Suite 600 Washington, DC 20005	202-289-3100 Fax: 202-289-3199 www.ahma.com:80	Will mediate disputes if you have first contacted the management of the hotel in question and (if need be) the corporate office of the hotel's chain.
The American Resort Development Association 1220 L St. NW, 5th Floor Washington, DC 20005	202-371-6700 Fax: 202-289-8544 www.ari.net:80/arda.	Comprised of time-share sellers who operate under a stringent code of ethics. Free tips to help you avoid potential time-share scams.
The Federal Maritime Commission Office of Informal Inquiries and Complaints 800 N. Capitol St. NW Washington, DC 20573	202-523-5807 Fax: 202-523-0014	Monitors the solvency of cruise lines sailing from U.S. ports and will assist you if you are having trouble receiving settlement for injuries on board any cruise ship embarking from U.S. ports.
The American Society of Travel Agents Consumer Affairs Department 1101 King St., Suite 200 Alexandria, VA 22314	703-739-2782 Fax: 703-684-8319 www.ASTAnet.com.	Mediates travel agencies disputes involving members only. They also keep files on complaints regarding non-member agencies and offer free consumer brochures.
The U.S. Tour Operators Association 342 Madison Ave., Suite 1522 New York, NY 10173	212-599-6599 Fax:212-599-6744 www.ustoa.com. e-mail: ustoa@aol.com	Free consumer information on avoiding fraudulent tour packages. Also makes referrals to companies who abide by certified escrow account procedures.

Total annual global spending on tourism by national governments: over $1.2 billion.

OTHER CONSUMER ALLIES		
ORGANIZATION & ADDRESS	**PHONE/FAX/NET**	**SERVICES OFFERED**
Chief Postal Inspector of the U.S. Postal Service 475 L'Enfant Plaza SW Washington, DC 20260	202-268-2000	National contact point for victims of mail fraud. Also notify your local postal inspector.
Federal Communication Commission Informal Complaints and Public Inquiries Branch Mail Stop Code 1600 A2 Washington, DC 20554	202-418-1500 www.fcc.gov.	Investigate excessive phone charge or surcharge complaints. Offers a free brochure, *Know The Phone Facts Before You Hit The Road.*
Call for Action 5272 River Rd., Suite 300 Bethesda, MD 20816	800-647-1756	A consumer advocacy group that assists victims of fraud.
The National Fraud Information Center P.O. Box 65868 Washington, DC 20590	800-876-7060 www.fraud.org	Free brochures including *Telemarketing Travel Fraud* and *Telephone Scams and Older Consumers.* Consumer hotline operates weekdays from 8 a.m. to 5 p.m. EST.
The U.S. Office of Consumer Affairs 750 17th St. NW, Suite 600 Washington, DC 20006	800-664-4435	A White House office that will intervene on travel scams if you have explored all other reasonable options. They also offer a free 128-page book, the *1997 Consumer's Resource Handbook.*
American Association of Retired Persons Consumer Affairs Section 601 E St. NW Washington, DC 20049	202-434-6030 www.aarp.org:80	Catalogs and assists in scams directed at seniors. Free consumer publications.
The Federal Trade Commission 6th Avenue & Pennsylvania Avenue NW Washington, DC 20580	Written communication only	Travel industry complaints; free publications on travel and time-share fraud.

The only state in the U.S. without incorporated cities: Hawaii.

SAFE TRAVEL

TRAVELERS' OVERVIEW

Most studies show that you are safer traveling than at home. In an attempt to cut down on crimes against tourists, many cities have developed special segments of their police forces dedicated solely to serving and protecting tourists. In the U.S., we saw what happened to tourism in Miami after the murder of a German tourist and other tragic incidents. The city mobilized law enforcement efforts and crimes against tourists are now on the decline. Miami provides a special airport car rental lot patrol. It is illegal to display any signs on rental cars or use common-sequence license plate numbers that would make it easy for predators to target tourists.

Tourism is important to most cities and vital to others. City leaders know that an unsafe reputation can be disastrous. Increase your odds for safe travel by preplanning and maintaining an air of alertness throughout your trip.

PROTECT YOUR HOME

Don't let your home take on an abandoned appearance. Arrange for yard care if your trip is lengthy. Don't forget winter concerns. An unshoveled walk is as revealing as unmowed grass. Program light timers and alarm systems, and have someone check to make sure an electric surge or momentary blackout hasn't disrupted either system.

Crimes against travelers in the U.S. compared to crimes against the general population: 40% less.

Notify trusted neighbors and ask one to help keep watch in your absence. Have mail and newspapers picked up daily, or suspend delivery until you return. Don't forget the circulars that get hung on doorknobs or thrown on the porch.

Leave a complete copy of your itinerary so you can be contacted in case of emergencies. Leave numbers for a plumber, electrician and any other contact your neighbor might need in an emergency situation.

Don't leave answering machine messages that reveal that you are out of town. If you use an answering service, instruct operators that your out-of-town information is for their use only. Callers should just be told you are currently unavailable.

PREPARE FOR YOUR OWN SECURITY

List credit card and travelers check numbers. Make copies of tickets, travel vouchers, confirmations and any hard-to-replace documents. Pack this material apart from the originals.

Share your excitement with discretion. Talking publicly about an upcoming trip alerts everyone, including strangers, to your upcoming absence. They can easily obtain your address and plan an effective burglary while you're gone.

Identify luggage inside and out. Using a business address protects your home's security. Consider adding your destination address to your luggage tags.

Leave your vehicle at home to avoid the dangers (and expense) of unattended airport lots. Take public transport, an airport shuttle or ask a friend or family member to drop you off. Leaving your car at home also helps give it an occupied look that deters burglars.

WHILE YOU TRAVEL

Keep alert by resting up from travel and time-zone changes, and avoiding substances that slow down your thinking and reaction time.

Choose shoes and clothing that won't inhibit quick escapes from risky situations. Don't tempt muggers with expensive jewelry and watches.

Travelers checks and credit cards are safer than cash, but they are still popular targets for thieves. Carry cash in unusual places, a money belt or a neck pouch. In high crime areas, consider carrying a decoy wallet with a small amount of cash inside.

The worst places to carry money are handbags and back hip pockets. If you are wearing a coat or jacket, put it on over the handbag. If you carry your wallet in a back pocket, wrap a thick rubber band around it so it can not be slipped out as easily.

Public transportation in most cities is reasonably safe if you avoid low-traffic times and high risk areas.

Keep keys in hand when heading for your car or hotel room, to avoid delays that increase vulnerability.

Caution in subway cars and elevators comes down to instinct. Wait for the next one if your suspicions are aroused.

Walk against the flow of traffic. It makes pickpockets' lives more difficult. When possible, explore with a companion. Know where you're going and the best way to get there. Try to keep from being weighted down by packages.

Restroom stalls find you at your most vulnerable. Position belongings so they can't be grabbed from outside or by the occupant of the next stall.

Violent crime rate in Hawaii: less than half the mainland average.

Name tags should not be worn in public. A smart thief can find out your room number and be in and out of your room before you return.

Beware of well-dressed con artists. The better the appearance, the higher the degree of sophistication.

Distraction theft is becoming a big problem. The distractor spills a drink on you, or asks the time. Some crooks even fake illnesses and solicit your assistance. The accomplice takes the opening, *and* your handbag or briefcase.

INTERNATIONAL CONCERNS

The Office of American Citizens Service (a division of the Department of State), **202-647-5225**, provides frequently updated, automated information on any unusual dangers associated with travel to specific foreign countries. Request information by fax, dialing **202-647-3000** on your fax machine phone. Recorded prompts will take it from there allowing you to request exactly what you need, and have it faxed right back to you.

Another free State Department benefit is *Your Trip Abroad*, a 30-page pamphlet that addresses safety issues. Request it from the Bureau of Consular Affairs, Room 6811, Department of State, Washington, DC 20520; call **202-647-1488**.

> *"Go to U.S. government sources for accurate safety information on travel destinations worldwide. Tourism officials in other countries are in the business of attracting tourists and may be tempted to downplay safety concerns."*

American Embassy and Consulate phone numbers should be noted for each country you visit. Embassy and Consulate staffers are your local advocates in many unsafe or threatening situations. They can also be trustworthy sources for information about your destination, because of the firsthand knowledge they have developed while living in the country.

Guard your passport. You have to carry it while in transit, checking into hotels, renting cars or cashing travelers checks. Leave it in the hotel safe the rest of the time, or carry it in a passport pouch, available for about $10. Since the pouch is worn under your clothing, most thieves won't detect it. Keep a photocopy of the data page in a safe place. U.S. passports are highly valued documents.

Be an informed border crosser. Learn exactly what you are allowed to carry. An over-the-counter medication approved in one country can be deemed contraband in another. This is even true for travel across the U.S.-Canadian border.

Understand basic cultural differences and be aware of legal penalties that can easily take a U.S. citizen by surprise. Singapore, for example, has severe punishments for littering.

Transact currency exchanges only at authorized facilities. Avoid the helpful stranger who offers unasked-for assistance or unusual exchange rates.

Learn key emergency words for countries you are visiting. There are times when you may not have time to fumble with a language guide.

Feature of Shanghai's American Dream Park: a theme section called Miami Beach.

LUGGAGE LOGIC

AIRLINE POLICIES

Standardized policies with minor variations exist on most major U.S. air carriers. Some low cost and niche airlines, commuters and charter flights have their own policies. Check specific policies when you purchase tickets on carriers new to you, or when flying to a new destination. Aloha Airlines, for example, prohibits wheeled luggage as carry-ons because they take up overhead bin room that is needed for life vests.

AIRLINE CARRY-ONS

Rules for carry-on items are changing. For years, major carriers allowed two carry-on items. United tested a one carry-on limit in Des Moines, then took the policy systemwide in North America. Other carries are following suit. Northwest is the major exception, limiting budget travelers to just one carry-on. Passengers flying on full-fare tickets receive more leniency. While some passengers abuse carry-on privileges, we would have rather seen a combination of better unilateral enforcement of the two carry-on policy and addition room for carry-on storage.

Southwest took a very reasonable approach, by maintaining a limit of two carry-on items but enforcing size limits more stringently. On full flights, they may call for a one carry-on item limit one hour before flight time.

Items not included in carry-on limits comprise an ever-shrinking list. Lately, we have seen purses, camera bags and diaper bags count against the limit. Many airlines count laptop computers and some include briefcases. The most stringent policies exempt only canes, crutches and infant

Job aspect gate agents dislike the most: enforcing carry-on limits.

seats. General rules include:

- **Linear size** (height plus length plus width) must not equal more than 45 inches, and weight must be 40 pounds or less, per piece.
- **All carry-ons must fit** in the overhead bins or under the seat.
- **Garment bag dimensions** must not surpass 4" x 23" x 45" (16" x 10" x 24" when folded, on Southwest).

Rules are more strict on airlines with quick-turnarounds and on commuter flights. Sizing boxes—metal-framed devices at boarding gates—are often used. Average dimensions are 16" x 10" x 24" and any carry-on must fit inside. Soft-sided pieces can more easily be made to fit. Other airlines rely on visual checks by gate attendants. If you have to gate-check luggage, be consoled in knowing that it will be among the first items unloaded when your flight arrives.

> *"If your itinerary includes multiple airlines, gear your luggage to the one with the most restrictive policies or be prepared to pay additional fees. Choose direct and non-stop flights when feasible and allow adequate check-in time (45-minutes domestic and 90-minutes international) to make sure there is plenty of time for the ground crew to load your luggage."*

CHECKED LUGGAGE ON AIRLINES

Most airlines permit three total pieces of luggage, including carry-ons. Usually, checked pieces may not weigh more than 70 pounds each. Airlines measure luggage in linear inches: height plus width plus length. The largest piece must not exceed 62 linear inches. The second piece has a limit of 55 linear inches and the third has a limit of 45 linear inches. Additional pieces can usually be checked at $50 per bag. Strollers, infant seats and two-wheeled luggage carts do not count against your allowance.

Most sports equipment can be carried if packed appropriately. Golf clubs and ski equipment usually are free, and count as one piece of checked luggage. Fees for transporting bicycles domestically average $50, including the cost of the carrier box. International flights often allow bicycles at no fee as part of checked luggage. Allow a little extra check-in time.

Special-care items can be carried under specific conditions. Unloaded weapons can be packed in locked, checked luggage, but they must be declared. Ammunition is subject to quantity limits. Fragile items and some musical instruments may require special packing, and you're likely to be asked to sign a waiver releasing the airline from liability should they be damaged in flight.

INTERNATIONAL AIRLINES

International luggage limits roughly parallel domestic rules as long as you remain on a U.S.-based carrier. Destination-specific variances include flights to the Caribbean—the total weight of your three pieces cannot exceed 140 pounds.

International flights are generally more weight sensitive, and luggage limits are more strictly enforced.

Travel on foreign based airlines is subject to rules as varied as their home countries and the type of aircraft they fly. On some flights between two international

Passengers handled by the international terminal at LAX each year: over ten million.

cities, luggage allowance is based on weight rather than number of pieces.

LOST LUGGAGE

Most luggage arrives without mishap. If your luggage is lost, you have an 80 percent chance of getting it back within 24 hours; a 90 percent chance of getting it back within five days. Only one percent of all lost luggage is never recovered. Add-on insurance is available at $1-2 per $100 in coverage. Check to see if you already have coverage from your credit or charge card company. Added coverage is most valuable on overseas flights when the carrier's maximum liability inadequately covers luggage contents.

If your luggage is lost, airline liability is limited to $1,250 per passenger on domestic flights. Efforts are being made to raise this limit to $1,850. International liability averages $645 per passenger and is based on weight. File a lost luggage claim before leaving the airport. Airlines with computerized tracking can locate luggage the fastest. Get a copy of the claim and a toll-free number. Be persistent and ask for the small emergency kit most airlines can issue to passengers with lost luggage. After 24 hours, you may request an emergency advance of $25-75. You must ask for the money and go to the airport to pick it up. Be prepared to explain why you want the higher amount. If your luggage is later located, the money is yours to keep. If they are not, the advance is deducted from your final settlement. After 48 hours you're entitled to an additional $25. Again, you have to ask.

- **Be a strong negotiator.** Claims generally take three to four weeks to settle. Payment is based on depreciated value, not replacement cost. List the contents of your luggage and provide any receipts that will substantiate your claim. Items not covered include cash, negotiable documents, jewelry, furs, cameras and electronics. Airlines routinely try to deduct 20-30 percent from your requested settlement.
- **Formal complaints** should be made to the customer relations division of the airline, with a copy sent to the U.S. Department of Transportation, Consumer Affairs, 400 7th Street S.W. Room 407, Washington, DC 20590; call **202-366-2220**.

STOLEN LUGGAGE

Your luggage is far more likely to end up in the hands of thieves than lost by the airline. Luggage theft has increased now that many travelers carry laptops, cellular phones and other easily fenced items.

- **Lock all luggage** and tie an identifying scarf or ribbon on common-appearing pieces to make it stand out at a glance.
- **The shuttle bus** from the parking lot to the terminal is your first area of vulnerability. A quick-acting thief can grab your luggage and get off at an early stop. You won't know the theft has occurred until you have reached your terminal.
- **If you use a skycap** make sure you watch him place your luggage on the conveyer belt. Most skycaps are honest, but they are also busy. If they load luggage on a cart, thieves can seize the opportunity. Make sure skycaps and gate agents tag your luggage correctly. Know the three letter airport code for your destination.
- **If you check in at the ticket counter** or stop to purchase a ticket, don't set your bags down and forget about them. It just takes a second for a thief to pick them up and disappear. Don't be

U.S. residents who stay in the country for their winter vacations: 70 percent.

assured just because the closest people to you are dressed in business-like attire. Thieves have a dress code too.

- **Thieves often work in unison** at security check-in points. One creates a diversion while the other snatches your laptop or luggage. For example, you place your luggage on the conveyor belt and step toward the scanner gate but someone cuts in front of you. Maybe they drop their keys and apologize profusely. By the time you make it through the scanner, your luggage has been picked up and whisked away by a partner-in-crime at the other end of the conveyor belt.
- **There is not a lot in-flight theft**, but that is no consolation if you are one of the unlucky few. Thieves sit in the forward seats to assure that they'll be among the first to deplane. Flight attendants can't remember which garment bag or carry-on goes with every passenger. If you stow luggage in overhead compartments, use compartments in line with your seat or toward the rear of the plane.
- **The final test is the luggage claim area.** Always go to baggage claim immediately. It may take a while for your luggage to arrive, but the crooks will be waiting. Few domestic airports have security guards who check to see that all claim tickets match.

CRUISE, RAIL & BUS

Cruise luggage limits are essentially determined by the carrier that flies you to the port city. Cruise lines set weight limits on luggage (usually 200 pounds total), but they are not likely to be enforced unless you visibly exceed it in excess. Liability for lost or damaged luggage is minimal, averaging $100 per passenger. Most lines offer a multi-use insurance option that includes lost or damaged luggage.

Amtrak luggage policies are contingent on whether or not the train has a luggage car. Without one, you're limited to two carry-ons, with no specific weight or size limit except their ability to fit in overhead compartments. Trains with baggage cars also allow three checked pieces per passenger, with 50 pounds per piece maximum. The weight allowance can be raised to 75 pounds if you pay an additional $10 per item. Check three more pieces for $10 per item. Total per passenger liability is $500. Amtrak carries skis at no extra cost, and bicycles (dismantled and in boxes) for $10.

Interstate bus lines allow two pieces of checked luggage and two carry-ons. Total weight of all four pieces must not exceed 120 pounds. Maximum liability is $250 per passenger.

NEW LUGGAGE

Buy the best luggage you can afford. Increased instances of damaged luggage are caused, in part, from the use of ultra-economy pieces not designed to withstand the rigors of travel.

Hard shell luggage provides extra protection, but each piece can be as much as 20 pounds heavier than soft-sided versions. Check the manageability by carrying the empty bag around the luggage department. If you have trouble carrying it while it is empty, opt for wheeled luggage.

Soft-sided luggage is most durable when it is made of "ballistic" fabric similar to that used for bulletproof vests. Second best is fabric made of nylon or polyester yarn of at least 1,000 denier for checked-pieces; 450 denier for carry-ons.

Semi-soft luggage combines some benefits of hard shell and soft-sided luggage.

Garment bags should open book-style

and have pouches and compartments to keep items from jumbling at the bottom.

Look for features that are durable and convenient.

- **Plastic frames and wheels** are more durable then metal. Four-wheel designs provide easier navigation than two-wheel designs. Look for wheels which are protected by housings or are partially recessed.
- **Handles** should be padded and riveted rather than attached by D-rings or screws. Retractable handles are best. Detachables tend to get misplaced.
- **Shoulder straps** should be wide, fully-adjustable and have comfort pads.
- **Self-repairing zippers** eliminate costly repairs.
- **Divided sections** and waterproof pouches make packing easier.
- **Attachments** for carrying multiple pieces are useful if their design holds each piece securely.

A CLEVER PACKER'S CASE STUDY

Frequent travelers know there is a science to packing. Follow their lead and make their tips second nature.

- **Remove old destination tags** and make sure your luggage is well identified inside and out. Retrievable luggage tags have a notice in eight languages alerting people to the itinerary inside their pouch. They are ideal for lengthy trips, and cost $4.85 for two tags. You can get them from Magellan's, **800-962-4943**.
- **Decide your best luggage strategy.** Most convenient: carry-ons. When using checked pieces, consider using two smaller pieces rather than one hard-to-carry piece. You'll also minimize wrinkles and lessen the odds of being totally inconvenienced by lost luggage. Plan to pass laptops and computer discs through security via the conveyor belt. Security arches and hand-held wands are the most hazardous to their magnetic fields.
- **Make a list** to remind you of things to be done before you pack, such as picking up cleaning and shopping for new items. Save packing room by omitting what you can get or use for free at any good hotel: an alarm clock, hair dryer, iron or basic toiletries. Allow room for purchases made at your destination.
- **Set everything out, then put half back.** Remember the limited reimbursement you get for lost luggage. Never carry anything you deem irreplaceable.
- **Place heavier items** on the bottom of your suitcase. If you are going on a long trip, start by packing what you need for the last destination, and place clothing you'll want first at the top.
- **Roll clothes** into cylinders to eliminate creasing. Fill up empty spaces by packing socks, belts and accessories inside shoes.
- **Couples** traveling together can place one outfit in each other's suitcase. If one suitcase is lost, you each have a change of clothes.
- **Pack essentials in carry-on pieces**: a change of clothes or as close as you can get with space limitations; prescriptions in original containers and over-the-counter medicine you take regularly; toiletries in spill-proof container; your address book and contact information; keys—but just the ones you'll need.

Business travelers who carry laptops: over 50 percent.

ITEMS THAT TRAVEL WELL

Get the style you need without sacrificing comfort. Travel is not the time to try new looks, new shoes or fabrics that may not stand up to travel demands. Clothes with usable pockets provide extra convenience. Vests come in fabrics from wool to satin and produce a finished look. Pack two pairs of shoes. One pair does not allow for broken heels or other footwear emergencies.

Consider a color scheme. Black and white are classic, easily dressed up or down with accessories.

Fabrics blended with a little polyester resist wrinkles best. Light-weight fabrics work for most climates if you dress in layers. You'll also have a much easier time doing emergency laundry in your hotel room. Learn the keep-cool lessons of the locals. Thin, natural fiber fabrics that cover the body loosely are actually cooler than exposing your skin to the sun.

Convertible shorts/pants are available in mens sizes at about $69. They have deep, cargo pockets, button-closed back pockets and khaki-type styling. A hidden zipper converts them from long pants to shorts. Call TravelSmith, **800-950-1600**.

Pack your swimsuit or trunks even in winter, so you'll be able to use hotel pool and spa facilities.

Limit jewelry to a few signature items. Don't be a glittering target for thieves or risk leaving a piece behind when you check out of your hotel.

Make light work of packing with inflatable items.

- **Puffy hangers** for hotel laundry chores cost about $2 each and are widely available in travel and discount stores.
- **The Sports Pouch** keeps your keys, wallet and watch from sinking when you're on the water. Prices range from $13-25 at travel and sporting goods stores.

> *"Many travelers forget to remove or secure garment bag hooks before placing their bags on security conveyor belts. The first time you make that mistake, you know you will never repeat it. If you are carrying a lot of carry-on luggage try to board early. Stow it in line with your seat to avoid going against the traffic flow when the flight lands. If you're traveling to a cold climate, carry your coat with you. I live in Texas but I carry my coat when I'm heading to colder climates. It's handy when I land and I don't have to worry about it disappearing if my luggage gets lost."*

HEALTHY TRAVEL

SHOULD YOU GO?

Minor illnesses easily managed at home can become greater problems when traveling. Minor ear infections will almost always be aggravated by air travel. Colds and sinus problems can produce additional discomfort when you are airborne, but decongestants provide some relief.

Medical certificates are not required as a condition of air travel unless the passenger is on a stretcher, in an incubator or requires oxygen. If you do require oxygen, you must make advance arrangements with the airline. Get a free update on major airline policies as well as travel by ship, train and bus in *Traveling With Oxygen*, available from the American Association for Respiratory Care, 11030 Ables Lane, Dallas, TX 75229; call **972-243-2272**; fax **972-484-2720**. The American Lung Association offers *Airline Travel With Oxygen*. Write to 2625 Third Avenue, Seattle, WA 98121; call **800-586-4872**; fax **206-441-3277**.

If you wear a pacemaker or have any metal implanted in your body, carry a physician's letter that will allow you to by-pass the security scanning device.

Medical-alert tags are recognizable signals of chronic conditions and specific medical needs. They can save your life in unfamiliar surroundings. You pay a $35 fee for the tag and access to a 24-hour number for emergency situations and $15 each subsequent year. Call the Medic Alert Foundation, **800-825-3785**.

Pregnancy does not have to be a barrier to any form of travel. Consult your obstetrician when planning a trip during the last trimester. Obtain written permission from your doctor. Comfort options for pregnant travelers include aisle seats and loose clothing and shoes. Don't be afraid to fasten your seat belt. Studies show that seat belts decrease risk of injury to both mother and baby.

Don't attempt to travel if you have a serious disease transmitted by airborne bacteria. Let your conscience and your need to travel be your guide when you have a minor communicable illness. Divers should not attempt air travel within 24 hours of their last dive. Get a physician's approval for travel if you have had recent surgery or suffer from heart disease, severe high blood pressure, bleeding disorders or other acute conditions.

BEFORE YOU GO

Prescription medicines should be carried in original containers. This is particularly important when you travel internationally. It's preferable that the name on the prescription label exactly matches the name on your passport. Copy all the information on the label and keep it in a safe place in case your medicine is lost. Synchronize your dosage times when you travel to different time zones.

Out-of-state prescriptions may be difficult to obtain. Your physician may not be licensed to authorize certain medications outside of his or her licensing state. Carry a replacement prescription.

Out-of-area medical care usually requires advance HMO or insurance approval for anything other than immediate threat to life. Carry the 24-hour authorization number of your plan.

People with immune system and allergy problems can benefit by booking "green rooms," available at an increasing number of hotels. Many use special air and water purifiers, all natural soaps and shampoos and natural fiber carpets. All are nonsmoking. Some are even cleaned with chemical-free products.

DIETARY CONCERNS

Most intestinal upsets run their course with minimal treatment, usually with the same over-the-counter medicine you take at home. Dehydration is almost always remedied by rapid fluid intake or rehydration powders available at all pharmacies.

Low-sanitation areas are best handled by using bottled water for drinking and brushing your teeth. Avoid ice cubes; peeled, uncooked fruits and vegetables; shellfish and undercooked foods. Many resort area hotels have thoroughly safe, treated water.

Treat questionable water by boiling it or adding iodine or halazone tablets. Follow package recommendations and double the amount used if the water you're treating is unusually cloudy or very cold. If you are on medication, consult your physician before using water additives.

Splurge on regional specialties, but keep good overall eating habits by sticking to the healthier aspects of each area's cuisine.

ACCLIMATING YOUR BODY

Extra demands made on your body include changes in climate, food and time zone. Adapt to new climates gradually. For example, expose yourself gradually to sun or extremely high elevations to allow your body time to adapt. Sunburn can even occur on the ski slopes. Restrict your first day's exposure and wear products that block harmful rays (usually strongest between 11 a.m. and 3 p.m.).

Decrease stress by swimming in the hotel pool, taking a sauna, relaxing in a whirlpool, exercising in the fitness center or having a massage.

Increase your activity level only to a reasonable degree. Most people come home from trips exhausted because they try to fit a two-week vacation into one.

Stay aware of the time in your hometown. Even though travel activities occur in another time zone, your body needs some notice paid to its customary schedule. You can slowly move your body into the effect of a new time zone to temper the tiring effects of time zone travel.

Out-of-town/out-of-shape is not an inevitable pairing. Walking gives you the best views, increases energy and strengthens your immune system. You also get more exposure of your destination.

People with diabetes can get valuable information on insulin adjustments by time zone and worldwide diabetic organizations. *The Diabetic Traveler Newsletter*, published quarterly, is $18.95 per year. Get a back issue copy for $1 and a self-addressed stamped envelope. Write to P.O. Box 8223-RW, Stamford, CT 06905; call **203-327-5832**.

> *"If your cup of tea is alcohol-free, you may want to check out three specialized vendors offering alcohol-free tours and cruises: Sober Vacations International at **818-878-0008** and Serenity Trips, **800-615-4665**."*

Accidents are a greater risk than travel-incurred disease. Exhaustion from long trips, all-day meetings and late nights are some of the greatest causes of mishaps. Head off exhaustion with adequate rest. A 15-minute nap can rejuvenate you. If the hotel tub doesn't have an anti-skid bottom lay a bath towel on it before you bathe or shower.

Water mishaps are best avoided by heeding posted warnings. Be particularly careful of unknown ocean tides and currents. Check to see if other people are in the water. Some of the world's most tempting beaches are for sunbathing only, with currents too strong for most swimmers. Always heed warnings posted on beaches and avoid swimming spots that do not have lifeguards on duty.

HELP IN THE U.S.

HotelDocs offers free membership that provides referrals to 1,500 physicians in over 130 cities. The standard hotel call fee averages $150-195 vs. walk-in clinics charges of about $50. Use this specialized service when a hotel call is worth the added cost. Call **800-468-3537**.

Inn Care of America gives you a number to call for non-emergency care. One of 2,200 physicians will call you within an hour to set up an office visit. The annual fee for membership only is $39.95. Call **800-489-6277**.

INTERNATIONAL TRAVEL

Updated immunization information is available from The Center For Disease Control, **404-332-4559**. Some immunizations are required, some are optional and a few that used to be mandatory, are now simply recommended. Health advisories are issued when an epidemic-level of a specific disease is present.

Polio and tetanus boosters and hepatitis immunizations are always good ideas if you're heading for tropical or developing countries. No regulatory agency demands them but, particularly if you have chronic illnesses or are of a certain age, discuss them with your doctor.

English-speaking doctors in 130 countries (trained in the U.S., the U.K. or

Center of the Texas wine industry: Grapevine.

Canada) can be located via a free list from The International Association for Medical Assistance, **716-754-4883**. This non-profit organization sets average fees for physician's services: $55 for an office visit, $75 for a house or hotel call; $95 evenings and holidays.

911 (the U.S. emergency phone number) translates differently in most countries that have an emergency number system. Britain uses 999; Germany, 110; Sweden, 90000; Peru, 05. Know the emergency access number for each country on your itinerary.

Foreign-made medicines should be approached with caution. Some countries sell over-the-counter products designed to look like their U.S. counterparts, but they can differ in composition and quality. Don't assume that common over-the-counter medicines are available worldwide. Pack an adequate amount and keep medication in original containers to avoid problems with customs.

Foreign medical care varies in quality from poor to excellent. Some countries will give you free medical care via excellent public health systems. Others are to be avoided for anything other than emergency interim care. An accurate quality rating can usually be given by resident American Embassy and Consulate staff members. They can also direct you to local physicians known by the Embassy and Consulate staffs.

After-hour pharmacies can be found in Europe by checking the placard on the door of any pharmacy. They all list the closest after-hours prescription source. Many are identified by green crosses.

Premium level charge and credit cardholders can call 24-hour assistance lines for help in medical emergencies. The credit card company's toll-free number will work from some Caribbean countries. In other countries call their regular traveler assistance number collect and tell the operator that you have a medical emergency.

Some unusual illnesses acquired while traveling don't exhibit symptoms for two to 12 months. If hard-to-diagnose rashes, fever or diarrhea develop, be sure to tell your doctor where you have traveled during the past year, even if you have just traveled domestically. If you require medical care while traveling, request copies of your records so your primary care physician can add them to your file and review any procedures or prescriptions.

Year in which the U.S. State Department lifted the ban on travel to China: 1971.

SPECIAL CATEGORIES OF TRAVEL

BUSINESS TRAVEL

Technology Is On Your Side

A wealth of gadgets and gizmos are being developed and marketed to business travelers. The new technology is also providing services to make life on the road easier for people who spend a significant portion of their work week away from home.

- **Smart Phones** dial up the internet, send and receive messages and download data. AT&T's PocketNet cellular weighs 11.5-ounces, uses analog service and features a three-line LED display. Find details at **www.airdata.com.** Nokia's 9000 Communicator, launched in Europe, uses all-digital technology. Visit **www.nokia.com**.
- **New pagers let you send messages as well as receive them.** Motorola's 6.3 ounce PageWriter communicates via e-mail, fax, internet and other pagers. It retails for about $400. Call **800-548-9954**; go online at **www.mot.com/PageWriter**.
- **U.S. cellular phones often won't work in other countries.** Rent a cellular phone that will function in Africa, Asia, the Caribbean and Europe from CellHire, **800-561-0610**. Rates begin at $69 per week.
- **Telephone modems**, as small as credit cards, cost $100-150 and give you access to bank account balances, online services and bulletin boards with a wealth of city-specific information.
- **The Pocket Tone Dialer** can be held to a telephone voicepiece and will dial up to 13 numbers on command, making you less vulnerable to shoulder-surfers. The cost is $24.85. Call **800-962-4943**.
- **Carry appropriate adapters** for modems and electrical appliances. If you are not a seasoned international traveler, you may not be aware that many countries have separate adapter needs. In The U.K., for example, you need one special type for shavers only. A $9 pack of adapters covers Australia, Europe, India, New Zealand and South America. Call **800-338-4962**.
- **The In-Car Notebook Charger** lets you power your laptop battery by connecting it to your cigarette lighter. The $59.95-79.95 device has a locking mechanism that keeps it connected and an LED power indicator. Call **800-242-3133**.

Item frequently left behind by air travelers: pagers.

> *"Long phone cords aren't exactly high-tech items but a 150-foot cord is one of my travel essentials. Until true two-phone-line hotel rooms are more prevalent, I have to be prepared for connecting to a phone jack in another room if I need to power my computer for a radio show. IBM has just released a cordless modem that can operate within 100 feet of any phone jack. For details check* ***www.research.ibm.com.****"*

Laptops are essential tools for many business travelers. Make sure your battery is fully charged and carry a spare for contingencies. We will see increased availability of laptop power sources for travelers in years to come but it is going to take some time for their availability to completely eliminate your need for battery power.

Insure your laptop under your homeowner's or renter's policy. Independent insurance is available from sources including Safeware, **800-800-1492**.

Savings Strategies

Leasing a car internationally may save you money on stays of two weeks or longer. Several companies offer leased vehicles at rates substantially lower than rentals—plus you will be driving a brand new car (see *Car Rentals* for details).

If your company has discontinued cash advances for travel, they are part of a nationwide trend. When possible, use your corporate card for cash advances (keep itemized expense records) to avoid dipping into your own funds.

Use per diems wisely. Taking a hotel shuttle or mass transit into the city can free funds for an exceptional dinner or a relaxing room service meal.

Cut the cost of business entertaining by using two-for-one dining coupons, but use them discretely unless your client is more likely to be impressed than offended by your thriftiness. Some people prefer to use dining programs that rebate 20 to 25 percent of the cost of your meal. Take clients to breakfast to avoid hefty lunch and dinner tabs and get a productive start on the day.

Take advantage of every travel tax deduction you qualify for. A tax-savvy CPA should more than pay for his or her services with the money you save by using the latest strategies.

- **Deduct the full cost** of travel and lodging and 50 percent of meal costs.
- **Don't stimulate auditor attention** with expenses far outside the framework of the type of business you conduct. A renowned entertainment lawyer can justify suites and gourmet meals. A just-starting-out sales representative probably cannot.
- **Travel expenses equal to the first two percent of your income** are not generally deductible. If you make $75,000 per year, for example, the first $1,500 in travel expense is not deductible.
- **Business-with-pleasure combination trips** allow reasonable deductions. The strictest requirements are on international travel. The total trip must be seven days or less and 75 percent of your time must be spent on business. Travel time and holidays and week-

ends between business days count toward the 75%.

- **Spouses get travel deductions** only if officially employed with bona fide reasons to travel.
- **Airline club dues** can be deducted if a convincing case is made that they are used primarily for business purposes.
- **The cost of airline upgrades** is deductible if you can establish that the extra room and quiet are necessary to the preparation of presentations and business material. Keep journal entries citing specific projects worked on per flight.
- **Free-lancers** must demonstrate a profit for three of the past five years to claim work related travel deductions.
- **Educational trips** are only deductible if they contribute to your current area of employment.
- **Conventions** (excluding investment, political and social) are deductible. If they're held abroad there must be a valid business reason for choosing the location. If they're held on a cruise ship, you can deduct a maximum of $2,000 per year if the ship is of U.S. registry and all ports-of-call are domestic.
- **Get a deduction in advance** by charging advance travel at the end of the year on any major credit card. You can claim the full transaction even if you haven't made payment.
- **If you get stuck with non-refundable airline tickets** you can deduct taxes, terminal and fuel surcharges and passenger facility charges. On international tickets, you can also deduct immigration, customs and agriculture inspection fees.
- ***IRS Publication 463*** details tax rules for travelers. Contact your regional office or write to Internal Revenue Service Mail Editor, 3041 Sunrise Blvd., Rancho Cordova, CA 95742.

Business Travel For Parents

Parents who travel on business learn to say goodbye a lot. There are ways to make leaving the children home easier on everyone.

- **Maps and calendar markings** help children visualize your trips.
- **Surprise them with overnight letters.** Brief notes can be supplemented with small gifts—even the comics from the local paper.
- **Be in two places at once via technology.** Make audio or video tapes of bedtime stories. Keep in touch by phone, fax and e-mail.

Parents take their children on business trips 63 percent more often than five years ago.

- **If your child travels often**, be sure he or she is enrolled in frequent flyer programs.
- **Stay away from night flights** if you are traveling with younger children. Maneuvering through airports with a sleepy child, a briefcase, garment bag and laptop is difficult.
- **Many major hotels offer children's activities** and many of them do so throughout the week. Over 100 of the 169 Hyatt Hotels have Camp Hyatt, including childcare, activities, supervised programs and second rooms at half price.
- **Keep your child's normal schedule in mind** when traveling to different time zones.

Common El Salvador vacation times: two weeks before & after Christmas and Easter, plus August.

- **Take your nanny** if your budget allows. It frees you from relying on unresearched childcare options.

General Strategies

Be sure to pack enough items to ensure your good appearance in case of lost luggage. Pack your own lost luggage insurance by wearing a business suit on your outbound flight and carrying a change of undergarments and a clean shirt or blouse in your briefcase. Take a second pair of shoes even on short trips. Being late for a meeting because you're trying to get your only pair of shoes repaired is an avoidable headache.

Allow some small indulgences to make business trips less grueling. Taking time out to have a relaxing dinner, attend a play or explore an interesting neighborhood can actually increase your productivity by making you more relaxed and focused when you return to work. Repeat trips to favorite cities may eventually feel like visits to second homes.

Don't doom international deals by ignorance of country-specific protocol. For example, white is the color of mourning in Japan. Shaking hands, particularly offering the left hand, is ill-received in several countries.

- *Culturegrams* are available from the David M. Kennedy Center for International Studies, **800-528-6279**. Each four-page briefing is written by someone who has lived in the country they cover for at least three years. *Culturegrams*, updated yearly, are $6 and cover one country of your choice. Get a 164 country pack for $120.
- *Kiss, Bow, or Shake Hands* ($19.95) offers over 400 pages of information on doing business in 60 countries. It is published by Bob Adams, Inc. Look for it in major bookstores. If it's not in stock, ask them to order it under ISBN number 9-781558-504448.

Several internet sites offer helpful information for frequent travelers.

- **Biztravel** at **www.biztravel.com** offers many valuable features for business travelers, including Flyte Trax, which charts the progress of commercial airline flights. It updates you on arrival and departure times and tells you exactly where any commercial flight is while in the air.
- **WebFlyer**, at **www.webflyer.com** updates you on frequent flyer programs and bonus mile offers.
- **Find names and numbers** of local airport limousine services at **www.thetrip.com**.
- **Epicurious Travel** on *Conde Naste's* site at **http://travel.epicurious.com** may amuse you with features including *How Annoying Is Your Airline?* and monthly rankings of the "least irritating" airlines.

> *"Don't forget **www.bestfares.com**. It's full of ideas and strategies to help you fight the high prices business people traditionally pay for travel. Travel sellers count on getting maximum revenue from you, but you don't have to play the game their way. You will find deals on Coach airfares, ways to fly First Class at prices that may amaze you, bonus offers, scam alerts on crimes that target businessmen and much more."*

SOLO TRAVEL

Accentuate The Positive

Solo travel can be one of the finest luxuries in life. Select the destination, set the pace and answer only to your own desires. Once you've tried it, you may consider it the ultimate form of travel.

Spur-of-the-moment travel offers amazing discounts and is easiest to take advantage of if you don't have to check anyone's schedule but your own. Take the last available seat on a charter to Las Vegas and you are likely to get it for about 75 percent less. Pick up on a last minute, weekend internet special from one of the airlines, couple it with low weekend rates at city center hotels and you've made weekend travel affordable.

Great theater seats and tickets to sold-out events are easier to acquire if you only need one. Build a trip around the Broadway season or a concert by a favorite group or performer.

Meeting people can be easier when you're solo. Safe meeting grounds include flights and airport and hotel clubs. You're no more likely to step into a dangerous situation on a trip than you are at home. Just use normal precautions.

Build a network of friends by exchanging addresses with people you meet along the way. If you feel a little uncertain, use a business address or post office box. Soon you will have friends to welcome you wherever you go.

Support is just a phone call away. If you get lonely, a phone call to someone you care for will usually cure your loneliness. Don't get discouraged by people who can't imagine solo travel. With careful planning, good choices and an adventuresome spirit, a wonderful trip is almost guaranteed.

Consider destinations where you have a connection. You may not choose to stay with them, but they can keep you from feeling entirely alone in a new city.

Foreign travel? Why not? Learn as much of the language as you can or select destinations where English is a strong second language.

Solo Strategies

Choose cities with vital centers and concentrations of activities, unless your expertise and courage allow you to tackle the great unknown.

Consider bed & breakfasts and hostels for built-in camaraderie plus budget advantages.

If you are driving, join an auto club and carry a cellular phone. Don't try to get around in a strange city after dark. Plan your arrival for a time when daylight lets you explore with greater safety.

Dine alone without apology. Some restaurants are reticent to tie up a table for one person, but most restaurants know better than to alienate you with anything other than their best service. Taking a book to dinner provides a margin of comfort for the timid. You can also ask to be seated at an inconspicuous table. Takeout lunches can be enjoyed in parks or wherever office workers congregate. While dining in Europe, don't be surprised if another solo diner is seated with you. It's a common and generally pleasant experience.

Most popular bedtime for business travelers: 11-11:59 p.m.

If You Want A Companion

Look for travel companions through groups or organizations or at your religious center. You are assured of at least one common interest.

Travel partners known to you or arranged by a service should be thoroughly checked and reasonably compatible. Are you extravagant or budget conscious; neat or messy; timid or adventurous; night owl or early riser; punctual or always late?

Match-up services include:

- **Travel Companion Exchange**, part of Golden Companies Network, is the biggest and oldest service of its kind. An six month membership is $99; a three year membership is $159. Both include bi-monthly newsletters with about 500 updated listings of travelers seeking companions. Write to P.O. Box 833, Amityville, NY 11701; Call **800-392-1256**.

Solo Travel Specialists include:

- **Backroads**, offering active tours. Single supplements are waived if you book at least 60 days in advance, ask for an assigned roommate and no suitable match can be made. Call **800-462-2848**.
- **Women-only services** including Shared Adventures, 420 W. 75th St., Downers Grove, IL; call **630-852-5533** and Rainbow Adventures, 15033 Kelly Canyon, Bozeman, MT 59715; call **800-804-8686**.

Periodicals for solo travelers include:

- ***Connecting: News For Solo Travelers***, a bi-monthly at $30 a year. Write to P.O. Box 29088, 1996 W. Broadway, Vancouver, BC V6J 5C2, Canada; call **800-557-1757** or **604-737-7791**.
- ***The Single Traveler Newsletter***, a bi-monthly at $29 a year. Write to P.O. Box 682, Ross, CA 94957; call **415-389-0227**.
- ***Travel Companions***, a bi-monthly at $48 a year. Write to P.O. Box 833, Amityville, NY 11701; call **516-454-0880**.
- ***Travelin' Woman***, a monthly at $48 a year. Write to 111 1/2 Park Place, Venice, CA 90219; call **800-871-6409** or **310-399-6246**.

> *"Woodswomen is a non-profit group (based in Minnesota) that arranges adventure travel for solo travelers as well as groups of women and children and (on request) co-ed groups. They've been organizing getaways for over two decades—usually about 70 different options each year. There is mountaineering in St. Croix, biking in Ireland, dog sledding in Minnesota, backpacking in the Cascade Mountains and many other interesting options. While Woodswomen packages appeal to a wide range of people, they have a special appeal for solo travelers who like the companionship of an amenable group. For more information, call **800-279-0555.**"*

SENIOR TRAVEL

Why You Are All VIPs

Remember when you first entered high school and longed to be a senior? When you reach the senior travel discount age, the benefits are just as exciting. Seniors are vibrant, energetic and as diverse as Jane Fonda and Margaret Thatcher; George Mitchell and Bob Dole; Elizabeth Taylor and Charlton Heston. Being a senior brings a special travel status. Take a look around on any cruise or vacation and you're likely to see that seniors are often the people who are having the best times.

Know your clout as the most powerful consumer group in America. You account for 80 percent of all leisure travel expenditures. You control more than half the discretionary income and own 80 percent of the savings. You hold almost 40 percent of all U.S. passports. Age discrimination tends to disappear when you travel. You get special discounts, and, particularly when traveling abroad, your age generates either additional respect or is encompassed in a spirit of camaraderie.

Travel vendors will cater to you because many of you are flexible—you are the people who fill the mid-week period and the seasons when travel is difficult for others. You also purchase one-third of all domestic travel and travel to Europe and Africa. About 90 percent of you have traveled before. You have the knowledge and sophistication that makes life easier for anyone selling or providing a travel-related service.

Discount Basics

Here are some basic rules to follow, no matter what type of travel you're buying.

- **Check the minimum age for discounts.** We have seen senior rates offered to people as young as 45 years of age. Some discounts only require that one member of your party meet the age minimum. There are age maximum advantages too. Some European hotels discount your room by a percentage equal to your age.
- **Always ask for senior discounts.** They aren't always advertised, and the reservation desk may not readily offer them, because they are reticent about implying that you're of a certain age.
- **Check out the discount possibilities** before you make your reservation. If you wait until you are ready to make payment, it may be too late. Many companies offer nominal discounts to seniors but increase the discount with advance booking. If you can plan ahead, your ten percent discount could turn into 50 percent.
- **Ask about restaurant discounts** offered by your hotel. Large chains are most apt to offer them, and they can apply to your companion as well. Discounts are sometimes limited to off-peak hours.
- **Enjoy the highest savings** during off-peak travel times. September is special for seniors. Many locations offer dis-

count rates or plan events designed to attract seniors and keep the summer vacation season going a month longer. Check the newspapers and call tourism offices in places you'd like to visit.

- **Weigh the senior discount** against other promotions and discount offers. You may get a better deal or, in some cases, be able to take a senior discount off the promotional rate.
- **Always carry proof of age** and applicable membership cards. You may not be asked to show them, but be prepared to verify your age or club membership.

Membership Savings

Consider a membership organization that provides the card you sometimes need to acquire senior discounts. Their affiliated travel clubs may not always offer the best value, but their cards are always worth having, particularly at the low annual rates charged for membership. If you join the American Association for Retired Persons (AARP), for example, you get a membership card that opens many discount doors. You may also be inundated with enticements by mail both from AARP and companies that utilize AARP's mailing lists. Be sure to evaluate all discount offers. Senior membership options and annual membership fees include:

- **The American Association for Retired Persons** at $8 per household. Write to 601 E St. NW, Washington, DC 20049; call **800-424-3410** or **202-434-2277**.
- **The Canadian Association of Retired Persons** at $10 per couple. Write to 27 Queen St. East, Toronto M5C 2M6 Canada; call **416-363-8748**.
- **Catholic Golden Age** at $8 per couple. Write to P.O. Box 3658, Scranton, PA 18540; call **800-233-4697**.
- **The National Association of Retired Credit Union People** at $12. Call **800-937-2644**.
- **The National Association of Retired Federal Employees** at $21. Write to 1533 New Hampshire Ave. NW, Washington, DC 20036; call **202-234-0832**.
- **The National Council of Senior Citizens** at $13 a year, $33 for three years and $175/lifetime. Call **301-578-8800**.

Many organizations sell their membership list to marketing firms. All legitimate organizations give you the option of being excluded from any mailing list sold outside the company. If you can't find a box to check on the membership form, advise the organization in writing and attach the note to your check where it can't be missed.

Travel With Grandchildren

Grandparents and grandchildren make such great travel partners that special organizations provide new ideas and creative itineraries. GrandTravel, **800-247-7651**, offers specially designed grandchild/grandparent tours. Last minute weekend discount airfares by internet provide great opportunities for travel year-round that won't interfere with older children's schoolwork. Many senior airfare discount programs allow companions to travel at the same discount enjoyed by the senior.

Savvy Seniors

Make a friend in a country you plan to visit. International Pen Pals offers reduced rates to people 60 and above. Send a stamped, self-addressed envelope to P.O. Box 290065, Homecrest Station,

Brooklyn, NY 11229. Golden Pen-Pal Association offers the same service in the U.S. Send a stamped, self-addressed envelope to 1304 Hedgelawn Way, Raleigh, NC 27615.

Get free admission to all U.S. National Parks, monuments and recreation areas with the *Golden Age Passport*, available at age 62. Camping, boat launching, tours and parking are half price. You can buy one at any National Park for $10. It's not available by mail, but you can request information from The National Park Service, Box 37127, Washington, DC 20013. Each state also offers its own discounts. Contact state tourism offices for details.

Canadian National and Provincial Parks give you free entry if you're 62 or above just for showing your driver's license and vehicle registration. Camping is half price on weekends for seniors.

The Golf Card ($95 a year for single membership; $145 per couple) includes free membership in the Quest discount program, two free 18-hole rounds of golf at your choice of 2,700 courses worldwide, a bi-monthly magazine and resort discounts on golf packages. Write to The Golf Card, P.O. Box 7020, Englewood, CO 80155; call **800-453-4260**.

Sears Mature Outlook, open to people 50 and above, provides free membership in a dining and hotel discount club and discounts on merchandise and insurance. Annual dues for a family are $14.95. Call **800-336-6330**.

Montgomery Ward's Years Of Extra Savings, open to people 55 and above, provides ten percent off any merchandise, even sale items, every Tuesday, plus a five to ten percent rebate on travel booked through the company's travel service. Annual dues are $34.99. Call **800-421-5396**.

Universal Studios Florida Silver Stars Club is free to people 55 and above. You get 15 percent off on up to six passes as well as food and merchandise discounts. Call **407-363-8217**.

First Class travel in Europe is available from TraveLearn, **800-235-9114**. All-inclusive two- to three-week tours cost about $3,000 including air and all accommodations, and amenities are superb.

The Evergreen Bed & Breakfast Club, open to people 50 and above, provides rooms in other members' private homes for as little as $25 a night. Membership is $50 per year including directories updated two times a year. Call **800-383-7473**.

Tourism agencies worldwide offer special packages and discounts to seniors. You can stop by their offices after you arrive, but a phone call when you're making travel plans will yield new ideas and bargains you may want to know about before you go. There are city, state and national offices listed in our *Know Who To Contact* section and specific offerings in *More Dollars & Cents*.

Club Med's Forever Young Club for travelers age 55 and above offers a $140 discount on a week's stay at select Club Med locations in the Bahamas, Guadalupe and Mexico. For more details, see your travel agent or call Club Med at **800-258-2633**.

The ninth edition of *Unbelievably Good Deals and Great Adventures That You Absolutely Can't Get Unless You're Over 50* by Joan Heilman's guide covers information on all forms of senior travel. It's available in major bookstores or order by mail for $14 (including shipping and handling): Morton Booksellers, 812 Stuart Avenue, Mamaroneck, NY 10543.

Miles of border shared by the U.S. & Canada: 300.

Educational vacations are economical and interesting, Sometimes you sleep in dormitories and eat college cafeteria food. Sometimes the surroundings are elegant.

- **Study in Victorian ambiance** at the Chatauqua Institute on a lake setting outside of Buffalo. The per week cost includes room and meals. Call the Program Center for Older Adults, **716-357-6200**.
- **The Folkways Institute** offers non-profit study opportunities that require no previous training or knowledge. They offer a range of programs from exotic cultural treks to overland trips where you stay in small hotels and guest houses. Call **800-225-4666**.
- **Senior Adventures** is a network of nine colleges and universities in Western states that combine education with travel. Topics range from Shakespeare to Southwestern ecology. Call **800-257-0577**.
- **University Vacations** includes students of all ages with seven to 12-day sessions at Oxford, Cambridge, Trinity College (Ireland) and the Sorbonne. Mornings are spent in study; afternoons and evenings, in exploration. Call **800-792-0100**.

Active senior vacations focus on adventure.

- **The National Senior Sports Association** sponsors competitive golf holidays in the U.S. and abroad. The $25 fee includes a monthly newsletter, discounts on sports equipment and names and addresses of members so you can organize sports holidays on your own. Call **800-282-6772**.
- **The 70+ Ski Club** offers organized ski trips, a newsletter, locations offering free skiing for club members and other locations offering discounts. Lifetime membership is $5. Write to Lloyd Lambert, 70+ Ski Club, 104 Eastside Dr., Ballston Lake, NY 12019; call **518-399-5458.**
- **The Over The Hill Gang International** sponsors ski trips and theme trips including diving, hiking, camping and surfing. Annual membership is $40; $65 for couples. The age minimum is 50. Go online at **www.skiersover50.com**.
- **Retreads Motorcycle Club** has 30,000 members with no membership fee and a club newsletter. Call **913-235-3893**.
- **Roads Less Traveled Fabulous Fifties** division schedules bicycle trips in Colorado, Utah and New Mexico. Call **800-488-8483**.

> *"Be sure to check the senior deals in our airline section. There are some excellent membership programs available. You'll save on airfare* ***and*** *on hotels and rental cars. Most programs also allow for any-age companion travel at a reduced rate."*

CHILDREN & TRAVEL

Think Before You Go

Your parenting style matters when making decisions about traveling with children. Should vacations be geared toward fun? Should they be learning experiences? Do you want to spend the entire vacation as a family or do you prefer some childcare options? Any answer is the right answer if it's right for you.

Leaving children at home while you take a vacation does not make you a bad parent. It's sometimes the best decision for everyone. Arrange alternate activities for your children or split your vacation into adults-only and family segments.

Take age levels into consideration. If you're traveling with an infant or toddler, make sure you're able to carry the child for long periods. Account for the increased independence of teenagers. Don't count on children liking the same travel activities they enjoyed last year.

Minor childhood illnesses don't have to cause canceled trips if the illness is not readily contagious and is easily managed. Slowing down the pace for the first few days gives your child time to rest. Children with ear infections are prone to painful flights which often intensify their symptoms. Consult your doctor.

There may be legal issues to consider.

- **Solo parents and children** traveling to Mexico, Brazil, Australia and other countries must have a letter of consent from the absent parent. This is designed to guard against kidnapping. One parent or grandparent may be asked to provide proof that the other parent is aware of and approves the trip.
- **Travel with anyone other than the custodial parent** requires written permission for medical treatment. This is even true for grandparents and other close relatives. A simple sentence authorizing medical care will suffice. Have the statement notarized for extra assurance.

- **International travel** (including travel to Canada) requires the proper documents for all children, including infants. Check on up-to-date requirements with the U.S. Tourism Office or the embassy of the country you plan to visit.

Prepare Your Child

Allow children choices about what to pack, activities and even some budget matters. Don't try to meet every expectation. If their spending money will be limited, let them know in advance so they can plan for what is most important.

Discuss rule changes. Will bedtime remain the same? Will more snacks be permitted? What new rules are required to deal specifically with the trip?

Make the unknown known. Take the time to explain the trip to your children. Use brochures, library books and online travel information to inform them about new destinations.

Size of Walt Disney World: 43 square miles—twice the size of Manhattan.

> *"Kids love train travel. Sleeping berths, dining cars and observation cars are interesting novelties to them. They get to move around and aren't stuck in a car or plane for extended periods of time. That's reason enough to consider the train, but here's another incentive—Amtrak offers half-price tickets for kids two through 15 and their recently expanded Student Advantage program offers high school students 16 and over 15 percent off most fares year-round. Call* ***800-962-6872*** *for more information."*

Program free time into your travel. Underplanning can be your best friend.

Taking your child's friend on a family trip can add to everyone's enjoyment, but be aware of special needs and of your own liability. Be sure your guest is compatible with your child for extended periods of time. A good test is a weekend sleepover.

Children taking their first flights should be prepared by conversation, books or even a trip to the airport.

- **Just Planes Videos** offers three videos that answer most fears and questions. They cost $14.95 each (plus shipping and handling). Call **800-752-6376**; fax **617-539-3224**.
- ***How To Fly For Kids*** covers the same ground in book form for $10.95 plus shipping and handling. It also offers games and in-flight activities. It's available in bookstores or order by calling **800-729-6423**.

What To Take

A common misconception about traveling with children is that you have to carry an enormous amount of extra luggage. Pack the essentials and rent or improvise when you arrive. Essentials include:

- **Prescription medicine** and copies of the prescription in case of loss or spillage plus an easy-to-read pediatric thermometer.
- **Easy-care clothing** that the child likes to wear and that can easily be laundered in a hotel room.
- **Plastic bags of various sizes**, for soiled clothes, special finds, crayons, small toys and a dozen other things you can't predict in advance.
- **The stuffed toy or blanket** necessary to sleep. Try to take your child's second-best comfort item or purchase a duplicate. Many travel tears are shed when well-loved comfort items are lost during travel.

Carry infants up to five months old in canvas slings that rest against your chest. Backpack-style carriers for older infants keep your hands free and provide them with a secure view of the world.

Surprise kits packed with treats and travel activities provide you with anti-boredom ammunition.

Personal backpacks or carry-ons allow children to take along personal treasures and favorite toys and books. As much as possible, leave this space free for what they select and what they might find interesting along the way.

Travel By Car

Make essential safety guidelines unbreakable rules of the road.

- **Never allow a young child to travel**

in the front seat. Observe all manufacturers' guidelines on air-bags.

- **Approved car seats are mandatory** in all states for children four and under. Bring your own or look for a rental (about $5 a day) that is certified to meet Federal Motor Vehicle Safety Standards.
- **Carry a locking clip** to use on free-sliding latches common on foreign and domestic rental cars.
- **Check all seat belts and shoulder harnesses** to make sure they are arranged and function in a fashion that protects every family member.

Relieve car travel monotony to make your trips more enjoyable:

- **Head for back roads** for scenery that will awaken children's interest.
- **Leave early in the morning** so you can cover distances by mid-afternoon and take full advantage of hotel pools and recreational facilities.
- **Invest in inexpensive peace of mind.** Small cassette players with headphones can produce instant quiet as your four-year-old listens to a story tape and your 12-year-old tunes in to music. A child who usually reads little more than a cereal box can be fascinated by a road map or atlas.
- **Portable armrests,** available at auto supply stores, have storage compartments with lift-up lids. They create separate kid-zones when two children share a back seat.

Lodging

Use *Kids Stay Free* and *Kids Eat Free* programs. Many hotels offer free accommodations for children sharing a room with parents. Some hotels discount a second room so families with older children can enjoy privacy at bargain rates. Holiday Inns and other hotels frequently offer three free meals a day to children under 12 who are dining with their parents. Hotel Reservations Network, **800-964-6835**, is a clearinghouse for special values for family hotels. Check our chapter on hotels for information by chain.

Ask for child-proof rooms to make vacation life easier. They include special safety features and equipment. Safety check rooms where small children will be staying. Remember that most hotels (even grandma's house) are not set up for small children. The routine protection you are used to at home is not likely to be present when you travel. Cribs provided by hotels may not be up to safety standards.

Supervised activities are increasingly available at hotels and resorts. They can be free or cost as much as $65 per day at ultra luxury properties. Inquire about the ratio of counselor to child, first aid training and activities provided.

Childcare options exist at most major hotels, but often they consist of referral numbers with minimal reference checks. Make sure you are satisfied that your children are being left in trustworthy hands.

Caution children about added hotel expenses like in-room refrigerator items and using the hotel phone. In their eyes, every service may seem as free as the complimentary shampoo.

Consider condo rentals and suite hotels with kitchen facilities, room to spread out and separate sleeping areas.

Hostels offer inexpensive lodging options. Some have family rooms with private baths. Some are in lighthouses or restored downtown buildings. Get a complete list of hostels in the U.S. and Canada

#1 dream vacation of 433 kids surveyed at Sea World: a coast-to-coast theme park tour.

by sending $3, payable to Jim Williams at Sugar Hill International House, 722 St. Nicholas Ave., New York, NY 10031.

Almost 800 U.S. colleges offer accommodations, mostly on a summer season basis. About 50 offer year-round availability. Call Campus Travel Service, **800-525-6633**. Be sure your selection is child-friendly.

Child-Friendly Dining

Dining with children is simplified if you eat at restaurants that welcome them. Call ahead to see if they offer highchairs and booster seats.

Create your own room service. Milk, cereal and fresh fruit are great in-your-room alternatives to expensive restaurant breakfasts. Nested plastic bowls take up little luggage space and many hotels have nearby shopping areas where prices approach reason.

Consider a fast food meal. It may not be your idea of regional cuisine, but it can be comforting to smaller children already overloaded with change. Take the food back to your hotel and let your children enjoy their food while you order from room service. Chances are they'll think they got the better deal.

Surviving Disney

A trip to Disneyland or Walt Disney World is a highlight for most families.

- ***Birnbaum's Walt Disney World*** is the official guide to Walt Disney World. It's updated annually, contains a wealth of information and comes with discount coupons that make the $12.95 price a steal. It's published by Hyperion and is available in major bookstores.
- **Get a free Orlando Magicard** with over $1,000 in discounts on lodging, attractions, dining, transportation and shopping. Call **800-646-2092**.
- **Afternoons are generally the most crowded.** If you plan your park time for mornings and evenings, you can see twice as much. Go against the flow of traffic. Most people turn right at intersections. Turn left, and watch the crowd thin out.
- **Don't be scared away by a rainy day.** The parks are arranged to allow for all but downpours. A little wet weather is a small price to pay for lines that may take half the time.
- **Consider renting a small refrigerator** for your hotel room to save on meal and snack costs. The going rate from hotels that offer them (including on-site properties) is $5 a day.
- **Bring your own snacks** but be discreet. Disney does not allow food or drink to be taken into the park, but they rarely search backpacks or strollers. Compare prices for in-park food. A hotdog that costs $5 at one Magic Kingdom stand costs $2.35 at Casey's Coke Corner on Main Street USA.
- **Walt Disney World Resort guests** who take advantage of the Food 'n Fun Plan receive the equivalent of a $5 food credit per adult ($3 per child) for each day's Food 'n Fun Plan purchased. You pay $50 per adult per day for Food 'n Fun; $22 per child (ages three-nine). Your actual credit will be $55 and $25, respectively, usable toward any food or beverage purchase at any Walt Disney World Resort restaurant. The program operates on a debit system so you don't have to carry vouchers or cash. As a bonus you also receive free use of water sprites (small boats), horseback trail rides and tennis. Call **800-647-7900** or purchase

#2 dream vacation of 433 kids surveyed at Sea World: a trip under the ocean.

through your travel agent.

- **Don't try to see everything in one day.** One of the saddest sights is impatient parents rushing children from ride to ride while wondering why they don't seem to be having a great time.
- **Dress the whole family in the same bold-colored t-shirts or caps** for easier identification in crowds. Whistles worn around the neck make good alarms and calling signals.

A Bag Of Travel Tricks

Take advantage of printed materials that offer information, tips and discounts. If you are on a tight budget, check your library for the titles we suggest.

- **All major cities offer free information** on attractions for children. *New York For Kids*, for example, is available from the NYC Convention and Visitors Bureau, 2 Columbus Circle, New York, NY 10019. Similar information is available from state and national tourism organizations. Be sure to ask specifically for material pertaining to children.
- ***Family Travel Times*,** a quarterly at a $40 per year, is a compact source of information on traveling with children. Write to 45 W. 18th St., 7th Floor, New York, NY 10011; call **212-477-5524**.
- ***The Family & Travel Directory*** includes family travel discounts and extensive information on over 500 hotels and resorts oriented toward family stays. The cost is $19.95.

Make children's high energy levels work for you by planning hiking tours and outdoor-oriented vacations. Let the smallest walking child set the pace. There's a lot to be seen from a kid's-eye view. Teach children low impact tourism by emphasizing respect for the environment and the creatures living in it.

Hands-on programs at Sea World and Busch Gardens offer specialized programs for all children—from pre-schoolers to teenagers. Camp Sea World, **407-363-2380**, focuses on science and conservation. Busch Garden's Zoo Camp and Safari Classes, **813-987-5555**, offers a more limited variety of activities for groups.

Living history recreations and hands-on museums recognize that children like to learn by doing. Colonial Williamsburg in Virginia, Mystic Seaport in Connecticut and the six-floor Hands-On Museum in Ann Arbor are just a few places where destinations can define your trip.

Trips to visit relatives are great but don't expect your children to instantly bond with people they see infrequently. Allow them time to get over initial shyness. Plan a nostalgia trip to show your children where you went to school and the park you used to play at.

International travel is more affordable and manageable than you may think. A big plus is the opportunity for your kids to interact with children from other cultures. Take your child to a neighborhood park. You are likely to find other English-speaking parents who will be happy to share tips on top attractions for local children.

> *"Let your children feel some sense of familiarity. A visit to McDonald's is not what you traveled 2,000 miles for, but it may be a comfort to children trying to absorb major changes in culture, food and language."*

ACCESSIBLE TRAVEL

Getting What You Need & Want

The upside—With a little pre-planning, most people with physical disabilities can see as much of the world as they like. New legislation in several countries (and the Americans with Disabilities Act in the U.S.) compel travel vendors to open the doors to all people. Know your legal rights and insist on them. Almost 50 million Americans have physical disabilities. You are becoming a valued target market. Special agencies develop accessible tour and travel opportunities. Choose one of them or choose the same sources used by most travelers. The choice is yours.

The downside—Seven years after the passage of the Americans with Disabilities Act, compliance is lagging. When booking accommodations, book with hotels that value your business enough to provide free and accessible airport shuttles. An able-bodied traveler routinely enjoys that added value; people in wheelchairs can end up paying $50 or more to use a private service.

Hopeful signs—Hilton hotels have committed to remodeling 2,700 of its 90,000 U.S. rooms to improve accessibility. The plan will not be completed until 2002 but, at a $22,000 per room cost, it's a move in the right direction. Princess Cruises doubled the number of accessible cabins on its new *Sun Princess*. There are 19 cabins designed for people with physical disabilities.

The needs of travelers with disabilities vary. Travelers in wheelchairs need ramp access and wide doorways while travelers who are blind may benefit from Braille signs and menus. When you book accessible travel, spell out your needs clearly and ask for details on all areas of accessibility.

Travel vendors specializing in accessible travel offer a variety of travel planning (except where noted).

- **Able to Travel** at **800-986-0053**.
- **Accessible Journeys** at **800-846-4537**.
- **Action Whitewater Adventures** at **800-453-1482**.
- **Alaska Snail Trails**, operating out of Anchorage, offers accessible travel in Alaska via minibus. Call **800-348-4532**.
- **Flying Wheels Travel**, the oldest agency with a special emphasis on accessible travel. Call **800-535-6790**.
- **Le Boat** offers three to six night bookings on the 12-passenger *La Reine Pedauque*, a French river cruise barge with a staff including a Cordon-Bleu-trained chef. Call **800-922-0291**.
- **Mobility International USA** at **541-343-1284** is a non-profit group that sponsors trips that link you with disability activists worldwide and serves as a clearinghouse for work-study travel programs.
- **Nautilus Tours & Cruises** at **800-**

Material used by the posh La Costa Spa in its treatments: 2,000 year old mud.

797-6004.

- **Neverland Adventures** at **800-717-8226**.
- **Sundial Special Vacations** at **800-547-9198**.
- **Turtle Tours** at **800-453-9195**.

Ski programs with special services for skiers with disabilities include:

- **Adaptive Skiers Program**, covering Telluride, CO. Call **970-728-7533**.
- **Adaptive Sports Center**, covering Crested Butte, CO. Call **970-349-2296**.
- **Blind Outdoor Leisure Development**, covering Aspen Highlands, Aspen Mountain, Buttermilk and Snowmass, CO. Call **970-923-0578**.
- **California Adaptive Ski School**, covering Bear Mountain, CA. Call **909-585-2519**.
- **Disabled Skiers Program**, covering Beaver Creek, CO. Call **970-479-3264**.
- **Disabled Skiers Program**, covering Steamboat Springs, CO. Call **970-879-6111**.
- **The National Sports Center for the Disabled**, covering Winter Park, CO. Call **970-726-1540**.
- **Outdoor Education Center**, covering Arapahoe Basin, Breckenridge, Copper Mountain and Keystone, CO. Call **970-453-6422**.
- **The Tahoe (CA) Adaptive Ski School**. Call **916-581-4161**.

Enlightened Allies

A free bi-monthly newsletter is offered by the U.S. Architectural and Transportation Barriers Compliance Board. Call **202-272-5434**; visit **www.access-board.gov**.

The Society for the Advancement of Travel for the Handicapped engages in lobbying for increased accessibility and offers several free information sheets plus a quarterly newsletter at $13 a year. Write to 347 Fifth Ave., New York, NY 10016; call **212-447-7284**.

Disabilities Express: Travel & Disability Resource Directory lists worldwide sources for travel vendors and associations. The cost is $40. Call **417-836-4773**.

Twin Peaks Press publishes a quarterly on accessible travel at $25 a year and the 192-page *Travel for the Disabled: A Handbook of Travel Resources and 500 Worldwide Access Guides* at $23.45, including shipping. Call **360-694-2462** for more information; **800-637-2256** to order.

Travelin' Talk provides information on over 800 accessible travel advisors. The cost is $35. Call **615-552-6670**.

> *"We love New York and hope more cities, states and countries will follow their lead. The City of New York's Department of Cultural Affairs offers an international toll-free number for information on accessibility. Call* ***888-424-4685*** *from 9 a.m. to 5 p.m. ET Monday through Friday. The service is a clearing-house for city-wide information, previously only available by calling dozens of numbers."*

Accessible Vehicle Rentals In The U.S.

This chart shows services available for vehicle rentals. Most agencies will allow additional drivers at no extra charge. Policies and vehicle availability vary by location. It's best to reserve with as much advance as possible to help ensure that you will be able to get the vehicle you want.

ACCESSIBLE VEHICLE RENTALS			
COMPANY	**SERVICES**	**ADVANCE**	**TTY NUMBER**
ADVANTAGE 800-777-5500	Hand controls must be requested when you make your reservation; wheelchair-equipped vans are available at 800-828-1736.	48-72 hours	N/A
ALAMO 800-462-5266	Hand controls in the U.S. and Canada; wheelchair access to all Rental Plazas; pickup and delivery services.	24-48 hours	800-522-9292
AVIS 800-331-1212	Hand controls in the U.S.; wheelchair accessible mini-vans with ramps and lifts.	24 hours	800-331-2323
BUDGET 800-527-0700	Hand controls (right or left hand) and accessible parking at corporate rental locations.	24-72 hours	800-826-5510
DOLLAR 800-800-4000	Hand controls at major locations; lift-equipped shuttles are being introduced.	24 hours	800-232-3301
HERTZ 800-654-3131	Hand controls at 900 corporate locations in the U.S. and Canada; spinner knobs for travelers with decreased upper body strength; accessible parking at corporate locations; lift-equipped buses at some airports.	24-48 hours	800-654-2280
NATIONAL 800-328-4567	Hand controls at major locations.	24 hours	800-328-6323
THRIFTY 800-367-2277	Hand controls at major locations.	24-72 hours	800-358-5836
WHEELCHAIR GETAWAYS 800-642-2042.	Lift-equipped van rentals in 80 cities in the U.S. and Puerto Rico. Rent daily, weekly or monthly.	72 hours	N/A

INTERNATIONAL TRAVEL

You can take a trip across the ocean for the same amount (or less) than you would spend on some trips from state to state. Now that international travel is financially within the reach of most travelers, let's cut the paperwork and question marks down to size, and get in position to take advantage of great international deals. This is the year to see places you have always longed to see. Take a bargain airfare, add an international hotel special and you are on your way.

Start by taking advantage of Uncle Sam's library, courtesy of the U.S. Superintendent of Documents. Dozens of publications are available. You can order them by mail for $1 each (U.S. Government Printing Office, Washington, DC 20402). You can get them for free by fax by calling **202-647-3000** and entering the appropriate four number code. Current offerings (and their codes) include *A Safe Trip Abroad* (1000), *Tips for Travelers to the Caribbean* (1003), *U.S. Consuls Help Americans Abroad* (1004), *Tips for People's Republic of China* (1010), *Tips for Travel to Russia and the NIS* (1011), *Travel Warnings on Drugs Abroad* (1014), *Tips for Central and South America* (1039) and *Tips for Mexico* (1042).

Passports

A U.S. Passport is essential for most foreign travel and the best proof of citizenship for all travelers. Every U.S. citizen, including infants, must carry a passport when traveling abroad. You can travel to Mexico, Canada and the Caribbean Islands with an original or certified copy of your birth certificate, a photo ID and a travel ticket, but you can prevent any possible problem on returning to the U.S. by carrying a passport instead.

U. S. Passports are valid for ten years. If you plan to do a lot of travel, request a passport with extra pages at no additional charge. You won't have to renew early simply because you've used up all the pages.

Apply for all passports by one of the following methods:

- **Any U.S. Passport Agency office** (listed in *Know Who To Contact*).
- **Any of 2,500 courthouses and 900 post offices** that accept applications.
- **Send mail applications** to the National Passport Center, P.O. Box 371971, Pittsburgh, PA 15250.
- **Download application forms** at **http://travel.state.gov/passport_services.html**.

Passport applications require proof of identity, such as a driver's license or state ID (credit cards and social security cards are not acceptable) plus one of the following documents:

- **An expired passport** regardless of the date of expiration.
- **A certified birth certificate copy** or naturalization papers.
- **A baptismal certificate or** record of elementary school enrollment.
- **A U.S. citizen appearing in person** to sign a statement attesting to your identity.

Location of the Statue of Liberty in Paris: two blocks southwest of the Eiffel Tower.

You will also need two identical passport photos taken within the past six months. It's best to have them taken by a company that specializes in passport photos. Some large travel agencies offer this service in house.

Passport applications fees are $65 if you apply in person, $55 if you apply by mail and $40 for children under 18 applying by mail or in person.

Routine issuance of passports takes two to six weeks depending on time of year (February through July is busiest) and how you apply. U.S. Passport Agency expedited service (one week or less) is available for an additional $30. You must have a ticket in hand showing that you are traveling within ten days or need your passport urgently in order to apply for visas. Private expediting services can get you a passport in as little as 24 hours, but the cost can be $150 or more. They can be very helpful in emergency situations, but try to plan ahead to avoid this often avoidable expense. Find them in the classified directory under *Passport and Visa Services*.

Guard your passport carefully, both at home and when you travel. A valid U.S. passport can be more valuable to certain types of thieves than a wallet stuffed with cash and credit cards.

Report lost passports immediately and request a temporary replacement while traveling from the American embassy or consulate. If you locate your passport after it's been reported missing, don't use it. Immigration will stop you for traveling on what they have listed as a lost or stolen document.

Visa Requirements

Visa requirements can change fairly often. Countries that participate in the U.S. Visa Waiver Program (covering stays of up to 90 days) include Andorra, Argentina, Australia, Austria, Belgium, Brunei, Denmark, Finland, France, Germany, Iceland, Ireland, Italy, Japan, Liechtenstein, Luxembourg, Monaco, the Netherlands, New Zealand, Norway, San Marino, Spain, Sweden and Switzerland.

Some embassies do not charge for issuing visas, but policies vary by country. Some Middle Eastern countries or former Soviet satellites may charge hundreds of dollars for the privilege of visiting. The current range runs from 42-cents to over $400.

A chart listing fundamentals on obtaining entry into 78 countries is offered at no charge through Trans-World Visa Service, which expedites visas on a fee basis. Send a stamped, self-addressed envelope to Trans-World Visa Service, 790 27th Ave., San Francisco, CA 94121.

The State Department fax information line, 202-647-3000, provides information on your choice of three countries. Request the "foreign entry requirements" option. Get the same data by recording by calling **202-647-5226**.

Most visas take two to three weeks to acquire and you must have a passport before you apply. Expedited service is available from the same companies that expedite passports. These services are not inexpensive and can cost as much as several hundred dollars for one-day passport service. Visa services are useful for their proximity to embassies and their daily contact with them. Passport expediters should be reserved for emergency situations only.

The chart on the following page lists select visa and passport expediters and typical fees.

Three countries that border East Africa's Lake Victoria: Kenya, Tanzania & Uganda.

Visa & Passport Expediters

Fees listed reflect agency service charges only. Government fees for visas and passports, and shipping charges are additional.

VISA & PASSPORT EXPEDITERS		
SERVICE PROVIDERS	AVERAGE TOURIST VISA FEE	PASSPORTS FEES
ALL POINTS VISA Bethesda, MD 301-652-9055	$35	$120 – less than 24 hours $60 – more than 24 hours
ATLAS VISA Arlington, VA 703-418-0800	$50	$75 – one to five days $50 – six or more days
CAPITOL VISA Silver Spring, MD 301-942-8576	$30	$110 – under two and a half weeks $55 – over two and a half weeks
DMS VISA INTERNATIONAL Washington, DC 202-745-3815	$40	$85 – 24 hour service $65 – more than 24 hours
EXPRESS VISA Washington, DC 202-337-2442	$40	$125 – less than three days $65 – more than three days

Customs

The basics of customs are simple. In 1995 Customs set a goal of getting most people through the system within five minutes of picking up their luggage at the carousel. For the most part, they succeed.

Duty-free allowances vary by country of origin and destination, existing trade policies, tax policy and in some countries, trade sanctions. You must have been out of the country at least 48 hours to be eligible to bring in any duty-free items. You can't save unused allowances from trip to trip, and there must be a 30-day period between exemptions.

- **You will pay generally ten percent** on the first $1,000 in purchases above your $400 allowance and various rates on purchases exceeding that limit.
- **You can carry up to $10,000** in cash and negotiable instruments. Higher amounts must be reported on Customs form 4790 when entering and leaving the U.S. Remember that carrying high amounts of cash can incite custom inspector's interest. Be prepared to explain why you are carrying it.
- **Carry receipts** on new-looking, foreign-made items that you purchased before your trip to prove that they are not subject to duty.

The Generalized System of Preference applies to 125 countries and exempts certain items from duty. *GSP & The Traveler* provides an updated list. Get it from any regional customs office or write to U.S. Customs Services, Box 7407, Washington, DC 20044.

The newest customs technology is INSPass, available by enrollment to residents of the U.S., Canada and Bermuda who travel internationally at least three times a year. Members can check in on ATM-like machines and proceed directly to Customs. INSPass is in use in Chicago, Honolulu, Houston, Los Angeles, Miami, Montreal, Newark, New York (JFK), San Francisco, Toronto and Vancouver. To request an application write to U.S. Immigration & Naturalization Service INSPass, P.O. Box 300766, JFK Airport Station, Jamaica, Queens, NY 11430; call **800-870-3676**, **212-206-6500** or **201-645-4400**. Request form I833.

Factors that could subject you to intense scrutiny include having your name in a government alert data base, travel from known drug-source countries or popular shopping destinations, bulky or unusual clothing, a nervous demeanor or obvious signs of wealth. The sensitive snout of a drug-sniffing dog can single you out for attention even if you are the picture of innocence. An incredible percentage of all U.S. currency carries trace amounts of cocaine. Don't panic, but do avoid carrying large sums of cash, particularly when visiting countries with high levels of drug activity.

There are 45 regional U.S. Customs Offices. Get the complete list at **www.customs.ustreas.gov**. A selection covering most areas of the country:

Anchorage – 907-271-2675

Chicago – 312-353-6100

Dallas – 214-574-2170

Detroit – 313-226-3177

El Paso – 915-540-5800

Honolulu – 808-522-8068

Los Angeles – 310-514-6030

Miami – 305-536-4321

New Orleans – 504-670-2082

New York – 212-466-5817

Portland (ME) – 207-780-3326

St. Louis – 314-428-2662

Seattle – 206-553-0554

Washington (DC) – 703-318-5900

Know Before You Go is a free publication offered by the U.S. Customs Service. It offers a traveler's insight into customs' rules and regulations. Write to U.S. Customs Service, KBYG, P.O. Box 7407, Washington, DC 20044; call **202-927-6724**.

> *"The North American Free Trade Agreement (NAFTA) calls for no or very low duty on certain items imported from Canada and Mexico. For other items you get a $400 exemption, then pay seven percent for the first $1,000 in goods from Mexico; two percent from Canada. Customs will confiscate certain items purchased abroad despite the assurances of shopkeepers eager to make a sale. Don't purchase lizard, snake or crocodile skin products, feathers or feather products, furs from spotted cats or marine mammals, sea-turtle products, ivory, live birds, decorative items made from wildlife or unlicensed copies of brand name products."*

Keynote speaker at a recent American Tourism Society convention: Latvian president Guntis Ulmanis.

> *"Don't try to avoid paying duty. If you get caught you may have to pay more than you would have been charged had you declared your purchases. Customs agents are authorized to multiply the duty if you exhibit a lack of cooperation. They are well versed in tricks people use to try to cover up purchases made overseas. If they choose to, they can check serial and registration numbers. If you got a deal on your purchase (and you should limit your purchases to real deals and unusual finds), the legal duty is a small price to pay. Purchases made in duty-free shops are exempt from tax only in the country of purchase. They're still subject to U.S. duty."*

Legal Pitfalls

Learn local laws and customs when you travel internationally. What is merely frowned on in the U.S. can be prosecuted under the laws of other countries. Carrying or holding a package for a stranger could open you to drug charges in countries with laws that include the death penalty for contraband offenses.

If you are arrested, notify the American Embassy and retain a lawyer immediately. Embassies do not provide direct legal assistance. They guarantee that your rights as a detained U.S. citizen are protected, but those rights are defined by the laws of the country you're in. The best source for an international lawyer referral is your own attorney in the U.S. The best time to get that referral: before trouble strikes. If he or she cannot provide information on representation in countries you plan to visit, contact the International Legal Defense Council, **215-977-9982** or (for U.S. and Latin America only) the Inter-American Bar Association, **202-393-1217**.

Never purchase endangered species products or antiquities. Shop owners may assure you that you'll encounter no problems but many countries—primarily Peru, Mexico, China, Greece and other Mediterranean countries—have strict laws protecting their national treasures.

Exchange currency only through authorized channels. The small amount of money you might save is not worth risking the harsh penalties some countries impose.

Dissolving Language Barriers

You may find that language problems encountered by Americans in Paris are no more confusing than conversation between a Texan and a person from the Bronx. An impressive number of citizens of other countries have a reasonable command of English as a second language. Even if your grade in high school Spanish 101 was barely passing, there are ways for you to get through language barriers.

- **Learn four words or phrases a day** before you go. Two weeks gives you 56 new ways to communicate.
- **Speak distinctly and avoid slang or colloquialisms.** Don't make the common mistake of speaking louder when you are not immediately understood. They hear you loud and clear—they just are having trouble understanding what you are saying.
- **Use commonly understood gestures** to emphasize what you're trying to say and don't try to over-communicate. Keep it simple and clear.

Best breed for sniffing out illegal agricultural products: beagles.

> *"Our Embassies and Consulates can do a lot but they are not miracle workers. They can provide a list of English-speaking physicians, authorize 90-day special circumstance replacement passports and provide support services (not legal representation) for U.S. citizens incarcerated in foreign countries. They will even get you back home in some dire financial circumstances. They can't provide loans, cash your checks or enforce U.S. standards of justice. You are under the legal domain of your host country."*

- **One picture can be worth a dozen words** if you know how to read internationally accepted symbols. Quickpoint takes this idea a step further with the creation of easy to comprehend symbols to convey things like specific meal requests, the need for a haircut or a place to develop film. A folding card the size of a standard business envelope increases your worldwide communications skills at a $5 cost. Write to Gaia Communications, Box 239, Alexandria, VA 22313.
- **Learn a foreign language** where it's spoken. Universities and private schools offer language programs for foreigners. Contact The American Institute for Foreign Study, **800-727-2437** or Language Studies Abroad, **800-424-5522**.

International Travel Tips

Three Seasons of European Travel each offer their own advantages.

- **Peak season** (late June, July and August) offers travel when most leisure travelers are best able to go. The crowds can even be advantageous. Pick a good vantage point and get the benefit of several tour guides' interpretations within 30 minutes.
- **Shoulder season** (May, early June, September and early October) has the best mix of rates, weather and uncrowded conditions.
- **Off-season** (all remaining months) offers the best bargains. Budget hotels throughout Europe are readily available, though some hostels will be closed for the season.

Americans are generally welcome travelers. Do your part by understanding indigenous customs. Be observant enough to gauge what's appropriate. Soothe first-trip jitters with videos to introduce you to new destinations. Watch them for free in some large travel agencies, rent them from video shops or purchase them from retailers and tourism offices. Free or almost free travel information comes from many sources, including car rental agencies and airlines. Brochures geared toward attracting customers include helpful information on destinations they service. Tourism offices listed in *Know Who To Contact* will send you free information.

Prepare for the unexpected before you take your trip. Foreign holidays and holy days can take you by surprise with crowded streets and businesses that are closed for the day. Countries where political and economic climates are in flux present special challenges. Make as many arrangements as possible from the U.S., but don't take your confirmations too seriously. Traveling in such countries requires a special sort of

The four official languages of Switzerland: French, German, Italian & Romansch.

flexibility. On the bright side, travel to some countries has opened up and become much easier for the average traveler.

Save with Hot Cards and other destination-specific promotions. See *Dollars & Cents* for a selection of what is available. Don't forget free attractions. London, for example, has no standard admission charge at the National Gallery and the Tate Gallery.

Save by heading for smaller towns rather than big international centers. You can visit them by train or rental car with a home base in a place where lodging and food are one-third to one-half cheaper. You'll also get perspectives not available to travelers who stick to the biggest tourist destinations.

Shopping Internationally can be an adventure.

- **Visit outdoor markets** for bargains and a panoramic look at local culture. Whether it's a *souk* in Morocco or a *mercato* in Italy, you'll find a feast for all your senses.
- **Get a gem of a bargain** in countries where your favorite stone is king. Best bets: opals from Australia and New Zealand, diamonds from Belgium, jade from Hong Kong, pearls from Japan, sapphires from Thailand, emeralds from South Africa, agate and turquoise from Mexico, rubies from India, amber from Russia.
- **Check out each country's specialty items:** alpaca and leather items from Argentina, chocolates from Belgium, silk from China, made-to-order suits from England, electronics from Hong Kong, batik from Bali, beaded jewelry and clothing from Nepal, sweaters and linens from Ireland. Check out public marketplaces like Ho Chi Minh City's Thanh Market where an intricately embroidered blouse is yours for about $10.

Simplify taxi travel by writing out the address of your destination to show your driver, or have someone familiar with the local language call it in when you request the taxi. Pick up a book of matches from the front desk and you have a convenient cue-card for your return trip.

Currency adapters may take care of differences in plug styles, but they don't convert electrical currents that can cause shocks, smoke and sizzled appliances. *Electric Current Abroad*, published by the U.S. State Department, lists voltage and currency fluctuations around the world. Ask for document #003-008-00203-2. The cost is $3. Order from the Superintendent of Documents, Washington, DC 20402.

Departure taxes are charged by some countries. Keep enough local currency to pay them without taking another trip through the currency exchange labyrinth.

> *"Here are two practical tips. Don't count on free beverage refills in cafes. Most countries charge the same for the second cup or glass as they did for the first. After you've quenched your thirst and head for the facilities, you may be surprised to discover that not all toilets flush. You might have to push or pull, twist, step-on or squeeze a handle—or you might be surprised by an electric-eye that does the work for you. Coin-operated water closets await your need on street corners in London and Amsterdam."*

TRAVEL WITH ANIMALS

Can You?/Should You?

Pets are family and an increasing number of vacation-goers want to take along the *whole* family – even those with paws. Your teenage son may not be jumping with joy at the thought of your two-week road trip through the Ozarks, but Shooby and Spike will probably be thrilled to go anywhere you go.

Sometimes taking pets with us when we travel is not the best decision. Animals who are easily stressed or have special health considerations can suffer greatly from travel, particularly if you use air travel. If you think the air in Coach is bad, you should check out the air in the cargo hold. Air travel for animals is covered extensively in Chapter One's *On Board Basics.*

Assistance and certified companion dogs are allowed to accompany you anywhere in the U.S. You don't have to receive permission, but it is a good idea to let the reservation desk know so you can be given any information available to make travel easier for both of you.

Quarantine laws are applicable anytime you travel outside the continental U.S. In most cases, the mandatory length of quarantine (as long as six months) effectively prohibits the vacationing pet. The baggage department of the airline you're flying can give you specific quarantine requirements. Assistance and certified companion dogs should be exempt from quarantine rules, but they aren't always.

Pets are not allowed on bus lines or in Amtrak passenger cars. Some trains allow pets to travel in baggage compartments, but you are responsible for feeding, watering and exercising your pet during stops.

Travel By Car

Car trips with pets require that you carry proof of immunization if you are crossing state lines and, in rare instances, when you cross county lines.

- **Don't set out on a long trip** unless you know your pets travel well. If Winkie hides every time he's scheduled for a short trip to the vet, he isn't going to be a very happy cat on a weekend vacation drive. Size and breed of your animal matters less than temperament.

> *“The U.K. finally seems ready to relax its excessive six month quarantine rule on all pets arriving from overseas—including guide and companion dogs. New legislation should cut the time requirement to one month (still unnecessarily long) for animals coming from rabies-free countries or certified as healthy by a microchip implant.”*

> *"Some dogs can go anywhere. Rocky, a 120-pound Old English Sheepdog, is a legend in our office building. When Rocky travels by car, he changes radio stations with his paw if he doesn't like what's coming out of the speaker. If he's left in the car too long, he beeps the horn."*

- **Take short rest stops** every two to three hours and, as much as possible, keep Helga or Gypsy on leash. Most dogs are used to leashes. If you plan to travel with cats, a little leash training before you go is a good idea.
- **Take a jug of water** from home, and add to it as your animals drink. This helps them get accustomed to different water supplies gradually.
- **Don't let your dogs hang their heads out of the open windows** of fast-moving vehicles. Flying debris can permanently injure eyes. Foreign material can lodge in their ears and noses.

Pet-Friendly Lodging

Pet-friendly lodging is available at about 15 percent of U.S. hotels. You don't have to make a reservation for your "children," Cora and Simon, and hope no one will notice that they are covered with fur. Protect your pets when you stay at hotels and motels. Try not to leave them alone in the room. They can be out the door the second the maid opens it.

Chains that are particularly pet-friendly include:

- **Best Western**—Almost 70 percent welcome pets. Call **800-528-1234**.
- **Four Season and Regent Hotels**—This canine and cat conscious company provides a welcome tray of rawhide chews for dogs and litter boxes for cats at all hotels. Dinner may be served on a silver tray. Pets (and kids) stay free. Call **800-332-3442**.
- **Holiday Inns**—Over 1,000 accept pets and some offer dog-walking services. Call **800-465-4329** for a free directory.
- **Loews**—Annapolis and Washington, DC locations have a Very Important Pets Program that delivers treats on a silver tray and donates five percent of the room rate to a local humane society. Call **800-235-6397**.
- **Motel 6** —Most accept one pet per room. Call **800-466-8356**.

> *"England's White Topps Hotel in Southbourne will not accept human guests unless they bring their dogs along. The decor features paw-print wallpaper and curtains and clocks with wagging tails. The proprietor (who has six dogs of her own) provides doggy bags with all meals and offers a special room for aged or arthritic pets. Britain has over 900 animal-lodging facilities that put out the welcome mat for Lord Gizzmo and his human friend."*

Guide Books & Periodicals

Periodicals include:

- *DogGone* at $24 annually is a bi-monthly offering travel tips and information on dog-friendly destinations. Call **561-569-8434**.
- *The Furry Traveler* has a $25 annual subscription rate. Call **301-495-4823**.

Extensive guides are also available. Be sure to ask when the book was last revised. If you get an out-of-date book, you'll miss being able to take advantage of the latest information.

- *Vacationing With Your Pet* by Eileen Barish lists over 23,000 hotels, inns, ranches and bed & breakfasts in the U.S. and Canada that welcome guests with pets. In the words of the *Wall Street Journal*, it "helps travelers avoid fax paws." You'll find listings as varied as New York's Regency Hotel and Beverly's Log Guest House in Plymouth, Wisconsin. Each listing includes phone number, address and rate range. Many do not charge extra for pets. Others charge a refundable deposit. The book suggests you reserve in advance and confirm current pet policies when you call. Keep in mind that policies may vary by the type and size of your pet. The book is available directly from Pet Friendly Publications at a cover price of $19.95. Call **800-496-2665**.
- ***Great Vacations for You & Your Dog Abroad*** is available for $22.70 (including shipping) from Martin Management Books. Order by phone at **808-244-4187**.
- ***Pets-R-Permitted*** lists over 10,000 lodging options, including prices, restrictions and additional charges at hotels in the U.S., Canada and Mexico. The $16.95 price includes shipping. Call **800-274-7297**.
- ***Take Your Pet USA*** is available for $13.95, including shipping, from Artco Publishing, 12 Channel St., Boston, MA 02210.

Pet Protective Publications

Send for free pet-friendly publications, enclosing a self-addressed, stamped envelope.

- ***Air Travel For Your Dog Or Cat*** from the Air Transport Association of America, 1301 Pennsylvania Ave. NW, Suite 1100, Washington, DC 20004; call **202-626-4000**.
- ***Pet Travel Tips*** from People For The Ethical Treatment Of Animals (PETA), P.O. Box 42516, Washington, DC 20015; call **757-622-7382**.
- ***Travel Tip Sheets*** from the American Society for the Prevention of Cruelty to Animals (ASPCA) Education Dept., 441 E. 92nd St., New York, NY 10128; call **212-876-7700**. Also available, ***Traveling With Your Pet,*** a $5 ASPCA publication.

Major benefit dogs give humans: lowering their blood pressure and anxiety levels.

KNOW WHO TO CONTACT

Have you ever headed for a bank of airport pay phones, reached for the telephone directory and found an empty holder? It's hard to let your fingers do the walking when there's nowhere for them to go.

This section will help you avoid that annoyance and many others with an updated list of phone numbers, mailing addresses and key internet site addresses. Some information—such as Airport Paging numbers—are unique to this book.

Some 800 numbers may not be accessible from one specific state. If you run into that glitch, make a free call to 800 directory assistance (**800-555-1212**) and they'll be happy to give you a number that will work from your location. Please note that numbers with an 888 prefix are also toll-free.

Check **www.bestfares.com** for additional internet URL's and direct links to many travel sites.

AIRLINES

Vacation Package Divisions are listed after main reservation numbers.

DOMESTIC & DOMESTIC/INTERNATIONAL RESERVATIONS

Air Nevada 800-634-6377
www.pcap.com/airnev.htm
AirTran Airways 800-247-8726
www.airtran.com
Alaska Airlines 800-426-0333
www.alaska-air.com
Aloha Airlines 800-367-5250
www.alohaair.com
Aloha Islandair 800-323-3345
America West Airlines 800-235-9292
www.americawest.com
America West Vacations 800-356-6611
American/American Eagle 800-433-7300
www.aa.com
American FlyAAway Vacations 800-321-2121
American Trans Air 800-225-2995
www.ata.com
Cape Air 800-352-0714
www.capecod.com/capeair/index.html
Comair 800-354-9822
www.fly-comair.com
Continental Airlines 800-525-0280
www.flycontinental.com
Continental Vacations 800-634-5555
Corporate Express 800-555-6565
Delta Air Lines 800-221-1212
www.delta-air.com
Delta Dream Vacations 800-872-7786
Delta Express 800-325-5205
www.delta-air.com/express/index.html
Eastwind 800-644-3592
Frontier 800-432-1359
www.flyfrontier.com
Great Lakes Airlines 800-367-5320
www.greatlakesav.com
Gulfstream 800-992-8532
Hawaiian 800-367-5320
Kiwi 800-538-5494
www.jetkiwi.com
Midway Airlines 800-446-4392
Midwest Express 800-452-2022
www.midwestexpress.com
MetroJet 888-638-7653
Nations Air 800-248-9538
Northwest Airlines 800-225-2525
www.nwa.com
Paradise Island Airways 800-786-7202
www.paradiseair.com
Reno Air 800-736-6247
www.renoair.com
Reno Quick Escape Vacation Packages . 800-736-6247
Skywest Airlines 800-453-9417
Southwest Airlines 800-435-9792
www.southwest.com
Southwest Fun Pack Vacations 800-423-5683
SunJet 800-478-6538
Tower Air 800-221-2500
TriStar Airlines 800-218-8777
www.infosys.de/tristar
TWA (Trans World Airlines) 800-221-2000
www.twa.com
TWA Getaway Vacations 800-438-2929
United Airlines 800-241-6522
www.ual.com
United Vacations 800-328-6877
US Airways/US Airways Shuttle 800-428-4322
www.usairways.com
US Airways Vacations 800-455-0123
Vanguard Airlines 800-826-4827

INTERNATIONAL AIRLINE RESERVATIONS

Aer Lingus 800-223-6537
www.aerlingus.ie
Aer Lingus Discover Ireland 800-223-6537
Aero California 800-237-6225
Aeroflot 800-995-5555
www.aeroflot.org/aeroflot.html
Aerolineas Argentinas 800-333-0276
www.aerolineas.com.ar
Aeromexico 800-237-6639
www.wotw.com/aeromexico
Aeromexico Vacations 800-245-8585
AeroPeru 800-777-7717
www.aeroperu-usa.com
Air Afrique 800-456-9192
Air Aruba 800-882-7822
www.interknowledge.com/air-aruba
Air Canada 800-776-3000
www.aircanada.ca
Air Canada Vacations 800-774-8993
Air France 800-237-2747
www.airfrance.fr
Air India 212-751-6200
www.allindia.com/airindia
Air Jamaica 800-523-5585
www.airjamaica.com
Air Mauritius 800-537-1182
Air New Zealand 800-262-2468
www.airnz.com
Air New Zealand Pacific Vacations 800-722-4342
Air Zimbabwe 800-742-3006
Alitalia Airlines 800-223-5730
www.italia.com

Fine for importing chewing gum into Singapore: $1,000.

ALM-Antillean Airlines 800-327-7197
www.empg.com/alm
ANA-All Nipon Airways 800-235-9262
www.ana.co.jp/index-e.html
Ansett Airlines 800-366-1300
www.ansett.com.au
Austrian Airlines 800-843-0002
www.aua.co.at/aua
Avensa 800-428-3672
Avianca Airlines 800-284-2622
Aviateca 800-327-9832
www.flylatinamerica.com/acc_aviateca.html
Bahamasair 800-222-4262
Balkan Airlines 800-852-0944
British Airways 800-247-9297
www.british-airways.com
British Airways Holidays 800-876-2200
British Midland Airways 800-788-0555
www.iflybritishmidland.com
BWIA International 800-538-2942
Canadian Airlines 800-426-7000
www.cdnair.ca
Cathay Pacific Airways 800-233-2742
www.cathay-usa.com
Cathay Pacific Tours 800-762-8181
Cayman Airways 800-422-9626
www.caymans.com/~caymans/Cayman_Airways.html
China Airlines 800-227-5118
www.china-airlines.com
CityBird 888-248-9247
Copa Airlines 800-359-2672
www.copaair.com
CSA-Czech Airlines 800-223-2365
www.csa.cz
El Al 800-223-6700
www.elal.co.il
Emirates Airlines 800-777-3999
www.ekgroup.com
Ethiopian Airlines 800-433-9677
EVA Airways 800-695-1188
www.evaair.com.tw
Faucett Airlines 800-334-3356
Finnair 800-950-5000
www.us.finnair.com
Garuda-Indonesian Airways 800-247-8380
Guyana Airways 800-242-4210
Gulf Air-Golden Falcon 800-553-2824
Iberia Airlines 800-772-4642
Icelandair 800-223-5500
www.centrum.is/icelandair
Japan Airlines 800-525-3663
www.jal.co.jp
Kenya Airways 800-343-2506
KLM 800-374-7747
www.klm.nl
Korean Air Lines 800-438-5000
www.koreanair.com
Kuwait Airways 800-458-9248
LACSA Airline of Costa Rica 800-225-2272
www.flylatinamerica.com/acc_lasca.html
Lan Chile Airlines 800-735-5526
www.lanchile.com
Lan Chile Tours 800-995-4888
Lloyd Aero Boliviano 800-327-7407
LOT-Polish Airlines 800-223-0593
www.lot.com
LTU International Airways 800-888-0200
www.ltu.com
Lufthansa 800-645-3880
www.lufthansa.com
Malaysia Airlines 800-552-9264
www.MalaysiaAir.com
Malev Hungarian Airline 800-223-6884
www.osgweb.com/airlines/malev
Martinair Holland 800-366-4655
Mexicana Airlines 800-531-7923
www.mexicana.com
Mexicana MexSeaSun 800-531-9321
Olympic Airways 800-223-1226
agn.hol.gr/info/olympic1.htm
Philippine Airlines 800-435-9725
www.sequel.net/PAL
Polynesian Airlines 800-272-5042
Qantas Airways 800-227-4500
www.qantas.com
Qantas Vacations 800-641-8772
Royal Air Maroc 800-344-6726
Royal Jordanian Airlines 800-223-0470
www.rja.com.jo
Sabena Airlines 800-955-2000
www.sabena.com
Sabena Eurostarters 800-955-2000
SAS 800-221-2350
www.sas.com
SAS Tours 800-221-2350
Saudi Arabian Airlines 800-472-8342
www.saudiarabian-airlines.com
Singapore Airlines 800-742-3333
www.singaporeair.com
Singapore Asian Affair Holidays 800-742-3133
Solomon Airlines 800-677-4277
South African Airways 800-722-9675
www.saa.co.za/saa/welcome2.htm
Swissair 800-221-4750
www.swissair.com
TACA International Airlines 800-535-8780
www.flylatinamerica.com/acc_taca.html
TAP Air Portugal 800-221-7370
Thai Airways International 800-426-5204
www.thaiair.com
Thai Royal Orchid Holidays 800-426-5204

Dublin hotel owned by the rock group U2: The Clarence.

Transbrasil Airlines 800-872-3153
www.transbrasil.com.br
Trans Jamaican Airlines 800-523-5585
Varig Brazilian Airlines 800-468-2744
Virgin Atlantic Airways 800-862-8621
www.fly.virgin.com
Virgin Vacations 800-364-6466

> *"For frequent flyer programs, please see pages 125 to 147 for full contact information."*

AIRLINE CLUBS

Aer Lingus Gold Circle Club 800-223-6537
Air Canada Maple Leaf Club 800-813-9237
Alaska Airlines Board Room 800-654-5669
Aloha Executive Club 800-367-5250
America West Phoenix Club 602-693-2994
American Admirals Club 800-237-7971
Canadian Empress Lounge 800-426-7000
Continental Presidents 800-322-2640
Delta Crown Room 800-221-1212
Hawaiian Premier Club 800-367-7637
JAL Global Room 800-525-3663
KLM Premium Class Lounge 800-374-7747
Northwest WorldClubs 800-692-3788
Swissair/Austrian Airlines Travel Club . 800-388-2878
TWA Ambassadors Club 800-527-1468
United Red Carpet Club 602-881-0500
US Airways Club 800-828-8522

AIRLINE COMPLAINTS

Address all correspondence to Customer Relations

Aer Lingus 800-223-6537
122 E. 42nd St.
New York, NY 10168

Air Canada 800-813-9237
fax: 514-422-5077
221 N. Lasalle St.
Chicago, IL 60601

Air France 800-872-3224
fax: 914-365-1150
125 W. 55th St.
New York, NY 10019

Air New Zealand 310-648-7917
1960 E. Grand Ave., Ste. 900
El Segundo, CA 90245

AirTran 800-925-8538
1800 Phoenix Blvd., Ste. 126
Atlanta, GA 30349

Alaska Airlines 800-426-0333
fax: 206-439-4477
P.O. Box 68900
Seattle, WA 98168

Alitalia 800-903-9991
fax: 212-903-3507
666 5th Ave.
New York, NY 10103

All Nippon (ANA) 212-956-8200
fax: 212-969-9022
630 5th Ave., Ste. 537
New York, NY 10111

Aloha 808-836-4115
fax: 808-836-4206
Box 30028
Honolulu, HI 96820

America West 800-235-9292
fax: 602-693-3707
4000 E. Sky Harbor Blvd.
Phoenix, AZ 85034

American 817-967-2000
fax: 817-967-4162
P.O. Box 619612, M.D. 2400
D/FW Airport, TX 75261-9612

American Trans Air 800-225-2995
fax: 317-487-4808
P.O. Box 51609
Indianapolis, IN 46251

Austrian Airlines 718-670-8600
17-20 Whitestone Expy.
Whitestone, NY 11357

British Airways 800-422-9101
fax: 718-397-4395
75-20 Astoria Blvd.
Jackson Heights, NY 11370

Canadian Airlines 800-661-3311
fax: 403-569-4180
Calgary Administration Bldg.
615-18 St. SE
Calgary, Alberta T2E 6J5

Cathay Pacific 310-640-8551
fax: 310-615-0042
300 N. Continental Blvd., Ste. 500
El Segundo, CA 90245

Continental 800-932-2732
fax: 713-590-2150
3663 N. Sam Houston Pkwy. E
Ste. 500
Houston, TX 77032

Delta 404-715-1450
fax: 404-715-1400
P.O. Box 20980
Atlanta, GA 30320-2980

Home to more airline headquarters and maintenance bases than any other state: Texas.

El Al 212-852-0600
120 W. 45th St.
New York, NY 10036

EVA Air 310-521-6000
260 W. 5th St.
San Pedro, CA 90731

Finnair 800-950-4768
fax: 212-499-9037
8th Floor
228 E. 45th St.
New York, NY 10017-3303

Hawaiian Airlines 808-835-3424
Box 30008
Honolulu, HI 96820

Iberia 305-267-7747
fax: 305-262-0594
6100 Blue Lagoon Dr., Ste. 200
Miami, FL 33126

Icelandair 410-715-1600
fax: 410-715-3547
5950 Symphony Woods Rd.
Columbia, MD 21044

Japan (JAL) 212-310-1309
fax: 212-310-1258
655 5th Ave.
New York, NY 10022

Kiwi International 800-538-5494
fax: 201-624-0537
Hemisphere Center
U.S. Routes 1 & 9S
Newark, NJ 07114

KLM 800-556-1800
fax: 914-784-2545
565 Taxter Rd.
Elmsford, NY 10523

Korean Airlines 310-417-5200
fax: 310-417-8841
6101 W. Imperial Hwy.
Los Angeles, CA 90045

Lufthansa 800-645-3880
fax: 212-479-8817
1640 Hempstead Tpke.
East Meadow, NY 11554

Mexicana 800-353-8245
9841 Airport Blvd., Ste. 200
Los Angeles, CA 90045

Midway 800-564-5001
300 W. Morgan St., Ste. 1200
Durham, NC 2770

Midwest Express 800-452-2022
fax: 414-570-0199
P.O. Box 37414
Milwaukee, WI 53237-9977

Northwest 612-726-2046
fax: 612-726-0776
Dept. C5270
5101 Northwest Dr.
St. Paul, MN 55111-3034

Qantas 310-726-1407
fax: 310-726-1401
841 Apollo St., Ste. 400
El Segundo, CA 90245-4741

Reno Air 702-686-3835
fax: 702-858-4957
P.O. Box 30059
Reno, NV 89520

Sabena 516-562-9303
fax: 516-562-9323
1155 Northern Blvd.
Manhasset, NY 11030

SAS Scandinavian Airlines 800-345-9684
fax: 201-896-3735
9 Polito Ave.
Lyndhurst, NJ 07071

Singapore Airlines 213-934-8833
fax: 213-939-6727
5670 Wilshire Blvd.
Los Angeles, CA 90036

Southwest Airlines 214-904-4223
fax: 214-792-5099
P.O. Box 36611
Dallas, TX 75235-1611

Swissair 800-221-4750
fax: 310-335-5935
3391 Peachtree Rd. NE, Ste. 210
Atlanta, GA 30326

Thai Airways International 800-426-5204
fax: 310-335-5935
22 N. Sepulveda Blvd., Ste. 1950
El Segundo, CA 90245

Tower Air 718-553-3598
fax: 718-553-4312
JFK Int'l Airport
Hanger #17
Jamaica, NY 11430

TWA 800-221-2000
fax: 610-631-5280
1415 Olive St., Ste. 100
St. Louis, MO 63103

United 847-700-6796
fax: 847-700-2214
P.O. Box 66100
Chicago, IL 60666

US Airways 910-661-0061
fax: 910-661-8031
P.O. Box 1501
Winston Salem, NC 27102-1501

Amenity for travelers at Miami International Airport: an outdoor pool ($8 admission).

Virgin Atlantic 800-496-6661
fax: 203-750-6490

747 Belden Ave.
Norwalk, CT 06850

Dept of Transportation Aviation Consumer Protection 202-366-2220

FAA Consumer Hotline 800-322-7873

AIRPORT PAGING

Some airports have a central paging number. Others ask that you call the airline's main reservation number and request a page at the specific airport. Letters in parentheses indicate airport codes.

ALABAMA

Birmingham (BHM) 205-599-0500
Mobile (MOB) 334-633-4510
Montgomery (MGM) .... CALL AIRLINE

ALASKA

Anchorage (ANC) .... CALL AIRLINE
Fairbanks (FAI) .... CALL AIRLINE

ARIZONA

Phoenix (PHX) 602-273-3455
Tucson (TUS) 520-573-8000
Flagstaff (FLG) 520-556-1234

ARKANSAS

Little Rock (LIT) 501-375-1509

CALIFORNIA

Burbank (BUR) .... CALL AIRLINE
Long Beach (LGB) 310-425-5555
Los Angeles (LAX) .... CALL AIRLINE
Monterey (MRY) 408-648-7002
Oakland (OAK) 510-577-4000
Ontario (ONT) 909-988-2700
Orange County (SNA) 714-252-5006
Sacramento (SMF) 916-929-5411
San Diego (SAN) 619-231-2294
San Francisco (SFO) 415-876-2377
San Jose (SJC) 408-277-4759

COLORADO

Colorado Springs (COS) 719-550-1919
Denver (DIA) 303-342-2000

CONNECTICUT

Hartford (BDT) .... CALL AIRLINE
New Haven (HVN) .... CALL AIRLINE

DELAWARE

Wilmington (ILG) 302-328-4097

DISTRICT OF COLUMBIA

Dulles (IAD) 703-661-8636
Reagan National (DCA) 703-419-3972

FLORIDA

Fort Lauderdale (FLL) .... CALL AIRLINE
Fort Myers (RSW) 941-768-4700
Jacksonville (JAX) 904-741-3044
Gainesville (GNV) .... CALL AIRLINE
Miami (MIA) 305-876-7000
Orlando (MCO) 407-825-2000
St. Petersburg (PIE) 813-535-7600
Sarasota/Bradenton (SRQ) 941-359-5225
Tampa (TPA) 800-767-8882
West Palm Beach (PBI) 407-471-7420

GEORGIA

Atlanta (ATL) .... CALL AIRLINE
Macon (MCN) 912-788-6310
Savannah (SAV) 912-964-0514

HAWAII

Hilo, Hawaii (ITO) 808-934-5838
Lihu, Kauai (LIH) .... CALL AIRLINE
Kahului, Maui (OGG) .... Departing 808-872-3894
.... Arriving 808-872-3893
Honolulu, Oahu (HNL) .... CALL AIRLINE

IDAHO

Boise (BOI) 208-383-3135

ILLINOIS

Chicago Midway (MDW) 312-767-0500
Chicago O'Hare (ORD) 312-686-2200
Moline (MLI) 309-757-1530
Peoria (PIA) 309-697-4741
Rockford (FRD) 815-987-3390

INDIANA

Evansville (EVV) .... CALL AIRLINE
Fort Wayne (FWA) .... CALL AIRLINE
Indianapolis (IND) 317-487-7243
South Bend (SBN) 219-282-4590

IOWA

Cedar Rapids (CID) 319-362-8336
Des Moines (DSM) 515-256-5050

KANSAS

Kansas City (MCI) 816-243-5237
Wichita (ICT) .... CALL AIRLINE

KENTUCKY

Lexington (LEX) 606-255-4143
Louisville (SDF) 502-367-4636

Shortest major airline scheduled airline flight: American's LAX-John Wayne at 35 miles.

LOUISIANA

Monroe (MLU) 318-329-2461
New Orleans (MSY) 504-464-0831
Shreveport (SHV) 318-673-5370

MAINE

Bangor (BGR) 207-947-0384
Portland (PWM) 207-775-5809

MARYLAND

Baltimore/Washington (BWI) 410-859-7111

MASSACHUSETTS

Boston/Logan (BOS) ....CALL AIRLINE

MICHIGAN

Detroit (DTW) ....CALL AIRLINE
Flint (FNT) ....CALL AIRLINE
Grand Rapids (GRR) ....CALL AIRLINE
Lansing (LAN) 517-321-6121

MINNESOTA

Duluth (DLH) 218-727-3201
Minneapolis/St. Paul (MSP) ....CALL AIRLINE
Rochester (RST) ....CALL AIRLINE

MISSISSIPPI

Jackson (JAN) 601-939-5631

MISSOURI

Kansas City (MCI) 816-243-5237
St. Louis (STL) ....CALL AIRLINE

MONTANA

Billings (BIL) ....CALL AIRLINE
Bozeman (BZN) 406-388-8321
Great Falls (GTF) 406-727-3404

NEBRASKA

Lincoln (LNK) 402-475-7243
Omaha (OMA) 402-422-6817

NEVADA

Las Vegas (LAS) 702-261-5733
Reno (RNO) 702-328-6789

NEW HAMPSHIRE

Manchester (MHT) 603-624-6556

NEW JERSEY

Atlantic City (AIY) ....CALL AIRLINE
Newark (EWR) ....CALL AIRLINE

NEW MEXICO

Albuquerque (ABQ) 505-842-4379

NEW YORK

Albany County (ALB) 518-869-3021
Buffalo (BUF) ....CALL AIRLINE
New York Kennedy (JFK) ....CALL AIRLINE
New York LaGuardia (LGA) ....CALL AIRLINE
Rochester (ROC) ....CALL AIRLINE
Syracuse (SYR) ....CALL AIRLINE

NORTH CAROLINA

Charlotte (CLT) 704-359-4027
Greensboro/Piedmont (GSO) 910-665-5688
Raleigh/Durham (RDU) 919-840-2123
Winston-Salem (INT) ....CALL AIRLINE

NORTH DAKOTA

Bismarck (BIS) ....CALL AIRLINE
Fargo (FAR) 701-241-1501
Minot (MOT) 701-857-4724

OHIO

Akron/Canton (CAK) 216-499-4221
Cincinnati (CVG) ....CALL AIRLINE
Cleveland (CLE) 216-265-6030
Columbus (CMH) ....CALL AIRLINE
Dayton (DAY) ....CALL AIRLINE

OKLAHOMA

Oklahoma City (OKC) 405-680-3317
Tulsa (TUS) 918-838-5046

OREGON

Eugene (EUG) 541-341-5870
Portland (PDX) 503-335-1040

PENNSYLVANIA

Harrisburg (MDT) ....CALL AIRLINE
Philadelphia (PHL) 215-937-6937
Pittsburgh (PIT) 412-472-3525

RHODE ISLAND

Providence (PVD) 401-737-4000

SOUTH CAROLINA

Charleston (CHS) 803-767-7009
Columbia (CAE) 803-822-5002

SOUTH DAKOTA

Rapid City (RAP) 605-393-9924
Sioux Falls (FSD) ...605-336-0762 (9 a.m. to 2 p.m.)
....................605-331-3733 (after 2 p.m.)

TENNESSEE

Chattanooga (CHA) 423-855-2200

Miles of skyways in St. Paul: five.

Knoxville (TYS) .... CALL AIRLINE
Memphis (MEM) .... CALL AIRLINE
Nashville (BNA) 615-275-1675

TEXAS

Austin (AUS) 512-472-3321
Corpus Christi (CRP) 512-289-2675
Dallas Love Field (DAL) 214-904-5559
Dallas/Fort Worth (DFW) .... CALL AIRLINE
El Paso (ELP) 915-772-4271
Harlingen (HRL) 210-430-8600
Houston Hobby (HOU) .... CALL AIRLINE
Houston Intercontinental (IAH) 713-230-3000
Lubbock (LBB) .... CALL AIRLINE
San Antonio (SAT) 210-207-3411

UTAH

Salt Lake City (SLC) 801-575-2600

VERMONT

Burlington (BTV) .... CALL AIRLINE
Rutland (RUT) 802-747-7101

VIRGINIA

Norfolk (ORF) . . 804-857-3351 (8:30 a.m.-5 p.m. M-F)
.... 804-444-3040 (other times)
Richmond (RIC) .... CALL AIRLINE

WASHINGTON

Seattle/Tacoma (SEA) .... CALL AIRLINE
Spokane (GEG) 509-455-6455

WISCONSIN

Green Bay (GRB) .... CALL AIRLINE
Madison (MSN) 608-246-3380
Milwaukee (MKE) 414-747-5245

WYOMING

Casper (CPR) .... CALL AIRLINE
Cheyenne (CYS) 307-635-6623
Jackson Hole (JAC) 307-733-7682

HOTEL/MOTEL RESERVATIONS

Adam's Mark 800-444-2326
Admiral Benbow Inns 800-451-1986
Allegro Resorts 800-858-2258
www.allegroresorts.com
Americana 800-634-3444
AmeriSuites 800-833-1516
ANA Hotels 800-262-4683
Aston Hotels & Resorts 800-922-7866
Best Inns of America 800-237-8466
Best Western Inn Suites/Hotels 800-752-2204
Best Western International 800-528-1234
www.bestwestern.com/best.html
Budget Host Inns 800-283-4678
Budgetel Inns 800-428-3438
Camberley Hotels 800-866-7666
Canadian Pacific 800-441-1414
Choice Hotels 800-424-6423
www.hotelchoice.com
- **Clarion** 800-252-7466
- **Comfort Inn** 800-228-5150
- **Econo Lodges** 800-553-2666
- **MainStay Suites** 800-660-6246
- **Quality Inns** 800-228-5151
- **Rodeway Inns** 800-228-2000
- **Sleep Inns** 800-228-2000

ClubHouse Inns 800-258-2466
Colony Resorts 800-777-1700
Comfort Inns 800-228-5150
Concorde Hotels 800-888-4747
www.concorde-hotels.com
Country Hearth Inns 800-848-5767
Country Inns & Suites 800-456-4000
Crown Sterling 800-433-4600
Days Inns 800-325-2525
www.daysinn.com
Delta Hotels 800-877-1133
www.deltahotels.com
- Canada 800-268-1133

Doubletree 800-222-8733
www.doubletreehotels.com
- **Club Hotels** 888-444-2582
www.clubhotels.com
- **Guest Quarters** 800-424-2900
- **Red Lion** 800-547-8010

Drury Inns 800-325-8300
Econo Lodge 800-424-6423
Economy Inns of America 800-826-0778
Embassy Suites 800-362-2779
www.embassy-suites.com
Exel Inn 800-356-8013
Fairmont Hotels 800-522-3437
Fiesta Americana 800-343-7821
Flag International 800-624-3524
www.flag.com.au/flag
Forte, Grand & Le Meridien 800-225-5843
www.forte-hotels.com
Four Seasons and Regent 800-332-3442
www.fshr.com
Friendship Inns 800-453-4511
Golden Tulip 800-344-1212
Grand Heritage 800-437-4824
www.grandheritage.com
Hampton Inns 800-426-7866
www.hampton-inn.com
Handlery Hotels 800-223-0888
Harley Hotels 800-321-2323

Average 737 Coach passenger to lavoratory ratio: 102 to 8; First Class, 1 to 10.

Hawthorn Suites 800-527-1133
www.hawthorn.com
Hilton 800-445-8667
International 800-445-8667
www.hilton.com
Holiday Inn 800-465-4329
www.holiday-inn.com
Crowne Plaza www.crowneplaza.com
Homewood Suites 800-225-5466
www.homewood-suites.com
Hospitality International 800-251-1962
Hotel Sofitel 800-221-4542
Howard Johnson 800-446-4656
www.hojo.com
Hyatt 800-233-1234
www.hyatt.com
Inter-Continental 800-327-0200
www.interconti.com
ITT Sheraton .800-325-3535
www.sheraton.com
Kempinski 800-426-3135
www.dusit-kempinski.com
Knights Inns .800-843-5644
La Quinta 800-531-5900
www.laquinta.com
Lennox House Suites 800-445-3669
Lexington Hotels/Suites/Inns 800-537-8483
Loews 800-223-0888
www.loewshotels.com
Luxbury Hotels 800-252-7748
Mandarin Oriental Hotels 800-526-6566
Marriott 800-228-9290
www.marriott.com
Courtyard by Marriott 800-331-3131
Fairfield Inn & Suites 800-241-3333
Residence Inns 800-228-2800
Microtel 888-771-7171
www.microtelinn.com
Miyako Hotels .800-336-1136
Motel 6 800-466-8356
National 9 800-524-9999
New Otani Hotels 800-421-8795
Nikko Hotels .800-645-5687
Omni Hotels 800-843-6664
www.omnihotels.com
Outrigger Hotels 800-462-6262
www.outrigger.com
Pan Pacific 800-327-8585
www.panpac.com
Park Lane Hotels 800-338-1338
Piccadilly Inns 800-468-3587
Preferred Hotels & Resorts 800-323-7500
www.preferredhotels.com/preferred.html
Prince Hotels .800-542-8686
Princess Hotels 800-223-1834
Quality Inns 800-228-5151
Radisson 800-333-3333
www.radisson.com
Ramada Domestic 800-272-6232
International 800-854-7854
Red Carpet Inns 800-251-1962
Red Roof Inns .800-843-7663
www.redroof.com
Regent International Hotels 800-545-4000
Registry Hotels & Resorts 800-247-9810
Renaissance 800-228-9898
www.renaissancehotels.com
Ritz-Carlton 800-241-3333
Rodeway Inns .800-228-2000
Shilo Inns & Resorts 800-222-2244
Shoney Inns 800-222-2222
www.shoneysinn.com
Signature Inns 800-822-5252
Sonesta International Hotels 800-766-3782
Sterling Hotels 800-637-7200
Super 8 800-800-8000
www.super8motels.com/super8.html
Susse Chalet 800-524-2538
Swissotel 800-637-9477
Tara Hotels 800-843-8272
Thistle Hotels .800-847-4358
Thriftlodge Hotels 800-525-9055
Travelers Inns 800-633-8300
Travelodge 800-578-7878
Utell 800-448-8355
Vagabond Inns 800-522-1555
Walt Disney World Resorts 407-934-7639
Warwick International 800-203-3232
Westin 800-228-3000
www.westin.com
Wingate Inns .800-228-1000
Wyndham 800-996-3426

HOTEL COMPLAINTS

Some hotel chains do not have separate numbers for customer relations. In those cases, call the reservation number.

AmeriSuites 800-525-5864
fax: 615-452-5355
ANA 213-955-7688
fax: 213-955-7678
Aston Hotels & Resorts 800-922-7866
fax: 808-931-1409
Best Western International 800-528-123
fax: 602-780-6199
Budget Host Inns 800-283-4678
fax: 817-861-6089
Budgetel Inns .800-428-3438
fax: 414-302-1310

Price you can be charged for ruining a bedspread at Las Vegas' New York New York: $140.

Choice Hotel International 800-228-505
fax: 301-593-2069

Clarion 602-953-7513
fax: 301-649-7286

Comfort Inns 602-953-7513
fax: 301-649-7286

Econo Lodges 800-637-9605
fax: 602-953-7514

MainStay Suites 800-228-5050
fax: 301-649-7286

Quality Inns 800-228-5151
fax: 301-649-7286

Rodeway Inns 800-228-5050
fax: 301-649-7286

Sleep Inns 800-228-5050
fax: 301-649-7286

ClubHouse Inns 800-258-2466
fax: 913-451-6072

Colony Resorts 412-920-5700
fax: 412-920-5770

Days Inn 602-389-5539
fax: 602-780-6199

Doubletree 800-528-0444
fax: 602-244-0213

Club Hotels 800-528-0444
fax: 602-244-0213

Red Lion Hotels & Inns 360-696-0001
fax: 360-604-5132

Embassy Suites 800-362-2779
fax: 901-680-7350

Exel Inns 608-241-5271
fax: 608-241-3224

Fiesta Americana 800-679-3748
fax: 214-891-3158

Forte, Grand & Le Meridien 800-224-1644
fax: 619-258-6619

Four Seasons and Regent 416-449-1750
fax: 416-441-4381

Hampton Inns 800-426-7866
fax: 901-680-7350

Hilton 800-445-8667
fax: 310-205-3640

Holiday Inn & Crowne Plaza 800-621-0555
fax: 801-975-1846

Homewood Suites 800-225-5466
fax: 901-680-4350

Hospitality International 800-251-1962
fax: 770-270-1077

Howard Johnson 800-544-9881
fax: 602-389-5588

Hyatt 800-233-1234
fax: 402-593-9838

Inter-Continental 212-852-6400
fax: 212-852-6463

La Quinta 800-642-4241
fax: 210-302-6151

Marriott Hotels 301-380-7600
fax: 801-468-4088

Courtyard 800-831-0224
fax: 301-897-9014

Fairfield Inn & Suites 800-831-0224
fax: 301-897-5629

Marriott Hotels 800-831-0224
fax: 301-897-5629

Residence Inns 800-899-7224
fax: 402-397-9218

Motel 6 800-466-8356
fax: 214-716-6540

Nikko Hotels 800-645-5687
fax: 312-527-2650

Omni Hotels 512-884-6664
fax: 602-926-1049

Outrigger Hotels 800-688-7444
fax: 808-921-6901

Radisson 800-333-3333
fax: 402-498-9166

Ramada 800-828-6644
fax: 216-349-3159

Red Roof Inns 800-554-4555
fax: 614-777-8927

Ritz-Carlton 404-237-5500
fax: 404-365-9643

Shoney Inns 800-222-2222
fax: 615-442-5355

Super 8 800-800-8000
fax: 605-229-8908

Susse Chalet 603-654-2000
fax: 603-654-2664

Thriftlodge 800-525-9055
fax: 619-258-6619

Travelers Inns 714-256-2070
fax: 714-256-2165

Travelodge 800-255-3050
fax: 619-258-6619

Vagabond Inns 800-522-1555
fax: 310-643-6135

Westin 800-228-3000
fax: 206-443-3142

Wingate Inns 800-449-3716
fax: 602-389-5588

Wyndham 800-996-3426
fax: 214-863-1342

FREQUENT GUEST PROGRAMS

Adam's Mark Gold Club 800-627-6275
Best Western Gold Crown Intl. 800-873-4653
ClubHouse Inns BestGuest 800-258-2466
Courtyard Club 800-321-2582
Crowne Plaza Preferred 800-277-4567
Days Inn-Credible Card 800-344-3636

Location of Super 8's 1,500th motel: Cranberry, PA.

Fairfield INNsiders Club 800-443-7200
Fairmont President's Club 800-553-3658
Hilton HHonors Worldwide 800-446-6677
Holiday Inn Priority Club 800-272-9273
Howard Johnson Business Club 800-547-7829
Hyatt Gold Passport 800-544-9288
Inter-Coninental Six Continents Club . .800-462-6686
ITT Sheraton Hotels Club International 800-247-2582
La Quinta Returns Club 800-642-4258
Loews First 800-563-9712
Marriott Honored Guest Awards & Marriott Miles 800-367-6453
Ramada Business Card 800-672-6232
Red Lion Frequent Guest Dividends . . .800-547-8010
Renaissance Club Express 800-824-3571
Westin Premier 800-521-2000

HOSTELS

American Association of International Hostels 505-988-1153
ElderHostel 617-426-7788
Hostelling International 202-783-4943
International Travelers Club 310-399-7649

CAR RENTAL COMPANIES

Ace Rent-A-Car 800-243-3443
Advantage Rent-A-Car 800-777-5500
Alamo Rent-A-Car 800-327-9633
www.goalamo.com
International rentals 800-522-9696
Corporate accounts 800-328-8018
Roadside service 800-803-4444
Auto Europe .800-223-5555
www.autoeurope.com
Avis Car Rental 800-331 1212
www.avis.com
International rentals 800-331-1084
Corporate account 800-331-1082
Spanish speaking 800-874-3556
Roadside service 800-354-2847
Bon Voyage 800-272-3299
Budget Rent-A-Car 800-527-0700
www.budgetrentacar.com
International rentals 800-472-3325
Corporate accounts 800-527-0700
Roadside service 800-527-0700
Dollar Rent-A-Car 800-800-4000
www.dollarcar.com
Corporate accounts 800-800-0088
Roadside service 800-235-9393
Enterprise Rent-A-Car 800-325-8007
Roadside service 800-325-8007
www.pickenterprise.com
EuroDollar (International) 800-800-6000
www.eurodollar.co.uk
Hertz Rent-A-Car 800-654-3131
www.hertz.com
International rentals 800-654-3001
Corporate accounts 800-654-4405
Roadside service 800-654-5060
Holiday Autos (International) 800-422-7737
I.T.S. (International) 800-521-0643
Kemwel Group 800-678-0678
www.kemwel.com
National InterRent 800-328-4567
www.nationalcar.com
International rentals 800-227-3876
Corporate accounts 800-777-6285
Roadside service 800-367-6767
Payless Car Rentals 800-729-5377
www.paylesscar.com
International rentals 800-237-2804
Corporate accounts 800-729-5255
Renault International 800-221-1052
Rental Car Guide www.bnm.com
Rent-A-Wreck .800-535-1391
www.rent-a-wreck.com:80/raw
Thrifty Car Rental 800-367-2277
www.thrifty.com
Corporate accounts 800-331-3550
Roadside Service 800-367-2277
U-Save Auto Rental 800-272-8728
Ugly Duckling Rent-A-Car 800-843-3825

FREQUENT RENTER PROGRAMS

Advantage Frequent Renter 800-777-1374
Alamo Express True Blue 800-882-5266
Avis Preferred Renter 800-831-8000
Budget AwardsPlus 800-972-3414
Hertz Number One Club 800-654-3131
National Emerald Club 800-962-7070
Payless Championship Club 800-729-5255

CAR RENTAL COMPLAINTS

Ace Rent-A-Car 800-243-3443
fax: 317-248-7251
Advantage Rent-A-Car 800-777-5524
fax: 210-341-9716
Alamo Rent-A-Car 800-445-5664
fax: 954-468-2108
Auto Europe .800-223-5555
fax: 800-235-6321
Avis Car Rental 800-331-1212
fax: 918-621-4819
Budget Rent-A-Car 800-621-2844
fax: 214-404-7067

Average cost incurred by car rental companies on a 500 mile frequent flyer bonus: $8.06.

Dollar Rent-A-Car 800-800-5252
fax: 918-669-3009
Enterprise Rent-A-Car 314-512-5000
fax: 314-512-4722
Hertz Rent-A-Car 800-654-4173
fax: 405-728-6516
Kemwel Group 800-678-0678
fax: 914-835-5126
National InterRent 800-468-3334
fax: 612-830-2936
Payless Car Rentals . . . . .813-321-6352 ext 137
fax: 813-323-3529
Rent-A-Wreck .800-535-1391
fax: 410-581-1566
Thrifty Car Rental 800-334-1705
fax: 918-669-2765
U-Save Auto Rental . . . . .800-438-2300 ext 100
fax: 410-760-0452
Ugly Duckling Rent-A-Car 800-843-3825
fax: 520-322-7833

CRUISE LINES

Use these numbers for brochure requests and general information. Book your cruise through a large cruise agency or discounter to get the best deal.

American Hawaii Cruises 800-765-7000
fax: 312-466-6001
www.cruisehawaii.com
Carnival Cruise Line 800-327-9501
fax: 800-532-9225
www.carnival.com
Celebrity Cruises 800-437-3111
fax: 800-437-9111
www.celebrity-cruises.com
Commodore Cruise Line 800-237-5361
fax: 800-654-9031
Costa Cruise Line 800-462-6782
fax: 305-375-0676
Crystal Cruises 800-446-6620
fax: 310-785-0011
Cunard Line 800-528-6273
fax: 718-786-0038
www.cunardline.com
Holland America Line 800-426-0327
fax: 206-281-0627
www.hollandamerica.com
Norwegian Cruise Line 800-327-7030
fax: 305-443-2464
www.ncl.com
Orient Lines .800-333-7300
fax: 954-527-6657
Premier Cruise Line 800-327-7113
fax: 407-783-4925
www.bigredboat.com
Princess Cruise Line 800-421-0522
Radisson Seven Seas Cruises 800-333-3333
fax: 800-935-5440
Renaissance Cruises 800-525-5350
fax: 800-243-2987
Royal Caribbean International 800-327-6700
fax: 305-530-8397
www.royalcaribbean.com
Seabourn Cruise Line 800-929-9595
fax: 415-391-8518
Silversea Cruises 800-722-6655
fax: 954-522-4499

CRUISE LINE COMPLAINTS

American Hawaii Cruises 800-765-7000
fax: 312-466-6001
Carnival Cruise Line 305-599-2600
fax: 305-471-4718
Celebrity Cruises 800-242-6374
fax: 305-267-3523
Commodore Cruise Line 800-327-5617
fax: 800-654-9031
Costa Cruise Line 305-358-7325
fax: 305-375-0676
Crystal Cruises 310-785-9300
fax: 310-785-3891
Cunard Line 800-528-6273
fax: 718-786-2350
Delta Queen Steamboat 800-458-6789
fax: 504-585-0630
Holland America Line 206-270-6290
fax: 800-628-4855
Norwegian Cruise Line 800-327-7030;
fax: 305-567-9173
Premier Cruise Line 407-783-5061
fax: 407-784-0954
Princess Cruise Line 310-553-1770
fax: 310-277-6175
Radisson Seven Seas Cruises 800-333-3333
fax: 800-935-5440
Renaissance Cruises 800-525-2450
fax: 954-356-0146
Royal Caribbean International 800-327-6700
fax: 800-722-5329
Seabourn Cruise Line 415-391-7444
fax: 415-391-8518
Silversea Cruises 800-722-6655
fax: 954-522-4499

RAIL TRAVEL

Alaska Railroad 800-544-0552
Amtrak (U.S.) .800-872-7245
www.amtrak.com
Customer Service 202-906-2121

Honored guests at an annual November vegetarian feast in Thailand: 600 monkeys.

BritRail 888-274-8724
www.Britrail.com
DER Rail (Europe) 800-782-2424
Europe through the Back Door 206-771-8303
www.ricksteves.com
Eurostar 800-659-7602
www.eurostar.com
German Rail 800-782-2424
www.bahn.de/Home_e/f-engl.html
Mexico Tours 800-722-2296
Online Travel (Europe) 800-722-7151
www.eurorail.com
Rail Australia 800-423-2880
Rail Europe 800-848-7245
www.raileurope.com
VIA Rail Canada 800-563-6166
www.viarail.ca
White Pass & Yukon Route (Alaska) .. 800-343-7373

BUS LINES & OTHER GROUND OPTIONS

Cruise America RV Rentals 800-327-7778
Eurobus 800-517-7778
Gray Line Sightseeing Assoc. 972-934-8700
Greyhound Bus Lines 800-231-2222
www.greyhound.com
Greyhound Canada 403-260-0877
Recreation Vehicle Rentals 800-336-0355

U.S. TOURISM INFORMATION

The first phone number provides statewide information. City and regional tourism bureaus and the number to call for information on road conditions follows.

ALABAMA

Alabama 800-252-2262
Auburn/Opelika 800-321-8880
Bessemer 205-425-3253
Birmingham 800-962-6453
Calhoun County 800-489-1087
Colbert County 205-383-0783
Decatur 205-350-2028
Dolthan/Houston Counties 334-794-6622
Huntsville 800-772-2348
Mobile 800-566-2453
Montgomery 334-240-9437
Mountain Lakes 205-350-3500
Road conditions 334-242-4378

ALASKA

Alaska 907-465-2010
Anchorage 800-446-5352
Fairbanks 800-327-5774
Juneau 907-586-2201
Sitka 907-747-5940
Road conditions 907-273-6037

ARIZONA

Arizona 800-842-8257
Flagstaff 800-842-7293
Mesa 602-827-4700
Phoenix 602-254-6500
Scottsdale 800-877-1117
Tucson 602-624-1817
Road conditions 602-241-3100 ext.7623

ARKANSAS

Arkansas 800-828-8974
Eureka Springs 800-638-7352
Hot Springs 800-772-2489
Little Rock 800-844-4781
North Little Rock 800-643-4690
Road conditions 501-569-2374

CALIFORNIA

California 800-862-2543
Anaheim 714-999-8999
Beverly Hills 800-345-2210
Carlsbad 800-227-5722
Lake Tahoe North 800-468-2463
Lake Tahoe South 800-288-2463
Los Angeles 800-228-2452
Newport Beach 800-942-6278
Oakland 800-262-5526
Palm Springs 800-967-3767
Sacramento 916-264-7777
San Diego 619-232-3101
San Francisco 415-391-2000
Sonoma Valley 707-996-1090
Road conditions 916-445-7623

COLORADO

Colorado 800-265-6723
Boulder 303-442-1044
Colorado Springs 800-368-4748
Denver 800-645-3446
Durango 800-525-8855
Greeley 970-352-3566
Southwest Colorado 800-933-4340
Road conditions 303-639-1234

CONNECTICUT

Connecticut 800-282-6863
Hartford 800-446-7811
Housatonic Valley 800-841-4488
New Haven 800-332-7829
Road conditions 203-594-2650

Length of the Trans-Siberian railway: over 5,000 miles.

DELAWARE

Delaware 800-441-8846
Rehoboth/Dewey Beaches 800-441-1329
Wilmington 800-422-1181
Road conditions 302-739-6677

DISTRICT OF COLUMBIA

District of Columbia 202-789-7000
Road conditions 202-936-1111

FLORIDA

Florida 904-487-1462
Central Florida 800-828-7655
Daytona 800-854-1234
Everglades 800-388-9669
Florida Keys 800-352-5397
Fort Lauderdale 800-227-8669
Lakeland 941-688-8551
Lee County 800-237-6444
Lee County/Fort Myers 800-533-4753
Miami 800-283-2707
Naples 941-262-6141
Orlando 800-365-2860
Palm Beach 561-655-3282
Panama City 800-722-3224
Pensacola 800-874-1234
St. Augustine 904-829-5681
Space Coast 800-872-1969
Surfside 800-327-4557
Tallahassee 904-413-9200
Tampa/Hillsborough 800-448-2672
Road conditions 904-488-8676

GEORGIA

Georgia 800-847-4842
Amicalola Falls State Park 706-265-8888
Andersonville/Perry 912-987-1234
Atlanta 800-285-2682
Augusta 800-726-0243
Jekyll Island 800-841-6586
Lake Lanier Islands 800-768-5253
Macon/Bibb County 800-768-3401
Savannah 800-444-2427
Road conditions 404-624-7890

HAWAII

Hawaii 808-923-1811
Hilo 808-961-5797
Kauai 800-245-2824
Kona 808-329-7787
Maui 800-525-6284
Molokai 800-800-6367
Lanai 808-565-7600
Waikiki/Oahu 808-524-0722
Wailea 800-782-5642
Road conditions 808-536-6566

IDAHO

Idaho 800-635-7820
Boise 800-635-5240
Sun Valley/Ketchum 800-634-3347
Road conditions 208-336-6600

ILLINOIS

Illinois 800-487-2446
Bloomington 309-829-1641
Carbondale 800-526-1500
Champaign/Urbana 217-351-4133
Chicago 312-567-8500
Chicago Southland 800-873-9111
Kankakee River Valley 800-747-4837
Peoria 309-676-0303
Rockford 800-521-0849
Springfield 800-545-7300
Road conditions 312-368-4636
Road conditions May-Oct 800-452-4368

INDIANA

Indiana 800-289-6646
Evansville 618-826-5000
Indianapolis 800-323-4639
Laporte County 219-872-5055
Muncie 317-284-2700
Nashville/Brown County 812-988-7303
Richmond/Wayne County 317-935-8687
Terre Haute 800-366-3043
Road conditions 317-232-5533

IOWA

Iowa 800-345-4692
Burlington 319-752-7004
Cedar Rapids 800-735-5557
Des Moines 800-451-2625
Dubuque 319-557-9200
Iowa City/Coraville 319-337-6592
Waterloo 319-233-8350
Road conditions 515-288-1047

KANSAS

Kansas 800-252-6727
Emporia/Lyon County 316-342-1600
Finney County 316-276-3264
Lawrence 913-843-4411
Overland Park 800-262-7275
Salina 913-827-9301
Topeka 800-235-1030
Wichita 316-265-2800
Road conditions 800-585-7623

KENTUCKY

Kentucky 800-225-8747

Side benefit of cruise ship growth spurt: lower Caribbean hotel rates.

Ashland 606-329-1007
Bowling Green 502-782-0800
Cave City 502-773-3131
Kentucky State Parks 800-255-7275
Lexington 800-845-3959
Louisville 800-626-5646
Northern Kentucky 800-354-9718
Paducah 502-443-8783
Richmond 606-626-8474
Road conditions 800-459-7623

LOUISIANA

Louisiana 800-334-8626
Baton Rouge 800-527-6843
Houma/Terrebonne 504-868-2732
Iberia Parish 318-365-1540
Lafayette 800-346-1958
Lake Charles 800-456-7952
New Orleans 504-566-5085
Shreveport/Bossier 800-551-8682
St. Mary's Parish 800-256-2931
St. Tammany Parish 800-634-9443

MAINE

Maine 800-533-9595
Road conditions 207-287-3427
Road conditions May-Oct 207-287-2672

MARYLAND

Maryland 800-543-1036
Annapolis 410-280-0445
Baltimore 800-282-6632
Frederick County 301-663-8687
Montgomery County 301-588-8687

MASSACHUSETTS

Massachusetts 800-447-6277
Berkshire 800-237-5747
Boston 617-536-4100
Cape Cod 508-362-3225
Nantucket Island 508-228-1700
Pioneer Valley 413-787-1548
Plymouth County 617-826-3136

MICHIGAN

Michigan 800-543-2937
Ann Arbor 313-995-7281
Bay County 517-893-1222
Detroit 800-338-7648
Grand Rapids 616-459-8287
Kalamazoo 616-381-4003
Lansing 517-487-6800
Muskegon County 616-722-3751
Plymouth 313-453-1540
Saginaw County 800-444-9979
Traverse City 616-947-1120
Upper Peninsula 800-562-7134
West Michigan 616-456-8557
Road conditions/lansing 517-332-2521

MINNESOTA

Minnesota 800-657-3700
Bloomington 800-346-4289
Duluth 800-892-4997
Grand Rapids 800-472-6366
Minneapolis 800-445-7412
St. Paul 800-627-6101
Road conditions 800-542-0220

MISSISSIPPI

Mississippi 800-927-6378
Gulf Coast 800-237-9493
Metro Jackson 800-354-7695
Vicksburg 800-221-3536
Road conditions 601-987-1212

MISSOURI

Missouri 800-877-1234
Branson 417-334-4136
Cape Girardeau 800-777-0068
Columbia 573-875-1231
Hannibal 573-221-2477
Kansas City 800-767-7700
Springfield 800-678-8766
St. Charles 314-946-7776
St. Joseph 800-785-0360
St. Louis 800-325-7962
Road conditions 573-526-8828

MONTANA

Montana 800-541-1447
Road conditions 800-226-7623

NEBRASKA

Nebraska 800-228-4307
Lincoln 800-423-8212
Omaha 800-332-1819
Road conditions 402-479-4512
Road conditions (winter) 402-471-4533

NEVADA

Nevada 800-638-2328
Carson City 800-638-2321
Incline Village Crystal Bay 800-468-2463
Las Vegas 800-882-3157
Pony Express Territory 702-423-4556
Reno/Tahoe 800-367-7366
Road conditions/Northeast/Elko ... 702-738-8888
Road conditions/South/Las Vegas .. 702-486-3116
Road conditions/Northwest/Reno ... 702-793-1313

Size of New Orleans' French Quarter: 80 small square blocks.

NEW HAMPSHIRE

New Hampshire 603-271-2343
Mt. Washington Valley 603-356-3171
Road conditions 603-271-6900

NEW JERSEY

New Jersey 800-537-7397
Atlantic City 609-348-7130
Cape May County 800-227-2297
Monmouth County 800-523-2587
Ocean City 800-232-2465
Princeton 609-520-1776
Shore Region 800-365-6933
Trenton 609-777-1770
Road conditions 908-727-5929

NEW MEXICO

New Mexico 800-545-2040
Alamagordo 800-545-4021
Albuquerque 800-284-2282
Farmington 800-448-1240
Gallup 800-242-4282
Grants 800-748-2142
Las Cruces 800-343-7827
Raton 800-638-6161
Red River 800-348-6444
Ruidoso 800-253-2255
Santa Fe 800-777-2489
Silver City 800-548-9378
Taos 800-732-8267
Road conditions 505-827-5118

NEW YORK

New York 800-225-5697
New York State Visitors Info 800-225-5697
1000 Islands 800-847-5263
Albany County 518-434-1217
Broome County 800-836-6740
Buffalo 800-283-3256
Catskills 800-882-2287
Chautauqua/Allegheny 800-242-4569
Dutchess County 800-445-3131
Finger Lakes 800-548-4386
Hudson Valley 800-232-4782
Long Island 800-441-4601
New York City 800-692-8474
Niagara Falls 800-338-7890
Oneida County 800-426-3132
Ontario County 800-654-9798
Syracuse 800-234-4797
Wayne County 800-527-6510
Westchester 800-833-9282

NORTH CAROLINA

North Carolina 800-847-4862
Asheville 800-257-1300
Cape Fear Coast 800-222-4757
Charlotte 800-231-4636
Fayetteville 800-255-8217
Greensboro 800-344-2282
Henderson County 800-828-4244
High Point 910-884-5255
Pinehurst Area 800-346-5362
Raleigh Area 800-849-8499
Wilmington 800-222-4757
Winston/Salem 800-331-7018
Road conditions 919-549-5100

NORTH DAKOTA

North Dakota 800-435-5663
Bismarck/Mandan 701-222-4308
Fargo/Moorhead 800-235-7654
Grand Forks 701-746-0444
Minot 800-264-2626
Road conditions 800-472-2686

OHIO

Ohio 800-282-5393
Akron/Summit 800-245-4254
Athens County 800-878-9767
Canton/Stark County 800-533-4302
Cincinnati 800-246-2987
Cleveland 800-321-1001
Columbus 800-345-4386
Dayton Area 800-221-8235
Geuga County 800-775-8687
Mansfield/Richland County 800-642-8282
New Philadelphia 800-527-3387
Ohio Valley 800-765-6482
Ottawa County 800-441-1271
Portage County 800-648-6342
Sandusky/Erie County 800-255-3743
Toledo 800-243-4667
Trumbull County 800-672-9555
Warren County 800-433-1072
Zanesville 800-743-2303
Road conditions 888-264-7623

OKLAHOMA

Oklahoma 800-652-6552
Cherokee Heritage 918-456-6007
Oklahoma City 800-225-5652
Tulsa 918-585-1201
Road conditions 405-425-2385

OREGON

Oregon 800-547-7842
Coos Bay/Bend/Charleston 800-824-8486
Eugene/Springfield 800-547-5445

Derivation of the name Illinois: confederated Indian tribes known as the Iliniwek (superior men).

Newport 800-262-7844
Oregon Coast 800-858-8598
Pendleton 800-547-8911
Portland 800-345-3214
Salem 800-874-7012
Road conditions 541-889-3999

PENNSYLVANIA

Pennsylvania 800-847-4872
Allegheny Mountains 800-842-5866
Berks County 800-443-6610
Brandywine Valley 800-228-9933
Cumberland Valley 717-261-1200
Endless Mountain 717-836-5431
Gettysburg 717-334-6274
Lehigh Valley 800-747-0561
Lycoming County 800-358-9900
Mercer County 800-637-2370
Pennsylvania Dutch 800-735-2629
Philadelphia 800-537-7676
Pittsburgh 800-366-0093
Pocono Mountains 800-762-6667
Valley Forge 610-834-1550
York County 800-673-2429
Road conditions 717-939-9551
Turnpike conditions 800-331-3414
Interstate Highway conditions ... 814-355-6049

RHODE ISLAND

Rhode Island 800-556-2484
Newport 401-849-8048
Providence 800-233-1636
South County 800-548-4662
Road conditions .... 401-444-1000 or 401-277-2468

SOUTH CAROLINA

South Carolina 803-734-0122
Charleston 800-868-8118
Columbia 800-264-4884
Greenville 864-233-0461
Myrtle Beach 800-356-3016
Seabrook Island 800-845-2475
Road conditions 803-737-1030

SOUTH DAKOTA

South Dakota 800-732-5682
Aberdeen 605-225-2414
Black Hills/Bad Lands 605-341-1462
Pierre 605-224-7361
Rapid City 800-487-3223
Sioux Falls 605-336-1620
Road conditions 605-394-2255

TENNESSEE

Tennessee 800-322-3344
Clarksville/Montgomery 615-648-0001
Gatlinburg 800-568-4748
Kingsport 800-743-5282
Knoxville 800-727-8045
Memphis 800-447-8278
Nashville 615-259-4755
Pigeon Forge 800-251-9100
Smokey Mountains 423-983-2241
Upper Tennessee 423-753-5961
Williamson County 615-794-1225

TEXAS

Texas .... 800-452-9292 or 800-888-8839
Abilene 800-727-7704
Amarillo 800-692-1338
Arlington 800-342-4305
Austin 800-888-8287
Bandara 800-364-3833
Beaumont 800-392-4401
Big Bend National Park 915-477-2251
Big Thicket 409-839-2689
Brownsville 800-626-2639
Corpus Christi 800-678-6232
Dallas 214-746-6677
Del Rio 210-775-3551
East Texas 903-757-4444
El Paso 800-351-6024
Fort Davis 800-524-3015
Fort Worth 800-433-5747
Fredicksburg 210-997-6523
Galveston 800-351-4237
Granbury 800-950-2212
Grapevine 800-457-6338
Guadalupe Mountains 915-828-3251
Houston 800-231-7799
Irving 800-247-8464
Kerrville 800-221-7958
Kilgore 903-984-5022
King Ranch 512-592-8055
Laredo 800-292-2122
Lubbock 800-692-4035
McAllen 210-682-2871
Midland 800-624-6435
Nacogdoches 409-564-7351
New Braunfels 800-572-2626
Odessa 800-780-4678
Port Aransas 800-452-6278
Port Arthur 800-235-7822
San Angelo 800-375-1206
San Antonio 800-447-3372
San Marcos 512-396-2495
South Padre Island 800-343-2368
Tyler 800-235-5712
Waco 800-922-6386
Wichita Falls 817-723-2741
Road conditions 800-452-9292

The United States capital for Tejano music: San Antonio.

UTAH

Utah 801-538-1030
Mountainland 801-377-2262
Moab/Green River 800-635-6622
Park City Area 800-453-1360
Salt Lake City 801-538-1467
Road conditions 801-964-6000

VERMONT

Vermont 802-828-3236
Kellington/Pico Area 802-773-4181
Stowe Area 800-247-8693
Sugarbush 800-828-4748
Road conditions 802-295-9276

VIRGINIA

Virginia 800-847-4882
Alexandria 703-838-4200
Arlington 800-677-6267
Charlottesville 804-293-6789
Colonial Williamsburg 800-447-8679
Eastern Shore 804-787-2460
Fairfax County 800-732-4732
Fredericksburg 540-373-1776
Hampton 800-800-2202
Lexington 540-463-3777
Lynchburg 804-847-1811
Newport News 800-333-7787
Norfolk 800-368-3097
Prince William/Manassas 800-432-1792
Richmond 800-365-7272
Virginia Beach 800-446-8038
Williamsburg 800-368-6511
Road conditions 800-367-7623

WASHINGTON

Washington 800-544-1800
Seattle 206-461-5840
Road construction 360-705-7070
Road conditions Nov.-Apr. 206-368-4499

WEST VIRGINIA

West Virginia 800-225-5982
Charleston 800-733-5469
Harpers Ferry 800-848-8687
Northern West Virginia 800-458-7373
Parkersburg 304-428-1130
Road conditions 304-558-2889

WISCONSIN

Wisconsin 800-432-8747
Eau Claire 800-344-3866
Fond Du Lac 414-923-3010
Green Bay 414-494-9507
Hayward/Sawyer Counties 800-724-2992
Indian Head Country 800-826-6966
La Crosse 608-782-2366
Madison 608-255-2537
Milwaukee 800-231-0903
Oshkosh 414-236-5250
Racine 414-634-3293
Wisconsin Dells 800-223-3557
Road conditions 800-372-2737

WYOMING

Wyoming 800-225-5996
Cheyenne/Laramie County 800-426-5009
Jackson Hole 307-733-3316
Riverton 307-856-4801
Road conditions 307-635-9966

SKI AREAS

ALASKA

Ayeska 800-880-3880
Eaglecrest 907-586-5284

ARIZONA

Snowbowl 520-779-1951
Sunrise 800-554-6835

CALIFORNIA/NEVADA

Alpine Meadows 800-441-4423
Bear Mountain 909-585-2519
Diamond Peak 800-468-2463
Heavenly Valley/Tahoe 800-243-2836
Kirkwood 800-967-7500
Mammoth 800-228-4947
Mt. Rose 702-849-0704
Northstar-at-Tahoe 800-466-6784
Sierra-at-Tahoe 800-288-2463
Snow Valley 909-867-2751
Squaw Valley 800-545-4350

COLORADO

Colorado Ski Resorts www.colorado.net
Aspen Highlands 800-525-6200
Aspen Mountain 800-262-7736
Beaver Creek 800-525-2257
Breckenridge 800-800-2732
Copper Mountain 800-458-8386
Crested Butte 800-544-8448
Keystone Resort 800-222-0188
Purgatory 800-525-0892
SilverCreek 800-448-9458
Snowmass 800-598-2005
Steamboat Springs 800-525-2628
www.steamboat-ski.com/ski
Telluride 800-525-3455

Town that adopted the name of a world renowned Native American athlete in 1954: Jim Thorpe, PA.

Vail 800-525-2257
www.vail.net
Winter Park 800-525-3538
www.skiwinterpark.com

IDAHO

Bogus Basin 800-367-4397
Schweitzer Mountain 800-831-8810
Sun Valley 800-786-8259

MAINE

Sugarloaf 800-843-5623
Sunday River 800-543-2754

MASSACHUSETTS

Jiminy Peak 800-882-8859
Wachusett 508-464-2300

MONTANA

Big Mountain 800-858-5439
Big Sky 800-548-4486
Bridger Bowl 800-223-9609
Showdown 406-236-5522

NEW HAMPSHIRE

Attitash Bear Peak 800-223-7669
Bretton Woods 800-258-0330
Gunstock 800-486-7862
King Pine Ski Area 800-367-8897
Loon Mountain 800-227-4191
Ski Cranmore 800-786-6754

NEW JERSEY

Vernon Valley/Great Gorge 201-827-2000

NEW MEXICO

New Mexico Ski Resorts www.nets.com/skinm
Angel Fire 800-633-7463
Santa Fe 800-776-7669
Ski Apache 800-253-2255
Taos 800-821-2437

NEW YORK

Greek Peak 800-955-2754
Holiday Valley 800-323-0020
Hunter Mountain 800-524-2655
Whiteface 800-447-5224
Windham 518-734-4300

OREGON

Mt. Bachelor 541-382-2442
Mt. Hood Meadows 800-929-2754
Mt. Hood Skibowl 503-272-3206
Timberline 800-452-1335

PENNSYLVANIA

Camelback 717-629-1661
Seven Springs 800-452-2223

UTAH

Utah Ski Resorts www.skiutah.com
Alta 801-742-3333
Brighton 800-873-5512
Brian Head 800-272-7426
Deer Valley 800-424-3337
Park City 800-222-7275
Powder Mountain 801-745-3772
Snowbird 800-453-3000
Solitude 800-748-4754
Sundance 800-892-1600

VERMONT

Bolton Valley 800-451-3220
Jay Peak 800-451-4449
Killington 800-621-6867
Mt. Snow/Haystack 800-245-7669
Okemo 800-786-5366
Pico 800-225-7426
Smuggler's Notch 800-451-8752
Stowe 800-253-4754
www.stowe.com/smr
Stratton 800-787-2886
Sugarbush 800-537-8427

VIRGINIA

Bryce 540-856-2121
Homestead 800-838-1766
Massanutten 800-207-6277
Wintergreen 800-325-2200

WASHINGTON

Crystal Mountain 360-663-2265
Mission Ridge 509-663-7631

WEST VIRGINIA

Snowshoe/Silvercreek 304-572-5252
Timberline 304-866-4801

WYOMING

Alpine Meadows/Tahoe City 800-441-4423
Grand Targhee 800-827-4433
Jackson Hole 800-443-6931
www.jacksonhole.com/ski
Snow King 800-522-5464

FALL FOLIAGE HOTLINES

Alabama 800-252-2262
Connecticut 800-282-6863
Delaware 800-441-8846
Indiana 317-232-4002
Kentucky 800-225-8747
Maine 800-533-9595
Maryland 800-532-8371
Massachusetts 800-227-6277
Michigan 800-644-3255
Minnesota 800-657-3700
New Hampshire 800-258-3608
New Jersey 609-292-2470
New York 800-225-5697
North Carolina 800-847-4862
Ohio 800-282-5393
Rhode Island 800-556-2484
South Carolina 800-849-4766
Tennessee 800-697-4200
Vermont 802-828-3239
Virginia 540-999-3500
West Virginia 800-225-5982
Wisconsin 800-432-8747

ADVENTURE TRAVEL

BICYCLE TRAVEL

Alaskan Adventures 800-770-7242
American Wilderness Experience 800-444-0099
Backroads Touring 800-462-2848
Chateaux Tours 800-678-2453
Country Cycling Tours 212-874-5151
Easy Rider Tours 800-488-8332
Gerhard's Odysseys 503-223-2402
Timberline Tours 303-759-3804
Vermont Touring 802-453-4811

RIVER TRAVEL

All Rivers Adventures 800-743-5628
American Adventures 800-288-0675
Arkansas River Tours 800-321-4352
Buffalo Joe River Trips 800-356-7984
Canyon Marine Whitewater 800-643-0707
Down Stream River Runners 800-234-4644
Dvorak's Kayak & Rafting 800-824-3795
Glacier Raft Company 800-332-9995
Performance Tours 800-328-7238
Raft Masters 800-568-7238
Royal Gorge Rafting 800-758-5161
White Water Adventure 800-366-2004

WILDERNESS TOURS

Murray's Tickets, Worlwide 800-542-4466
Outward Bound Trips 800-243-8520
Wilderness Inquiry 612-379-3858
Wilderness Southeast 912-897-5108

CANADIAN TOURISM INFORMATION

Alberta 800-661-8888
Calgary 403-263-8510
Chinook 800-661-1222
Road conditions 403-246-5853
British Columbia 800-663-6000
Vancouver 604-683-2000
Victoria 800-663-3883
Manitoba 800-665-0040
Winnipeg 204-943-1970
Road conditions 204-945-3704
New Brunswick 800-561-0123
St. John 506-658-2855
Newfoundland/Labrador 800-563-6353
Cornerbrook 709-637-2280
Gander 709-256-5000
St. John 709-729-4521
Wabush 709-282-3011
Road conditions 709-466-7953
Northwest Territories 800-661-0788
Road conditions 403-874-2208
Nova Scotia 800-341-6096
Dartmouth 902-490-5948
Halifax 902-421-8736
Road conditions 902-424-3933
Ontario 800-668-2746
Hamilton 905-546-4111
Kingston 613-548-4415
Kitchener 800-265-6959
London 519-661-5000
Niagara/Midwestern Ontario 519-756-3230
Ottawa 613-237-5158
Toronto 800-363-1990
Road conditions 800-668-2746
Prince Edward Island 800-565-0267
Road conditions 902-368-4770
Quebec 800-363-7777
Montreal 800-363-7777
Quebec City 418-692-2471
Road conditions 514-873-4121
Saskatchewan 800-667-7191
Regina 306-789-5099
Saskatoon 800-567-2444
Road conditions 306-787-7623
Thunder Bay 800-667-8386
Yukon 403-667-5340
Road conditions 403-667-8215

Location of a tourist-popular gas chamber (inoperable): Rawlins Territorial Prison, Wyoming.

CANADIAN SKI AREAS

Big White 800-663-2772
Fortress Mountain 403-591-7108
Lake Louise 800-258-7669
Mont-Sainte-Ane 800-463-1568
Nakiska 403-591-7777
Panorama 604-342-6941
Silver Star 800-663-4431
Stoneham 800-463-6888
Sun Peaks 800-663-2838
Sunshine Village 800-661-1676
Tremblant 800-567-6760
Whistler 800-944-7853

INTERNATIONAL TOURISM INFORMATION

AFRICA

Egypt 312-280-4666
Ethiopia 212-421-1830
Gabon 212-447-6701
Gambia 212-949-6640
Kenya 310-274-6635
Liberia 212-687-1033
Mali 212-737-4150
Mauritius 201-871-8381
Morocco 212-557-2520
Nigeria 212-850-2200
Senegal 212-517-9030
Sudan 212-573-6033
South Africa 800-822-5368
Tanzania 212-972-9160
Tunisia 202-862-1850
Uganda 212-949-0110
Zambia 212-972-7200
Zimbabwe 800-621-2381

ASIA/SOUTH PACIFIC

Australia 800-333-0199
Bhutan 800-950-9908
China 212-760-9700
Fiji 800-932-3454
Guam 800-873-4826
Hong Kong 630-575-2828
India 213-380-8855
Indonesia 213-387-2078
Japan 212-757-5640
Korea 312-819-2560
Macau 213-851-3402
Malaysia 212-754-1113
Nepal 202-667-4550
New Zealand 800-388-5494
Pakistan 212-879-5800
Papua New Guinea 202-745-3680
People's Republic of China 212-760-9700
Philippines 212-575-7915
Singapore 800-283-9595
Sri Lanka 202-483-4025
Tahiti 310-414-8484
Taiwan 212-466-0691
Thailand 213-382-2353

BERMUDA & THE CARIBBEAN

Anguilla 800-553-4939
Aruba 800-862-7822
Bahama Islands 800-422-4262
Barbados 800-221-9831
Bermuda 800-237-6832
Bonaire 800-826-6247
British Virgin Islands 800-835-8530
Caribbean 212-682-0435
Cayman Islands 800-346-3313
Cuba 212-986-1500
Curacao 800-332-8266
Dominica 212-475-7542
Dominican Republic 212-575-4966
Guadeloupe 888-448-2335
Grenada 800-927-9554
Haiti 212-661-3757
Jamaica 800-233-4582
Martinique 212-838-6887
Montserrat 800-646-2002
Puerto Rico 800-223-6530
St. Kitts/Nevis 800-582-6208
St. Lucia 800-456-3984
St. Maarten 800-786-2278
St. Vincent/The Grenadines 800-729-1726
Trinidad & Tobago 201-662-3403
Turks & Caicos Islands 800-241-0824
US Virgin Islands 212-332-2222

CENTRAL AMERICA

Belize 800-624-0686
Costa Rica 800-327-7033
Guatemala 305-442-0651
Nicaragua 202-939-6570
Panama 305-371-7031

EUROPE/MIDDLE EAST

Austria 212-944-6880
Belgium 212-758-8130
Bulgaria 212-822-5900
Croatia 800-247-5353
Cyprus 212-683-5280
Czech Republic 212-288-0830
Denmark 212-949-2333
Estonia 212-247-1450
Finland 212-949-2333
France 212-838-7800

What to wear under a kilt: nothing (unless you are a dancer).

Georgia (former USSR) 212-757-3884
Germany 212-661-7200
Great Britain .800-462-2748
Greece 212-421-5777
Hungary 212-355-0240
Iceland 212-949-2333
Ireland 800-223-6470
Israel 800-596-1199
Italy 212-245-4822
Jordan 202-265-1606
Latvia 202-726-8213
Lithuania 202-234-5860
Luxembourg 212-935-8888
Malta 212-695-9520
Monaco 800-753-9696
Netherlands 312-819-0300
Northern Ireland 212-922-0101
Norway 212-949-2333
Poland 212-338-9412
Portugal 800-767-8842
Romania 212-697-6971
Russia 212-758-1162
Saudi Arabia .212-752-2740
Scotland 800-462-2748
Slovakia 212-737-3971
Slovenia 212-358-9686
Spain 305-358-1992
Sweden 212-949-2333
Switzerland 212-757-5944
Syria 713-622-8860
Turkey 212-687-2194
Ukraine 212-741-0033
Wales 800-462-2748

MEXICO

Mexico 800-446-3942

SOUTH AMERICA

Argentina 212-603-0443
Bolivia 202-483-4410
Brazil 800-544-5503
Chile 800-244-5366
Colombia 202-387-8338
Ecuador 202-234-7200
Paraguay 202-483-6960
Peru 202-833-9860
Surinam 305-593-2163
Uruguay 305-593-2163
Venezuela 202-342-2214

REGIONAL PASSPORT OFFICES

Boston 617-565-6990
Chicago 312-353-7155
Honolulu 808-522-8283
Houston 713-209-3153
Los Angeles 310-235-7070
Miami 305-536-4681
New Orleans 504-589-6728
New York City 212-399-5290
Philadelphia 215-597-7480
San Francisco .415-744-4444
Seattle 206-220-7777
Stamford 203-325-3530
Washington 202-647-0518

U.S. CUSTOMS OFFICES

Anchorage 907-271-2675
Baltimore 410-962-2666
Boston 617-565-6147
Buffalo 716-551-4373
Charleston 803-727-4312
Charlotte 704-329-6100
Chicago 312-353-6100
Cleveland 216-891-3800
Dallas/Fort Worth 214-574-2170
Detroit 313-226-3177
District of Columbia 703-318-5900
Duluth 218-720-5201
El Paso 915-540-5800
Great Falls 406-453-7631
Honolulu 808-522-8060
Houston 281-985-6700
Laredo 210-726-2267
Los Angeles 310-514-6001
Miami 305-869-2603
Milwaukee 414-571-2860
Minneapolis 612-348-1690
Mobile 334-441-5107
New Orleans 504-589-6353
New York City 212-330-2912
Jamaica (NY) .718-553-1585
Newark 201-645-3633
Nogales (AZ) .520-287-1410
Norfolk 757-543-2033
Ogdensburg (NY) 315-393-0660
Pembina (ND) 701-825-6201
Philadelphia 215-597-4605
Port Arthur (TX) 409-724-0087
Portland (ME) 207-780-3326
Portland (OR) 503-326-2865
Providence 401-941-6326
St. Albans (VT) 802-524-6527
St. Louis 314-428-2662
San Diego 619-557-5360
San Francisco .415-744-7741
San Juan (Puerto Rico) 809-729-6950
Savannah 912-652-4256
Seattle 206-553-0554
Tampa 813-228-2381

City with streets named Chocolate & Cocoa: Hershey, Pennsylvania.

LOST OR STOLEN CREDIT CARDS

The first number listed is for calling within the U.S. The second number is for international calling; you may call collect.

American Express 800-992-3404
910-333-3211
www.americanexpress.com
AT&T Universal Card 800-423-4343
904-448-8661
www.att.com/ucs/
Diners Club/Carte Blanche 800-234-6377
www.dinersclub.com
Discover Card .800-347-2683
801-568-0205
www.discovercard.com
MasterCard 800-826-2181
314-275-6690
www.mastercard.com
Visa 800-336-8472
410-581-9994
www.visa.com

TRAVELERS CHECKS

Use these numbers to report lost or stolen travelers checks. The first number is for calling within the U.S.; the second is for international calls.

American Express 800-221-7282
801-964-6665
Citicorp 800-645-6556
813-623-1709
Thomas Cook/MasterCard 800-223-7373
609-987-7300
Visa 800-227-6811
410-581-7931

AUTOMATED TELLER NETWORKS

Also see credit card internet sites.

ATM Locators .800-248-4286
Cirrus 800-424-7787
www.mastercard.com/atm
Plus System 800-843-7587
www.visa.com/cgi-bin/vee/vwproductsatm/world/html?2+0

CABLEGRAMS/TELEGRAMS

Moneygrams 800-926-9400
Western Union/U. S. & Canada 800-325-6000
www.westernunion.com

TRAVEL INSURANCE

Access America 800-284-8300
International SOS Assistance 800-523-8930
www.intsos.com
Medic Alert 800-344-3226
Mutual of Omaha 800-228-9792
Travel Assistance International 800-821-2828
Travel Guard International 800-782-5151
TravMed Travel Insurance 800-732-5309
Wallach & Company, Inc. 800-237-6615

SHIPPING & AIR FREIGHT

Airborne Express 800-247-2676
www.airborne-express.com
America West Air Cargo 800-292-2274
American Airlines Cargo 800-227-4622
British Airways 214-574-4842
Continental Airlines 800-421-2456
Delta Dash 800-638-7333
DHL Worldwide Express 800-225-5345
www.dhl.com
Federal Express 800-238-5355
www.fedex.com
Northwest Airlines Cargo 800-692-2746
Southwest Airlines Cargo 800-533-1222
TWA 800-892-2746
United Airlines .800-621-5647
UPS 800-742-5877
www.ups.com
US Airways Cargo 214-574-5577

INTERNATIONAL WEATHER

National Weather Service 301-763-8155
www.nws.noaa.gov
USA Today's Weather Hotline 900-555-5555
www.usatoday.com/weather/wfront.htm

TRAVELER'S ASSISTANCE & INFORMATION

AIRLINES

U.S. Department of Transportation . . .202-366-2220
www.dot.gov/affairs.index.htm
400 7th St. SW
Washington, DC 20590

Federal Aviation Administration 800-322-7873
www.faa.gov
800 Independence Ave. SW
Washington, DC 20591

The capital city with the highest elevation: La Paz, Bolivia.

Aviation Consumer Action Project 202-638-4000
Box 19029
Washington, DC 20036

CREDIT CARDS

Federal Trade Commission
Information 202-326-2222
Complaints 202-326-2418
www.ftc.gov
Correspondence Branch
Washington, DC 20580

CRUISES

National Association of Cruise-Only Agencies
. 305-663-5626
fax: 305-663-5625
7600 Red Rd., Ste. 128, Dept. CN
South Miami, FL 33143

Cruise Lines International Association .212-921-0066
fax: 212-921-0549
www.ten-io.com/clia/index.html
500 5th Ave. Ste. 1407
New York, NY 10110

Federal Maritime Commission 202-523-5807
fax: 202-523-0014
www.fmc.gov
Office of Informal Inquiries and Complaints
800-N. Capitol St. NW
Washington, DC 20573

HOTELS

American Hotel & Motel Association . .202-289-3100
fax: 202-289-3199
www.ahma.com:80
1201 New York Ave. NW, Ste. 600
Washington, DC 20005-3931

PHONE OVER-CHARGES

Federal Communications Commission .202-418-1500
www.fcc.gov
Informal Complaints and Public Inquiries Branch
Mail Stop Code 1600 A2
Washington, DC 20554

TRAVEL AGENTS/TOUR COMPANIES

American Society of Travel Agents 703-706-0387
fax: 703-684-8319
www.ASTAnet.com
Consumer Affairs Department
1101 King St., Ste. 200
Alexandria, VA 22314

Institute of Certified Travel Agents 800-542-4282
617-237-0280
www.icta.com
148 Linden St., Box 812059
Wellesley, MA 02181

National Tour Association 800-682-8886
fax: 606-226-4414
546 E. Main St.
Lexington, KY 40508

U.S. Tour Operators Association 212-599-6599
fax: 212-599-6744
www.ustoa.com
342 Madison Ave., Ste. 1522
New York, NY 10173

TRAVEL FRAUD

National Fraud Information Center 800-876-7060
www.fraud.org
Box 65868
Washington, DC 20035

Largest consumer of Girl Scout cookies in 1998: United Airlines.

TRAVEL
SECRETS
ALROD